MW01131976

# Translating Buddhism from Tibetan

# *Translating Buddhism from Tibetan*

Joe Bransford Wilson

Snow Lion Publications

Ithaca, New York USA

Snow Lion Publications
P.O. Box 6483
Ithaca, New York 14851
USA

Printed in the USA

**Library of Congress Cataloging-in-Publication Data**

Wilson, Joe (Joe Bransford)
    Translating Buddhism from Tibetan / Joe Bransford Wilson.
      p. cm.
    Includes bibliographical references, glossary, and index.
    ISBN 0-937938-34-3 :
    3. Buddhist literature, Tibetan—Translating.  4. Tibetan language-Readers—Buddhism.
    5. Tibetan language—Style.  I. Title.
    PL3621.W55  1992
    495',482421—dc20
                                       92-9582
                                         CIP

Cassette tapes to accompany the drills and exercises presented in this book may be ordered from Snow Lion Publications, P.O. Box 6483, Ithaca, NY 14851. Tel: 800-950-0313 or 607-273-8519.

This book is dedicated to
the people of Tibet and the survival
of the Tibetan cultural heritage.

# *Table of Contents*

## Section One

*The Phonemic and Lexical Dimensions of Tibetan
Patterns in Letters, Syllables, and Words*

---

**Chapter One**
*The Tibetan Alphabet • The Thirty Consonants*

---

---

**Chapter Two**
*The Four Vowels • Modification of Vowel Sounds*

---

## Chapter Three
### *Aspiration and Tone • Writing Tibetan Letters*

## Chapter Four
### *The Root Letter • The Thirty Consonants*

## Chapter Five
### *Suffixes and Secondary Suffixes • Levels of Analysis*

## Chapter Six
### *Letters that Precede the Root Letter • Structural Patterns & Dimensions of Meaning*

## Chapter Seven
### *Subscribed Letters • Rules for Finding Root Letters •*
### *The Doctrinal Dimension of Tibetan*

## Chapter Eight
### *Pronunciation: Rules and Exceptions • Syllables and Words •*
### *Tibetan Numbers • Doctrinal Dialects*

# Section Two
*The Lexical and Syntactic Dimensions of Tibetan*
*Patterns in Syllables and Words*
*Patterns in Phrases, Clauses, and Sentences*

## Chapter Nine
### Words • *The Existent and the Nonexistent*

## Chapter Ten
### *Lexical, Syntactic, & Case Marking Particles •*
### *The Science of the Dots • Cyclic Existence*

## Chapter Eleven
### *Phrases, Clauses, and Sentences • Noun Phrases • Cyclic Existence and Enlightenment*

## Chapter Twelve
*Declension • Nominative and Connective Case Paradigms •*
*Classes of Nominative Verbs • Linking Verbs*

## Chapter Thirteen
*Verbs of Existence • Agentive Case Marking Particles • Locative and*
*Objective Case Paradigms • The Four Truths: True Sufferings*

# Section Three
*The Syntactic and Rhetorical Dimensions of Tibetan*
*Nominative, Agentive, and Specialized Verbs*
*The Rules of Buddhist Logic*

## Chapter Fourteen
*Specialized Verbs of Possession & Necessity • Purposive-Beneficial*
*and Originative Cases • First Person Pronouns • Simple Syllogisms*

## Chapter Fifteen
### *Syntactic Particles • Verbs of Living • Case Particles Indicating Means and Reasons • Reflexive and Second Person Pronouns*

## Chapter Sixteen
### *Syntactic Elements • Verbs of Dependence • Third Person and Reflexive Pronouns • Tenet Systems*

## Chapter Seventeen
### *Action Verbs • Agentive-Nominative Verbs • Originative Case: Separation, Comparison, Inclusion • Interrogative Pronouns*

## Chapter Eighteen
### *Agentive-Objective Verbs • Objective Complements • Nominative-Objective Verbs • The Objective Case*

## Chapter Nineteen
*Rhetorical Verbs • Attitude Verbs • Nominative-Syntactic Verbs • Objective Case Identity • Classes and Types of Verbs*

# Appendices

## Appendix Five
### *Case Marking Particles*

## Appendix Six
### *Adverbs and Postpositions*

## Appendix Seven
### *Lexical and Syntactic Particles*

## Answers to Drills

## Notes

## Bibliography

## Glossary

# *Preface*

The roots of *Translating Buddhism from Tibetan* are in the methods of teaching Tibetan originally developed by Jeffrey Hopkins at the University of Virginia in the 1970's. Using these methods to teach Tibetan in the early 1980's, the present author expanded them to include the diagramming of Tibetan phrases, clauses, and sentences with boxes and arrows (as seen throughout this book) and, later, revised the analysis of parts of speech, especially that of grammatical particles and verbs.

The philosophy of *Translating Buddhism from Tibetan* is to balance traditional Tibetan grammatical and syntactic analysis with a use of terminology that reflects English preconceptions about sentence structure. Although it is a book written for beginners, the analysis of grammar and syntax should be of interest to advanced students as well.

> Teachers using this book as a textbook and students who already know the basics of Tibetan may prefer to begin their reading with the appendices. They have been arranged systematically as an advanced introduction to the analysis of Tibetan presented in this book.

*Translating Buddhism from Tibetan* begins with rules for reading, writing, and pronouncing Tibetan, gradually carrying the reader through the patterns seen in the formation of words, and into the repeating patterns of Tibetan phrases, clauses, and sentences. It discards the Latin- and Sanskrit-based categories used in other Western grammars of Tibetan in favor of an approach to learning and translating Tibetan based on identifying repeating patterns in phrases and sentences.

The focus in this book is on Buddhist texts, especially those dealing with philosophy and meditation. It provides the student with vocabulary basic to a wide variety of Tibetan texts, as well as with the special terminology and patterns used in Buddhist logic, essential for reading many philosophical works.

*Translating Buddhism from Tibetan* is, in significant ways, the creation of many hands and many minds. As mentioned above, it had its origin in the materials used by Jeffrey Hopkins to teach Tibetan, materials to which Donald Lopez and Elizabeth Napper (both then students at Virginia) also contributed, and which benefitted as well from the suggestions of a decade of University of Virginia Tibetan students. I used these materials when I taught Tibetan at Virginia (from 1981-85) and, in the six years since then, have collected and analyzed lexical and syntactic data from a number of different genres of Tibetan Buddhist literature. The presentations of case marking particles and syntactic particles and the classification of verbs into three categories and eight classes is based on the analysis of this data, as is the theoretical structure (summarized in the Introduction) of nine levels of analysis and seven dimensions of meaning.

Not only is this book a dependent arising (རྟེན་ཅིང་འབྲེལ་པར་འབྱུང་བ་ **dên-jíng-ḍél-war-jung-wa**—Sanskrit, *pratītyasamutpāda*), but so is my own understanding of Tibetan, nurtured as it has been by study with a number of teachers, each with their own approach to the translation of Tibetan texts into English. My study of Tibetan began at the University of Wisconsin in the late 1960's under the tutelage of Géshé Lhundup Sopa and Stephan Beyer, and continued during a three year tenure with Géshé Wangyal at what is now the Tibetan Buddhist Learning Center in Washington, New Jersey, and during study with Venerable Khetsun Sangpo, now Director of Orgyen Donghag Choeling in Kathmandu, Nepal. From 1976 to 1979, I studied much of the doctrinal material presented in this book at the University of Virginia with Tibetan scholars including Lati Rinboché, Denma Lochö Rinboché, Géshé Gendün Lodrö, and Gusho Gëlsang Yéshé. I subsequently taught Tibetan at Virginia from 1981-85. I am grateful to all of my students there for helping me to formulate and clarify many of the ideas seen in *Translating Buddhism from Tibetan*, especially Bill Magee, Jules Levinson, Diane Short, Daniel Cozort, Craig Preston, Leah Zahler, Guy Newland, Karen Saginor, and John Powers. I would also like to thank the students at the Tibetan Buddhist Learning Center—especially Nancy Long and Amy Sims—for their assistance in proofreading and their suggestions. I am grateful to Bill Magee of the Center for South Asian Studies at the University of Virginia and to his students for testing this material in the classroom. Along with Craig Preston and Paul Hackett, he provided valuable corrections for the second edition.

Elizabeth Napper and Jeffrey Hopkins read earlier versions of this book, providing valuable corrections and suggestions, as well as many hours of discussion and debate on difficult points of Tibetan grammar and syntax. Jules Levinson read through much of the book and Diane Short, taking time from her own career, read through several versions of *Translating Buddhism from Tibetan* in their entirety— the two of them saving the reader from much confusion and the author from many errors, both typographic and factual. Whatever is of use in this book is owed to the efforts of these teachers, colleagues, and students. The remaining errors are mine alone.

Special thanks go to Richard Martin, late curator of the Tibetan collection at Alderman Library of the University of Virginia, whose unfailing hospitality and generosity over fifteen years and whose expertise in the bibliography of Buddhism and Tibet have helped immeasurably in this and many other projects.

Gratitude is also extended to Joshua and Diana Cutler of the Tibetan Buddhist Learning Center for their support of this project anf for allowing me the use of the facilities there. Tupden T. Taikhang and Geshé Tupden Gyatso—also of the Tibetan Buddhist Learning Center—provided valuable comments and assistance on the Tibetan examples and the drills, as did Geshé Jambël Tarndö of Charlottesville, Virginia.

I wish also to thank Venerable Samdong Rinboché, director of the Central Institute of Tibetan Higher Studies in Sarnath, India, for his hospitality during my visit there in 1990 and for allowing me the use of the facilities of the Central Institute, and to the faculty and staff there for assistance in locating grammatical treatises. Special thanks goes to Venerable Ngawang Samden for his critique of my analysis of Tibetan grammar and syntax. I am also grateful to Doboom Rinboché, director of Tibet House (New Delhi, India), who allowed me the use of the library facilities there and whose International Seminar on Buddhist Translations enabled me to travel to India.

Both the Faculty Research and Development program and the Department of Philosophy and Religion at the University of North Carolina at Wilmington have also generously supported me in the research and writing of this book in the United States, India, and Nepal.

I am appreciative of the patience that Jeffrey Cox and Sidney Piburn of Snow Lion Publications have shown over the past six years while I wrote, edited, and rewrote *Translating Buddhism from Tibetan*. They—and the readers who have awaited this book for so long—have truly shown a perfection of patience.

Finally, I wish to record my appreciation to my parents, Joe and Dorothy Wilson, for their support and encouragement during the many years I have pursued my studies of Tibetan and of Buddhism, to my children, Jason and Gareth (Denzin Dorjé and Denzin Söba), for their inspiration, and to my wife, Diane Short, for her patience and support, as well as for many hours of proofreading.

## *Technical Note*

The final version of *Translating Buddhism from Tibetan* was written on a Macintosh SE, using Microsoft Word 4.0, Chet Wood's Wylie Edit, QuicKeys, and Superpaint. The fonts are Pierre Robillard's DTimes and LTibetan (that is, Times with diacritics and Laser Tibetan). All the box and arrow diagrams were constructed in Word using postscript.

## *Conventions Used in the Text*

The names of places, persons, and lineages are written in a modified version of the phonemic transcription used throughout *Translating Buddhism from Tibetan*, one using only é, ü, and ö as special characters. In those cases where a particular usage is well known, it has been used in preference to a more accurate pronunciation. For example, Tsong-kha-pa is used instead of D̄zong-kha-b̄a. Pronunciation is noted in bold, with special characters for some vowels (as in **yîn**, **shé-rap**, and **pö'**), for high and low tones (as in **D̄zong-kha-b̄a** and **dzok-chên**), and for retroflex consonants (as in **ḍum-tha**). In addition to their systematic presentation in the beginning of the book, these phonemic equivalents are outlined in Appendix One.

Reference to persons and texts in the notes use the Wylie system of transcription (also presented in Appendix One), modified through the capitalization of the first pronounced letter at the beginning of the name.

Rules of grammar, syntax, and sometimes doctrinal principals are presented enclosed in boxes with heavy borders.

---

| |
|---|
| Rules and principals seen for the first time will be found in boxes like this one. |

Reviews of such rules, as well as more minor points, are in boxes with light borders.

| |
|---|
| Reviews of rules and principals will be found in boxes like this one. |

Suggested assignments and references to works on Buddhist doctrine and Tibetan history and culture have a grey background.

References to further readings and suggested assignments look like this.

In the diagrams, adjectives and verbs are preceded by leftward pointing arrows ( ← ) and declined nouns, adverbs, and postpositions are followed by rightward pointing arrows ( → ), indicating their syntactic functions. Syntactic particles are diagrammed with arrows or dots *underneath* them, depending on whether they bring together two parts of a sentence, phrase, or clause ( ⇔ ), terminate a sentence ( • ), or connect a clause or phrase to material that comes before it ( ⇐ ) or after it ( ⇒ ).

# *Introduction*

*Translating Buddhism from Tibetan* analyzes Tibetan at a number of levels. It provides analysis and instruction in the **phonemic dimension** of Tibetan (the pronunciation of letters, syllables, and words). In the **lexical dimension**, it provides the student with a grounding in basic Buddhist vocabulary. In the **syntactic dimension**, it classifies everything on a Tibetan page into words, syntactic particles, and case marking particles and presents in diagrammed form the patterns that occur with the various classes of verbs. In the **conceptual dimension**, it expands the student's understanding of vocabulary to encompass the definitions and categories of important terms, knowledge that the authors of Tibetan texts assume their readers will have. In the **rhetorical dimension**, it introduces and analyzes the patterns seen in the larger structures of logical analysis (structures consisting of many clauses or many sentences).

## The Tibetan Language

Tibetan is the language spoken and written throughout the Himalayan region, the language of Tibet, Ladakh, Sikkim, and Bhutan, as well as of Tibetan refugees in India, Nepal, and elsewhere.

It is traditional, within Himalayan culture, to speak of two forms of Tibetan: the colloquial language of everyday discourse (ཕལ་སྐད་, **phël-ḡë'**) and the doctrinal language (ཆོས་སྐད་, **chö>-ḡë'**).

> Pronunciation equivalents (**phonemics**) such as **phël-ḡë'** are explained in Chapters Two and Three and in Appendix One.

Both the colloquial and the doctrinal language have spoken and literary forms. There are various dialects of spoken Tibetan, including those of Central Tibet (དབུས་, ü>), Kham (ཁམས་, **kham**), and Amdo (ཨ་མདོ་, **am-do**). Dialects, however, are not treated in *Translating Buddhism from Tibetan*. The phonemic equivalents used here correspond to Tibetan as spoken by those native to Lhasa (**Hla-s̄a**) and Central Tibet. Experience has shown that Westerners who learn to speak the Lhasa dialect are better able to communicate with Tibetans (whatever their origin) than are those who learn provincial dialects.

Roy Andrew Miller ("Review of A. Róna-Tas, *Tibeto-Mongolica*," in *Language* 44.1, pp. 147-149), basing himself on the work of Nishida Tatsuo, distinguishes six periods in the history of Tibetan language:

1  the Proto-Tibetan of the period prior to the advent of a Tibetan written language in the seventh century;

2  Old Tibetan (seventh and eighth centuries);

3  Late Old Tibetan—after the time of Tridé Songdzen (ཁྲིད་ཕྱེ་སྲོང་བཙན་, *T̩í-dé-s̄ong-d̄zën*), that is, from 825 into the tenth century;

4  Middle Tibetan—including the writings of Rinchen Sangbo (རིན་ཆེན་བཟང་པོ་, *Rîn-chên-s̩ang-b̄o*) and Pudön (བུ་སྟོན་, *Pu-dön*), and later the writings of Tsong-kha-pa (ཙོང་ཁ་པ་, *D̄zong-ka-b̄a*) and his followers;

5  the New Tibetan of the seventeenth to nineteenth centuries;

6  the modern Tibetan of the twentieth century, which shows evidence of exposure to Hindi, English, and Chinese.

One might, based roughly on this chronology, divide Tibetan Buddhist literature into the following five periods:

1  early literature—including early translations of Buddhist texts into Tibetan (ca. 625-825);

2  translations after the linguistic reforms of Tridé Songdzen (that is, from 825 to approximately 1300), as well as indigenous Tibetan writings of that period;

3  classical literature from the time of Pudön (approximately 1300-1600);

4    modern literature (1600-1950);

5    contemporary literature showing evidence of exposure to modern, non-Tibetan cultures.

*Translating Buddhism from Tibetan* is based on an analysis of Tibetan as it is used in Buddhist texts of the classical and modern periods, drawing from literature deriving from the fourteenth through the twentieth centuries.

> The material in the remainder of the Introduction is a brief overview of the theory behind the presentation of Tibetan in this book. It is not necessary for a practical understanding of Tibetan and, at any rate, will be presented later as it becomes relevant. Although teachers of Tibetan and advanced students may wish to read this material, beginners are advised to begin their reading with Chapter One.

## Approaches to Tibetan Grammar

In writing this book, I have attempted to hold to a middle way between two extremes—those of (1) a conservatively traditional approach and (2) an interpretive academic approach. The conservatively traditional approach presents Tibetan grammar and syntax using the categories and explanations of traditional Tibetan grammarians. While this seems on the surface to be appealing, for who would know Tibetan better than the Tibetan grammarians themselves, there are drawbacks. Traditional grammars, for example, spend a great deal of time on the nature of letters (whether they are masculine, feminine, and so on) and what this means in terms of how they combine to make syllables, what particles may follow them, and so forth. Much less is said about how nouns and verbs operate within sentences.

Led by the grammars of Csoma de Körös, Jäschke, and Das, the interpretive academic approach—while it does not ignore the traditional Tibetan grammarians—bases itself on what had become standard in the presentation of Sanskrit grammar, the use of grammatical terms and concepts from Latin.

See Alexander Csoma de Körös, *Grammar of the Tibetan Language in English* (1834), H. A. Jäschke, *Tibetan Grammar* (1865), Herbert Bruce Hannah, *A Grammar of the Tibetan Language* (1912), and Sarat Chandra Das, *An Introduction to the Grammar of the Tibetan Language* (1915).

The use of Latin grammar as a paradigm has a long history in the grammar of English. There the famous example of the way in which such an approach is overly prescriptive is the rule that infinitives may not be split. Saying *to clearly explain* is incorrect and should be revised to become *to explain clearly* so that the adverb *clearly* is not inserted between the words of the infinitive, *to explain*. Why is splitting infinitives incorrect? Because in Latin, seen to be the model language, it is impossible to split an infinitive, an infinitive being one word and not two.

What I wish specifically to avoid in the traditional Western approach to Tibetan is the use of Latin grammatical categories, for example the use of the terms *accusative, instrumental, dative, ablative* and so on as names for the Tibetan declensions. These came into Western grammars of Tibetan by way of Western grammars of Sanskrit. The rationale for using these terms for Tibetan is clear and seems sensible but, in fact, is not. Sanskrit and Latin are both Indo-Aryan languages; they share a common root, and thus are grammatically similar. The use of the Latin terms listed above to identify the Sanskrit declension of nouns thus has an intuitive propriety.

Tibetan, however, is a member of the Tibeto-Burman group of languages, a group not related to the Indo-Aryan group. Unlike Latin and Sanskrit, it is not an inflected language. In Sanskrit, for example, the word *buddha* is transformed in order to show its usage in a sentence, becoming *buddhaḥ* (in the nominative singular case typically showing a noun to be the subject of a sentence), *buddhaṃ* when it is in the second or accusative case (meaning *to a buddha*), and *buddhena* in the third or instrumental case (*by a buddha*). The word itself is changed, much as *he* becomes *him* and *his* in English. Tibetan, on the other hand, is an agglutinative language—a language where particles (much like English prepositions) are attached to the ends of words in order to show their use in a sentence.

That traditional Tibetan grammarians do explain their own language in terms of the Sanskrit categories brought from India is not being disputed here. The grammatical analysis that forms the core of *Translating Buddhism from Tibetan* is based on their explanations of these categories. However, it is based equally on an examination of Tibetan as it is actually used in books on the theory and practice of Buddhism. I have attempted to balance the traditional categories and terminology of Tibetan grammar with an analysis of Tibetan syntax as it appears in Tibetan Buddhist writings and to present this analysis in a way accessible to contemporary English speaking people.

## The Analysis of Patterns

The presentation and analysis of Tibetan seen in *Translating Buddhism from Tibetan* is organized around three basic concepts.

1  **Levels of analysis** include the sounds symbolized by letters, the way these sounds change when letters are made into syllables, the building of words out of syllables, the ways in which words are combined to make sentences, and so on. Each level acts as the basis for the next level, the simpler serving as the basis for the more complex.

2  **Structural patterns** are the repeating patterns seen at the various levels just mentioned, including the way in which letters are arranged in orderly patterns to form syllables and the way in which nouns and verbs are arranged in certain standard patterns to make sentences. Because these patterns are repeated, they may be learned.

3  **Dimensions of meaning** are the types of meaning communicated at the various structural levels. At the level of letters and syllables, the meanings communicated are not ideas but sounds. At the level of words, ideas begin to be conveyed. The higher and more complex the level, the more complex is the meaning that may be communicated.

Thus, as presented in *Translating Buddhism from Tibetan*, the study of Tibetan involves:

1    analysis of the language at levels of greater and greater complexity,
2    identification of distinctive, repeating patterns within each level, and

3   development of the ability to see how each level contributes a new dimension
to the overall meaning of what is being read.

## *Levels of Analysis*

Looking at Buddhist Tibetan in terms of the patterns in which it is arranged, there
are nine possible **levels of analysis**, each level being more complex than the ones
before it. The first six of these levels are basic to any study of Tibetan.

1   **Letters** are consonants with or without vowels (for example, ཀ) and are
dealt with in Chapters One through Three.

2   **Syllables** range from those of a single letter to those with six consonants
and a vowel marker. The final syllable པ is a common single letter
syllable, whereas the verb བསྒྲུབས་ (meaning *achieved*—in transliteration,
*bsgrubs*, but pronounced ḍu̱p) has—in addition to its root letter ག— a
prefix, a superscribed letter, a subscribed letter, a vowel marker, a suffix,
and a secondary suffix. The patterns of pronunciation seen when letters
are combined to form syllables is the subject matter of Chapters Four
through Nine.

3   **Particles** and **words** are built from syllables. The word བུམ་པ་ (**pum-b̄a**,
*pot*) is a noun and the particle གལ་དེ་ (**kël-d̄é**), which marks the beginning
of a conditional clause and may be translated *if*, is a syntactic particle.
Most words have more than one syllable, whereas many particles (for
example, the case marking particle གྱི་ [**gyí**, *of*]) have only one. There
are, however, quite common words of only one syllable—for example,
དེ་ (**té**, *that*). Particles are introduced in Chapter Nine.

4   **Phrases** are made of words or of words and particles. བུམ་པ་དམར་པོ་
(**pum-b̄a mar-b̄o**, *red pot*) combines a noun and an adjective; མེ་དང་རླུང་
(**mé dang lung**, *fire and wind*) connects one noun with another; and ཤེས་
པར་བྱ་ (**s̄hé-b̄ar-ja**, *will know* or *should know*) combines a verbal
infinitive (ཤེས་པར་) and an auxiliary verb (བྱ་).

5   **Clauses** are made of words and phrases (for example, མི་རྟག་པ་ཡིན་པ་,
*being impermanent* and སངས་རྒྱས་ཀྱིས་བསྟན་པ་, *taught by Buddha*). Clauses
differ from sentences in that they do not end in terminal verbs.

6    **Sentences** are made of words, and often of phrases and clauses, but
     must end in a terminal verb. བུམ་པ་མི་རྟག་པ་ཡིན། (**pum-b̄a mí-d̄ak-b̄a yîn**),
     is a sentence meaning *Pots are impermanent*.

The seventh and eighth structural levels are not seen in all Tibetan texts, although the
seventh is very important in the present book.

7    **Rhetorical sequences** are groups of clauses and sentences linked
     together in a progression of theses and proofs. They are usually written
     in a rigidly formal structure, knowledge of which is essential to an
     understanding of a great deal of philosophical Tibetan writing. An
     example of a very simple rhetorical sequence is བུམ་པ་མི་རྟག་པ་ཡིན་ཏེ། རྟག་པ་མ་
     ཡིན་པའི་ཕྱིར། (**pum-b̄a mí-d̄ak-b̄a yîn-d̄é d̄ak-b̄a ma-yîn-b̄ë chír**), *Pots
     are impermanent because [they] are not permanent*.

8    **Sections** consist of groups of sentences and are introduced by an entry
     from a contents outline (ས་བཅད་, **s̄ap-j̄ë'**).

The ninth level is, by definition, relevant to all Tibetan literature.

9    The **work** as a whole (for example, an entire book) is constructed on a
     pattern—from the title page at the beginning to the publication informa-
     tion at the end.

## *Dimensions of Meaning*

At each progressively higher level, a language is capable of conveying progressively
more complex meanings. The philosophy behind *Translating Buddhism from
Tibetan* is that the Tibetan of Buddhist texts conveys seven dimensions of meaning:

1    the phonemic dimension,

2    the lexical dimension,

3    the syntactic dimension,

4    the doctrinal dimension,

5    the rhetorical dimension,

6    the tacit dimension,

7    the concrete dimension.

Of the seven, only the first five need be dealt with when reading and translating Buddhist texts. Of those, the first three—the phonemic, lexical, and syntactic dimensions—are relevant to all forms of Tibetan.

## The Phonemic Dimension

The meaning conveyed in the **phonemic dimension** is not one involving ideas. It has to do with the way that letters, both by themselves and when combined in syllables, 'mean'—that is, refer to—certain sounds. Sounds are not ideas: they are neither mental events nor are they naturally inextricably linked to mental events. However, they are—in human languages—generated by mental events (such as the intention to make a certain sound in order to communicate a certain idea) and, when heard by humans, they give rise to other mental events.

> For example, the symbol ད refers to the sound d̄a. Adding some other letters gives us དག, which—phonemically—means d̄ak. As you will see, there are many homophones in Tibetan; thus, phonemically, དག, དགས, བདགས, and བཏགས all equivalently mean d̄ak.

## The Lexical Dimension

The **lexical dimension** of meaning is more complex, arising from the combination of syllables into particles and words (nouns, pronouns, adjectives, adverbs, and verbs) and particles. Here the meanings communicated are those found in dictionaries, which are a form of lexicon—hence the term *lexical dimension*.

> The combination of དག (d̄ak) and the final syllable པ (b̄a), for example, produces དགཔ (*permanent, static*), but the addition of the negative particle མི (mí) creates མིདགཔ (*impermanent*), a word with exactly the opposite meaning.

Grammarians distinguish between lexical meaning and grammatical meaning. The lexical meaning of a word is the meaning of a base form of the word, the form before it is inflected (as opposed to the meaning of one or another inflection). Similarly, in *Translating Buddhism from Tibetan*, the lexical dimension of meaning is prior to the syntactic dimension, since it is in the syntactic dimension that a word is inflected to show its relation to other words in a sentence. The lexical dimension is defined rather narrowly, comprising only the basic dictionary meanings of terms without distinguishing between greater and lesser degrees of readers' education or literacy. As understood here, the lexical dimension of a word corresponds to Tzvetan Todorov's concept of linguistic encoding (Ducrot and Todorov, p. 254): "the linguistic meaning of a word is present in every use of the word and constitutes its very definition." Thus, the lexical dimension of a word is its meaning according to the general lexicon of a language and not as defined in the specialized lexicons of professional groups or subcultures. The technical use of terms by the various schools of Buddhist doctrine and within specialized areas of doctrine (epistemology, monastic discipline, etc.) is the province of the conceptual dimension of meaning.

The lexical dimension of a word or particle is abstract, in the sense that the word བུམ་པ་, for example, refers not just to a specific pot in a specific place at a specific time, but to all pots. What the word བུམ་པ་ conveys—its lexical dimension—is a reference to an idea shared, in a general way, by all who know Tibetan.

Tibetan epistemologists traditionally define the lexical dimension of the word བུམ་ པ་ to be "flat-based, bulbous thing able to hold fluids." Likewise, following *Webster's Ninth New Collegiate Dictionary*, the lexical dimension of the English word *pot* is "a usually rounded metal or earthen container used chiefly for domestic purposes (as in cooking or for holding liquids or for growing plants)."

## The Syntactic Dimension

The **syntactic dimension** of meaning is seen when words and particles are combined to make phrases, clauses, and sentences. This combination is capable of conveying more complex meanings than words. For the most part, this dimension becomes evident when words and particles are actually used in phrases and other larger units. However, all Tibetan words and particles are limited in their potential uses, even before they actually appear in a sentence.

Words, for example, are either nouns, verbs, pronouns, adjectives, postpositions, or adverbs. The most basic syntactic meaning of any Tibetan word is its functional type.

བུམ་པ་, for instance, is a noun. It may not be used as a verb, nor is it ever used as a pronoun, adjective, or grammatical particle. This is the basis of its syntactic dimension and limits its use.

However, the syntactic dimension of བུམ་པ་ is most clearly seen when it is used in a phrase, clause, or sentence along with other words and particles.

Saying བུམ་པ་མི་རྟག་པ་ཡིན། (*Pots are impermanent*) is a way of using the word བུམ་པ་ in a sentence to convey more about pots than is possible using merely the simple word བུམ་པ་. Likewise, inflected forms of the word བུམ་པ་—བུམ་པ་ ལ་ and བུམ་པ་ལས་, for example—define certain ways that the word བུམ་པ་ can and cannot relate to other words in a phrase, clause, or sentence.

## The Doctrinal Dimension

The next three dimensions of meaning—the doctrinal dimension, the rhetorical dimension, and the tacit dimension—are not as basic to Tibetan as the first three, but they are important for the study of Buddhist texts in Tibetan.

The **doctrinal dimension** is a specialized and enriched form of the lexical dimension. It comprises the meanings of words used technically to convey ideas about doctrine (that is, the theory and practice of Buddhism).

For example, whereas the translation *mind* is part of the lexical dimension of the noun བློ་ (**lo**), its inclusion (in some textbooks on བློ་རིག་—philosophy of mind and epistemology) among phenomena which have objects (ཡུལ་ཅན་, **yül-jēn**, literally *object-possessor*) is part of its doctrinal dimension. Its division into *conceptual* (རྟོག་བཅས་ **ḏok-jē>**) and *nonconceptual* (རྟོག་མེད་ **ḏok-mé'**) types further expands its doctrinal dimension, enriching the signification of the term well beyond its basic lexical meaning.

Technical vocabulary may be defined in different ways from one doctrinal system to another and may be used differently in different sorts of texts.

## *The Rhetorical Dimension*

The **rhetorical dimension** has to do with the special vocabulary and syntax used to link sentences in logical sequences of theses and proofs. Just as one can say more with a sentence than a single word, so more is conveyed in the formal statement of a thesis and a proof than in a single sentence. The rhetorical dimension includes statements of syllogisms and consequences, and the implications such statements have within Buddhist logic. It also includes the *critical analysis* (མཐའ་དཔྱོད་) genre of literature and the analysis of the differences between things in terms of their permutations (three permutations, four permutations, contradictory, or equivalent).

## *The Tacit Dimension*

The **tacit dimension** includes (1) the associations a given culture assigns to specific words, (2) the axioms upon which the doctrinal dimension is built, and (3) the assumptions a culture makes about language in general.

The association of the idea of loyalty or the concept of 'man's best friend' with *dog* is common among English speakers, but is not found in the dictionary definition of *dog* (and thus is not parts of *dog*'s lexical dimension). That dog as man's best friend would not easily appear to the mind of someone raised in traditional India is suggestive of the way in which it is tied to a particular culture. Although this dimension of the word *dog* is relevant to the way in which the word is understood, it is not usually articulated. It is, thus, tacitly present.

The second of the above three facets—the axioms upon which the doctrinal dimension is built—may be seen in the connotations of the word རྣམ་པར་རྟོག་པ་ (**ñam-bar-ḍok-ba**, Sanskrit *vikalpa*). རྣམ་པར་རྟོག་པ་ lexically means simply *thought* or *conceptualization*. However, there is a bias throughout Tibetan Buddhism against conceptual knowledge and in favor of nonconceptual understanding. Thus, even prior to being so defined in one or another doctrinal dimension, རྣམ་པར་རྟོག་པ་ connotes something to be transcended, something that is not ultimately compatible with knowledge of reality. One of the lexical meanings of རྣམ་རྟོག་ in colloquial Tibetan, *superstition*, suggests a derivation from the negative valuation given it in Buddhist Tibetan.

Another facet of the tacit dimension of a language is the overall attitude of those who read and speak it towards language and speech. One important assumption that Buddhism, and Tibetan Buddhism especially, makes about language in general is that the phonemic dimension has significant meaning beyond the one outlined above, one not related to the lexical and syntactic dimensions. This assumption is the basis for the use of mantras and of the belief in the importance of oral transmission. It is not the lexical meaning of a mantra, but rather its sound that has power. Similarly, the idea of oral transmission assumes that the ability to succeed in a certain practice (or, for that matter, even the ability to learn a certain subject) comes not only from rational understanding about it obtained from books, but also from actually hearing a text read aloud or a practice described by someone who has also, in his own time, heard it from his or her own teacher.

## *The Concrete Dimension*

From one viewpoint, the most important dimension of meaning is the **concrete dimension**. In some cases at least, this is something to which one can literally point. Let us take, as an example, the Tibetan word བུམ་པ་, the concrete dimension of which is any actual pot, an entity with a bottom and sides that can be used to cook in or to store things. This is not something that would be found in a dictionary, nor is it an idea; it is something that sits on a stove or table or floor and can be pointed to with a finger. Pointing to a pot conveys a far richer meaning than any definition or description of pot could, although that meaning is limited in time and space to a particular pot.

The concrete dimension of meaning is important in discussions of epistemology and philosophy of language, and it is also basic to Buddhist assumptions about the primacy of direct experience and the liberative potential of nonconceptual knowledge. However, it is not of primary importance in the analysis of the structures of Tibetan language.

# Section One

### The Phonemic & Lexical Dimensions of Tibetan

### Patterns in Letters, Syllables & Words

# *Chapter 1*

## *The Tibetan Alphabet*
## *The Thirty Consonants*

### The Tibetan Alphabet

The English word *alphabet* has its origin in the Latin *alphabetum*, a word which uses the first two Greek letters (*alpha* and *beta*) as a name for all the letters. Similarly, the Tibetan alphabet is called **ḡa-ka** (ཀ་ཁ་), after its first two letters. Another name for it is **a-lí-ḡa-lí** (ཨ་ལི་ཀ་ལི་—pronounced a-lee-ga-lee), *the vowels and consonants*.[1]

The Tibetan alphabet has thirty consonants and four vowels (see page 4).[2] In English, a consonant like 'c' has to be followed by a vowel—or by one of a limited group of consonants (such as the 'h' in 'ch')[3] —if it is the beginning sound in a syllable. *Cat* makes sense to us; *ct* does not. In English, *ct* might be an abbreviation for any word beginning in c and ending in t; in point of fact, it is the abbreviation for carat, cent, and count. In Tibetan, on the other hand, each consonant has an inherent vowel sound. Thus, if English syllables acted like Tibetan syllables, *ct* would be *cat* unless it was explicitly modified by a vowel marker.

The natural vowel sound of a Tibetan syllable is the sound of the 'a' in the English word *farther* and the 'o' in the American pronunciation of *opt*.[4]

> The basic Tibetan vowel sound, the one inherent in every consonant, will be represented in this book by **a**.

|  | Column 1 | Column 2 | Column 3 | Column 4 |
|---|---|---|---|---|
| **Row 1** | ཀ་ k͟a | ཁ་ kha̅ | ག་ k̲a | ང་ n̲ga |
| **Row 2** | ཙ་ j̄a | ཚ་ cha[5] | ཛ་ c̲ha | ཉ་ n̲ya |
| **Row 3** | ཊ་ d̄a | ཋ་ tha[6] | ཌ་ ta | ན་ n̲a |
| **Row 4** | པ་ b̄a | ཕ་ pha[7] | བ་ pa | མ་ m̲a |
| **Row 5** | ཙ་ d̄za | ཚ་ tsha | ཛ་ d̲za | ཝ་ wa |
| **Row 6** | ཞ་ s̲ha | ཟ་ s̲a | འ་ a | ཡ་ ya |
| **Row 7** | ར་ ra | ལ་ la | ཤ་ s̄ha | ས་ s̄a |
| **Row 8** | ཧ་ ha | ཨ་ a |  |  |
| **Vowels** | ཨི་ í | ཨུ་ u | ཨེ་ é | ཨོ་ o |

The Tibetan Alphabet

The **a** sound is represented separately in the Tibetan alphabet not by a vowel (although it is sometimes called such), but by the thirtieth consonant, ཨ་.

It is thus possible for a single letter, without vowel marking, to be an entire syllable in Tibetan, or even an entire word. An example of this is ཇ་ (pronounced <u>ch</u>a), meaning *tea*. As we shall see, however, the typical Tibetan word has two or more syllables, and it is likely that each syllable will be spelt with one or more silent letters (letters such as the k, g, and h in the English word *knight*).

## The Thirty Consonants

The thirty consonants of the Tibetan alphabet are arranged in seven and a half sets of four, indicated on page 4 by the seven and a half horizontal rows of letters (Rows 1-8).[8]

| Row 1 | ཀ་  ḡa | ཁ་  kha | ག་  ka | ང་  <u>n</u>ga |
|---|---|---|---|---|

The first set of four consonants are gutturals, sounds produced from the throat.[9] This row, as well as Rows 2, 3, and 4, and part of Row 5, follow a regular pattern.

- The first consonant in each of these rows is high in tone and lacks aspiration.
- The second is of middle tone and is strongly aspirated.
- The third consonant is low in tone and, by itself, is semi-aspirate.
- The fourth is a nasal and low in tone.

ཀ་ is always pronounced ḡa. (That is, it is always a high tone 'g'. The vowel, as will be seen in Chapter Two, may change.) Like the next four consonants in the first column, its phonemic equivalent is marked with a macron to show its high tone. ཁ་ is always pronounced kha. It may sometimes be heard with the same pitch as the ཀ་ (that is, a high pitch) or as a slightly lower tone; at any rate, the tone of the ཁ་ is higher than that of the third column ག་. ག་ is pronounced ka, but in some predictable contexts (discussed in Chapter Four), it is pronounced **ga**. In either case, ཀ is a low-tone consonant.

The letters in the fourth column of Rows 1 through 4 are the four nasals, all of which are low in tone. ང is the guttural nasal, a sound not heard at the beginning of English words, although one quite common at their ends. To learn this sound, take an English word ending in *-ing* (for example, *sing*) and add vowels to its end. Then, gradually drop the beginning of the word until the initial sound is **ng**.

| **Row 2** | ཅ **ja** | ཆ **cha** | ཇ **cha** | ཉ **nya** |
|-----------|----------|-----------|-----------|-----------|

The second set of four consonants are sounds produced with the tongue touching the hard palate. The **ch** sound is that in the English word *church*; it is not the hard initial sound of the word *chronic*. The second column ཆ is really a **chha** sound, but will be shown here as **cha**. (See the discussion of aspiration in Chapter Three.)

Note that the third-column ཇ is one of the few cases in which a low tone is shown with an underline (as **cha**). This is done in order to distinguish it from the middle-tone, aspirated **cha** of the second column.

The nasal of this group is ཉ, another sound not heard in the beginning of English syllables. Like ང, its natural tone is low. Unlike ང, it is not a sound that occurs at the end of Tibetan syllables—that is, it is not the **ny** of *pony*. Nor is it the **ny** of *nylon* or of *nymph*. The closest naturally occurring English equivalent (with the exception of the children's expression, 'Nyaah-nyaah') is heard at the boundary between the second and third syllables of the word *opinion* and the two syllables of the word *canyon*.[10] ཉ is this 'n'-'ya' combination said as one sound.

| **Row 3** | ཏ **da** | ཐ **tha** | ད **ta** | ན **na** |
|-----------|----------|-----------|-----------|-----------|

The third set are dentals—produced with the tongue touching the back of the front teeth. The second column **tha** sound is not the **th** sound of the English word *the*—a sound not heard in Tibetan—but more like the **th** combination in the word *boathouse*.

The fourth column is the nasal ང་, the sound heard in the English 'n'. It is pronounced with the tongue at the same position on the teeth as are ད་, ཐ་, and ཏ་. This rule holds for each of the first four rows: each of these rows contains four consonants, all four of which are pronounced with the tongue at the same position in the mouth.

**Row 4**

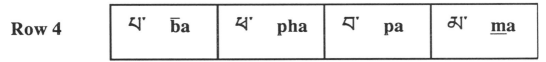

| བ་ b̄a | ཕ་ pha | པ་ pa | མ་ m̲a |
|---|---|---|---|

The fourth set of letters are labials—those made using the lips. The second column sound **pha** is not the **ph** of *phone* but a **p** sound with more aspiration than usual, as in the English *push*. There is no **f** in Tibetan. The **ma** is the same sound heard in the English 'm', for example in *martyr*.

**Row 5**

| ཙ་ d̄za | ཚ་ tsha | ཛ་ d̲za | ཝ་ wa |
|---|---|---|---|

The first three letters of the fifth set (ཙ་, ཚ་, and ཛ་) represent sounds not found in English; they are pronounced with the tip of the tongue touching the hard palate, as are the palatals, but at the same time making a **z** or an **s** sound. These sounds are heard in the English words *pizza* and *grits*.[11]

As before, the second column sound (here **tsha**) is not a soft sound but an aspirated form of the letter it follows. The last letter of the fifth row is like the English 'w' in *word*.

**Row 6**

| ཞ་ s̲ha | ཟ་ s̲a | འ་ a | ཡ་ ya |
|---|---|---|---|

The first two letters of row six (ཞ་ and ཟ་) are low-tone sibilants. (High and low tones will be discussed shortly.) The last two are the short **a** (called the "little a"— ཨ་ཆུང་ )[12] and the first of the series of three semivowels.

These three semivowels—**ya, ra,** and **la**—are pronounced as they are in English.

**Row 7**

| ར་ ra | ལ་ la | ཤ་ śha | ས་ ṣa |
|---|---|---|---|

The first two letters of Row 7 are the remaining two semivowels (ར་ and ལ་). The last two are the high-tone sibilants (ཤ་ and ས་). There is thus a symmetry in rows six and seven in that sibilants begin row six and end row seven, with **a**, **ya**, **ra**, and **la** in the middle.

**Row 8**

| ཧ་ ha | ཨ་ a |
|---|---|

The last row—really only half a row—contains only two letters. The last letter (ཨ་) is the prevalent **a** sound. Some grammarians have treated it as a vowel.[13]

Tibetan grammarians name these rows not by number (as has been done here), but by the letter that begins the row:

1   the **ḡa** row
2   the **j̄a** row
3   the **d̄a** row
4   the **b̄a** row
5   the **dz̄a** row
6   the **sha** row
7   the **ra** row
8   the **ha** row.

Memorize the alphabet (the thirty consonants and four vowels) in Tibetan alphabetical order, by rows.

*Recite it,* paying particular attention to the tones. Oral repetition is extremely important in learning a language, particularly one so different from English.

In the beginning *there is nothing the student is reading or writing that he or she should not speak aloud.* It is very important to establish a coordination between eye, mouth, and mind.

Never confuse the phonemic transcriptions **tha, pha,** and **tsha** for the English sounds 'th' (as in *the*), 'ph' (as in *phone*), and 'sh.'

## Drill 1

Recite the alphabet, row by row, working to build speed while retaining the distinctive pronunciation of each letter.

| | | | | |
|---|---|---|---|---|
| 1 | ཀ་ | ཁ་ | ག་ | ང་ |
| 2 | ཅ་ | ཆ་ | ཇ་ | ཉ་ |
| 3 | ཏ་ | ཐ་ | ད་ | ན་ |
| 4 | པ་ | ཕ་ | བ་ | མ་ |
| 5 | ཙ་ | ཚ་ | ཛ་ | ཝ་ |
| 6 | ཞ་ | ཟ་ | འ་ | ཡ་ |
| 7 | ར་ | ལ་ | ཤ་ | ས་ |
| 8 | ཧ་ | ཨ་ | | |

## *Vocabulary*

Beginning with the next chapter, each chapter will end with a vocabulary which should be memorized before the next chapter is begun. At this point, however, it is more important to memorize the letters of the Tibetan alphabet. Be able to write and speak them in the proper order.

# Chapter 2

*The Four Vowels*
*Modification of Vowel Sounds*

## The Four Vowels

There are four marks that can modify the inherent **a** of any consonant. The four modifications that result are the four vowels. When these vowels are written in the Roman alphabet used in English *without regard to their actual pronunciation* (that is, when they are *transliterated*), they are 'i,' 'u,' 'e,' and 'o'. However, their actual pronunciations are closer to the French pronunciations of these letters than to standard English pronunciation.

- The Tibetan 'i' is pronounced like the 'ee' in *keep*. *Gigu*
- The Tibetan 'u' is pronounced like the 'u' in *tune*. *Shabkyu*
- The Tibetan 'e' is usually pronounced like the 'a' in *fade*. *Drengbu*
- The Tibetan 'o' is pronounced like the 'o' in *bone*. *Naro*

**a**

> The Tibetan 'a' (written ཨ་) is usually pronounced like the 'a' in *farther* or the 'ah' in *shah*. In this book the 'a' sound will consistently be represented with an unadorned **a**.
>
> *Example.* ས་ is pronounced **sa** (and means *earth* and *ground*); ད་ is pronounced **ta** and means *now*. This is the normal vowel sound of a consonant without vowel modification.

In most instances the main or **root letter** of a syllable is pronounced with an **a** sound unless it is modified by one of the four vowel markers. However, Tibetan syllables are usually made up not only of a single consonant and its vowel sound but also of other consonants—called prefixes, superscriptions, subscriptions, and suffixes, depending on their placement in the syllable. (They will be discussed in Chapters Four through Seven.)

When the consonants ད་, ན་, ལ་, and ས་ occur as the final or suffix letter of a syllable, they modify the inherent **a**-vowel.

> When a ད་, ན་, ལ་, or ས་ occurs as a suffix or final letter in a syllable, it modifies the vowel sound of the letter preceding it. These four suffixes narrow the pronunciation of the inherent **a**-vowel of the syllable, causing it to become the vowel sound heard in the English word *edge*. This sound will be represented by an umlaut written over an 'e': **ë**.
>
> *Example.* The syllable ང་ is pronounced **nga**; it is the first person pronoun, meaning *I*. The addition of the consonant ན་ after the ང་ gives us ངན་ (meaning *bad*); however, ངན་ is pronounced not **ngan**, but **ngën**. Likewise, ལ་ (**la**) followed by the consonant ས་ becomes ལས་, pronounced not **las** but **lë** (like the beginning of the word *ledge*). Note that although ས་ as the main letter of a syllable is pronounced **s̄a**, here—as a suffix—it is silent; it merely changes the pronunciation of the vowel and its tone.

The line over the **s** in **s̄a** indicates that this letter has a high tone. This is a function of the consonant and not the vowel.

> A Tibetan letter may be high, medium, or low in tone. Tone is determined by the main *consonant* of a syllable (see Chapter Three), but may be modified by other letters in the syllable (see Chapters Five through Seven).

The second example—ལས་—is a very common word; its main meaning as a noun is *action*, or, in Sanskrit, *karma*.

Other examples of this process are དད་ (**të**), the first syllable of the word དད་པ་, meaning *faith*, and ངལ་ (**ngël**), meaning *fatigue*. In དད་, the first ད is the root letter and the second is the suffix. Similarly, in ངལ་, the ང་ is the root letter and the ལ་ is the suffix.

**í**

The Tibetan 'i' (written ཨི་) is usually pronounced like the 'ee' in *keep* or the 'i' in *machine*. Although many Western scholars use the letter 'i' to indicate the pronunciation of this sound, the average English speaker looks at **i** and thinks of the vowel sound in *bin* or in *fine*. Therefore, in this book, the accented letter **í** indicates the 'ee' sound of the basic Tibetan 'i.'

*Example*. Without vowel modification, མ་ is pronounced **ma**. མི་, on the other hand, is pronounced **mí**; it is a noun meaning *human being*. Notice that the vowel in the example མི་ is a mark written over the consonant མ་. Other examples are ར་ and རི་, ཁ་ and ཁི་, ད་ and དི་, and ཙ་ and ཙི་.

**î**

There is also a soft or short 'i' (see Chapter Six) whose pronunciation is like the 'i' in *bin*; that pronunciation will be represented by a circumflex written over the 'i': **î**. The mouth is held somewhat the same way when pronouncing **a** and **î**.

*Example*. Without vowel modification, ཡ་ is pronounced **ya**; with the 'i' mark it becomes ཡི་ and is pronounced **yí**, rhyming with the English word *me*. Adding a ན་ gives us ཡིན་, which is pronounced **yîn**, rhyming with the English *bin*. ཡིན་ is a verb meaning *is*.

**u**

The Tibetan 'u' (written ཨུ་) is usually pronounced like the 'u' in *tune*. Since this is a not uncommon English pronunciation of 'u,' the Tibetan sound is represented by an unaccented **u**.

Note that, like the **í**, the **u** is indicated in Tibetan by a curve, but this time under the consonant and rotated 180 degrees.

*Example*. Without vowel modification, ས་ is pronounced **s̄a**. However, སུ་ is pronounced **s̄u**—rhyming with *flu*—and means *who*.

The suffixes ད་, ན་, ལ་, and ས་ modify the sound of a preceding **u**. These four suffixes narrow the pronunciation of that vowel, causing it to become similar to the vowel sound heard in the first syllable of the English word *surprise*, but without the 'r.' This sound will be represented by an umlaut written over the 'u': **ü**.

*Example.* The combination of ཀ་ and the vowel གུ་ is pronounced **gu**. The addition of the consonant ན་ as a suffix gives us ཀུན་ (**gün**), a common adjective meaning *all*. Similarly, whereas ཡུ་ is **yu**, ཡུལ་ is **yül**, a noun meaning *region* or *object*.

The Tibetan 'e' (written ཤེ་) is pronounced like the 'a' in *fade*—that is, as what we often call a "long a." Since the English 'e' is not commonly pronounced in this manner (the first e in *melee* being one of the few examples), whereas this is the way in which the French 'é' is pronounced, the Tibetan sound is represented here by an 'e' with an acute accent: **é**.

*Example:* Without vowel modification, ད་ is pronounced **ta**. དེ་, on the other hand, is pronounced **té** (rhyming with *say*); it is an adjective, and sometimes a pronoun, meaning *that*.

In the phonemic system used here, **t** is pronounced like an English 't', but with less aspiration; in Tibetan ད་ is a semi-aspirate consonant. The more aspirate 't' (ཐ་) is shown here as **th**. ད་ is always pronounced with a low tone.

There is also a soft 'e' which is pronounced somewhere between **é** and **î**. Its pronunciation is indicated here by **ê**.

*Example.* སེམས་ is formed by first putting the é-marker ( ˆ ) on the letter ས་, changing the **sa** to **sé**, and then adding the suffix མ་ (pronounced **m**) and the secondary suffix ས་ (which is not pronounced). The combination is pronounced not **sém**, however, but **sêm**. It rhymes more with *hem* than with *same*. སེམས་ means *mind*.

O

The Tibetan 'o' (written ཨོ) is pronounced in Tibetan in the same way as it frequently is in English—like the 'o' in *bone*. For that reason it is represented by an unaccented **o**.

*Example.* Without vowel modification, ར is pronounced **ra**. རོ is pronounced **ro** and is a noun meaning *taste*.

Ö

Just as with **a** and **u**, the suffixes ད, ན, ལ, and ས modify the sound of a preceding **o**. They narrow the vowel, causing it to become the vowel sound of the English word *push*, pronounced with the lips fully rounded. This sound will be represented by an umlaut written over the 'o': **ö**.

*Example.* ཆོས is pronounced not **chos**, but **chö**. (A ས-suffix is always silent.) ཆོས is one of the most important terms in Tibetan literature; it translates the Sanskrit word *dharma* and has the same wide range of meanings as that word; the two most important are *religion* and *phenomenon*. Likewise, where དོ would be pronouned **to**, དོན—a frequently seen noun with many groups of meanings (*meaning*, *purpose*, *object*, etc.)—is pronounced **tön**.

Memorize the four vowels and their unmodified pronunciations:
the basic vowel sound of all consonants is **a**, the vowel in *shah*;
ཨི is **i** and rhymes with *ski*; gigu
ཨུ is **u** and rhymes with *flu*; shabkyu
ཨེ is **é** and rhymes with *day*; Drengbu
ཨོ is **o** and rhymes with *so*. Naro
Memorize the pronunciations of all the phonemic symbols used here:
**a** and **ë**, **i** and **î**, **u** and **ü**, **é** and **ê**, and **o** and **ö**.

## Drill 2

Practice reading and pronouncing letters with vowels. (All of the following are commonly occurring Tibetan syllables or words.)

| | | | | | | |
|---|---|---|---|---|---|---|
| 1 | གི་ | གྷི་ | ཙེ་ | ཇི་ | དྲི་ | མེ་ |
| | ཞི་ | ཨེ་ | རེ་ | ལི་ | ཧི་ | ཥི་ |
| 2 | གུ་ | ཌ་ | ཚུ་ | ཉུ་ | པུ་ | སུ་ |
| | ཝུ་ | ཡུ་ | རུ་ | ཤུ་ | ཧུ་ | |
| 3 | ཙེ་ | ཚེ་ | ཇེ་ | དེ་ | མེ་ |
| | ཞེ་ | ཨེ་ | རེ་ | ཧེ་ |
| 4 | ཁོ་ | གོ་ | ངོ་ | ཙོ་ | ཇོ་ | མོ་ |
| | ཞོ་ | རོ་ | ལོ་ | སོ་ |

---

## *Vocabulary*

---

Now that the alphabet has been memorized, practice reading and speaking these simple words from Chapters One and Two. Memorize them, drilling both from Tibetan to English and English to Tibetan.

| | | |
|---|---|---|
| ང་ | **nga** | I |
| ཆོས་ | **chö**[14] | religion; phenomenon |
| ཇ་ | **cha** | tea |
| དད་པ་ | **të-ba** | faith |
| དེ་ | **té** | that |

| དོན་ | **tön** | meaning, purpose, object |
| མི་ | **mi** | human being |
| ཡིན་ | **yîn** | is  [verb][15] |
| ཡུལ་ | **yül** | region, country, place, object |
| རོ་ | **ro** | taste |
| ལས་ | **lë** | action  (*karma*) |
| སུ་ | **s̄u** | who |
| སེམས་ | **s̄êm** | mind |

# Chapter 3

*The Tibetan Alphabet: Aspiration and Tone*
*Writing Tibetan Letters*

## Aspiration and Tone

In each of the first five rows, there is a repeated pattern of aspiration and tone. (The exception is the ཝ་ [**wa**] at the end of Row 5.)

- Column 1 is high-tone and unaspirated.
- Column 2 is middle-tone and aspirated.
- Column 3 is low-tone and semi-aspirated—with the exception of the Row 5 letter ཛ་ which, in the dialect presented in this book, is not aspirated; it is pronounced **dza**.
- Column 4 consonants are low-tone nasals.

**High-tone Unaspirated**. Taking Row 1 as an illustration of the first five rows, the consonant in column 1 (ཀ་ **ḡa**) is not aspirated in Hla-ša Tibetan (that is, it is a **ga** and not a **ka**) and has a high tone (**ḡa**). High tone means that the sound is pitched higher than normal—pronounced high in the throat and somewhat more sharply than lower tones. The high tone is represented in English phoneticization by a macron (the line over the **g** in **ḡa**).

**Middle-Tone Aspirated**. The consonant in the second column (ཁ་ **kha**) is closer in tone to the high tones of column 1 than to the low tones of column 3. It is of the same family of sounds as the consonants in this row—the letters in the first row, remember, are all gutturals—but unlike its cousin of column 3 it is fully aspirated;

when it is spoken, one can feel a puff of breath if the hand is held close to the mouth.

**Low-Tone <u>Semi-Aspirated</u>**. The consonant in the third column (ཀ **ka**) is semi-aspirate and of low tone; it is pronounced somewhat more softly than its counterpart in column 2 and farther down in the throat. The pronunciations of low tone consonants are not usually marked. However, three of the semi-aspirate consonants (ཀ **ka**, ཏ **ta**, and པ **pa**) occur *only* as low tones. Their fully aspirate cousins (ཁ **kha**, ཐ **tha**, and ཕ **pha**) occur *only* as middle tones. Neither group is ever pronounced with high tone. In those cases where confusion is possible an underline has been added to show lowness of tone: where ཚ (**cha**) is middle-tone and aspirated, ཆ (**<u>cha</u>**) is low-tone and semi-aspirate; where ཛ (**<u>dza</u>**) is high-tone, ཇ (**<u>dza</u>**) is low-tone.

As will be seen in Chapter Six, the first four Column 3 consonants (ཀ, ཇ, ཏ, and པ) do sometimes lose their aspiration. They are then pronounced **ga**, **ja**, **da**, and **ba**, respectively.

> The phonemic transcriptions **ga**, **ja**, **da**, and **ba** are always to be pronounced with low tone. When they represent the high-tone sounds of Column 1 consonants (ཀ, ཙ, ཏ, and པ) they will be written with macrons: **ḡa**, **j̄a**, **d̄a**, and **b̄a**.

**Low-Tone <u>Nasal</u>**. The first four Column 4 consonants (ང **nga**, ཉ **nya**, ན **na**, མ **ma**) are the nasal forms of the consonants of their respective rows. Thus, the nasal ending the **ḡa**-row is the guttural nasal **nga**. Like the first four Column 3 consonants, they are low in tone.

**Note**: you will see that in certain contexts the semi-aspirate consonants of column 3 can lose their aspiration and the low tone nasals can become high-tone.

The English equivalents on page 4 are phonemic equivalents and represent only the pronunciations of the letters when they are found by themselves. *Phonemic* equivalents should not be confused with the *transliteration* of Tibetan, a one-to-one substitution of English letters for Tibetan in which each Tibetan letter—whether or not it is pronounced—is represented by a letter of the Roman alphabet. This holds true for all transliteration schemes: the system formulated by René de Nebesky-Wojkowitz,[16] the one used by Turrell Wylie at the University of Washington,[17] the modification of the Wylie system by Jeffrey Hopkins that is used at the University of Virginia (and in this book),[18] or one of the European systems. Transliteration uses English "equivalents" that are related to, but different from, pronunciation—particularly in regard to the first column consonants. Thus, the phonemic equivalents shown on page 4 must be distinguished from such schemes of transliteration.[19]

> Memorize the pattern of aspiration and tone in the first five rows.
> Know which column of letters is high tone, which is middle, and which is low.
> Know which column is naturally unaspirated, which is aspirated, and which is semi-aspirate.
> Know which sibilants are high tone and which are low tone.

## Drill 3.1

Recite the following, working to build speed while retaining the distinctive pronunciation of each letter. The letters in lines 1 to 4 are similar in aspiration and tone to the other letters in their own line. Lines 5 through 11 are designed for the practice of alternation between different tones and aspirations.

| | | | | | | | |
|---|---|---|---|---|---|---|---|
| 1 | ཀ་ | ཙ་ | ཏ་ | པ་ | ཙ་ | | |
| 2 | ཁ་ | ཚ་ | ཐ་ | ཕ་ | ཚ་ | | |
| 3 | ག་ | ཇ་ | ད་ | བ་ | ཛ་ | | |
| 4 | ང་ | ཉ་ | ན་ | མ་ | | | |
| 5 | ཀ་ | ག་ | ཀ་ | ག་ | ཁ་ | ག་ | ཁ་ |

| | | | | | | | |
|---|---|---|---|---|---|---|---|
| 6 | ཙ' | ཇ' | ཙ' | ཇ' | ཚ' | ཇ' | ཚ' |
| 7 | ཏ' | ད' | ཏ' | ད' | ཐ' | ད' | ཐ' |
| 8 | པ' | བ' | པ' | བ' | ཕ' | བ' | ཕ' |
| 9 | ཛ' | ཇ' | ཛ' | ཇ' | ཚ' | ཇ' | ཚ' |
| 10 | ཞ' | ཤ' | ཞ' | ཤ' | ཟ' | ས' | ཟ' |
| 11 | ཤ' | ཟ' | ས' | ཞ' | ས' | ཤ' | ཞ' |

## Writing Tibetan

There are several ways in which to write the alphabet in Tibetan: a printed style, called **ū-jen** (དབུ་ཅན་) or "headed," and several forms of cursive. This book will confine itself to the ū-jen style.

Tibetan letters are written as if they *hang* from imaginary horizontal lines running across the page; this, of course, is just the reverse of the Roman alphabet used in English and European languages where the *bases* of most letters begin on the same line. With few exceptions, Tibetan letters incorporate pieces of this imaginary line from which they hang. All four letters in Row 1 (the **ḡa** row), for example, have a horizontal line at the top:

ཀ'   ཁ'   ག'   ང'

In Row 4 (the **b̄a** row), the line is somewhat abbreviated, or broken, but is still present:

པ'   ཕ'   བ'   མ'

The only things that are written above the line in Tibetan are the "flags" on the **d̄za**, **tsha**, and **dza**, and the marks indicating the vowels **í**, **é**, and **o**:

When writing Tibetan letters, one begins with the top line (that piece of the imaginary horizontal line from which they hang). This top line (which may be quite small, or even curved) is drawn from *left to right*. Then, beginning with the vertical line farthest to the left, the vertical lines are drawn in from *top to bottom*. The first and third letters are formed like this:[20]

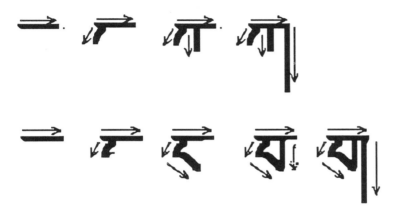

The general rule is that *the writing implement should not travel upwards.*

However, exceptions are made in the cases of the looped letters— ཏ་, ཆ་, ན་, མ་, ཙ་, ཚ་, ཤ་, and ཕ་. The loops are formed with a continuous motion, part of which moves upward.

The letters ༩་, ༴་, ༠་, ༑་ incorporate curves, but are not full loops. They should be written with downward strokes. This may be done by breaking the curves into parts.

## Drill 3.2

Write out the alphabet in Tibetan along with the phonetic equivalent of each consonant and vowel.

## Review of Phonemics

The Tibetan vowel sounds introduced so far are as follows:

- **a**     the vowel sound in the first syllable of *farther*, corresponding to the Tibetan ཨ;

- **ë**     the vowel sound in *edge*, as heard in ངན and ལས;

- **é**     the vowel sound in *say*, corresponding to the Tibetan ཨེ;

- **ê**     a sound between the vowels in *same* and *set*, as in སེམས;

- **í**     the vowel sound in *keep*, corresponding to the Tibetan ཨི;

- **î**     the vowel sound in *bin*, heard in the Tibetan ཡིན;

- **o**     the vowel sound in *boat*, corresponding to the Tibetan ཨོ;

- **ö**     like the vowel sound in the first syllable of *surprise* pronounced with pursed lips—as heard in དོན;

- **u**     the vowel sound in *tune*, corresponding to the Tibetan ཨུ;

- **ü**     like the vowel sound in *push* pronounced with pursed lips—as heard in ཚུལ.

The following are phonemic transcriptions of Tibetan consonants where differences in tone are potentially confusing:

whereas **b̄a** is pronounced with a high tone, **ba** has a low tone;

whereas **cha** is pronounced with a middle tone, **c̲ha** has a low tone;

whereas **d̄a** is pronounced with a high tone, **da** has a low tone;

whereas **ḡa** is pronounced with a high tone, **ga** has a low tone;

whereas **j̄a** is pronounced with a high tone, **ja** has a low tone;

**ka** is pronounced with a low tone;

**kha** is pronounced with a middle tone;

**pa** is pronounced with a low tone;

**pha** is pronounced with a middle tone and is not the English 'ph' in *phone*;

whereas **s̄a** is pronounced with a high tone, **s̲a** has a low tone;

whereas **s̄ha** is pronounced with a high tone, **s̲ha** has a low tone;

**ta** is pronounced with a low tone;

**tha** is pronounced with a middle tone and is not the 'th' in the English *the*.

---

In summary, when **b**, **d**, **g**, **j**, **k**, **p**, and **t** are seen with no diacritical marks, they are to be pronounced with a low tone. When the nasals—**ng**, **ny**, **n**, and **m**—are seen with no diacritics, they are pronounced with a low tone.

---

# *Vocabulary*

Practice reading and speaking these simple words. Memorize them, drilling both from Tibetan to English and English to Tibetan.

| | | |
|---|---|---|
| གཁ་ | **ḡa-kha** | alphabet |
| ཁ་ | **kha** | mouth |
| ཁོ་ | **kho** | he, it |
| ངན་པ་ | **ngën-b̄a** | bad |
| ཆུ་ | **chu** | water |
| འཆི་ | **chí** | die [verb] |
| ད་ | **ta** | now |

| བུ་ | **pu** | son |
| བུ་མོ་ | **pu-mo** | daughter |
| མེ་ | **mé** | fire |
| རི་ | **rí** | mountain |
| ས་ | **s̄a** | earth, ground, stage |
| ཨ་ལི་ཀ་ལི་ | **a-lí-ḡa-lí** | alphabet |

# *Chapter 4*

## *The Root Letter*
## *The Functions of Letters in Syllables*

## Words and Syllables

Some English words have only one syllable, but many have more. When English is taught, one begins with words and then, later on, turns to syllables. Moreover, in English, the division between syllables in a word is determined by the application of rules and is sometimes not at all obvious. In Tibetan, on the other hand, there is no difficulty in distinguishing syllables from one another because they are separated by dots; the difficulty for beginners lies in determining where one word ends and another begins. However, with practice and the internalization of certain rules, this will become second nature.

Because it is obvious where a Tibetan syllable begins and ends, and not so obvious where Tibetan words begin and end, we will begin with syllables.

## Syllables without Silent Letters

Most Tibetan syllables include letters that are not themselves pronounced (although, as will be seen below, they may modify the pronunciation of other letters). Setting aside spelling for the time being, in terms of *pronunciation* a typical simple Tibetan syllable has three parts:

1   an initial consonant;
2   one vowel sound;
3   an optional closing consonant (the suffix).

Here are examples of some very simple syllables—ones without silent letters—
where pronunciation follows spelling very closely.

| དུང་ | tung | མར་ | mar | བུམ་ | pum |
|---|---|---|---|---|---|

དུང་ means *conch*—the beginning of the study of philosophy in the Gé-luk-b̄a Order
uses *the color of a white religious conch*[21] as the first subject. མར་ means *butter*;
and བུམ་ is the first syllable of བུམ་པ་ (**pum-b̄a**) which means *pot*—another important
subject used in the study of philosophy in Tibetan.

> Remember that the vowel sounds in བུམ་ and དུང་ are like those in *moon* and
> *tune*.

Not all syllables end in a closing consonant:

| ཁ་ | kha | རོ་ | ro | སུ་ | s̄u |
|---|---|---|---|---|---|

ཁ་ means *mouth*; རོ་ means *taste* and *corpse*; སུ་ means *who*, and is also a "case
marking particle."  Tibetan case marking particles function similarly to English
prepositions in that they show how nouns and pronouns function in the sentences
and clauses in which they are found (see Chapter Ten).  Thus, here སུ་ means *at*, *to*,
*for*, and so on.

There are also some instances of syllables whose initial sound is a vowel:

| འུག་ | uk (ook) | འང་ | ang |
|---|---|---|---|

An འུག་པ་ (**uk-b̄a**) is an *owl*.  འང་ means *also*, *even*, and *but*.

And there are a few cases of syllables with two distinct vowels:

| ལེའུ་ | **lé-u (lay-oo)** | chapter |
|---|---|---|

Note that here each vowel is pronounced with its full value; they do not combine to make a new sound. By way of contrast, when the vowel འི་ is attached to a syllable without a suffix, a new sound *is* formed. In this example the combination of **a** and **í** forms the sound **ë** (the initial sound in *edge*):

| | | |
|---|---|---|
| བུམ་པའི་ | **pum-bë** | of the pot |

In English, the division of a word into syllables is not indicated in writing except in cases where a word is hyphenated at the end of a line. English *words*, however, are either separated from other words by a space or followed immediately by punctuation. In Tibetan, on the other hand, *syllables* are separated from one another by terminating dots (called ཚེག་ **tshék**—rhymes with shake). These dots are small pieces of that imaginary horizontal line at the top of the letters:

| | |
|---|---|
| བུམ་པ་མི་རྟག་པ་ཡིན། | **pum-b̄a  mí-d̄ak-b̄a  yȋn** |

The རྟ་ in མི་རྟག་པ་ is not one letter but two: a small, truncated ར་ written with a ཏ་ beneath it.

---

There are three letters that may be **superscribed** to other letters: ར་, ལ་, and ས་. (See Chapter Six.) A ར་ superscribed to the root letter ཏ་, for example, looks like རྟ་, means *horse*, and is pronounced **d̄a**. Note that only the top part of the ར་ is superscribed to the ཏ་. This example demonstrates that the root or main letter of the syllable does not have to be a letter whose top is part of the imaginary top line; here it is the superscribed ར་ whose top is on that line: ཏ་`````རྟ་.

---

In the example བུམ་པ་མི་རྟག་པ་ཡིན།, although there are six syllables, there are three words—a noun, an adjective, and a verb. The first word is བུམ་པ་ (**pum-b̄a**), meaning *pot*. The second word is མི་རྟག་པ་ (**mí-d̄ak-b̄a**), meaning *impermanent*. The third and final word in this sentence is ཡིན་, a verb meaning *be*. The most general translation of this sentence would thus be *Pots are impermanent*. Note that half of the dots in the sentence follow words, but half are only between the syllables within those words.  The dots that merely separate syllables are shown here with an S written above them.  (Dots are treated in more detail in Chapter Ten.)

---

| | |
|---|---|
| S    S  S    བུམ་པ་ མི་རྟག་པ་ ཡིན། | POTS IMPERMANENT ARE. <br> Pots are impermanent. |

---

The last "dot" in the sentence is not a dot at all but a ཤད་ (shë).  A ཤད་ is a vertical line ( | ) used to end a sentence, a clause, a line of poetry, or—in some cases—even a single word.  It's use varies according to context.  A single ཤད་ is used before and after a line of poetry, and after a sentence.  A double ཤད་ ( ‖ ) is used only after a complete sentence.

## The Root Letter

At the core of the Tibetan syllable is its **root letter**.  The root letter is the main letter of a syllable, and any of the thirty consonants may be a root letter.  Root letters occur in six contexts.

1    In syllables that have only one letter, with no vowel marker, the root letter occurs *by itself* (with its natural **a** sound as the vowel).
     An example is the syllable ད་ (**ta**), which means *now*.

2    A root letter may have a *vowel marker*.
     In the case of the root letter ས་ (**sa**), vowel markers change it into syllables such as སི་ (**si**), སོ་ (**so**), and སུ་ (**su**).

3    A root letter may be *preceded by one of five possible prefix* letters.
     An example is the word མཐུ་ (**thu**, *power*); its root letter is ཐ་ and its prefix letter is མ་.  Since the prefixed letters are always silent, it is pronounced **thu**—that is, like the English word *too* with an aspirated 't'—and not **m'thu** or **mathu**.

> Recall that the 'th' of **thu** is that heard in *boathouse* and is not the 'th' in *the*.

4    A root letter may be *topped by one of three possible superscripts*; like the prefixes, the superscribed letters are not pronounced.

An example is the word མི་རྟག་པ་ (**mí-d̄ak-b̄a**), meaning *impermanent*.

5    A root letter may be *subjoined with* (that is, it may have hanging underneath it) *one of four possible subscribed letters*. These subscripts usually affect the pronunciation of the root letter in a radical way.

An example is the word ཟླ་, composed of the subscript ལ་ hanging beneath the root letter ཟ་. Although ཟ་ is, by itself, pronounced <u>s</u>a, when it is written with a ལ་ underneath it, it becomes ཟླ་ (meaning *moon*)[22] and is pronounced **da** (that is, 'da' with a low tone).

6    A root letter may be *followed by one of the ten suffixes*, some of which are pronounced and some of which change the pronunciation of the root letter's vowel.

The root letter ད་ followed by the suffix ང་ makes དང་, meaning *and* or *or* and pronounced **tang** (with a low tone). The root letter ཆ་ (**cha**) modified by the vowel marker ˘ becomes ཆོ་ (**cho**); with a ས་ suffix it becomes ཆོས་ and is pronounced **chö**.

Suffixes will be explained in Chapter Five, the prefixes and superscripts in Chapter Six, and the subscripts in Chapter Seven.

## The Functions of Letters

Anything in Tibetan followed by a dot is a **syllable**. (Words are sometimes only one syllable long, but typically are longer.) In the smallest instance, a syllable may be only a single letter; in the largest, it may be composed of six consonants and a vowel modifying mark. An example of the smallest type of syllable, one that is also an example of the smallest possible word, is ད་ (**ta**, meaning *now*). An example of the longest type of syllable is the following word:

| བསྒྲུབས་ | **ḍup** | established [past tense verb] |

བསྒྲུབས་ is the past tense form of the verb meaning *prove [a thesis]* and *establish.*

The **ḍ** represents a 'd' pronounced with the tongue curled back, a sound in between an English 'd' and a 'dr.'

The most important letter of a Tibetan syllable is the root letter. In the first example (the word ད་), the root letter is the ད་. In the second example ( བསྒྲུབས་ ), the root letter is the ག་. The root letter is the initial *spoken* sound of the syllable and is the letter under which you would seek a word in a dictionary. The word བསྒྲུབས་ (or a word beginning with that syllable) would be found not under བ་ but under ག་.

The word བསྒྲུབས་ demonstrates the seven possible functions of Tibetan letters in a syllable. A letter in a syllable is either:

1     a root letter

2     a vowel marker

3     a prefix

4     a superscribed letter

5     a subscribed letter

6     a suffix

7     a secondary suffix.

Let us unpack this somewhat involved syllable. (The numbers in the diagram on the next page refer to the description of the construction of the syllable and the pronunciation changes that occur as each part is added.)

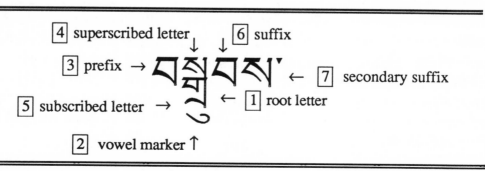

Functions of Letters

1    Any consonant can be a root letter. Here ཀ is the root letter.

2    The inherent **a** sound of the consonant is modified by a vowel marker, and thus ཀ **ka** becomes ཀུ **ku**.

3    The prefix བ is not itself pronounced but does alter the pronunciation of the root letter ཀ. བཀུ is pronounced not **ku** but **gu**.

4    The superscribed ས is not pronounced and in this word does not further alter the pronunciation of the root letter. བསྐུ remains **gu**.

5    The subscribed ར turns the བསྐུ into a བསྐྲུ and changes its pronunciation radically—from **gu** to **ḍu**. In Tibetan, a subscribed letter is called a "hanging" letter. ར, when it is a subscript, is written ྲ.

6    The suffix བ changes the **ḍu** into བསྐྲུབ **ḍup**.

7    The secondary suffix ས is not pronounced. Secondary suffixes are never pronounced in Hla-ŝa Tibetan, nor do they affect the pronunciation of other letters in a syllable.

You are already able to read syllables consisting of a root letter and vowel marker. Nearly as simple are syllables made of root letters followed by a suffix or a suffix and a secondary suffix. They are treated in Chapter Five. In Chapter Six the letters that precede the root letter—the superscribed letters and prefixes—are discussed. In Chapter Seven, subscribed letters are examined and the rules for determining the root letter in any syllable are set forth.

## Doctrinal Vocabulary and Grammar
### *Introduction*

In order to understand the essentials of the Tibetan language it is necessary to understand the rules of Tibetan grammar and syntax and at least a basic Tibetan vocabulary. Much of the material in this book is devoted to just that. However, a knowledge of Tibetan language alone is not enough to enable a person to read the philosophical and religious literature of Tibetan Buddhism.[23] There are other highly important elements:

1    knowledge of the technical vocabulary of the particular subject about which one is reading;

2    knowledge of the basic assumptions made in a particular subject and the basic definitions in that area of study—things that an author will assume a reader knows without being told;

3    in the case of much philosophical writing in Tibetan, specialized knowledge of the rules of logic that underlie the assertions being made;

4    knowledge of the abbreviated types of sentence structure used to present logical statements in philosophical writing (and of the different type of abbreviated writing used in different genres, for example, meditation instructions);

5    knowledge of the cultural and historical tradition within which a book is written.

This book seeks to present at least an introduction to the first four. The fifth is outside the scope of an introductory treatment such as this.

It would not be impossible for intelligent people who knew only the Tibetan alphabet and a few rules of grammar to be able to read a book written in clear and brief Tibetan sentences, providing they had dictionaries, a great deal of time, and endless patience. They could puzzle out the mechanics of the Tibetan sentences and hope that the vocabulary provided in the available dictionaries was adequate for the subject at hand.[24] Similarly, it is not impossible for someone who is not a Tibetan, but has a knowledge of Tibetan, to pick up a Tibetan book on Buddhist philosophy or a commentary on one of the basic Indian texts and, with diligent study and detective work, piece together at least part of the author's meaning.

Unlike most Western works, however, Tibetan books are not written to be accessible to every educated person. They are often much briefer than clear comprehension would call for, and they make constant use of abbreviations, both in vocabulary and sentence structure. The reason for this is that they are written not for beginners, but as scripts for oral instruction. Beginning with Chapter Eight, every chapter will have some material that introduces the technical vocabularies of focal areas of study within Tibetan Buddhist traditions. Later chapters will present the basic rules of Buddhist logic, rules that are taken for granted in most philosophical literature.

# *Vocabulary*

Memorize the spellings, pronunciations, and meanings of these basic words. Practice speaking them.

| | | |
|---|---|---|
| མཐུ་ | **thu** | power |
| རྟ་ | **d̄a** | horse |
| རྟག་པ་ | **d̄ak-b̄a** | permanent |
| དང་ | **tang** | and, or |
| དུང་ | **tung** | conch shell |
| བུམ་པ་ | **pum-b̄a**[25] | pot |
| ཞེམ་པོ་ | **pem-b̄o** | [physical] matter |
| མར་ | **mar** | butter |
| མར་མེ་ | **mar-mé** | butter lamp |
| མི་རྟག་པ་ | **mí-d̄ak-b̄a** | impermanent |
| ཟླ་བ་ | **da-wa** | moon |

བ་, as the final syllable of a word, is pronounced **wa**. Thus, ཟླ་བ་ is **da-wa**.

| | | |
|---|---|---|
| ཡོད་པ་ | **yö'-b̄a** | existent |

An **o** followed by the suffix letter ད་ is pronounced **ö'**—where **ö** is near to the vowel sound in the English word *push* and **'** indicates that the vowel sound is cut off. This rule will be explained in Chapter Five.

| | | |
|---|---|---|
| ལེའུ་ | **lé-u** | chapter |

# Chapter 5

*Suffixes and Secondary Suffixes*
*Levels of Analysis*

## Introduction and Review

We have seen that it is easy to identify syllables in Tibetan; you need not even know the language. What takes some experience is identifying words—determining where one word (or particle) ends and another begins. This will be explained beginning in Chapter Nine. However, it is necessary first to be able to read Tibetan, and to that end you must become familiar with the positions in which letters can occur within a syllable. A letter in a Tibetan syllable is either:

1  a root letter,
2  a vowel or vowel marker,
3  a prefix,
4  a superscribed letter,
5  a subscribed letter,
6  a suffix, or
7  a secondary suffix.

It is very frequently the case that a Tibetan syllable consists of a root letter with some *combination* of vowel marker, prefix, superscript, subscript, and suffix letter.

> Remember that while any letter may be a root letter, only four of the letters are vowels, and only certain consonants may function in the other positions.

Only ག, ད, བ, མ, and འ may serve as prefixes.
Only the letters ར, ལ, and ས may be superscribed.
The letters ག, ང, ད, ན, བ, མ, འ, ར, ལ, and ས are the only suffixes.
Only ད and ས may function as secondary suffixes.
Only ཡ, ར, ལ, and ཝ may be subscribed letters.

An example of the most complex type of Tibetan syllable was presented in Chapter Four, one with letters functioning in each of the seven possible ways. Fortunately, the more complex a syllable is, the easier it is to identify the root letter and to pronounce the syllable.

The letters that may follow the root letter—the four subscribed letters (ཡ, ར, ལ, and ཝ), the ten suffixes (ག, ང, ད, ན, བ, མ, འ, ར, ལ, and ས), and the two secondary suffixes (ད and ས)—are more important for pronunciation than the ones that precede the root letter. Whereas the letters that precede the root letter—the prefixes and superscripts—are almost never pronounced themselves, but affect only the aspiration or tone of the root letter,[26] the letters that follow the root letter—the subscribed letters and suffixes—have a much greater affect on pronunciation.

## The Ten Suffixes

Only ten letters may be suffixes:

- the five possible prefixes—ག, ད, བ, མ, and འ
- the three possible superscripts—ར, ལ, and ས
- the nasals of Rows 1 and 3—ང and ན.

Described another way, the ten suffixes are the last two letters of Rows 1, 3, and 4, and the letters འ, ར, ལ, and ས:

ག   ང   ད   ན   བ   མ   འ   ར   ལ   ས

Suffixes are usually pronounced, either as vowel modifications, as terminating sounds at the end of syllables, or as both.

## *Pronunciation Changes due to Suffixes*

Six of the ten suffixes are pronounced as would be expected. Using the root letter ཚ་ as an example, we have the following.

| ཚག་ | chak | ཚང་ | chang | ཚབ་ | chap |
|---|---|---|---|---|---|
| ཚམ་ | cham | འཚའ་ | cha | ཚར་ | char |

The initial འ in the example འཚའ་ is an unpronounced prefix letter.

In these six examples the root letter and its vowel remain unchanged, with the suffix merely adding its own sound after the vowel. It should be kept in mind that unlike the sound of the root letter, *a suffix has no inherent vowel sound.* Thus ཚར་ is pronounced **char** and not **chara**.

Here are some frequently seen words incorporating syllables consisting merely of a root letter, a vowel, and the suffix ག་.

| ནག་པོ་ | **nak-b̄o** | black |
|---|---|---|
| ལག་པ་ | **lak-b̄a** | hand |
| མིག་ | **mík** | eye |
| ཚིག་ | **tshík** | word |

The suffix ག་ sometimes transforms the Tibetan í into an î. (Whereas í represents the vowel sound in *seen*, î is the vowel in *bin*.)

Here are some useful words incorporating syllables with a ང་ suffix.

| མང་པོ་ | **mang-b̄o** | many |
|---|---|---|
| དང་ | **tang** | and |
| ཚང་མ་ | **tshang-ma** | all |
| མིང་ | **míng** | name |

| ཞིང་ | **shíng** | field |
|---|---|---|

The following are examples of words in which the suffix letter བ occurs.

| ཟབ་མོ་ | **sap-mo** | profound |
|---|---|---|
| ཡབ་ | **yap** | father [honorific form] |
| ཞིབ་མོ་ | **shíp-mo** | subtle |
| ནུབ་ | **nup** | west; disappear [as verb] |

Here are some useful words incorporating syllables ending in the suffix མ.

| བུམ་པ་ | **pum-b̄a** | pot |
|---|---|---|
| ཡུམ་ | **yum** | mother [honorific form] |
| ལམ་ | **lam** | path |
| རིམ་པ་ | **rîm-b̄a** | stage |
| ཚམ་ | **d̄zam** | mere, only |

Note that རིམ་ is not pronounced **rím** (which would rhyme with *seem*), but **rîm**, the vowel being that heard in the English word *him*. This follows the general rule seen with the other nasal suffix— ན་ —when it follows the vowel *i*.

---

The suffixes ན་ and མ་ regularly change an **í** into an **î**.

---

ཡབ་ in the previous group of examples and ཡུམ་ in the present group are honorific words. Honorifics will be introduced in the next chapter. For the time being, understand that whereas མ་ and ཡུམ་ both mean *mother*, the use of the honorific ཡུམ་ implies an attitude of respect towards the referent of the word.

There are no prefixless syllables ending in the suffix འ.

Here are some useful words incorporating the suffix ར.

| | | |
|---|---|---|
| མར་མེ་ | **mar-mé** | butter lamp |
| བར་མ་ | **par-ma** | intermediate |
| ཤར་ | **s̄har** | east; appear [as verb] |
| ཚོར་བ་ | **tshor-wa** | feeling |

བ as a final syllable is pronounced **wa** (as in **tshor-wa**).

The remaining four suffixes (ད, ན, ལ, and ས) change the sounds of the vowels they follow in regular manners.

- The ཨ inherent in every letter becomes **ë** (similar to the vowel in *edge*).
- The ཨོ becomes **ö** (the vowel sound in *push* pronounced with the lips fully rounded).
- The ཀུ becomes **ü**—the closest English sound is the vowel sound in the first syllable of *surprise*, but without the 'r.'
- The ཨི and ཨེ remain the same—**í** and **é**, respectively—except when followed by a ན.[27]

Two of these four— ད and ས —are not pronounced themselves, but they do affect the sound of the vowels they follow as described above. In addition to changing the pronunciation of the vowel it follows, ད brings about a glottal stop—a sharp cut-off of the sound of the vowel (shown in this book by an apostrophe):

| ཆད | chë' | ཆིད | chí' | ཆུད | chü' | ཆེད | ché' | ཆོད | chö' |
|---|---|---|---|---|---|---|---|---|---|

Here are some examples of useful words illustrating pronunciation changes due to the ད suffix.

| | | |
|---|---|---|
| དད་པ་ | **të'-b̄a** | faith |

| ཡིད་ | yí' | mind, intellect |
| ཡུད་ཙམ་ | yü'-dzam | an instant |
| མེད་པ་ | mé'-ba | nonexistent |
| བོད་ | pö' | Tibet |

In addition to altering the sounds of the vowels it follows, a ས་ suffix brings about a gradual fall-off in the tone of the vowel (shown by the symbol >):

| ཆས་ chë> | ཆིས་ chí> | ཆུས་ chü> | ཆེས་ ché> | ཆོས་ chö> |

Here are some words illustrating pronunciation changes due to the ས་ suffix.

| ལས་ | lë> | action, deed [Sanskrit *karma*] |
| རིས་མེད་ | rí>-mé' | impartial, nonsectarian |
| དུས་ | tü> | time |
| ཤེས་པ་ | shé>-ba | knowledge, perception |
| ཤེས་རབ་ | shé>-rap | wisdom [Sanskrit *prajñā*] |
| ཆོས་ | chö> | [Sanskrit *dharma*] |

The last example— ཆོས་ —for which no translation is given, is one of the richest terms in Buddhist Tibetan. It means the *doctrine* taught by Buddha, as well as the practice of that doctrine.[28] Another basic sense of ཆོས་ is *phenomenon* in the sense of 'something that exists.'

> The colloquial English usage of *phenomenon* (and *phenomenal*) in which the reference is to something unusual or extraordinary is not the one being invoked here. Phenomena are merely things that exist.

ད་ and ལ་, in addition to changing the pronunciation of the vowels they follow, are pronounced themselves.  ལ་ transforms the vowels in the same way as ད་ and ས་:

| ཆལ་ chël | ཆིལ་ chíl | ཆུལ་ chül | ཆེལ་ chél | ཆོལ་ chöl |
|---|---|---|---|---|

Here are some words illustrating pronunciation changes due to the ལ་ suffix.

Note, in the first example, that the prefix letter འ་ causes the root letter ག་ to lose its aspiration.

| འགལ་བ་ | **gël-wa** | mutually exclusive |
|---|---|---|
| ཡུལ་ | **yül** | place, region, object |
| སེལ་ | **sél** | purify, eradicate  [verb] |
| འཚོལ་ | **tshöl** | seek  [verb] |

ན་ differs from the other suffixes in that it alters not only the sounds of the vowels ཤ་ (a), ཁོ་ (o), and ཤུ་ (u) but also the sounds of the other two vowels, making them softer:

| ཆན་ chën | ཆིན་ chîn | ཆུན་ chün | ཆེན་ chên | ཆོན་ chön |
|---|---|---|---|---|

Thus, the copula ཡིན་ is not pronounced **yín** (which would rhyme with *seen*), but **yîn**, rhyming with the English word *bin*.  The word ཆེན་པོ་ (*large, great*) is not **chén-bo** (where ཆེན་ would would rhyme with *rain*) but rather **chên-bo** (closer to the vowel sound in the English word *den*).  Here are some additional examples.

| ཕན་པ་ | **phën-ba** | benefit, help |
|---|---|---|
| ཡིན་ | **yîn** | is  [verb] |
| ཀུན་ | **gün** | all |
| ཆེན་པོ་ | **chên-bo** | large, great |
| དོན་ | **tön** | meaning, aim, object |

## Secondary Suffixes

Only two letters may serve as secondary suffixes: ས and ད. Secondary suffixes do not occur by themselves but, when they do occur, follow the normal suffixes just discussed. They are never pronounced.

| སངས་ | s̄ang | ཞེནད་ | shên |
|---|---|---|---|

སངས་ is a verb meaning *wake up*. The first ས is the root letter; the ང—even though it is in the middle of the syllable—is a suffix; and the final ས is a secondary suffix.

ཞེནད་ (more often seen spelt ཞེན་) is the past tense of a verb meaning *be attached* and *crave*. The root letter is ཞ, ན is the suffix, and ད is the secondary suffix. Note that it is obvious that the ཞ is the root letter because it has a vowel; only root letters have vowels.

Although ས as a secondary suffix is fairly common, the secondary suffix ད is used mainly in works on grammar and lexicography, where it occurs in the past tenses of some verbs. Here are some examples of secondary suffixes.

| རིགས་ | rík | type, lineage |
|---|---|---|
| ཐབས་ | thap | method, means |
| ཐམས་ཅད་ | tham-jë' | all |
| ལུགས་ | luk | way, system |
| ཁམས་ | kham | realm, element, constituent |

# Drill 5

Pronounce the following syllables. Write out their pronunciation.

1   དག་      དོག་      ཞུགས་      རིག་

2   དང་      དུང་      སོང་

| 3 | དུད་ | ཆེད་ | རེད་ | ཟད་ | | |
|---|---|---|---|---|---|---|
| 4 | ཅུད་ | སིད་ | ཁོར་ | | | |
| 5 | མན་ | མིན་ | སུན་ | ཕོམ་ | ལིན་ | བོན་ |
| 6 | ཟབ་ | རིབ་ | ཏོབ་ | ཐུན་ | | |
| 7 | དམ་ | དོམ་ | དུམ་ | འབའ་ | འབད་ | |
| 8 | ཚར་ | ཚོར་ | གུར་ | ཁིལ་ | | |
| 9 | དུལ་ | ཁིལ་ | དུལ་ | ཐེལ་ | གོལ་ | |
| 10 | རས་ | ཀིས་ | གིས་ | དུས་ | ཆེས་ | ཚོས་ |

Practice pronunciation changes with ད་, ན་, ལ་, and ས་. Write out the pronunciations, showing glottal stops (') and falling tones (>).

| 11 | ཆ་ | ཆད་ | ཆན་ | ཆལ་ | ཆས་ |
|---|---|---|---|---|---|
| 12 | དུ་ | དུད་ | དུན་ | དུལ་ | དུས་ |
| 13 | གོ་ | གོད་ | གོན་ | གོལ་ | གོས་ |
| 14 | རེ་ | རེད་ | རེན་ | རེལ་ | རེས་ |

---

## Final Syllables

Many—if not most—nouns and adjectives in Tibetan end in simple syllables such as པ་ or བ་. These word-ending syllables are sometimes called 'nominalizing syllables.' This is because, as will be seen later, they may be added to verbs to make nouns.

For example, where འཆི་ (chí) is a verb meaning *die*, འཆི་བ་ (chí-wa) is a noun meaning *death*; where ཡིན་ (yîn) means *is*, ཡིན་པ་ (yîn-ba) means *being*.

However, since it is misleading to think that *any* Tibetan word ending in པ or a similar syllable is a case of a verb made into a noun or an adjective, the term 'nominalizer' will not be used here.

The full set of **final syllables** is comprised of three pairs of related endings: པ and པོ, བ and བོ, and མ and མོ. Not all nouns and adjectives end in one or another of these six, nor are the six interchangeable. However, most instances of one, two, or three syllables followed by one of these final syllables are nouns or adjectives.[29]

> A string of syllables ending in one of the following six syllables is a word, and most likely a noun or an adjective: པ, པོ, བ, བོ, མ, or མོ. As a final syllable, བ is pronounced **wa** and བོ, **wo**.

There is an anomaly here: as final syllables, བ and བོ are pronounced not **pa** and **po**, but **wa** and **wo**, with low tones. Here are examples of each of the six:

- བུམ་པ, pronounced **pum-b̄a**, means *pot*;
- ཆེན་པོ, pronounced **chên-b̄o**, means *great* and *large*;
- ཚོར་བ, pronounced **tshor-wa**, means *feeling*;
- གཙོ་བོ, pronounced **d̄zo-wo**, means *main* and *chief*;
- ཚང་མ, pronounced **tshang-ma**, means *all*;
- ཟབ་མོ, pronounced **s̱ap-mo**, means *profound*.

None of these examples, it may be noted, is an example of a verb being transformed into a noun.

> Note that there are many nouns and adjectives that do not end in one or another of these six terminal syllables. སེམས (*mind*) and ལས (*action*) illustrate this point.

## Patterns in the Tibetan Language
### *Doctrinal and Lexical Vocabularies*

Beginning with Chapter Eight, every chapter of *Translating Buddhism from Tibetan* will end with (1) a Doctrinal Vocabulary and Grammar section and (2) an ordinary Vocabulary section.

The **doctrinal vocabularies** will include both (1) lists of terms that are important in Buddhist texts and (2) explanations of the context in which they are found and their definitions and implications.

Some of these terms have been introduced already, for example ཐབས་ and ཤེས་རབ་. In general, ཐབས་ signifies *method* or *means* and ཤེས་རབ་, *wisdom*. Both are 'methods' for attaining enlightenment in that they are the two main causes for such an attainment. However, an examination of the definitions and explanations of ཐབས་ and ཤེས་རབ་ will tell us that ཐབས་ doctrinally means, for the most part, social and ethical activities influenced by, but outside of meditative wisdom. Thus, understood in their doctrinal dimensions, ཐབས་ mainly means compassionate activity and ཤེས་རབ་ mainly means the wisdom achieved through meditative vision of reality.

The other type of vocabularies—ordinary or **lexical vocabularies**—are lists of terms and simple translations along with an indication of their syntactic functions (that is, the way in which they may used in phrases, clauses, and sentences—as nouns, verbs, or word-modifying particles, for example).

## *Levels of Analysis*

Looking at Buddhist Tibetan in terms of the patterns in which it is arranged, there are nine possible **levels of analysis**, each level being more extensive (that is, longer) and more complex than the last.

> The nine levels are: letters, syllables, particles and words, phrases, clauses, sentences, logical sequences, sections, and works.

The first six of these levels are basic to any study of Tibetan.

1   **Letters** are consonants with or without vowels (for example, ཀ་);
    they were dealt with in Chapters One through Three.

2   **Syllables** are minimally a single letter and at most six consonants and a
    vowel marker. An example of a single-letter syllable is the pronoun ང་ (*I*
    and *me*); an example of the most complex type of syllable is the verb
    བསྒྲུབས་ (*achieved* or *proven*).

The patterns of pronunciation seen when letters are combined to form syllables is the subject matter of Chapters Four through Nine.

3    **Particles** and **words** are built from syllables—examples include the word ཆོས་ (*religion, doctrine, phenomenon*) and the particle ལ་ (which, depending on context, may be translated by English prepositions such as *on, in, at,* and *for*). Most words have more than one syllable, whereas many particles have only one. You have been learning words for several chapters, and will continue to look at patterns in the formation of words and particles through Chapter Ten.

4    **Phrases** are made of words or of words and particles. The phrase མེ་དང་ས་, *fire and earth*, for example, connects one noun with another using the particle དང་ (**tang,** *and*).

5    **Clauses** are made of words and/or phrases. They differ from sentences in that they do not end in terminal verbs—that is, clauses are themselves complex nouns, adjectives, or adverbs that are *parts* of sentences. They differ from phrases in that they are *almost* sentences and as such are much more complex than phrases. (See Chapter Eleven.)

6    **Sentences** are made of words, and often of phrases and clauses, but end in a terminal verb; a simple example is བུམ་པ་མི་རྟག་པ་ཡིན།, *Pots are impermanent.* (Changing the verb at the end into a verbal noun makes this sentence into a clause— བུམ་པ་མི་རྟག་པ་ཡིན་པ་ means *a pot's being impermanent.* This clause could then be used as part of a larger sentence such as *A pot's being impermanent is its nature.*)

The seventh and eighth structural levels (**logical sequences** and **sections of text**) are not seen in all Tibetan texts, although the seventh is very important in the present book. The ninth level—the **work** as a whole—is, by definition, relevant to all Tibetan literature.

# *Vocabulary*

Memorize the spellings, pronunciations, and meanings of these basic words. Practice speaking them. Honorific words are indicated with an **HON**.

## *Nouns*

| ཁམས་ | **kham** | realm, constituent |
| ཐབས་ | **thap** | method, means |
| དད་པ་ | **të'-ba** | faith |
| དུས་ | **tü>** | time |
| དོན་ | **tön** | meaning; goal; object |
| ཕན་པ་ | **phën-ba** | aid, help, benefit |
| བུམ་པ་ | **pum-ba** | pot |
| བོད་ | **pö'** | Tibet |
| མིག་ | **mík** | eye |
| མིང་ | **míng** | name |
| མེད་པ་ | **mé'-ba** | nonexistent |
| ཚིག་ | **tshík** | word |
| ཚོར་བ་ | **tshor-wa** | feeling |
| ཞིང་ | **shíng** | field |
| ཡབ་ | **yap** | father [HON] |
| ཡིད་ | **yí'** | mentality; intellect |
| ཡུམ་ | **yum** | mother [HON] |

| ཡོད་པ་ | yö'-b̄a | existent |
| རིགས་ | rík | type |
| རིམ་པ་ | rîm-b̄a | stage |
| ལམ་ | lam | path |
| ལས་ | lë> | action  [Sanskrit *karma*] |
| ལུགས་ | luk | way, system |
| ཤེས་པ་ | s̄hé>-b̄a | knowledge, consciousness |
| ཤེས་རབ་ | s̄hé>-rap | wisdom  [Sanskrit *prajñā*] |

## *Verbs*

| ནུབ་ | nup | disappear, [sun] set |
| མེད་ | mé' | am not, does not exist |
| འཚོལ་ | tshöl | search for, seek |
| ཡིན་ | yîn | is, am [linking verb] |
| ཡོད་ | yö' | am, are, is, exist[30] |
| ཤར་ | s̄har | appear, [sun] rise |
| སེལ་ | sél | eradicate, remove |

## *Adjectives*

| གུན་ | ḡün | all |
| འགལ་བ་ | gël-wa | mutually exclusive |
| ཆེན་པོ་ | chên-b̄o | large, great |

| | | |
|---|---|---|
| ཐམས་ཅད་ | **tham-jĕ'** | all |
| ནག་པོ་ | **nak-b̄o** | black |
| བར་མ་ | **par-ma** | intermediate |
| མང་པོ་ | **mang-b̄o** | many |
| ཙམ་ | **d̄zam** | only, mere |
| གཙོ་བོ་ | **d̄zo-wo** | principal, main |
| ཚང་མ་ | **tshang-ma** | all |
| ཞིབ་མོ་ | **s̱híp-mo** | subtle, fine |
| ཟབ་མོ་ | **s̱ap-mo** | profound |

## Particles

| | | |
|---|---|---|
| དང་ | **tang** | and |

# Chapter 6

*Letters that Precede the Root Letter*
   *Superscribed Letters*
   *Prefixes*
*Structural Patterns and Dimensions of Meaning*

## Introduction and Review

In Chapter Five the ten suffixes— ག་, ང་, ད་, ན་, བ་, མ་, འ་, ར་, ལ་, and ས་ — and the two secondary suffixes (ད་ and ས་) were introduced. With the exception of solitary root letters, syllables formed merely from a root letter followed by a suffix (or a suffix and a secondary suffix) are the simplest Tibetan syllables.

   Chapter Six introduces the letters that may precede the root letter of a syllable—the five possible prefixes and the three possible superscriptions. The four sub-scribed letters— ཡ་, ར་, ལ་, and ཝ་ —will be introduced in Chapter Seven.

   Unlike the suffix letters you have already seen, the letters that precede the root letter—the prefixes and superscripts—are almost never pronounced themselves. They typically affect only the aspiration or tone of the root letter.[31]

## Pronunciation Changes due to Prefixes and Superscripts

Tibetan is a living entity; the people who speak and write Tibetan shape it. Thus, all of the rules that have been or will be given in this book have exceptions. Moreover, there are many Tibetans who pronounce the letters, syllables, and words differently or with different "rules" than the ones given here. However, Westerners who learn Tibetan using these rules have proven able to communicate with Tibetans very well.

In the Hla-ŝa Tibetan being presented here, prefixes and superscribed letters are almost never pronounced. Note, however, that *prefixes and superscribed letters alter the pronunciation of eight root letters.* These eight letters are the first four third column consonants and the first four fourth column consonants—that is, the consonants in columns 3 and 4 of rows one through four:

ག་       ཇ་       ད་       བ་       ང་       ཉ་       ན་       མ་

ག་ which by itself is pronounced **ka** becomes **ga.**

ཇ་ which by itself is pronounced <u>c</u>**ha** becomes **ja.**

ད་ which by itself is pronounced **ta** becomes **da.**

བ་ which by itself is pronounced **pa** becomes **ba.**

ང་ which by itself is low tone becomes high tone—**n̄ga.**

ཉ་ which by itself is low tone becomes high tone—**n̄ya.**

ན་ which by itself is low tone becomes high tone—**n̄a.**

མ་ which by itself is low tone becomes high tone—**m̄a.**

---

When preceded by a prefix or superscribed letter, the first four low tone semi-aspirates (ག་, ཇ་, ད་, and བ་) lose their aspiration but retain their low tone, while the four nasals (ང་, ཉ་, ན་, and མ་) become high tone.

---

Thus, whereas ག་ alone is pronounced **ka**, the addition of a prefix or a super-scription, while having no affect on whether it is pronounced with high or low tone, makes it a **ga.**

For example, adding the prefix ད་ and the **u**-vowel marker to a ག་ creates the word དགུ་, which is pronounced **gu** and means *nine.*
Adding instead a superscribed ས་ and an **o**-vowel marker results in སྒོ་ (**go**), meaning *door.*
With a མ་ prefix instead of the superscript, we get མགོ་, which is pronounced in exactly the same way as སྒོ་, but means *head* and *beginning.*

Similarly, where ད་ is pronounced **ta**, the addition of a prefix or superscription changes it to a **da.**

Just as མགོ is **go**, so མདོ (Sanskrit, *sutra*—a *discourse* spoken by Buddha) is **do**.

Replacing the prefix with a superscription does not change the pronunciation: both མདོ and རྡོ (*stone*) are pronounced **do**.

Finally, a ད with both a prefix and a superscript is pronounced as it would be had it only one or the other: བསྡུ་བ (*collection* or *compendium*) is **du-wa**.

---

Recall, from Chapter Five, that when བ occurs as a final *syllable* it is pronounced **wa**.

---

It is only the semi-aspirated consonants of column three that lose their aspiration when preceded by a prefix letter or superscription. The first column consonants have no aspiration to lose, and the second column aspirates do not normally lose their aspiration.

---

The aspirated Column 2 letters—ཁ, ཆ, ཐ, ཕ, and ཚ— do not loose their aspiration when they are preceded by prefixes and superscriptions.

---

Thus, འཁོར་ལོ (*wheel*) is pronounced **khor-lo**.

The following is a schematic presentation of some of the examples used above.

| | | | | | | | |
|---|---|---|---|---|---|---|---|
| ཀ | ka | དགུ | gu | སྒོ | go | མགོ | go |
| ད | ta | མདོ | do | བསྡུ | du | རྡོ | do |
| ང | nga | ཉ | ṅga | ཌ | ṅga | སྔ | ṅga |

## Superscribed Letters

Only three of the thirty consonants may be superscribed letters ("superscripts" for short):

ᡘ·                          ལ·                          ས·

With only one exception, superscribed letters are never pronounced, although they do affect the pronunciation of some root consonants.

ᡘ· often loses some of its shape when superscribed;  when superscribed to a ཀ· it loses its bottom curve and looks like this: ཀ·. ᡘ· may be superscribed to twelve letters:[32]

ཀ·          ག·          ང·          ཇ·          ཉ·          ཏ·

ད·          ན·          བ·          མ·          ཙ·          ཛ·

The superscribed ᡘ· is fairly common in Tibetan.  Here are some frequently used words in which the superscribed ᡘ· is seen.

| རྙིང་མ· | n͞yíng-ma | *Nyingma* [Old (Translation) Order] |
|---|---|---|
| ཏག་པ· | d͞ak-b͞a | permanent |
| ཏོག་པ· | d͞ok-b͞a | thought, conceptual knowledge |
| རྡོ་རྗེ· | dor-jé | *vajra* [literally 'lord of stones'] |
| ཙ་བ· | d͞za-wa | root, basic |

རྙིང་མ· is one of the four orders (literally *doctrinal systems*—ཆོས་ལུགས· chö-luk) of Tibetan Buddhism.  The four are listed in the Doctrinal Vocabulary section of Chapter Eight.

Note the irregular pronunciation of the very frequently seen word རྡོ་རྗེ·; it is pronounced not **do-jé**, but **dor-jé**, with the superscribed ᡘ· pronounced as if it ended the previous syllable.  A རྡོ་རྗེ· is, most concretely, a ritual implement used in a great many Tibetan Buddhist rituals.  Symbolically it may signify method (ཐབས·—as opposed to ཤེས་རབ་, *wisdom*), but it symbolizes as often the nondual union of method and wisdom.

Unlike the superscribed ར་, the other two superscripts retain their shapes. A superscribed ལ་ is merely a smaller version of that letter written hanging from the top line, with a slightly smaller than normal root letter hanging beneath it: ཤ. There are ten letters to which ལ་ is superscribed:[33]

| ཀ་ | ཁ་ | ལྕ | ལྗ་ | ལྟ་ |
|------|------|------|------|------|
| ལྡ་ | ལྤ་ | ལྦ་ | ལྷ་ | ལྦ་ |

Here are some frequently used words in which a superscribed ལ་ is seen.

| ལྐོག་པ་ | **ḡok-b̄a** | hidden |
|---|---|---|
| ལྟ་བ་ | **d̄a-wa** | view, viewpoint |
| ལྕགས་ | **j̄ak** | iron |
| ལྗེ་ | **j̄é** | tongue |

The superscribed ས་ is is written as a small ས་ hanging from the imaginary top line with a slightly smaller than normal root letter written below it: ཤ. There are eleven superscribed ས་ combinations:[34]

| སྐ་ | སྒ་ | སྔ་ | སྙ་ | སྣ་ |
|------|------|------|------|------|
| སྤ་ | སྦ་ | སྨ་ | སྟ་ | སྩ་ | སྩ་ |

Here are some common words incorporating a superscribed ས་.

| སྐུ་ | **ḡu** | body [H] |
|---|---|---|
| སྒོ་ | **go** | door |
| སྡིག་པ་ | **dîk-b̄a** | misdeed, evil deed |

| སྙིང་པོ་ | ñyíng-bo | heart, essence |
| --- | --- | --- |

Note that a superscribed letter is never written above the imaginary top line. The three superscribed letters sit between the top line and the root letter; the root letters are said to hang from them. With experience the student will see that not all super-scripts and subscripts may be combined indiscriminately with all main letters. (All the possible combinations have been listed above.) For example, the second letter of the Tibetan alphabet— ཁ་ —never receives a superscript. It may be preceded by a prefix, or have a subscript or a suffix, but none of the superscribed letters may be superscribed to the letter ཁ་ .

## Prefixes

Of the thirty consonants, only five may be prefixes in a syllable:

ག་        ད་        བ་        མ་        འ་

Note that these five are the third members of Rows 1, 3, and 4, the fourth member of Row 4, and the "little a."

A prefix is a letter preceding the root letter of a syllable; it is not itself pro-nounced but—in certain cases—modifies the pronunciation of the root letter.

> Memorize these five letters, recognizing them to be the only possible prefixes.

It is helpful to know which of the letters can be used in the various positions; this is because a letter's pronunciation (or, often, its lack of pronunciation) is determined, among other things, by its position within a syllable. The prefixes themselves are never pronounced, but they affect the pronunciation of *some* root consonants. This will be explained in the following section.

Examples of syllables with prefixes are the following:

| བགོ་ | go | དམར་ | m̄ar | བད་ | da | དག་ | d̲a |
| --- | --- | --- | --- | --- | --- | --- | --- |

Note that unadorned root letters never have prefixes.

> Root letters without vowel markers, suffixes, superscriptions, or subscriptions never have prefixes.

In order for a syllable to begin with a prefix letter, one (or a combination) of the following must be true of that syllable:

- the root letter is marked with a vowel; in the first example—བགོ—the ག is marked with an ˘;

- the root letter is followed by a suffix; in the second example—དམར་—the root letter མ is followed by the suffix ར;

- the root letter has a letter superscribed to it; in the third example—བད་— the root letter ད hangs from a superscripted ར;

- the root letter has a letter subscribed to it; in the fourth example—དྲ་— the root letter ག has a ར hanging from it.

> The subscribed ར changes the pronunciation of its root letter—the one to which it is subscribed—to a sound whose closest English equivalent is 'dra' or 'tra.' Thus, དྲ་ (which means *enemy*) is pronounced ḍa.

This rule—that root letters without vowel markers, suffixes, superscriptions, or subscriptions never have prefixes—means that in the four examples given above, the first letter becomes the root letter in the absence, respectively, of a vowel marker, suffix, superscription, or subscription:

- whereas བགོ is pronounced **go**, the same syllable without the vowel marker—བག་—is pronounced **pak**;

- whereas དམར་ is pronounced m̄ar, ད and མ without a suffix—དམ་—is **tam**;

- whereas བད་ is pronounced **da**, the same syllable without the superscription—བད་—is pronounced **pë**;

- whereas དྲ་ is pronounced ḍa, removing the subscription leaves us with དག་, which is pronounced **tak**.

Here, in chart form, are common words incorporating examples of the pronunciation differences just explained:

|  |  |  |
|---|---|---|
| བག་ཆགས་ | **pak-chak** | latency, predisposition |
| དམར་པོ་ | **m̄ar-b̄o** | red |
| དམ་པ་ | **tam-b̄a** | ultimate, superior |
| བརྡ་ | **da** | sign, convention |
| དགྲ་ | **ḍa** | enemy |
| བད་ཀན་ | **pë'-g̈en** | mucus, phlegm |
| དག་པ་ | **tak-b̄a** | purified, purification |

The first example— བག་ཆགས་, *latency*—is a key term in many areas, as it is through the establishment of latencies in the mind that ordinary actions (*karma*) as well as religious practice affect experiences in future lifetimes. Likewise, whereas the term བད་ཀན་ may seem trivial, it is one of the three physical constituents according to the Tibetan medical system. The other two are རླུང་ (l̄ung, *wind*) and མཁྲིས་པ་ (tí>-b̄a, *bile*).

## Special Cases of Pronunciation Changes

There is one instance in which a superscription does radically affect the pronunciation of the root letter over which it is written. The superscription of a ལ་ to a ཧ་—ལྷ་—is pronounced **hla** . The word ལྷ་ itself means *god* or *deity*.

There is one instance in which a prefix radically changes the pronunciation of the root letter it precedes. ད་ as a prefix to the root letter བ་ causes the བ་ (normally pronounced as low tone **pa** or, with a prefix or superscription, **ba**) to be pronounced **w̄a** (or **ā**). This pronunciation change may be seen in the following examples.

|  |  |  |
|---|---|---|
| དབང་ | **w̄ang / āng** | empowerment / initiation |

| ད་ | ū | head |
| --- | --- | --- |
| དབེན་ | w̄én / én | isolation, solitary place |

Note that there are two ways to pronounce the ད་ - བ་ combination. Some Tibetans will pronounce དབང་ as āng; others will say w̄ang. Either is correct in Hla-śa Tibetan. It is only བ་ (the third column letter) that becomes w̄a in the above circumstances; the first column letter in the same row— པ་ —undergoes no such change. Thus, དཔེ་ (*example*) is pronounced b̄é and not w̄é.

The illustrations used above are frequently used words and should be learned.

● དབང་ (w̄ang or āng) means *empowerment* or *initiation*. However, it is very common as an abbreviation for དབང་པོ་, where it means *sense power*, i.e., sense faculty.

● ད་ (ū) means *head*, but when it is an abbreviation for དུ་མ་ (ū-ma), it means *center* or *middle*.

● དབེན་པ་ (w̄én-b̄a or én-b̄a) means *isolation* or a *solitary place*.

● དཔེ་ (b̄é) means *example*.

## Honorifics

Two words meaning *head* have been introduced in this chapter: མགོ་ and ད་. Like any other language, Tibetan has synonyms, different words that mean more or less the same thing. However ད་ and མགོ་ are special sorts of synonyms; where མགོ་ is a word I may use about my own head, ད་ refers only to the heads of those who are my social or spiritual superiors. ད་ is thus the **honorific** of མགོ་. Honorifics will be marked in the vocabularies with the abbreviation **H**.

## Homophony

At the beginning of this chapter, in the section describing the rules for pronouncing syllables with prefixes and superscriptions, the words མགོ་ and གོ་ were used as examples. They exemplify as well another characteristic of the Tibetan language, that of homophony. Many Tibetan words are pronounced alike (or, as in this case, identically) despite being spelt differently and having different meanings. This can be seen very clearly with the letter ང་. By itself, it is a very common word meaning *I*. It takes all three superscribed letters, making three words pronounced identically—ṅga—but having different meanings:

ལྔ་ means *five*.

རྔ་ means *drum*.

སྔ་ means *early*.

རྟོག་པ་ and རྟོགས་པ་ are also examples of this. While the first means *thought* (that is, *conceptuality*), the second means *realization*. Both are pronounced ḏok-b̄a.

---

# Drill 6

Practice reading and writing superscribed letters. The following examples exhaust the possible combinations of superscriptions and root letter.

| | | | | | | |
|---|---|---|---|---|---|---|
| 1 | རྐ་ | རྒ་ | རྔ་ | རྗ་ | རྙ་ | རྟ་ |
| 2 | རྡ་ | རྣ་ | རྦ་ | རྨ་ | རྩ་ | རྫ་ |
| 3 | ལྐ་ | ལྒ་ | ལྔ་ | ལྕ་ | ལྗ་ |
| 4 | ལྟ་ | ལྡ་ | ལྤ་ | ལྦ་ | ལྷ་ |
| 5 | སྐ་ | སྒ་ | སྔ་ | སྙ་ | སྟ་ |
| 6 | སྡ་ | སྣ་ | སྤ་ | སྦ་ | སྨ་ | སྩ་ |

Read the following, pronouncing the syllables aloud and writing them in their phonemic equivalents in the Roman alphabet.

| | | | | |
|---|---|---|---|---|
| 7 | གོ་ | སྒོ་ | མགོ་ | ཁོ་ |
| 8 | མགོ་ | དགེ་ | བསྒོ་ | གོ་ |

| | | | | |
|---|---|---|---|---|
| 9 | ཏུ་ | ཋུ་ | འཇི་ | ཐི་ |
| 10 | ང་ | སྨ་ | རྩེ་ | ཀླ་ |
| 11 | སྲུ་ | ཕུ་ | ཌ་ | ཚ་ |
| 12 | ནི་ | ཕྲ་ | ར་ | ཀླུ་ |
| 13 | སྨེ་ | ཕ་ | སྣུ་ | |
| 14 | དབུ་ | དཔང་ | དབང་ | དབེ་ |
| 15 | དཔལ་ | འབའ་ | དབུ་ | དབང་ |
| 16 | དཔག་ | དབུལ་ | དབུས་ | དཔའ་ |

# Patterns in the Tibetan Language
## *The Phonemic, Lexical, and Syntactic Dimensions*

The presentation and analysis of Tibetan seen in *Translating Buddhism from Tibetan* is organized around three basic principles, the first of which was introduced in Chapter Five:

**1 Levels of Analysis**

Languages may be analyzed at various levels. One may look at the sounds symbolized by letters, at the way these sounds change when letters are made into syllables, at the building of words out of syllables, at the ways in which words are combined to make sentences, and so on. Each level acts as the basis for the next level, the simpler serving as the basis for the more complex.

**2 Structural Patterns**

Repeating patterns or structures may be seen in each of these levels. The way in which letters are arranged in orderly patterns to form syllables has been the main topic in the last three chapters. On a more complex level, nouns and verbs are arranged in certain standard patterns to make sentences. Because these patterns are repeated, they may be learned. Learning the pat-

terns and the vocabulary that is arranged in these patterns, one learns the
language.

## 3  Dimensions of Meaning

Each structural level is capable of conveying meaning—of communicating.
At the level of letters and syllables, the meanings communicated are not
ideas but sounds. At the level of words, ideas begin to be conveyed. The
higher and more complex the level, the more complex the meaning that may
be conveyed.

> The nine levels are: letters, syllables, particles and words, phrases, clauses,
> sentences, logical sequences, sections, and works.

Beginners in a language must consciously analyze what they are reading at each
level. However, once the alphabet is memorized and drilled, the analysis of letters
(level 1) need no longer be done—it has become automatic. Likewise, once the
rules for the construction of syllables and their pronunciation have been internalized
and practiced, this analysis (level 2) will also have become redundant—that is, it will
take place without conscious effort. The same will eventually be the case with the
arrangement of particles and words in phrases, clauses, and sentences. This is the
reason for the **pattern analysis** which underlies most of this book. Some of it may
seem, perhaps, to be pedantic or petty. And it would be, if it were necessary to continue forever to be mindful of each level of analysis in order to understand Tibetan.
However, once the patterns have been internalized and practiced, they need not be
consciously attended to, unless one is engaged in the linguistic analysis of Tibetan
or in teaching it.

Languages, of course, are not merely patterns and structures, they refer to things
and ideas and they communicate meaning, although their structures do impose limi-
tations on the meanings they may communicate. In learning Buddhist Tibetan, it is
helpful to think of six dimensions of meaning in a text. The first three—the
phonemic, lexical, and syntactic dimensions—are relevant to all forms of Tibetan.

## The Phonemic Dimension

The **phonemic dimension** is the most basic of the six dimensions of meaning, but the meaning involved is not one involving ideas.[35] It operates at levels 1 and 2 and, as its name implies, has to do with the way that letters by themselves (level 1) and when combined in syllables (level 2) mean, or refer to, certain sounds .

The phonemic dimension of the letter ཁ, for example, is **kha**, that of the particle པ་ is **b̄a**, and that of the word སེམས་, **s̄êm**.

Likewise, ད་, in this dimension, means the sound **d̄a**. Adding a prefix letter and a superscription gives us རྟག་, which—phonemically—means **d̄ak**. As has been seen, there are many homophones in Tibetan; thus, phonemically, རྟག་, རྟགས་, བརྟགས་, and བརྟགས་ all equivalently mean **d̄ak**.

## The Lexical Dimension

The lexical[36] dimension of meaning is more complex; it arises (at level 3) from the combination of syllables into particles and words (nouns, pronouns, adjectives, adverbs, and verbs).  Here the meanings communicated are those found in dictionaries, which are a form of lexicon—hence the term *lexical dimension*.[37]

Whereas the phonemic meaning of དད་ is **të'** and that of པ་ is **b̄a**, the lexical meaning of དད་པ་ —the one found in a dictionary—is *faith*.

The combination of རྟག་ and the final syllable པ་, for example, produces རྟག་པ་ (*permanent*, *static*), but the addition of the negative particle མི་ creates མི་རྟག་པ་ (*impermanent*), a word with exactly the opposite meaning.

The lexical dimension of a word or particle is abstract, in the sense that the word བུམ་པ་, for example, refers not just to a specific pot in a specific place at a specific time, but to all pots.  What the word བུམ་པ་ conveys—its lexical dimension—is  a reference to an idea shared, in a general way, by all who know Tibetan.[38]

## The Syntactic Dimension

The syntactic dimension of meaning is seen when words and particles are combined (at levels 4, 5, and 6) to make phrases, clauses, and sentences.  This combination is capable of conveying more complex meanings than individual words can convey.

For the most part, this dimension becomes evident when words and particles are actually used in phrases and other larger units. However, all Tibetan words and particles are limited in their potential uses, even before they actually appear in a sentence. Words, for example, are one or another of six functional types: nouns, verbs, pronouns, adjectives, adverbs, or postpositions. The most basic syntactic meaning of any Tibetan word is its functional type.

བུམ་པ་, for instance, is a noun. It may not be used as a verb, nor is it ever used as a pronoun, adjective, or grammatical particle. This is the basis of its syntactic dimension and limits its use.

However, the syntactic dimension is most clearly seen when a noun such as བུམ་པ་ is used in a phrase, clause, or sentence along with other words and particles.

Saying བུམ་པ་མི་རྟག་པ་ཡིན། (*Pots are impermanent*) is a way of using the word བུམ་པ་ in a sentence to convey more about pots than is possible using merely the simple word བུམ་པ་.

---

The phonemic dimension is that of pronunciation, the sounds to which letters and syllables refer.

The lexical dimension is what people ordinarily mean when they speak of the meaning of a word.

The syntactic dimension involves the patterns in which words and particles are used in phrases, clauses, and sentences.

---

Chapters One through Eight of *Translating Buddhism from Tibetan* concentrate on the phonemic and lexical dimensions. The remainder of the book is concerned with syntactic patterns and the vocabulary and grammar of Buddhist texts. (The remaining three dimensions of Buddhist Tibetan will be introduced in the next chapter.)

# *Vocabulary*

Memorize the spellings, pronunciations, and meanings of these basic words, which include model examples of the use of the prefixes and superscripts. Practice speaking them.

## *Nouns*

| | | |
|---|---|---|
| འཁོར་ལོ་ | khor-lo | wheel |
| མགོ་ | go | head, beginning |
| སྒོ་ | go | door |
| ང་ | n̄ga | drum |
| ལྕགས་ | j̄ak | iron |
| ལྕེ་ | j̄é | tongue |
| རྙིང་མ་ | n̄yíng-ma | *Nying-ma* Order |
| སྙིང་པོ་ | n̄ying-b̄o | heart, essence |
| རྟོག་པ་ | d̄ok-b̄a | thought, conceptuality |
| རྟོགས་པ་ | d̄ok-b̄a | realization |
| ལྟ་བ་ | d̄a-wa | view, viewpoint |
| མདོ་ | do | discourse [Skt. *sūtra*] |
| རྡོ་ | do | stone |
| རྡོ་རྗེ་ | dor-jé | diamond [Skt. *vajra*] |
| སྡིག་པ་ | dîk-b̄a | misdeed, evil deed |
| བརྡ་ | da | sign, convention |

| དཔེ་ | b̄é | example |
| བག་ཆགས་ | pak-chak | latency, predisposition |
| དབང་ | āng / w̄ang | empowerment / initiation |
| དབུ་ | ū | head |
| དབུ་མ་ | ū-ma | center, middle, middle way |
| དབེན་པ་ | én-b̄a / w̄én-b̄a | isolation, solitary place |
| རྩ་བ་ | d̄za-wa | root, basic |
| ལྷ་ | hla | god, deity |
| ལྷ་ས་ | hla-s̄a | Lhasa  [city in Tibet] |

## Adjectives

| དགུ་ | gu | nine |
| དགེ་བ་ | gé-wa | virtuous, wholesome |
| ལྔ་ | n̄ga | five |
| རྙིང་པ་ | n̄yíng-b̄a | old |
| རྟག་པ་ | d̄ak-b̄a | permanent |
| དམ་པ་ | tam-b̄a | ultimate, superior |
| དམར་པོ་ | m̄ar-b̄o | red |
| གཙོ་བོ་ | d̄zo-wo | main, chief, principal |
| ཞིབ་མོ་ | s̱híp-mo | subtle, fine |

# Chapter 7

*Subscribed Letters*
*Rules for Finding the Root Letter of a Syllable*
*The Doctrinal Dimension of Tibetan*

---

## Subscribed Letters

There are only four letters that can be subscribed to other letters; these letters are called "subscripts" for short:

ཡ་　　　ར་　　　ལ་　　　ཝ་

In almost all instances, subscribed letters radically change the pronunciation of the root letter. Memorize this list of four letters.

---

## Subscribed ཡ་

ཡ་ is subscribed (in the form ྱ) to only seven letters. The seven letters are the first three letters of Row 1 (that is, of the **ḡa** row, the letters ཀ་, ཁ་, and ག་) and all the letters in Row 4 (the **b̄a** row—པ་, ཕ་, བ་, and མ་). The first three combinations are pronounced as might be expected:

ཀྱ་ is pronounced **ḡya,**

ཁྱ་ is pronounced **khya,**

གྱ་ is pronounced **kya** or (with a prefix or superscript) **gya.**

These three examples illustrate a general rule—subscribed letters do not alter the aspiration of the root letter. The གྱ་ combination, for example, is still a type of ག་ and so is affected by prefixes and superscripts in the same way as any other ག་. Thus, a ग्र་ with either a prefix or superscript is pronounced not **kya** but **gya**. Whereas ग्रུ་ would be **kyu**, ग्रུ་ (meaning *cause*) is pronounced **gyu**.

Here are some common illustrations of ﹈ subscribed to first row consonants.

| | | |
|---|---|---|
| ग्रུད་ | **gyü'** | continuum, *tantra* |
| དग्रིལ་འཁོར་ | **ḡyíl-khor** | mandala |
| ཁྱོད་ | **khyö'** | you |
| སྐྱེ་བ་ | **ḡyé-wa** | birth, arising |
| སངས་རྒྱས་ | **s̄ang-gyë>** | Buddha |

If it followed the general rules, དग्रིལ་འཁོར་ would be pronounced **ḡyíl-khor**; however, it is most often pronounced **ḡyín-khor**, following exception nine (as outlined in Chapter Eight).

The latter four instances of a subscribed ﹈ are not pronounced as would be expected.

> ﹈ subjoined to the consonants of Row 4 (the **b̄a** row) causes these letters to be pronounced as if they were the letters of Row 2 (the **j̄a** row).

ब्य་ is pronounced not **b̄ya** but **j̄a**;

फ्य་ is pronounced not **phya** but **cha**;

प्य་ is pronounced not **pya** but **cha** or **ja**;

म्य་ is pronounced not **mya** but **nya**.

As before, the Column 3 and Column 4 letters are liable to pronunciation changes if they are preceded by a prefix or superscript. A प्य་ with an འ་ prefix is pronounced not **cha** but **ja**, as in འབྱུང་བ་ (**jung-wa**—*arising*, *element*, etc.). A ब्य་ with an ས་ superscript is also pronounced **ja**: སྦྱོར་བ་ **jor-wa**) means *application*, *connection*, *endeavor*, *preparation*, and *syllogism*, among other things.

Note that both སྦྱོར་བ་ and འབྱུང་བ་ are nouns ending in a final བ་ syllable. In these cases, unlike the examples given in the previous chapter, the བ་ does serve to nominalize verbs. (The verb འབྱུང་ means *occur and arise*; སྦྱོར་ means *apply* and *connect*.)

It should be noted that when Tibetans transliterate Sanskrit words into their own language, as for example in the case of mantras, the subscribed ཡ་ occurs with other letters as well.

Here are some useful words illustrating the subscription of ཡ་ to the consonants of Row 4.

| | | |
|---|---|---|
| བྱིས་པ་ | **chí>-b̄a** | child, immature or foolish person |
| འབྱུང་བ་ | **jung-wa** | arising, element [e.g., air, water, etc.] |
| ཕྱག་འཚལ་བ་ | **chak-tshël-wa** | prostration [bowing down] |
| མྱ་ངན་ལས་འདས་པ་ | **nya-ngën-lë>d̲ë>-b̄a** | nirvana [Sanskrit: *nirvāṇa*] |

## Drill 7.1

Practice writing the subscribed ཡ་:

| 1 | ཀྱ་ | ཁྱ་ | གྱ་ | པྱ་ | ཕྱ་ | བྱ་ | མྱ་ |
|---|---|---|---|---|---|---|---|

Pronounce the following. Write out their pronunciations.

| 2 | ཀ་ | ཀྱ་ | ཁ་ | ཁྱ་ | ག་ | གྱ |
|---|---|---|---|---|---|---|

| 3 | ཁ་ | ཁྱ་ | ཁྱ་ | ཁྱ་ | འཁྱ་ | ཀྱ་ | ཀྱ་ |
|---|---|---|---|---|---|---|---|

| | | | | | | |
|---|---|---|---|---|---|---|
| 4 | ག་ | གུ་ | རྒུ་ | འགྱི་ | | |
| 5 | གུ་ | རྒུ་ | རྒྱེ་ | གུ་ | ཁུ་ | |
| 6 | པ་ | པུ་ | ཕ་ | པུ་ | བ་ | བུ་ |
| 7 | པ་ | པུ་ | དཔུ་ | སྤུ་ | ཕ་ | པུ་ | འཕུ་ |
| 8 | བ་ | བུ་ | འབྱེ་ | འབྱེ་ | མུ་ | སྨྱོ་ |

## A Special Case of the Subscribed ཡ་

We have seen that ད་ prefixed to the root letter བ་ regularly causes it to be pronounced w̄a or ā.. ད་ prefixed to the root-subscript combination བྱ་ also brings about
a radical change, one whereby it is pronounced not **cha** but **ȳa**.

| དབྱིབས་ | **ȳíp** | shape |
|---|---|---|
| དབྱེ་བ་ | **ȳé-wa** | division, category |

The root letter བ་ becomes a high tone **ȳa** only in those cases in which it has a ད་
prefix and a subscribed ཡ་. Thus, the syllable དབག་ is pronounced **ḍak** and not **w̄ak**.
All that the ད་ prefix does in that case is to remove the aspiration: བག་ (ṭak) becomes
དབག་ (ḍak). The general principle is that the combination of ད་ prefixed to a root བ་
which has either a non-ཡ་ subscript or no subscript at all is pronounced according to
the general rules and not this special one. Again, it is only the third column བ་ that
becomes **ȳa** in the above circumstances; the first column པ་ makes no such change.
Thus, དཔྱོད་ (a verb meaning *analyze*) is pronounced **ǰö'** and not **ȳö'**.

## Drill 7.2
Practice reading and speaking these syllables.

| | | | | | | |
|---|---|---|---|---|---|---|
| 1 | བར་ | འབའ་ | དབུ་ | དབང་ | དཔལ་ | དབྱེ་ |

2    དབལ་      དབྱིན་      དཔྱོད་      དགྱུག་

3    དཔག་      དགུལ་      དབུས་      དཔའ་      དཔྱིབས་

---

## Subscribed ར་

ར་ is subscribed (in the form ▵ ) to thirteen letters:

the first three letters of Row 1 and Row 3—ཀ་, ཁ་, and ག་, and ཏ་, ཐ་, and ད་;

all four letters of Row 4—པ་, ཕ་, བ་, and མ་;

and three other letters, ས་, ཧ་, and ཏ་ (**ha**).

In this case, however, it is more important to look at columns than at rows. Nine of these thirteen letters fall naturally into three groups—each group corresponding to one column in the alphabet—and each group represents only one sound.

In Column 1, ཀ་, ཏ་, and པ་ are all an unaspirated, high tone *ḍa*.

In Column 2, ཁ་, ཐ་, and ཕ་ are all a fully aspirated *ṭha*.

In Column 3, ག་, ད་, and བ་ are all a semi-aspirated and low tone *ḍa*.

The dot under each letter of the phoneticization indicates a **retroflex** letter. These are similar to the dentals—ད་ (**d̄a**), ཐ་ (**tha**), and ཏ་ (**ta**)—but, instead of touching the back of the upper front teeth, the tongue is turned backwards on the roof of the mouth, a little behind the upper front teeth. The closest English approximations of these sounds are **dra** (as in *drama*) and **tra** (as in *trawl*), but pronounced with the tongue curled back.

Like the subscribed ཡ་, a subscribed ར་ has no effect on the aspiration of its root letter. However, prefixes and superscriptions change the aspiration of the column 3 letters here as they do elsewhere.

● Whereas གྲིབ་མ་ (*shadow*) is pronounced *ṭíp-ma*,
　 སྒྲིབ་པ་ (*obstruction*) is *ḍíp-b̄a* and དགྲ་ (*enemy*), *ḍa*.

● Whereas གྲོལ་བ་ (*liberation*) is *ṭöl-wa*,
　 སྒྲོལ་མ་ (*Tara, the name of a female Buddha*) is *ḍöl-ma*.

- Whereas རྡི་མ (*stain*) is pronounced *ṭi-ma*,
  འདྲི་བ (*question*) is *ḍ́i-wa*.

- Whereas སྤལ་བ (*separation*) is pronounced *ṭël-wa*,
  འབྲས་བུ (*effect* and *fruit*) is *ḍ́ë-bu* and འབྲེལ་བ (*relationship* and *connection*) is *ḍ́ël-wa*.

Note that the first, second, and fourth sets of examples incorporate suffix letters. The effects of suffix letters on pronunciation will be detailed in the next chapter.

> Recall that when a ལ occurs at the end of a syllable, an **a** becomes an **ë**—the vowel sound heard in the English word *edge*—and an **o** becomes an **ö** (the vowel sound in the English *push*, pronounced with the lips fully rounded). The suffix འ, on the other hand, does not alter the pronunciation of the vowel.

The exceptions to the regularity outlined above are the following.

- སྨ is pronounced like མ, with no change.

- སྲ is usually pronounced with no change (that is, as **śa**); examples are སྲས (**śë>**, *son* or *child* [HON]) and སྲིད་པ (**śí'-ba**, *existence*). Sometimes, however, it is pronounced like ཊ and the other column one retroflexes—as a high tone **ḍa**.

- ཧྲ is not used in indigenous Tibetan words but in the transliteration of the Sanskrit *śra* (**shra**) into Tibetan.

- ཧྲ is pronounced **hra**.

---

## Drill 7.3

Practice writing the subscribed ར.

| 1 | ཀྲ | ཁྲ | གྲ | ཏྲ | ཐྲ | དྲ |    |
|---|----|----|----|----|----|----|----|
| 2 | པྲ | ཕྲ | བྲ | མྲ | ཤྲ | སྲ | ཧྲ |

Pronounce the following.

| 3 | ग་ | གང་ | གི་ | | | |
|---|---|---|---|---|---|---|
| 4 | ཁ་ | ཁག | ཁོ་ | | | |
| 5 | གྱ་ | གྱག་ | གྱངས་ | གྱི་ | གྱུབ | གྱོ་ |
| 6 | ཅ་ | ཅམ་ | ཅི་ | ཐ་ | | |
| 7 | ད་ | དག་ | དང་ | དེ་ | དུང་ | དྲེའ་ |
| 8 | པ་ | པོག་ | ཕ་ | ཕག་ | ཕིང་ | |
| 9 | བ་ | བང་ | བུག་ | བམས་ | བེ་ | |
| 10 | སྨ་ | འཕ་ | ས་ | སྱེ་ | སྱུང་ | |
| 11 | ཅ་ | ཅེ་ | ཅག་ | ཅོབ་ | | |

Practice distinguishing between dentals and retroflex letters. You must eventually
be able not only to speak the difference but to hear it.

| 12 | ཏ་ | ཊ་ | ཐ་ | ཋ་ | ད་ | ཌ་ |
|---|---|---|---|---|---|---|
| 13 | ས་ | སྲ་ | ཅ་ | ཅ་ | ཐ་ | ཐ་ |
| 14 | ད་ | ཌ་ | འདའ་ | འཌ་ | ཏ་ | པ་ |
| 15 | ཐ་ | ཕ་ | ད་ | བ་ | ས་ | སྲ་ |

---

## Subscribed ལ་

ལ་ is subscribed to six letters only and does not undergo any change of shape when
it is subscribed. In the cases of five of the letters, the root letters become completely
silent and only the ལ་ is sounded, but high, as **la**.

ཟླ་, ཟླ་, ཟླ་, ནོ་, and ཟླ་ are all pronounced **la**.

- ཀླུ་ is pronounced **lu** and translates the Sanskrit *nāga* (*serpent* or *dragon*).
- གླུ་ is pronounced **lu** and means *song*.
- བློ་ is pronounced **lo** and means *mind*.
- བླ་མ་ is pronounced **la-ma** and translates the Sanskrit *guru*.
- རླུང་ is pronounced **lung** and means *wind* or *energy wind* (Sanskrit: *prāṇa*).

When ཟ་ takes this subscription—as ཟླ་—it is pronounced, strangely enough, as a low tone **da**. An example is ཟླ་བ་ (**da-wa**), which means *moon*.

ཝ་ is subscribed to many letters (as ◄ ) but does not significantly affect their pronunciation. An example is ཀྭ་ which is pronounced identically with ཀ་. ཝ་ is sometimes subscribed to a root letter which already has a subscription. The most frequent instance of this is གྲྭ་, which—following the rule that a subscribed ཝ་ does not alter pronunciations—is pronounced the same as གྲ་—*ṭa*. གྲྭ་པ་ (**ṭa-ba**) means *monk* (in the broad sense of one who lives in a monastic community).

---

## Drill 7.4
Practice writing the subscribed ལ་ and ཝ་.

| | | | | | |
|---|---|---|---|---|---|
| 1 | ཟླ་ | ཟླ་ | ཟླ་ | ཟླ་ | ཟླ་ |
| 2 | ཀླ་ | ཁླ་ | གླ་ | མླ་ | ཙླ་ |
| 3 | དྭ་ | ཌྭ་ | ཚྭ་ | ཚྭ་ | ཞྭ་ |
| 4 | ཟྭ་ | རྭ་ | ལྭ་ | ཤྭ་ | སྭ་ |

Pronounce the following syllables.  Write out their pronunciation.

| | | | | |
|---|---|---|---|---|
| 5 | གླ་ | གླུ་ | གླིང་ | |
| 6 | གླ་ | གློ་ | གླང་ | ཀླུ་ |
| 7 | བླ་ | བླང་ | བློ་ | |
| 8 | ཧྲེ་ | ཧྲག་ | ཧྲམ་ | ཧྲུང་ |
| 9 | ས་ | སེ་ | སོང་ | སོབ་ |
| 10 | ཟླ་ | ཟློག་ | ཟླུམ་ | |
| 11 | ཁ་ | ག་ | དང་ | ཚོ་ |

## Finding the Root Letter of a Syllable

Let us review what has been said so far about the most important letter in the pronunciation of the syllable, the root letter.

- The root letter is almost always sounded first; prefixes and superscribed letters, although written prior to a root letter, are never themselves pronounced.

- The root letter carries the vowel—either the ཨ་ (a) sound inherent in a Tibetan consonant or one of the four vowels (i, u, e, and o—pronounced í, u, é, and o).

- If there is a subscript in the syllable, it can only be subscribed to the root letter.

- If there is a superscript in the syllable, it is superscribed to the root letter.

There are five basic rules for finding the root letter of any syllable.[39]

## *Rules for Finding the Root Letter: Rule One*

In some cases the root letter of a syllable is obvious.  For example, any letter with a vowel marker is a root letter—bearing in mind that subscripts and superscripts may never themselves be root letters. Thus the most basic rule is that if one or more of the following conditions is true about a letter, then that letter must be a root letter:

1    there is a vowel marker either above or below it;[40]

2    there is a letter superscribed to it;

3    there is a letter subscribed to it.

| | | | |
|---|---|---|---|
| བགོ་ | *go* | root letter | ག་ —condition 1 |
| འདུ་ | *ḍa* | root letter | ད་ —condition 3 |
| བཅགས་ | *ḍak* | root letter | ཅ་ —condition 2 |
| བསྒྲུབས་ | *ḍup* | root letter | ག་ —conditions 1, 2, 3 |

## Rule Two

In the case of *syllables of two letters* with no vowel markers, no superscripts, and no subscripts, the following is true. If the initial letter is *not* included among the permissible prefixes, it must be the root letter.

| | | | |
|---|---|---|---|
| ཆད་ | *chë'* | root letter | ཆ་ |
| རང་ | *rang* | root letter | ར་ |
| མན་ | *mën* | root letter | མ་ |

## Rule Three

Sometimes *syllables of two letters* occur in which the first letter is one of the five possible prefixes and the second is one of the ten possible suffixes. In the case of such syllables, the *first letter is the root letter* and the second is its suffix *if* the following condition is true: the second letter is not marked by a vowel, superscript, or subscript.

The rule that has priority is that *a letter marked by a vowel, superscript, or subscript must be the root letter.*

| | | | |
|---|---|---|---|
| དག | *tak* | root letter | ད |
| དང | *tang* | root letter | ད |
| བག | *pak* | root letter | བ |
| མར | *mar* | root letter | མ |

Suppose, however, that one wanted a syllable in which the *second* of two letters fitting the above description was the root letter, and not the first. It would then be necessary either to have a vowel marker on the second letter or, if the vowel is to be an **a**, to affix an འ suffix to the end.

In the syllable དག, the ད is the root letter and not the ག. In order for the ག to be the root letter, the syllable must either become དགེ or དགའ or something similar.

## Rule Four

In a *syllable composed of three letters* which has no vowel marker, superscription, or subscription, the middle letter is usually the root letter.

| | | | |
|---|---|---|---|
| མནར | *ñar* | root letter | ན |
| བསམ | *sam* | root letter | ས |

However, if the last letter of the syllable is either ས or ད, that is, if it is one of the two that may be a secondary suffix, it is then possible for the first letter to be the root letter. (Remember that the secondary suffix ད is normally used only by grammarians and lexicographers.)

| | | | |
|---|---|---|---|
| སངས | *sang* | root letter | ས |
| དངས | *tang* | root letter | ད |

Note that in the first case, the initial ཤ *cannot* be a prefix—not being one of the five permissible prefixes—and so must be the root letter. In the second case, the initial ད —which *is* a permissible prefix—is marked with a subscribed ཤ to indicate that it is not a prefix in this syllable.

## *Rule Five*

In a syllable composed of four letters, the role played by each is fixed.

1  The first letter must be a prefix.

2  The second letter must be the root letter.

3  The third letter must be a suffix.

4  The last letter must be one of the two secondary suffixes.

| | | | |
|---|---|---|---|
| བཤགས་ | *shak* | root letter | ག |
| དཔརད་ | *bar* | root letter | པ |
| འཇབས་ | *jap* | root letter | ཇ |

# Drill 7.5

Identify the root letters of these syllables. Read them aloud. Write out their pronunciation.

| | | | | | |
|---|---|---|---|---|---|
| ① | དག་ | ② | སྟེག་ | ③ | འདྲིལ་ |
| ④ | དག་ | ⑤ | སུད་ | ⑥ | པ་ |
| ⑦ | སྤག་ | ⑧ | གད་ | ⑨ | སྨ་ |
| ⑩ | སློམ་ | ⑪ | འབྱུར་ | ⑫ | སྐྱུར་ |
| ⑬ | དབྱུར་ | ⑭ | དམར་ | ⑮ | རྣལ་ |

16 ཚོས་    17 ཟད་    18 སད་

19 བ་ཕད་    20 བཞིད་    21 སྒྲུབ་

22 དངར་    23 དང་    24 དམངས་

25 དྲངས་    26 གྲུབ་

# Doctrinal Vocabulary and Grammar
## *The Doctrinal, Rhetorical, and Tacit Dimensions of Tibetan*

Of the six dimensions of Tibetan, the first three—the phonemic, lexical, and syntactic dimensions—were introduced in Chapter Six. The remaining three dimensions of meaning—the doctrinal dimension, the rhetorical dimension, and the tacit dimension—are not as basic, but an understanding of them is indispensible when translating Buddhist texts from Tibetan. (The doctrinal dimension was introduced in Chapter Five in terms of the doctrinal meanings of སྒྲབས་ and ཤེས་རབ་.)

## *The Doctrinal Dimension*

The doctrinal dimension is built on the lexical dimension, but goes beyond it. And just as a term may have a number of different lexical meanings, so it may have different technical meanings. The doctrinal dimension includes—as separate, but interrelated, facets—the specialized vocabularies of areas such as epistemology, liturgy, psychology, and meditative technique, as well as the ways terms are defined and used in different doctrinal systems. (The doctrinal systems of Buddhism are discussed in Chapters Eight and Sixteen.)

This dimension, in principle, is not limited to Buddhist doctrine. All specialized professional groups have their own technical vocabularies, even, presumably, yak herders. Thus, in general, the term *technical dimension* is the generic one, with *doctrinal dimension* referring to only certain technical vocabularies, the ones seen in Buddhist doctrine. (The term *doctrine* translates the Tibetan ཚོས་, a term which includes not only the theory of Buddhism but its practice as well.)[41]   In this book, however, the terms *technical dimension* and *doctrinal dimension* are used interchangeably.

The doctrinal dimension may be seen very clearly in the literary genre known as ཡིག་ཆ་ (**yík-cha** or **yîk-cha**, *textbooks*), commentaries on specific texts or on particular topics.   In these textbooks, key terms are defined, concrete illustrations are given, the ranges of each term are set and divisions into categories and subcategories are made.   These areas of analysis are the heart of the doctrinal dimension examined in this book.

Basic   doctrinal   analysis   includes   definitions   of   key   terms, lists of their equivalents, illustrations (that is, examples), and their divisions—divisions which are in turn divided into categories and subcategories.

| | | |
|---|---|---|
| མཚན་ཉིད་ | **tshën-nyí'** | definition [Sanskrit: *lakṣana*] |
| དོན་གཅིག་ | **tön-jîk** | equivalent |
| མཚན་གཞི་ | **tshën-shí** | illustration |
| དབྱེ་བ་ | **yé-wa** | division, category, subcategory |

For example, according to the Gé-luk textbooks, the definition of མི་རྟག་པ་ (*impermanent*) is that which is momentary.   Illustrations of མི་རྟག་པ་ include ཤེས་པ་ (*knowledge*—that is, sense and mental perceptions), ཆུ་ (*water*), and བུམ་པ་ (*pots*). The divisions of མི་རྟག་པ་—the categories of impermanent things—are (1) the physical, (2) the mental, and (3) those impermanent things that are neither physical nor mental (called non-associated compositional factors).

For more on the doctrinal dimension of impermanence from a philosophical viewpoint, see Daniel Perdue, *Debate in Tibetan Buddhism*, pp. 272-76 and Jeffrey Hopkins, *Meditation on Emptiness*, pp. 219-20.

Impermanence as it ought to be recognized in an individual's everyday experiences and in conjunction with meditation on death is a related, but different, aspect of this dimension that may be seen in books on *stages of the path* (ལམ་རིམ་ lam-rîm) and *preliminary practices* (སྔོན་འགྲོ་ ngön-do).

See, for example, Khetsun Sangpo, *Tantric Practice in Nyingma*, pp. 57-63 and Sonam Gyatso, *Essence of Refined Gold*, pp. 68-71.

| | | |
|---|---|---|
| སྐད་ཅིག་མ་ | ḡë'-jík-ma | momentary |
| བེམ་པོ་ | pém-b̄o | [physical] matter |
| ཤེས་པ་ | s̄hé>-b̄a | knowledge, mental phenomena |
| ལྡན་མིན་འདུ་བྱེད་ | dën-mîn-du-jé' | non-associated compositional factors |

However, not just ཡིག་ཆ་, but all Buddhist texts have doctrinal dimensions. If, for instance, a text uses the terms ཤེས་པ་ (s̄hé>-b̄a, *knowledge*), མ་རིག་པ་ (ma-rík-b̄a, usually translated *ignorance*), and ཡེ་ཤེས་ (yé-s̄hé>, *wisdom* or *pristine knowledge*), then an analysis of that text should be able to suggest the ways in which these terms are used in relation to (or in distinction from) one another and what characteristics are posited of them or assumed about them.

## The Rhetorical Dimension

The **rhetorical dimension** has to do with the special vocabulary and syntax used to link sentences together in logical sequences of theses and proofs (level 7).

An English translation of such a logical sequence might read as follows. *It follows that sound is impermanent because it is a product. This follows because sound is created [from causes]. Whatever is created [from causes] is necessarily a product because being created [from causes] is the definition of product.*

On the formal aspects of proof statements, see Daniel Perdue, *Debate in Tibetan Buddhism*, pp. 33-60 (especially pp. 34-35, 49-50, and 55).

The rhetorical dimension also includes other explanatory devices such as the analysis of words (སྒྲ་བཤད་, ḍa-shë'—literally, *explanation of words*).

Just as one can say more with a sentence than a single word, so more is conveyed in the formal statement of a thesis and a proof than in a single sentence.[42] The rhetorical dimension will be discussed in more detail later.

## The Tacit Dimension

The tacit dimension includes (1) the associations that people within a given culture have to specific words (for example, associating the idea of loyalty with the word *dog*),[43] (2) the axioms upon which the doctrinal dimension is built, and (3) the assumptions a culture makes about language in general. The connotations of the word རྣམ་པར་རྟོག་པ་ (ñam-bar-dok-ba, Sanskrit *vikalpa*) illustrate the first and second of these facets.

Whereas རྣམ་པར་རྟོག་པ་ lexically means simply *thought* or *conceptualization*, Buddhists tend to see conceptual knowledge as a stepping stone to nonconceptual understanding.[44] Thus, even prior to being so defined in one or another doctrinal dimension, རྣམ་པར་རྟོག་པ་ connotes something to be transcended, something that is ultimately incompatible with knowledge of reality. Two of the lexical meanings of རྣམ་རྟོག་ in colloquial Tibetan, *superstition* and *paranoia*, suggest a derivation from the negative valuation given it in Buddhist Tibetan.[45]

On the general differences between conceptual and nonconceptual, see Lati Rinbochay, *Mind in Tibetan Buddhism*, pp. 130-34. The progression from ordinary perception to meditative wisdom is outlined in the same book on pp. 26-7. The Géluk tradition holds correct conceptual minds (such as inference) to be somewhat more useful than I have indicated above; on the value of conceptuality, see Anne Klein, *Knowledge and Liberation*, pp. 206-216.

Another facet of the tacit dimension of Buddhist Tibetan is the overall attitude towards language and speech. One important assumption that Buddhism, and Tibetan Buddhism especially, makes about language in general is that the phonemic dimension has significant meaning beyond the one outlined in Chapter Six, one not dependent on the kind of conceptual interpretation that is done when syllables are combined to make words and words combined to make phrases, clauses, and sentences. This is the principle underlying the use of mantras and the belief in the importance of oral transmission. It is not the lexical meaning of a mantra but its sound that has power. Similarly, the idea of oral transmission assumes that the ability to succeed in a certain practice (or, for that matter, even the ability to learn a certain subject) comes not only from rational understanding about it obtained from books, but also from actually hearing a text read aloud or a practice described by someone who has heard it from his own teacher (and who has experienced success in it's practice). Tradition dictates the necessity of giving and receiving such spoken transmissions, which in many cases are said to originate (through a long line of transmitters and recipients) from Śākyamuni Buddha.

On oral transmission, see Tulku Thondup Rinpoche, *Hidden Teachings of Tibet*, pp. 45-49 and Sonam Gyatso, *Essence of Refined Gold*, pp. 36-37, 38-39, and 41-43.

Of these three more specialized dimensions of meaning, the doctrinal dimension is particularly important for an understanding of Buddhist Tibetan and cannot be ignored when translating texts from Tibetan into other languages. Once the basics of the phonemic and syntactic dimensions have been presented, a great deal of emphasis will be placed not just on the lexical dimension (which began with Chapter Two) but also on this technical dimension of Tibetan.

# Vocabulary

Memorize the spellings, pronunciations, and meanings of these nouns, among which are included model examples of the use of subscripts. Practice speaking them.

## Nouns

|  |  |  |
|---|---|---|
| ཀླུ་ | lu | *nāga* |
| དཀྱིལ་འཁོར་ | g̱yíl-khor or g̱yín-khor | mandala |
| དགྲ་ | ḍa | enemy |
| རྒྱུ་ | gyu | cause |
| རྒྱུད་ | gyü' | continuum |
| སྒྲ་ | ḍa | sound |
| སྒྲ་བཤད་ | ḍa-s̄hë' | explanation of words |
| སྒྲིབ་པ་ | ḍíp-b̄a | obstruction |
| སྒྲོལ་བ་ | ḍöl-wa | liberation |
| སྒྲོལ་མ་ | ḍöl-ma | Tara (*Tārā*) |
| དོན་གཅིག་ | tön-ĵik | equivalent |
| འདྲི་བ་ | ḍi-wa | question |
| རྣམ་པར་རྟོག་པ་ | ñam-b̄ar-ḏok-b̄a | conceptuality, thought |
| ཕྱག་འཚལ་བ་ | chak-tshël-wa | prostration [bowing down] |
| བྱིས་པ་ | c̱hí>-b̄a | child, immature person |
| བླ་མ་ | l̄a-ma | guru |

| བློ་ | lo | mind |
|---|---|---|
| དབྱིབས་ | yíp | shape |
| དབྱེ་བ་ | yé-wa | division, category |
| འབྱུང་བ་ | jung-wa | arising, element |
| འབྲས་བུ་ | ḍë>-bu | fruit, effect |
| འབྲེལ་བ་ | ḍél-wa | relationship, connection |
| སྦྱོར་བ་ | jor-wa | application, connection, endeavor, preparation, syllogism |
| མ་རིག་པ་ | ma-rík-b̄a | ignorance, unawareness |
| མྱ་ངན་ལས་འདས་པ་ | nya-ngën-lë>-dë>-b̄a | nirvana (*nirvāṇa*) |
| མཚན་ཉིད་ | tshën-nyí' | definition, characteristic |
| མཚན་གཞི་ | tshën-s̱hí | illustration |
| ཟླ་བ་ | da-wa | moon |
| ཡིག་ཆ་ | yík-cha or yîk-cha | textbook |
| ཡེ་ཤེས་ | yé-s̄hé> | wisdom, pristine awareness |
| ཡུལ་ཅན་ | yül-j̈en | subject |
| རླུང་ | lung | wind; energy wind (*prāṇa*) |
| སངས་རྒྱས་ | s̄ang-gyë> | Buddha |
| སྲས་ | s̄ë> | son or child [H] |
| སྲིད་པ་ | s̄í-b̄a | existence |

### Pronouns

| ཁྱོད་ | khyö' | you |
|---|---|---|

### Adjectives

| སྐད་ཅིག་མ་ | ḡë'-ĵîk-ma | momentary (made of moments) |
|---|---|---|

### Particles

| ལ་ | la | to, in, at, for |
|---|---|---|
| ལས་ | lë> | from |

# CHAPTER 8

*Pronunciation: Rules and Exceptions*
*Syllables and Words*
*Tibetan Numbers*
*Doctrinal Dialects*

## Summary and Review of Pronunciation Rules

Here is a summary of the main rules of pronunciation that have been covered so far.

- The Tibetan alphabet has thirty consonants and four vowels which are combined to make syllables; it is more the rule than the exception for syllables to have silent letters.

- Each syllable has a central letter, called the root letter. Whether it is the first letter of the syllable or not, this root letter is the first letter to be pronounced in the syllable. (It is also under this letter that a syllable will be found in the dictionary.)

- In addition to being the root letter, there are six other functions that a letter can perform in a syllable. A Tibetan syllable usually has a single vowel sound and, sometimes, a terminating consonant. A syllable can be anything from a single consonant (with its inherent vowel sound **a**) to an aggregate of six consonants and a vowel modification.

- Prefixes and superscribed letters are not pronounced with even part of their full value but do alter the pronunciation of some root letters (in that they remove aspiration from Column 3 root letters).[46]

- Subscribed letters differ in their effect on pronunciation. A subscribed ཡ is pronounced with part of its value; it adds a **y** but not a full **ya** to most of the root letters with which it is used. (That is, a ཁ with a subscribed ཡ— ཁྱ —is **kya** and not **kaya**. The ཁ retains its vowel **a**, being the root letter, and the ཡ does not add another vowel.)

  A subscribed ལ, however, typically changes the root letter to a **la** and so is pronounced with its full value. And a subscribed ར radically alters the pronunciation of the letters from which it hangs, changing them to *ḍa, ṭha,* or *ṭa.*

- Some suffixes are pronounced with part of their value—a མ suffix adds an **m** (not a **ma**) to the end of a syllable. Similar effects occur with the suffixes ག, ང, བ, and ར. Other suffixes are not themselves pronounced, but alter the sound of the vowels that precede them; examples are ས and ད. The suffixes ན and ལ both alter the pronunciation of the vowels preceding them and are pronounced as **n** and **l**.

## Exceptions to the Pronunciation Rules

Some of the following exceptions have already been discussed; others are introduced here for the first time.

### *Exception One*

ལ superscribed to ཧ— ལྷ —is pronounced **hla**. This is the only case in which a superscribed letter is pronounced. Note that the pronunciation is not **l** followed by **h**, but **hla**—**h** followed by **l**. ལྷ means *god* or *deity.* The term refers to two different kinds of beings:

1   the gods who comprise the upper tiers of cyclic existence (འཁོར་བ **khor-wa**—see Chapter Ten), beings who are superior to humans neither in morals nor in wisdom, but mainly in pleasure and length of lifetime;

2   enlightened beings (Buddhas).

The second usage is from tantra and gives rise to terminology such as *deity yoga* (ལྷའི་རྣལ་འབྱོར་ [hlë ñen-jor]—see Exception Nine), meditation in which the practitioner creates him or herself as a Buddha through visualization and conviction.

ལྷ་ས་ —**hla-ṣa**, *place of the gods*—is the main city in Tibet.

## Exception Two

ཥ་ is pronounced **ma** and not *ṭa*.    ཥ་ is normally pronounced ṣa; only sometimes is it pronounced **ḍa**.  This follows no discernible pattern.

| | | |
|---|---|---|
| སྨྲ་བ་ | **m̄a-wa** | speaking, propounding |

The combination of ར་ subscribed to ས་ is more common and is seen in words such as the following.

| | | |
|---|---|---|
| སྲིད་པ་ | **ṣí'-b̄a** | existence (rebirth) |

## Exception Three

ཧྲ་ is pronounced as it is spelt—**hra**. (It is pronounced neither *ṭa*, following the general rule, nor **ha** (on the model of ཥ་ being pronounced ṣa). ཧྲིལ་པོ་ is an adjective meaning *complete* and *round*.

## Exception Four

ཟླ་ is pronounced **da** and not **l̄a**.  The word ཟླ་བ་ (**da-wa**) means *moon*.

## Exception Five

ད་ as a prefix to the root letter བ་ causes the pronunciation of the  བ་ to change in surprising, but regular, ways.  This is probably the most common exception to the general rules; it may, in fact, be so common that it should be called a rule and not an exception.  In any event, the pronunciation changes are seen in the following examples.

| དབང་པོ་ | w̄ang-b̄o or āng-b̄o | empowerment / initiation |
| དབྱིབས་ | ȳíp | shape |

These changes occur only in certain well defined cases. The root letter བ་ becomes a high tone w̄a only when it has a ད་ prefix *and has no subscript*. It becomes a high tone ȳa only in those cases in which it has a ད་ prefix and a subscribed ྱ. Thus, the syllable དབག་ is pronounced ḍak and not w̄ak. Similarly, it is only the third column བ་ that becomes w̄a (or ȳa) in the above circumstances; the first column པ་ makes no such change. Thus, དཔའ་བོ་ is pronounced b̄a-wo (*hero*).

Note in the first example (དབང་པོ་)—where the root letter བ་ is prefixed by a ད་ but not subscribed by a ྱ—there are two options for pronouncing the letter. Both are correct in Hla-s̄a Tibetan.

## Exception Six

Many Tibetan nouns and adjectives have one of the **generic suffix syllables**— པ་, པོ་, བ་, བོ་, མ་, or མོ་ —as a concluding syllable. When བ་ is the concluding *syllable* of a word, it is pronounced **wa**; བོ་ in the same situation is pronounced **wo**.

| རུང་བ་ | **rung-wa** | suitable, proper |
| ཆུ་བོ་ | **chu-wo** | river |

## Exception Seven

The Tibetan syllables that we have been examining are made of words and particles, where **particles** are one or two syllable units whose only function is to relate words to one another. (Particles are introduced in Chapters Nine and Ten.) Among the particles are **case marking particles**—single-syllable particles that are placed after nouns, pronouns, and adjectives to show how they relate to other words around them in phrases, clauses, and sentences.

When a Tibetan word ends in a syllable that has a suffix, case marking particles follow that final syllable. Adding the connective[47] case marking particle ཀྱི to the word སྲས་ produces the following.

| སྲས་ཀྱི | **së>-ḡyí** | of the child, child's |

Adding the agentive particle to སངས་རྒྱས་ yields the following construction.

| སངས་རྒྱས་ཀྱིས་ | **s̄ang-gyë>-ḡyí>** | by Buddha |

*By Buddha* is a literal translation of སངས་རྒྱས་ཀྱིས་. In most cases, agentive case marking particles merely serve to mark the subject of certain types of verbs and are not to be translated as separate words in English.

However, in the case of syllables that do not end in suffixes—such as པ་, པོ་, བ་, and བོ་—the very common agentive and connective **cases** are indicated by adding letters to the syllable itself.

- པ་ becomes པས་ in the agentive case; it is pronounced **bë>**, with a falling tone.

- པ་ becomes པའི་ in the connective case, and is pronounced **bë**, with a flat high tone.

- Analogously, པོ་ in the agentive case—པོས་—is **bö>**, pronounced with a falling tone.

- In the connective case པོ་ becomes པོའི་ and is pronounced **bö**, with a flat high tone.

The above holds true as well when བ་ and བོ་ are final syllables of words, and the same principle is seen with **u**-syllables: སུས་ is **s̄ü>** and སུའི་ is **s̄ü**.

The other two vowels are affected in the following ways.

- རི་ (**rí**, *mountain*) becomes རིའི་ in the connective case and is pronounced with a lengthened **í**: **ríi**. In the agentive case it becomes རིས་ and is pronounced **rí>**.

- དེ་ (**té**, *that*) becomes དེའི་ in the connective case and will be heard either without recognizeable change (as **té**) or as **téí** (that is, **té-í**). The agentive དེས་ is pronounced **té>**.

## *Exception Eight*

Syllables other than the first syllable in a word tend not to be stressed. In many cases, this causes column 3 aspirates (ཀ་, ཅ་, ཏ་, and པ་) to lose their aspiration when they are the root letters of second, third, or fourth syllables in words.

An example would be ཡི་དམ་, meaning *personal deity*. It is pronounced **yí-dam** and not **yí-tam**, whereas the word དམ་པ་ by itself is pronounced **tam-b̄a**. The difference lies in the fact that in the first case, the ཏ་ is the root letter of the unstressed second syllable (and thus loses its aspiration), while in the second case it is the root letter of a stressed syllable.

The strongly aspirated letters of column 2, by the way, usually do not lose their aspiration when they are the root letters of unstressed syllables. An example is ཆོས་ འཁོར་ meaning *wheel of doctrine*; it is pronounced **chö-khor** and not **chö-gor**. The word ཉན་ཐོས་, on the other hand, is pronounced both **nyën-thö** and **nyën-d̄ö**. ཉན་ཐོས་ means *Hearer* (Sanskrit: *śrāvaka*).

## *Exception Nine*

Sometimes an འ་ prefix beginning a syllable "assimilates" to the end of the previous syllable and causes the suffix of that previous syllable to be pronounced as a nasal. An example is རྣལ་འབྱོར་, a term meaning *yoga*. Although it is sometimes pronounced **n̄ël-jor**, following the rules, more often it is pronounced **n̄ën-jor**. Likewise, the Tibetan translation of the Sanskrit word *mandala*—དཀྱིལ་འཁོར་—whose pronunciation following the rules is **ḡyíl-khor**, is more often pronounced **ḡyín-khor**. Here are two other examples of this principle.

| ། | | |
|---|---|---|
| སྒྲུབ་འཇུག་ | ḍum-juk | complete engagement[48] |
| དགེ་འདུན་ | gén-dün | spiritual community (*sangha*) |

The same sort of effect is seen with the prefix མ་. It can cause the syllable before it to be pronounced as if it had a མ་ suffix. An example is རྒྱ་མཚོ་ (*ocean*), which—following the rules—is pronounced **gya-tso,** but may also—in accordance with this exception—be pronounced **gyam-tso.**

---

# Drill 8.1
Practice reading and speaking these syllables and words.

| | | | | | |
|---|---|---|---|---|---|
| 1 | གླུ་ | ཀླུ་ | ཁྱུན་གྲུབ་ | ལྱ་པོ་ | | |
| 2 | འདྲ་བ་ | ཕྱལ་པོ་ | ཅམ་པ་ | ཀླག་པ་ | རྩིབ་ | སྲོག་ |
| 3 | སྐུ་དྲན་ | སྐུར་ | སྨྲིན་ | སྒྲུ་གུ་ | སྐྲོས་ | སྒྲོན་པ་ |
| 4 | དཔེ་ | དཀྱི་ | དབག་ | དབང་ | བྱང་ | སྒྲག་ |
| 5 | ཆེན་མོ་ | ཆེན་མོས་ | ཆེན་མོའི་ | དབང་པོའི་ | དབང་པོས་ | སྙིང་མོ་ |

---

# Patterns in the Tibetan Language
## *Letters, Syllables, and Words*

---

The nine levels of Tibetan were introduced in Chapter Five. You have reached the point where you know the letters, the ways in which they may be combined to form syllables, and their pronunciation when they are so combined. Levels 1 and 2 have thus been understood and level 3—the combination of syllables to form particles and words—is about to be introduced. By way of review, the first three levels are as follows.

1 **Letters** are consonants with or without vowel markers. They function only as constituents of syllables (although there are some single-letter syllables).

- ང་ is a letter.
- ཀྵི is a letter.

2  **Syllables** are minimally a single letter and at most six consonants and a
vowel marker. Syllables are separated from one another with dots.

- ང་, དང་, and རེམ་ are examples of relatively simple syllables involving only root letters, vowel markers, and suffix letters.

- དབང་ is a syllable with a prefix and a suffix letter.
བཤགས་ has a prefix, a suffix, and a secondary suffix.

- སྐོ་ has a superscript, and སྐྲ་ has both a superscript and a subscript.

- བསྒྲུབས་ has letters in all possible positions: prefix, suffix, secondary
suffix, superscript, subscript, and vowel-marker.

3  **Particles** and **words** are built from syllables. Most words have more
than one syllable, whereas many particles have only one. There are,
however, quite a few single-syllable words in Tibetan.

- ང་ (*I*) is an example of the simplest sort of syllable as well as the
simplest sort of word. དེ་ (*that*) is also a single-syllable word, as
is ཆོས་ (*phenomenon*).

- གྱི་ (*of*) is a single-syllable particle. པ་ and དང་ are also particles.
གྱི་ belongs to a class of particles—called **case marking particles**—that are used with nouns, pronouns, and adjectives to show
how they relate to other words around them. པ་, on the other
hand, is a particle used to form nouns and adjectives and is found
only within words; it is a **lexical particle**. དང་ (*and*) would in
English be a conjunction, but in Tibetan belongs with the **syntactic particles**.

Many Tibetan words, and some particles, have two syllables.

- བུམ་པ་ (*pot*) is a two-syllable word ending in the lexical particle པ་;
དབུ་མ་ (*middle* or *middle way*) is a two-syllable word ending in the
lexical particle མ་. ཁ་དོག་ (*color*) is a two-syllable word that incorporates no lexical particles.

- གཞན་ཡང་ (*moreover*) is a two-syllable syntactic particle.

Many Tibetan words, and a few particles, have three syllables.

- མི་རྟག་པ་ (*impermanent*) is a three-syllable word ending in the lexical particle པ་ and beginning with the lexical particle མི་.

- དེ་བས་ན་ (*therefore*) is a three-syllable syntactic particle.

Quite a few Tibetan words—especially words created to translate Buddhist Sanskrit terms—have four or more syllables.

- རྣམ་པར་ཤེས་པ་ (*consciousness*—Sanskrit *vijñāna*) is a four-syllable word ending in the lexical particle པ་ and beginning with the lexical particle རྣམ་པར་.

- རྣམ་པར་མི་རྟོག་པ་ (*nonconceptual*) also begins with the lexical particle རྣམ་པར་, and incorporates a མི་ and a པ་ as well.

- མྱ་ངན་ལས་འདས་པ་ translates the Sanskrit word *nirvāṇa*. This term is usually translated into English as *nirvana*.

## Syllables and Words

The rules for identifying root letters are part of the analysis of levels 1 and 2, letters and syllables. Level 3 is that of particles and words, considered in themselves and not taking into account their uses in phrases, clauses, and sentences. Tibetan syllables make up words and particles in three ways:

- as entire single-syllable words or particles,

- as the final syllables of multi-syllable words or particles,

- as the beginning or middle syllables of multi-syllable words or particles.

The first and second kinds are syllables that end words. The fact that they end a word (or particle) means, in Tibetan, that they are the place at which a word or particle makes a connection to other words and particles. Thus, if one wanted to connect the word དབུས་ (*middle, center*) to another word or to some part of a sentence, it would be at, or more precisely, *after* the ས་ syllable that this would be done.

> It is at its end that a syllable or particle is connected to the remainder of a sentence.

In English, on the other hand, we say things like *to the middle* and *in the middle*, where both the article (*the*) and the prepositions (*to* and *in*) *precede* the word. In Tibetan both articles (which are much less frequently used than in English), adjectives, and the particles that connect a word such as དྲུལ་ to other parts of the sentence are placed *after the word*.

## *Syllables at the Beginning or in the Middle of a Word*

A syllable at the beginning or in the middle of a multi-syllable word or particle is just a building block. Its relation to what follows it—the other syllables in the word or particle—is fixed. Most importantly, it has no relation of its own to anything outside the word or particle. Such a syllable may be the first syllable of a two-syllable word or particle:

| ཏག་པ་ | ཁ་དོག་ | ཡོད་པ་ |
|:---:|:---:|:---:|
| ↑ | ↑ | ↑ |

Again, it may be the first or second syllable in a three-syllable word, or the first, second, or third syllable in a four-syllable word:

| མི་ཏག་པ་ | རྣམ་པར་བཞག་པ་ | རྣམ་པར་ཤེས་པ་ |
|:---:|:---:|:---:|
| ↑ ↑ | ↑ ↑ ↑ | ↑ ↑ ↑ |

རྣམ་པར་བཞག་པ་ means *presentation*; རྣམ་པར་ཤེས་པ་ means *consciousness*.

The importance of these syllables is limited. They are merely components of words or particles and have *no* relationship with any syllable *outside* of the word or particle of which they are parts.

This type of syllable may be considered to be *enclosed within* a word or particle. In the word དྲུལ་, the enclosed syllable would be དྲུ་. Think of a word as a box containing smaller boxes; these smaller boxes are the syllables of the word, *only the last of which* determines how a word relates to the remainder of a sentence or a clause.

The use of boxes nested one within another to diagram Tibetan is very helpful—especially as it will be done later on, showing the relationship not between syllables within words, but between words and clauses within sentences. At this point, however, we are dealing only with syllables within words—diagramming words as large boxes containing smaller syllable-boxes. Here are some examples of word diagrams:

Note that the box surrounding the last syllable also surrounds all the other syllables. This symbolizes the function performed by the syllable at the end of a word. This final syllable is the interface to the rest of the sentence. Another way of speaking about the importance of the end of a Tibetan word will be seen in Chapter Ten when the functions performed by the dots at the end of words are described.

## Syllables at the End of Words

The syllable that ends a multi-syllable word is, like the other syllables, a building block of that word. However, it is more—it is the key syllable where the reader is shown the way in which the word is used in a clause or sentence. It is at this syllable that the word will be modified—through the addition of a particle—to show the relationship of the word to the rest of the sentence. In many instances this modification is done by placing a particle immediately after that syllable.

བུམ་པ་ (**pum-b̄a**) becomes, for example:

བུམ་པ་ལ་ (**pum-b̄a-la**)—*to the pot,* (also *in, for, at the pot*) and
བུམ་པ་ལས་ (**pum-b̄a-lë>**)—*from the pot.*

Sometimes, however, (as has been seen in pronunciation exception seven), the particle merges into the final syllable itself and changes it.

Illustrations of this are:

ཕུམ་པའི་ (**pum-bë**)—*of the pot*,

ཕུམ་པས་ (**pum-bë>**)—*by the pot*, and

ཕུམ་པར་ (**pum-bar**)—*to the pot* or *as the pot* or *in the pot*.


## Tibetan Numbers

The numerals and their names, from one to ten, are as follows:

| | | | |
|---|---|---|---|
| 1 | ༡ | གཅིག་ | *jĭk* |
| 2 | ༢ | གཉིས་ | *ñyĭ>* |
| 3 | ༣ | གསུམ་ | *sum* |
| 4 | ༤ | བཞི་ | *shĭ* |
| 5 | ༥ | ལྔ་ | *ñga* |
| 6 | ༦ | དྲུག་ | *ṭuk* |
| 7 | ༧ | བདུན་ | *dün* |
| 8 | ༨ | བརྒྱད་ | *gyë»* |
| 9 | ༩ | དགུ་ | *gu* |
| 10 | ༡༠ | བཅུ་ | *ju* |

Actually, when counting, ten can occur as བཅུ་ཐམ་པ་. However, often when talking about ten of something, the word is just བཅུ་.

These are the first ten cardinal numbers. The ordinal numbers are formed, with one important exception, by adding a second syllable to the names of the cardinal numbers: thus, where *two* is གཉིས་, *second* is གཉིས་པ་. The exception is that whereas *one* is གཅིག་, *first* is དང་པོ་. གཅིག་པ་ means not *first*, but *same*.

## Drill 8.2

Here are some words and particles from the vocabularies of previous chapters.

- Draw boxes around words as shown above.
- Each numbered group of words (or words and particles) is a meaningful unit, either a phrase or a complete sentence. Try to translate each into English. (Answers to this and all subsequent drills are given at the end of the book, after the appendices.)

1. ཞིམ་པོ་ཤེས་པ་ལྷུན་མིན་འདུ་བྱེད་གསུམ་

2. ཡོད་པ་མེད་པ་གཉིས།

3. གཟུགས་སེམས་འགལ་བ་

4. འཁོར་བ་རྒྱུ་ངན་ལས་འདས་པ་

5. བུམ་པ་དེ་མི་རྟག་པ་ཡིན།

6. སངས་རྒྱས་ལ་མ་རིག་པ་མེད།

7. འཁོར་བ་ལས་སྒྲོལ་བ་ཡོད།

8. ལས་དགེ་བ་དང་མི་དགེ་བ་

9. ཡེ་ཤེས་མ་རིག་པ་རྣམ་པར་རྟོག་པ་ལྱལ་ཅན་ཡིན།

10. སེམས་ཡིད་རྣམ་པར་ཤེས་པ་དོན་གཅིག་ཡིན།

## Doctrinal Vocabulary and Grammar
### *Dialects of the Doctrinal Dimension*

It was pointed out in Chapter Four that translation of Buddhist texts from Tibetan requires more than a lexical understanding of Tibetan words. At least as important is an understanding of the technical usage of terms—called here the doctrinal dimension of Tibetan.

However, the best sort of translation relies not only on the general doctrinal meanings of Tibetan Buddhist terms, but on their meanings as understood by the author of the text being translated and, later, by Tibetan readers of that text. (This is a theoretical norm, and not an attainable one, since the author's understanding of a text is not retrievable, and readers' understandings change with distance in time and space from the author.)

What is needed is a middle way between, on the one hand, the sort of literal translation that assumes that any given term has one meaning (or a limited group of meanings) that remains static over all texts and across the centuries and, on the other hand, the philosophy of translation that claims that the modern Western reader's critical understanding of a text is as valid (or more valid) as any other. One approach to that middle way is to be aware that there are as many dialects of Buddhist Tibetan as there are writers of Buddhist texts or, for that matter, as there are texts (since authors may change their minds over the course of their lives). Another is to attempt to balance the Western method of historical analysis of texts, in which traditional claims are looked at with great suspicion, with the Tibetan use of a text as a skeleton for the oral transmission of its subject matter. Both methods provide valuable insights to the translator.

The idea of variant dialects of Doctrinal Tibetan has its roots in two traditional Tibetan ways of thinking about different varieties of Buddhism. The first is a way of ordering the Buddhist philosophies seen in Indian texts dating from about the first century onwards; the traditional name for this taxonomy is the **four tenet systems** (གྲུབ་མཐའ་ *ṭup-tha*). The other way of looking at Buddhism is to look at systems of practice and of textual transmission and commentary as they evolved in Tibet. This latter way is not based purely on either texts or practices, since many of the defining factors of this evolution were political, social, and geographical. Here, speaking of the main types of Tibetan Buddhism—as seen in monastic institutions—are the **four orders of Tibetan Buddhism** (ཆོས་ལུགས་ **chö>-luk**—literally, *systems of religion*).

## The Four Buddhist Tenet Systems

As seen from Tibet, there are four main Indian schools of Buddhist tenets, listed here according to the Tibetan assessment of their profundity relative to one another. The Middle Way School is held to be most correct and the *Great Exposition* School to be farthest from reality.

| | | |
|---|---|---|
| དབུ་མ་པ་ | **ū-ma-b̄a** | Middle Way School<br>Skt: *Mādhyamika* |
| སེམས་ཙམ་པ་ | **s̄êm-d̄zam-b̄a** | Mind Only School<br>Skt: *Cittamātra* |
| མདོ་སྡེ་པ་ | **do-dé-b̄a** | Sutra School<br>Skt: *Sautrāntika* |
| བྱེ་བྲག་སྨྲ་བ་ | **c̱hé-ḍak-m̄a-wa** | *Great Exposition* School<br>Skt: *Vaibhāṣika* |

In terms of practice, Tibetan Buddhists are followers of the Middle Way School (although the Mind Only School had decisive influence on tantric practice). In terms of Tibetan commentaries on earlier texts, the matter is somewhat more complex, with writers often taking a tenet system other than the Middle Way School as normative for the sake of commenting on a particular text or genre of texts. For example, works on epistemology are often written from a Sutra School perspective. It is for this reason that translators must be aware that these four tenet systems present them with at least four different dialects of doctrinal vocabulary.

> For a thoughtful discussion of the pros and cons of the doxographic approach embodied in the study of tenet systems, see Geshe Lhundup Sopa and Jeffrey Hopkins, *Cutting Through Appearances*, pp. 111-13 and 117-20. For a detailed overview of the four systems following contemporary traditional accounts, see Hopkins, *Meditation on Emptiness*, pp. 335-351 and 365-439.

More academically oriented overviews of Buddhist doctrine may be seen in Paul Williams, *Mahāyāna Buddhism: the Doctrinal Foundations* and Hirakawa Akira, *A History of Indian Buddhism: From Śākyamuni to Early Mahāyāna.* Nakamura Hajime's *Indian Buddhism: A Survey with Bibliographical Notes* is a valuable source for bibliographic information and synopses of scholarly works.

Tenet systems and the Indian Buddhist thinkers associated with them are presented in more detail in Chapter Sixteen.

## *The Four Orders of Tibetan Buddhism*

There are currently four main orders in Tibetan Buddhism—where an order is understood as an institutionalized lineage in which Buddhist teachings, empowerments, and vows are passed down from generation to generation.

| རྙིང་མ་ | **ñyíng-ma** | Nyingma [Ancient (Translations)] |
|---|---|---|
| བཀའ་བརྒྱུད་ | **ḡa-gyü'** | Gagyu [Transmission of the Word] |
| ས་སྐྱ་ | **ṡa-ḡya** | Sagya [Grey Earth] |
| དགེ་ལུགས་ | **gé-luk** | Géluk [Way of Virtue] |

A member of the རྙིང་མ་ order is called a རྙིང་མ་པ་. Likewise, a follower of བཀའ་བརྒྱུད་ is called a བཀའ་བརྒྱུད་པ་, and those associated with the ས་སྐྱ་ and དགེ་ལུགས་ lineages are known, respectively, as ས་སྐྱ་པ་ and དགེ་ལུགས་པ་.

The final syllables པ་, པོ་, བ་, and བོ་ may be used—as seen here—as **subjective suffix syllables** showing agency, ownership, or membership. (See Chapter Eleven.)

Thus, where དགེ་ལུགས་ is the name of a lineage of teaching and monastic ordination centered in certain monasteries, a དགེ་ལུགས་པ་ is a member of that lineage. This same process is seen in the creation of the names of the tenet systems.

The རྙིང་མ་པ་ are so named because they follow the earlier translations of tantras from Indic languages into Tibetan, whereas the other three—in relation to the རྙིང་མ་ —are གསར་མ་པ་, that is, *New Ones*, since they follow the "new" (which means "later") translations of the tantras. The ས་སྐྱ་པ་ are named for the seat of their order, which is at a place named ས་སྐྱ་ or *Grey Earth*. བཀའ་བརྒྱུད་ and དགེ་ལུགས་, on the other hand, are descriptive terms in the same way that the terms མདོ་སྡེ་པ་ and དབུ་མ་པ་ are. Just as all Buddhists—not just the Sūtra School—are followers of Buddha's discourses (མདོ་སྡེ་—the *sūtras*), and all Buddhists attempt to follow a middle way (དབུ་ མ་), not just the Middle Way School, so all four orders of Tibetan Buddhism, not only the བཀའ་བརྒྱུད་, are lineages in which Buddha's Word (བཀའ་) is transmitted, and all four orders teach the importance of virtue (དགེ་བ་)—the observance of ethics and vowed commitments—not merely the དགེ་ལུགས་.

> For brief overviews of the four orders, see Stephen Batchelor, *The Jewel in the Lotus: A Guide to the Buddhist Traditions of Tibet*, pp. 58-63, and Marylin Rhie and Robert Thurman, *Wisdom and Compassion: The Sacred Art of Tibet*, pp. 26-30. For more detailed academic approaches, see David Snellgrove, *Indo-Tibetan Buddhism* (vol. II), pp. 485-508 and Giuseppe Tucci, *The Religions of Tibet*, pp. 33-39.

## *Principal Figures in the History of Buddhism in Tibet*

Although there are many important authors and meditators in the history of Tibetan Buddhism, there are some who stand out as major innovators or systematizers. The three listed immediately below are Indians who traveled to Tibet and were important for the initial introduction of Buddhism there.

སློབ་དཔོན་པདྨ་འབྱུང་གནས་

**lo-bön bë-ma-jung-ñë>**

Ācārya (སློབ་དཔོན་) Padmasambhava founded the Nyingma lineage. He is remembered for his yogic powers, especially his subjugation and conversion of the indigenous spirits of Tibet.

Padmasambhava's activities in Tibet are are recounted by Dudjom
Rinpoche in *The Nyingma School of Tibetan Buddhism*, pp. 512-21.
On the life of Padmasambhava, see Rhie and Thurman, *Wisdom and
Compassion*, pp. 168, 176-179; for the iconographic dimension of
Padmasambhava's life, see pp. 169-175 and 180-183.

| | |
|---|---|
| མཁན་ཆེན་ཞི་བ་འཚོ་<br>**khën-chên s̱hi-wa-tsho** | The Great Abbot (མཁན་ཆེན་) Śāntarakṣita came from India during the time of Padmasambhava, but as a scholarly defender of Buddhism. |
| དཔལ་ལྡན་ཨ་ཏི་ཤ་<br>**b̄ël-den a-d̄i-s̱ha** | Atīśa came to Tibet in 1042. He founded the བཀའ་གདམས་ (*Instruction in the Word*) lineage, a predecessor of the Géluk and Gagyu orders. |

Tibetans dislike calling spiritual teachers and leaders by their 'bare names.'
Thus, instead of saying ཨ་ཏི་ཤ་, they say དཔལ་ལྡན་ཨ་ཏི་ཤ་, *the glorious Atisha.*
Likewise, པདྨ་འབྱུང་གནས་ becomes སློབ་དཔོན་པདྨ་འབྱུང་གནས་, and ཞི་བ་འཚོ་ is མཁན་ཆེན་ཞི་
བ་འཚོ་.

For a synopsis of the activities of Atisha in Tibet, see Snellgrove, *Indo-
Tibetan Buddhism*, pp. 479-84. A contemporary traditional account
(deriving from the Géluk *Stages of the Path* tradition) may be seen in
Pabongka Rinpoche, *Liberation in Our Hands* (Tharchin and Engle
translation), Part One, pp. 31-57.

The name Padmasambhava (པདྨ་འབྱུང་གནས་) means Lotus-Born—literally *he whose
origin* (འབྱུང་གནས་) *is a lotus* (པདྨ་). པདྨ་ is a transliteration of the Sanskrit *padma*, with
the *d + m* written in Tibetan as if the མ were subscribed to the ད. Note that whereas
the Sanskrit word is *padma*, Tibetans pronounce it **b̄e-ma**, following the rules for
pronouncing their own language.

Famous Tibetan teachers and authors are often known by their titles, names
based on their institutional seats or places of origin, or other epithets, rather than by
their proper names. Thus Padmasambhava is referred to more often as གུ་རུ་རིན་པོ་ཆེ་

(**gu-ru-rîn-b̄o-ché**—*Precious Guru*) and Atīśa as ཇོ་བོ་རྗེ་ (**jo-wo-jé**—*Foremost Lord*).

Although there are both scholars and yogis in each of the four orders, the Sagya and Géluk traditions emphasize rational philosophical study more than the Nyingma and Gagyu. Those of the Nyingma and Gagyu lineages, on the other hand, see themselves as continuations of the lineages of the Indian *siddhas* (གྲུབ་ཐོབ་ **t̥up-thop**—*adepts, accomplished ones*), practitioners of Vajrayāna Buddhism known for their magical powers and their poetic expressions, sometimes in song, of their meditative experiences. An understanding of both traditions—the rational and the nonrational—is essential to an understanding of Tibetan Buddhism, since, in fact, all Tibetan Buddhists combine the two in a distinctive way.

The term 'nonrational' does not mean 'irrational'—although there are many instances in which Buddhist teachers, especially the tantric gurus, act in seemingly irrational ways in order to *train* (འདུལ་ **dül**—literally *tame*) their *disciples* (གདུལ་བྱ་ **dül-ja**—literally *those to be tamed*). I use the term 'nonrational' in order to avoid the term 'mystical,' a term not well suited to the translation of Buddhist accounts of meditative experience, accounts which emphasize knowledge and clarity rather than mystery.

> For an example of the way in which the rational and nonrational are blended in the life and philosophy of the most well known Tibetan Buddhist of modern times, the fourteenth Dalai Lama, see *Freedom in Exile: the Autobiography of the Dalai Lama* (New York: HarperCollins, 1990).

---

| | | |
|---|---|---|
| བསྟན་འཛིན་རྒྱ་མཚོ་ | **d̄en-d̠zîn-gya-tsho** | Tenzin Gyatso, the fourteenth Dalai Lama, was born in 1935. |

---

Again, བསྟན་འཛིན་རྒྱ་མཚོ་ is another bare name. A traditional Tibetan Buddhist would preface it with a ceremonial title, saying in this case, རྒྱལ་དབང་བསྟན་འཛིན་ རྒྱ་མཚོ་ or རྒྱལ་བ་བསྟན་འཛིན་རྒྱ་མཚོ་.

Note that in this case D̄enzin Gyatso is Tenzin Gyatso.

---

Where a widely known Western spelling varies from the phonemic romanization usually used in this book, the widely accepted usage will be followed. Thus, D̄zong-ka-b̄a (see below) becomes Tsong-kha-pa.

---

*Dalai Lama* is not a Tibetan term; it is a title bestowed in the sixteenth century by the Mongolian leader, Altan Khan.[49] To Tibetans the Dalai Lama is རྒྱལ་བ་རིན་པོ་ཆེ་ (**gyël-wa rîn-b̄o-ché**—*precious conqueror*, where *conqueror* means Buddha) or ཡིད་བཞིན་ནོར་བུ་ (**yí'-s̲hí-nor-b̲u**, *wish-fulfilling jewel*).

Listed below are representative seminal figures from the four orders.

Rhie and Thurman, in *Wisdom and Compassion: The Sacred Art of Tibet*, present us with yet another dimension of Tibetan Buddhism, that of art and its symbolism. Discussions of each of the four orders along with visual representations of their principal figures and meditative visions may be found beginning on pages 165-167 (for the Nyingma tradition), 199 (Sagya), 236 (Gagyu), and 262-263 (Géluk).

---

| | | |
|---|---|---|
| མར་པ་ཆོས་ཀྱི་བློ་གྲོས་ <br> མི་ལ་རས་པ་ | **mar-b̄a chö>-ḡyí-lo-d̲ö>** <br><br> **mi-la-rë>-b̄a** | Marpa and Mila Repa are the quintessential Tibetan guru and disciple; the Gagyu lineages originate with them. |

---

Mila Repa (instead of Mi-la Ré-ba) and Marpa (instead of Mar-b̄a) are Western spellings used because of their currency rather than their phonemic accuracy.

The life of Mila Repa is well known in the West through the French translation of his biography by Jacques Bacot and the English version by Kazi Dawa-Samdup and W. Y. Evans-Wentz. A more modern translation is Lobsang Lhalungpa's *The Life of Milarepa*. The iconographic dimension of Mila's life may be seen in Rhie and Thurman, *Wisdom and Compassion*, pp. 237-245.

| ཀུན་དགའ་སྙིང་པོ | **ḡün-ga-ñyíng-b̄o** | Gunga Nyingbo (1092-1158) was the first of the great Sagya masters; Gunga Gyeltsen is better known as ས་ སྐྱ་པཎྜི་ཏ་ (s̄a-ḡya pan-ḍi-d̄a). |
| ཀུན་དགའ་རྒྱལ་མཚན་ | **ḡün-ga-gyël-tshën** | |

Most Tibetan religious names have a meaning apart from their use as names. Thus, whereas མར་པ་ merely means *person from the Mar region*, ཆོས་ཀྱི་བློ་གྲོས་ means *doctrinal intellect*. The ཀུན་དགའ་ in ཀུན་དགའ་སྙིང་པོ་ and ཀུན་དགའ་རྒྱལ་མཚན་ means *delight* or *bliss* and is no doubt a reference to Buddha's attendant and closest disciple, Ānanda (ཀུན་དགའ་པོ་ in Tibetan). A རྒྱལ་མཚན་ is a *victory banner*.

Sakya Pandita lived from 1182 to 1251.

> The spelling *Sakya Pandita* is the commonly accepted Western spelling.

པཎྜི་ཏ་ is a Tibetan transliteration of the Sanskrit *paṇḍita* (*scholar*). Written in a less compact form, we have the following:

པཎ་ཌི་ཏ་ — where ཎ་ is a reversed ན་ and ཊ་ is a reversed ཏ་.

In པཎྜི་ཏ་, the ཌ་ is simply written as if it were subscribed to the ཎ་.

ཌ་ and ཎ་ are retroflex letters; ཌ་ is pronounced like the Tibetan ད་.

> On the role of Sakya Pandita in Tibetan Buddhism, see the references to descriptions of the Sagya Order given above. See also Rhie and Thurman, pp. 210-211.

| ཀློང་ཆེན་དྲི་མེད་འོད་ཟེར་ <br><br> **l̄ong-chên ṭí-mé'-ö'-s̱ér** | The most respected writer in the Nyingma lineage, he is better known as ཀློང་ཆེན་རབ་འབྱམས་ or just as ཀློང་ཆེན་པ་. |

ཀློང་ཆེན་རབ་འབྱམས་ (l̄ong-chên ram-jam) lived from 1308 to 1364.

རྡུ་མེད་འོད་ཟེར་ means *stainless* (རྡུ་མེད་— literally 'stain not existing,' or 'without stain') *luminance* (འོད་ཟེར་—literally 'light rays'). Note that རབ་འབྱམས་ is an example of the assimilation of the འ-prefix to the end of the previous syllable as a nasal;  in this case the suffix བ is nasalized and the རབ་ becomes **ram.**

> A lengthy account of Long-chen-ba's life appears in *The Nyingma School of Tibetan Buddhism*, pp. 575-596.

---

| | |
|---|---|
| ཙོང་ཁ་པ་བློ་བཟང་གྲགས་པ་<br><br>**dzong-kha-ba lo-sang-dak-ba** | Tsong-kha-pa was the founder of the Géluk order, in which scholarship and monastic discipline are emphasized;  it became the most politically powerful of the four orders. |

---

Tsong-kha-pa lived from 1357 to 1419.  The name ཙོང་ཁ་པ་ alludes to his birth in the ཙོང་ཁ་ region of northeastern Tibet.

ཀློང་ཆེན་པ་ and ཙོང་ཁ་པ་ illustrate the use of subjective suffix syllables. ཙོང་ཁ་པ་ means *the one from Dzong-ka*, a region in Amdo. ཀློང་ཆེན་པ་ means *one of the great expanse*, referring to one of the core Great Completion (རྫོགས་པ་ཆེན་པོ་) teachings.  Both ཀློང་ཆེན་པ་ and ཙོང་ཁ་པ་ are also known—within their respective traditions—as, respectively, ཀུན་མཁྱེན་ཀློང་ཆེན་པ་ and རྗེ་བདག་ཉིད་ཆེན་པོ་:

ཀུན་མཁྱེན་ means *omniscient*;

རྗེ་བདག་ཉིད་ཆེན་པོ་ means, literally, *foremost great being*, where བདག་ཉིད་ཆེན་པོ་ would in Sanskrit be *mahātma*.

> On the life of Tsong-kha-pa, see Robert Thurman, *The Life and Teachings of Tsong Khapa*, pp. 4-34.  See also Rhie and Thurman, *Wisdom and Compassion*, pp. 266-267 and 372-373.

# *Vocabulary*

Memorize the spelling and pronunciation of these words; practice speaking them. In addition, learn the names of the four Buddhist tenet systems, the four orders of Tibetan Buddhism, and the numbers and numerals from one through ten.

## *Nouns*

| | | |
|---|---|---|
| ཀུན་མཁྱེན་ | **ḡün-khyên** | omniscient one |
| ཀློང་ | **l̄ong** | expanse |
| བཀའ་ | **ḡa** | speech, Word [H] |
| ཁ་དོག་ | **kha-dok** | color |
| མཁན་པོ་ | **khën-b̄o** | abbot |
| འཁོར་ལོ་ | **khor-lo** | wheel |
| གྲུབ་ཐོབ་ | **t̞up-thop** | [tantric] adept |
| གྲུབ་མཐའ་ | **t̞up-tha, t̞um-tha** | tenets [Skt. *siddhānta*] |
| དགེ་འདུན་ | **gén-dün** | spiritual community |
| རྒྱ་མཚོ་ | **gya-tsho, gyam-tsho** | ocean |
| ཆོས་ལུགས་ | **chö>-luk** | order ['system of doctrine'] |
| ཇོ་བོ་ | **jo-wo** | lord |
| རྗེ་ | **jé** | master, foremost one |
| དྲི་མ་ | **t̞í-ma** | stain, defilement |
| དྲི་མ་མེད་པ་ | **t̞í-ma-mé'-b̄a** | stainless |
| གདུལ་བྱ་ | **dül-ja** | disciple |

| བདག་ཉིད་ | **dak-nyi'** | being, nature |
| རྣམ་པར་རྟོག་པ་ | **ñam-b̄ar-d̄ok-b̄a** | conceptuality |
| རྣམ་པར་ཤེས་པ་ | **ñam-b̄ar-s̄hé>-b̄a** | consciousness |
| རྣལ་འབྱོར་ | **ñël-jor, ñën-jor** | yoga |
| ཤེམ་པོ་ | **pém-b̄o** | matter |
| བློ་གྲོས་ | **l̄o-ḍö>** | intelligence, intellect |
| དབང་པོ་ | **wang-b̄o** | empowerment, sense power |
| སྨྲ་བ་ | **m̄a-wa** | speaking, propounding |
| རྫོགས་པ་ | **ḏzok-b̄a** | completion |
| ཟླ་བ་ | **da-wa** | moon |
| འོད་ | **ö'** | light |
| འོད་ཟེར་ | **ö'-s̱ér** | radiance, luminance ['light rays'] |
| ཡི་དམ་ | **yí-dam** | personal deity |
| ལུགས་ | **luk** | system, way |
| སློབ་དཔོན་ | **l̄o-b̄ön** | *ācārya* |
| སྲིད་པ་ | **s̄í'-b̄a** | existence [rebirth] |
| ལྷ་ | **hla** | god, deity |
| ལྷ་ས་ | **hla-s̄a** | Lhasa [city] |

## Verbs

| | | |
|---|---|---|
| འདུལ་ | **d̠ül** | tame, subdue, train |
| སྨྲ་ | **m̄a** | speak, propound |
| སྲིད་ | **s̄í'** | be possible, exist |

## Adjectives

| | | |
|---|---|---|
| དང་པོ་ | **tang-b̄o** | first |
| རྫོགས་པ་ | **d̠zok-b̄a** | complete |
| རིན་པོ་ཆེ་ | **rîn-b̄o-ché** | precious |
| རུང་བ་ | **rung-wa** | suitable, proper |

Memorize the names of these four colors; they are the four primary colors (ཚ་བའི་ཁ་ དོག་ — **d̄za-wë kha-dok**).

| | | |
|---|---|---|
| སྔོན་པོ་ | **n̄gön-b̄o** | blue |
| སེར་པོ་ | **s̄ér-b̄o** | yellow |
| དཀར་པོ་ | **ḡar-b̄o** | white |
| དམར་པོ་ | **m̄ar-b̄o** | red |

## Lexical Particles

The asterisk (*) indicates where the remainder of the word would be in relation to the particle.

| | | |
|---|---|---|
| རྣམ་པར་ * | **n̄am-b̄ar** | [prefix syllable] |
| * པ་ | **b̄a** | [final syllable] |

| | | |
|---|---|---|
| * པོ་ | **b̄o** | [final syllable] |
| * བ་ | **wa** | [final syllable] |
| * བོ་ | **wo** | [final syllable] |
| མི་ * | **mí** | [negative] |
| * ་མེད་ | **mé'** | without … |

## Syntactic Particles

| | | |
|---|---|---|
| གྱི་ | **gyí** | of |
| དང་ | **tang** | and, or |
| གཞན་ཡང་ | **s̲hën-yang** | moreover, furthermore |

# Section Two

## The Lexical and Syntactic Dimensions of Tibetan

## Patterns in Syllables and Words

## Patterns in Phrases, Clauses, and Sentences

# CHAPTER 9

*Words*
   *Verbs and Syntactic Patterns*
   *Nouns, Pronouns, and Adjectives*
   *Adverbs and Postpositions*
*The Existent and the Nonexistent*

## Introduction and Review

Beginning at the most general level, one can say that any written symbol on a Tibetan page is one of the following four:

   1   a word (such as ཤེས་ or ཤེས་པ་);
   2   a case marking particle (such as ལ་ or གྱི་);
   3   a syntactic particle (such as དང་);
   4   a punctuation mark (such as the ཚེག་ or the གད་).

Both particles and words are made of syllables. The third type of particles—not listed here, since they do not occur outside of words—are lexical particles. While lexical particles are merely special sorts of syllables, syntactic and case marking particles operate at the same level as words to create phrases, clauses, and sentences. Letters and syllables (some of which are lexical particles) generate the phonemic dimension, whereas words and particles operate in the lexical dimension and, when they are put together, in the syntactic dimension.

   The syntactic dimension of a language is expressed in the patterns in which words and particles are used in phrases, clauses, and sentences. There are certain basic functions that words and particles play in these patterns.

The six categories of words—categories that describe in general their basic functions—are introduced in this chapter:

1  nouns,
2  pronouns,
3  adjectives,
4  verbs,
5  adverbs,
6  postpositions.

In Chapter Eight, the basic presentation of letters and syllables (the first and second structural levels of Tibetan) was concluded.

> The seven functions of letters—actually, their locations within a syllable—are: root letter, vowel marker, prefix, superscript, subscript, suffix, and secondary suffix. However, only five of the thirty consonants may be prefixes, only three may be superscripts, only four may be subscripts, only ten suffixes, and only two secondary suffixes.

Also in Chapter Eight, the way in which syllables function as the building blocks of words and particles was introduced.

> Tibetan words and particles are constructed of syllables, as few as one syllable but typically no more than four or five.

Longer words—such as the seven syllable མངོན་པར་རྫོགས་པར་སངས་རྒྱས་པ་ (n̄gön-b̄ar-dzok-b̄ar-s̄ang-gyë>-b̄a, *complete, perfect enlightenment as a Buddha*) or the even longer verb form, མངོན་པར་རྫོགས་པར་སངས་རྒྱས་པར་འགྱུར་ (n̄gön-b̄ar-dzok-b̄ar-s̄ang-gyë>-b̄ar-gyur, *will become a complete, perfect Buddha*)—are often translation equivalents for Sanskrit terms.[50]

མངོན་པར་རྫོགས་པར་སངས་རྒྱས་པ་ literally means *complete, perfect Buddhahood*, with the neologism *Buddhahood* following the model of English words such as *sainthood*. The alternative is a translation on the order of *enlightenment as a Buddha*, which is more cumbersome.

All that remains to be explained about how syllables make up words are the **lexical particles**—frequently reoccurring syllables that are found within words (although not all words contain lexical particles).

You have already been introduced to one class of these—the **final syllables** (པ་, པོ་, བ་, བོ་, མ་, and མོ་) that terminate many nouns and adjectives.

**Negative particles** (མ་ and མི་) are another example of these lexical particles. Whereas the verb ཡིན་ means *is*, for example, མ་ཡིན་ means *is not*.

The syllables མངོན་པར་ and རྟོགས་པར་ in མངོན་པར་རྟོགས་པར་སངས་རྒྱས་པ་ are also lexical particles of a type called **prefix particles**; these are especially common in words whose origins are in Sanskrit terminology.

Lexical particles will be examined in detail beginning in Chapter Ten, where the other groups of particles—the **case marking particles** and **syntactic particles**—will also be introduced.

The present chapter, after concluding an analysis of how the words of a sentence relate to each other at their ends, focuses on the types of **words** in Tibetan, with an emphasis on the basic characteristics of nouns, adjectives, and verbs. In the doctrinal vocabulary section at the end of this chapter, the Tibetan Buddhist presentation of the basic categories of existence is examined.

## Syllables at the Ends of Words
### *The Use of Syntactic and Case Marking Particles*

In Tibetan it is at the end of a word, and not at the beginning, that the word is connected to the rest of the sentence. In English we often use prepositions such as *to, at, from*, and so on to show how a word fits into a clause or sentence. As the term '*pre*position' implies, they are placed in front of the words they connect to the rest of the sentence:

He went *to the store*.

He read a book *before breakfast*.

In Tibetan, matters are different. For one thing, even "prepositions" *follow* the word or phrase that they connect to the sentence; thus, they are really *post*positions.

Thus, not only the actual postpositions (words such as མདུན་ [dün, *front*] and སྟེང་ [dḗng, *top*]), but all syntactic and case marking particles are postpositions as well.

The first sentence in the above example would read like this if written in Tibetan word order, which we can call "Tenglish":

| HE |    | STORE | -TO |    | WENT |

Notice that the TO follows the noun STORE, connecting it to the verb WENT. In Tibetan TO would be a case marking particle. Notice also that except for the subject, HE, this sentence makes better sense to the English speaker *if it is read backwards*, from right to left. More will be said on this later, but never forget that Tibetan, like English, is *actually* written from left to right. Tibetans read their language as we do, from left to right, and the flow of ideas is from left to right. However, sometimes it is easier, for someone used to English syntax, to read at least part of a sentence or clause backwards from the verb at its end.

More important than the fact that Tibetan "prepositions" *follow* nouns is the fact that prepositions are not as commonplace in Tibetan as they are in English. Many, but by no means all of the connections shown by prepositions in English are shown in Tibetan by **declension of nouns**—that is, by case marking particles.

---

**Declension** is a grammatical term which refers to the modification of a noun, pronoun, or adjective to show its use in a sentence. Declension is a type of **inflection**, a term which refers to all types of modifications—modifying verbs to show tense, modifying nouns to show number, modifying pronouns to show gender, and so on. (In Tibetan, number and gender are shown by lexical particles.)

---

In English, for example, the pronoun *she* becomes *her* when it is an object of a verb or preposition. Thus, if one sees *she* in a sentence, one knows that it is the subject of the sentence and not an object. Again, while *does* is a present tense verb (*He does it now*), *did* is a past tense form (*He did it yester-day*). The words *he* and *she* may be modified to show number as well, both becoming *they*. Many such inflections are shown in Tibetan by the use of particles.

There are, traditionally, eight declensions (or **cases**) in Tibetan. Six of the cases are marked by particles. In the Tenglish example, HE STORE-TO WENT, the TO is a case marking particle, that is, a case marking particle that shows which of the declensions is operative.

> The terms 'declension' and 'case' are merely a way of talking about a range of possible functions that a noun, pronoun, or adjective may perform in a phrase, clause, or sentence. Cases are forms that nouns, pronouns, and adjectives assume to show how they are related to other words in a sentence.

Thus, the particle TO following the word STORE shows how that word fits into the sentence. The fact that HE has *no* case marking particle following it tells us almost as much as if it did; here it tells us that it can be the subject of the verb WENT.

Sometimes the syllable at the end of a word is modified to connect it to another word or clause. The word བུམ་པ་, which means *pot*, can be modified by the addition of a **connective case** particle to form a word meaning, in its most common use, *of the pot*. In this instance, the case particle is made a part of the suffixless syllable པ་.

| | | | |
|---|---|---|---|
| བུམ་པའི་ | **pum-b̄ë** | POT-OF | *of the pot, pot's* |

Connectives connect nouns, pronouns, or adjectives to words that follow them.

| | | | |
|---|---|---|---|
| བུམ་པའི་ཁ་དོག་ | **pum-b̄ë kha-dok** | POT-OF COLOR | *the color of a pot* |

In some instances, however, the case particle follows the word as a separate syllable.

| | | | |
|---|---|---|---|
| བུམ་པ་ལ་ | **pum-b̄a-la** | POT-IN | *in the pot, at the pot, for the pot* |
| བུམ་པ་ལས་ | **pum-b̄a-lë>** | POT-FROM | *from the pot, from among the pots* |

If one were to diagram these examples of འབྲས་པ་ modified by case particles, this would be the result:

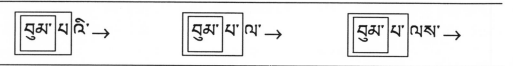

Case marking particles are like hooks that are used to attach the word or phrase they follow to other words and phrases in a sentence. In these examples, the arrows following the case particles show the way in which they connect the word འབྲས་པ་ to the remainder of the sentence. Note that in the first example (འབྲས་པའི་), the boundary of the box is drawn *between* the letters of the second syllable in order to show the way in which the case particle acts to connect the word to something outside itself.

Only in this chapter are individual syllables enclosed in their own boxes. (In later chapters boxes will surround only words, phrases, and clauses.) Words are being diagrammed in this way here to emphasize the way in which their last syllables are their interface to clauses and sentences.

Sometimes a word is neither modified nor followed by a particle. This is also significant.

འབྲས་པ་ standing alone, with no particle—if it is not part of a phrase (for example, a list of nouns or a noun followed by an adjective)—is in the **nominative case**. As such, it may be used in many different ways, *depending mainly on the type of verb ending the sentence or clause in which it is found.* Nominatives are objects of one type of verb, agents of other types, and subjects or complements of yet another type.

The cases, their names, their uses, and the particles used to mark them will be introduced in Chapter Twelve.

## Drill 9.1

Which of the following Tenglish sentences mirror proper Tibetan syntax? Correct the ones that do not.

1. MOUNTAINS EXIST
2. THERE ARE MOUNTAINS
3. BUDDHA TURNED WHEEL-OF DOCTRINE
4. BUDDHA DOCTRINE-OF WHEEL TURNED
5. ATISHA TRAVELLED TO TIBET
6. ATISHA TRAVELLED TIBET-TO
7. RED IS COLOR
8. IS RED COLOR
9. RED COLOR IS
10. FROM-EMPTINESS BODY-OF BUDDHA ARISES
11. EMPTINESS-FROM BUDDHA-OF BODY ARISES
12. FROM-EMPTINESS BODY-OF BUDDHA ARISES

## Patterns in Tibetan Language
### *Words*

Traditional English grammar speaks of **parts of speech**. Nouns, adjectives, adverbs, and verbs are parts of speech. So are articles (such as *a* and *the*), demonstratives (*that* and *this*), pronouns, prepositions (*of, at, in spite of*), conjunctions (*and, when*), and interjections (*oh*).[51] In English, all of these are words. However, the functions performed in English by prepositions and conjunctions are handled in Tibetan by particles (including both the case marking and syntactic varieties). Thus, the term **word** is used in this book not as a cover term for all parts of speech (as it is in English), but as a term excluding particles.

Words may easily be distinguished from syllables and particles in that words mean something in their own right. Syllables, of course, are merely parts of words, and particles are either parts of words or serve only to connect words (or groups of words) to other words.

> **Words** are comprised of one or more syllables and have their own, independent lexical meanings.

Some of the syllables that go to make up words may be lexical particles.

Since there are many single-syllable words, it is not uncommon for single syllables to have ideas associated with them, that is, to have not merely a phonemic but a lexical dimension as well.

An illustration of this is the construction of the word གུན་ཏུ་བཟང་པོ་ (*Samantabhadra*, the name of both a Buddha and a Bodhisattva) from the prefix particle གུན་ཏུ་, meaning *thoroughly*, and the adjective བཟང་པོ་ (*good*). Prefix particles such as གུན་ཏུ་ are a type of lexical particle.

Furthermore, many Tibetan words are built by combining not merely syllables, but short words.

The word མར་མེ་, meaning *butter lamp*, is a compound of མར་ (*butter*) and མེ་ (*fire*), both words in their own right.

Thus, whereas only words have full-fledged lexical meanings, their syllables often contribute something to these meanings.

A Tibetan word performs one of six basic syntactic functions. That is, with one major exception, any given word can play only one sort of role in a phrase, clause, or sentence.

> Any Tibetan word is either a noun, a verb, a pronoun, an adjective, an adverb, or a postposition.

For example, the word ཐུམ་པ་ is always a noun—never a pronoun, adjective, adverb, or verb. Similarly, the word ཡིན་ is a verb; it may be made into a noun with the addition of a final པ་, but as ཡིན་ it is a verb.

The one major exception to this rule are those nouns and adjectives made from verbs—the **verbals**. They often act both as verbs (ending clauses which have their own subjects, complements, and objects) and as nouns (when they—and the clause that they end—are the subject, object, or complement of a later verb).

> The equivalent of a Tibetan clause ending in a verbal would be an English phrase such as *[the person] who had come yesterday from Lhasa*. In Tenglish, that would read LHASA-FROM YESTERDAY CAME with a པ་ or བ་ syllable ending the Tibetan verb represented by CAME.

(Clauses are discussed in more detail in Chapter Eleven.)

Some of the roles played by the six categories of words, moreover, are closely related. Nouns and pronouns act similarly in Tibetan phrases, clauses, and sentences. (Pronouns, after all, are merely words that substitute for nouns.) Adjectives—although their basic use is as modifiers of nouns—may also sometimes substitute for nouns, and act as the subject, object, or complement of a sentence.

## *Verbs*

The verb is the syntactic heart of a Tibetan clause or sentence, but always occurs at its end.

> Verbs occur only at the end of a Tibetan clause or sentence, with their subjects and objects before them, never after them.

This simple looking statement has many implications. First, a **sentence** is defined by the fact that a verb ends it.[52]

> A Tibetan sentence is a series of words that completely expresses a thought, ends in a verb, and is not itself a part of a clause or sentence.

Verbs in their most basic forms look like ཡིན་ (*is*) and བྱེད་ (*do, make, perform*); only in exceptional circumstances do they end in པ་ or བ་.[53] **Verbal nouns** and **verbal adjectives** (collectively known as **verbals**), on the other hand, usually do end in པ་ or བ་, although they need not (especially in verse).

The simplest sort of Tibetan verbs are **existential verbs** such as ཡིན་ (a linking verb) and ཡོད་ (a verb of existence). They indicate no action, merely that something *is* something (ཡིན་) or that something *exists* (ཡོད་).

The most basic syntax—the deepest pattern—seen in Tibetan clauses and sentences is that used with verbs of existence such as ཡོད་:

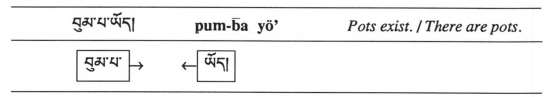

An example of this syntax is the following, where Tibetan and English word order coincide.

---

| བུམ་པ་ཡོད། | **pum-ba yö'** | *Pots exist. / There are pots.* |

| བུམ་པ་ → | ← ཡོད། | |

---

This could also mean, depending on context, *There is a pot.*

Slightly more complex is the following pattern, which serves as the basis of most Tibetan sentences and clauses.[54]

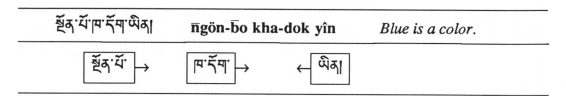

(Objects occur with some action verbs—as in *Buddha taught **the doctrine***. Linking verbs, although they have no objects, do have complements—as in *Sound is **impermanent***.) Thus, the SUBJECT + COMPLEMENT + VERB pattern is seen in the following sentence ending in a linking verb.

---

| སྔོན་པོ་ཁ་དོག་ཡིན། | **ngön-bo kha-dok yin** | *Blue is a color.* |

| སྔོན་པོ་ → | ཁ་དོག་ → | ← ཡིན། |

---

སྔོན་པོ་ is the subject, ཁ་དོག་ is the complement, and ཡིན་ is the verb. The word order is important. Although reversing the order of the nouns and saying ཁ་དོག་སྔོན་པོ་ཡིན། is acceptable grammatically, it expresses a mistaken idea, since it is not the case that colors are blue.

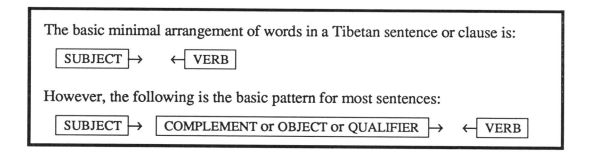

The basic minimal arrangement of words in a Tibetan sentence or clause is:

SUBJECT → ← VERB

However, the following is the basic pattern for most sentences:

SUBJECT → COMPLEMENT or OBJECT or QUALIFIER → ← VERB

## Categories of Verbs

A useful way of classifying verbs is to categorize them in terms of the syntax that must be used in the clauses and sentences they end—that is, to categorize them on the basis of the case marking particles that are used to mark their subjects, objects, and so on. There are, thus, three main categories of verbs in Tibetan.

1  **Nominative verbs** take subjects in the first (nominative) case.

2  **Agentive verbs** take subjects in the third (agentive) case.

3  **Specialized verbs** take subjects in the seventh (locative) or fourth (purposive-beneficial) cases.

The third category, with one significant exception, comprises verbs that are in most other instances either agentive or nominative verbs. It is only in certain specialized applications that their subjects are locative or purposive.

The exception is the verb དགོས་ (gö>, *need, require*), the verb of necessity. It is discussed in Chapter Fourteen along with the specialized usage of ཡོད་ (normally a nominative verb) as a verb of possession (meaning *have*).

Since the eight cases and the particles used to mark them will not be explained until Chapter Twelve, it is not possible to present this classification in detail now. However, here are paradigmatic illustrations of the three types of verbs with their subjects marked.

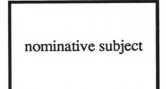

SOUND IMPERMANENT IS.
**Sound** *is impermanent.*

ཡིན་ is a **linking verb** that requires a nominative subject and a nominative **complement** (in this example, མི་རྟག་པ་). The nominative case is "marked" by the *absence* of a case marking particle.

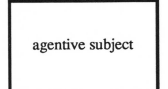

BUDDHA DOCTRINE TAUGHT.
**Buddha** *taught the doctrine.*

The case marking particle ཀྱིས་ is an agentive case marker. The verb is བསྟན་, meaning *taught*. Note that the case marking particle is not translated with a separate English word, a not unusual occurrence. In the present instance, one could say—in order to make the Tenglish translation capture even more the syntax of the Tibetan— BUDDHA-BY DOCTRINE TAUGHT, since agentive case marking particles sometimes do translate as *by*.

The final paradigm illustrates the way in which a verb that is normally a nominative verb of existence (མེད་, *does not exist*) is used with a locative subject in a specialized way.

locative subject  དགྲ་བཅོམ་པ་ལ་  ཉོན་མོངས་ མེད།

ARHATS AFFLICTIONS NOT-HAVE
**Arhats** *do not have afflictions.*

The ལ་ particle here marks the seventh case. As in the previous example, it does not require a separate word in English, but in Tenglish could be ARHATS-AT AFFLICTIONS NOT-EXIST.

Note that the verb མེད་ (whether it means *does not exist* or *does not have*), is an inherently negative verb. Its affirmative form is ཡོད་ (*exist, exists, has, have*).

## *Diagramming Tibetan*

Diagramming phrases, clauses, and sentences is a useful tool for learning Tibetan. Two Tibetan sentences have already been diagrammed in this chapter.

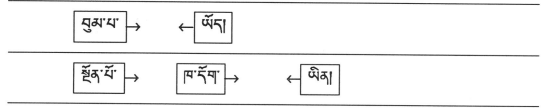

In box-diagramming the sentences under analysis, their main parts are indicated by separate boxes.

An arrow attached to a box shows the direction in which the word (or phrase or clause) within that box connects to the rest of the sentence. Nouns, pronouns, and adverbs connect "forward" in the sentence, or to the right; verbs connect "backward" or to the left.

To put it another way, verbs relate to words, clauses, and phrases that precede them, that is where their subjects, objects, complements, and qualifiers are found. Nouns and pronouns are the subjects, objects, or complements of verbs that follow them. Adjectives will be discussed later in this chapter.

## *Verb Forms*

Verbs themselves appear in a number of different forms, all of which are subsumed under two types:

1    final (or terminal) forms,
2    open forms.

The **final forms** of verbs are those that close sentences. They range from the very simple basic form (such as ཤེས་) to lengthy verb phrases (such as the VERB + AUXILIARY mentioned at the beginning of this chapter, མཚན་པར་རྟོགས་པར་སངས་རྒྱས་པར་ འགྱུར་). Final forms include:

1    basic verbs (for instance, ཤེས་ *know*) by themselves,

2    compound verb phrases (such as ཤེས་ནུས་ *able to know*),

3    phrases composed of verbs and auxiliary verbs (for example, ཤེས་པར་བྱ་ *one should know*).

Verbs also occur in non-final, or **open**, contexts. As such they do not end sentences but either (1) act to end clauses within a sentence or (2) function within verb phrases. Clauses are like small sentences that function as parts of larger sentences.

1    Some clauses end in basic verbs (like ཡིན་) followed by syntactic particles such as the conditional particle ན་ (*if* or *when*) or the continuative particle ནས་. The following clause means *given that pots are impermanent*— བུམ་པ་མི་རྟག་པ་ཡིན་ན་.

2    Many clauses end in verbs made into nouns—the so-called **verbal nouns** and **adjectives** (explained in Chapter Ten). Where སངས་རྒྱས་ཀྱིས་ ཆོས་བསྟན་ is a sentence meaning *Buddha taught the doctrine*, the following clause (ending in the verbal བསྟན་པ་) means *what Buddha taught*— སངས་རྒྱས་ཀྱིས་བསྟན་པ་.

In the first example, ཡིན་ is followed by a syntactic particle and *in that context* is an open verb; in the second, བསྟན་པ་ is open.

The internal parts of verb phrases are often open verbs. For example, the ཤེས་པར་ in the verb phrase ཤེས་པར་བྱ་ is an example of an open construction. ཤེས་པར་ by itself is incomplete and may not end a sentence.

This has been merely a summary introduction to verbs. Because verbs are the determinants of the syntaxes of the construction in which they are found, much of the remainder of *Translating Buddhism from Tibetan* will be centered on verbs, the forms in which they occur, and the syntaxes they govern.

## Drill 9.2

Without looking up any words, identify the verbs in the following sentences—both final and open forms. (The vocabulary used may be found in the glossary at the end of this chapter; the sentences are translated at the end of the book.)

1. བདག་གིས་ཐིག་པ་བྱུས།

2. མི་དྲག་པ་ཚོགས་པར་བྱ།

3. སངས་རྒྱས་ཀྱིས་བསྟན་པ་ནི་ཆོས་ཡིན།

4. སངས་རྒྱས་སྟོན་པ་ཡིན།

5. དགྲ་བཅམ་པས་ཞི་བ་བཅས།

---

## *Nouns, Pronouns, and Adjectives*

Tibetan has many words that are formed from verbs and that, in some ways, still act like verbs—the verbal nouns and adjectives. The following chart illustrates this process.

| | VERB | | | VERBAL NOUN OR ADJECTIVE | |
|---|---|---|---|---|---|
| ཡོད་ | yö' | *exist* | ཡོད་པ་ | yö-b̄a | *existence, existent* |
| ཡིན་ | yîn | *is* | ཡིན་པ་ | yîn-b̄a | *being, occurrence* |
| ཤེས་ | s̄hé> | *know* | ཤེས་པ་ | s̄hé>-b̄a | *knowledge, known* |
| བྱེད་ | chÉ' | *do, make* | བྱེད་པ་ | chÉ'-b̄a | *action, agent* |
| འགྲོ་ | do | *go* | འགྲོ་བ་ | do-wa | *going, migration* |

The last example—འགྲོ་བ་—is the common Tibetan word for a person in cyclic existence, someone *going* from one lifetime to another. འགྲོ་བ་ in that case then translates literally either as *migrator* or *migration*, depending on whether the text is speaking of a person or a potential state of rebirth.

Tibetan also has many nouns that are *just* nouns, that is, not derivatives of verbs.

| | | |
|---|---|---|
| བུམ་པ་ | **pum-ba** | *pot* |
| མི་ | **mí** | *human* |
| བོད་ | **pö'** | *Tibet*[55] |

Notice in the last example that there are no capital letters in Tibetan to set off proper nouns. *Tibet* in Tibetan is *tibet*.

## Ordinary and Honorific

Nouns and pronouns are either ordinary or honorific. An ordinary-honorific pair that has already been introduced is that of མགོ་ and དབུ་, *head*. Ordinary (non-honorific) nouns are neutral as regards social and spiritual status, and in some cases their use is disrespectful (and would thus be considered poor Tibetan). Honorific (**H**) nouns are used about things (both physical and mental) relating to Buddhas and others held to be spiritually superior and to those of higher social status. The three most basic ordinary-honorific pairs are those describing the full range of human and other sentient activity.

| ORDINARY | | HONORIFIC | | TRANSLATION |
|---|---|---|---|---|
| ལུས་ | **lü>** | སྐུ་ | **ḡu** | *body* |
| ངག་ | **ngak** | གསུང་ | **ṡung** | *speech* |
| ཡིད་ | **yí'** | ཐུགས་ | **thuk** | *mind* |

Thus, a Buddha's mind is ཐུགས་, and not ཡིད་ or སེམས་.

These three honorific forms are often prefixed to other nouns to create new honorifics.

Whereas the ordinary term for compassion is སྙིང་རྗེ་, a Buddha's compassion is ཐུགས་རྗེ་. The ordinary term for the core of Mahāyāna Buddhist ethics is སེམས་བསྐྱེད་—*generation of the mind [aspiring to (or acting towards) enlightenment]*. The honorific term is ཐུགས་བསྐྱེད་.

Note in these examples that the honorific ཕྱག་ replaces a number of different ordinary nouns. There are, in general, fewer honorific than ordinary words.

Verbs also occur in honorific forms. Thus, of the following two sentences, only the second is correct Tibetan. The first, although grammatically correct, is lexically incorrect, because ཤེས་ means an ordinary person *knows* and not a Buddha *knows*. མཁྱེན་, on the other hand, is not used except in honorific situations.

| སངས་རྒྱས་ཀྱིས་ཤེས་བྱ་ཐམས་ཅད་ཤེས། | *Buddhas know all objects of knowledge.* |
|---|---|
| སངས་རྒྱས་ཀྱིས་ཤེས་བྱ་ཐམས་ཅད་མཁྱེན། | *Buddhas know all objects of knowledge.* |

ཤེས་བྱ་ means *object of knowledge* and is the equivalent of *existent*.

## Pronouns

Pronouns are words that take the place of nouns.[56] There are personal pronouns such as ང་ (**nga** *I*). There are relative pronouns such as གང་ (**kang**, *which, who, whom, that which* or *he/she who*) and སུ་ (**śu**; *who, whom*). སུ་ and གང་ are also used as interrogative pronouns (*what, which, who*). Personal pronouns vary according to person. Thus, whereas ང་ is a first person pronoun, ཁྱོད་ (**khyö'**, *you*) is a second person pronoun.[57] Like nouns, pronouns occur in ordinary-honorific pairs.

The most common pronouns are དེ་ (**té**, *that*) and འདི་ (**dí**, *this*). Similar to their English counterparts, they are adjectives which, when used alone—that is, when they do not modify nouns—function as pronouns.[58] དེ་ means *that*, but also *he/she/it*. དེ་དག་ means *these* and also *they*.

| དེ་མི་རྟག་པ་ཡིན། | **té mí-ḍak-ḅa yín** | That is impermanent. |
|---|---|---|

This sentence follows the standard syntax of a sentence ending in a linking verb: དེ་ is the subject; མི་རྟག་པ་ is the complement; ཡིན་ is the verb.

> Unlike the verbs of many other languages, Tibetan verbs—in the literary language that is being explained in this book—do not vary according to person.

(In colloquial Tibetan, on the other hand, the first, second, and third persons—I, you, and he/she—are marked by different verbal endings.) In English we say *I am a sentient being* but *He is a sentient being*. *I is* and *She am* are incorrect. In literary Tibetan, however, ཡིན་ means both *is*, *am*, and *are*.

| | |
|---|---|
| ང་སེམས་ཅན་ཡིན། | *I am a sentient being.* |
| དེ་སེམས་ཅན་ཡིན། | *He/she is a sentient being.* |
| དེ་དག་སེམས་ཅན་ཡིན། | *They are sentient beings.* |

## Adjectives

Adjectives modify nouns. Many adjectives follow the nouns they modify, creating **noun-adjective phrases**.

| | | |
|---|---|---|
| བུམ་པ་དམར་པོ་ | **pum-ba m̄ar-b̄o** | *red pot* |
| སེམས་ཅན་ཀུན་ | **sêm-jĕn ḡün** | *all sentient beings* |
| མི་བདུན་ | **mí dün** | *seven humans* |

Some adjectives, however, typically precede the nouns they modify, connected to them by the case marking particles marking the sixth, or connective, case.

---

Recall from the exceptions to the pronunciation rules (Exception Seven) that the final syllables པ་ and བ་ become པའི་ and བའི་ in the connective case. Of the five connective case marking particles, here འི་ (í) is the one used.

---

What result are **adjective-noun phrases**.

| | | |
|---|---|---|
| དགེ་བའི་སེམས་ | **gé-wë sêm** | *virtuous mind(s)* |
| དམ་པའི་ཆོས་ | **tam-b̄ë chö>** | *holy doctrine* |

Both combinations—noun followed by adjective and adjective connected to noun—create phrases that are themselves nouns. Like any noun, a noun phrase may be modified by an adjective.

| བུམ་པ་དམར་པོ་དེ་ | pum-ba mar-bo té | *that red pot* |
|---|---|---|
| དགེ་བའི་ཆོས་ཀུན་ | gé-wë chö> gün | *all virtuous phenomena* |

Here, the noun-adjective phrase བུམ་པ་དམར་པོ་ has been further qualified by adding a དེ་ (*that*) to create བུམ་པ་དམར་པོ་དེ་. The adjective-noun phase དགེ་བའི་ཆོས་ has been modified with the adjective ཀུན་ (*all*), becoming དགེ་བའི་ཆོས་ཀུན་.

## Drill 9.3

Translate the following noun-adjective or adjective-noun phrases into English.

1. ཡིག་ཆ་རིང་པ་

2. བློ་གྲོས་ཆེན་པོ་

3. དུང་དཀར་པོ་

4. ཀླུང་ལྷ་

5. བླ་མ་དམ་པ་

Translate the following into Tibetan.

1. the first effect
2. red light
3. a white horse
4. nonvirtuous minds
5. permanent phenomena

## *Adverbs*

Adverbs are words that modify either verbs or adjectives. They are not, however, a separate category in traditional Tibetan grammar, and are often included in lists of particles.

| ཇི་ལྟར་ | ji-dar | *how* [literally, 'like what'] |
|---|---|---|
| དེ་ལྟར་ | té-dar | *in that way* [literally, 'like that'] |
| ཅུང་ཟད་ | jung-së' | *a little* |
| དེ་བཞིན་དུ་ | té-shin-du | *thus* |

> As mentioned earlier, this book uses English grammatical terms and concepts to explain Tibetan grammar. Some of the distinctions being made here are distinctions not made in traditional Tibetan grammar. Nonetheless, it has proven helpful to think of certain Tibetan particles as adverbs, if—following the definition of an adverb in English grammar—they are words that modify verbs, adjectives, or other adverbs.

Actually, there are two types of Tibetan adverbs:

1  words that are always adverbs,

2  words that are themselves nouns and adjectives, but have been modified for use as adverbs.

འབའ་ཞིག་ (ba-shík), for example, is an adjective meaning *only*. If the case marking particle དུ་ is added to it, it becomes an adverb, འབའ་ཞིག་དུ་, also meaning *only*, but now a modifier of verbs and verbals. Here are some examples of the process. Note in the examples of this process shown below, that when the final syllable is suffixless, the adverb marking particle used is ར་, and it becomes part of that syllable.

| NOUN or ADJECTIVE | | ADVERBIAL CONSTRUCTION | | |
|---|---|---|---|---|
| སྐད་ཅིག་མ་ | momentary | སྐད་ཅིག་མར་ | g̱ë'-jík-mar | moment by moment |
| རྫོགས་པ་ | completion | རྫོགས་པར་ | d̲zok-b̄ar | completely |
| རྟག་པ་ | permanent | རྟག་པར་ | d̄ak-b̄ar | permanently, always |
| གཙོ་བོ་ | main, chief | གཙོ་བོར་ | d̄zo-wor | predominantly |
| དང་པོ་ | first | དང་པོར་ | tang-b̄or | first |

The words སྐད་ཅིག་མར་ and so on are not adverbs *per se*. They function in the same way as adverbs like ཅུང་ཟད་, but are still merely inflected nouns or adjectives.

## Postpositions

The final type of words are the postpositions, so called because they occur after the words they relate to the rest of the phrase, clause, or sentence in which they are found. The category of postpositions is something of a grab-bag, and many post-positions are, in fact, something like syntactic particles. However, syntactic particles cannot be declined, and postpositions are—that is, they are typically marked by case marking particles.

> Recall that syntactic and case marking particles serve only to connect words (or groups of words) to other words (or groups of words).

Moreover, postpositions are connected to the word or phrase that precedes them with a connective case particle. (The connective case was seen in the section on adjective-noun phrases.)

Postpositions commonly indicate relations involving time, place, and purpose.

| | | |
|---|---|---|
| མདུན་ | dün | front |
| སྟེང་ | d̄éng | top |

| ཇེས་ | jé> | *after* |
|---|---|---|
| ཆེད་ | ché' | *purpose* |

In the following examples of usage, the adjective དེ་ (*that*) is used as a pronoun, a connective case marker (ཡི་ *of*) is placed between the དེ་ and the postposition, and the postposition is followed by the appropriate case marking particles.

| དེ་ཡི་མདུན་ལ་ | té-yí dün-la | in front of that |
|---|---|---|
| དེ་ཡི་སྟེང་དུ་ | té-yí déng-du | on top of that |
| དེ་ཡི་ཇེས་སུ་ | té-yí jé>-su | after that |
| དེ་ཡི་ཆེད་དུ་ | té-yí ché'-du | for the sake of that |

## Numbers and Numerals

Above ten, the names of the Tibetan numbers are formed in a regular way. From ten to nineteen, they are merely a reflection of the numeral—the first syllable is བཅུ་ (*ten*) and the second, whatever number is added to ten to make the number in question. The first three are illustrative of the names for the numbers ten through nineteen:

| 10 | ༡༠ | བཅུ་ | ju |
|---|---|---|---|
| 11 | ༡༡ | བཅུ་གཅིག་ | ju-jík |
| 12 | ༡༢ | བཅུ་གཉིས་ | ju-ñyí> |
| 13 | ༡༣ | བཅུ་གསུམ་ | juk-sum |

Twenty through twenty-nine follow the same model, with two modifications: the word for twenty is not གཉིས་བཅུ་ but ཉི་ཤུ་, and there is an intermediate connecting syllable. This will be the model for the numbers from twenty through ninety-nine.

| | | | |
|---|---|---|---|
| 20 | ༢༠ | ཉི་ཤུ་ | nyi-s̄hu |
| 21 | ༢༡ | ཉི་ཤུ་རྩ་གཅིག་ | nyi-s̄hu-d̄za-jík |
| | | ཉི་ཤུ་ཉེར་གཅིག་ | nyi-s̄hu-nyér-jík |
| 22 | ༢༢ | ཉི་ཤུ་རྩ་གཉིས་ | nyi-s̄hu-d̄za-n̄yí> |
| | | ཉི་ཤུ་ཉེར་གཉིས་ | nyi-s̄hu-nyér-n̄yí> |

As shown above, there are two ways of naming the numbers from twenty-one through twenty-nine. Thus, twenty-one occurs as both ཉི་ཤུ་རྩ་གཅིག་ and ཉི་ཤུ་ཉེར་གཅིག་. The latter may also be abbreviated, producing numbers such as ཉེར་གཉིས་ and so forth.

The names for the numbers from thirty through thirty-nine follow the same pattern, but with a different intermediate syllable.

| | | | |
|---|---|---|---|
| 30 | ༣༠ | སུམ་ཅུ་ | s̄um-j̄u |
| 31 | ༣༡ | སུམ་ཅུ་སོ་གཅིག་ | s̄um-j̄u-s̄o-jík |
| | | སུམ་ཅུ་རྩ་གཅིག་ | s̄um-j̄u-d̄za-jík |

The intermediate syllable རྩ་ may be used in numbers from twenty-one through ninety-nine, although in numbers above thirty it is more common to see a different intermediate syllable for every set of ten. The remaining numbers are formed in accordance with the following model:

| | | | |
|---|---|---|---|
| 40 | ༤༠ | བཞི་བཅུ་ | s̲híp-j̄u |
| 41 | ༤༡ | བཞི་བཅུ་ཞེ་གཅིག་ | s̲híp-ju-s̲hé-jík |
| 50 | ༥༠ | ལྔ་བཅུ་ | n̄gap-ju |
| 51 | ༥༡ | ལྔ་བཅུ་ང་གཅིག་ | n̄gap-ju--nga-jík |
| 60 | ༦༠ | དྲུག་བཅུ་ | ṭuk-j̄u |
| 61 | ༦༡ | དྲུག་ཅུ་རེ་གཅིག་ | ṭuk-ju-ré-jík |

| 70 | ཉ༠ | བདུན་ཅུ་ | **dün-ju** |
| 71 | ཉ༡ | བདུན་ཅུ་དོན་གཅིག་ | **dün-ju-dön-jík** |
| 80 | ༨༠ | བརྒྱད་ཅུ་ | **gyë'-ju** |
| 81 | ༨༡ | བརྒྱད་ཅུ་གྱ་གཅིག་ | **gyë'-ju-gya-jík** |
| 90 | ༩༠ | དགུ་བཅུ་ | **gu-ju** |
| 91 | ༩༡ | དགུ་བཅུ་གོ་གཅིག་ | **gu-ju-go-jík** |

The Tibetan for hundred is བརྒྱ་ (gya) and for thousand is སྟོང་ (ḏong). A set of a hundred is བརྒྱ་ཕྲག་ and, similarly, a set of a thousand is སྟོང་ཕྲག་. The hundreds are counted in the same way as the tens: བརྒྱ་, ཉིས་བརྒྱ་, སུམ་བརྒྱ་, and so on, and the thousands are ཅིག་སྟོང་, ཉིས་སྟོང་, སུམ་སྟོང་, and so forth. Alternately, one hundred may be བརྒྱ་ ཕྲག་གཅིག་, two hundred, བརྒྱ་ཕྲག་གཉིས་, and so on, with the thousands counted in the same way, སྟོང་ཕྲག་གཅིག་ and so on.

| 100 | ༡༠༠ | བརྒྱ་ | **gya** |
| 1000 | ༡༠༠༠ | སྟོང་ | **ḏong** |
| 10,000 | ༡༠༠༠༠ | ཁྲི་ | **ṭhí** |
| 100,000 | ༡༠༠༠༠༠ | འབུམ་ | **bum** |
| 1,000,000 | ༡༠༠༠༠༠༠ | ས་ཡ་ | **s̄a-ya** |
| 10,000,000 | ༡༠༠༠༠༠༠༠ | བྱེ་བ་ | **c̱hé-wa** |

Here are some examples of numbers used as adjectives.

| སྒྲོལ་མ་ཉེར་གཅིག་ | **ḏöl-ma nyér-jík** | *the twenty-one Tārās* |
| གནས་བརྟན་བཅུ་དྲུག་ | **ñë-ḏën ju-ḍuk** | *the sixteen Sthaviras* |
| ཡི་གེ་བརྒྱ་ | **yí-gé gya** | *one hundred syllables* |

| ཡི་གེ་བརྒྱ་པ་ | **yí-gé gya-b̄a** | *that having one hundred syllables* |
| འབུམ་ལྔ་ | **bum n̄ga** | *five [sets of] one-hundred-thousand* |

The པ་ in ཡི་གེ་བརྒྱ་པ་ is an example of a subjective suffix syllable. Where ཡི་གེ་ བརྒྱ་ means *one hundred syllables* (or *one hundred letters*), ཡི་གེ་བརྒྱ་པ་ means *that having one hundred syllables* (or *that composed of one hundred syllables*). (See Chapter Eleven.)

The number འབུམ་ (*hundred thousand*) is used both literally, as above, and figuratively (as a metaphor for a great number of something). In the first example below, འབུམ་ is used as a syllable within a word, in the second, it is used metaphorically.

| གསུང་འབུམ་ | **s̄ung bum** | *collected works* <br> [literally: *hundred thousand proclamations*] |
| སྐུ་འབུམ་ | **ḡum bum** | *Gum-bum [Monastery]* <br> [literally: *hundred thousand images*] |

# Doctrinal Vocabulary and Grammar
## *Categories of Existence and Nonexistence*

Introduction to the technical vocabulary used in Tibetan texts treating the philosophy, practice, and history of Buddhism begins with this chapter. The logical place to start such an introduction is with an overview of the basic categories about which Indo-Tibetan Buddhist writers speak. Thus, this chapter is mainly an examination of the divisions of the existent, some of the terminological equivalents, and a few illustrations of each.

Although much of the material presented in these Doctrinal Vocabularies is based on Gé-luk texts, the material itself is so basic to all forms of Buddhism that there is not much significant difference in other presentations.

Basic doctrinal analysis—as outlined in Chapter Seven—includes:

མཚན་ཉིད་ (**tshën-nyí'** [Sanskrit: *lakṣana*])—*definitions*;

དོན་གཅིག (**tön-jík**, literally *meaning +one*)—*equivalents* ;

མཚན་གཞི་ (**tshën-shí**)—*illustrations*, that is, examples;

དབྱེ་བ་ (**yé-wa**)—*divisions*, that is, categories and subcategories.

In terms of the basic categories discussed in Indo-Tibetan Buddhism, the broadest category is not what exists, but what is selfless (བདག་མེད་པ་, **dak-mé-ba**—Sanskrit: *nairātmya*), since everything, whether it exists or not, is—in Buddhism—selfless.

Selflessness is one of the traditional four key doctrines of Buddhist philosophy.[59] There are various types of selflessness, but they all refer to the absence of an imagined form of existence, an exaggeration. Thus, བདག་མེད་ refers sometimes to the absence of a person that is partless, permanent, and independent, at other times to the absence of a self-sufficient person, at yet others to the absence of intrinsic identity in either persons or other phenomena.

The adjective *selfless* (and the corresponding noun *selflessness*) are literal translations of Sanskrit and Tibetan terms and are the words used by most English writers, although a few prefer terms such as *no self*. To the average English-speaker, however, these terms are, at least in the beginning, misleading, since in English *selfless* behavior is unselfish behavior—seen in the action of someone who throws himself into an icy river to save a drowning child, for example. A person who had understood Buddhist selflessness and lived according to that understanding would act selflessly in the English sense, but selfless action would not necessarily be a sign that a person had realized (or even, for that matter, believed in the truth of) Buddhist selflessness.

## The Nonexistent

Buddhist writers speak of what exists (ཡོད་པ་—the *existent*) and what does not exist (མེད་པ་—the *nonexistent*). While it is difficult to identify a single, most important existent in a way that would be acceptable in all forms of Indo-Tibetan Buddhism—except, possibly, *mind* (སེམས་ s̄ēm—Sanskrit: *citta*)—it is clear that the most important nonexistent in Buddhism is *self* (བདག་). Buddhism is, after all—both in terms of its theory and its practice—a doctrine of selflessness.

There are three groups of nonexistents.

- Some phenomena do not exist because they are logically impossible, for example a མོ་གཤམ་གྱི་བུ་ (**mo-s̄ham-gyi pu**)—the *child* (བུ་ *son* or *child*) *of a barren woman.* (གྱི་ is a connective case marking particle.)

- Some phenomena, while they are logically possible, do not exist in the world as we know it, assuming that we know it correctly. An example would be a གངས་རི་སྔོན་པོ་ (**gang ri n̄gön-b̄o**—*snow + mountain + blue*), a *blue snow mountain.* Another example, and the one most used as an example of the nonexistent, is རི་བོང་ར་ (**ri-bong-ra**—*rabbit + horn[s]*), *the horns of a rabbit.*

| མོ་གཤམ་ | **mo-s̄ham** | *barren woman* |
|---|---|---|
| བུ་ | **pu** | *son, child* |
| གངས་ | **kang** | *snow* |
| རི་བོང་ | **rí-bong** | *rabbit* |

- The most important category of nonexistents are the various forms of nonexistent self (བདག་ **dak**—Skt. *ātman*). According to the standard Tibetan analysis, all Buddhists agree that there are no རྟག་གཅིག་རང་དབང་ཅན་གྱི་གང་ཟག་ (**d̄ak jík rang-wang-jën-gyi kang-s̄ak**)—no *persons that are permanent, partless, and independent.*

The grammar here is that of a noun—གང་ཟག་ (**kang-s̄ak**, *person*)—qualified by a phrase consisting of adjectives in a list (similar to the noun-list that will be introduced in Chapter Ten): རྟག་ (**d̄ak**) meaning *permanent*, གཅིག་, *one*, and རང་དབང་ཅན་, *independent* (literally, *own-power-possessing*). (As above the གྱི་ is a connective case particle.) This is the least subtle of the selves rejected by Buddhist philosophers.

> Concerning nonexistents in general, see Jeffrey Hopkins, *Meditation on Emptiness*, pp. 213-214. On the different usages of the term *self* (བདག), see Joe Wilson, *Chandrakīrti's Sevenfold Reasoning: Meditation on the Selflessness of Persons*, pp. 13-30 and Hopkins, *Meditation on Emptiness*, pp. 35-46.

The members of the first group (logically impossible nonexistents) are used as easy to understand examples of nonexistence. The members of the second group (logically possible, but still not seen) are brought up as examples of perceptual error and as similes for the self rejected in the doctrine of selflessness. The third group of nonexistents is the most important of the three, and is also the one generative of most controversy within Buddhism.

## The Existent

Existents (ཡོད་པ) are also called ཆོས, ཤེས་བྱ, and གཞི་གྲུབ. These are the phenomena that are *equivalent* (དོན་གཅིག, **tön-jík**) to existents.

| ཆོས | **chö>** | *phenomenon* |
|---|---|---|
| ཤེས་བྱ | **s̄hé>-ja** | *object of knowledge* |
| གཞི་གྲུབ | **s̱hí-ḍup** | *basic existent* |

Their equivalence means that whatever is a phenomenon is necessarily an existent, and vice versa.

> Concerning the category of existence, see Perdue, *Debate in Tibetan Buddhism*, pp. 269-272.

Existents are categorized in a number of different ways. The most basic division is into རྟག་པ (**ḏak-ba**, *permanent*) and མི་རྟག་པ (**mí-ḏak-ba**, *impermanent*). The emphasis in Buddhism, in many ways, is on the impermanent, with the mental superimposition of permanence on what is, in fact, impermanent being seen as a major obstacle to practice. On the other hand, one of the most important meditation objects is བདག་མེད་ (*selflessness*), and selflessness is a permanent phenomenon.

> The term *permanent* is misleading, but has been used here because most writers use it to translate རྟག་པ་ (Sanskrit: *nitya*). Permanent phenomena are not necessarily eternal, that is, they may come into and go out of existence. What makes them 'permanent' is that they do not change while they exist; that is, they are not *momentary* (སྐད་ཅིག་མ་, ḡë'-jík-ma). *Static* might be a better term for རྟག་པ་. On the other hand, impermanent phenomena arise and cease every moment and are thus constantly disintegrating.

Selflessnesses are permanent because they are merely absences, absences of some sort of self (for instance, the permanent, partless, and independent self spoken of above). Since such a self never existed in the first place, it is never present and, thus, always absent. Its absence does not change. (This differs from, say, the absence of an elephant in a given place. Leading an elephant to that place then destroys the 'temporarily permanent' elephantlessness. However, while elephantlessness exists there, it remains static and unchanging.)

   This illustrates one problem involved in translating between languages. Whereas the term *static* is closer to the sense of རྟག་པ་, there is no corresponding English negative; neither *nonstatic* nor *unstatic* are words.

> As a rule, neologisms (in this context, words invented by the translator) should be avoided when possible. *Nonstatic* is a neologism, as is *elephantlessness*.

The opposite of *static* is *dynamic*, but if one uses these as the translations of རྟག་པ་ and མི་རྟག་པ་, respectively, the clear opposition between the two seen in both Sanskrit and Tibetan ( where རྟག་པ་ and *nitya* oppose མི་རྟག་པ་ and *anitya*) is almost completely lost. This is also the case if *static* and *impermanent* are used.

## The Permanent

The example of a permanent phenomenon most commonly used in Tibetan text-books on philosophy is འདུས་མ་བྱས་ཀྱི་ནམ་མཁའ་ (**dü>-ma-jë>-g̱yí nam-kha**), *uncompounded space*, defined as an absence of obstructive contact.[60]

Note that འདུས་མ་བྱས་ is the negative of འདུས་བྱས་, and མི་རྟག་པ་ is the negative of རྟག་པ་. མ་ and མི་ are two particles used to negate words in Tibetan. Their usage will be discussed in Chapter Ten.

Whereas འདུས་བྱས་, compounded things, are impermanent, འདུས་མ་བྱས་ are permanent. The existence of permanent phenomena is not contingent on an aggregation (འདུས་) of causes and conditions.

> See Hopkins, *Meditation on Emptiness*, pp. 215-219, and Perdue, *Debate in Tibetan Buddhism*, pp. 279-284.

## The Impermanent

To be impermanent is to be momentary (སྐད་ཅིག་མ་), to distintegrate moment by moment. Things that are impermanent are causes and effects; they are produced from causes and conditions. They are put together from parts, that is *compounded*. They are *functioning things*.

| | | |
|---|---|---|
| རྒྱུ་ | **gyu** | *cause* |
| རྐྱེན་ | **g̱yên** | *condition* |
| འབྲས་བུ་ | **ḏë>-bu** | *effect* |
| བྱས་པ་ | **c̠hë>-b̄a** | *produced, product* |
| འདུས་བྱས་ | **dü>-c̠hë>** | *compounded* |
| དངོས་པོ་ | **n̄gö>-b̄o** | *functioning thing* |

See *Meditation on Emptiness*, pp. 219-220, and *Debate in Tibetan Buddhism*, pp. 272-279.

There are three main categories of impermanent things: forms (physical things), knowledge (that is, consciousness, including both nonconceptual types, such as sense perception, and conceptual, mental awareness), and a third category of impermanent phenomena that are neither mental nor physical called non-associated compositional factors.

| | | |
|---|---|---|
| གཟུགས་ | <u>su</u>k | *form* |
| ཞིམ་པོ་ | pém-b̄o | *matter* |
| ཤེས་པ་ | s̄hé>-b̄a | *knowledge, consciousness* |
| ལྡན་མིན་འདུ་བྱེད་ | dën-mîn-du-jé' | *non-associated compositional factors* |

Forms include all physical phenomena, knowledge includes all mental phenomena, and non-associated compositional factors, everything else that exists but is not permanent.

On the threefold division of impermanent things, see Perdue, *Debate in Tibetan Buddhism*, pp. 353-355.

# *Vocabulary*

Memorize the spelling and pronunciation of these words and of the numbers from ten through one-hundred, along with the names for the larger numbers. Practice speaking them.

## *Nouns*

| ཀུན་ཏུ་བཟང་པོ་ | **ḡün-ḏu-s̱ang-b̄o** | Samantabhadra |
|---|---|---|
| རྐྱེན་ | **ḡyên** | condition |
| སྐུ་ | **ḡu** | body [H] |
| གངས་ | **kang** | snow |
| ངག་ | **ngak** | speech |
| དངོས་པོ་ | **ṉgö>-b̄o** | functioning thing |
| ཉོན་མོངས་ | **nyön-mong** | affliction [Skt. *kleśa*] |
| ཐུགས་ | **thuk** | mind [H] |
| ཐུགས་རྗེ་ | **thuk-jé** | compassion [H] |
| འདུ་བྱེད་ | **du-jé'** | compositional factor |
| འདུས་མ་བྱས་ | **dü>-ma-jé>** | uncompounded phenomenon |
| ལྡན་མིན་འདུ་བྱེད་ | **dën-mîn-du-jé'** | nonassociated compositional factor |
| ནམ་མཁའ་ | **nam-kha** | space |
| གནས་བརྟན་ | **ṉë>-ḏën** | elder [Skt. *sthavira*] |
| བུ་ | **pu** | child, son |

| བྱས་པ་ | chë>-ba | product, that which has been made |
| མོ་གཤམ་ | mo-sham | barren woman |
| ཞི་བ་ | shí-wa | peace, pacification |
| གཞི་གྲུབ་ | shí-dup | basic existent |
| རང་དབང་ | rang-wang | independence |
| རི་བོང་ | rí-bong | rabbit |
| ར་ | ra | horn |
| ལུས་ | lü> | body |
| ཡི་གེ་ | yí-gé | letter |
| ཡིད་ | yí' | mind, mentality |
| ཤེས་བྱ་ | shé>-ja | object of knowledge |
| གསུང་ | sung | speech [H] |
| གསུང་འབུམ་ | sung-bum | collected works |

## Verbs

Verbs not identified as past, future, or imperative forms are present tense forms. NOM identifies nominative verbs, AG agentive verbs, and SV specialized verbs.

| མཁྱེན་ | khyên | know, realize [H] [AG] |
| འགྲོ་ | do | go [NOM] |
| བརྙེས་ | ñyé> | [past form of རྙེད་] |
| རྙེད་ | ñyé' | find [AG] |
| རྟོགས་ | dok | realize, understand [AG] |

| ཕྱ་ | c͟ha | [future form of བྱེད་] |
| ཕྱས་ | c͟hë> | [past form of བྱེད་] |
| བྱེད་ | c͟hé' | do, make, perform, act [AG] |
| ཕྱོས་ | c͟hö> | [imperative form of བྱེད་] |
| ཤེས་ | s͞hé> | know [AG] |

## Pronouns

| དེ་ | té | that one |
| དེ་དག་ | té-dak | those |

## Adjectives

| དཀའ་ | g͞a | difficult |
| དེ་ | té | that |
| དེ་དག་ | té-dak | those |
| འབའ་ཞིག་ | ba-s͟hík | only |
| རང་དབང་ཅན་ | rang-wang-j͟ën | independent |

## Adverbs

| ཅུང་ཟད་ | j͞ung-s͟ë' | a little |
| ཇི་ལྟར་ | c͟hí-d͞ar | how |
| དེ་ལྟར་ | té-d͞ar | thus |

## Postpositions

| | | |
|---|---|---|
| ཆེད་ | **ché'** | purpose, [for] the sake [of] |
| རྗེས་ | **jé>** | after |
| སྟེང་ | **dēng** | top, [on] top [of] |
| མདུན་ | **dün** | front, [in] front [of] |

## Lexical Particles

The asterisk identifies where the remainder of the word stands in relation to the lexical particle.

| | | |
|---|---|---|
| ཀུན་ཏུ་ * | **ḡün-ḏu** | [prefix particle] |
| མངོན་པར་ * | **n̄gön-b̄ar** | [prefix particle] |
| * ཅན་ | **jën** | [subjective suffix syllable] |
| མ་ * | **ma** | [negative prefix syllable] |
| མི་ * | **mi** | [negative prefix syllable] |
| རྫོགས་པར་ * | **d̲zok-b̄ar** | [prefix particle] |

## Syntactic and Case Marking Particles

| | | |
|---|---|---|
| ན་ | **na** | if, when [conditional] |
| ནས་ | **në>** | [continuative—after verb] |
| ནི་ | **ni** | [punctuational] : |
| ཡི་ | **yí** | of [case marking particle] |

# CHAPTER 10

*Lexical, Syntactic, and Case Marking Particles*
*Pattern Analysis: the Science of the Dots*
*Cyclic Existence*

## Patterns in Tibetan Language
### Particles

The term 'particle' as it is used in *Translating Buddhism from Tibetan* has its origin in traditional Tibetan grammar. However, the concept of the particle is not as simple as that of the word. Tibetan grammarians tend to include so many different sorts of items among particles (ཚིག་ཕྲད་, *tshík-ṭhë'*) as to make the traditional understanding not very useful for the English speaker.[61] Thus, the particles in this book, while they sometimes coincide with the traditional ཚིག་ཕྲད་, are defined somewhat more narrowly.

> There are three classes of **particles**: lexical particles, case marking particles, and syntactic particles.

Unlike words, the meanings that particles bring to a phrase, clause, or sentence are either ambivalent or general. For example, some particles merely show plurality, while others are conjunctions indicating relations such as *and* or *but*. They gain fuller, more specific meanings only when they are used in specific contexts.

The particle ལ་, for example, is a case marking particle placed after nouns to indicate, among other things, the place where an action is done or where something exists.

ཕུམ་པ་ལ་ (pum-b̄a-la) means *in the pot*, as well as many other things (*at the pot*, *for the pot*, etc.) depending on context.

ལས་ is one of two particles used to indicate origins.

ཕུམ་པ་ལས་ (pum-b̄a-lë>) means *from the pot*, *from among the pots*, and so on, again depending on context.

Particles are just that: particles. They are pieces, spare parts that need to be used with words to make sense. Thus, although particles may have lexical or dictionary meanings, those meanings are minimal.

Particles such as ལ་ and ལས་ have minimal lexical meaning in that they have no more concrete meaning than their English counterparts, *in* and *from*. It should be noted that ལ་ may also occur as a word meaning *[mountain] pass*, but it is much more frequently a case marking particle. ལས་, on the other hand, is frequently seen as a word meaning *action* (Sanskrit: *karma*).

One can think of case marking and syntactic particles as being similar to the symbols called operators used in mathematics: + - =. These mathematical symbols mean nothing by themselves but, like particles, show how other things are related to one another.

## Lexical Particles

Lexical particles are so called because they do not function, as do the other two sorts of particles, to show how words in phrases, clauses, and sentences are related to one another. They operate merely at the lexical level, serving as constituents of words and particles.

> **Lexical particles** are units, usually made of one or two syllables, that serve as parts of words. They do not function independently of words.

Lexical particles perform such functions as indicating plurality in nouns and negating verbs.

For example, the word ཕུམ་པ་ may be made explicitly plural by adding the particle རྣམས་ to form ཕུམ་པ་རྣམས་ (pum-b̄a-ñam, *pots*).

The terms ཡུལ་ཅན་, རྟོག་བཅས་, and རྟོག་མེད་—important in the doctrinal dimension of བློ་—are also illustrations of the use of lexical particles.

| བློ་ | **lo** | *mind* |
|---|---|---|
| ཡུལ་ | **yül** | *object* [also: *place, region*] |
| ཡུལ་ཅན་ | **yül-jën** | *subject* |
| རྟོག་པ་ | **dok-ba** | *thought, conceptuality* |
| རྟོག་བཅས་ | **dok-jë>** | *conceptual* |
| རྟོག་མེད་ | **dok-mé'** | *nonconceptual* |

The final syllable of ཡུལ་ཅན་ (**yül-jën**, *subject*), for instance, is a particle that means *possessing*; ཡུལ་ཅན་ literally translates as *possessing an object*. The final syllable of རྟོག་བཅས་ (**dok-jë>**, *conceptual*), བཅས་, also means *possessing*, but is actually an abbreviated form of དང་བཅས་པ་—རྟོག་པ་དང་བཅས་པ་ (literally, *possessing conceptuality*) being the expanded form of the word. The final syllable མེད་, likewise, is a particle which, when it ends a word, means *without*—in this case, རྟོག་མེད་, *without conceptuality*, or *nonconceptual*.

## Types of Lexical Particles

There are five classes of lexical particles:

1.  **prefix particles** such as the རྣམ་པར་ in རྣམ་པར་ཤེས་པ་ (*consciousness*);
2.  **negative prefix syllables** such as the མ་ in མ་ཡིན་ (*is not*);
3.  **final syllables**—for example, the པ་ in བུམ་པ་ and ཡོད་པ་ and the three-syllable particle དང་བཅས་པ་ in རྟོག་པ་དང་བཅས་པ་ (*possessing conceptuality*—abbreviated རྟོག་བཅས་);[62]
4.  **optional suffix syllables** such as the pluralizers དག་ and རྣམས་—where, for example, བུམ་པ་རྣམས་ means *pots*;
5.  **negative verbal particles** such as the མེད་པ་ in རྟོག་པ་མེད་པ་ (*without conceptuality*—abbreviated as རྟོག་མེད་).

The first two classes of lexical particles are seen in verbs, nouns, and adjectives.

In general, Tibetan words beginning with prefix particles (two-syllable[63] lexical particles such as རྣམ་པར་, རྗེས་སུ་, ཀུན་ཏུ་, and མངོན་པར་) are Tibetan translations of Sanskrit Buddhist terms. Whereas མངོན་པར་རྟོགས་ (n̄gön-b̄ar-d̄ok, *realize*) is a verb, མངོན་པར་རྟོགས་པ་ (n̄gön-b̄ar-d̄ok-b̄a, *realization*) is a noun. Likewise, whereas མ་ཡིན་ (*is not*) is a verb, མ་ཡིན་པ་ is a noun meaning *not being* (as seen in རྟག་པ་མ་ཡིན་པ་, *not being permanent* or *non-permanent*).

---

Although verb-and-auxiliary phrases such as རྟོགས་པར་བྱ་ (*will/should realize*) and verbs such as མངོན་པར་རྟོགས་ (which begin with prefix particles) may appear to the beginner to be confusingly similar in structure, they are not. There are a limited number of auxiliary verbs and, even more important, a limited number of prefix syllables—none of which are also verbs.

---

The latter three classes of lexical particles are seen only in nouns and adjectives, not in verbs.

Optional suffix syllables (such as the pluralizing particle རྣམས་) only follow nouns or adjectives (although they often follow noun and adjective *phrases*).

All final syllables (such as པ་) and negative verbal particles (such as མེད་པ་) end in syllables in which final verbs never end.

## Verbal Nouns and Adjectives

There is a class of nouns and adjectives that, while they *are* nouns and adjectives, in some ways function as verbs. However, they may never be final verbs.

---

Any word ending in one of these six final syllables—པ་, པོ་, བ་, བོ་, མ་, and མོ་—is either a noun or an adjective (or, rarely, a pronoun). Final verbs never end in these syllables.

There are many nouns and adjectives made by affixing these six syllables to verbs; such words are called **verbal nouns** and **verbal adjectives**. These words—generically called **verbals**—are seen very frequently in Tibetan.

Where མེད་, for example, is a verb meaning *not to exist*, མེད་པ་ is a verbal noun meaning *nonexistence* and *nonexistent*.

These verbal nouns and adjectives act like verbs in many ways—they may have subjects and objects, for example—but they are nouns (or adjectives); they are themselves the subjects or objects of other verbs. For example, the verb བསྟན་, which means *taught*, *have taught*, or *has taught*, may be made into the verbal བསྟན་པ་. In Chapter Nine, you were presented with a model sentence ending in the verb བསྟན་: སངས་རྒྱས་ཀྱིས་ཆོས་བསྟན། (BUDDHA + *AGENTIVE-CASE-MARKER* + DOCTRINE + TAUGHT— *Buddha taught the doctrine*). Transforming the terminal verb བསྟན་ into the verbal བསྟན་པ་ creates clauses that act, themselves, as complex nouns or adjectives.

| | |
|---|---|
| སངས་རྒྱས་ཀྱིས་ ཆོས་ བསྟན་པ་ | Buddha's having taught the doctrine |
| སངས་རྒྱས་ཀྱིས་ བསྟན་པ་ | taught by Buddha,  that taught by Buddha |
| ཆོས་ བསྟན་པ་ | the doctrine taught, [who] taught the doctrine |

Such constructions will be explained in detail in later chapters.[64]

## Syntactic Particles

Like lexical particles, and unlike words, syntactic and case marking particles do not have their own distinct lexical meanings. Unlike lexical particles, however, they do not normally become parts of words. Rather, they are used to connect words, and even phrases and clauses, to one another.

> **Syntactic particles** (or **grammatical particles**) are units of one or two syllables that have only a grammatical function. Although, unlike lexical particles, they are not parts of words, they too cannot function independently of words, but must be used with words in phrases, clauses, and sentences.[65]

● Some syntactic particles are used only with nouns, pronouns, and adjectives, for example, the conjuction དང་ (*and*):

དཀར་པོ་དང་དམར་པོ་                    *white and red*

རྟག་པ་དང་མི་རྟག་པ་                    *permanent and impermanent.*

● Others are used to introduce phrases, clauses, and sentences:

གཞན་ཡང་                                *moreover*

དེས་ན་                                    *therefore*

ཡང་ན་                                    *alternatively.*

● Still others are similar to punctuation marks:

མི་རྟག་པ་ནི་                    —where the ནི་ is like a colon ( : ).

The particle ནི་ may be placed after a noun (as in མི་རྟག་པ་ནི་) or after a noun phrase to indicate that the noun or noun phrase denotes the topic to be discussed and that the discussion immediately follows. The translation of ནི་ depends mainly on context, but options include translating it as a colon or making the noun or noun phrase a section heading.

● Finally, some of the most important end clauses or sentences:

ཡོད་པའི་ཕྱིར་                        *because of existing*

བུམ་པ་མི་རྟག་པ་ཡིན་ནོ།            —where the ནོ་ is like a period.

The particle ཕྱིར་ is one of the most common syntactic particles in philosophical texts, since it ends clauses that present reasons. Like the postpositions, it is connected to the clause it ends with a connective case marking particle. Unlike the postpositions, it is not declined.[66]

The particle ནོ་ is a member of a group of eleven **terminators**, one for each of the suffix letters. Thus, the terminator གོ་ follows words ending in the suffix letter ག. Likewise, the terminating syntactic particles ངོ་, དོ་, ནོ་, བོ་, མོ་, འོ་, རོ་, ལོ་, and སོ་ follow, respectively, words ending in the suffix letters ང་, ད་, ན་, བ་, མ་, འ་, ར་, ལ་, and ས་. The terminator ཏོ་ follows the secondary suffix ད་. The secondary suffix ས་ is followed by the terminator ཪོ་. Words that do not end in a suffix may be terminated with the particle འོ་.    ( ཤེས་པ་, for instance, may in this way be terminated as ཤེས་པའོ། .)

Syntactic particles are also used within verb phrases (between verbs and auxiliary verbs) and after verbs to mark the ends of clauses, imperative constructions, and the like.[67]

## Analyzing Patterns in Tibetan Language
### *The Science of the Dots*

Diagramming phrases, clauses, and sentences with boxes and arrows was introduced in Chapter Nine. Before such diagramming can be done, however, the categories of words and types of particles must first be properly identified. This most basic level of syntactic analysis—identifying which words are nouns, which are verbs, what sorts of particles are used, and so on—has been termed by Jeffrey Hopkins, the "science of the dots."[68]

The science of the dots is a way of speaking about the relationships between syllables within words and between words and the remainder of the phrases, clauses, and sentences in which they are found *as if the dots following syllables and words actually had different functions*. It is possible to identify each dot in a Tibetan sentence in terms of either:

1   the type of syllable it follows, or
2   the relationship between the syllable it follows and the rest of the phrase, clause, or sentence in which it is found.

> Dots actually perform no other function than to separate syllables or to end words. The "functions" of dots, therefore, are merely metaphors for the relationships among the syllables, particles, and words that precede and follow the dots.

The main purpose in identifying the functions of the dots is to facilitate the reading of complex sentences by providing background knowledge of the possible relationships between words. This knowledge is gained naturally through exposure to a language over many years. For those who want to learn a language more quickly, however, it is helpful to be exposed to the range of possible relationships between syllables, particles, and words through the grammatical analysis presented here. Such an analysis begins with simple sentences that seemingly require no analysis. For beginners this will pose no problem; they will be learning Tibetan vocabulary, syntax, and grammatical analysis at the same time. However, readers who already know Tibetan may be put off by the repetitiveness of this material. Many of the beginning analyses are of sentences and phrases that are so simple that such an analysis seems at best redundant and, at worst, a needless superimposition of complexity onto what is already simple and clear. However, years of experience with this system have shown that it facilitates rapid reading and clear understanding of Tibetan; thus, more advanced readers are urged to approach this material with patience and flexibility.

The following is a complete list of the "functions" of dots. Preceding the description of the context in which a dot occurs is its abbreviation, used in the analysis of phrases, clauses, and sentences.

| | |
|---|---|
| S | between syllables within words, particles, and verb phrases |
| OM | indicating an omitted syllable in a contraction or abbreviation |

| | |
|---|---|
| NA | between a noun and an adjective modifying that noun |
| NN | between nouns in a list |
| APP | between two words or phrases in an appositional relationship |

| | |
|---|---|
| VB | after a final verb (either a simple verb or a verb phrase) |
| V | after an open verb (infinitives, verbals at the ends of clauses, etc.) |
| ADV | after an adverb or after a particle marking adverbial identity |

| | |
|---|---|
| NOM | after a noun in the nominative case |
| VOC | after a noun in the vocative case or an interjection |
| C | before or after a case marking particle |
| UP | indicating an understood case marking or syntactic particle |

| | |
|---|---|
| SP | before or after a syntactic particle |

The following is a list of the five most basic "functions" of dots.

| | |
|---|---|
| S | between syllables within words, particles, and verb phrases |
| VB | after a final verb (either a basic verb or a verb phrase) |
| NOM | after a noun in the nominative case |
| C | before or after a case-marking syntactic particle |
| SP | before or after a syntactic particle other than a case marking particle |

Memorize the mnemonic abbreviations for these five types of dots.

## Lexical Dots

The first group of dots—S and OM dots—are found only within words and particles, in the lexical dimension of Tibetan. Thus, they do not act in the syntactic dimension of Tibetan; that is, they do not serve to connect words with other words or with particles. The purpose in identifying them is that once they have been identified, they may be eliminated from grammatical analysis. The remaining dots are syntactic—they follow (or precede) particles and words and are named after the ways in which those particles and words relate to other words in phrases, clauses, and sentences.

You have already seen quite a few S dots; all dots after syllables in the beginning or middle of words and particles are instances of either S dots or OM dots.

 བུམ་པ་མི་རྟག་པ་ཡིན། means *Pots are impermanent.*

The OM (OMitted syllable) dots are not as common as S dots, but they are found frequently. As will be seen later in this chapter, Tibetan words are often abbreviated by means of omitting syllables.

Here are dot analyses of two examples of abbreviation.

| S   S   S | | OM |
|---|---|---|
| རྣམ་པར་ཤེས་པ་ | — | རྣམ་ཤེས་ |

| S   S   S | | OM |
|---|---|---|
| ཡོངས་སུ་གྲུབ་པ་ | — | ཡོངས་གྲུབ་ |

Note that although རྣམ་པར་ and ཡོངས་སུ་ are lexical particles (specifically, prefix particles), there is no separate lexical particle dot. རྣམ་པར་ཤེས་པ་ means *consciousness* and ཡོངས་སུ་གྲུབ་པ་ means *perfect phenomenon* (a Mind Only term for emptiness).

The dots between the two syllables in the abbreviated forms are **OM** dots. The dots at the ends of words, however, cannot be classified without seeing the rest of the sentence, clause, or phrase in which those words are found.[69]

## *Dots within Noun Phrases*

The second group of dots—**NA**, **NN**, and **APP** dots—occur within certain types of noun phrases (respectively, noun-adjective phrases, list phrases, and appositional phrases).

| NA |
|---|
| between a noun and its adjective |

NA   S
རྟ་ དཀར་པོ་
↑

The first dot in རྟ་དཀར་པོ་ (*white horse*) is an **NA** (Noun-Adjective) dot, one between a noun and an adjective. The second dot is an **S** (Syllable) dot.

| NN |
|---|
| between nouns in a list |

NN  NN  NN
ས་ ཆུ་ མེ་ རླུང་
↑   ↑   ↑

The first three dots in ས་ཆུ་མེ་རླུང་ are **NN** dots, separating nouns in a list (that is, a Noun and a Noun).

ས་, ཆུ་, མེ་, and རླུང་ are the four physical elements: *earth, water, fire,* and *wind.*

---

## Dots Used with Verbs and Adverbs

The third, fourth, and fifth groups of dots are true syntactic dots. They help show how words relate to one another in clauses and sentences.

Dots in the third group occur after verbs, within verb phrases, or after adverbs. The **VB** (terminal VerB) dot is found only after complete verbs—that is, final verbs such as ཤེས། or final verb phrases (such as ཤེས་པར་བྱ་).

| | | | |
|---|---|---|---|
| **VB**<br>after a final verb | | **VB**<br>སངས་རྒྱས་ ཀྱིས་ ཆོས་ བསྟན།<br>↑ | |

The **V** (open or incomplete Verb) dot occurs after verbs that are not terminal:

1   after infinitives (such as the རྟོགས་པར་ in རྟོགས་པར་དཀའ་ **d̄ok-b̄ar-g̱a,** *difficult to realize*),

2   between the components of verb phrases
     (for example, the ཤེས་པར་ in ཤེས་པར་བྱ་ **s̄hé>-b̄ar-cha,** *will know*),

3   after verbals at the ends of clauses,

4   after verbs preceding continuative syntactic particles
     (as seen in བསྟན་ནས་ **d̄ën-në>,** *having taught,* and in བསྟན་ན་ **d̄ën-na,** *if* or *when taught*).

| | |
|---|---|
| **V**<br>after an open verb | **V**<br>ཤེས་པར་བྱ།<br>↑ |

The final dot in the phrase ཤེས་པར་བྱ་ is a **VB** dot.

## *Dots and Declension*

The fourth group—the **NOM**, **VOC**, **C**, and **UC** dots—are used when nouns, pronouns, and adjectives are declined. **NOM** and **VOC** dots follow nouns, pronouns, and adjectives in the nominative and vocative cases, respectively. These are the two cases that are identified by the fact that no case particle is used to mark them.

| | |
|---|---|
| **NOM**<br>nominative case | NOM    NOM<br>བུམ་པ་ མི་རྟག་པ་ ཡིན།<br>↑        ↑ |

The other six cases are marked by case marking particles, and the dots before and after these Case particles are **C** dots. Sometimes case particles are dropped, and in those instances, the dot where the case-marking particle would normally have been seen is an **Understood Case** dot.

| | |
|---|---|
| **C**<br>before or after a case<br>marking particle | C  C<br>སངས་རྒྱས་ ཀྱིས་ ཆོས་ བསྟན།<br>↑  ↑ |

## *Dots Used with Syntactic Particles*

The fifth group of dots is actually only one type—the dots found before and after Syntactic Particles.

| | |
|---|---|
| **SP**<br>before or after<br>syntactic particles | SP  SP<br>ལས་དང་ཉོན་མོངས་<br>↑ ↑ |

དང་ is a conjunction usually meaning *and* but also seen with the meaning *or*. ལས་དང་ཉོན་མོངས་—*actions (karma) and the afflictions*—are the two causes of cyclic existence.

## Pattern Analysis
### Nouns in a List

Since there are no real punctuation marks in Tibetan, lists of nouns are often just a group of nouns strung together. Take as an example the sentence, *Mind, mentality, and consciousness are equivalent.* Sometimes the writer (or, more precisely, the scribe or secretary—the person who is actually putting pen to paper) will separate the individual items with lines instead of dots. In that case, you will see the following.

| སེམས། | ཡིད། | རྣམ་པར་ཤེས་པ་ | དོན་གཅིག | ཡིན་ནོ། |
|---|---|---|---|---|
| sêm | yí' | ñam-b̄ar-s̄hé>-b̄a | tön-j̄ík | yîn-no |
| MIND I | MENTALITY I | CONSCIOUSNESS I | EQUIVALENT | ARE I |

(The bottom line is a Tenglish translation of the sentence.)

More often than not, however, what you will be confronted with is this, with no punctuation to separate the words:

སེམས་ཡིད་རྣམ་པར་ཤེས་པ་དོན་གཅིག་ཡིན་ནོ།

The two sentences are essentially the same and mean the same thing: *Mind, mentality, and consciousness are equivalent.*

Here is a dot analysis of that sentence. The numbers above the dots have been added as an aid to discussing them.

| 1 | 2 | 3 4 5 6 | 7 8 | 9 10 |
|---|---|---|---|---|
| NN | NN | S S S NOM | S NOM | VB SP |
| སེམས་ | ཡིད་ | རྣམ་པར་ཤེས་པ་ | དོན་གཅིག | ཡིན་ ནོ། |

Had the word རྣམ་པར་ཤེས་པ་ been used in its abbreviated form རྣམ་ཤེས་, the dot between those two syllables would have been an **OM** dot and not an **S** dot.

Classifying the dots in this way tells you what function the *syllable prior to the dot* performs in the sentence. The **NN** after the first word, སེམས་, tells you that you have a noun that is a member of a list of nouns, as does the next **NN** dot. Notice that the last item of the three in this list is not followed by an NN dot; NN dots occur *between* the items in a list, not after the list as a whole.

Moreover, the list as a whole is one unit in Tibetan. Lists are units in which the parts—the words within it—do not relate to anything outside of the list. Just as a word is a unit made of syllables, a unit connecting to the other words of the sentence only at its end, so a list is a unit connecting to the other words of the sentence only at one place, its end. In the example above, this is the last syllable of the final item in the list (the syllable prior to dot 6). Dot 6 is a nominative dot. Of the traditional eight cases in which nouns can be declined, this list-unit is in the first, or nominative case.

How do you know that this dot is a nominative dot? First, the word རྣམ་པར་ཤེས་པ་ is neither an adverb, a verb, or a postposition. Therefore, it is either an internal component of a phrase, or it is declined.

> Only nouns, pronouns, and adjectives are declined.[70]

Second, རྣམ་པར་ཤེས་པ་ is a noun that has no case particle following it. Third, as is often the case, the context of the sentence provides clues for determining when a noun is a nominative and when it is not. The main clue is the verb that comes at its end. You know that the verb ཡིན་ requires both a nominative subject and a nominative complement. The **subject** of such a sentence is the first word or group of words in the sentence, whereas the **complement** follows it and immediately precedes the verb. Thus, they are both easy to find.

དོན་གཅིག་—the word just prior to the verb—means *equivalent*. This ought immediately to make you suspect that the subject of this sentence, that which is equivalent, is going to be not one thing but, rather, a number of things. It does not make any sense to say that one thing is equivalent (or, for that matter, mutually exclusive); there must be at least two. Thus, in this case we should look for either a compound subject ('X and Y') or nouns in a list ('X, Y, Z').

The last two dots of the sentence (dots 9 and 10) follow the syllables ཡིན་ and ནོ་, respectively. ཡིན་ is a verb, the terminal verb of this sentence. Thus, the dot after it is a VB dot. The final syllable, ནོ་, a syntactic particle called a terminator, emphasizes the completion of the sentence.  In the present example it is redundant because ཡིན་ is obviously a terminal verb.  Such redundancy is not uncommon in terminators.

Notice that the SP dot following the terminator is defined as a dot "before or after a syntactic particle."  Technically speaking, the dot preceding it is also an SP dot. However, the fact that this dot (dot 9) also follows the verb is much more significant than the fact that it precedes a syntactic particle.  Thus, being after a verb takes precedence and the dot is identified as a VB dot.

When the sentence is diagrammed, it looks like this.

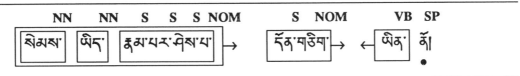

Since this is a sentence ending in a linking verb, it has three main parts:

1   a **subject**—three nouns in a list,
2   a **complement** (the word དོན་གཅིག),
3   a **verb** ( ཡིན་, with a terminating syntactic particle ནོ་).

---

Syntactic particles are not boxed.  The one here is marked with an oversized period underneath it to indicate that it moves grammatically neither to the left nor to the right, but, rather, terminates the sentence.

---

## Lexical Particles
### *Final Syllables*

There are five types of final syllables, using the term narrowly and not just as a description of any syllable that ends a word.  These particles are found only in nouns, adjectives, and a few pronouns:

1   generic suffix syllables (པ་, པོ་, བ་, བོ་, མ་, or མོ་),
2   subjective suffix syllables (པ་, པོ་, བ་, བོ་, ཅན་, and མཁན་),
3   restrictive suffix syllables (ཚམ་ and ཅིག),

4    possessive suffixes (དང་བཅས་པ་ and དང་ལྡན་པ་),

5    separative suffixes (དང་བྲལ་བ་).

Generic suffix syllables are discussed in this chapter. Subjective and restrictive suffix syllables will be introduced in Chapter Eleven.

## Generic Suffix Syllables

You have already seen many generic suffix syllables. Nouns and adjectives ending in a པ་, པོ་, བ་, བོ་, མ་, or མོ་ are illustrations of the use of these lexical particles. In some, but by no means all cases, these syllables have been placed after verbs—as true **nominalizing syllables**—to create nouns and adjectives.

The following are illustrations of common words of this type, the first example in each pair being a noun or an adjective with no obvious relation to a verb, the second being a noun or adjective deriving from a verb.

| རྣམ་པ་ | **ñam-b̄a** | *aspect, type* |
| ཡོད་པ་ | **yö'-b̄a** | *existent, existence* |
| དཀར་པོ་ | **ḡar-b̄o** | *white* |
| རྒྱལ་པོ་ | **gyël-b̄o** | *king* |
| རྩ་བ་ | **d̄za-wa** | *root* |
| སྐྱེ་བ་ | **ḡyé-wa** | *birth* |
| ཆུ་བོ་ | **chu-wo** | *river* |
| སྐྱེ་བོ་ | **ḡyé-wo** | *being, person* |
| དབུ་མ་ | **ū-ma** | *middle* |
| སྲུང་མ་ | **sung-ma** | *guardian, protector* |
| ཆེན་མོ་ | **chên-mo** | *great, large* [feminine form] |
| རྒྱལ་མོ་ | **gyel-mo** | *queen* |

པ་ and བ་ are by far the most common concluding syllables.

ཆེན་མོ་ and རྒྱལ་མོ་, incidentally, are *feminine* words, insofar as any Tibetan words may be said to have gender. The more universal (that is, genderless) form of ཆེན་མོ་ is ཆེན་པོ་—as seen in ཐེག་པ་ཆེན་པོ་ (*Mahāyāna* or *Great Vehicle*) and the masculine form of རྒྱལ་མོ་ is རྒྱལ་པོ་ (*king*). Nouns in languages such as Sanskrit, Latin, and French are either feminine, masculine, or neuter, and in these languages adjectives must agree in gender with nouns. Tibetan, on the other hand, is ambiguous as to number (བུམ་པ་ sometimes means *pot*, sometimes *pots*) and it is also ambiguous as to gender, except in certain instances when the feminine is specified through the use of the final syllables མ་ and མོ་.

There are, however, certain specifically feminine names.

| སྒྲོལ་མ་ | **ḍöl-ma** | *Tārā* [a female Buddha] |
|---|---|---|
| རྡོ་རྗེ་རྣལ་འབྱོར་མ་ | **dor-jé-ñen-jor-ma** | *Vajrayoginī* [a female Buddha] |

In general, where རྣལ་འབྱོར་པ་ means *yogin* (that is, a practitioner of yoga—in Buddhism, a meditator), a རྣལ་འབྱོར་མ་ is a *yoginī*, a woman who is a meditator.

Books are also often given feminine titles, especially in the case of abbreviated titles.

| ལམ་རིམ་ཆེན་མོ་ | **lam-rim-chên-mo** | *Great Stages of the Path* |
|---|---|---|

ལམ་རིམ་ཆེན་མོ་ means *great [exposition of the] stages of the path [to enlightenment]*. ལམ་ means *path* and རིམ་ is an abbreviated form of རིམ་པ་, meaning *stage*. This is the abbreviated title, and the one usually used, of Tsong-kha-pa's famous systematic presentation of Buddhist practice from the viewpoint of the texts of Indian Buddhism.

Liturgical texts are sometimes known by abbreviated feminine titles based on their first few words. For example, a short prayer whose first line is དམིགས་མེད་བརྩེ་བའི་གཏེར་ ཆེན་སྤྱན་རས་གཟིགས། (*Avalokiteshvara, a great repository of the compassion [that] does not objectify* ...) is given a brief title made from the first syllables of its first two words (དམིགས་མེད་ and བརྩེ་བ་) and the feminine suffix syllable མ.

| | | |
|---|---|---|
| དམིགས་བརྩེ་མ་ | m̄ík-d̄zé-ma | *The Non-Objectifying Compassion* |

Non-objectifying compassion is compassion that does take inherently existing sentient beings as its objects, but rather sees only beings empty of inherent existence.[71] The non-objectified is emptiness, that is, reality.

In the phrase དམིགས་མེད་བརྩེ་བའི་གཏེར་ཆེན་སྤྱན་རས་གཟིགས, བརྩེ་བ་ means compassion, a གཏེར་ is a treasure, a vein of ore, or a place for storing things, and སྤྱན་རས་ གཟིགས་ is Avalokiteshvara, the Buddha epitomizing compassion (see Chapter Eleven).

However, it is not the case that any noun or adjective ending in མ or མོ should be construed as referring to the feminine. The very common adjectives ཟབ་མོ་ (*profound*) and ཕྲ་མོ་ (*subtle, fine*) are used without reference to gender, as are དྲུ་མ་ and ཤུང་མ་.[72]

# Lexical Particles
## *Pluralizing Suffix Syllables*

It is not always the case that words as found in use in a text will correspond identically to words defined in dictionaries. In many cases, lexical particles may be used on an *ad hoc* basis to modify the meanings of extant nouns, pronouns, and adjectives. The generic suffix syllables just examined, for instance, may be used in this way to form verbal nouns and adjectives from any verb. However, some lexical particles are always used in this way and, for this reason, may be called **optional suffix syllables.**

They are optional because they do not form part of the basic noun, pronoun, or adjective. That is, whereas the noun བུམ་པ་ is found in a dictionary, བུམ་པ་ རྣམས་ (meaning *pots*) is not.

Included in this group are the pluralizing suffix syllables རྣམས་, དག་, ཅག་, and ཚོ. Pluralizing particles are used to make plurality explicit.

Tibetan nouns and pronouns which lack pluralizing suffix syllables are not singular nouns and pronouns. They are ambiguous as to number.

Thus, བུམ་པ་ means *pot* or *pots*, *a pot* or *the pot*—depending on context. བུམ་པ་རྣམས་, on the other hand, explicitly says *pots*. དེ་ means *that* and *those*, but དེ་རྣམས་ and དེ་དག་ just mean *those*.

They are included among the lexical particles because the plural nouns, pronouns, and adjectives they are used to create may then be marked with case marking particles or followed by syntactic particles, like any other nouns, pronouns, and adjectives.

Of the two classes of particles, lexical particles modify words—usually by becoming part of them—and syntactic particles indicate how words relate to one another within phrases, clauses, and sentences.

བུམ་པ་ means *pot* or *a pot* or *the pot* or *pots*. The addition of the pluralizing lexical particle རྣམས་ creates བུམ་པ་རྣམས་, explicitly meaning *pots* in the plural. This word is then connected to other words with the addition of syntactic particles: བུམ་པ་རྣམས་ལ་, བུམ་པ་རྣམས་ལས་, and so on.

Pluralizing particles are found after nouns, pronouns, and adjectives. In many noun phrases, however, they may occur only at the end.

Thus, although བུམ་པ་རྣམས་ means *pots*, adding དམར་པོ་ (*red*) to the end—making བུམ་པ་རྣམས་དམར་པོ་—does not produce a phrase meaning *red pots*. The grammatically correct construction is བུམ་པ་དམར་པོ་རྣམས་, where the noun-adjective phrase བུམ་པ་དམར་པོ་ (*red pot*) functions as single unit, which is then pluralized through the addition of the particle རྣམས་.

## Lexical Particles
### Negative Particles

Traditional Tibetan grammars list four negating particles—མ་, མི་, མིན་, and མེད་. Two of them—མ་ and མི་—are placed before the word being negated and are called here negative prefix syllables. The other two—མེན་ and མེད་—are placed after it. མེན་ and མེད་ are, in fact, verbs—མེན་ is the negative linking verb (*is not*) and མེད་ is the negative verb of existence (*does not exist*). They have been categorized here (as negative suffix syllables) following tradition, although they are actually not lexical particles, but verbal nouns or adjectives.

## *Negative Prefix Syllables*

The primary use of these two negative particles is prior to verbs, negating their meanings.

Thus, where ཡིན་ means *is*, མ་ཡིན་ means *is not* (and *are not*). Where སྐྱེ་ means *is born*, མི་སྐྱེ་ means *is not born* (and *are not born*).

In the case of verbs that have prefix particles—for example, རྣམ་པར་རྟོག་—the negating particle is placed in front of the core verb (རྟོག་), which means, in effect, that it is placed in the middle of the word, producing a new word, རྣམ་པར་མི་རྟོག་.

Although negating particles are used mainly with verbs (and verbals), they are used with other types of words as well.

The word དགེ་བ་ is an adjective meaning *virtuous* (or *wholesome*). Adding the negative particle མི་ creates a new word, མི་དགེ་བ་, which means *non-virtuous*. Similarly, where རྟག་པ་ means *permanent*, མི་རྟག་པ་ means *impermanent*.

Like some other particles, the syllables མ་ and མི་ also have usages as words. Used as a word and not a particle, མ་ is a noun meaning *mother*. As a word, མི་ is a noun meaning *human being*. མ་ is also one of the generic suffix syllables. In most instances, however, མ་ as a negative prefix will not be mistaken for མ་ as a generic suffix, since one occurs before a word, whereas the other only after it.

Here are some other useful examples of words embodying negative particles. Although most are verbals, they are all given as nouns or adjectives rather than in their core verb forms.

- Whereas འཇིག་པ་ means *disintegrating*, མི་འཇིག་པ་ means *non-disintegrating*.

- Whereas རིག་པ་ means *awareness*, མ་རིག་པ་ means *lacking awareness* or (following the by-now standard translation), *ignorance*.

- Whereas དམིགས་པ་ means *observed* and *observation* (and also *object of observation*), མི་དམིགས་པ་ means *not observed* and *non-observation*. In an exception to the general rule that a given word is negated by either མ་ or མི་ but not both, the term མ་དམིགས་པ་ is also used.[73]

- Whereas ཐ་དད་ means *different*, ཐ་མི་དད་ means, literally, *non-different*, that is, *same*. This is not a case of placement of the negating particle before the core verb; rather, this is an exception. Most adjectives that are not constructed from verbs are negated by a negative *suffix* (མིན་ or མེད་), not a prefix.

- Finally, an example of a word that has within it a negating particle but which is only etymologically a negative is མ་འོངས་པ་. འོངས་ is the past tense of the verb འོང་ (*come*); མ་འོངས་པ་ thus is literally *the not come*—that which has yet to come. However, in actual usage མ་འོངས་པ་ means simply *future*.

## Doctrinal Vocabulary and Grammar
### The Buddhist Universe: Cyclic Existence

In Chapter Nine you were introduced to the main divisions of the selfless. By way of review, here is a chart of what has been presented up to now.

This sort of taxonomy is at the heart of the Tibetan Buddhist examination of the universe. I will return to the discussion of impermanent phenomena, their divisions, and the definitions of these categories in later chapters. For now, the focus will be not on a philosophical analysis of phenomena according to whether they are permanent or impermanent, or whether they are physical or mental, but in terms of the value given them in the practice of Buddhism. In this chapter and the next you will be introduced to the basic terminology used to discuss cyclic existence and nirvana.

## Cyclic Existence

The Buddhist cosmos—viewed cosmologically or psychologically (the two are hard to separate in Buddhism)—consists of cyclic existence (འཁོར་བ་—Sanskrit *saṃsāra*) and nirvana (མྱ་ངན་ལས་འདས་པ་—Sanskrit *nirvāṇa*), together abbreviated as འཁོར་འདས་ (**khor-dë>**)—literally, *cycling/turning [and] transcended*.

འཁོར་བ་ is a verbal noun constructed from the verb འཁོར་ (which means *turns*), as is the noun འཁོར་ལོ་ (Sanskrit *cakra*), meaning *wheel*. འཁོར་ is a verb of the nominative class, meaning that it has no objects, just a subject followed by no case marking particle. This is seen in the sentence འཁོར་ལོ་ འཁོར། *The wheel turns*. (See Chapter Twelve.)

འཁོར་བ་ thus refers to the involuntary cycling of the individual from one form of sentient life to another that characterizes the Buddhist cycle of birth, death, and rebirth. མྱ་ངན་ལས་འདས་པ་ literally means *transcended suffering* (མྱ་ངན་ *suffering, pain* + SYNTACTIC PARTICLE ལས་ *from, beyond* + འདས་པ་ *passed/transcended*). The reference of suffering is to the first of the four truths (see Chapter Thirteen), where cyclic existence is equated with suffering (སྡུག་བསྔལ་, **duk-ngël**), or more broadly, *unsatisfactoriness*.

| | | |
|---|---|---|
| འཁོར་ | **khor** | *turn* [verb] |
| འཁོར་བ་ | **khor-wa** | *cyclic existence* |
| འཁོར་ལོ་ | **khor-lo** | *wheel* |
| མྱ་ངན་ལས་འདས་པ་ | **nya-ngën-lë>-dë>-ba** | *nirvana* |

There are, in cyclic existence, three main 'regions.' Cosmologically, these three are generic categories of rebirth. Psychologically, they are levels of mental function—ranged not from least to most valuable, but from those bound in desire and hatred to those absorbed in trance. All three, from the Buddhist perspective, are flawed.

| འདོད་པའི་ཁམས་<br>འདོད་ཁམས་ | *Desire Realm* | Sanskrit: *kāmadhātu* |
|---|---|---|
| གཟུགས་ཀྱི་ཁམས་<br>གཟུགས་ཁམས་ | *Form Realm* | Skt.: *rūpadhātu* |
| གཟུགས་མེད་པའི་ཁམས་<br>གཟུགས་མེད་ཁམས་ | *Formless Realm* | Skt.: *ārūpyadhātu* |

The second member of each set of Tibetan terms is the standard abbreviation of the first. Thus, འདོད་ཁམས་ is the abbreviation of འདོད་པའི་ཁམས་.

> On the three realms and their subdivisions, see Lati Rinbochay et al, *Meditative States in Tibetan Buddhism*, pp. 23-47.

The Desire Realm includes humans and gods (male and female), while only various types of gods and goddesses live in the Form and Formless Realms.[74] Note the form of the construction གཟུགས་མེད་པའི་ཁམས་.

1 Begin with the phrase གཟུགས་མེད་ (*Forms do not exist*).

2 Make the verb མེད་ into a verbal with addition of the generic nominalizing syllable པ: མེད་པ་.

  The verbal phrase གཟུགས་མེད་པ་ then means [*somewhere*] *forms do not exist* or [*something or someone*] *without form.*

3 Add the connective case marking particle particle འི་ (which connects nouns, pronouns, and adjectives with other nouns).

  The resulting phrase is གཟུགས་མེད་པའི་. (The ཀྱི་ in གཟུགས་ཀྱི་ཁམས་ is also a connective particle.)

4   Add what is, syntactically, the main word of the entire construction, ཁམས་.

The term གཟུགས་མེད་པའི་ཁམས་ is thus actually a brief phrase meaning *a realm [where] there is no form*. Grammatically, it is an ADJECTIVE + NOUN phrase (discussed in Chapter Eleven): *formless realm*. ཁམས་ is syntactically the main word because གཟུགས་མེད་པའི་ is a phrase that modifies it as an adjective.

Although only gods and goddesses are born in the Form and Formless Realms, one finds all six principal types of rebirth in the Desire Realm, not just humans and gods. The six types of rebirth are the following—listed from the most unpleasant to the most pleasant.

| དམྱལ་བ་པ་ | **n̄yël-wa-b̄a** | *hell beings* |
|---|---|---|
| ཡི་དགས་ | **yi-dak** | *hungry ghosts* |
| དུད་འགྲོ་ | **tün-d̤o** | *animals* |
| མི་ | **mí** | *humans* |
| ལྷ་མ་ཡིན་ | **ḣla-ma-yîn** | *demigods* |
| ལྷ་ | **ḣla** | *gods* |

Note that a hell being is a དམྱལ་བ་པ་. དམྱལ་བ་ means *hell*; the addition of a generic suffix syllable (here, པ་) to a noun already ending in a generic suffix (དམྱལ་བ་) creates a new, derivative noun. Thus, the reader who is not familiar with the term དམྱལ་བ་པ་ should expect it to refer to something or someone related in some way to དམྱལ་བ་. In point of fact, དམྱལ་བ་པ་ means *hell-being*, a person born in a hell. Note also that a demigod is a ལྷ་མ་ཡིན་, a 'non-god'—the noun ལྷ་མ་ཡིན་ literally meaning *is not a god*.

Tibetan does not often speak of the six types of rebirth as *rebirths*.[75] They are sometimes referred to as *births* (སྐྱེ་བ་, ḡyé>-wa), but more often the term འགྲོ་བ་ (d̤o-wa) is used. འགྲོ་བ་ is from the verb འགྲོ་ (go) and thus literally means *going* or *goer*, or, in this case, *migrations* (or *migrators*). Everyone from gods to hell beings is such a migrator in cyclic existence. (Neither hells nor heavens are eternal in Buddhism; those born there eventually die and travel on to another rebirth.)

Everyone in cyclic existence is also a *sentient being* (སེམས་ཅན་, **sêm-jën**—Sanskrit *sattva*) and a *person* (གང་ཟག་, **kang-sak**—Sanskrit *pudgala*).

> Those who know colloquial Tibetan should not confuse the use of སེམས་ཅན་ there (where it means *animal*) with its meaning in literary Tibetan at the doctrinal level, which is much broader.

There are a number of subdivisions within these six types of rebirth. Texts on the stages of the path to enlightenment (a genre of literature called ལམ་རིམ་—from ལམ་ *path* + རིམ་པ་ *stages*) speak of many types of hells, including eight hot hells and eight cold hells. There are also various types of hungry ghosts, and many different levels of gods. Although these need not concern us at this point, it will be useful to be aware of some of the Tibetan names of animals, as these occur in all varieties of Tibetan literature.

| | | |
|---|---|---|
| རྟ་ | **ḏa** | *horse* |
| བྱ་ | **c̱ha** | *bird* |
| བ་གླང་ | **pa-lang** | *ox* |
| ཕག་པ་ | **p̱hak-ḇa** | *pig* |
| གླང་པོ་ཆེ་ | **lang-ḇo-ché** | *elephant* |
| སྟག་ | **ḏak** | *tiger* |
| སྦྲུལ་ | **ḍül** | *snake* |
| ཉ་ | **nya** | *fish* |
| ཁྱི་ | **khyi** | *dog* |
| སེང་གེ་ | **s̱éng-gé** | *lion* |

Buddhist cosmology holds that these animals, as well as the other five types of sentient beings, inhabit a world-system (འཇིག་རྟེན་, **jík-ḏên**—Sanskrit *loka*) centered on a huge mountain, རི་རབ་ལྷུན་པོ་ (**rí-rap hlün-b̄o**, Meru or Sumeru in Sanskrit). རི་ རབ་ལྷུན་པོ་ is often referred to in abbreviated form as རི་རབ་ and, metaphorically, as རིའི་ རྒྱལ་པོ་ (**rí gyël-b̄o**), *king of mountains*.

རི་ means *mountain*. འི་ is a connective case marking particle used when the last syllable of a word has no suffix letter. རྒྱལ་པོ་ means *king*.

---

The connective particles (technically the particles marking the sixth or connective case—see Chapter Twelve) are some of the most frequently seen syntactic particles. There are five connective particles: གི་ (**kí**), གྱི་ (**ḡyí**), ཀྱི་ (**kyí**), འི་ (**í**), and ཡི་ (**yí**).

---

Note (in རིའི་རྒྱལ་པོ་) that the fourth particle—the འི་—does not follow the word it connects, but becomes part of its final syllable.

---

Recall that according to Exception Seven of the pronunciation rules, པའི་ is pronounced **b̄ë**, པོའི་ is pronounced **b̄ö**, དེའི་ is **téí**, སུའི་, **s̄ü**, and རེའི་, **ríí**.

---

Very often Tibetan texts speak of the part of the universe where we live as འཛམ་ བུའི་གླིང་ or as the southern continent. The reference is to the four continents of this world system, where འཛམ་བུའི་གླིང་—in Sanskrit, *Jambudvīpa*—is the continent to the south of Mount Meru.

| | | |
|---|---|---|
| འཛམ་བུའི་གླིང་ | **d̲zam-bü-líng** | Jambu Continent |
| གླིང་ | **líng** | island, continent |

The various realms and levels of cyclic existence—in terms of the people who experience them—are discussed in more detail in Perdue, *Debate in Tibetan Buddhism*, pp. 367-373.

Cyclic existence is treated psychologically as well as cosmologically in Tibetan texts. From that perspective, cyclic existence is a result of *actions* (ལས་ **lë>** — Sanskrit *karma*) and *afflictions* (ཉོན་མོངས་ **nyön-m̄ong**—Sanskrit *kleśa*). Action here means not just any action, but that done by humans and other sentient beings, and then (as a cause of cyclic existence) only when it is intended and when it is motivated by attachment, aversion, or ignorance.

| འདོད་ཆགས་ | **dö'-chak** | attachment or desire |
|---|---|---|
| ཞེ་སྡང་ | **<u>s</u>hé-dang** | aversion or hatred |
| གཏི་མུག | **d̄í-muk** | obscuration, equivalent to མ་རིག་པ་ (*ignorance*) |

These are the three main negative attitudes in Buddhist psychology; they are also known as the *three poisons*—དུག་གསུམ (**tuk s̄um**—*poisons + three*).

Just as the phrase meaning *cyclic existence and nirvana* may be abbreviated as འཁོར་འདས་, so the causes of cyclic existence— ལས་དང་ཉོན་མོངས་ (*karma + and + afflictions*)—may be abbreviated: ལས་ཉོན་. Not just any intended action (ལས་) leads to cyclic existence, only ones that are contaminated (ཟག་བཅས་ **<u>s</u>ak-j̄é>**) by being motivated by afflictions such as attachment, aversion, and ignorance.

See Geshe Rabten, *Treasury of Dharma*, pp. 36-38, 53-60.

# *Vocabulary*

Memorize the spelling and pronunciation of these words.  Practice speaking them.

## *Nouns*

| | | |
|---|---|---|
| འཁོར་འདས་ | **khor-dë>** | cyclic existence and nirvana |
| འཁོར་བ་ | **khor-wa** | cyclic existence |
| གླང་པོ་ཆེ་ | **lang-bo-ché** | elephant |
| གླིང་ | **líng** | island, continent |
| རྒྱལ་པོ་ | **gyël-bo** | king |
| རྒྱལ་བ་ | **gyël-wa** | conqueror |
| རྒྱལ་མོ་ | **gyël-mo** | queen |
| འཇིག་པ་ | **jík-ba** | disintegration |
| ཉ་ | **nya** | fish |
| གཏི་མུག་ | **di-muk** | obscuration |
| ཐེག་པ་ཆེན་པོ་ | **thék-ba-chên-bo** | great vehicle  [Skt. *mahāyāna*] |
| ཐེག་པ་ | **thék-ba** | vehicle |
| རྟོག་བཅས་ | **dok-jë>** | conceptual |
| རྟོག་མེད་ | **dok-mé'** | nonconceptual |
| སྟག་ | **dak** | tiger |
| དུག་ | **tuk** | poison |

| | | |
|---|---|---|
| དུད་འགྲོ་ | tün-ḍo | animal |
| འདོད་ཁམས་ | dö'-kham | Desire Realm |
| འདོད་ཆགས་ | dö'-chak | desire, attachment |
| ཕག་པ་ | phak-b̄a | pig |
| ཕྲ་མོ་ | ṭha-mo | subtle |
| བ་གླང་ | pa-lang | ox |
| བྱ་ | c̱ha | bird |
| སྦྲུལ་ | ḍül | snake |
| མ་འོངས་པ་ | ma-ong-b̄a | future |
| དམིགས་པ་ | m̄ík-b̄a | observation, object of observation |
| དམྱལ་བ་ | ñyël-wa | hell |
| ཚིག་ | tshík | word |
| ཚིག་ཕྲད་ | tshík-ṭhë' | particle |
| འཛམ་བུའི་གླིང་ | ḏzam-bü-líng | Jambu Continent |
| ཟག་པ་ | s̱ak-b̄a | contamination |
| ཟག་བཅས་ | s̱ak-jë> | contaminated |
| ཟབ་མོ་ | s̱ap-mo | profound |
| གཟུགས་ཁམས་ | s̱uk-kham | Form realm |
| གཟུགས་མེད་ཁམས་ | s̱uk-mé'-kham | Formless Realm |
| ཞེ་སྡང་ | s̱hé-dang | hatred |
| ཡི་དགས་ | yí-dak | hungry ghost [Skt. *preta*] |

| ཡུལ་ | yül | object, place |
| ཡུལ་ཅན་ | yül-jën | subject |
| རིམ་པ་ | rîm-b̄a | stage |
| སེང་གེ་ | s̄éng-gé | lion |
| སྲུང་མ་ | s̄ung-ma | guardian |
| ལྷ་མ་ཡིན་ | hla-ma-yîn | demigod [Skt. *asura*] |

## Verbs

Verbs not identified as past, future, or imperative forms are present tense forms. NOM identifies nominative verbs, AG agentive verbs, and SV specialized verbs.

| སྐྱེ་ | ḡyé | is born, arises [NOM] |
| འཇིག་ | jík | disintegrates [NOM] |
| འདའ་ | da | pass [beyond], transcend [NOM] |
| འདས་ | dë> | [past form of འདའ་] |
| འདོད་ | dö' | wish, assert, claim [that] [AG] |
| མིན་ | mîn | is not [NOM—linking] |
| མེད་ | mé' | does not exist [NOM] |
| དམིགས་ | m̄ík | observe, take as object [AG] |
| འོང་ | ong | come [present & future] [NOM] |
| འོངས་ | ong | [past form of འོང་] |
| རིག་ | rîk | know, experience [AG] |

## Adjectives

| དགེ་བ་ | gé-wa | virtuous, wholesome |
|---|---|---|
| ཆེན་མོ་ | chên-mo | large, great [feminine] |
| འཇིག་པ་ | jík-b̄a | disintegrating |
| ཐ་དད་ | tha-dë' | different |
| ཐ་མི་དད་ | tha-mí-dë' | non-different, not different |
| མི་དགེ་བ་ | mí-gé-wa | non-virtuous, unwholesome |
| མི་འཇིག་པ་ | mí-jík—b̄a | non-disintegrating |

## Lexical Particles

The asterisk identifies where the remainder of the word stands in relation to the lexical particle.

| * ཙག་ | j̄ak | [pluralizing suffix syllable] |
|---|---|---|
| * དག་ | dak | [pluralizing suffix syllable] |
| * དང་བཅས་པ་ | dang-jë>-b̄a | [possessive suffix] |
| རྣམ་པར་ * | n̄am-b̄ar | [prefix particle] |
| * རྣམས་ | n̄am | [pluralizing suffix syllable] |
| * པ་ | b̄a | [generic suffix syllable] |
| * པོ་ | b̄o | [generic suffix syllable] |
| * བ་ | wa | [generic suffix syllable] |
| * བོ་ | wo | [generic suffix syllable] |
| * མ་ | ma | [generic suffix syllable] |

| | | |
|---|---|---|
| * མོ་ | **mo** | [generic suffix syllable] |
| * ཚོ་ | **tsho** | [pluralizing suffix syllable] |

## *Syntactic Particles*

| | | |
|---|---|---|
| གྱི་ | **g̱yí** | [connective case marking particle] |
| གོ་ | **go** | [terminator following ག་ suffix] |
| ངོ་ | **ngo** | [terminator following ང་ suffix] |
| དོ་ | **d̄o** | [terminator after ད་ secondary suffix] |
| དེས་ན་ | **té>-na** | therefore [syntactic particle] |
| དོ་ | **do** | [terminator following ད་ suffix] |
| ནོ་ | **no** | [terminator following ན་ suffix] |
| ཕྱིར་ | **chír** | because [of] [syntactic particle] |
| བོ་ | **bo** | [terminator following བ་ suffix] |
| མོ་ | **mo** | [terminator following མ་ suffix] |
| འོ་ | **o** | [terminator following འ་ suffix] |
| གཞན་ཡང་ | **s̱hën-yang** | moreover [syntactic particle] |
| ཡང་ན་ | **yang-na** | alternatively [syntactic particle] |
| རོ་ | **ro** | [terminator following ར་ suffix] |
| ལོ་ | **lo** | [terminator following ལ་ suffix] |
| སོ་ | **s̄o** | [terminator following ས་ suffix] |

# *Chapter 11*

*Phrases, Clauses, and Sentences*
*Noun Phrases*
*Cyclic Existence and Enlightenment*

## Introduction and Review

In the last chapter, a technique for analyzing sentence structure was introduced, that of identifying the functions played by the dots that end every Tibetan syllable, particle, word, clause, and sentence.

> The functions of dots are actually the ways in which particles, words, and phrases relate, as units, to the words around them.

The principle of Tibetan grammar underlying this method of analysis cannot be repeated too often: a noun or pronoun should be considered a unit that connects with or leads to what comes after it and not what comes before it.

> Only at the end of its last syllable does a noun or pronoun relate to the phrase, clause, or sentence in which it occurs. This relationship, with a few regular exceptions, is one that moves to the right—towards the end of the sentence.

This principle holds true for entire clauses as well; only at their end are they connected to the sentences in which they occur. A verb, however, is a part of a sentence that relates (as a verb) only to the nouns and adverbs that precede it—words that are to its left. These principles of Tibetan syntax are diagrammed as follows.

$$\boxed{\text{NOUN or PRONOUN}} \rightarrow \quad \boxed{\text{ADVERB}} \rightarrow \quad \leftarrow \boxed{\text{VERB}}$$

Tibetan clauses and sentences all have a subject, and most have an object or a complement—and these are all nouns, pronouns, or noun phrases.

The way in which adjectives work will be discussed later in this chapter.

## Patterns in Tibetan Language
### *Phrases, Clauses, and Sentences*

Words, syntactic particles, and case marking particles are the building blocks for the construction of phrases (level four), clauses (level five), and sentences (level six). **Sentences** are the most complex of these units, often incorporating within themselves phrases and clauses. Sentences have subjects and predicates, and they end in verbs. **Clauses** may be thought of as sentences modified so that they may be used as components of other, larger sentences. Clauses often end in verbals (instead of the terminal verbs that end sentences). **Phrases** are groups of words (or words and particles) that are more complex than simple words by themselves but not complex enough to be considered clauses. Phrases are often merely lists of nouns, or nouns modified by adjectives.

### *Sentences*

Sentences are constructed minimally of a subject and a predicate, although Tibetan is much more lenient than English in terms of what must be explicitly stated. For example, many Tibetan sentences have implicit subjects—that is, unstated subjects that are implied by the context in which the sentence is found. (See Chapter Twelve.)

---

The **subject** of a verb or verbal is, in most instances, its agent, the thing or person that performs the action indicated by the verb. In the case of the existential verbs, the subject is the thing or person that is something, that exists, and so on.

---

| | |
|---|---|
| agentive subject | 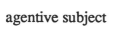 ཆོས་ བསླབ། |

***Buddha*** *taught the doctrine.*

| | |
|---|---|
| subject of existential verb | སྒྲ་ མི་རྟག་པ་ ཡིན་ནོ། |

***Sound*** *is impermanent.*

> The predicate of a sentence includes its closing verb, phrases qualifying that verb, and its object or complement.

Whereas action verbs have **objects**—the *doctrine* that Buddha taught—linking verbs have **complements**, for example, the word *impermanent* in *Sound is impermanent.*

| | |
|---|---|
| predicate of action verb | སངས་རྒྱས་ཀྱིས་ ཆོས་ བསླབ། |

*Buddha **taught the doctrine**.*

| | |
|---|---|
| predicate of linking verb | སྒྲ་ མི་རྟག་པ་ཡིན་ནོ། |

*Sound **is impermanent**.*

Most sentences are composed not merely of words, but also of case marking particles and syntactic particles. Sentences may also incorporate phrases and many incorporate clauses.

A Tibetan sentence is a meaningful group of words, particles, phrases, and clauses that ends in a verb, but is not a part of some larger clause or sentence. Sentences may end either in verbs in their basic forms, in verbs followed by a terminating syntactic particle, or in verb phrases formed of verbs followed by auxiliary verbs.

A sentence could end, for example, in a basic verb like ཤེས་ (*know, knows*) or a basic verb followed by a syntactic particle like ཤེས་སོ།, a compound verb like ཤེས་ནུས་ (*able to know*), or a verb phrase such as ཤེས་པར་བྱ་ (*will know*). Until the essentials of syntax have been completely understood, however, *Translating Buddhism from Tibetan* will concentrate on basic verbs.

Remember that a group of words ending in the mark | is not *necessarily* a sentence, although sentences are often so terminated.

The pattern of words and particles seen in a sentence is determined by the type of verb that ends the sentence. This is exemplified in the following two sentences, the first of which ends in a nominative verb, the second in an agentive verb.

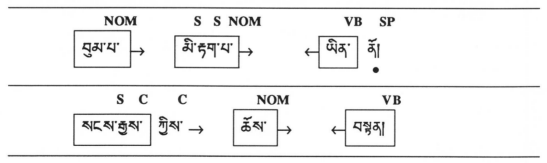

ཡིན་ is a linking verb, that is, a **nominative-nominative** verb—one whose subject and complement are both in the nominative case. Thus, the subject (བུམ་པ་) is a simple noun with no case marking particle following it, and the complement—a simple adjective (མི་རྟག་པ་)—also lacks a case marking particle.

In the second example, the verb མཐོང་—seen in its past tense form, མཐོང་—is an **agentive-nominative** verb. The subject (སངས་རྒྱས་) is marked by an agentive case particle. The object (ཆོས་) is a simple noun in the nominative case.

## Clauses

Like sentences, clauses are constructed of a subject and a predicate—although, with clauses, it is even more the case that the subject, object, or complement of the verb may be not be explicitly stated. Clauses often incorporate phrases and may incorporate other clauses.

> Clauses are sentences that have been modified for use *within* other sentences. Instead of ending in terminal verbs, they end either (1) in a verbal noun or adjective or (2) in a syntactic particle which leads to a continuation of the thought expressed in the clause.

The first type of clause is a meaningful group of words that ends in a verbal such as ཡོད་པ་, བྱས་པ་, or སྟོན་པ་. Where སངས་རྒྱས་ཀྱིས་ཆོས་བསྟན། is a sentence, སངས་རྒྱས་ཀྱིས་བསྟན་པ་ is a clause which is actually a complex adjective, *taught by the Buddha.*

| | |
|---|---|
| སངས་རྒྱས་ཀྱིས་ ཆོས་ བསྟན། | SENTENCE |
| སངས་རྒྱས་ཀྱིས་ བསྟན་པ་ | CLAUSE |

The clause itself—as a self-contained unit—thus becomes a noun or an adjective and, as such, may serve as the agent or object of a verb, or even as a noun in a list of nouns. In the following sentence, the clause སངས་རྒྱས་ཀྱིས་བསྟན་པ་, set off by the syntactic particle ནི་, serves as the nominative subject of the verb ཡིན་.

| | |
|---|---|
| སངས་རྒྱས་ཀྱིས་བསྟན་པ་ནི་ ཆོས་ ཡིན། | *That taught by Buddha is the doctrine.* |

When diagrammed, a clause is contained within its own box and has its own internal grammar.

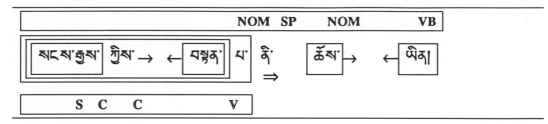

The box diagram clarifies the way in which the clause སངས་རྒྱས་ཀྱིས་བསྟན་པ་ acts as a single unit and is connected only at its end to the sentence in which it is found. The double arrow under the syntactic particle ནི་ indicates that it operates to the right; that is, the ནི་ marks སངས་རྒྱས་ཀྱིས་བསྟན་པ་ as a unit that will be explained further by material following, or to the right of the ནི་.

> In general, a mark underneath a particle indicates that it is a syntactic particle. *Double arrows* (⇐, ⇔, and ⇒) are used only to mark syntactic particles.

Note the way in which the dots within the clause are labelled—within a box and on their own line. *Within* the clause, the verbal noun བསྟན་པ་ acts as a verb, relating to the words that *precede* it. (Nouns, on the other hand, relate to the words that *follow* them.) The **V** (Verbal) dot that follows the verbal acknowledges that. The བསྟན་པ་ acts as a noun to its right, but as a verb to its left.

Clauses may have their own subjects, complements, and objects. The agentive case marking particle (marked with the Case-marker dots) marks the subject of the clause.

> One of the principles of Tibetan easily seen in box diagrams is that the grammar inside a phrase or a clause is isolated from the sentence in which that phrase or clause is found.

The second type of clause ends not in a verbal, but in a verb followed by one among certain sorts of syntactic particles. Clauses may end in verbs followed by continuative particles such as ནས་, and they may end in verbs followed by the rhetorical syntactic particle ན་. Whereas the sentence སངས་རྒྱས་ཀྱིས་ཆོས་བསྟན། expresses a complete thought and ends in a terminal verb, the addition of the syntactic particle

ནས་ opens the sentence up, making it merely the beginning of a larger unit, and often implies a sequence of activities.

| | |
|---|---|
| སངས་རྒྱས་ཀྱིས་ ཆོས་ བསྟན། | SENTENCE |
| སངས་རྒྱས་ཀྱིས་ ཆོས་ བསྟན་ ནས་ | CLAUSE |

སངས་རྒྱས་ཀྱིས་ཆོས་བསྟན་ནས་ is a clause meaning *Buddha, having taught the doctrine ...*, a clause which sets the stage for the next statement to be made. Thus, the syntactic particle ནས་ is marked with a forward-pointing arrow.

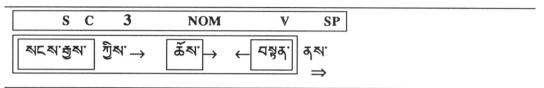

Note the **3** dot after the case marking particle ཀྱིས་. Case dots following case marking particles may be replaced by the number of the case they indicate. (Replacing the dot following but not the dot preceding the case marking particle highlights the way in which the case markers operate, connecting the substantive or adjective they mark to what *follows* them.)

Likewise, where བུམ་པ་ མི་རྟག་པ་ཡིན། is a sentence, the addition of the syntactic particle ན་ creates a conditional clause meaning *if pots are impermanent* or *given that pots are impermanent*.

| | |
|---|---|
| བུམ་པ་ མི་རྟག་པ་ ཡིན། | SENTENCE |
| བུམ་པ་ མི་རྟག་པ་ ཡིན་ ན་ | CLAUSE |

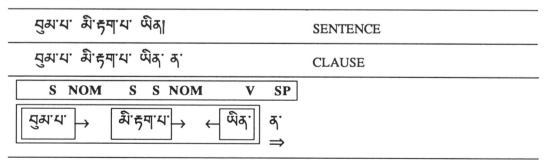

The clause བུམ་པ་མི་རྟག་པ་ཡིན་ན་ implies that something consequent to the fact that pots are impermanent will be stated.

> Since clauses are actually sentences modified for use as parts of other sentences, most of what has been and will be said about the syntax of sentences also applies to clauses.

## *Phrases*

Phrases are groups of words and syntactic particles that function as nouns, adjectives, verbs, or adverbs within clauses and sentences (and, occasionally, even within larger phrases).  However, phrases are the simplest groups of words and particles; they are much less complex than clauses and sentences.

> Phrases are meaningful groups of words that, unlike clauses and sentences, have neither subjects nor predicates.

There are phrases made of lists of nouns, noun and adjective phrases, and groups of words ending in syntactic particles that function as adverbs. There are also verb phrases consisting, for example, of compound verbs or verbs with auxiliaries.

Here are some of the phrases already seen in previous chapters.

|  |  |  |
|---|---|---|
| དགེ་བའི་སེམས་ | *virtuous mind(s)* | ADJECTIVE - NOUN |
| དམ་པའི་ཆོས་ | *holy doctrine* | ADJECTIVE - NOUN |
| སེམས་ཅན་ཀུན་ | *all sentient beings* | NOUN - ADJECTIVE |
| བུམ་པ་དམར་པོ་དེ་ | *that red pot* | NOUN - ADJECTIVE |
| དཀར་པོ་དང་དམར་པོ་ | *white and red* | ADJECTIVE + ADJECTIVE |
| ལས་དང་ཉོན་མོངས་ | *actions and afflictions* | NOUN + NOUN |
| ཤེས་པར་བྱ་ | *will know* | VERB + AUXILIARY VERB |
| ཤེས་ནུས་ | *able to know* | COMPOUND VERB |

Unlike clauses and sentences, phrases do not *have* subjects and predicates. Rather, they act *as* subjects of clauses and sentences, or as parts of their predicates.

## Noun Phrases

Nouns may occur as simple nouns or as noun phrases. An example of a simple noun is the word བུམ་པ་.

Phrases are the simplest sort of pattern using words and particles. There are five types of noun phrases:

1   noun-adjective phrases,

2   lists of nouns,

3   nouns modified by nouns or pronouns preceding them,

4   appositive phrases,

5   nouns modified by adjectives preceding them.

| | |
|---|---|
| noun-adjective phrase | བུམ་པ་དམར་པོ་ *red pot*<br><br>NOUN followed by an ADJECTIVE |

As seen in the section on adjectives in Chapter Nine, this is the way in which most adjectives modify nouns and noun phrases.

| | |
|---|---|
| list phrase | ས་དང་ཆུ་ *earth and water*<br><br>NOUN + CONJUNCTION + NOUN<br><br>ས་ཆུ་མེ་རླུང་ *earth, water, fire, and wind*<br><br>NOUN + NOUN + NOUN + NOUN ... |

Conjunctions such as དང་ are a type of syntactic particle. Note in the second example that Tibetan does not *require* a conjunction in a list of nouns (as English does).

| | |
|---|---|
| noun-noun phrase | སངས་རྒྱས་ཀྱི་ཐུགས་ *Buddha's mind*<br><br>NOUN (or PRONOUN) + CONNECTIVE + NOUN |

There are similar PRONOUN + NOUN phrases (for example, དེ་ཡི་སེམས་—*that one's mind*).

| | |
|---|---|
| adjective-noun phrase | དམ་པའི་ཆོས་          *holy doctrine*<br><br>ADJECTIVE + CONNECTIVE + NOUN |

This translates the Sanskrit *saddharma*. Adjectives usually follow the nouns they modify (as in the first example in this section, ཐུགས་པ་དམར་པོ་). In those instances when they do precede their nouns, however, they must be connected to those nouns with a connective case particle.

---

The connective case particles are གི་ (ḵí), གྱི་ (ḡyí), ཀྱི་ (kyí), འི་ (í), and ཡི་ (yí).

---

| | |
|---|---|
| appositive phrase | སངས་རྒྱས་ཚེ་དཔག་མེད་ *the Buddha Amitāyus*<br><br>NOUN followed by a NOUN in apposition to it |

In an appositive phrase, the second noun qualifies the first—that is, among the many Buddhas, here Amitāyus is being discussed.

Nouns are used within these phrases, but the phrases themselves—as single units—are also nouns. It is for the second reason that they are called noun phrases—they function as nouns in the larger patterns of which *they* form a part.

---

A noun phrase is a group of words, or of words and particles, that, as a unit, functions as a noun. This unit connects only at its end to the remainder of the larger phrase, clause, or sentence in which it is found.

---

You should be aware that where བུམ་པ་རྣམས་ means *pots*, neither བུམ་པ་རྣམས་དམར་པོ་ nor བུམ་པ་རྣམས་དམར་པོ་རྣམས་ are seen. The correct construction is བུམ་པ་དམར་པོ་རྣམས་.

There are exceptions to this. One such exception is the appositive phrase དེ་དག་ཐམས་ཅད་, *all of those* (those + all—literally, '[among] those, all'). As in English, since ཐམས་ཅད་ is a collective noun, it does not become plural.

> In many instances, a pluralizing particle is a sign that a noun or noun phrase has terminated. This is a useful piece of information in the syntactic dimension—that is, it helps in the interpretation of the structure of clauses and sentences.

## Pattern Analysis
### *The Syntactic Particle* དང་

Sometimes a list of nouns is separated not only by dots but also by a conjunction. The following example translates *Shape and color are impermanent.*

| | SP | SP | S NOM | S S NOM | VB |
|---|---|---|---|---|---|
| | དབྱིབས་ | དང་ | ཁ་དོག་ | མི་རྟག་པ་ | ཡིན། |

དང་ is a conjunction; it usually means *and*, but can sometimes mean *or*. In certain, well-defined constructions, it translates into English as *with* or *from*.[76] As a conjunction, དང་ is a syntactic particle. Notice that the dot after the first of the two nouns in this list (དབྱིབས་ —*shape*) is an SP dot. The entire list is in the nominative case, but *not* the separate members of that list.[77] Whereas the phrase དབྱིབས་དང་ཁ་དོག་ as a whole is in the nominative case, དབྱིབས་ and ཁ་དོག་ are not separately in the nominative.

Notice also that the SP dot is a dot that is *either* before or after a syntactic particle. All the other dots—the SP dot and the C dot (the dot before or after a case marking particle) being the exceptions—are determined only by what they *follow*, never by what follows them.

The example looks like the following when diagrammed.

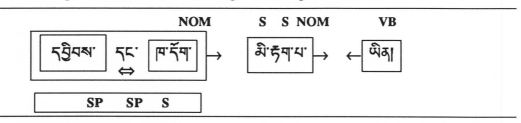

Note the double arrow (pointing both left and right) under the དང་. It indicates that དང་ is a syntactic particle connecting what comes before it with what follows it.

Another example of a sentence with a compound subject, a simple complement, and the verb ཡིན་ is the sentence *Permanent and impermanent are mutually exclusive.*

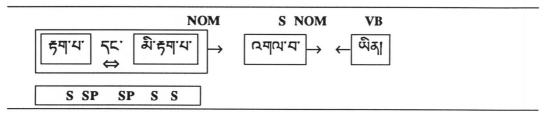

Continuing with the subject of སངས་རྒྱས་ཀྱི་ཆོས་ yields another phrase incorporating the syntactic particle དང་. In this sentence the subject is a clause and the complement is a compound.

སངས་རྒྱས་ཀྱི་ ཆོས་ ནི་    ལུང་ དང་ རྟོགས་པའི་ ཆོས་ ཡིན།

*Buddha's doctrines are the scriptural and realized doctrines.*

The phrase ལུང་དང་རྟོགས་པའི་ཆོས་ illustrates the usage of the connective case to show type. What type of ཆོས་? The ཆོས་ which is scripture and the ཆོས་ which is the individual Buddhist's realization of what Buddha taught in scripture.

ཨུང་ (Sanskrit: *āgama*) is an important word in Tibetan. In general it means scripture, but not in the Western sense of revelation. ཨུང་ has the sense of *transmission*, of a *tradition* of understanding passed down verbally from one generation to another—from teacher to student. And in Tibetan Buddhism, as in Buddhism in general, scripture is not so much something read (and therefore visual) as it is something spoken and heard.

> The *locus classicus* (that is, the original textual source) for this distinction is Vasubandhu's *Abhidharmakośa* (*Treasury of Advanced Knowledge*), 8:39 (that is, Chapter Eight, verse 39). The context in which this is appropriated in Tibetan Buddhism is the explanation of taking refuge. The actual refuge from the suffering of cyclic existence is the doctrine, specifically the realized doctrine. See, for example, H. H. Tenzin Gyatso, *The Dalai Lama at Harvard*, p. 16, and Geshe Rabten, *Treasury of Dharma*, pp. 78-79.

## Pattern Analysis
### *Nouns and Adjectives*

Adjectives are exceptions to the rule that all words except for verbs relate to what follows them and not to what precedes them. Adjectives most often *follow* the nouns they modify; thus, they relate directly to what immediately precedes them.

The བུམ་པ་དམར་པོ་ paradigm presented in the section on noun phrases is diagrammed with the adjective in a smaller box and the noun in a relatively larger box that completely contains the smaller adjective box. The fact that the adjective modifies a noun to its left is symbolized by the left-pointing arrow.

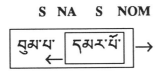

```
     S  NA  S  NOM
```

Note that the entire phrase, noun and adjective, is surrounded by one box which, since *the phrase is itself a noun*, points to the right. This is the simplest type of noun phrase in Tibetan.

The NA dot is a dot between a Noun and an Adjective. Since there is no case ending, let us provisionally say that the phrase is in the nominative case.[78]

> It is the phrase as a whole, and not just the last part of it, that functions in a nominative way in the sentence.

It is possible for an adjective to precede a noun in Tibetan. When the ADJECTIVE + NOUN construction is viable, the adjective must be joined to the noun with the sixth (or connective) case particle. Thus, the syntax is *not* merely ADJECTIVE + NOUN, but rather ADJECTIVE + CONNECTIVE PARTICLE + NOUN. This is less common than the NOUN + ADJECTIVE construction.

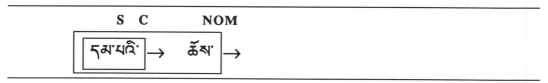

Joining an adjective to a noun with a connective particle is not always viable. དམར་པོའི་བུམ་པ་, for example, means not *red pot* but *pot of* [that is, *belonging to*] *the red one.*

Tibetan adjectives are modifiers and, as such, they must modify a noun. However, as in English, they can act as substantives. The adjectives དེ་ and འདི་ often act as pronouns meaning *that* and *this.* Adjectives like དམར་པོ་ can do this as well: where བུམ་པ་དམར་པོ་ means *red pot*, ཁ་དོག་དམར་པོ་ means *the color red.* As in English, this depends on context.

> The phrase ཁ་དོག་དམར་པོ་ is an appositive phrase.

Here is one more example, this time of an adjective occurring by itself.

| | |
|---|---|
| དེ་ དམར་པོ་ ཡིན། | *That is red.* |

Here དམར་པོ་ is not a case of an adjective used as a noun; it is merely a predicate adjective, that is an adjective that occurs (in the present instance) as the complement of a linking verb. The ད་, on the other hand, *is* a case of an adjective being used as a pronoun.

However, the context in which this sentence appears can dictate a different grammatical evaluation. If the subject being discussed is color and the sentence means *That one is [the color] red*, then, in fact, དམར་པོ་ is a case of an adjective being used as a noun.

Nonetheless, in either case the construction is the standard linking verb construction: SUBJECT + COMPLEMENT + VERB, and the sentence is diagrammed in the same way.

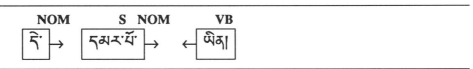

Adjectives can be used to qualify not only simple nouns, but also noun-adjective phrases, as in the phrase བུམ་པ་དམར་པོ་དེ་. The basic NOUN + ADJECTIVE phrase is བུམ་ པ་དམར་པོ་, which then, as a unit, is modified by the adjective དེ་.

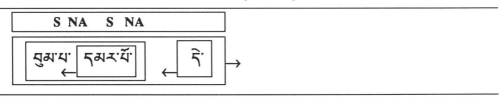

Thus, the དེ་ is an adjective modifying not the word immediately preceding it (that is, དམར་པོ་), but the phrase immediately preceding it (བུམ་པ་དམར་པོ་). The word order is not arbitrary; making དེ་ the first adjective and saying བུམ་པ་དེ་དམར་པོ་ means not *that red pot* (or even *red that pot*), but rather *That pot [is] red*.

Note that བུམ་པ་དེ་དམར་པོ་ is, in the proper context, a full sentence in Tibetan—one in which the verb (ཡིན་, *is*) is "understood." Thus, བུམ་པ་དེ་ དམར་པོ་ is a shorter, but still acceptable form of the sentence བུམ་པ་དེ་དམར་པོ་ ཡིན།.

## Drill 11.1

Translate the following into Tibetan.

1. This is a white conch shell.
2. this white horse
3. many phenomena
4. All fish are sentient beings.

## Drill 11.2

Identifying the dots, translate the following sentences. Diagram the first three with boxes and arrows.

1. སེམས་མི་རྟག་པའི་ཆོས་ཡིན།

2. སངས་རྒྱས་མང་པོ་ཡོད།

3. སེམས་ཅན་ཐམས་ཅད་མི་རྟག་པ་ཡིན།

4. ཁྱིའུ་ལྔ་ཡོད།

5. འདི་རྟ་དཀར་པོ་ཡིན།

## Pattern Analysis
### *Appositives*

There is one other dot that is especially relevant when discussing nouns in a list, and that is the appositive dot (**APP**). English examples of appositives are *my friend George*, *King Henry*, and *the Buddha Amitāyus*. In the first example, *George* qualifies *my friend* (Which of my friends?—George), but is a noun, not an adjective. Most words that qualify or modify nouns are adjectives.

As with nouns in a list, here we have two nouns, one after the other (appositive means placed alongside of). However, the relationship is very different from that of nouns in a list. In the case of appositives, one noun identifies the other, narrowing down the field so to speak. I have many friends, but here I am speaking of one in particular—George. There are many buddhas, but here we are speaking of Amitāyus. Thus, the relationship between appositives is not necessarily that of synonyms, although it can be.[79]

Like a list of nouns, a set of appositives acts as a unit that attaches to the rest of a sentence at its end, and only at its end. Here are two examples of such appositive blocks.

| སངས་རྒྱས་ཚེ་དཔག་མེད་ | the Buddha Amitāyus |
|---|---|
| ཁ་དོག་དམར་པོ་ | the color red |

The latter diagrams as follows.

Note that in this example the main word is *color*. *Color* is the general term that is clarified by the word *red*. (Which color?—Red.) Thus, the box around ཁ་དོག་ also encloses the appositive དམར་པོ་.

> Unlike the NOUN-ADJECTIVE phrase, here there is no arrow; *red* does not modify the noun *color* as it modifies *apple* in *red apple*, but is almost at the same level as *color*.

> It would be **incorrect** to diagram this appositive phrase (as is done immediately below) with two separate boxes; for they do not act separately in a sentence, but as one unit.

Such a diagram is incorrect because if the two words are truly appositives, the first will never relate to any other word or particle in the sentence without the second being related in precisely the same way. The two appositives are, in fact, one *compound* construction.

In the above example, the more general of the words in apposition was the first (*color*), however this is not always the case. An example of a common construction in which the opposite is true is that in which a number is appended to a list of nouns as an indication of how many things are in that list. We can construct such an example based on the list of three synonyms—mind, mentality, and consciousness—we examined earlier. Adding the number *three* in apposition to that list makes the sentence in which they are described as synonyms clearer: ***The three—mind, mentality, and consciousness—are equivalent.***

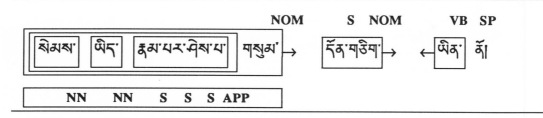

When diagrammed, it is easy to see that the word གསུམ་ (*the three things*) is in apposition not merely to the word immediately before it (རྣམ་པར་ཤེས་པ་), but to the *box* immediately preceding it—that is, to the entire list.

## Drill 11.3

Identify the dots and translate the following phrases.

1. དཀར་པོ་སྟོན་པོ་དམར་པོ་སེར་པོ་

2. སངས་རྒྱས་དང་ཡི་དམ་

3. མི་ཏ་གཉིས་

4. ཡུལ་དབང་པོ་རྣམ་ཤེས་གསུམ་

## Lexical Particles
### *Subjective Suffix Syllables*

The generic suffixes པ་, པོ་, བ་, and བོ་ are also used as subjective suffix syllables: particles added to the ends of words that create new words specifying agency, ownership, composition, or membership—sometimes literally, sometimes metaphorically. In some cases these subject nouns are indistinguishable from ordinary nouns ending in པ་, པོ་, བ་, or བོ་.

> For example, where མཁས་ is a verb meaning *be skilled*, the verbal noun མཁས་པ་ means *scholar*—that is, *one who is skilled, one who possesses skill.* Likewise, where རྒྱལ་ is a verb meaning *conquer*, the noun རྒྱལ་པོ་ (*king*) clearly originally meant *one who conquers.* The noun རྒྱལ་བ་, on the other hand, does mean *conqueror* and is a term used of Buddhas.

However, some subject nouns are easier to identify. Words with an *extra* པ་ or པོ་ (and sometimes བ་ or བོ་) are examples of the use of subjective suffix syllables.

> For example, based on the core verb ཤེས་ (*know*), one can form a verbal, ཤེས་པ་ meaning *knowledge.* The addition of the suffix syllable པོ་ creates the agent noun ཤེས་པ་པོ་, *knower.* Similarly, the verbal noun འཆད་པ་ (*explanation*) is based on the verb འཆད་, meaning *explain.* Adding the subjective suffix syllable པོ་ creates the agent noun འཆད་པ་པོ་ (*explainer* or *commentator*). And whereas the noun-adjective phrase ཐེག་པ་ཆེན་པོ་ means *Great Vehicle* (*Mahāyāna*), a ཐེག་པ་ཆེན་པོ་པ་ is a *Mahāyānist*, that is, *one associated with the Great Vehicle.*

The rule of thumb for translating words like this is to attempt a generic translation first: *something or someone having to do with X.* Thus, if དབུས་ means *middle*, དབུ་མ་པ་ means, in the broadest sense, *something or someone having to do with the middle.* In fact, དབུ་མ་པ་ refers to the Middle Way tenet system and its adherents.

The two other subjective suffix particles are ཅན་ and མཁན་, with the former being quite common and the latter being used mainly, but not exclusively, in the spoken language. They are attached to the end of words, like the other subjective particles. And, as in the case of the others, the entire word is then declined (by adding a particle after the suffix particle) if needed.

> For example, adding the particle ཅན་ to the word སྐྱོན་ (*fault*) makes སྐྱོན་ཅན་, meaning *possessing fault(s)* or *flawed.* Syntactic particles may then be added to this—སྐྱོན་ཅན་ལ་, སྐྱོན་ཅན་གྱི་, and so on—to indicate its function in a clause or sentence.

ཅན་ shows only "ownership," it never shows agency. མཁན་, on the other hand, is used to help designate a wide range of subjects.

བྱེད་མཁན་ means *one who does* and is agentive. ཡིན་མཁན་, however, means *that which is [something]* and (in the colloquial language) ཡིག་མཁན་ (built not on a verb but a noun, ཡིག་, which means *letter*) means *scribe* or *secretary*.

## Lexical Particles
### *Restrictive Suffix Syllable*

There is one true restrictive suffix syllable—ཉིད་. As a final syllable, ཉིད་ sometimes means *just* and sometimes creates abstract nouns.

For example, where དེ་ means *that*, དེ་ཉིད་ means *just that* or *that itself*. Sometimes a ཉིད་ merely intensifies what is already stated, and is untranslatable—རང་ means *itself* and so does རང་ཉིད་.

ཉིད་ also often creates abstract nouns—words that express an ideal or characteristic by itself, without speaking of something having that characteristic. The rule of thumb here is to translate the Tibetan word as an English word ending in *-ness*.

Thus, སྟོང་པ་ (Sanskrit *śūnya*) is an adjective meaning *empty* and སྟོང་པ་ཉིད་ (Sanskrit *śūnyatā*) means *emptiness*. Besides meaning *just that*, དེ་ཉིད་ may also mean *reality* (Sanskrit *tattva*), literally *thatness*. བདག་ means *self*, but བདག་ཉིད་ (*self-ness*) means *nature* or *essence*.

Many Tibetan words ending in ཉིད་ translate Sanskrit abstract nouns ending in *-tva* or *-tā* (སྟོང་པ་ཉིད་ translating *śūnyatā*, and དེ་ཉིད་, *tattva*). The very common word མཚན་ཉིད་ (*characteristic, definition*) is an example of one that does not. It normally translates *lakṣaṇa*. མཚན་ཉིད་ also demonstrates that not all words ending in ཉིད་ are either abstract nouns or *just* something.

There are two other particles—ཙམ་ and ཁོན་ (both mean *just* or *only* or *merely*)—that appear to function restrictively.

An example that has already been introduced is སེམས་ཙམ་, the name for the *Cittamātra* or *Mind Only* tenet system—སེམས་ meaning *mind* and ཙམ་, *only*.

Similarly, yet another name for ultimate reality (in addition to སྟོང་པ་ཉིད་ and དེ་ ཉིད་) is དེ་ཁོ་ན་ཉིད་, literally *just-that-ness*.

Most occurrences of ཙམ་ and ཁོ་ན་, however, are not as lexical particles ending nouns, but in noun-adjective combinations, where ཙམ་ and ཁོ་ན་ are adjectives meaning *just* or *only*. It also common to see ཉིད་ used not as a lexical particle, but as an adjective modifying a noun.

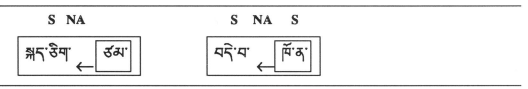

Where སྐད་ཅིག་ means *instant* or *moment*, སྐད་ཅིག་ཙམ་ is a NOUN-ADJECTIVE phrase meaning *only a moment*. བདེ་བ་ཁོ་ན་, likewise, is a noun qualified by the adjective ཁོ་ན་, meaning *happiness* (or *bliss*) *alone*. And, whereas ཆོས་ཉིད་ (Sanskrit: *dharmatā*) means *reality* (literally, *phenomena-ness*—that is, the nature of phenomena, or what it means to be a phenomenon), ཆོས་གསུམ་ཉིད་ does not mean *being-three-phenomena-ness* (nor does it mean *the nature of three phenomena*), but rather *just the three phenomena*.[80]

## Doctrinal Vocabulary and Grammar
### *The Buddhist Universe: Cyclic Existence and Enlightenment*

As explained in Chapter Ten, the Buddhist universe consists of cyclic existence and nirvana. The primary reference of these terms is psychological, but they also refer to places and people. This may be seen, for instance, in the use of the term འཇིག་རྟེན་ (*world*): སྣོད་ཀྱི་འཇིག་རྟེན་ (where སྣོད་ means *receptacle* or *vessel*) is the physical universe, whereas བཅུད་ཀྱི་འཇིག་རྟེན་ (where བཅུད་ means *sap* or *essence*) is the world of sentient beings. (In fact, the two are often listed as སྣོད་ཀྱི་འཇིག་རྟེན་ and བཅུད་ཀྱི་སེམས་ཅན་.)

སྣོད་ཀྱི་འཇིག་རྟེན་ does not mean *environment*, since that would include non-human animals, and, for Buddhists, animals are sentient beings included in the བཅུད་ཀྱི་འཇིག་རྟེན་. Nor is the བཅུད་ཀྱི་འཇིག་རྟེན་ the biosphere, since plants are not

deemed to be sentient.  The words *inanimate* and the *animate*, on the other
hand, do seem to approximate the sense of these Tibetan terms.

| | | |
|---|---|---|
| འཇིག་རྟེན་ | **jík-dēn** | *world* |
| སྣོད་ | **n̄ö'** | *vessel, receptacle* |
| སྣོད་ཀྱི་འཇིག་རྟེན་ | **n̄ö'-ḡyí jík-dēn** | *physical world, inanimate world* [Skt. *bhājanaloka*] |
| བཅུད་ | **jü'** | *sap, essence* |
| བཅུད་ཀྱི་འཇིག་རྟེན་ | **jü'-ḡyí jík-dēn** | *animate world* |

Note that the word འཇིག་རྟེན་ is constructed, without lexical particles, from
syllables that—when used separately—are words in their own right.  འཇིག་
means *disintegrate* and རྟེན་ means *basis* (or *support*).

སྣོད་ཀྱི་འཇིག་རྟེན་ and བཅུད་ཀྱི་འཇིག་རྟེན་ are **noun phrases**.

Earlier in this chapter,  you saw that among the noun phrases there were two
types that contained connective particles.  However, སྣོད་ཀྱི་འཇིག་རྟེན་ differs
from སངས་རྒྱས་ཀྱི་ཕྱགས་ (the example given earlier) in that the connective does
not show possession—སྣོད་ཀྱི་འཇིག་རྟེན་ does not mean *receptacle's world*.  Nor
is it similar to དམ་པའི་ཆོས་, since སྣོད་—unlike དམ་པ་—is not an adjective.  སྣོད་ཀྱི་
འཇིག་རྟེན་ is an example of one of the more common usages of a connective
particle in NOUN-NOUN phrases to show apposition.  Thus, a སྣོད་ཀྱི་འཇིག་རྟེན་ is
a world *which is* a receptacle.

Here is a chart of noun phrases utilizing connective case particles.  The connective
particles perform different functions in each.

| | |
|---|---|
| སངས་རྒྱས་ཀྱི་ཕྱགས་ | POSSESSIVE NOUN-NOUN |
| དམ་པའི་ཆོས་ | ADJECTIVE-NOUN |
| སྣོད་ཀྱི་འཇིག་རྟེན་ | APPOSITIVE NOUN-NOUN |

Tibetan often adds redundant nouns or adjectives in order to emphasize the meaning of terms. Here, the སྣོད་ཀྱི་འཇིག་རྟེན་ is the *external* (ཕྱི་) world and the བཅུད་ཀྱི་སེམས་ཅན་ are the *inner* (ནང་) world.

The physical world, as ordinary people experience it, is part of cyclic existence, since this is where sentient beings are reborn by the power of actions motivated by afflictions. A pure land (དག་ཞིང་ **tak-shíng**—*pure + field*), on the other hand, is created by a Buddha and is not part of cyclic existence. Rebirth there is through a Buddha's power, not by way of desire, hatred, and ignorance.

> Concerning pure lands, see Rhie and Thurman, *Wisdom and Compassion*, pp. 311-313, 361ff.

People who are not in cyclic existence are called སངས་རྒྱས་ (*buddha*) and དགྲ་བཅོམ་པ་ (Sanskrit *arhat*—literally, *foe destroyers*).

| | | |
|---|---|---|
| སངས་རྒྱས་ | **sang-gyë>** | *buddha* |
| དགྲ་བཅོམ་པ་ | **da̱-jom-b̄a** | *arhat* [literally, *one who has destroyed the enemy*] |

> Recall that, in Buddhism, even animals and gods are 'people'—that is, they are གང་ཟག་, *persons*. Thus the terms *person* and *people*, while they do refer to human beings, do not refer exclusively to human beings.

People who are in cyclic existence are called སོ་སོའི་སྐྱེ་བོ་ (*ordinary beings*—Sanskrit *pṛthagjana*) until they have seen selflessness in direct meditative vision; they are then called འཕགས་པ་ (Sanskrit *ārya*), literally *superior [beings]*. (Buddhas and arhats are also འཕགས་པ་.)

| གང་ཟག་ | **kang-ṣak** | *person* |
|---|---|---|
| སོ་སོའི་སྐྱེ་བོ་ | **ṣo-ṣö-ḡyé-wo** | *ordinary beings* [literally, *individual beings*] |
| འཕགས་པ་ | **phak-b̄a** | *superior* |

Concerning persons and their types, see Daniel Perdue, *Debate in Tibetan Buddhism*, pp. 363-365.

Here are abbreviations for some terms relevant to this discussion.

| འཁོར་བ་དང་མྱ་ངན་ལས་འདས་པ་ | འཁོར་འདས་ | **khor-dë>** |
|---|---|---|
| སོ་སོའི་སྐྱེ་བོ་ | སོ་སྐྱེ་ | **ṣo-ḡyé** |
| མྱ་ངན་ལས་འདས་པ་ | མྱང་འདས་ | **nyëng-dë>** |

In most cases, it is possible intuitively to understand just what a given abbreviation is abbreviating.  For example, གསེར་བུམ་ (**ṣér-bum**) abbreviates གསེར་གྱི་བུམ་པ་ (**ṣér-gyí pum-b̄a**, *golden pot*—where གསེར་ means *gold*).

In the chart below, མྱ་ངན་ལས་འདས་པ་ is given in its abbreviated form as མྱང་འདས་ (**nyëng-dë>**).

$$
\text{འཁོར་འདས་}
\begin{cases}
\text{མྱང་འདས་}
\begin{cases}
\text{སངས་རྒྱས་} \\
\text{དགྲ་བཅོམ་པ་}
\end{cases} \\
\text{འཁོར་བ་}
\begin{cases}
\text{འཕགས་པའི་སློབ་པ་} \\
\text{སོ་སོའི་སྐྱེ་བོ་}
\end{cases}
\end{cases}
\text{འཕགས་པ་}
$$

འཕགས་པའི་སློབ་པ་ are འཕགས་པ་ who are still *training* (སློབ་པ་), that is, not yet Buddhas.

In the Tibetan tradition, nirvana is spoken of mainly in contrast to cyclic existence—since it is, most basically, the cessation of cyclic existence for the individual. However, it is not the most common Tibetan designation for the goal of the Buddhist path. The most common term is བྱང་ཆུབ་ (chang-chup—Sanskrit *bodhi*), usually translated *enlightenment*.

> The Sanskrit verb *budh* means *understand, know, notice, think, wake up,* and *regain consciousness*.[81] The words *buddha* and *bodhi* are derived from it and are thus closely related in meaning, *buddha* meaning *something understood, someone awake,* and, by extension, *a wise person* and *bodhi* meaning *understanding, judgement, return to consciousness*, and so on. However, when they were translated into Tibetan, *budh* was translated by cognitive terms such as རྟོགས་ (dok, a verb meaning *understand*),[82] *bodhi* became བྱང་ཆུབ་, and *buddha* became སངས་རྒྱས་. Both བྱང་ཆུབ་ and སངས་རྒྱས་ are used in very specific ways, the former referring to enlightenment in general and the latter to a particular type of enlightened person.

One of the rhetorical tools in Buddhist literature is the སྒྲ་བཤད་ (da-shë', *etymology*—literally, *word + explanation*). Tibetan སྒྲ་བཤད་, however, typically do not spring from the historical and linguistic concerns that motivate modern, scientific etymologies. For this reason, some modern writers have translated this term as *folk etymology* or *heuristic etymology*. While the composition of the Tibetan term བྱང་ཆུབ་ does not tell us much about the roots of the Sanskrit term *bodhi*, it does tell us something about the understanding of the term in Indian Mahāyāna Buddhism at the time that Sanskrit texts were being translated into Tibetan, and it tells us, more importantly, what image appears to the minds of Tibetan writers and their readers when they see, hear, or think བྱང་ཆུབ་.

The traditional etymology of བྱང་ཆུབ་ (*enlightenment*) presents the reader with something that is བྱང་ and something else that is ཆུབ་. Enlightenment thus refers to the purification (བྱང་བ་) of all obstructions (such as the three poisons) and the internalization or realization (ཁོང་དུ་ཆུབ་པ་) of all virtues.[83]

The term སངས་རྒྱས་, on the other hand, presents to the Tibetan Buddhist two possible images. The first syllable, སངས་, means *dispell*, in the sense of *waking up* (dispelling sleep), of *purifying* (cleaning impurities out of water, for example), and of *dispelling* darkness and obstructions.[84] One can, therefore, take a སངས་རྒྱས་ to be someone who has woken up from the sleep of ignorance. In another way, one can think of a Buddha as someone who has dispelled the darkness of cognitive and afflictive obstructions. In either case, the རྒྱས་ (most basically meaning *extended*) suggests that a Buddha's mind has opened up (like a flower opening) in the sense of being omniscient and compassionate.[85]

## Buddhas

The following is a partial list of Buddhas important to all the orders of Tibetan Buddhism.

| | | | |
|---|---|---|---|
| ཤཱཀྱ་ཐུབ་པ་ | **śha-ḡya thu-b̄a** | *Shakyamuni* [Skt. *Śākyamuni*] |
| སྒྲོལ་མ་ | **ḍöl-ma** | *Tara* [*Tārā*] |
| རྡོ་རྗེ་འཆང་ | **dor-jé-chang** | *Vajradhara* [*Vajradhāra*] |
| རྡོ་རྗེ་སེམས་དཔའ་ | **dor-jé-ṣêm-b̄a** | *Vajrasattva* [*Vajrasattva*] |
| ཀུན་ཏུ་བཟང་པོ་ | **ḡun-d̄u-ṣang-b̄o** | *Samantabhadra* [*Samantabhadra*] |

The mark under the ཀ in ཤཱཀྱ་ཐུབ་པ་ is the letter འ. ཤཱཀྱ is not a translation of the Sanskrit *śākya*, but, rather, a **transliteration** in which the subscribed འ indicates the long vowel in Sanskrit.

This list of buddhas is continued in the doctrinal vocabulary of Chapter Twelve.

Translations aimed at the academic world should employ correct Sanskrit spelling and diacritics (e.g., *Śākyamuni* and *Cittamātra*). Translations that are intended to be accessible to those who do not know Sanskrit, however, are more effective if they employ phonemic spellings (such as *Shakyamuni* and *Chittamatra*).

On the various buddhas important in Tibetan Buddhism, see David Snellgrove, *Indo-Tibetan Buddhism*. The visual representations of these buddhas is as integral a part of the doctrinal dimensions of their names as are their descriptions and histories. Dudjom Rinpoche's *The Nyingma School of Tibetan Buddhism* contains many line drawings of buddhas and other awakened beings. In Rhie and Thurman, *Wisdom and Compassion: The Sacred Art of Tibet*, see especially the material beginning on pp. 72-73 (on Śākyamuni) and on pp. 124-134 (Tārā); Vajradhāra is discussed on pp. 358-360.

# VOCABULARY

## Nouns

Learn the names of the Buddhas listed in the Doctrinal Vocabulary section.

| ཀྱོན་ | **ḡyön** | fault |
| མཁས་པ་ | **khë>-b̄a** | skill, scholar |
| སྒྲ་བཤད་ | **ḍa-s̄hë'** | etymology [literally 'explanation of word'] |
| བཅུད་ | **j̄ü'** | essence |
| འཆད་པ་པོ་ | **chë'-b̄a-b̄o** | explainer |
| འཇིག་རྟེན་ | **jík-d̄ên** | world |
| སྟོང་པ་ཉིད་ | **d̄ong-b̄a-nyí'** | emptiness |
| དེ་ཁོ་ན་ཉིད་ | **te-kho-na-nyí'** | suchness |
| དེ་ཉིད་ | **te-nyí'** | thatness, reality |

| བདག་ཉིད་ | **dak-nyí'** | nature |
| སྣོད་ | **n̄ö'** | vessel, receptacle |
| འཕགས་པ་ | **phak-b̄a** | superior  [Skt. *ārya*] |
| བདེ་བ་ | **dé-wa** | bliss |
| དབུ་མ་པ་ | **ū-ma-b̄a** | Mādhyamika |
| བྱང་ཆུབ་ | **c̲hang-chup** | enlightenment |
| ཚེ་དཔག་མེད་ | **tshé-b̄ak-mé'** | Amitāyus |
| ཤེས་པ་པོ་ | **s̄hé>-b̄a-b̄o** | knower |
| སོ་སོའི་སྐྱེ་བོ་ | **s̄o-s̄ö-ḡyé-wo** | ordinary person |
| གསེར་ | **s̄ér** | gold |

## Verbs

**NV** are verbs requiring nominative subjects, **AV** are agentive subject verbs, and **SV**, specialized verbs.

| མཁས་ | **khë>** | be skilled [in] [NV] |
| རྒྱས་ | **gyë>** | extend, develop  [NV] |
| འཆད་ | **chë'** | explain, present  [AV] |
| བཤད་ | **s̄hë'** | [past & future of འཆད་] |
| སངས་ | **s̄ang** | be dispelled, be purified  [NV] |

## Adjectives

| ཁོ་ན་ | **kho-na** | only, merely |
| སྟོང་པ་ | **d̄ong-b̄a** | empty |

| ནང་ | **nang** | internal |
| ཕྱི་ | **chí** | external |
| ཙམ་ | **d̄zam** | only, merely, just |

## *Lexical Particles*

| * ཁོ་ན་ | **kho-na** | [restrictive suffix syllable] |
| * མཁན་ | **khën** | [subjective suffix syllable] |
| * ཅན་ | **jën** | [subjective suffix syllable] |
| * ཉིད་ | **nyí'** | [restrictive suffix syllable] |
| * པ་ | **b̄a** | [subjective suffix syllable] |
| * པོ་ | **b̄o** | [subjective suffix syllable] |
| * བ་ | **wa** | [subjective suffix syllable] |
| * བོ་ | **wo** | [subjective suffix syllable] |
| * ཙམ་ | **d̄zam** | [restrictive suffix syllable] |

# Chapter 12

*Declension*
*Nominative and Connective Case Paradigms*
*Classes of Nominative Verbs*
*Linking Verbs*
*Types of Enlightenment*

## Patterns in Tibetan Language
### The Eight Cases

Case marking particles are placed after nouns, pronouns, adjectives, and postpositions to show how they are connected to words that come after them. Modifying words, phrases, and clauses in this way to show their relationship to other parts of a phrase, clause, or sentence is called **declension**.

> Case particles make no sense by themselves; they serve only to indicate the relationships between words in a phrase, clause or sentence.

Tibetan grammar models itself on Sanskrit, in which there are **eight cases**. Following the lead of European and American Sanskritists, many scholars use the Latin grammatical terms for the Tibetan declensions. Some of these have been retained here, but only where they adequately translate the Tibetan term. At any rate, the declensions are traditionally identified less often by their names than by their numbers (རྣམ་དབྱེ་དང་པོ་ [*case + first*, or *first case*], རྣམ་དབྱེ་གཉིས་པ་, and so forth). The more common English names for the eight are noted here in parentheses, mainly for the convenience of Sanskritists. They will not be used in this book.[86]

| | | | |
|---|---|---|---|
| 1 | first case | **nominative** | (nominative) |
| 2 | second case | **objective** | (accusative) |
| 3 | third case | **agentive** | (instrumental) |
| 4 | fourth case | **beneficial-purposive** | (dative) |
| 5 | fifth case | **originative** | (ablative) |
| 6 | sixth case | **connective** | (genitive) |
| 7 | seventh case | **locative** | (locative) |
| 8 | eighth case | **vocative** | (vocative) |

Note that they may be known *either* by numbers (*first* and so forth) or by names (*nominative* and so forth). The fourth case will be identified sometimes as beneficial and sometimes as purposive, depending on how it is being used at the time.

Here is the same list, but this time in Tibetan. The word རྣམ་པར་དབྱེ་བ་, abbreviated as རྣམ་དབྱེ་, translates *case* and *declension*.

| | | | |
|---|---|---|---|
| 1 | རྣམ་དབྱེ་དང་པོ་ | **nominative** | ངོ་བོ་ཙམ་བརྗོད་པ་ |
| 2 | རྣམ་དབྱེ་གཉིས་པ་ | **objective** | ལས་སུ་བྱ་བའི་སྒྲ་ |
| 3 | རྣམ་དབྱེ་གསུམ་པ་ | **agentive** | བྱེད་སྒྲ་ |
| 4 | རྣམ་དབྱེ་བཞི་པ་ | **beneficial-purposive** | དགོས་ཆེད་ཀྱི་སྒྲ་ |
| 5 | རྣམ་དབྱེ་ལྔ་པ་ | **originative** | འབྱུང་ཁུངས་ཀྱི་སྒྲ་ |
| 6 | རྣམ་དབྱེ་དྲུག་པ་ | **connective** | འབྲེལ་སྒྲ་ |
| 7 | རྣམ་དབྱེ་བདུན་པ་ | **locative** | རྟེན་གནས་ཀྱི་སྒྲ་ |
| 8 | རྣམ་དབྱེ་བརྒྱད་པ་ | **vocative** | བོད་སྒྲ་ |

The following chart lists the **case particles** according to the declensions they mark.

| | | |
|---|---|---|
| 1 | first or nominative | — marked by no particle |
| 2 | second or objective | — either སུ་, རུ་, དུ་, ཏུ་, ན་, ར་, or ལ་ |
| 3 | third or agentive | — either གིས་, ཀྱིས་, གྱིས་, འིས་, or ཡིས་ |

| 4 | fourth or beneficial-purposive | — either སུ་, ར་, རུ་, དུ་, ན་, ར་, or ལ་ |
| 5 | fifth or originative | — either ནས་ or ལས་ |
| 6 | sixth or connective | — either གི་, ཀྱི་, གྱི་, འི་, or ཡི་ |
| 7 | seventh or locative | — either སུ་, ར་, རུ་, དུ་, ན་, ར་, or ལ་ |
| 8 | eighth or vocative | — marked by no particle |

Two particles are listed by grammarians as particles denoting the eighth case; they are ཀྱེ་, and ཀྭ་ཡེ་. However, unlike the others, they occur before the word and not after it.[87] In English, they would be interjections and they are so called here.

- Note that the agentive particles are merely the connective particles with the addition of the suffix ས་.

- Note that the particles marking the second, fourth, and seventh cases are the same.

There are rules (which will be presented in later chapters) that determine which particles follow what words. Many of these particles (and some of the other syntactic particles) follow only syllables ending in certain suffix letters and not others.

> There are actually only three sets of case marking particles. One set of seven particles— སུ་, ར་, རུ་, དུ་, ན་, ར་, and ལ་—mark the second, fourth, and seventh cases. The particles marking the third and sixth cases are nearly the same (གི་ and གིས་, ཀྱི་ and ཀྱིས་, གྱི་ and གྱིས་, འི་ and འིས་, and ཡི་ and ཡིས་). Finally, there are two particles that mark the fifth case (ནས་ and ལས་).

To summarize, there are two types of case marking particles, one the **actual case markers** themselves, whereas the other would be, in English, **interjections**. These interjections are identified by traditional Tibetan grammarians as case particles but in reality are not used in the same way as the others.

Each of the eight declensions will be examined in some detail in subsequent chapters. It will become clear in the course of this examination that there are many more than eight different usages of substantives (that is, nouns or pronouns) and adjectives within phrases, clauses, and sentences.

There are five main sorts of nominatives, four types of objective case usages, three agentives, three beneficial-purposives, seven originative case usages, six primary categories of connectives, and six locatives. These usages are listed, with examples, in Appendix Five.

For the time being, it will be enough to be aware of a few important usages of each case. Memorizing this set of examples will provide you with a very basic set of Tibetan phrase and sentence structures. Remember, however, that this is a set of representative examples and not an exhaustive list.

## Case Marking Particles
### *Nominative Case Paradigms*

If a word is followed by a case marking particle, it cannot be in the nominative case. However, not all nouns, pronouns, and adjectives without case marking particles are nominatives—for instance, you have already seen nouns in a list and noun-adjective phrases. The individual nouns in these phrases are not nominatives, but the phrase as a whole may be.

   Nominatives perform in a variety of ways, but the most basic are as the subject or the complement of sentences or clauses ending in **linking verbs**.

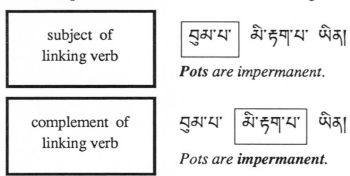

| subject of linking verb | བུམ་པ་ མི་རྟག་པ་ ཡིན། |
|---|---|
| | *Pots are impermanent.* |

| complement of linking verb | བུམ་པ་ མི་རྟག་པ་ ཡིན། |
|---|---|
| | *Pots are **impermanent**.* |

Recall that there are three basic groups of verbs in Tibetan. Linking verbs belong to the first category—the nominative verbs (verbs whose subjects are in the nominative case)—as do verbs of existence.

The other nominative verbs—verbs of existence, verbs of living, verbs of dependence, and verbs expressing mental attitudes—also take nominative subjects. What follows is an example of a sentence ending in a verb of existence. (Paradigms of the other nominative verbs are given later in this chapter.)

| | |
|---|---|
| subject of verb of existence | **S NOM   VB**<br>བུམ་པ་ ཡོད། <br><br>*Pots exist.* |

Many of the agentive verbs take nominative *objects*. This is one of the more common usages of the nominative.

| | |
|---|---|
| object of agentive verb | **S  C  3     NOM   VB**<br>སངས་རྒྱས་ཀྱིས་ ཆོས་ བསྟན། <br><br>*Buddha taught **the doctrine**.* |

> Recall that Case dots *following* case marking particles may be replaced by the number of the case they indicate. Thus the **3** dot is one following an agentive particle.

Finally, a nominative standing alone at the beginning of a sentence may be unrelated grammatically to the sentence, serving as what in English might be a title or section heading. This corresponds to the **block language** of English grammar.[88]

| | |
|---|---|
| topical nominative | **NN NN APP   C   5      S NOM SP**<br>གཞི་ལམ་འབྲས་གསུམ་ལས། དང་པོ་ ནི། <br><br>*From among the three—bases, paths, and fruits—<br>**the first** is as follows.* |

You have seen ལས་ elsewhere in its use as a noun meaning *karma* (*action*). Here it is a particle marking the fifth or originative case, specifically its use to show separation (the first item among three).

# Case Marking Particles
## *Connective Case Paradigms*

There are five connective case marking particles: གི་, གྱི་, ཀྱི་, འི་, and ཡི་.

> Remember that there are two ways in which a syllable's third-column root letter may lose its aspiration: when it has a prefix or superscribed letter and when it is in an unstressed position in a word.
>
> གི་ and གྱི་—because they are merely particles—are naturally unstressed syllables. They are, therefore, pronounced **gí** and **gyí**, respectively.

The sixth case relates nouns, pronouns, and adjectives not to verbs, but to other substantives or to postpositions. It indicates many sorts of connections; there are six major types of usage, within which there are (at least) seventeen differentiable uses. One of the more important is that showing **possession**.

| possessive connective | བདག་ཅག་གི་ སྟོན་པ་ |
|---|---|

*our Teacher*

*Teacher* is capitalized because it is an epithet of Buddha. བདག་ (*I*) is a first person pronoun.

ང་ is the more common first person pronoun. བདག་ is an elegant form, and is often seen in Buddhist Tibetan. Neither pronouns are honorific, as honorifics may be used only for others, never for oneself.

Adding the pluralizing lexical particle ཅག་ to བདག་ produces བདག་ཅག་ (*we, us*). Applying the connective particle གི་ then yields བདག་ཅག་གི་ (*our*).

The possessive connective is closely related to the type connective. Type connectives, however, answer the question, "Which?" and not "Whose?"

| type connective | ཐེག་ཆེན་གྱི་ | ཆོས་ |

*doctrine of the Mahāyāna*

Other connectives imply relationships of origin, agency, effect and cause, time, or place. The following example indicates a relationship of causality or, more literally, destination.

| destination connective | བྱང་ཆུབ་ཀྱི་ | ལམ་ |

*path to awakening*

What sort of path? A path that leads to བྱང་ཆུབ་ (*awakening*—Skt. *bodhi*)—not a path made of awakening (*bodhi* is the goal), nor a path that belongs to awakening, but one that leads there.

Thus, whereas the general rule-of-thumb translation of a connective case particle is *of*, just about every English preposition will be appropriate in some instance of connective case use.

## The Lexical Dimension of Connective Case Markers

Although the five connective case marking particles (གི་, གྱི་, ཀྱི་, འི་, and ཡི་) have the same syntactic meaning (that is, they mark the same sorts of relationships between nouns, pronouns, adjectives, and postpositions), they are not interchangeable *lexically*. For example, གི་ (**gí**) may be used only after a word whose final syllable ends in either ག་ or ང་.

Recall that because a case marking particle is an unstressed syllable, it is pronounced with no aspiration.

Thus, the following example is pronounced **rang-gi dün-du**.

| རང་གི་ | མདུན་དུ་ | *in front of one* |

གྱི་ (gyí) is used after a word whose final syllable ends in either ད་, བ་, or ས་.

| ཤར་ཕྱོགས་ཀྱི་ | ཡུལ་ | *a land in the east* |

The above example illustrates a relationship of type, one in which the noun, ཡུལ་, is narrowed from places in general to a specific type of land—one in the east.

གྱི་ (gyí) is used after a word whose final syllable ends in either ན་, མ་, ར་, or ལ་. In the following example the connective indicates apposition.

| ལམ་གྱི་ | བདེན་པ་ | *truths [which are] paths* |

འི་ (í) merges with final syllables that end in འ་ or that have no suffix letter.

| འཕགས་པའི་ | དགེ་འདུན་ | *a spiritual community of superiors* |

| བྱང་ཆུབ་སེམས་དཔའི་ | སྙིང་རྗེ་ཆེན་པོ་ | *great compassion of bodhisattvas* |

The connective case is often used with appositives. Frequently the generalizing lexical particle ལ་སོགས་པ་ (*and so forth, et cetera*) terminates the word to which the connective marker is applied. དུད་འགྲོ་ལ་སོགས་པ་ means *animals and so forth*, and is the usual way to indicate a list by stating only a representative member of that list.

| དུད་འགྲོ་ལ་སོགས་པའི་ | ངན་འགྲོ་ | *bad migrations such as animals* |

The following example illustrates the use of connective case marking particles to link adjectives and the nouns they qualify.

| ཨེ་དགེ་བའི་ | བསམ་པ་ | ***nonvirtuous*** *attitude* |

ཨེ་ (**yí**) is used *after* a word whose final syllable either ends in འ་ or has no suffix letter. Thus, any of the examples of འི་ usage could be restated with a ཨེ་. This is most frequently seen in verse when an extra syllable is needed to complete the meter of the line.

| འཕགས་པ་ཡི་ | དགེ་འདུན་ | *a spiritual community **of superiors*** |

## Summary

Memorize these rules for the proper usage of connective case marking particles.

- གི་ (**gí**) is used after a word whose final syllable ends in either ག་ or ང་.

- གྱི་ (**ḡyí**) is used after a word whose final syllable ends in either ད་, བ་, or ས་.

- ཀྱི་ (**gyí**) is used after a word whose final syllable ends in either ན་, མ་, ར་, or ལ་.

- འི་ (**í**) merges with final syllables that end in འ་ or that have no suffix letter.

- ཡི་ (**yí**) is used *after* a word whose final syllable either ends in འ་ or has no suffix letter.

## Drill 12.1

Translate the following into English.

1. ལས་ཀྱི་སྒྲིབ་པ་

2. སངས་རྒྱས་ཀྱི་སྲས་

3  དངུལ་གྱི་མཆོན་ཅིད་

4  སྨྱིག་པའི་ལས་

5  འགྲོ་འོངས་ཀྱི་ཆོས་

6  ཐིག་པ་ཆེན་པོའི་ལམ་

7  བླ་བའི་འོད་ཟེར་

8  སེམས་ཅམ་པའི་ལུགས་

9  བྱིས་པའི་རྒྱུད་ཀྱི་ཉིན་མོངས་

10  ཕག་པོའི་མགོ་

11  སྲུང་མའི་ཁང་

12  རྙུང་སེམས་ཀྱི་འཕྲུལ་བ་

---

## Drill 12.2

Use the appropriate connective case marking particle after each word.

1  ཨེ་ཤེས་

2  ཁ་དོག་

3  སྙིད་པ་

4  གྲུབ་ཐོབ་

5  ཇ་བོ་

6  ཀུན་མཁྱེན་

7  ཨེ་དམ་

8 ཆོད་ཉེར་

9 སྒྲ་

10 གངས་

11 ཡིན་

12 དེ་

# Verbs and Verb Syntax
## *Types of Verbs*

There are many ways of categorizing Tibetan verbs; the classification used in this book—which is based on the sentence patterns dictated by various verbs—was introduced in Chapter Nine:

1. **nominative verbs**—whose subjects are in the first (nominative) case;

2. **agentive verbs**—whose subjects are in the third (agentive) case;

3. **specialized verbs**—most of whose subjects are in the seventh (locative) case, but including one class of verbs with fourth case subjects.

Another useful classification divides verbs into two basic types:

1. **existential verbs** such as ཡིན་ (*is*) and ཡོད་ (*exists*);

2. **action verbs** such as བྱེད་ (*do, make*) and སྟོན་ (*teach, show*).

In that classification, the second type (action verbs) also divides into two subtypes.

1. Verbs expressing an action in which an agent acts on something other than itself, as in *Buddha taught the doctrine*, require an agentive subject:
   སངས་རྒྱས་ཀྱིས་ ཆོས་ བསྟན།.

2. Action verbs that do not speak of objects distinct from their agents, as in *The wheel turns*, require a nominative subject:
   འཁོར་ལོ་ འཁོར།.

Most existential verbs also take a nominative subject, but a few take a locative subject (as specialized verbs) and one (དགོས་, *need*—also a specialized verb) takes a fourth case subject.

Nominative existential verbs are discussed in Chapters Twelve and Thirteen. Locative existential verbs are discussed in Chapter Fourteen.

> It is crucial, when analyzing and translating a Tibetan sentence, to find the verb and to then identify what type of verb it is. The type of verb determines the syntax used in the clause or sentence it ends.

## Nominative Verbs
### *Classes of Nominative Verbs*

There are—from the viewpoint of the syntax typically seen in the clauses and sentences they end—four classes of nominative verbs:

I   **nominative-nominative verbs**, requiring a nominative (first case) subject and a nominative complement;

II   **nominative-locative verbs**, requiring a nominative subject and (optionally) a locative (seventh case) qualifier;

III   **nominative-objective verbs**, with nominative subjects and objective (second case) qualifiers or objects;

IV   **nominative-syntactic verbs**, with nominative subjects and qualifiers marked by syntactic particles instead of case marking particles.

The fact that a nominative-locative verb takes a qualifier marked by a locative case marking particle does not mean that it must have a qualifier, *nor does it mean that all the qualifiers in the clauses and sentences it ends must be in the locative case.*

> The case particles marking the subject of a given verb, its object, and its complement are fairly (although not invariably) predictable. However, there are many different types of qualifiers possible in a given clause or sentence.

The same holds true for nominative-objective and nominative-syntactic verbs.

There is only one type of Class I or nominative-nominative verb—the **linking verbs** whose syntax has been discussed since Chapter Nine.

| | | |
|---|---|---|
| Class I Verbs Nominative-Nominative | NOM    NOM    VB བུམ་པ་ མི་རྟག་པ་ ཡིན། | |

*Pots are impermanent.*

There are a number of different types of Class II (nominative-locative) verbs:

1  simple **verbs of existence** (such as ཡོད་, *exist*) for which the locative qualifier (marking the place where there is existence) is optional;

2  **verbs of living**—that is, verbs of continuing existence such as གནས་ (*stay, live*)—with the place where or time during which existence continues being in the locative case;

3  **verbs of dependence** (such as རྟེན་, *depend on*) in which the thing or person upon which there is dependence is marked by a locative case particle;

4  **attitude verbs** expressing mental attitudes taken about something (where the *about* translates a referential locative) such as འཇིགས་ (*fear*) and ཆགས་ (*is attached to*), as well as verbs such as མཁས་ (*is skilled in*).

The following is an example of a Class II verb.

| | | |
|---|---|---|
| Class II Verbs Nominative-Locative | NOM    7    VB འབྲས་བུ་ རྒྱུ་ལ་ བརྟེན། | |

*Effects **depend** on causes.*

Class III verbs have objective case qualifiers or objects. Verbs that express actions without allowing separation of subject and object are found among these verbs. In the following example of such a **nominative action verb,** the light rays are both the agent and the object of the verb—they do the dissolving, but they are also what dissolves.

| Class III Verbs Nominative-Objective | NOM    C 2      VB<br>འོད་ཟེར་ རང་ལ་ ཐིམ།<br>*Light rays **dissolve** into us.* |
|---|---|

There are a number of other different types of Class III verbs; all have nominative subjects and, sometimes optionally, objective case qualifiers.

> Remember that the objective and locative case marking particles are the same. Moreover, although the main qualifier in a sentence ending in a Class III verb is in the objective case, there may be other qualifiers marked in other ways.

Class IV is something of a grab bag. These nominative-syntactic verbs mainly show separation or conjunction. The verb in the following example shows the latter. Notice that its qualifier—མི་སྡུག་པ་དང་ (*with the unpleasant*)—ends in the syntactic particle དང་, which in other situations means *and* or *or*.

| Class IV Verbs Nominative-Syntactic | NOM    SP SP   V   SP<br>ང་རང་ མི་སྡུག་པ་དང་ ཕྲད་ ན་<br>*If we **meet** with the unpleasant, ...* |
|---|---|

> Although there are only three **categories** of verbs (nominative, agentive, and specialized), each category includes a number of different **classes** (for example, the four classes of nominative verbs), within which there may be different **types**.

Thus, verbs of existence (such as ཡོད་) are a type of nominative-locative verb. Nominative-locative verbs are Class II verbs, a class found within the nominative verb category.

---

There are eight classes of verbs, numbered consecutively. Thus, Classes I to IV are nominative verbs, Classes V and VI are agentive verbs, and Classes VII and VIII, specialized verbs. (See Appendix Four.)

---

## Nominative Verbs
### *Linking Verbs*

The simplest Tibetan verb is ཡིན་, the most common copula (or linking verb), usually translated *is* or *are*.[89] A **linking verb** does one of two things:

1   links a noun, pronoun, or adjective with another noun or pronoun;
2   links a noun, pronoun, or adjective with another adjective.

Since nouns and pronouns can be grouped under the name **substantive**, another way of putting this is to say the following.

---

Linking verbs connect a substantive or an adjective with another substantive or adjective.

---

Here are two examples of sentences ending in linking verbs. The first example refers to the Buddhist concept of personhood, which is far wider than that accepted by either scientists or philosophers in the Western tradition. In Buddhism, any sentient being is a person, and thus not only humans, but also animals, hungry ghosts, hell-beings, and gods are persons. Buddhas, likewise, are persons, but it is considered philosophically incorrect to say that a Buddha is a person, since included in the concept of Buddha is the cessation of all afflictions, and cessations (as will be seen in Chapter Sixteen) are permanent (that is, unchanging) phenomena, whereas persons are impermanent. Thus, the convention is to refer to Buddha the person as སངས་རྒྱས་འཕགས་པ་ (*buddha superior*) or, as abbreviated here, སངས་འཕགས་.

| སངས་འཕགས་གང་ཟག་ཡིན། | śang phak kang-ṣak yîn | A Buddha superior is a person. |
| ཁ་དོག་གཟུགས་ཡིན། | kha-dok ṣuk yîn | Colors are forms. |

Diagrammed, the first sentence looks like this:

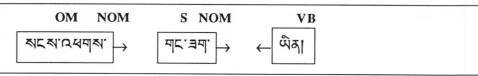

In this sentence, སངས་འཕགས་ is the subject and གང་ཟག་ is the complement.

Two rules help to diagram this type of sentence, both of which should be familiar to the reader by this point. The first is this.

> The structure of a sentence ending in a linking verb is:
> SUBJECT [nominative case] + COMPLEMENT [nominative case] + VERB.

In Tenglish the two examples given above would look like the following.

BUDDHA SUPERIOR    PERSON    IS.

COLORS    FORMS    ARE.

Notice that the verb ཡིན་ can mean either *is* or *are*. And, depending on context, it may also mean *was* or *will be*.

> Tibetan is ambiguous as to number (singular and plural) and does not require indefinite or definite articles as English does.

The second rule that is relevant here is the following.

> Nouns or adjectives in the nominative case have no case ending—that is, they are followed by no case particles.

True, this makes it hard for the novice to differentiate nouns or adjectives in the nominative from, say, nouns in a list or nouns followed by adjectives; in both of those cases nouns also do not have case endings. However, you *can* exclude any word with a *case* marking particle following it from being in the nominative case.

The word order in sentences ending in linking verbs is not arbitrary. Take, for example the following two sentences.

| སངས་འཕགས་གང་ཟག་ཡིན། | BUDDHA SUPERIOR PERSON IS | *A Buddha superior is a person.* |
|---|---|---|
| གང་ཟག་སངས་འཕགས་ཡིན། | PERSON BUDDHA SUPERIOR IS | *A person is a Buddha superior.* |

The first nominative in such a sentence is the subject and the second is the complement; the second says something about the first. Thus, when the second sentence reverses the order of the words prior to the verb, the meaning is changed, and the sentence—while still grammatically correct—expresses an incorrect proposition.

The following two sentences exemplify this same principle.

| སེར་པོ་ཁ་དོག་ཡིན། | YELLOW COLOR IS | *Yellow is a color.* |
|---|---|---|
| ཁ་དོག་སེར་པོ་ཡིན། | COLOR YELLOW IS | *Colors are yellow.* |

Reversing the order of the nouns in the first sentence to say ཁ་དོག་སེར་པོ་ཡིན། is to say—in the most general case—*Colors are yellow* (and, again, to be incorrect).

ཁ་དོག་སེར་པོ་ཡིན། can have other meanings as well. The meaning of a Tibetan sentence is dependent on its context to a much greater degree than the meaning of an English sentence. Thus, if the context in which this sentence is found was as an answer to the question, "What is that color?"—then it would clearly be an appositive construction (in which the subject was *not* stated), *[That color] is the color yellow.* Stating the implied subject of that sentence yields the following.

| ཁ་དོག་དེ་ ཁ་དོག་སེར་པོ་ ཡིན། | COLOR THAT COLOR YELLOW IS |
|---|---|

Other grammatically possible translations of ཁ་དོག་སེར་པོ་ཨིན། are:

*Colors are yellow.*
*A color is yellow.*
*The color is yellow.*

However, in every case, the meaning of a sentence or clause has to be translated in context. Thus, a sentence such as the one above—*which, standing by itself, has no context*—must be translated in the broadest, most general context: *Colors are yellow* or *Color is yellow*. More specific translations would be appropriate only in the proper context.

> Tibetan grammar does not require—as English does—that all the major parts of a sentence be stated in words. In many cases, for example, the subject will be dropped if it has already been made clear in an earlier sentence.

Understood elements in clauses and sentences are discussed later in this chapter.

## Drill 12.3

These sentences have been constructed using words from the vocabularies of previous chapters. Practice reading and speaking them. Identify the dots. Translate into English, diagramming the first and eighth with boxes and arrows.

1. སློན་པོ་ཁ་དོག་ཨིན།

2. ང་གང་ཟག་ཨིན།

3. སེམས་མི་རྟག་པ་ཨིན།

4. དེ་ང་ཨིན།

5. རྒྱུ་མཚོ་ཆུ་ཨིན།

6 དབྱིབས་ཚོས་ཡིན།

7 དམར་པོ་མི་རྟག་པ་ཡིན།

8 བུམ་པ་ཡོད་པ་ཡིན།

## *Negating Linking Verbs*

The linking verb ཡིན་ is negated with the negative prefix syllable མ་, a lexical particle (see Chapter Ten). Whereas ཁ་དོག་དེ་སྔོན་པོ་ཡིན། means *That color is blue*, placing a མ་ before the verb ཡིན་ gives us a sentence meaning *That color is not blue*.

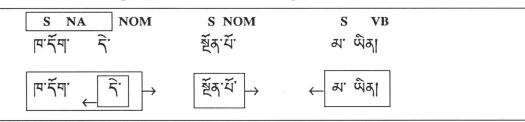

The མ་ is diagrammed along with the verb, in a single box. For our purposes, མ་ཡིན་ can be considered to function as a single word: *isn't*.[90] The མ་ really means nothing by itself.[91]

Here are some examples of the use of མ་ཡིན་. Note the compound subject in the first example.

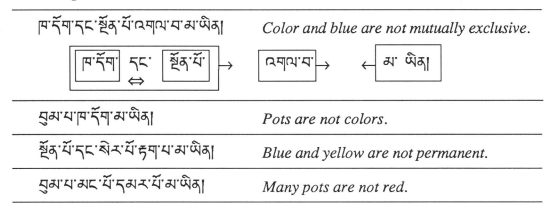

| | |
|---|---|
| ཁ་དོག་དང་སྔོན་པོ་འགལ་བ་མ་ཡིན། | *Color and blue are not mutually exclusive.* |
| བུམ་པ་ཁ་དོག་མ་ཡིན། | *Pots are not colors.* |
| སྔོན་པོ་དང་སེར་པོ་རྟག་པ་མ་ཡིན། | *Blue and yellow are not permanent.* |
| བུམ་པ་མང་པོ་དམར་པོ་མ་ཡིན། | *Many pots are not red.* |

| ཁ་དོག་སྔོན་པོ་རྟག་པ་མ་ཡིན། | *The color blue is not permanent.* |
|---|---|

མ་ཡིན་ can be contracted to མེན་. Thus, one can say that there are two main forms of linking verbs—exemplified by ཡིན་ (meaning *be [something]* ) and མེན་ (or མ་ཡིན་— meaning *not to be [something]* ).

## Drill 12.4

Translate the following into Tibetan.

1. Minds and forms are mutually exclusive.
2. Many phenomena are not colors.
3. Humans are not horses.
4. All sentient beings are not humans.
5. Five pots are blue; two pots are yellow.

## Drill 12.5

Translate the following, diagramming the first and fourth and marking their dots.

1. རྟ་དང་མི་སེམས་ཅན་ཡིན།

2. ཕྱམ་པ་མང་པོ་སེར་པོ་ཡིན།

3. ཕྱན་མེན་འདུ་བྱེད་སེམས་མ་ཡིན།

4. ཆོས་ཀྱི་དུང་དཀར་པོ་ཁ་དོག་དམར་པོ་མེན།

5. དངོས་པོ་ཐམས་ཅད་མི་རྟག་པ་ཡིན།

6. སྟེང་རྗེ་ཆེན་པོ་སེམས་ཡིན།

## *Linking Verbs Other than* ཡིན་

ཡིན་ and its negation མིན་ are the most frequently used linking verbs in all periods of Tibetan literature. In the modern colloquial language ཡིན་ and མིན་ are used only for the first person declarative (*I am, I am not*) and the second person interrogative (*Are you?, Aren't you?*). In the written language being analyzed in this book, however, they are used without regard to person.

In addition to ཡིན་ and མིན་, there are other linking verbs. The verbs ལགས་ and མ་ ལགས་ are common occurrences in translations of *sūtra*s from Sanskrit. The following example is from the *Diamond Cutter Sūtra*:[92]

བཅོམ་ལྡན་འདས་ ངོ་མཚར་ ལགས་སོ།

**ȷom-dën-dë> ngo-tshar lak-so (OR la'-so)**

*O Transcendent Victor, [it] is amazing.*

བཅོམ་ལྡན་འདས་ refers to Buddha(s) and is often translated as *Blessed One*, a rendering that is not appropriate in translating Buddhism. It is inappropriate because it misleads the reader, implying as it does that Buddhas are believed to be blessed by some greater power.[93] There are two traditional Buddhist etymologies of the Sanskrit term *bhagavan*; one suggests a translation of *Fortunate One*.[94] However, the one followed by Tibetan translators when they rendered Indian Buddhist texts into Tibetan a thousand years ago resulted in the term བཅོམ་ལྡན་འདས་, suggesting that a Buddha (1) *has conquered* (བཅོམ་) desire, hatred, and ignorance, (2) *possesses* (ལྡན་) positive qualities such as wisdom, and (3) *has gone beyond* (འདས་) both cyclic existence and nirvana.[95] Thus, a translation from the Tibetan should give us something such as *Transcendent Victor*.[96]

ངོ་མཚར་ means *amazing*. As we have seen before, the verb is followed by a terminating syntactic particle (here, སོ་).

Based on the sentences that have been analyzed so far and on the standard syntax of sentences ending in linking verbs (SUBJECT + COMPLEMENT + VERB), the logical translation would be *The Transcendent Victor is amazing*. As always, however, context must be taken into account. Because sutras are dialogues between Buddha and his listeners, it is not uncommon to find statements addressed to people. When someone is addressed in a Tibetan sentence, the name of the person addressed is in the vocative case which, like the nominative case, has no case marker (with rare exceptions). These vocative constructions are much more common in translations of sutras and tantras than in more modern writings on philosophy and meditation. Thus, here we see a sentence beginning with a vocative, བཙོམ་ལྡན་འདས་: *Transcendent Victor, [it] is amazing.* The context of this sentence tells us that the understood subject, *it*, refers to the assistance given to Bodhisattvas by the Buddha.

This sentence is an example of the syntax VOCATIVE + [UNDERSTOOD SUBJECT] + COMPLEMENT + VERB.

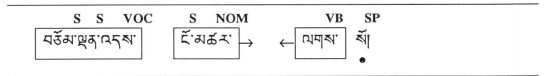

> Note that there is no arrow attached to the vocative. Vocatives are neither
> subjects, objects, nor qualifiers of verbs, nor do they modify other words,
> as do adjectives, adverbs, and phrases in the connective case.

Vocatives can occur in other positions as well, as long as they precede the verb. They do not occur frequently in expository philosophical and meditative literature; however, they do occur in poetic treatments of philosophy and meditation (treatises in verse being much more common in Tibetan than they are in English).

The verbs རེད་ and མ་རེད་ are also linking verbs, but they are typically used in more modern, colloquially oriented writing.[97]

# Patterns in Tibetan Language
## *Understood Elements in Clauses and Sentences*

In the proper contexts, when communication of meaning does not require their presence, parts of a sentence may be omitted. Those omitted parts are then said to be 'understood.' The following sentence, which takes sound (སྒྲ་ **ḍa**) as an illustration of an impermanent phenomenon, is one of the standard examples used in presenting logic in the Indian and Tibetan Buddhist traditions.

| སྒྲ་ མི་རྟག་པ་ ཡིན། | *Sound is impermanent.* |
|---|---|

In this case, all three basic elements of the sentence ending in a linking verb—subject, complement, and verb—are present. But suppose that the occasion for this statement is as an answer to the question, "Is sound permanent or impermanent?" In that case, it is not necessary to repeat the subject, and therefore the answer could be abbreviated as follows.

| མི་རྟག་པ་ ཡིན། | *[Sound] is impermanent.* |
|---|---|

This answer states only a complement and a verb; the subject is understood.

The sentence can be abbreviated even further in the event that the question being answered is "What is an example of something impermanent?" The answer could be as brief as a single word.

| སྒྲ། | *Sound [is impermanent].* |
|---|---|

Here there is only a subject; the complement and the verb are both understood.

## Drill 12.6

The following sentences have understood elements. Translate the sentences into English, supplying the understood elements in brackets as necessary.

1. སངས་རྒྱས་ཆེ་དཔག་མེད་མ་ཡིན།

2. འདོད་ཆགས་ནི་སྡང་གདེ་ཕྱུག་གསུམ་ཡིན།

3. འཁོར་འདས་ཀྱི་ཆོས་ཟག་བཅས་དང་ཟག་མེད་ཡིན།

4. ཤེས་བྱ་ཐམས་ཅད་མཁྱེན།

5. ཁྱོད་ཀྱིས་བསྐྱེད།

# Lexical Particles
## *Prefix Particles*

Buddhist Tibetan began not as a spoken language, but as a translation language. It was devised to assure accurate translation of Indian Buddhist texts into Tibetan. The vocabulary of Buddhist Tibetan, combined with the syntax of colloquial Tibetan, became the language of philosophic and religious discourse in the Tibetan cultural area, even among those whose native language was not Tibetan (for example, the Mongols).

Understanding the original purpose of Buddhist Tibetan vocabulary helps to explain why so much of it consists of words that begin with prefix particles. They are translations of Sanskrit prefix syllables (for example, the *abhi-* of *abhisamaya*, the *vi-* of *vijñāna*, and the *prati-* of *pratimokṣa*). An analysis of the translation equivalents shows, however, that whereas some Tibetan prefix particles usually translate certain Sanskrit prefix syllables, there is no invariable one-to-one equivalence.

There are thirteen very frequently seen Tibetan prefix particles. They are listed here with examples of words in which they are used and with the Sanskrit originals they translate. It should be noted that these Sanskrit "equivalents" are only equivalent in the sense of being one of, usually, many Sanskrit words translated by a single Tibetan term.

The Indian and Tibetan Buddhist traditions often assign a lexical value, a meaning, to each syllable of a word. Thus, it is not out of place here (although not entirely accurate) to indicate a rule of thumb translation for each of these prefix particles. These rough translations of the prefix particles are often enough not borne out by the definitions of the words of which they form parts, and they do not always tally with the accepted definitions of their Sanskrit "originals" in that language.

- རྣམ་པར་ occurs in many words, usually translating the Sanskrit prefix *vi-*:
  - རྣམ་པར་གྲོལ་བ་ (ñam-bar-döl-wa) translates *vimokṣa* and *vimukta* and means *liberation* and *liberated*.
  - རྣམ་པར་རྟོག་པ་ (ñam-bar-dok-ba) translates *vikalpa* and *vitarka* and means *conceptuality* or *thought*.
  - རྣམ་པར་དབྱེ་བ་ (ñam-bar-yé-wa) translates *vibhakti* and means *distinction* (and *declension*).

- རྣམ་པར་བཞག་པ་ (ñam-b̄ar-s̱hak-b̄a) translates *vyavasthāpana* and means *presentation.*

The prefix རྣམ་པར་ is sometimes thought of as indicating separation or distinction (as in རྣམ་པར་དབྱེ་བ་) and sometimes as an emphasizing or intensifying particle (as may be the case in རྣམ་པར་གྲོལ་བ་).[98] Thus, a rough and tentative translation of an unknown word (X) beginning in རྣམ་པར་ would be either *separately X* or *very X.*

- ཀུན་ཏུ་ occurs in many words, usually—but not always—translating the Sanskrit prefix *sam-*:
    - ཀུན་ཏུ་འབྱུང་བ་ (ḡün-d̄u-jung-wa) translates *samudaya* and means *origin.*
    - ཀུན་ཏུ་བཟང་པོ་ (ḡün-d̄u-ẕang-b̄o) translates *Samantabhadra*—the ཀུན་ཏུ་ (*thoroughly*) translating *samanta.*
- ཀུན་ནས་ also translates the Sanskrit prefix *sam-*:
    - ཀུན་ནས་ཉོན་མོངས་པ་ (ḡün-në>-nyön-mong-b̄a), *thoroughly afflicted,* translates *samkliṣṭa.*

A tentative translation of an unknown word (X) beginning in ཀུན་ཏུ་ or in ཀུན་ ནས་ might be *thoroughly X* or *extensively X.*

- མངོན་པར་ occurs in many words, translating the Sanskrit prefix *abhi-*:
    - མངོན་པར་ཤེས་པ་ (ṉgön-b̄ar-s̱hé>-b̄a), *clairvoyance* (that is, *super-normal power*), translates *abhijñā.*
    - མངོན་པར་རྟོགས་པ་ (ṉgön-b̄ar-d̄ok-b̄a), *realization,* translates *abhisamaya.*

A tentative translation of an unknown word (X) beginning in མངོན་པར་ might be *exceptionally X* or *manifestly X.*

- ངེས་པར་ also occurs in many words, translating some uses of the Sanskrit prefix *nir-* (which also occurs as *niḥ-* and *niś-*):
    - ངེས་པར་འབྱུང་བ་ (ngé>-b̄ar-jung-wa), *renunciation* (literally, *definite emergence*), translates *niḥsaraṇa.*

- ངེས་པར་ཤེས་པ་ (**ngé>-bar-shé>-ba**) translates *niścaya* and means *ascertainment*.

A rough translation of an unknown word (*X*) beginning in ངེས་པར་ is *definitely X*.

- ཡོངས་སུ་ translates the Sanskrit prefix *pari-*:
  - ཡོངས་སུ་གྲུབ་པ་ (**yong-su-dup-ba**) translates *parinispanna* and means *thoroughly established* (and, by implication, *completely existent*).
  - ཡོངས་སུ་དག་པ་ (**yong-su-tak-ba**), *thoroughly pure* or *thoroughly purified*, translates *pariśuddhi*.

A rule of thumb translation for words beginning in ཡོངས་སུ་ is *completely* or *thoroughly X*.

- རྗེས་སུ་ translates the Sanskrit prefix *anu-*:
  - རྗེས་སུ་དཔག་པ་ (**jé>-su-bak-ba**) translates *anumāna* and means *inference*.
  - རྗེས་སུ་མཐུན་པ་ (**jé>-su-thün-ba**), *concordant* (or, sometimes, *similitude*), translates *anulomika* and *anukūla*.

The prefix རྗེས་སུ་ suggests *after* and *along with*.

- ཉེ་བར་ translates the Sanskrit prefix *upa-*:
  - ཉེ་བར་ལེན་པ་ (**nyé-war-lên-ba**), *appropriation*, translates *upadāna*.
  - ཉེ་བར་ཞི་བ་ (**nyé-war-shi-wa**), *pacified* or *pacification*, translates *vyupaśama* (the ཉེ་བར་ doing double duty for the Sanskrit *vi* + *upa*).[99]

The prefix ཉེ་བར་ suggests nearness—both in the sense of being close to something and in the sense of approximation. However, it also is used as an intensifier.

- སོ་སོར་ occurs as a translation of the Sanskrit prefix *prati-*:
  - སོ་སོར་ཐར་པ་ (**so-sor-thar-ba**) means *individual emancipation* (or *liberation*) and translates *pratimokṣa*.

A tentative translation of an unknown word (*X*) beginning in སོ་སོར་ is *separately X* or *individually X*.

- རབ་ཏུ་ translates the Sanskrit prefix *pra-*:
    - རབ་ཏུ་དགའ་བ་ (**rap-ḍu-ga-wa**), *joyous*, translates *pramudita*.
    - རབ་ཏུ་བྱུང་བ་ (**rap-ḍu-jung-wa**), literally *going forth* (*becoming a monk*), translates *pravrajita*.

A tentative translation of an unknown word (*X*) beginning in རབ་ཏུ་ is *thoroughly X* or *exceptionally X*.

རྣམ་པ་, ངེས་པ་, and སོ་སོ་ (lacking the final ར་ seen in the prefixes), and ཀུན་ (without the ཏུ་) are also words in their own right—རྣམ་པ་ meaning *type, aspect,* and *form*, ངེས་པ་, *certainty* or *ascertainment*, ཀུན་, *all*, and སོ་སོ་, *each one* and *individual*.

The remaining three Tibetan prefix particles are not as frequently translations of Sanskrit prefixes as the others. (Sometimes they translate adjectives or are without a separate Sanskrit equivalent.) ཡང་དག་པ་ and ལེགས་པ་ (when they lack that final ར་) are also adjectives, meaning *correct* and *good*, respectively. ཤིན་ཏུ་ is sometimes used as an intensifying adverb (meaning *very*).

- ཡང་དག་པར་ occurs in many words, usually translating the Sanskrit *samyak-*:
    - ཡང་དག་པར་སྤོང་བ་ (**yang-dak-ḇar-ḇong-wa**) means *correct elimination* or *complete abandonment* and translates *samyakprahāṇa*.
- ཤིན་ཏུ་ sometimes translates the Sanskrit prefix *pra-*, and translates some cases of the prefix *su-*:
    - ཤིན་ཏུ་སྦྱངས་པ་ (**shîn-ḍu-jang-ḇa**), *pliant, thoroughly practiced*, translates *prasrabdhi*.
    - ཤིན་ཏུ་ཆེ་བ་ (**shîn-ḍu-ché-wa**) means *very great* and translates *sumahat*.
- ལེགས་པར་ translates some instances of the Sanskrit prefix *su-*:
    - ལེགས་པར་བཤད་པ་ (**lék-ḇar-shë'-ḇa**) means *well explained* and *good explanations* and translates *subhāṣita*.

It should be noted that, although the examples given above are all nouns or adjectives, they are all—with the two exceptions of ཀུན་ཏུ་བཟང་པོ་ and ཀུན་ནས་ཉོན་མོངས་པ་— *verbal* nouns or adjectives, and thus there are cognate verb forms for each in both Tibetan and Sanskrit.

For example, the verb form of the noun ལེགས་པར་བཤད་པ་ is ལེགས་པར་བཤད་, and the verb form of རབ་ཏུ་བྱུང་བ་ is རབ་ཏུ་བྱུང་.

It must be kept in mind that not all instances of one or another of these prefix particles followed by a verb or verbal are actually examples of words made with prefix particles.

Although ངེས་པར་ is a prefix particle and འཆི་བ་ is a verbal noun, the combination ངེས་པར་འཆི་བ་ is a phrase meaning *definitely dying* (or, in better English, *will definitely die*). ངེས་པར་ here is an adverb.[100]

Finally, it is useful to be able to identify the simple verb from which a larger word is constructed, be that larger word a verbal noun (such as ཏོག་པ་) or a prefixed verb such as རྣམ་པར་ཏོག་པ་. The simplest form of the verb from which other words may be built may be called the **core verb**. In the two examples just given (ཏོག་པ་ and རྣམ་པར་ཏོག་པ་), the core verb is the verb ཏོག་.

## Abbreviated Nouns and Adjectives

Longer Tibetan words are often abbreviated by means of omitting syllables. All of the above examples of words made with prefix particles may be, and frequently are, shortened. In the following examples, the words on the left are words in their full forms and the words on the right are their abbreviated forms.

| | | | |
|---|---|---|---|
| རྣམ་པར་བཞག་པ་ | ñam-bar-s̲hak-b̄a | རྣམ་བཞག་ | ñam-s̲hak |
| རྣམ་པར་ཤེས་པ་ | ñam-b̄ar-s̄hé>-b̄a | རྣམ་ཤེས་ | ñam-s̄hé> |
| ངེས་པར་འབྱུང་བ་ | ngé-b̄ar-jung-wa | ངེས་འབྱུང་ | ngé-jung |
| ལེགས་པར་བཤད་པ་ | lék-b̄ar-s̄hë'-b̄a | ལེགས་བཤད་ | lék-s̄hë' |

| ཡོངས་སུ་གྲུབ་པ་ | **yong-sū-dup-ba** | ཡོངས་གྲུབ་ | **yong-dup** |
| རབ་ཏུ་བྱུང་བ་ | **rap-du-jung-wa** | རབ་བྱུང་ | **rap-jung** |

The longer, four-syllable words are often seen in the abbreviated forms given here. The abbreviation process is symmetrical—the shorter and less important second and fourth syllables have been lost in each of these words. Note that the second syllable of the third example— འབྱུང་ —has an འ prefix, allowing the alternative (and more common) pronunciation **ngén-jung**. Recall that the འ prefix can cause the end of the previous syllable (if that syllable is in the same word) to be nasalized.

The ཉེ་བར་ and སོ་སོར་ prefixes are abbreviated in the following ways.

| ཉེ་བར་ལེན་པ་ | **nyé-war-lên-ba** | ཉེར་ལེན་ | **nyér-lên** |
| སོ་སོར་རྟོགས་པ་ | **sō-sor-dok-ba** | སོར་རྟོགས་ | **sor-dok** |
| སོ་སོར་ཐར་པ་ | **sō-sor-thar-ba** | སོ་ཐར་ | **sō-thar** |

Whereas ཉེ་བར་ collapses into ཉེར་, སོ་སོར་ is less predictable. In some cases it becomes སོར་, in others, སོ་.

# Doctrinal Vocabulary and Grammar
## *Paths to Enlightenment*

The most basic format for speaking of paths to enlightenment is that of the three trainings: ethics, concentration, and wisdom. However, since the discussion begun in the previous chapter is not on paths but on their results, here only the terminology describing the ways of practicing these paths will be examined, since the way in which the paths are practiced determines the type of enlightenment to be attained.

The three trainings are discussed in Chapter Fifteen.

## *Vehicles*

In general, there are two main ways of practicing Buddhism according to Indian and Tibetan Mahāyāna Buddhists. One is their own way (ཐེག་པ་ཆེན་པོ་, **thék-ba-chên-**

b̄o—Sanskrit *Mahāyāna*), while the other they have traditionally called Hīnayāna (ཐེག་པ་དམན་པ་, **thék-b̄a-m̄en-b̄a**), a term which literally translates as *inferior vehicle* or *lower vehicle*. Because this obviously pejorative term is distasteful to many modern Buddhists, there have been attempts to tone down the terminology in English translation, using words such as *Modest Vehicle*.

- ཐེག་པ་ཆེན་པོ་ is a NOUN-ADJECTIVE phrase, where ཐེག་པ་ is a noun meaning *vehicle* and ཆེན་པོ་ is an adjective meaning *large* or *great*. It is abbreviated (and occurs most frequently) as ཐེག་ཆེན་. Those who practice the Great Vehicle are called བྱང་ཆུབ་སེམས་དཔའ་ (**c̲hang-chup-s̄ēm-b̄a**—Sanskrit *bodhisattva*); the goal they seek is the enlightenment of a Buddha.

- ཐེག་པ་དམན་པ་—abbreviated ཐེག་དམན་— is another NOUN-ADJECTIVE phrase, where དམན་པ་ means *lower* or *inferior*. There are two types of Lower Vehicle practitioners, ཉན་ཐོས་ (**nyën-thö>**—Sanskrit *śrāvaka*) and རང་རྒྱལ་ (**rang-gyël**—Sanskrit *pratyekabuddha*). Both attain the enlightenment of an Arhat.

ཉན་ཐོས་ and རང་རྒྱལ་ are *hearers* and *solitary conquerors*, respectively. Normally a conqueror (རྒྱལ་བ་ **gyël-wa**—Sanskrit *jina*) is a buddha, and in this case the Tibetan actually translates the *buddha* of *pratyekabuddha* as *conqueror*. However, despite the name, རང་རྒྱལ་ are not buddhas.

| ཉན་ཐོས་ | **nyën-thö>** | *hearer* |
|---|---|---|
| རང་རྒྱལ་ | **rang-gyël** | *solitary conqueror* |
| དགྲ་བཅོམ་པ་ | **d̲a-jom-b̄a** | *arhat* |
| བྱང་ཆུབ་སེམས་དཔའ་ | **c̲hang-chub-s̄ēm-b̄a** | *bodhisattva* |
| སངས་རྒྱས་ | **s̄ang-gyë>** | *buddha* |
| རྒྱལ་བ་ | **gyël-wa** | *conqueror [buddha]* |

Unlike the terms ཉན་ཐོས་ and རང་རྒྱལ་, which refer to both paths and goals, the word བྱང་ཆུབ་སེམས་དཔའ་ refers not to the goal but to the practitioner of the path. The goal is སངས་རྒྱས་. Further, although the Sanskrit word *sattva* by itself translates into Tibetan as སེམས་ཅན་ (*sentient being*), when *sattva* occurs in *bodhisattva* it is hierophanized as སེམས་དཔའ་, where དཔའ་ derives from དཔའ་བོ་ (b̄a-wo, *hero*). Thus, a བྱང་ཆུབ་སེམས་དཔའ་ is a *mind-hero [for the sake of] enlightenment*—or, less literally, a 'hero aspiring to enlightenment.'

Concerning hearers, solitary conquerors, and bodhisattvas, see Perdue, *Debate in Tibetan Buddhism*, pp. 365-367. For a more technical discussion, see Hopkins, *Meditation on Emptiness*, pp. 296-303.

## Results of the Paths

Another way of talking about cyclic existence and nirvana is to talk about embodiment. Sentient beings in cyclic existence take rebirth contingently, under the power of ignorance. Arhats have left cyclic existence, but do not take embodiment. Buddhas embody themselves voluntarily, both physically and mentally, in the three bodies (སྐུ་གསུམ་, ḡu s̄um) of buddhas:

- A ཆོས་སྐུ་ (abbreviating ཆོས་ཀྱི་སྐུ་, chö>-ḡyí ḡu—Sanskrit *dharmakāya*) is a *truth body*. Not a physical embodiment, it is a buddha's mind and its emptiness of inherent existence, that is, its selflessness.

- A ལོངས་སྐུ་ (abbreviating ལོངས་སྤྱོད་རྫོགས་པའི་སྐུ་, long-jö'-d̲zok-b̈ë ḡu—Sanskrit *sambhogakāya*) is a *complete enjoyment body*. Having its origin in the ཆོས་སྐུ་, it creates a *pure land* (དག་ཞིང་) outside of cyclic existence and appears to (and teaches) meditators in visions.

- སྤྲུལ་སྐུ་ (abbreviating སྤྲུལ་པའི་སྐུ་, ḍül-b̈ë ḡu—Sanskrit *nirmāṇakāya*) are *emanation bodies*. Creations of the ལོངས་སྐུ་, they are seen by ordinary people in cyclic existence. The historical buddha, Śākyamuni, is an example of a སྤྲུལ་སྐུ་.

སྤྲུལ་སྐུ་ (ḍül-ḡu) is the Tibetan word seen in English as 'tulku.'

On the embodiment of a buddha, see Jeffrey Hopkins, *Meditation on Emptiness*, pp. 117-123, Lobsang Lhalungpa, *The Life of Milarepa*, pp. xix-xxiv, and Rhie and Thurman, *Wisdom and Compassion: The Sacred Art of Tibet*, p. 35.

## Buddhas

There are three buddhas who epitomize the wisdom, compassion, and energy—མཁྱེན་ བརྩེ་ནུས་པ་—of the buddhas, the རིགས་གསུམ་མགོན་པོ་ (*protectors of the three lineages*): Manjushri, Avalokiteshvara, and Vajrapani.

| | | |
|---|---|---|
| འཇམ་དཔལ་ | **jam-bë(l)** | *Manjushri [Mañjuśrī]* |
| སྤྱན་རས་གཟིགས་ | **jën-rë>-s̲í(k)** | *Avalokiteshvara [Avalokiteśvara]* |
| ཕྱག་ན་རྡོ་རྗེ་ | **cha-na-dor-jé** | *Vajrapani [Vajrapaṇi]* |
| རིགས་ | **rík** | *family, lineage, type* |
| མགོན་པོ་ | **gön-b̄o** | *protector* |
| མཁྱེན་པ་ | **khyên-b̄a** | *knowledge, wisdom* [H] |
| བརྩེ་བ་ | **d̄zé-wa** | *compassion* |
| ནུས་པ་ | **nü>-b̄a** | *ability, power, energy* |

འཇམ་དཔལ་ (Sanskrit *Mañjuśrī*) is also known as འཇམ་པའི་དབྱངས་ (Skt. *Mañjughoṣa*). The two names are as often as not combined and written འཇམ་དཔལ་དབྱངས་. Manjushri symbolizes wisdom, Vajrapani energy, and Avalokiteshvara compassion. These three also appear—as bodhisattvas—in the *retinues* (འཁོར་) of other buddhas.

> The རིགས་གསུམ་མགོན་པོ་ are discussed collectively in Rhie and Thurman, *Wisdom and Compassion*, p. 68, and individually on pp. 68-69 (Vajrapani), 136-138 and 143 (Avalokiteshvara), and 139-140 (Manjushri).

The following table continues the listing of the names of buddhas (begun in Chapter Eleven) with a list of the principal meditational deities (ཡི་དམ་ **yi-dam**). Meditational deities are templates for meditators' generation of themselves (བདག་ བསྐྱེད་, *self generation*) in meditation as Buddhas.

| གསང་བ་འདུས་པ་ | **s̄ang-wa-dü>-b̄a** | *Guhyasamaja [Guhyasamāja]* |
| འཁོར་ལོ་སྡོམ་པ་ | **khor-lo-dom-b̄a** | *Chakrasamvara [Cakrasaṃvara]* |
| རྡོ་རྗེ་འཇིགས་བྱེད་ | **dor-jé-jík-jé'** | *Vajrabhairava [Vajrabhairava]* |
| ཀྱེ་རྡོ་རྗེ་ | **ḡyé dor-jé** | *Hevajra [Hevajra]* |
| རྡོ་རྗེ་རྣལ་འབྱོར་མ་ | **dor-jé ñël-jor-ma** | *Vajrayogini [Vajrayoginī]* |
| རྡོ་རྗེ་ཕག་མོ་ | **dor-jé pha-mo** | *Vajravarahi [Vajravarāhī]* |
| དུས་འཁོར་ | **tü>n-khor** | *Kalachakra [Kālacakra]* |
| རྟ་མགྲིན་ | **d̄an-d̂in** | *Hayagriva [Hayagrīva]* |
| རྡོ་རྗེ་ཕུར་པ་ | **dor-jé phur-b̄a** | *Vajrakila [Vakrakīla]* |

འཁོར་ལོ་སྡོམ་པ་ is also known as བདེ་མཆོག་ (*supreme bliss*) and as ཧེ་རུ་ཀ (Sanskrit *Heruka*). Vajrabhairava is also called གཤིན་རྗེ་གཤེད་ (Sanskrit *Yamāntaka*)—*slayer of the lord of the dead.* ཀྱེ་རྡོ་རྗེ་ is also called དགྱེས་པ་རྡོ་རྗེ་—*happy vajra.*

| བདེ་བ་ | **dé-wa** | *bliss* |
| མཆོག་ | **chok** | *supreme* |
| གཤིན་པོ་ | **s̄hîn-b̄o** | *those who have passed, the dead* |
| གཤིན་རྗེ་ | **s̄hîn-jé** | *Yama (lord of the dead)* |
| གཤེད་མ་ | **s̄hé'-ma** | *slayer* |
| དགྱེས་པ་ | **gyé>-b̄a** | *pleased, happy* |

The various meditational deities are discussed throughout Rhie and Thurman, *Wisdom and Compassion.* On Kalachakra, see also H. H. Tenzin Gyatso, *The Kālachakra Tantra: Rite of Initiation,* and Geshe Lhundup Sopa et al., *The Wheel of Time.*

# VOCABULARY

In addition to the words listed below, learn the names of the Buddhas listed in the
Doctrinal Vocabulary section.

## *Nouns*

| | | |
|---|---|---|
| ཀུན་ནས་ཉོན་མོངས་པ་ | ḡün-në>-nyön-mong-b̄a | thoroughly afflictive |
| མཁྱེན་པ་ | khyên-b̄a | knowledge, wisdom  [H] |
| དགོས་ཆེད་ | gö>-ché' | purposive-beneficial [case] |
| དགོས་པ་ | gö>-b̄a | purpose |
| མགོན་པོ་ | gön-b̄o | protector |
| ངེས་པ་ | ngé>-b̄a | certainty, definiteness, ascertainment |
| ངེས་པར་འབྱུང་བ་ | ngé>-b̄ar-jung-wa | renunciation |
| ངེས་པར་ཤེས་པ་ | ngé>-b̄ar-s̄hé>-b̄a | ascertainment, certain knowledge |
| མངོན་པར་རྟོགས་པ་ | n̄gön-b̄ar-d̄ok-b̄a | realization |
| མངོན་པར་ཤེས་པ་ | n̄gön-b̄ar-s̄hé>-b̄a | clairvoyance, paranormal knowledge |
| བཅོམ་ལྡན་འདས་ | j̄om-dën-dë> | Transcendent Victor |
| ཆོས་སྐུ་ | chö>-ḡu | truth body |
| རྗེས་སུ་དཔག་པ་ | j̄é>-s̄u-b̄ak-b̄a | inference |
| ཉེ་བར་ལེན་པ་ | nyé-war-lên-b̄a | appropriation, appropriated |
| ཉན་ཐོས་ | nyën-thö> | hearer [Skt. *śrāvaka*] |

| ཐེག་པ་ | **thék-b̄a** | vehicle  [Skt. *yāna*] |
| ཐེག་པ་དམན་པ་ | **thék-b̄a m̄ën-b̄a** | modest vehicle  [Skt. *hīnayāna*] |
| ནུབ་ | **nup** | west |
| ནུས་པ་ | **nü>-b̄a** | ability, power, energy |
| རྣམ་པ་ | **n̄am-b̄a** | aspect, type |
| རྣམ་པར་གྲོལ་བ་ | **n̄am-b̄ar-ḍöl-wa** | liberation |
| རྣམ་པར་རྟོག་པ་ | **n̄am-b̄ar-ḍok-b̄a** | conceptuality, thought |
| རྣམ་པར་དབྱེ་བ་ | **n̄am-b̄ar-ȳé-wa** | distinction, declension [case] |
| རྣམ་པར་བཞག་པ་ | **n̄am-b̄ar-s̲hak-b̄a** | presentation |
| རྣམ་པར་ཤེས་པ་ | **n̄am-b̄ar-s̄hé>-b̄a** | consciousness |
| སྤྲུལ་སྐུ་ | **ḍül-ḡu** | emanation body |
| སྤྲུལ་པ་ | **ḍül-b̄a** | emanation |
| ཕྱོགས་ | **chok** | direction, side, position [in debate] |
| བྱང་ | **c̲hang** | north [also verb meaning *purify*] |
| བྱེད་པ་པོ་ | **c̲hé'-b̄a-b̄o** | agent  ['doer'] |
| འབྱུང་ཁུངས་ | **jung-khung** | origin, source |
| འབྲེལ་བ་ | **ḍél-wa** | connection, relation |
| མིང་ | **míng** | name |
| མིང་ཙམ་ | **míng-ḏzam** | nominative [case] |
| བརྩེ་བ་ | **ḏzé-wa** | compassion |
| ཡོངས་སུ་གྲུབ་པ་ | **yong-s̄u-ḍup-b̄a** | thoroughly established [also adj.] |

| | | |
|---|---|---|
| ཡོངས་སུ་དག་པ་ | **yong-s̄u-tak-b̄a** | thoroughly pure [also adj.] |
| རབ་ཏུ་བྱུང་བ་ | **rap-d̄u-jung-wa** | going forth [becoming a monk] |
| རང་རྒྱལ་ | **rang-gyël** | solitary conqueror |
| རིགས་ | **rík** | family, lineage, type |
| ལས་སུ་བྱ་བ་ | **lë>-s̄u-cha-wa** | object, objective [case] |
| ལོངས་སྐུ་ | **long-ḡu** | complete enjoyment body |
| ལོངས་སྤྱོད་རྫོགས་པའི་སྐུ་ | **long-jö'-dzok-b̄ë-ḡu** | complete enjoyment body |
| ཤར་ | **s̄har** | east  [also verb meaning *appear*] |
| སོ་སོར་ཐར་པ་ | **s̄o-s̄or-thar-b̄a** | individual emancipation [Skt. *pratimokṣa*] |
| ལྷོ་ | **hlo** | south |

## Verbs

Verbs are marked by the Roman numeral indicating the class to which they belong—that is, the syntax they require.

| | | | |
|---|---|---|---|
| I | nominative-nominative | V | agentive-nominative |
| II | nominative-locative | VI | agentive-objective |
| III | nominative-objective | VII | purposive-nominative |
| IV | nominative-syntactic | VIII | locative-nominative |

The first part of the name of each class identifies the case of the subject and the second, that of the object, complement, or principal qualifier.  Thus, class **V** verbs are agentive verbs (that is, verbs whose subjects are marked by agentive case marking particles) with nominative or first case objects, whereas class **IV** verbs have nominative subjects and qualifiers marked by syntactic particles, and so on.

| | | |
|---|---|---|
| བཅོམ་ | **j̄om** | vanquished, defeated **V** |
| གནས་ | **n̄ë>** | stay, remain **II** |

| ལགས་ | la, lak | is I |
|---|---|---|

## Pronouns

| བདག་ | dak | I, me; self |
|---|---|---|
| བདག་ཅག་ | dak-jak | we, us |

## Adjectives

| ངོ་མཚར་ | ngo-tshar | amazing |
|---|---|---|
| ཀུན་ནས་ཉོན་མོངས་པ་ | ḡün-në>-nyön-mong-b̄a | thoroughly afflicted |
| ངེས་པ་ | ngé>-b̄a | definite, certain |
| སྡུག་པ་ | duk-b̄a | pleasant, attractive |
| རྣམ་པར་གྲོལ་བ་ | ñam-b̄ar-ḍöl-wa | liberated |
| མི་སྡུག་པ་ | mi-duk-b̄a | unpleasant, ugly |
| དམན་པ་ | m̄ën-b̄a | lesser, inferior, low |
| སོ་སོ་ | s̄o-s̄o | individual |

## Lexical Particles

| ཀུན་ཏུ་ ∗ | ḡün-d̄u- | [prefix particle] |
|---|---|---|
| ཀུན་ནས་ ∗ | ḡün-në>- | [prefix particle] |
| ངེས་པར་ ∗ | n̄gé>-b̄ar- | [prefix particle] |
| མངོན་པར་ ∗ | n̄gön-b̄ar- | [prefix particle] |
| རྗེས་སུ་ ∗ | jé>-s̄u- | [prefix particle] |
| ཉེ་བར་ ∗ | nyé-war- | [prefix particle] |

| ༚ དང་ལྡན་པ་ | dang-dën-b̄a | possessing * |
| རྣམ་པར་ ༚ | ñam-b̄ar- | [prefix particle] |
| ཡོངས་སུ་ ༚ | yong-s̄u- | [prefix particle] |
| ༚ ལ་སོགས་པ་ | la-s̄ok-b̄a | * and so on, such as * |

## Syntactic Particles

Learn the agentive and connective case marking particles listed in the chapter. Memorize the way in which they follow suffix letters.

# *Chapter 13*

*Verbs of Existence*
*Agentive Case Marking Particles*
*Locative and Objective Case Paradigms*
*The Four Truths: True Sufferings*
  *Aggregates • Sources • Constituents*

---

## Nominative Verbs
### *Verbs of Existence*

---

One of the great merits of the Tibetan language is that the verb of existence is *not* also a linking verb. In English one can use—it might be better to say, one *has* to use—the same verb (*be*) in two different and often confusing ways.

- *I think, therefore I am* is a case of the verb *be* used to indicate existence; it means *I think, therefore I exist.*

- *I am a human being*, on the other hand, is a case of the same verb used as a linking verb.

An interesting point about the English verb *be* is that one can use it in this second way—as a linking verb—without necessarily implying existence. One can say *A square circle is a strange shape* without the verb *is* implying that square circles exist.[101] In Tibetan, on the other hand, there are two different verbs.

ཡིན་, the linking verb, does not imply existence.

ཡོད་, the verb of existence, cannot be used as a linking verb.

The simplest examples of ཡོད་ sentences have only two parts, exemplifying the most basic Tibetan syntax:  SUBJECT + VERB.

| | | |
|---|---|---|
| གཟུགས་ཡོད། | **s̲uk yö'** | *Forms exist.* |
| ང་ཡོད། | **nga yö'** | *I exist.* |
| ལྔ་ཡོད། | ** n̄ga yö'** | *Five exist.*  [literal]<br>*There are five.*  [English syntax] |

Their analysis is equally simple:

## Drill 13.1

These sentences have been constructed using words from the vocabularies of previous chapters.  Practice reading and speaking them.  Identify their dots and translate them.  Diagram the third and fourth with boxes and arrows.

[1]  སངས་རྒྱས་ཡོད།

[2]  མེ་དང་རྟ་ཡོད།

[3]  སངས་རྒྱས་དང་དགྲ་བཅོམ་པ་བྱང་ཆུབ་སེམས་དཔའ་གསུམ་ཡོད།

[4]  ཆོག་བཅས་དང་ཆོག་མེད་ཀྱི་བློ་ཡོད།

[5]  ས་ཆུ་མེ་རླུང་ཡོད།

## Patterns in Tibetan Clauses and Sentences
### *Qualifiers*

Since a sentence ending in a verb of existence is so simple, it is an ideal foundation for introducing something a bit more complex. Many clauses and sentences add at least one qualifying element to their minimal syntax. In the case of verbs of existence, this gives us the following (with the optional qualifying element enclosed in brackets):

[ QUALIFIER ]→       SUBJECT →       ← VERB

**Qualifiers** (also called **modifiers**) are typically either:

1    words, phrases, or clauses stating such qualifications as the time when or the place where something exists or is done (for example, བོད་ལ་ in བོད་ལ་རི་ཡོད། —*There are mountains in Tibet*);

2    adverbs or adverbial words, phrases, or clauses (such as the བདེན་པར་ in ཆོས་བདེན་པར་མེད། —*Phenomena do not truly exist*);

3    phrases or clauses stating conditions or reasons (for example, སྒྲ་རྟག་པ་ཡིན་ ན་ —*If sound were permanent, ...*);[102]

4    words, phrases, or clauses ending in continuative syntactic particles that indicate either a contemporaneous action or a previous action (such as སངས་རྒྱས་ཀྱིས་ཆོས་བསྟན་ནས་ —*Buddha, having taught the doctrine, ...*).

The following illustrates the simplest sort of nominative verb construction, SUBJECT + VERB.

| | | |
|---|---|---|
| བྱང་ཆུབ་སེམས་དཔའ་ཡོད། | **c̱hang-chup-s̄ēm-b̄a  yö'** | *Bodhisattva(s) exist.* |

Adding a modifier explaining where Bodhisattvas exist yields the following, which could be translated either *There are Bodhisattvas in Tibet* or *Bodhisattvas are present in Tibet*. As before, the numbers at the top are for reference purposes.

| | |
|---|---|
| བོད་ལ་  བྱང་ཆུབ་སེམས་དཔའ་  ཡོད། | TIBET-IN  BODHISATTVA  EXIST |

| 1 2 | | 3 4 5 6 | | 7 |
|---|---|---|---|---|
| C  C | | S   S   S   NOM | | VB |
| བོད་ལ་ → | | བྱང་ཆུབ་སེམས་དཔའ་ → | | ← ཡོད། |

Dots 1 and 2—C dots—here bracket the case marking particle ལ་.

> The cases or declensions indicated by the particle ལ་ are the second, fourth, and
> seventh—the objective, beneficial, and locative cases.

Fortunately, these cases are used in specifically defined situations, and indicate a
limited number of relationships between a noun, pronoun, or adjective and the rest
of the sentence. In fact, they almost always relate one of those words to a verb. The
options in the present example may be narrowed very quickly.

> Most instances of a noun or pronoun followed by the case particle ལ་ in a sen-
> tence ending in ཡོད་ are instances of those usages of the locative case indicating
> possession or place of existence.

Since the noun in question is བོད་ (*Tibet*), it is not reasonable to speak of possession. (The convention used here will be that people possess things, whereas places
and things do not.)

> Verbs of possession are specialized verbs. In the sentences that they end,
> the locative case marking particle marks the subject, not the qualifier. Verbs
> of possession are analyzed in Chapter Fourteen.

This leaves us with that usage of the locative indicating a place of existence.
Translated in a slavishly literal manner, the sentence reads *In Tibet Bodhisattvas exist*. This is better expressed as *There are Bodhisattvas in Tibet*.

བོད་ལ་བྱང་ཆུབ་སེམས་དཔའ་ཡོད། exemplifies the pattern QUALIFIER + SUBJECT + VERB.
However, it is also syntactically permissible to say བྱང་ཆུབ་སེམས་དཔའ་བོད་ལ་ཡོད།, that is,
SUBJECT + QUALIFIER + VERB. There are two rules to be learnt from this. Rule
one has to do with the position taken in a clause or sentence by subjects, objects,
and qualifiers.

> The general rule is that the subject of a sentence comes first.

Nonetheless, the subject of the sentence བོད་ལ་ཤུང་ཆུབ་སེམས་དཔའ་ཡོད།, the noun ཤུང་ཆུབ་ སེམས་དཔའ་, is not the first element in this sentence. The first new rule that this construction introduces, then, is one that in some instances modifies the general rule.

> Placing a word at the beginning of a clause or sentence *may* indicate emphasis.

Thus, if a writer or speaker wishes to stress the subject, as would often be the case, it most likely will come first. However, if an object or qualifier is being emphasized—if the object or qualifier of the sentence is what that sentence is really about—then that object or qualifier might precede the subject, taking the initial position in the sentence.

There is one common situation in which this modification does not apply, and that is in the case of sentences or clauses ending in linking verbs such as ཡིན་.

> The complement of a linking verb may not be stated before its subject, so their positions are fixed.

The second new rule has specifically to do with the syntax of clauses and sentences ending in verbs of existence like ཡོད་. Such verbs have no object—they do not perform an action on something else. Nor do such verbs have a complement as do the linking verbs—you cannot use them to say that something is something. Thus, the syntax operative with verbs of existence is one of the following two:

[ QUALIFIER ]→    SUBJECT →    ← VERB

SUBJECT →    [ QUALIFIER ]→    ← VERB

A syntax you will *never* see is VERB + SUBJECT (ཡོད་ཤུང་ཆུབ་སེམས་དཔའ།); nor will you see SUBJECT + VERB + QUALIFIER (ཤུང་ཆུབ་སེམས་དཔའ་ཡོད་བོད་ལ།).[103]

Here is another example of a locative qualifier with ཡོད.

| ཕུམ་པ་ འདིར་ ཡོད། | **pum-ba dír yö'** | *The pot is here.* *There is a pot here.* |

The qualifier in this sentence is the adjective འདི (*this*) marked by the case ending ར.

---

ར is one of the so-called ལ-particles, the case particles used to mark the second, fourth, and seventh cases. The particle ར (which is actually a suffix) is used when a word ends in a suffixless syllable.

---

In the present example, the case-marking suffix ར marks འདི as being in the seventh or locative case; it then no longer means *this*, but *here*.

## Adverb Qualifiers

In the following illustration the qualifier is an adverb.

| ཕུམ་པ་ བདེན་པར་ ཡོད། | **pum-ba dên-bar yö'** | *The pot truly exists.* *Pots exist truly.* |

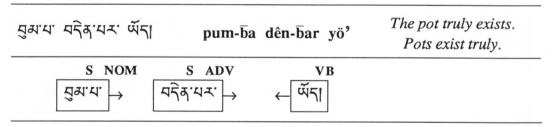

This is an instance of a noun (བདེན་པ, *truth*) made into an adverb with the addition of the suffix ར. This is technically an instance of the usage of the second case; however, it is such a specialized usage that it is labelled here with the **AD**Verb dot, not the Case or the **2** dot.

> This sentence, by the way, states an assertion unacceptable to most Tibetan Buddhist philosophers, who, following the Consequentialist Middle Way School (*Prāsaṅgika Mādhyamika*—in Tibetan, དབུ་མ་ཐལ་འགྱུར་བ), deny that anything exists truly or exists independently of any relation to its parts.

## *Negating the Verb* ཡོད།

The negative of ཡོད་ is མེད་. Unlike the negation of ཡིན་ (as མ་ཡིན་), one does not add a syntactic particle to ཡོད་ in order to negate the verb.

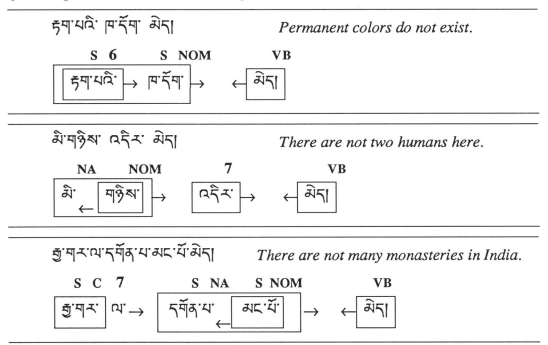

In the first example— རྟག་པའི་ཁ་དོག་མེད། —the connective particle འི་ in རྟག་པའི་ indicates an adjectival relationship: *colors which are permanent* or *permanent colors*.

Remember that *permanent colors* in Buddhist philosophy are not colors that do not wash away with water, but rather colors that do not disintegrate moment by moment. Thus, in fact, there are no permanent colors.

Although some feel that the connective case ought always to be translated *of*, it has in fact eighteen documented usages, only some of which are properly translated as *of*.[104] Were the connective translated as *of* in the present example, we would have *the color of permanence*; such a translation makes literal sense (and is grammatically parallel to བུམ་པའི་ཁ་དོག་, *the color of a pot*), but does not exhaust the possibilities of the phrase. Here, རྟག་པའི་ཁ་དོག་ is parallel to རྟག་པའི་དངོས་པོ་ (*permanent thing—a thing* which is permanent) and this is how a reader trained in Buddhist philosophy (མཚན་ ཉིད་, *definitions*) would understand it.

Like རྟག་པའི་ཁ་དོག་, རྟག་པའི་དངོས་པོ་ is a contradiction in terms (for all except the Great Exposition School). There are no permanent དངོས་པོ་; དངོས་པོ་ and མི་རྟག་ པ་ are equivalents.

In the second example— མི་གཉིས་འདིར་མེད་ —the qualifier is འདིར་; it means *here* and is in the locative case. (Locatives are discussed in more detail later in this chapter.) In the last example— རྒྱ་གར་ལ་དགོན་པ་མང་པོ་མེད་ —the qualifier is རྒྱ་གར་ལ་, where the ལ་ again indicates the locative case.

## Drill 13.2

Translate the following into Tibetan.

1. There are no humans in the formless realm.
2. There are not many elephants in the West.
3. There are no hungry ghosts in a pure land.

## Drill 13.3

Translate the following sentences. Diagram the first and identify its dots.

1. བྱང་ཕྱོགས་ལ་གླང་ཆེ་མེད།
2. འཕགས་པའི་ཡི་གེས་ལ་ཟག་བཅས་ཀྱི་བློ་མེད།
3. ཁོངས་སྐྱེད་ཚོགས་པའི་སྐུ་ལ་དྲི་མ་མེད།
4. སོ་སོའི་སྐྱེ་བོའི་རྒྱུད་ལ་སྙིང་རྗེ་ཆེན་པོ་མེད།

## *Verbs of Existence Other than* ཡོད་

Other verbs of existence include འདུག་, མཆིས་, གདའ་ and མངའ་. The first may also be used to mean *sit* (not the action of sitting down, but rather sitting in place—as, for example, in a discussion of meditative posture).[105] It is used (in its meaning of *existence*) more in colloquial language than in the literary and religious language, and it is used colloquially in a more precise way—as a verb of existence in second and third person situations (***There are nomads in Tibet***) and as a verbal modifier marking second and third person present tense actions (*She is sowing barley*).

In the literary language, you may see འདུག་ in the same contexts in which ཡོད་ is found, and also as a verbal modifier used to intensify other verbs. For example, you may see not just ཡིན་, but ཡིན་པར་འདུག་. Such an addition of འདུག་ is read as emphasizing or adding certainty to the verb.

The negative of འདུག་ is མི་འདུག་, pronounced **mîn-duk**.

More frequently seen are མཆིས་ and མ་མཆིས་ used with the meaning of ཡོད་ and མེད་, respectively.[106]

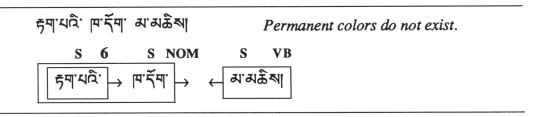

Permanent colors do not exist.

---

## Drill 13.4

Translate the following into Tibetan.

1. There are oceans and mountains in the world.
2. There are large rivers in Tibet.
3. There is a middle way.
4. There are no afflictions in a Buddha's truth body.

## Drill 13.5

Identify the dots in the following and translate. Diagram the third.

1   ལས་དགེ་བ་དང་མི་དགེ་བ་གཉིས་ཡོད།

2   བལ་ཡུལ་ལ་རྒྱ་མཚོ་མ་མཆིས།

3   རྒྱ་པོ་ཆེན་པོ་རྒྱ་གར་ལ་མི་གདའ།

4   དངོས་པོ་ལ་རྒྱུ་དང་འབྲས་བུ་མང་པོ་ཡོད།

5   སྙིང་རྗེ་ཆེན་པོ་ཉིན་ཐོས་ལ་མེད།   བྱང་ཆུབ་སེམས་དཔའ་ལ་ཡོད།

## Pattern Analysis
### *Reading a Sentence by Analyzing Dots*

Although very useful, dot analysis can become complicated. Before getting too far, it might be good to lay out a few guidelines for this kind of analysis. These guidelines are presented with the idea that as a beginner you should read through a sentence several times, each time looking for something different.

1   In the first pass through a Tibetan sentence you should identify as many of the **S** dots as you can. This is a function of your vocabulary—what you are really doing is picking out the multi-syllable words and particles you know and identifying their internal syllables.

---

        **S**                     **S   S**

འདོད་ པའི་ ཁམས་ ལ་ ལྷ་ དང་ ལྷ་ མ་ ཡིན་ གཉིས་ ཡོད།

---

2   In the second pass through the sentence, identify the syntactic particles and case marking particles;  mark the dots before and after them as **SP** and **C** dots, respectively. Since connective, agentive, and originative case marking particles are unique (that is, each is used to mark only one

case—although they may also be used as syntactic particles), they may be marked **6**, **3**, and **5**, respectively.

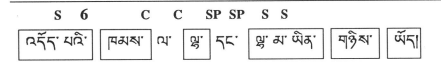

3    In the third pass, put small boxes around the words. Words include substantives (nouns and pronouns), adjectives, and verbs. Case and syntactic particles should not be put in boxes by themselves.

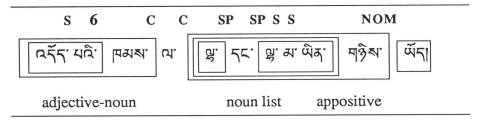

4    In the fourth pass, identify the noun phrases and box them. (The arrows have been left off in this illustration due to lack of space.) Mark the noun phrases that have no case marking particles after them with the **NOM** dot.

adjective-noun                noun list        appositive

5    In the fifth pass, identify the terminal verbs at the ends of sentences and the open verbs at the ends of clauses. Tibetan sentences always end in verbs although, as you have seen, sometimes the verb is not visible—it may be hidden or "understood." For the present, assume that a sentence will always end in a visible verb. The dot after the verb is a **VB** dot, and the box around the verb has an arrow on its left side, one pointing towards the beginning of the sentence. The dot after an open verb (for example, the verbal at the end of a clause) is a **V** dot.

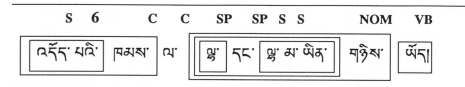

At this point you must determine what *type* of verb ends the sentence, for this in turn determines how the subject, complement (or object), and any modifiers function in the sentence. Once you know what type of verb ends the sentence, you will know what case particles to look for in the rest of the sentence.

6   Based on your knowledge of the basic syntaxes used with the three categories of verbs and, within that, the nine classes of verbs, identify the subjects, objects, complements, and qualifiers. Mark the dots after ambivalent case marking particles (such as ལ་) with the most likely case numbers.

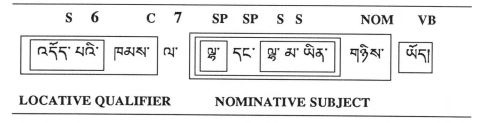

In actual practice, once you have developed a reasonable vocabulary and have some experience with different types of sentences and clauses, you will be able to do this analysis in one or two passes. You may also find that a different order of analysis suits you better.

> Memorize the order to be followed in an analysis of dots:
> Pass 1: **S** dots;
> Pass 2: **SP** and **C** dots;
> Pass 3: box the words;
> Pass 4: identify the noun phrases and mark the **NOM** dots;
> Pass 5: mark the **VB** and **V** dots; identify verb type;
> Pass 6: identify the syntactic elements (subject, etc.) of the sentence.

# Case Marking Particles
## *Agentive Case Paradigms*

There are five agentive case marking particles: གིས་, ཀྱིས་, གྱིས་, འིས་, and ཡིས་.

> Like the connective case particles གི་ and ཀྱི་, the agentive particles གིས་ and ཀྱིས་ are naturally unstressed syllables and, therefore, are pronounced **gí>** and **gyí>**, respectively.

Agentive case marking particles have three usages *as case marking particles*.

1  Agentives are used to mark the subjects of many action verbs; as such, they often do not require translation as separate words, although in some contexts they may be translated as *by*.

2  They are used to indicate the means by which something is done, translating, as a rule of thumb, into *by*, *through*, or *by means of*.

3  They are used to show reasons—translating into *because of*.

## *Agentive Agents*

The strongest way to express action in Tibetan is to use an agentive verb. In the following construction, the agent (or subject) is in the agentive case and the object is in the nominative case.

| subject of agentive verb | སངས་རྒྱས་ཀྱིས་ ཆོས་ བསྟན། |
|---|---|

***Buddha** taught the doctrine.*

The case marking particle ཀྱིས་ (**gyí>**) placed after the noun སངས་རྒྱས་ marks it as a word in the agentive case.

Note in the predicate of this sentence that ཆོས་ (*dharma, doctrine*) is the object of the verb བསྟན་ (**dën**, *taught*) and is in the first case. This introduces another type of nominative usage: the nominative object of an agentive-nominative verb.

While all agentive verbs take objects, not all require those objects to be in the nominative case. There are two classes of verbs whose subjects are indicated by agentive case marking particles:

Class V      agentive-nominative verbs (such as བསྟན་);

Class VI     agentive-objective verbs (such as ལྟ་, *look*).

The following is an example of a sentence with an agentive subject and an object in the objective case.

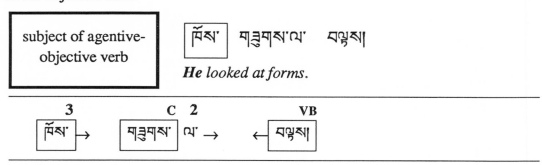

*He looked at forms.*

The first word, ཁོ་, is the subject (becoming ཁོས་ in the agentive). The objective case is marked by one or another of the *la*-group of particles: སུ་  ར་  ཏུ་  དུ་  ན་  ར་  ལ་. བལྟས་ is the past tense form of the verb ལྟ་, a verb that regularly takes an agentive subject and a second case object.

## *The Lexical Dimension of Agentive Case Markers*

There are five agentive case markers—the connective case endings with the addition of ས་ suffixes. Although they have the same syntactic meaning (that is, they mark the same relationships—agency, means, and logical entailment), they are not inter-changeable *lexically*. The criteria for their use—that is, what suffix letters they follow—are identical to those of the connective case markers. གིས་ (**gí>**) is thus used after a word whose final syllable ends in either ག་ or ང་.

ཁ་ཅིག་གིས་    འདོད་པ་                               *asserted **by someone** / **someone's** assertion*

This is a very common construction in philosophical literature, usually with an object or complement between the ཁ་ཅིག་ (*someone, a certain person*) and the འདོད་ (*assert, wish*).

ཀྱིས་ (ḡyí>) is used after a word whose final syllable ends in either ད་, བ་, or ས་.

| སངས་རྒྱས་ཀྱིས་ | གསུངས་པ་ | *said by Buddha* / what *Buddha* said |

གྱིས་ (gyí>) is used after a word whose final syllable ends in either ན་, མ་, ར་, or ལ་.

| ལས་ངན་གྱིས་ | འཕངས་པ་ | *propelled by bad actions* |

*Propulsion* (literally, *being shot*—as one shoots an arrow with a bow) refers to the way in which present experience is the result of previous *karma* (ལས་).

ཞིས་ (í>) merges with final syllables that end in འ་ or that have no suffix letter. In so doing, the འི་ is lost and only the ས་ remains.

| འཕགས་པས་ | མཁྱེན་པ་ | *understood by the Superiors* / *that which* Superiors *understand* |

ཡིས་ (yí>) is used *after* a word whose final syllable either ends in འ་ or has no suffix letter. Thus, any situation in which ཞིས་ may be used also allows the use of ཡིས་. This is most frequently seen in lines of verse that require an extra syllable to complete the meter.

| འཕགས་པ་ཡིས་ | མཁྱེན་པ་ | *understood by the Superiors* / *that which* Superiors *understand* |

## *Summary*

Memorize these rules for the proper usage of agentive case marking particles.

- གིས་ (**gí>**) is used after a word whose final syllable ends in either ག་ or ང་.

- གྱིས་ (**g̱yí>**) is used after a word whose final syllable ends in either ད་, བ་, or ས་.

- ཀྱིས་ (**gyí>**) is used after a word whose final syllable ends in either ན་, མ་, ར་, or ལ་.

- འིས་ (**í>**) merges with final syllables that end in འ་ or that have no suffix letter.

- ཡིས་ (**yí>**) is used *after* a word whose final syllable either ends in འ་ or has no suffix letter.

## Case Marking Particles
### *Locative Case Paradigms*

Whereas the third (agentive), sixth (connective), and fifth (originative) case marking particles are unique in that each set marks only one case, the *la* group of particles mark more than one case.

---

སུ་, ཙུ་, དུ་, རུ་, ན་, ར་ and ལ་ are the *la* group of particles. They are used to mark the second, the fourth, *and* the seventh case.

---

The situation, unfortunately, is not quite that clear. Many of the *la* group, all of the connective and agentive particles, and both originative particles may sometimes be used in non-case-marking ways. (See Appendix Seven.)

At any rate, the particles སུ་, ཙུ་, དུ་, རུ་, ན་, ར་, and ལ་ have five usages *as particles marking the locative case.*

1    Locatives are used to mark the **place** where something exists (but *not* the place where something is *done*).

2    More universally, locatives indicate both the **time** when something exists
     *and* the time when something is done.

3    Locatives are used to mark the **subject who possesses** something (the *I*
     in *I have a book*).

4    The **'place' upon which something depends** (the *causes* in *Effects de-
     pend on causes*) is indicated by a locative case marking particle.

5    There is also a set of **referential** locative usages that mark very broad
     relations with other parts of clauses and sentences—one that marks what
     in English would be section headings or chapter titles, and one that
     translates roughly as *about*, *with regard to*, or *in the context of*.

The usage of the locative with verbs of existence and verbs of living is clearly a
'locative'—in the sense that the locative particle marks the place where someone or
something exists or lives or remains.

| place of existing or living | བོད་ལ་ | རི་མང་པོ་ ཡོད། |

*There are many mountains **in Tibet**.*

Unlike the locative place of existence or living—which is used only with those two
types of verbs—the locative of time may be used with any verb.  In the following
example, it is used with the verb བསྟན་.

| locative of time | ཉི་མ་ཕར་བ་ན་ | ཆོས་ བསྟན། |

*[He] taught the doctrine **when the sun rose**.*

The locative clause modifies the verb བསྟན་, telling the reader when the doctrine was taught.  Within the clause itself, the syntax is NOMINATIVE
SUBJECT + NOMINATIVE ACTION VERB.

As you will see in Chapter Fourteen, in Tibetan one uses the same verb to speak of
both what would in English be possession and existence.  Verbs of possession have
locative subjects—that is, the possessor is stated in the locative case.

| | |
|---|---|
| subject of verb of possession | དགྲ་བཅོམ་པ་ལ་ ཉོན་མོངས་ མེད། <br> **Arhats** *do not have afflictions.* |

The qualifiers in clauses and sentences ending in verbs of dependence are in the locative case. The example below was introduced previously (in Chapter Twelve) as a paradigm for Class II nominative-locative verbs.

| | |
|---|---|
| place of dependence | འབྲས་བུ་ རྒྱུ་ལ་ བརྟེན་ནོ། <br> *Effects depend* **on causes.** |

The topical locative indicates block language—a word or phrase that is not connected grammatically to the material following it.

| | |
|---|---|
| topical locative | དང་པོ་ལ་ <br> **The first** *[is as follows].* |

## The Lexical Dimension of Case Marking Particles
### *Second, Fourth, and Seventh Case Markers*

There are seven locative case markers: སུ་, ར་, ཏུ་, དུ་, ན་, ར་, and ལ་. As noted earlier, they are identical to the markers used to mark the second (objective) and fourth (purposive-beneficial) cases. The criteria for their use—that is, the suffix letters each follows—differs from those determining proper use of the agentive and connective case markers. Whereas, for example, the connective case marker ཀྱི་ follows a word whose final syllable ends in either ད་ བ་, or ས་, syllables ending in ད་ are followed by the *la*-particle དུ་, those ending in བ་ are followed by ཏུ་, and those ending in ས་ are followed by སུ་.

སུ་ (**su**) is used only after a word whose final syllable ends in ས་—either the suffix or the secondary suffix.

---

| ཤར་ཕྱོགས་སུ་ |
|---|

*in the eastern direction*

---

དུ་ (**du**) is used after a word whose final syllable ends in ག་, བ་, or the secondary suffix ད་.

---

| ཀུན་རྫོབ་ཏུ་ | ཡོད་པ་ |
|---|---|

*conventionally existent*

---

The phrase ཀུན་རྫོབ་ཏུ་ illustrates the adverbial use of the second case. How does it exist? Conventionally—or, alternatively, *as a convention*.

ཀུན་རྫོབ་ literally means *thoroughly covered*, but its central use in Buddhist philosophy is in the term ཀུན་རྫོབ་ཀྱི་བདེན་པ་ (*conventional truths*). ཀུན་རྫོབ་བདེན་པ་ and དོན་དམ་བདེན་པ་ (*ultimate truths*) are the two truths, a way of talking about all phenomena in terms of how they exist.

དུ་ (**du**) is used after a word whose final syllable ends in either ང་, ད་, ན་, མ་, ར་, or ལ་.

---

> Recall that because a case marking particle is an unstressed syllable, it is pronounced with no aspiration.

---

Thus, the following example is pronounced **rang-gi dün-du** and not **dün-tu**.

---

| རང་གི་ | མདུན་དུ་ |
|---|---|

*in front of one*

---

Be aware that not all syllables end as they seem to, at least as far as lexicographers are concerned. Thus, whereas the suffix ན་ is to be followed by the case marking particle དུ་ (as seen just above), and not by ཏུ་, you have already seen the following usage.

| གུན་ཏུ་བཟང་པོ་ | | *Samantabhadra,* **thoroughly** *good* |

Clearly the word གུན་ is actually གུནད་. The secondary suffix ད་ is rarely spelled out. ར་ merges with final syllables that end in འ་ or that have no suffix letter.

| རྒྱ་མཚོར་ | ཡོད་པ་ | *exists* **in the ocean** |

རུ་ (**ru**) follows final syllables that end in འ་ or that have no suffix letter.

| བདེན་པ་རུ་ | ཡོད་པ་ | *exists* **truly** |

ན་ and ལ་ may be used after any suffix letter.

| ཉི་མ་ཤར་བ་ན་ | | **when the sun rose** |
| བོད་ལ་ | | **in Tibet** |

## Summary

Memorize these rules for the proper usage of the *la*-group of case marking particles.

- སུ་ (**su**) is used after a word whose final syllable ends in ས་, that is, the suffix letter and the root letter of the particle are the same.
- ཏུ་ (**du**) is used after a word whose final syllable ends in either ག་, བ་, or the secondary suffix ད་.
- དུ་ (**du**) is used after a word whose final syllable ends in any of the nasal suffix syllables—ང་, ན་, or མ་—or in ད་, ར་, or ལ་.
- ར་ merges with final syllables that end in འ་ or that have no suffix letter.
- རུ་ (**ru**) is used *after* a word whose final syllable either ends in འ་ or has no suffix letter.
- ན་ and ལ་ may be used after any suffix syllable.

# Case Marking Particles
## *Objective Case Paradigms*

The place where something is done (that is, the place where an action verb's action is done) is not in the locative, but the objective case.

| | |
|---|---|
| objective place of activity | རྒྱ་གར་ལ་ *Buddha taught the doctrine in India.* |

The phrase རྒྱ་གར་ལ་ (*in India*) is syntactically the QUALIFIER in this sentence. The objective case is also used to mark the OBJECT of certain types of verbs (including, but not limited to, agentive-objective verbs), and the DESTINATION of verbs of motion.

Some agentive action verbs regularly take their object not in the nominative, but in the objective case. These are the agentive-objective verbs.

| | |
|---|---|
| object of agentive-objective verbs | གཟུགས་ལ་ *He looked at forms with [his] eye[s].* |

Given the name of the second case—ལས་སུ་བྱ་བ་ or *objective*—the syntax just exemplified would seem to be the normal manner in which verbs operate. Nevertheless, they do not. Many agentive verbs take nominative, and not objective objects.

Verbs of motion are distinguished from other verbs of the nominative class in that they have destinations. These destinations are marked not by locative, but by objective case particles.

| | |
|---|---|
| destination of a verb of motion | བོད་ལ་ *The Foremost Lord [Atiśa] arrived in Tibet.* |

བྱོན་ (**chön**) is the past tense form of the verb འབྱོན་ (*come, arrive*).

For a list of all usages of the objective case, with examples, see Appendix Five.

## Lexical Particles
### *Possessive and Separative Particles*

There are two groups of **verbal particles** among the lexical particles. One group, discussed in the next section, is that of the negative verbal particles མེན་ and མེད་. The other group consists of the particles ending in the verbals བཅས་པ་ (jë>-ba, *possessing, along with*), ལྡན་པ་ (dën-ba, *possessing*), and བྲལ་བ་ (tël-wa, *lacking* or *separated from*). Of the three, བྲལ་ especially is used as a verb, but the other two are technically verbs as well, even though their main usage is in their verbal forms, as parts of the constructions being analyzed now.[107] Thus, the constructions དང་བཅས་པ་, དང་ལྡན་པ་, and དང་བྲལ་བ་ are **verbal** particles.

These three lexical particles make words that are either nouns or adjectives.

- བློ་གྲོས་དང་ལྡན་པ་ (abbreviated བློ་ལྡན་) is, depending on context, either a subject noun meaning *one possessed of intelligence* or an adjective meaning *intelligent*. The word བློ་གྲོས་ means *intelligence*.
- ཟག་པ་དང་བཅས་པ་ (ཟག་བཅས་) is an adjective meaning *contaminated*. ཟག་པ་ means *contamination*, in the sense that desire, hatred, and their objects contaminate the mind.
- ས་བོན་དང་བཅས་པ་ is an adjective meaning *along with [their] seeds*. For example, the phrase ཉོན་མོངས་ས་བོན་དང་བཅས་པ་ means *the afflictions* (ཉོན་མོངས་— Sanskrit *kleśa*) *together with their seeds* (ས་བོན་—Sanskrit *bīja*). ས་བོན་དང་བཅས་པ་ is here an adjective, modifying the noun ཉོན་མོངས་.
- མཐའ་དང་བྲལ་བ་, or མཐའ་བྲལ་, means *free of extremes*. Buddhism presents itself as a middle way, *free from the two extremes* (མཐའ་གཉིས་དང་བྲལ་བ་).
- བདེ་བ་དང་བྲལ་བ་, in the same way, means *bereft of happiness*. Following the seventh exception to the pronunciation rules, བྲལ་—as part of the particle དང་བྲལ་བ་—loses its aspiration, becoming **dël-wa**, and དང་, when it is part of a larger unit such as བདེ་བ་དང་བྲལ་བ་, becomes **dang**.

Some words are given special meanings by these constructions. For example, དགའ་ ལྡན་ (**gan-dën**, literally *possessing joy*) is the Tibetan for *Tuṣita, The Joyous,* the name of the heaven in which a Buddha lives before appearing in the human world as a Buddha. It does not occur as དགའ་བ་དང་ལྡན་པ་. མཚན་ཉིད་ means *characteristic* and *definition,* and thus མཚན་ཉིད་དང་ལྡན་པ་ does mean *possessing characteristics,* but has the sense of having all the requisite characteristics to be or do something. For example, a བླ་མ་མཚན་ཉིད་དང་ལྡན་པ་ is a *fully qualified guru.*

## Lexical Particles
### *Negative Verbal Particles*

The negative *verbal* particles are མིན་ and མེད་—derived from the negative linking verb མིན་ (*is not*) and the negative verb of existence མེད་ (*does not exist*). The two are used widely.[108]

- ● བདག་མེད་ (**dak-mé'**, *selfless, the selfless, selflessness*—Sanskrit *anātma*) is the key term in Buddhist philosophy and meditation. It literally means *self* (བདག་) *not existing.*

- ● གཉིས་མེད་, really གཉིས་སུ་མེད་པ་, means *non-dual.* The syntactic particle སུ་ is, in this instance, an adverbial marker showing how something does not exist—*not as two.*

- ● Where བཅོས་མ་ is an adjective meaning *artificial,* བཅོས་མ་མ་ཡིན་པ་—abbreviated བཅོས་མིན་—means *genuine.*

- ● Just about any word may be negated with མ་ཡིན་པ་ or མིན་—བུམ་པ་མ་ཡིན་པ་, for example, means *non-pot.* An illustration of a word always incorporating མིན་ is འོག་མིན་ (translating the Sanskrit *Akaniṣṭha,* the name of a pure land). འོག་མིན་ literally means *the not low* (where འོག་མ་ means *low*).

## Doctrinal Vocabulary and Grammar
### *The Four Truths*

In Chapters Ten, Eleven, and Twelve, the vocabulary of cyclic existence and nirvana was introduced. Another more traditional way of presenting the same material is in the context of the four truths (བདེན་པ་བཞི་, **dên-b̄a shí**). Most English writers speak of the *four noble truths*, but in the Tibetan tradition they are the *four truths of superiors* (འཕགས་པའི་བདེན་པ་བཞི་, **phak-b̄ë dên-b̄a shí**), in the sense that those who have seen selflessness directly teach these as truths.[109]

| | | |
|---|---|---|
| སྡུག་བསྔལ་གྱི་བདེན་པ་ | **duk-n̄gël-gyí dên-b̄a** | *truths* (that is, *true things*) *that are unsatisfactory* |
| ཀུན་འབྱུང་གི་བདེན་པ་ | **ḡün-jung-gí dên-b̄a** | *truths that are sources* |
| འགོག་པའི་བདེན་པ་ | **gok-b̄ë dên-b̄a** | *truths that are cessations* |
| ལམ་གྱི་བདེན་པ་ | **lam-gyí dên-b̄a** | *truths that are paths* |

> ཀུན་འབྱུང་ is the abbreviated form of the word ཀུན་ཏུ་འབྱུང་བ་.

The first two truths include the phenomena of cyclic existence, while the latter two include the phenomena of nirvana. Within the first two, the first is the result of the second. Likewise, the third is the result of the fourth.

In many (if not most) English-language books on Buddhism, these four terms are translated as if they referred to abstract principles: 'the truth of suffering,' 'the truth of the path,' and so forth. However, in Tibetan Buddhism they are treated not as general propositions ('truths'), but, rather, as categories of specific phenomena.

Thus, སྡུག་བསྔལ་གྱི་བདེན་པ་ is not a broad principle stating that life is misery; instead སྡུག་བསྔལ་གྱི་བདེན་པ་ are the bodies and minds of everyone in cyclic existence and, in a derivative way, the physical universe as the environment formed by those past actions (karma) motivated by afflictions (attachment, aversion, and ignorance). Likewise, ལམ་གྱི་བདེན་པ་ is not the assertion that there is a way to attain nirvana; ལམ་གྱི་ བདེན་པ་ are, rather, the actual *paths* (ལམ་) that lead there. (The understanding that these paths exist does, of course, lead to the inference that there is a way to nirvana.)

སྡུག་བསྔལ་གྱི་བདེན་པ་, therefore, does not mean 'the truth of suffering,' it means *truths which are sufferings*, where *truths* means phenomena that are true (that is, phenomena that are seen to exist). Moreover, there are those who would say that སྡུག་བསྔལ་ ought not to be translated *suffering*, because a significant number of སྡུག་བསྔལ་གྱི་བདེན་པ་

are not suffering as suffering is normally understood. (For example, even food and water are སྡུག་བསྔལ་གྱི་བདེན་པ་ because, although they normally sustain life and thereby bring happiness or prevent suffering, they can potentially lead to illness and death.) Some advocate *unsatisfactoriness* here, giving us *unsatisfactory truths* or *true unsatisfactorinesses*. On the other hand, the noun སྡུག་བསྔལ་ does mean *suffering*. Thus, saying that even happiness is *unsatisfactory* because it cannot be sustained and eventually changes into the suffering of loss does not have the force of saying that even happiness is *suffering*.

> On the four truths, see Hopkins, *Meditation on Emptiness*, pp. 287-304. For a less technical and distinctively Tibetan formulation, see Geshe Rabten's *Treasury of Dharma* (which is structured according to the four truths). For the traditional Tibetan philosophical formulation, see H. H. Tenzin Gyatso, *The Dalai Lama at Harvard*, especially pp. 23-28 and 36-38.

## True Sufferings

The first of the four truths is synonymous with cyclic existence. In the traditional, person-oriented presentation, the most important unsatisfactory phenomena are the psycho-physical aggregates—the aggregates (ཕུང་པོ་ **phung-b̲o**) of body and mind. There are five aggregates.

| | | | |
|---|---|---|---|
| གཟུགས་ | <u>s</u>uk | *form* | Skt. *rūpa* |
| ཚོར་བ་ | tshor-wa | *feeling* | *vedanā* |
| འདུ་ཤེས་ | du-<u>s</u>hé> | *discrimination* | *saṃjñā* |
| འདུ་བྱེད་ | du-<u>c</u>hé' | *compositional factors* | *saṃskāra* |
| རྣམ་པར་ཤེས་པ་ | ñam-b̲ar-<u>s</u>hé>-b̲a | *consciousness* | *vijñāna* |

Identified explicitly as aggregates, the five are the གཟུགས་ཀྱི་ཕུང་པོ་, ཚོར་བའི་ཕུང་པོ་, འདུ་ཤེས་ཀྱི་ཕུང་པོ་, འདུ་བྱེད་ཀྱི་ཕུང་པོ་, and the རྣམ་པར་ཤེས་པའི་ཕུང་པོ་.

These five are NOUN-NOUN phrases with connective particles, but, unlike the phrase གཟུགས་ཀྱི་འཇིག་རྟེན་, in which the connective shows apposition, here it shows composition. གཟུགས་ཀྱི་ཕུང་པོ་ is neither *form's aggregate* nor *physical aggregate*; it means *aggregate of form* in the sense of 'aggregate [composed of] forms.'

It should be noted, however, that there is no Tibetan adjective corresponding to the English *physical*. Clearly, གཟུགས་ཀྱི་ and ལུས་ཀྱི་—which literally must be taken as *of forms* and *of the body*—convey the sense of the adjective *physical* and should often be translated in that way.

---

The four main uses of connective particles that have been seen so far are the **possessive connective** (as in སངས་རྒྱས་ཀྱི་ཕྱགས་), the **adjectival connective** (as in དམ་པའི་ཆོས་), the **appositional connective** (སྟོད་ཀྱི་འཇིག་རྟེན་), and the **compositional connective** (གཟུགས་ཀྱི་ཕུང་པོ་).

---

The *five aggregates* (ཕུང་པོ་ལྔ་ phung-bo nga) may in general be called 'aggregates of body and mind'—where body refers to the first aggregate and mind to the latter four—but that designation is not strictly accurate. The fourth aggregate (འདུ་བྱེད་ཀྱི་ཕུང་ པོ་) includes, along with many mental phenomena, a group of impermanent phenomena that are neither physical nor mental.

Concerning the aggregates, see Perdue, *Debate in Tibetan Buddhism*, pp. 363-64 and Hirakawa, *History of Indian Buddhism*, pp. 43-44.

---

The divisions of མི་རྟག་པ་—the categories of things that are impermanent—are ཤེམ་པོ་ (pém-bo, *matter*), ཤེས་པ་ (shé>-ba, *mental phenomena*), and ལྡན་མིན་འདུ་བྱེད་ (dën-mîn-du-chḗ', *non-associated compositional factors*). This third category (Skt. *viprayuktasaṃskāra*) is a group of impermanent things that are neither physical nor mental.

---

*Impermanence* (མི་རྟག་པ་) is itself neither physical nor mental. However, impermanence is impermanent, not some sort of abstract, unchanging quality. Thus, impermanence is put in the category of non-associated compositional factors. Likewise, *person* (གང་ཟག་) is a designation for a collection (that is an 'aggregation') including both physical and mental phenomena, but is itself neither physical nor mental. Thus, it is also a non-associated compositional factor.

## Aggregates and Sources

In abhidharma language, there are two main usages of གཟུགས་—a broad sense in which it is equivalent to ཤེས་པོ་ (*matter*) and a narrower sense in which it means merely one type of matter, visible *color* (ཁ་དོག་) and *shape* (དབྱིབས་). The first sense is that seen in གཟུགས་ཀྱི་ཕུང་པོ་, the first of the five aggregates. The second, narrower sense is seen in a different context, as one of the twelve *sources* (སྐྱེ་མཆེད་—Sanskrit *āyatana*).

| ཁ་དོག་ | **kha-dok** | *color* |
|---|---|---|
| དབྱིབས་ | **yíp** | *shape* |
| ཤེས་པོ་ | **pém-b̄o** | *matter* |
| སྐྱེ་མཆེད་ | **ḡyé-ché' or ḡyém-ché'** | *source [produce + increase]* |

Concerning visible forms, colors, and shapes, see Hopkins, *Meditation on Emptiness*, pp. 223-26 and Perdue, *Debate in Tibetan Buddhism*, pp. 192-200.

The twelve sources (སྐྱེ་མཆེད་)—so-called because they are sources of consciousness—are the six *sense powers* (དབང་པོ་ **w̄ang-b̄o**—Sanskrit *indriya*) and their *objects* (ཡུལ་ **yül**—Sanskrit *viṣaya*). The first five sense powers are physical, but the sixth is mental, being any of the six consciousnesses insofar as they act as causes of the next moment of consciousness.

| མིག་གི་དབང་པོ་ | **mík-gí w̄ang-b̄o** | *eye sense power* |
|---|---|---|
| རྣ་བའི་དབང་པོ་ | **ña-wë w̄ang-b̄o** | *ear sense power* |
| སྣའི་དབང་པོ་ | **ñë w̄ang-b̄o** | *nose sense power* |

| ཞེའི་དབང་པོ་ | **jé w̄ang-b̄o** | *tongue sense power* |
| ལུས་ཀྱི་དབང་པོ་ | **lü>-ḡyí w̄ang-b̄o** | *body sense power* |
| ཡིད་ཀྱི་དབང་པོ་ | **yí'-ḡyí w̄ang-b̄o** | *mental sense power* |

One might wish to translate མིག་གི་དབང་པོ་ as *visual sense power*. However, the literal meaning of the term is *sense power of the eye*, as is clear in the Tibetan. Likewise, if ལུས་ཀྱི་དབང་པོ་ is translated *physical sense power*, one runs the risk of misleading the reader, since four other sense powers are also physical (in the sense of being material phenomena).

The six objects of these six sense powers are the following.

| གཟུགས་ | **s̲uk** | *form* |
| སྒྲ་ | **ḍa** | *sound* |
| དྲི་ | **ṭi** | *odor* |
| རོ་ | **ro** | *taste* |
| རེག་བྱ་ | **rék-ja** | *tangible object* |
| ཆོས་ | **chö>** | *phenomena* |

As mentioned above, གཟུགས་ is used in its narrower sense here. Here it means color and shape. The traditional way of putting this is the following.

གཟུགས་ཀྱི་སྐྱེ་མཆེད་ལ་དབྱེ་ན་    *When form sources are divided,*
དབྱིབས་དང་ཁ་དོག་གཉིས་ཡོད།         *there are two: shapes and colors.*

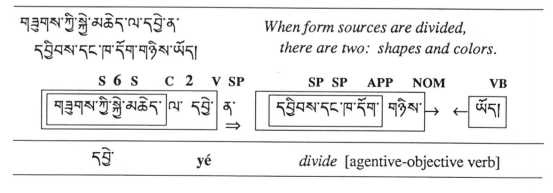

| དབྱེ་ | **yé** | *divide* [agentive-objective verb] |

| ན་ | **na** | *if, when* [syntactic particle] |
|---|---|---|
| ཡོད་ | **yö'** | *exist* [nominative-locative verb] |

*Form sources* are sources which are forms. The connective case marking particle (གྱི་) between གཟུགས་ and སྐྱེ་མཆེད་ indicates apposition. དྱེ་ is technically an agentive-objective verb but is most commonly used as it is here, with no subject, merely an object in the second case.

ཆོས་ or *phenomenon* refers to the entire range of existents (as objects of consciousness), for, although the sense consciousnesses know only impermanent phenomena such as forms and sounds, mental consciousnesses are capable of knowing permanent phenomena.

Expanding the sixth sense power, the ཡིད་ཀྱི་དབང་པོ་, into its individual members—the six རྣམ་པར་ཤེས་པ་ (abbreviated རྣམ་ཤེས་)—the twelve sources become the eighteen *constituents* (ཁམས་).

| མིག་གི་རྣམ་ཤེས་ | **mík-gí ñam-s̄hé>** | *eye consciousness* |
|---|---|---|
| རྣ་བའི་རྣམ་ཤེས་ | **ña-wë ñam-s̄hé>** | *ear consciousness* |
| སྣའི་རྣམ་ཤེས་ | **ñë ñam-s̄hé>** | *nose consciousness* |
| ལྕེའི་རྣམ་ཤེས་ | **jé ñam-s̄hé>** | *tongue consciousness* |
| ལུས་ཀྱི་རྣམ་ཤེས་ | **lü>-ḡyí ñam-s̄hé>** | *body consciousness* |
| ཡིད་ཀྱི་རྣམ་ཤེས་ | **yí'-ḡyí ñam-s̄hé>** | *mental consciousness* |

The first five are *sense consciousnesses* (དབང་ཤེས་) whereas the sixth is the *mental consciousness* (ཡིད་ཤེས་).

Note that both རྣམ་པར་ཤེས་པ་ and ཤེས་པ་ are translated here as *consciousness*. In general, the latter (ཤེས་པ་) is broader than the former. (In the five aggregates, the second, third, and much of the fourth are included in ཤེས་པ་ but are distinct from རྣམ་པར་ཤེས་པ་, the fifth.) The basic problem is that English, while enjoying a much richer vocabulary than Tibetan in many areas, lacks the range of psychological terminology developed in Buddhism.

On the twelve sources and eighteen constituents, see *Meditation on Emptiness*, pp. 220-38 and *Debate in Tibetan Buddhism*, pp. 187-221.


# *VOCABULARY*

## *Nouns*

| གུན་དུ་འབྱུང་བ་ | ḡün-ḏu-jung-wa | source, origin |
|---|---|---|
| སྐྱེ་མཆེད་ | ḡyém-ché' | source [Skt. *āyatana*] |
| ཁམས་ | kham | constituent |
| དགའ་ལྡན་ | gan-dën | Tuṣhita [a pure land] |
| དགའ་བ་ | ga-wa | happiness, joy |
| དགོན་པ་ | gön-ḇa | monastery |
| རྒྱ་གར་ | gya-gar | India |
| ལྗེ་ | jé | tongue |
| མཐའ་ | tha | end, extreme |
| བདེན་པ་ | dên-ḇa | truth |
| འདུ་བྱེད་ | du-jé' | compositional factor |
| འདུ་ཤེས་ | du-s̄hé> | discrimination |
| དྲི་ | ṭí | odor, scent |
| རྣ་བ་ | ña-wa | ear |
| སྣ་ | ña | nose |

| ཕུང་པོ་ | **phung-b̄o** | aggregate [Skt. *skandha*] |
| བློ་གྲོས་ | **lo-d̲ö>** | intelligence |
| དབྱིབས་ | **yíp** | shape |
| ཚོར་བ་ | **tshor-wa** | feeling |
| འོག་མིན་ | **ok-mîn** | Akaniṣṭha [a pure land] |
| རེག་བྱ་ | **rék-ja** | tangible object |
| རོ་ | **ro** | taste, corpse |
| ས་བོན་ | **s̄a-bön** | seed |

## Verbs

Verbs are marked by the Roman numeral indicating the class to which they belong—that is, the syntax they require.

| | | | |
|---|---|---|---|
| **I** | nominative-nominative | **V** | agentive-nominative |
| **II** | nominative-locative | **VI** | agentive-objective |
| **III** | nominative-objective | **VII** | purposive-nominative |
| **IV** | nominative-syntactic | **VIII** | locative-nominative |

The first part of the name of each class identifies the case of the subject and the second, that of the object, complement, or principal qualifier. Thus, class **V** verbs are agentive verbs (that is, verbs whose subjects are marked by agentive case marking particles) with nominative or first case objects, whereas class **IV** verbs have nominative subjects and qualifiers marked by syntactic particles, and so on.

| མཁྱེན་ | **khyên** | know [H] **V** |
| མངའ་ | **n̄ga** | exist **II** |
| ཆགས་ | **chak** | attached to **III** |
| མཆིས་ | **chí>** | exist **II** |
| འཇིགས་ | **jík** | fear, be afraid **II** |

| ཐིམ་ | **thîm** | dissolve III |
|---|---|---|
| རྟེན་ | **d̄ên** | depend on II |
| བརྟེན་ | **d̄ên** | past and future of རྟེན་ II |
| ལྟ་ | **d̄a** | look VI |
| བལྟས་ | **d̄ë>** | past of ལྟ་ VI |
| གདའ་ | **da** | exist II |
| འདུག་ | **duk** | exist II |
| འཕངས་ | **phang** | past of འཕེན་ V |
| འཕེན་ | **phên** | propel, throw, shoot V |
| ཕྲད་ | **ṭhë'** | meet with IV |

## *Adjectives*

| ཀུན་རྫོབ་པ་ | **ḡün-d̲zop-b̄a** | conventional<br>[lit. 'thoroughly covered'] |
|---|---|---|
| བཅོས་མ་ | **j̄ö>-ma** | artificial |
| གཉིས་སུ་མེད་པ་ | **ñyí>-s̄u-mé'-b̄a** | nondual |
| དོན་དམ་པ་ | **tön-tam-b̄a** | ultimate<br>[lit. 'highest object'] |
| འོག་མ་ | **ok-ma** | lower, later, following |

## *Lexical Particles*

| * དང་བཅས་པ་ | **dang-j̄ë>-b̄a** | possessing * |
|---|---|---|
| * དང་ལྡན་པ་ | **dang-dën-b̄a** | possessing * |
| * དང་བྲལ་བ་ | **dang-ḍël-wa** | free from *, lacking * |

# Section Three

## The Syntactic and Rhetorical Dimensions of Tibetan

## Nominative, Agentive, and Specialized Verbs

## The Rules of Buddhist Logic

# Chapter 14

*Specialized Verbs of Possession & Necessity*
*Purposive-Beneficial and Originative Cases*
*First Person Pronouns*
*Simple Syllogisms*
*The Sources of Cyclic Existence*
 *Actions and Afflictions • Causes and Effects*

## Verbs and Verb Syntax
### Specialized Verbs

Thus far only the simplest verbs— ཡིན་ and ཡོད་—have been examined in any detail. The syntax used with these verbs is straightforward. That seen in sentences and clauses ending in linking verbs appears in the following example.

| SUBJECT ⟼ | COMPLEMENT ⟼ | ⟵ LINKING VERB |
|---|---|---|

སྔོན་པོ་ཁ་དོག་ཡིན།    **n̄gön-b̄o kha-dok yîn**    *Blue is a color.*

The syntax used in sentences and clauses ending in verbs of existence is seen in the following example.

| [ QUALIFIER ]⟼ | SUBJECT ⟼ | ⟵ VERB OF EXISTENCE |
|---|---|---|

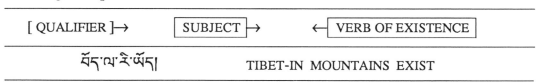

བོད་ལ་རི་ཡོད།      TIBET-IN  MOUNTAINS  EXIST

Both of these are patterns used with nominative verbs, even when—as in the latter illustration—the locative qualifier is the initial element of the clause or sentence.

On the surface, the following sentence also exemplifies this pattern, as its syntax is also LOCATIVE + NOMINATIVE + VERB OF EXISTENCE.

---

དགྲ་བཅོམ་པ་ལ་ ཉོན་མོངས་ མེད།           ARHATS-AT AFFLICTIONS NOT-EXIST

---

However, this sentence has already been seen as the paradigm for specialized verbs—specifically, those whose subjects are in the locative case.

> There are three categories of Tibetan verbs: nominative verbs, agentive verbs, and specialized verbs.

Strictly in terms of *Tibetan* grammar, specialized verbs are technically either nominative or agentive verbs. In the above example, what does not exist is not arhats, but afflictions; arhats are where they do not exist—just as Tibet is where mountains do exist. From that viewpoint, the subject is in the nominative case and, as with verbs of existence, a locative case particle marks a word or phrase that in some way qualifies the situation.

In English, however, the one who possesses something is the subject of a sentence, not its qualifier: ***Arhats do not have afflictions.*** The disparity lies in the fact that, in Tibetan, the verb indicating existence and that indicating possession are the same verb, ཡོད་, whereas in English the two are different verbs, namely *exist* and *have*. For this reason, it is useful to consider constructions such as དགྲ་བཅོམ་པ་ལ་ཉོན་ མོངས་མེད། to have locative subjects, following the pattern LOCATIVE SUBJECT + NOMINATIVE OBJECT + VERB.

---

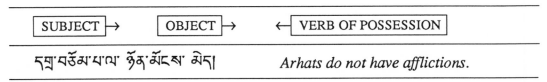

|  | | |
|---|---|---|
| SUBJECT → | OBJECT → | ← VERB OF POSSESSION |

དགྲ་བཅོམ་པ་ལ་ ཉོན་མོངས་ མེད།           *Arhats do not have afflictions.*

---

There are two classes of specialized verbs, one whose subjects are in the seventh or locative case, and one whose subjects are in the fourth case.

There are four principal sorts of nominative verbs (verb classes I through IV) and two main sorts of agentive verbs (classes V and VI). Specialized verbs make up the seventh and eighth classes of verbs.

VII   The purposive-nominative verb of necessity (དགོས་) has a fourth case (purposive-beneficial) subject.

VIII  Locative-nominative verbs (including verbs of possession and attributive verbs [such as ཟེར་ when it means *is called*]) have locative subjects.

Since the particles that mark the seventh and fourth cases (the *la*-group of particles) are the same, both classes are structurally similar.

Verbs of possession are locative-nominative verbs. The following is an example of such a verb.

| Class VIII Verbs Locative-Nominative | དག་བཅོམ་པ་ལ་ ཉོན་མོངས་ མེད། |
|---|---|

*Arhats **have** no afflictions.*

Saying that these verbs have subjects marked by a *la*-particle reflects the orientation of the grammatical analysis in *Translating Buddhism from Tibetan*. As a matter of convenience to those who think in English, the locative qualifier of ཡོད་ as *exist* becomes the locative subject of ཡོད་ as *have*.

The syntactic pattern seen in clauses and sentences ending in verbs of necessity (Class VII) appears to be identical to that seen with verbs of possession. The subject is marked by one of the *la*-group of particles and the object is nominative.

| Class VII Verbs Purposive-Nominative | མྱུ་གུ་ལ་ ཆུ་ དགོས། |
|---|---|

*Sprouts **need** water.*

In fact, however, verbs of necessity—following traditional Tibetan grammar— require fourth case subjects, since the fact of needing something shows purpose (དགོས་ པ་) or potential benefit. They are, therefore, **purposive-nominative** verbs.

Verbs of possession and verbs of necessity are similar in that neither, from the viewpoint of traditional Tibetan grammar, are verbs. Neither express actions, that being the traditional criterion for verbs. Moreover, if this book were describing strictly how Tibetan grammar operates, without concern for its translation into English, both would be nominative verbs. Class VIII verbs of possession would then be a species of nominative-locative verb (requiring a seventh case qualifier) and the Class VII verb of necessity would be a nominative-purposive verb (requiring a fourth case qualifier). Where do afflictions not exist? *At* (or *in*) *arhats*. For whom or what is water needed? *For sprouts*.

| དགྲ་བཅོམ་པ་ལ་ ཉོན་མོངས་ མེད། | AT-ARHATS  AFFLICTIONS  NOT-EXIST |
|---|---|
| མྱུ་གུ་ལ་ ཆུ་ དགོས། | FOR SPROUTS  WATER  IS-NEEDED |

The difference between the two types of verbs is that whereas the verbs ཡོད་ and མེད་ are basically nominative verbs of existence being used in a specialized way, with the qualifier being the focus of the sentence, this is the *only* way the verb དགོས་ is used. Although བུམ་པ་ཡོད། is a complete sentence, expressing general existence with no locative qualifier being necessary, བུམ་པ་དགོས། is incomplete, since there is no universal need for pots. There is always the implication that someone needs pots, or that somewhere pots are needed.

The other type of specialized verbs—the attributive verbs (verbs that attribute a meaning to a word or phrase)—are somewhat more complex. They are normally agentive verbs (such as ཟེར་ and བྱེད་) which are being used in a specialized way, translating into English as *is called*, *refers to*, or *is taken to mean*.[110] Such a usage of verbs belongs to Class VIII.

| Attributive Verbs | ཚོར་བའི་མྱོང་བྱ་ལ་ རྣམ་པར་སྨིན་པ་ ཟེར། |
|---|---|

*The experienced object of feeling **is called** a fruition.*

This could also be translated, *[The term] fruition refers to objects experienced by feeling.*

| S 6 | SC 7 | | S S S NOM | | VB |
|---|---|---|---|---|---|

ཚོར་བའི་ | མྱོང་བྱ་ | ལ་ → | རྣམ་པར་སྨིན་པ་ → | ← ཟེར

མྱོང་བྱ་ is a verbal noun built in the same way as ཤེས་བྱ་; and just as ཤེས་བྱ་ means *object of knowledge*, so མྱོང་བྱ་ means *object of experience*.

The literal translation of ཚོར་བའི་མྱོང་བྱ་ is *experienced objects of feelings*, based on the Tenglish FEELING-OF OBJECT-OF-EXPERIENCE. In English syntax this becomes *objects experienced by feeling*. Note the translation of the connective case marking particle as *by*.

As in sentences ending in verbs of possession, so here as well the actual syntax is somewhat farther away from English than the LOCATIVE + NOMINATIVE + VERB being used here. A more literal translation would read: *[We] say 'fruition' about experienced objects of feeling*—or [WE] FEELING-OF OBJECT-OF-EXPERIENCE-ABOUT FRUITION SAY.[111]

---

Calling a verb a specialized verb is a heuristic device. Verbs of possession, necessity, and attribution are so designated as a convenience for those who speak and think in English, so that they may look at such a construction and think SUBJECT MARKED BY *LA*-PARTICLE + NOMINATIVE OBJECT + VERB.

---

# Specialized Verbs
## *Verbs of Possession*

Tibetan verbs of possession and verbs of existence are thus actually not different groups of verbs; they are the same words used in different ways. Using the category 'verbs of possession' is really just a different way of looking at verbs such as ཡོད་ and མཆིས་. The Tenglish sentences TIBET-IN MOUNTAINS EXIST (*There are mountains in Tibet*) and HE BOOKS HAS (*He has books*) share a common syntax:

| LOCATIVE → | NOMINATIVE → | ← VERB OF EXISTENCE |
|---|---|---|

However, when ཡོད་ and the like are used to show possession, the possessor is marked by the locative case and the thing possessed is in the nominative case.

---

སངས་རྒྱས་ལ་ཡོན་ཏན་ཡོད།                              *Buddhas have good qualities.*

---

Whereas linking verbs, verbs of existence, verbs of living, and verbs of dependence have nominative subjects, verbs of possession have locative subjects.

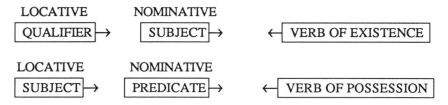

In Tibetan one uses a verb of existence (such as ཡོད་ or མངའ་) to say that someone *has* something. What is literally being said is that a thing exists in some relationship to a certain person. Since one may speak of having an arm, a mind, children, or external things such as books, there are obviously different sorts of relationships that may be implied. The standard syntax is:

AT A CERTAIN PERSON →      A THING →      ←EXISTS

The locative qualifier (literally a **place of existence**) comes first, followed by the nominative thing that exists in that "PLACE" (really a person).[112] However, it is misleading to analyze such a sentence this literally. Such an analysis mistakenly implies that the Tibetan language has built into it an idea of possession in which the thing possessed must be in the presence of the person who possesses it, or that it must be part of that person, or exist for that person.

In fact, when a verb such as ཡོད་ or མངའ་—verbs we have seen as verbs of existence—are used to show possession, this is really a different usage of the verb. The two uses are related, but they are not the same, and the syntax used with verbs of possession is distinctive.

> **Verbs of existence** take nominative subjects and, sometimes, locative quali-
> fiers. When these same verbs are used as **verbs of possession**, they take **loca-
> tive subjects** and **nominative objects**.

It must be kept in mind that this description of syntax is based on the English conception of subject and object. *Translating Buddhism from Tibetan* is an attempt to
balance Tibetan grammar and syntax with a use of terminology that reflects English
preconceptions about sentence structure.

Here are some examples of possessive constructions.

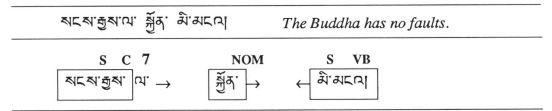

སངས་རྒྱས་ལ་ སྐྱོན་ མི་མངའ།          *The Buddha has no faults.*

Note the translation. Literally this sentence reads *A Buddha does not have a fault.*
སངས་རྒྱས་ is the subject and it is marked by the locative case particle ལ་. Specifically,
this is a **locative subject of a verb of possession or necessity.** The object possessed—སྐྱོན་—is in the nominative case: a **nominative object of a verb of possession or necessity.** (The most common verb of necessity is དགོས་; it translates *need* in
the same way that ཡོད་ here translates *have.*)

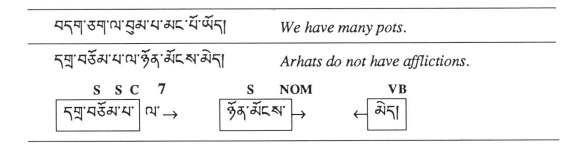

བདག་ཅག་ལ་བུམ་པ་མང་པོ་ཡོད།          *We have many pots.*

དགྲ་བཅོམ་པ་ལ་ཉོན་མོངས་མེད།          *Arhats do not have afflictions.*

---

There are three main afflictions (Skt. *kleśa*) in Buddhist psychology: འདོད་ཆགས་ —attachment or desire; ཞེ་སྡང་—aversion or hatred; གཏི་མུག་—obscuration, equivalent to མ་རིག་པ་ (*ignorance*). They are the principal causes of cyclic existence. One who has irreversibly eliminated them is called an *arhat*.

---

Verbs of possession typically have persons as subjects, not places or things. However, this is not a strict rule. The following two examples may be thought of either in terms of possession or existence in a place. The first translations of each use verb of existence syntax; the second are based on the syntax of verbs of possession.

---

| | |
|---|---|
| བོད་ལ་རི་མང་པོ་ཡོད། | *In Tibet there are many mountains.*<br>*Tibet has many mountains.* |
| འདོད་ཁམས་ལ་ལྷ་དང་མི་ཡོད། | *There are gods and humans in the Desire Realm.*<br>*The Desire Realm has gods and humans.* |

---

Note that the second example sounds better when translated using *there are* than when translated using *have*.

The syntax of sentences ending in verbs of existence is that (1) the things or people that exist are in the nominative case, as they are with verbs of possession, and (2) the places they exist are in the locative case, as is the possessor in the possession sentence. The reason for analyzing the syntax differently (distinguishing between existence and possession) is, again, for the benefit of those who mainly think and speak in English.

---

Recall from Chapter Ten that there are, in cyclic existence, three main areas of rebirth: the Desire Realm (འདོད་པའི་ཁམས་ or འདོད་ཁམས་); the Form Realm (གཟུགས་ ཀྱི་ཁམས་ or གཟུགས་ཁམས་); the Formless Realm (གཟུགས་མེད་པའི་ཁམས་ or གཟུགས་མེད་ཁམས་). This is mainly an abhidharma concern, not a soteriological one. Liberation occurs only from within a rebirth in the Desire Realm.

Whereas there are both gods and humans in the Desire Realm, there are only gods in the Form and Formless Realms.

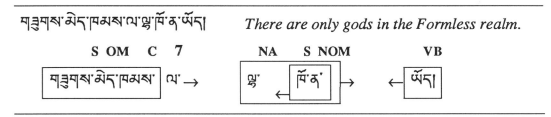

*There are only gods in the Formless realm.*

Recall, again from Chapter Nine, that the verbal phrase གཟུགས་མེད་པ་ means *some-where forms do not exist* or *someone who has no form* or *something without form*. This could be said in Tibetan with a relative pronoun (as it is in the third line below, which means *a realm in which forms do not exist*). གང་ལ་ here means *in which* or *where*.

| གཟུགས་མེད་ | *Forms do not exist.* [sentence] |
|---|---|
| གཟུགས་མེད་པ་ | *forms not existing* [clause] |

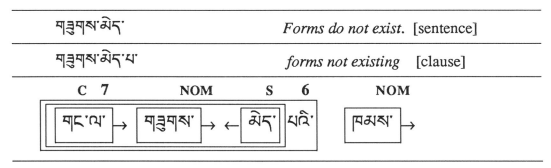

# Drill 14.1

Translate the following into Tibetan.

1   Foe destroyers have many virtuous phenomena.

2   They have yellow pots.

3   Buddhas have love and compassion.

4   Those monks have no food.

5   You have no elephants.

## Drill 14.2

Identify the dots in the following and translate.  Diagram the third.

1  དགྲ་བཅོམ་པ་ལ་སངས་རྒྱས་ཀྱི་ཡོན་ཏན་ཐམས་ཅད་མེད།

2  དེ་དག་ལ་དབྱིབས་དང་ཁ་དོག་ཡོད།

3  འཁོར་བ་ལ་ཡོད་པའི་གང་ཟག་ལ་རང་དབང་མ་མཆིས།

4  བདག་གཞན་ལ་ལུས་དང་ལོངས་སྤྱོད་མཆིས།

5  བྱང་ཆུབ་སེམས་དཔའ་ལ་དགེ་བའི་ཆོས་མང་པོ་ཡོད།

## Nominative Verbs
### *Verbs of Existence Indicating Inclusion*

So far you have seen verbs of existence used in a variety of ways:

- indicating mere existence (or nonexistence): གཞི་གྲུབ་ཡོད།;
- indicating existence in a place: བོད་ལ་རི་ཡོད།;
- indicating possession by persons: ང་ལ་རྟ་ཡོད།;
- indicating possession by entities that are not persons: བུམ་པ་ལ་དབྱིབས་དང་ཁ་དོག་ཡོད།.

The difference between verbs of existence and verbs of possession is a nominal one, actually based on the grammar of English and not that of Tibetan.  In English, it is necessary to translate a sentence such as the last of the above four not as *There are shapes and colors in pots*, but rather as *Pots have shapes and colors*.

One might, however, want to say something such as *Among basic existents there are two [types], impermanent ones and permanent ones.* (Basic existents [གཞི་གྲུབ་] and existents are equivalent.)  This would be done with a verb of existence as well.

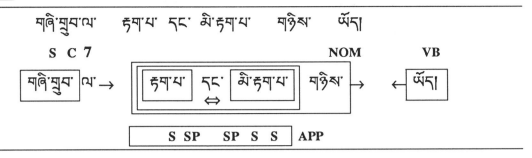

The grammar here is superficially the same: LOCATIVE + NOMINATIVE + VERB OF EXISTENCE. However neither the translation *There are two—permanent and impermanent—in established bases* nor the translation *Established bases have two, permanent and impermanent* is correct.

This locative is neither the locative place of existence (such as marks a qualifier in a typical sentence ending in a verb of existence) nor the locative subject of a verb of possession or necessity. Here we have a **locative of inclusion**—marking a place (or basis) of inclusion, in this example, basic existents. The rule-of-thumb translation (or rough translation) of the ལ in such a construction is *among* or *within*. The things included (in the example, permanent and impermanent phenomena) are all instances of the basis of inclusion. That is, all permanent and impermanent phenomena *are* basic existents. This is not radically different from a sentence such as བོད་ལ་རི་ཡོད། because the mountains are Tibet or at least parts of Tibet. However, it does differ from a sentence such as ཉ་མཚོ་ལ་ཉ་འདུག, since the fish are not oceans. They are found within the ocean without being examples of oceans themselves.

# Drill 14.3

Translate the following sentences. Beginning with this drill, vocabulary will be included to which you have not been introduced. Look for unknown words in the vocabulary at the end of the chapter.

1. ཕུམ་པ་ལ་གསེར་ཕུམ་དང་ཟངས་ཕུམ་གཉིས་ཡོད།

2. གཟུགས་ལ་དཔྱིབས་དང་ཁ་དོག་གཉིས་ཡོད།

3  ཕྱུང་ཆུབ་ལ་གསུམ་ཡོད།

4  བདེན་པ་ལ་ཀུན་རྫོབ་བདེན་པ་དང་དོན་དམ་བདེན་པ་གཉིས་ཡོད།

5  མེ་ཏོག་པ་ལ་རྩྭ་དང་འབྲས་བུ་ཡོད།

## Specialized Verbs
### *Verbs of Necessity*

Sentences ending in the verb of necessity དགོས་ (*must, needs, needs to*) have the appearance of those ending in verbs of possession (SUBJECT marked by a ལ་-particle + NOMINATIVE OBJECT + VERB). However, as noted before, their subjects are in the fourth case (which, in general, shows purpose or benefit).[113]

The fact that verbs of possession take locative subjects whereas verbs of necessity take fourth case subjects may be of little interest to anyone not a grammarian. The case marking particles used for the fourth and seventh cases are the same.

| | |
|---|---|
| ང་ལ་བུམ་པ་དགོས། | *I need a pot.* |
| མྱུ་གུ་ལ་ཆུ་དགོས། | *A sprout needs water.* |

Like any other phrase, clause, or sentence, one ending in a verb of necessity need not have an explicitly stated subject, and—as in the following illustration—what appears to be a purposive (fourth case) subject may actually be something else. You will see, for example, at the end of this chapter, that the two requisite causes of cyclic existence are actions (that is, contaminated actions) and afflictions. One way to put this is the following.[114]

འཁོར་བའི་ རྒྱུ་ལ་     ལས་ དང་ ཉོན་མོངས་པ་     གཉིས་     དགོས།

*As causes of cyclic existence, the two—actions and afflictions—are needed* .

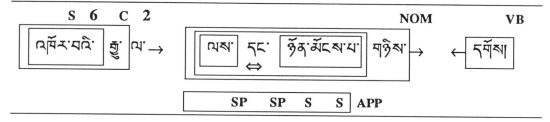

If this sentence followed the pattern seen above, it would mean *The cause[s] of cyclic existence need the two, actions and afflictions*, whereas the context tells you that the writer must have meant something like *The two—actions and afflictions—are needed as causes of cyclic existence*. The ལ་ ending the phrase འཁོར་བའི་རྒྱུ་ལ་ indicates identity, not the locative. It means *as a cause of cyclic existence*. In རུ་གུ་ལ་ཆ་ དགོས།, རུ་གུ་ is one thing and ཆ་ another; they are not identical. However, ལས་དང་ཉོན་ མོངས་པ་ *are* འཁོར་བའི་རྒྱུ་, and thus identity becomes a possibility.

Identity is one of the most frequently seen uses of the second case. Although identity is often adverbial (as in བདེན་པར་ཡོད་), here it is existential (translating into *as ...*).

More frequently than identity, however, a phrase ending in ལ་ (found in a clause or sentence that ends in a verb of necessity) will indicate purpose—especially if the ལ་ follows a verbal. The ལ་ is still a case-marking particle, and, as with the subjects of verbs of necessity, marks the fourth case, but here very clearly shows purpose.

In the following example, འཁོར་བའི་རྒྱུ་ has been altered to འཁོར་བ་འགྲུབ་པ་ (*establishment of cyclic existence*, where འགྲུབ་ is a nominative verb).

འཁོར་བ་ འགྲུབ་པ་ལ་ ལས་ དང་ ཉོན་མོངས་པ་ དགོས།

*In order for cyclic existence to be established* [that is, in order for it to exist], *actions and afflictions are needed.*

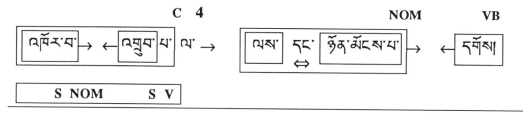

འཁོར་བ་འགྲུབ་ is a very short sentence meaning *Cyclic existence is established.* Its syntax is the basic nominative verb syntax seen earlier: NOMINATIVE SUBJECT + VERB. Adding a པ་ to the verb འགྲུབ་ creates the verbal noun འགྲུབ་པ་, *establishment* or *establishing*, a verbal noun ending what has then been transformed from a sentence into a clause: འཁོར་བ་འགྲུབ་པ་. འགྲུབ་པ་ལ་ would then best be translated *in order to establish* or *for the sake of establishing*.

In point of fact, this construction differs only slightly from the fourth case subject of the verb of necessity. One may consider འཁོར་བ་འགྲུབ་པ་ལ་ to be akin to an English **infinitive** phrase (meaning something like *to bring about cyclic existence*). Such a phrase may then be thought of as the subject which needs actions and afflictions.

Verbs of necessity are also often used in compound verb constructions. For example, where སྐྱེད་ is an agentive verb meaning *generate* and *produce*, and སྙིང་རྗེ་སྐྱེད། thus means *They [or he or she] generate compassion*, སྙིང་རྗེ་སྐྱེད་དགོས། is a sentence meaning *They must generate compassion.* The compound verb is སྐྱེད་དགོས།, *must generate* (in Tenglish, GENERATE MUST).[115]

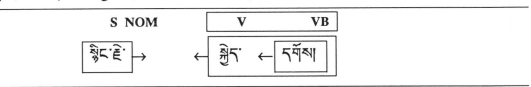

Note the manner in which the compound verb is diagrammed. Compound verbs must be distinguished from multi-syllable verbs (such as ཉམས་སུ་ལེན་, *experience*); thus, each verb requires its own box. Note that the main verb is སྐྱེད་—this is symbolized by the inclusion of the དགོས་-box within the སྐྱེད་-box.

སྙིང་རྗེ་ here is not the object of དགོས་, but rather the object of སྐྱེད་. The verb དགོས་ relates grammatically to སྐྱེད་, not to སྙིང་རྗེ་. It says something about སྐྱེད་—one *must generate*, not one *must [be] compassion*.

## Case Marking Particles
### *Beneficial-Purposive Case Paradigms*

The indirect object of an action verb—when that object clearly receives benefit—is in the fourth (beneficial-purposive) case.

| | |
|---|---|
| indirect object receiving benefit | སྨན་པས་ ནད་པ་ལ་ སྨན་ སྦྱིན། |

*A doctor gives medicine to the ill.*

སྨན་པ་ (*doctor*) is the AGENT in the agentive case; སྦྱིན་ (*give*) is an agentive dynamic verb; སྨན་ (*medicine*) is the direct or actual OBJECT; and ནད་པ་ (*ill person*), followed by the fourth case particle ལ་, is clearly benefitted by the giving of the medicine.

Any sentence (or clause) may include a qualifier which indicates the purpose of an action or state of being; these words or clauses are marked by fourth case particles.

| | |
|---|---|
| purpose or aim | དགེ་འདུན་ལ་ སྐྱབས་སུ་ མཆིའོ། |

*[We] go for refuge to the spiritual community.*

Verbs of motion like མཆི་ are nominative-objective verbs, with the subject in the first case and the destination in the second case. In the present example, there is a qualifying element indicating the purpose of the action of going—*for refuge*.[116]

Verbs of necessity—as seen earlier—take their subjects in the fourth case.

| | |
|---|---|
| subject of a verb of necessity | མྱུ་གུ་ལ་ ཆུ་ དགོས། |

***Sprouts*** *need water.*

## Case Marking Particles
### *Originative Case Paradigms*

The particles marking the fifth case are ལས་ and ནས་. Unlike the connective particles, agentive particles, and the *la*-group of particles, ལས་ and ནས་ may be used with any words; the suffix of a word's final syllable is not a criterion for choosing one over the other.

Originative case marking particles have six usages *as case marking particles*.

1    The fifth case particles are named after their usage to mark the **origin** or source from which something comes—such sources include books and persons (as the source of discourse or ideas), things, and places. Such a usage often translates into *from*, *out of*, or *in* (in the case of books).

2    Fifth case particles may also be used (but not as frequently as the agentive particles) to indicate the **means** by which something is done, translating, as a rule of thumb, into *by*, *through*, or *by means of*.

3    Like the agentive particles—but, again, not as often—they are used to show **reasons**—translating into *because of*.

4    One of the more significant usages of the fifth case is to show **comparison** (as in *this is greater than that*), a usage that, like the connective particles, relates adjectives and nouns.

5    Fifth case particles are also often used to indicate **inclusion**: *from Lhasa to Shigatse* or *from beginningless time*.

6    Finally, they may be used to show **separation** or **removal** (as in *from among the three* or *liberation from cyclic existence*).

Only the first usage will be examined in this chapter.

---

Always remember that ལས་ and ནས་ have significant uses both as words and as syntactic particles.

---

ལས་, as a word, means *action*—that is, *karma*.

ནས་—although meaning *barley* when it is a word—has its most significant use (more frequent than its use as a case marking particle) as a syntactic particle that is placed after verbs to indicate a continuation of the sentence (as in the following).

*In dependence on having accumulated unwholesome actions,*
  *one is born in a bad rebirth.*

མི་དགེ་བའི་ལས་བསགས་པ་ལ་བརྟེན་ནས་ངན་འགྲོར་སྐྱེ།

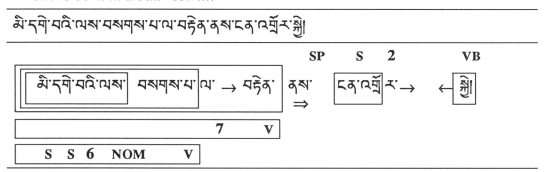

Note in this example that within the sentence there is a clause ending in the open verb བརྟེན་, and inside of that clause there is a smaller clause ending in the verbal བསགས་པ་ (which is, of course, another open verb).

བརྟེན་ is an open verb because it is followed by the continuative syntactic particle ནས་. བསགས་པ་ is an open verb because it ends in a generic suffix syllable.

The verb བསགས་ (*accumulated*), an agentive-nominative verb, has as its nominative object མི་དགེ་བའི་ལས་. The verb ending the sentence—སྐྱེ་ (*is born*)—is a nominative action verb with a second case qualifier (ངན་འགྲོར་, *in an evil migration*) indicating where someone is born. As is often the case in Tibetan, the subject (the one who accumulates actions and is born) is not stated.

## Source of Things and Actions

The originative case may indicate the actual source of something or, less directly, the means that cause something to come about.

In the first example below, the verb བྱུང་ (*arise*) is a nominative action verb. ཆུ་བུར་ (*bubbles*) is its subject.

| source<br>(place or substance) | ཆུ་ལས་ | ཆུ་བུར་ བྱུང་། |

*Bubbles come **out of the water**.*

ཆུ་བུར་ is not ཆུ་བུ་ with a ར་ particle. It is a noun ending in the suffix ར་.

Likewise, འར་, in the following example, is a nominative action verb meaning *arise* or *appear*. It is frequently used in discussions of meditation and epistemology.

---

*The sun rises **out of the east**.*

---

| ཤར་ཕྱོགས་ནས་ | ཉི་མ་ འར་ |

---

The syntax seen in both examples is QUALIFIER + SUBJECT + VERB.

| source<br>(speech) | རྩ་ཚིག་ལས་ | ··· ཞེས་ གསུངས་པ་ ལྟར་ |

*As is said **in the words of the basic text**, ...*

The example seen here is an abbreviated one; normally a passage taken from the basic text would be seen in place of the ellipsis. This construction is probably the most common use of the fifth case in Buddhist Tibetan. The closing ལྟར་ (*as, like*) is a particle that marks a phrase or clause as an adverb.

---

རྩ་ཚིག་ལས། འོང་བ་མེད་པ་འགྲོ་མེད་པ། ཞེས་གསུངས་པ་ ལྟར།

---

*As [Nāgārjuna] said in the basic text, "Without coming, without going"* ...

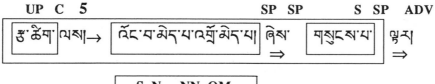

ཆོང་བ་མེད་པ་འགྲོ་མེད་པ་ is two nouns in a list, each noun being itself a clause. ཆོང་བ་ is the nominative subject in ཆོང་བ་མེད་པ་. འགྲོ་ (short for འགྲོ་བ་) is the nominative subject in འགྲོ་མེད་པ་.

Note that the verb གསུངས་ (*said, taught* [H]) here has an object (answering the question, 'What was said?') that is not in the nominative case, but, rather, is marked by a syntactic particle. ཞིས་ is one of a set of three punctuational syntactic particles—ཞིས་, ཅེས་, and ཤེས་—that are used to mark the *end* of a quotation.

- ཅེས་ follows words ending in the suffixes ག་, ད་, བ་, and the secondary suffix ད་.
- ཞིས་ follows words ending in the suffixes ང་, ན་, མ་, འ་, ར་, and ལ་, as well as syllables without suffixes.
- ཤེས་ follows words ending in the suffix ས་.

Tibetan has no special sign for the beginning of a quotation as English does.

> The quotation is from Nāgārjuna's *Verses on the Middle Way* (Sanskrit: *Mūlamadhyamikakārikā*—known in Tibetan as ཙ་བ་ཤེས་རབ་, *Basic Text on Wisdom*).

The grammar of the quoted material—whether it is a phrase, clause, sentence, or paragraph—is entirely self-contained, cut off from the sentence in which it is quoted by the syntactic particle ending it (here, ཞིས་).

> Note that the example given above is not a complete sentence. It ends in a verbal (གསུངས་པ་) followed by the syntactic particle སྟར་, indicating that it is a qualifier in some larger construction. སྟར་ and other similar syntactic particles make the words, clauses, or phrases they follow into adverbs. Thus, whereas the dot preceding it is an SP dot, the one following it is an ADV dot.

# Pronouns
## *Personal Pronouns*

Pronouns and nouns function in the same ways.

- They may be subjects or predicates of linking verbs.
- They may be subjects of verbs of existence, living, and dependence.

- They may be the subjects of nominative verbs.
- They may be the agents or objects of agentive verbs.
- They may find themselves connected to postpositions (such as སྔོན་, *before*) by connective case particles.

There are many varieties of pronouns in English grammar;[117] these English classifications may be used to help systematize Tibetan grammar. Thus, we may speak of:

1  personal pronouns (for example, ང་, *I*),
2  reflexive pronouns (for example, ང་རང་, *I* or *I myself*),
3  adjectives used as pronouns (for example, དེ་, *that*, and རེ་རེ་, *each*),
4  interrogative pronouns (for example, གང་, *which, what*),
5  relative pronouns (for example, གང་, *which*),
6  indefinite relative pronouns (for example, གང་ཡང་, *whichever*),
7  indefinite pronouns (for example, ཁ་ཅིག་, *whichever, whoever, someone*).

Note that there is a fair amount of double-duty being done here—interrogative pronouns, for instance, must be distinguished from relative pronouns by contextual clues.

Unlike verbs, Tibetan pronouns *do* differ according to person; persons, after all, is what they are all about. Thus, within the personal pronouns, there are first, second, and third person pronouns.

ང་ means *I* and is a first person pronoun;

ཁྱོད་ means *you* and is a second person pronoun;

ཁོ་ means *he* or *she* or *it* and is a third person pronoun.

ཁོང་ is a respectful word for *he* or *she*;
        it is an honorific third person pronoun.

## *First Person Pronouns*

First person pronouns in English include *I*, *me*, *my*, and *mine*.[118] The most common first person pronouns in Tibetan are ང་ and བདག་.

| | |
|---|---|
| ང་ སེམས་ཅན་ ཡིན། | *I am a sentient being.* |

Care must be taken in many philosophical contexts (especially those dealing with correct view—that is, wisdom and selflessness) not to confuse བདག་ used as a first person pronoun with the usage of བདག་ (*ātman*) that means *self* as that term is used in *selflessness* (བདག་མེད་པ་, Skt. *anātman*). In this case, བདག་ is not a pronoun but a generic term for various types of exaggerated existence that are mistakenly superimposed on persons and impersonal objects.

Two other first person pronouns, somewhat rarer, are ཁོ་བོ་ (**kho-wo**) and ཅད་.

The addition of the lexical syllables ཅག་ and ཚོ་ to these pronouns makes them explicitly **plural**. The following four words mean *we*.

| | | | |
|---|---|---|---|
| བདག་ཅག་ | ང་ཅག་ | ང་ཚོ་ | ཁོ་བོ་ཅག་ |

The lexical syllable རྣམས་, the most common mark of plurality in nouns, also pluralizes pronouns. It is sometimes redundantly combined with ཅག་, giving us plural pronouns such as ཁོ་བོ་ཅག་རྣམས་.

> Remember that in many instances plurality need not be explicitly indicated.

Pronouns are also used placed in apposition to numbers in order to show a more specific sort of plural— ང་གཉིས་ (*we two, the two of us*), ང་གསུམ་ (*we three*), ང་བདུན་ (*the seven of us*).

| APP | NOM | NOM | VB | |
|---|---|---|---|---|
| ང་ | གཉིས་ | མི་ | ཡིན། | *The two of us are humans.* |

The ང་གཉིས་ in this example is an appositive because ང་ and གཉིས་ are both nouns. Alternatively, ང་ and གཉིས་ could be considered a noun and an adjective; in that case the dot between them would be an **NA** dot. ངའཚིག, however, is one word—ཚིག has no meaning of its own and is merely a pluralizing particle.

When analyzing the dots of words marked by such lexical particles, the dot before the pluralizer is an **S** dot, not an **SP** dot. An **SP** dot occurs before or after a *syntactic* particle. The dot after a pluralizing particle is a dot that follows a *lexical* particle. Since such a dot ends a noun (or pronoun, or noun phrase), it might be a **NOM** dot, one before a case ending (**C**), or an appositive dot (**APP**).

---

|   S NOM    S NOM   VB            |                              |
|----------------------------------|------------------------------|
| བདག་ཅག་ སེམས་ཅན་ ཡིན།            | *We are sentient beings.*    |

---

| S S S  NOM  S NOM  VB            |                              |
|----------------------------------|------------------------------|
| ཁོ་བོ་ཅག་རྣམས་ དགེ་སློང་ ཡིན།    | *We are monks.*              |

---

> In most instances, a pluralizing particle is a sign that a noun or noun phrase has terminated. If there is then no case-marking particle, you may assume that the noun (or noun phrase) is in the nominative case.

---

## Drill 14.4

Translate the following into Tibetan.

1. We are not Buddhas.
2. I am not a horse.
3. We exist.
4. Self and others exist in the world.
5. I am a Tathāgata.

## Drill 14.5

Translate the following sentences.

1  ཁྱི་པོ་ཅིག་རྟ་མ་ཡིན།

2  བདག་དགྲ་བཙལ་པ་ལགས།

3  ང་བཞི་མི་མ་ཡིན། ལྷ་མ་ཡིན།

4  རྒྱ་གར་ལ་དགེ་སློང་མང་པོ་ཡོད།

5  བདག་ཅིག་རྒྱལ་བ་སྟོན་པ་མ་ཡིན།

## Rhetorical Tools
### *Syllogisms with Linking Verbs*

*Rhetoric* refers to persuasion and logical demonstration. The rhetorical dimension of Buddhist Tibetan has to do with the special vocabulary and syntax used to link sentences together in logical sequences of theses and proofs. It embodies a more sophisticated level of syntax, one seen principally in technical works (including systematic presentations of philosophy and practice).

In this chapter, the syllogism, one of the most basic rhetorical structures, is examined based mainly on vocabulary and ideas presented in Chapter Nine. One thing ought to stand out about these patterns from the very start.

> The formal style of stating proofs in syllogisms and consequences (Chapter Fifteen) in Tibetan violates the rule that all sentences end in final verbs.

The simplest sort of statement of proof makes this clear.

*A pot is impermanent because of being a product.*

བུམ་པ་མི་རྟག་པ་ཡིན་ཏེ་བྱས་པ་ཡིན་པའི་ཕྱིར།

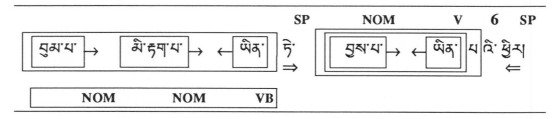

The sentence བུམ་པ་མི་རྟག་པ་ཡིན་ཏེ་བྱས་པ་ཡིན་པའི་ཕྱིར། may also be translated *Pots are impermanent because of being products.*

Although the main verb of the sentence is the ཡིན་ following བུམ་པ་མི་རྟག་པ, the sentence does not end there. *Being impermanent* is qualified by the statement that follows it, བྱས་པ་ཡིན་པའི་ཕྱིར.

The syntactic particle ཕྱིར་ is almost a postposition in that a connective case marking particle connects it to the word, phrase, or clause that it follows. However, it is not declined when it is used to mark a reason and, therefore, it is a syntactic particle and not a postposition. And, in this formal style of stating a reasoned proof, the phrase it ends relates to what has come before it, not what will follow it—thus, the leftward pointing double arrow.

The rightward pointing double arrow under the syntactic particle ཏེ་ serves to 'draw the reason' in Tibetan parlance. The leftward pointing double arrow under the ཕྱིར་ indicates that the clause that it ends refers to (in this case, proves) what has come before.

Here is another example of a simple syllogism, this one with a NOUN-ADJECTIVE phrase as a subject.

*A white conch shell is impermanent because [it] is not permanent.*

ཆོས་དུང་དཀར་པོ་མི་རྟག་པ་ཡིན་ཏེ་རྟག་པ་མ་ཡིན་པའི་ཕྱིར།

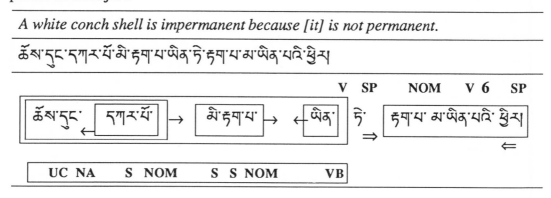

The following is a more complex rhetorical sequence.

---

རི་བོང་རུ་མེད་པ་ཡིན་ཏེ་ཡོད་པ་མ་ཡིན་པའི་ཕྱིར།

ཡོད་པ་མ་ཡིན་ཏེ་རྟག་པ་མ་ཡིན་པ་གང་ཞིག  མི་རྟག་པ་མ་ཡིན་པའི་ཕྱིར།

---

*The horns of a rabbit are nonexistent because [they] are not existent.*
*[They] are not existent because they are not permanent and are not impermanent.*

---

The second reason in this sequence is complex, having not one part but two. The two parts are separated by the syntactic particle གང་ཞིག and are both necessary in the proof. They are *not* to be read as alternative reasons: not being permanent and not being impermanent are both necessary for nonexistence.

- The first line—རི་བོང་རུ་མེད་པ་ཡིན་ཏེ་ཡོད་པ་མ་ཡིན་པའི་ཕྱིར—is a simple syllogism.

- The second line continues the argument. The understood subject of ཡོད་པ་ མ་ཡིན་ཏེ་ is རི་བོང་རུ, the subject of the first syllogism.

- The reason stated in the second line—རྟག་པ་མ་ཡིན་པ་གང་ཞིག མི་རྟག་པ་མ་ཡིན་པའི་ ཕྱིར—relates to the claim immediately preceding it (རི་བོང་རུ་ཡོད་པ་མ་ཡིན་ཏེ་); it does not relate grammatically to anything in the first sentence.

There is, however, a rhetorical (that is, logical) relationship between the two lines. Notice that what is being proven in the second syllogism is the reason of the first. Spelled out in its most complete form, then, we have the following.

1. རི་བོང་རུ་མེད་པ་ཡིན། — *The horns of a rabbit are not existent.*

2. Why? ཡོད་པ་མ་ཡིན་པའི་ཕྱིར — *because of not being existents.*

3. རི་བོང་རུ་ཡོད་པ་མ་ཡིན། — *The horns of a rabbit are not existents.*

4. Why? རྟག་པ་མ་ཡིན་པ་གང་ཞིག མི་རྟག་པ་མ་ཡིན་པའི་ཕྱིར — *because of [both] not being permanent [and] not being impermanent.*

---

The typical syntactic structure of a logical sequence is a statement of the form, SUBJECT + PREDICATE + REASON, followed often by another statement in which the first REASON becomes the new PREDICATE.

In ཕུམ་པ་མི་རྟག་པ་ཡིན་ཏེ་བྱས་པ་ཡིན་པའི་ཕྱིར, the subject is A POT, the predicate is IS IM-PERMANENT, and the reason is BECAUSE OF BEING A PRODUCT. One may then go on to state another syllogism in which the the old reason, བྱས་པ་ཡིན་པ, becomes what is being proven.

---

*A pot is a product  because of being created.*

---

ཕུམ་པ་བྱས་པ་ཡིན་ཏེ་སྐྱེས་པ་ཡིན་པའི་ཕྱིར

---

This reasoning invokes the fact that བྱས་པ is typically defined as སྐྱེས་པ (ḡyé-b̄a—*arisen, created*).

> Thus, a logical statement of the form **A** is **B** because of **C** is often followed in rhetorical sequence by the statement **A** is **C** because of **D**.

The terms **subject** and **predicate**, until now used grammatically, are also used doctrinally, as terms in the study of logic.  Such a study is seen in its most basic form in the རྟགས་རིགས (*Signs and Reasonings*) literature as well as in commentaries on Dharmakīrti's *Pramāṇavārttika* (ཚད་མ་རྣམ་འགྲེལ tshë'-ma-ñam-ḍél—literally a *commentary* [རྣམ་འགྲེལ] on *valid cognition* [ཚད་མ]).

The term ཚད་མ refers most basically to incontrovertible cognition.  Often translated *valid cognition*, it may also be translated *prime cognition*.  By ex-tension, the term ཚད་མ also refers to the study of epistemology and logic and to those texts that discuss these topics.  Thus, although ཚད་མ་རྣམ་འགྲེལ literally means *commentary* [རྣམ་འགྲེལ] on *valid cognition* [ཚད་མ], it is understood to mean "Commentary on Dignāga's *Compendium on Valid Cognition*" (*Pramāṇasamuccaya*—ཚད་མ་ཀུན་ལས་བཏུས་པ).

On ཚད་མ as *prime cognition*, see Lati Rinbochay, *Mind in Tibetan Buddhism*, pp. 31-32 and 116-129.

Technically—following the རྟགས་རིགས presentation—there are two parts to a syl-logism.  Using ཕུམ་པ་མི་རྟག་པ་ཡིན་ཏེ་བྱས་པ་ཡིན་པའི་ཕྱིར as an example, the two parts are as follows.

- The thesis (དམ་བཅའ་ **tam-ja**—Skt. *pratijñā*) is what is to be proven (བསྒྲུབ་ བྱ་ **ḍup-ja**—Skt. *sādhya*). In this case, བུམ་པ་མི་རྟག་པ་ཡིན་པ་ (*pot being impermanent*) is the thesis.

- The proof (སྒྲུབ་བྱེད་ **ḍup-jë'**—literally, *prover*) is the sign (རྟགས་ **d̄ak**— Skt. *linga*) or reason (གཏན་ཚིགས་ **d̄en-tshík**—Skt. *hetu*). In this case, བྱས་ པ་ is the reason.

The thesis itself (here, བུམ་པ་མི་རྟག་པ་ཡིན་པ་) also has two parts.

- The subject (ཆོས་ཅན་ **chö>-jën**—Skt. *dharmin*) is བུམ་པ་.

- The predicate to be proven (བསྒྲུབ་བྱའི་ཆོས་ **ḍup-jë-chö>**—Skt. *sādhya-dharma*) is མི་རྟག་པ་.

> See Daniel Perdue, *Debate in Tibetan Buddhism*, pp. 33-60.

All of these sentences may (and often do) occur with the subject formally marked as such. Setting off the logical (and also the grammatical) subject is the appositive ཆོས་ཅན་ (**chö>-jën**, *subject*—literally, ATTRIBUTE-POSSESSOR).

---

*The subject, a pot, is impermanent because of being a product.*

---

བུམ་པ་ཆོས་ཅན་མི་རྟག་པ་ཡིན་ཏེ་བྱས་པ་ཡིན་པའི་ཕྱིར།

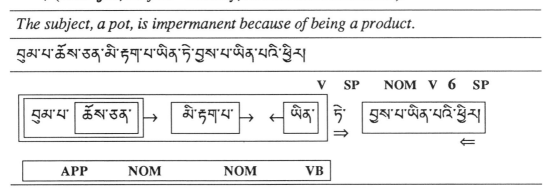

Examination of syllogisms and other rhetorical tools is continued in the next chapter.

## Drill 14.6

Translate the following into Tibetan.

1. The subject, the son of a barren woman, is not impermanent
   because of not existing.

2. The subject, a white horse, is a non-associated compositional factor
   because of being a person.

3. The subject, the color of a white horse, is a visible form
   because of being a color.

4. Conceptuality is a mental consciousness
   because of being a consciousness but not being a sense consciousness.

## Drill 14.7

Translate the following. Diagram the first and second, marking their dots.

1. མིག་གི་རྣམ་ཤེས་དབང་ཤེས་ཡིན་ཏེ་ཤེས་པ་ཡིན་པ་གང་ཞིག་ཡིད་ཤེས་མ་ཡིན་པའི་ཕྱིར།

2. གཟུགས་ཚོས་ཅན་གཞི་གྲུབ་ཡིན་ཏེ་མི་རྟག་པ་ཡིན་པའི་ཕྱིར།

3. ཤེས་པ་ཚོས་ཅན་རྟག་པ་མ་ཡིན་ཏེ་མི་རྟག་པ་མ་ཡིན་པའི་ཡོད་པ་མ་ཡིན་པའི་ཕྱིར།

4. རྩ་ཚོས་ཅན་འགྲོ་བ་ཡིན་ཏེ་འཕོར་བ་ལ་གནས་པའི་ཕྱིར།

## Doctrinal Vocabulary and Grammar
### *The Four Truths: Sources of Suffering*

The second of the four truths is the cause of the first—true sources (ཀུན་འབྱུང་, abbreviating ཀུན་ཏུ་འབྱུང་བ་) are the causes of true sufferings (that is, of rebirth in cyclic existence). In general, true sources are divided into actions (ལས་ lë>—Sanskrit *karma*) and afflictions (ཉོན་མོངས་ **nyön-mong**—Sanskrit *kleśa*). Here, *actions and afflictions* actually mean afflictions and the actions (called *contaminated actions*) that are motivated by those afflictions. (There are also actions not motivated by afflictions that do not act as causes of cyclic existence.)

| ཉོན་མོངས་ | **nyön-mong** | *affliction* [Skt. *kleśa*] |
| ལས་ | **lë>** | *action* [Skt. *karma*] |
| ཟག་བཅས་ | **ṣak-jë>** | *contaminated* |

The three main afflictions—attachment, aversion, and obscuration (equivalent to མ་རིག་པ་ [*ignorance*])—were introduced in Chapter Ten.

| འདོད་ཆགས་ | **dö'-chak** | *attachment* |
| ཞེ་སྡང་ | **ṣhé-dang** | *aversion, hatred* |
| ཁོང་ཁྲོ་ | **khong-ṭho** | *anger* [equivalent to ཞེ་སྡང་] |
| གཏི་མུག་ | **dí-muk** | *obscuration* |
| མ་རིག་པ་ | **ma-rík-ba** | *ignorance* |

These three, along with pride, doubt, and afflicted view, make up the six principal afflictions.

| རྩ་བའི་ཉོན་མོངས་ | **dza-wë nyön-mong** | *principal affliction* |
| ང་རྒྱལ་ | **nga-gyël** | *pride* |
| ཐེ་ཚོམ་ | **thé-tshom** | *doubt* |
| ལྟ་བ་ཉོན་མོངས་ཅན་ | **da-wa nyön-mong-jën** | *afflicted view* |

The last, ལྟ་བ་ཉོན་མོངས་ཅན་, is so qualified (as afflicted) to distinguish it from ཡང་དག་པའི་ ལྟ་བ་, the *correct view* (that is, understanding or realization of emptiness). There are five sorts of afflicted view; they are afflicted because they all derive from ignorance (མ་རིག་པ་). The most basic of these is the view of the transitory collection as a real I and mine; it sets up a self-other distinction through conceiving of one's own body and mind as I or as mine.

---

| འཇིག་ཚོགས་ལ་ལྟ་བ་ | **jík-tshok-la-d̄a-wa** | *view of the transitory collection* |

---

The *transitory collection* (འཇིག་ཚོགས་) is the aggregates of body and mind, the five aggregates presented in Chapter Thirteen. ལྟ་ is an agentive-objective verb; thus what is viewed is marked by a second case particle, here ལ་.

See Hopkins, *Meditation on Emptiness*, pp. 255-261, Rabten, *Treasury of Dharma*, pp. 53-60, and H. H. Tenzin Gyatso, *The Dalai Lama at Harvard*, pp. 77-79.

There are also a number of secondary afflictions. The following are some of the more useful, in terms of vocabulary.

---

| ཉེ་བའི་ཉོན་མོངས་ | **nyé-wë nyön-mong** | *secondary affliction* |
|---|---|---|
| ཕྲག་དོག་ | **ṭhak-dok** | *jealousy* |
| སེར་སྣ་ | **s̄ér-n̄a** | *miserliness* |
| རྒྱགས་པ་ | **gyak-b̄a** | *haughtiness* |
| རྨུགས་པ་ | **m̄uk-b̄a** | *lethargy* |
| རྒོད་པ་ | **gö'-b̄a** | *excitement* |
| ལེ་ལོ་ | **lé-lo** | *laziness* |
| རྣམ་པར་གཡེང་བ་ | **ñam-b̄ar-yéng-wa** | *distraction* |

---

See Hopkins, *Meditation on Emptiness*, pp. 261-268, Rabten, *Treasury of Dharma*, pp. 61-67, and H. H. Tenzin Gyatso, *The Dalai Lama at Harvard*, pp. 79-80.

As mentioned above, actions in general are not always the sources of suffering, only actions motivated by afflictions and, in particular, by ignorance. Such actions are called contaminated actions. Uncontaminated actions are actions not associated with ignorance.

| ཟག་བཅས་ཀྱི་ལས་ | **s̱ak-j̱ë>-ḡyí-lë>** | *contaminated actions* |
|---|---|---|
| ཟག་མེད་ཀྱི་ལས་ | **s̱ak-mé'-ḡyí-lë>** | *uncontaminated actions* |

There are three main sorts of actions: wholesome, unwholesome, and neutral.

| དགེ་བ་ | **gé-wa** | *virtuous, wholesome, positive* |
|---|---|---|
| མི་དགེ་བ་ | **mí-gé-wa** | *nonvirtuous, unwholesome, negative* |
| ལུང་དུ་མ་བསྟན་པ་ | **lung-du-ma-d̄en-b̄a** | *neutral* [literally: *not indicated in scripture*] |
| ལུང་མ་བསྟན་ | **lung-ma-d̄en** | *neutral* [abbreviated form] |

Wholesome or positive actions lead to the experience of pleasure (typically in a future lifetime, not this one). If they are uncontaminated, they bring about the pleasure experienced in enlightenment; if they are contaminated, they cause an experience of pleasure in cyclic existence. All unwholesome or negative actions are contaminated and, thus, lead only to the experience of suffering in one or another of the six types of rebirth. Neutral actions are inconsequential in terms of rebirth and the future experience of pleasure and pain.

> All phenomena are either wholesome, unwholesome, or neutral. However, only those included within a sentient being's body and mind may be wholesome or unwholesome.

See Rabten, *Treasury of Dharma*, pp. 33-36, and H. H. Tenzin Gyatso, *The Dalai Lama at Harvard*, pp. 59-61.

## *Cause and Effect*

There are various levels of explanation of cause and effect in Géluk doctrinal primers (བསྡུས་གྲྭ་—literally, *Collected Topics*). The most elementary explanation presents causality—that is, being a cause and an effect—as a primary characteristic of impermanent phenomena. (See the list of terms equivalent to མི་རྟག་པ་ in Chapter Nine.)

More advanced presentations list various types of causes, conditions, and effects.

| | | |
|---|---|---|
| རྒྱུ་ | **gyu** | *cause* |
| རྐྱེན་ | **g̱yên** | *condition* |
| འབྲས་བུ་ | **ḍë>-bu** | *effect* |

The standard categorization is into six causes, four conditions, and five effects.[119] This set of divisions is more of a discussion of terminology occurring in Indian texts than it is a taxonomy of causes and effects. Terminological division may be phrased in the following way.

*If causes are divided from the viewpoint of terminology, there are six.*

རྒྱུ་ལ་   སྒྲས་   བརྗོད་   རིགས་ཀྱི་   སྒོ་ནས་   དབྱེན་   དྲུག་   ཡོད།

C  2            3     UP      C 6 SP SP   V SP NOM VB

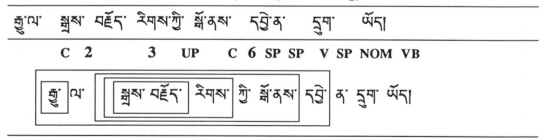

The core of the sentence is དྲུག་ཡོད་, *There are six*. The clause that states the condition that must be operative if there are to be six is (in *its* core form) རྒྱུ་ལ་དབྱེ་ན་—*when causes are divided*. Embedded within that is a smaller, adverbial clause: སྒྲས་བརྗོད་ རིགས་ཀྱི་སྒོ་ནས་ (*from the viewpoint of types expressed by terms*).

The dot between བརྗོད་ and རིགས་ is an Understood Particle dot, the phrase being a contraction of བརྗོད་པའི་རིགས་ (*types which are expressed*). སྒྲས་ is the noun སྒྲ་ (*sound, term*) in the agentive case. This is dictated by the verbal བརྗོད་པ་ which is derived from an agentive verb.

སྒོ་ནས་ is a commonly seen expression in which the particle ནས་ is not a case marking particle but a syntactic particle with an adverbial sense. This Tibetan expression, literally meaning *through the door [of]* has the sense of the English expression *from the viewpoint [of]*.

Of the six types of causes, the one most relevant here (in the discussion of the causes of cyclic existence) is the *fruitional cause*. There is a corresponding *fruitional effect*. There are two other effects that figure into discussions of *karma* as well, *causally concordant effects* and *dominant effects*.

| | | |
|---|---|---|
| རྣམ་སྨིན་གྱི་རྒྱུ་ | **ñam-m̄în-gyí gyu** | *fruitional cause* |
| རྣམ་སྨིན་གྱི་འབྲས་བུ་ | **ñam-m̄în-gyí ḍë>-bu** | *fruitional effect* |
| རྒྱུ་མཐུན་གྱི་འབྲས་བུ་ | **gyun-thün-gyí ḍë>-bu** | *causally concordant effect* |
| བདག་པོའི་འབྲས་བུ་ | **dak-b̄ö>- ḍë>-bu** | *dominant effect* |

Fruitional causes are either negative phenomena or afflicted positive phenomena—they lead to continued experience within cyclic existence. For example, the action of killing is a fruitional cause. Rebirth as a human—that is, with the contaminated psychophysical aggregates of a human being—is an example of a fruitional effect.

| | | |
|---|---|---|
| སྲོག་གཅོད་ཀྱི་ལས་ | **s̄ok-j̄ö'-ḡyí lë>** | *action of killing* |
| སྲོག་ | **s̄ok** | *life, life force* |
| གཅོད་ | **j̄ö'** | *cut* [agentive-nominative verb] |

Although born as a human, liking to kill is an example of a causally concordant effect issuing from killing in a previous lifetime. The physical environment in which one is born is an example of a dominant effect.

*although born in a pleasant migration, taking pleasure in killing*

བདེ་འགྲོར་ སྐྱེས་ཀྱང་ སྡུག་གཙོད་པ་ལ་ དགའ་བ་

| S | 2 | VB | SP | S | S C | 7 | S V |
|---|---|---|---|---|---|---|---|

| བདེ་འགྲོར་ | སྐྱེས་ | ཀྱང་ | སྡུག་གཙོད་པ་ | ལ་ | དགའ་བ་ |

| བདེ་འགྲོ་ | **dén-ḍo** | *pleasant migration* |
|---|---|---|
| སྐྱེས་ | **ḡyë>** | *born* [past tense] |
| ཀྱང་ | **ḡyang** | *even, also, but* |
| དགའ་ | **ga** | *delight in, enjoy* |

For a traditional account of the various karmic causes and effects, see Khetsun Sangpo, *Tantric Practice in Nying-ma*, pp. 86-100.

# *Vocabulary*

Memorize the spelling and pronunciation of these words; practice speaking them.

## *Nouns*

| རྐྱེན་ | **ḡyên** | condition |
|---|---|---|
| སྐྱབས་ | **ḡyap** | refuge |
| སྐྱེ་བ་ | **ḡyé-wa** | birth, arising |
| སྐྱེས་པ་ | **ḡyé>-b̄a** | born, arisen, created |
| སྐྱེས་བུ་ | **ḡyé>-bu** | being, man |
| ཁོང་ཁྲོ་ | **khong-ṭho** | anger |

| དགྲ་བཅོམ་པ་ | ḍa-jom-b̄a | arhat |
| འགྲེལ་པ་ | ḍél-b̄a | commentary |
| འགྲོ་བ་ | ḍo-wa | going, goer |
| གོད་པ་ | gö'-b̄a | excitement |
| རྒྱགས་པ་ | gyak-b̄a | haughtiness |
| ང་རྒྱལ་ | nga-gyël | pride |
| ཆུ་བུར་ | chu-bur | bubble |
| ཆོས་ཅན་ | chö>-j̈en | [logical] subject |
| ཉོན་མོངས་ | nyön-mong | affliction |
| གཏན་ཚིགས་ | d̄en-tshík | reason |
| གཏི་མུག་ | d̄i-muk | obscuration, bewilderment |
| རྟགས་ | d̄ak | sign, reason |
| ལྟ་བ་ | d̄a-wa | view, [wrong] view |
| ཐེ་ཚོམ་ | thé-tshom | doubt |
| དམ་བཅའ་ | tam-j̈a | thesis |
| དུང་ | tung | conch |
| འདོད་པ་ | dö'-b̄a | desire |
| འདོད་ཆགས་ | dö'-chak | attachment |
| ནད་པ་ | në'-b̄a | ill person |
| རྣམ་པར་སྨིན་པ་ | ñam-b̄ar-m̄in-b̄a | fruition |
| རྣམ་པར་གཡེང་བ་ | ñam-b̄ar-yéng-wa | distraction |

| རྣམ་སྨིན་ | ñam-m̄în | fruition |
| ཕྱོགས་ | chok | side, direction, position |
| ཕྲག་དོག | ṭhak-dok | jealousy |
| བྱས་པ་ | chë>-b̄a | produced, made, product |
| མ་རིག་པ་ | ma-rík-b̄a | ignorance |
| མྱུ་གུ | nyu-gu | sprout |
| མྱོང་བྱ་ | nyong-ja | object of experience |
| རྨུགས་པ་ | m̄uk-b̄a | lethargy |
| སྨན་ | m̄ën | medicine |
| སྨན་པ་ | m̄ën-b̄a | doctor |
| རྩ་བ་ | d̄za-wa | root, basis, principal |
| ཚད་མ་ | tshë'-ma | valid cognition, prime cognition |
| ཚོར་བ་ | tshor-wa | feeling |
| ཞེ་སྡང་ | s̱hé-dang | aversion, hatred |
| ཟངས་ | s̱ang | copper |
| འོང་བ་ | ong-wa | coming |
| ཡོན་ཏན་ | yön-d̄ën | good quality, virtues, qualities |
| རང་དབང་ | rang-wang | independence ('self-power') |
| ལུང་མ་བསྟན་ | lung-ma-d̄ën | neutral |
| ལུས་ | lü> | body |
| ལེ་ལོ་ | lé-lo | laziness |

| ཡོངས་སྤྱོད་ | **long-jö'** | resources |
| སེར་སྣ་ | **šér-ña** | miserliness |
| གསེར་ | **šér** | gold |
| སྲོག་ | **šok** | life, vitality |
| སྲོག་གཅོད་པ་ | **šok-jö'-ba** | killing |

## Verbs

Verbs are marked by the Roman numeral indicating the class to which they belong—that is, the syntax they require.

| | | | |
|---|---|---|---|
| **I** | nominative-nominative | **V** | agentive-nominative |
| **II** | nominative-locative | **VI** | agentive-objective |
| **III** | nominative-objective | **VII** | purposive-nominative |
| **IV** | nominative-syntactic | **VIII** | locative-nominative |

The first part of the name of each class identifies the case of the subject and the second, that of the object, complement, or principal qualifier.

| གྱེ་ | **ḡyé** | be born **III** |
| སྐྱེད་ | **ḡyé'** | generate, produce **V** |
| གྲུབ་ | **țup** | was established, proven **III** |
| དགོས་ | **gö>** | must, require **VII** |
| འགྲུབ་ | **ḍup** | is established, proven **III** |
| མངའ་ | **ṅga** | exist, have **II VIII** |
| མཆི་ | **chí** | go **III** |
| ཉམས་སུ་ལེན་ | **nyam-šu-lên** | practice **V** |
| སྦྱེར་ | **ḏér** | give **V** |

| ཉོང་ | nyong | experience V |
|------|-------|--------------|
| ཟེར་ | s̲ér | is called VIII |
| ཡོད་ | yö' | exist, have II VIII |
| ཤར་ | s̄har | appear, rise III |
| གསུངས་ | s̄ung | said, spoke V |
| བསགས་ | s̄ak | accumulated V |

## Pronouns

[HON] means honorific.

| ཁོ་ | kho | she, he, it |
|------|-----|-------------|
| ཁོ་བོ་ | kho-wo | I, me |
| ཁོ་བོ་ཅག་ | kho-wo-j̄ak | we, us |
| ཁོ་བོ་ཅག་རྣམས་ | kho-wo-j̄ak-n̄am | we, us |
| ཁོང་ | khong | he, she, it [HON] |
| ཁྱོད་ | khyö' | you |
| ང་ | nga | I, me |
| ང་ཅག་ | nga-j̄ak | we, us |
| ང་ཚོ་ | nga-tso | we, us |
| ང་རང་ | nga-rang | I, I myself |
| བདག་ | dak | I, me, self [ātman] |
| བདག་ཅག་ | dak-j̄ak | we, us |
| རང་ | rang | own, our own, its own |

| རང་ཅག་ | **rang-j̄ak** | we, ourselves |
|---|---|---|

## Adjectives

| ཁོ་ན་ | **kho-na** | only |
|---|---|---|
| གསལ་པོ་ | **s̄ël-b̄o** | clear |

## Syntactic and Case Marking Particles

| གང་ཞིག་ | **kang-s̲hík** | [punctuational syntactic particle] |
|---|---|---|
| ཅིང་ | **j̄íng** | [continuative syntactic particle] |
| ཅེས་ | **j̄é>** | [close quote (syntactic particle)] |
| དེ་ | **d̄é** | [continuative syntactic particle] |
| དུར་ | **d̄ar** | [adverb marking syntactic particle] |
| སྟེ་ | **d̄é** | [continuative syntactic particle] |
| དེ་ | **dé** | [continuative syntactic particle] |
| ནས་ | **në>** | [continuative syntactic particle] |
| ཞིང་ | **s̲híng** | [continuative syntactic particle] |
| ཞེས་ | **s̲hé>** | [close quote (syntactic particle)] |
| ལས་ | **lë>** | [fifth case marking particle] |
| ཤིང་ | **s̄híng** | [continuative syntactic particle] |
| ཤེས་ | **s̄hé** | [close quote (syntactic particle)] |

# Chapter 15

*Syntactic Particles*
*Nominative-Locative Verbs: Verbs of Living*
*Case Particles Indicating Means and Reasons*
*Reflexive and Second Person Pronouns*
*Four Truths: Cessations and Paths*

## Patterns in Tibetan Language
### Classes of Syntactic Particles

Like lexical and case marking particles, and unlike words, syntactic particles do not have their own lexical meanings. Unlike lexical particles, however, they do not become parts of words, but are used to connect words, and even phrases and clauses, to one another.

> Syntactic particles (or grammatical particles) are units of one or two syllables that have only a grammatical function. Although, unlike lexical particles, they are not parts of words, they too cannot function independently of words, but must be used with words in phrases, clauses, and sentences.

Because case marking particles are *technically* syntactic particles, there are—theoretically—two main types of syntactic particles: case marking particles and syntactic particles other than case marking particles. However, in *Translating Buddhism from Tibetan*, the term 'syntactic particle' is consistently used to mean 'a syntactic particle that is not a case marking particle.'

Excluding case marking particles, then, there are eight main categories of syntactic particles:

1    introductory particles;

2    terminating particles;

3    rhetorical particles;

4    punctuational particles;

5    conjunctive and disjunctive particles;

6    verb modifying particles;

7    continuational particles;

8    adverb marking particles.

**Introductory particles** such as དེས་ན་ (*therefore*) serve to begin phrases, clauses, and sentences.  Here are some common ones.

| | | |
|---|---|---|
| དེའི་ཕྱིར་ | **té-chír** | *therefore* |
| གཞན་ཡང་ | **shën-yang** | *moreover* |
| དེ་ཚེ་ | **té-tshé** | *then, at that time* |
| གལ་ཏེ་ | **kël-dé** | *if* |

**Terminating particles** such as the imperative marker ཤིག་ in འདིར་གཤེགས་ཤིག (*Come here!*) act as definite periods or exclamation marks in a Tibetan sentence. The most basic—terminators such as the ོ་ in འདི་ལས་འདི་འབྱུང་ངོ་། —were introduced earlier in the book.  Such particles are often redundant: འདི་ལས་འདི་འབྱུང་ངོ་། means the same thing as འདི་ལས་འདི་འབྱུང་།.

**Rhetorical particles** are used in conditional and logical constructions.  For instance, ཕྱིར་ means *because* and ན་ means *given that*.

| NOM | NOM | VB | SP | |
|---|---|---|---|---|
| བུམ་པ་ | རྟག་པ་ | ཡིན་ | ན་ | *If pots were permanent ...* |

The introductory particle གལ་ཏེ་ may be combined with the conditional ན to clarify the conditional nature of the construction.

| SP | NOM | NOM | VB | SP | |
|---|---|---|---|---|---|
| གལ་ཏེ་ | བུམ་པ་ | རྟག་པ་ | ཡིན་ | ན་ | *If pots were permanent ...* |

Some rhetorical particles—for example, ཅི་མ་རུང་ (which occurs at the end of a sentence)—are 'phrasal particles,' or particles that are actually phrases. ཅི་མ་རུང་ literally means *how would it not be suitable*, and—following a clause ending in ན—indicates that if something were the case, that would be great.

སེམས་ཅན་ཐམས་ཅད་ སྡུག་བསྔལ་དང་བྲལ་ན་ ཅི་མ་རུང་།

*Wouldn't it be great if all sentient beings were free from suffering?*

The verb བྲལ་ is a class IV nominative-syntactic verb. Its subject (in this sentence) is སེམས་ཅན་ཐམས་ཅད་ and its principal qualifier is སྡུག་བསྔལ་དང་, a word marked by the syntactic particle དང་.

**Punctuational particles** serve to show where a quote ends, or to set off a word or a phrase, functions that in English would be performed by punctuation marks. For example, the particles ཞེས་, ཅེས་, and ཤེས་ follow direct quotations.

ཅེས་ follows words ending in the suffixes ག, ད་, བ་, and the secondary suffix ད་.
ཞེས་ follows words ending in the suffixes ང་, ན་, མ་, འ་, ར་, and ལ་, as well as syllables without suffixes. ཤེས་ follows words ending in the suffix ས་.

The punctuational particle གང་ཞིག was used in the Rhetorical Tools section of Chapter Fourteen.

རི་བོང་རྭ་ ཡོད་པ་མ་ཡིན་ཏེ་ རྟག་པ་མ་ཡིན་པ་ གང་ཞིག མི་རྟག་པ་ མ་ཡིན་པའི་ཕྱིར།

*The horns of a rabbit are not existent*
    *because [they] are not permanent and [they] are not impermanent.*

The གང་ཞིག་ serves merely to separate the two parts of the reason here and is thus termed punctuational.

**Conjunctive** and **disjunctive particles** act to tie together phrases, clauses, and sentences, but are also used with individual words—sometimes conjunctively in the sense of *and*, sometimes disjunctively in the sense of *but* or *although*. These particles are very common in Tibetan, perhaps the most frequently used being གྱང་, ཡང་, and འང་ which mean *also, even,* or *but* (depending on context).

**Verb modifying particles** occur within verb phrases, connecting verbs in either their basic or verbal forms to auxiliary verbs following them. (Auxiliary verbs are treated beginning in Chapter Seventeen.)

**Continuational** (or **continuative**) **particles** tie phrases, clauses, and sentences together, sometimes by showing sequence in verbal action, sometimes by leading to a reason or a further elaboration of what has gone before. The most common have already been introduced. The continuative ནས་ follows any verb, no matter what its ending suffix letter.

| | C 2 | 2 | V | SP | VB | |
|---|---|---|---|---|---|---|
| ཉོན་མོངས་ལ་ དགྲར་ བཟུང་ནས་ འགོག | | | | | | *Holding the afflictions as enemies, stopping [them].* |

The continuatives དེ་, ཏེ་, སྟེ་ are used in specific lexical situations.

| དེ་ follows words ending in the suffix ད་.
| ཏེ་ follows only words ending in the suffixes ན་, ར་, ལ་, and ས་.
| སྟེ་ follows words without suffix letters as well as those ending in ག་, ང་, བ་, མ་, and འ་.

| NOM | NOM | V | SP | |
|---|---|---|---|---|
| བུམ་པ་ཆོས་ཅན་ མི་རྟག་པ་ ཡིན་ ཏེ་ | | | | *The subject, a pot, is impermanent.* |

ཅིང་, ཞིང་, and ཤིང་ are used mainly after verbs, but also after nouns and adjectives, as in the following example.

SP　SP
གསལ་ ཞིང་ རིག་པ་　　　　　　　　　　*clear and knowing*

གསལ་ཞིང་རིག་པ་ is the definition of ཤེས་པ་. This is an example of a continuative particle used between adjectives. ཅིང་, ཞིང་, and ཤིང་ follow the same suffix letters as ཅེས་, ཞེས་, and ཤེས་.

- ཅིང་ follows words ending in the suffixes ག་, ད་, བ་, and the secondary suffix ད་.
- ཞིང་ follows words ending in the suffixes ང་, ན་, མ་, འ་, ར་, and ལ་, as well as syllables without suffixes.
- ཤིང་ follows words ending in the suffix ས་.

This usage is also the case for the syntactic particles that emphasize imperative verbs, ཅིག་, ཞིག་, and ཤིག་.

**Adverb marking particles**—when placed after a word, clause, or phrase—make that word, clause, or phrase into an adverb. The particle ལྟར་, for example, means *like* and *according to*.

> Unlike the other syntactic particles, adverbial particles turn the word, clause, or phrase they end into an adverb and, thus, the dot after them should be identified as an **ADV** dot.

# Verbs and Verb Syntax
## *Nominative-Locative Verbs*

The simplest of the Class II verbs—verbs taking nominative subjects and locative qualifiers—are the verbs of existence examined in Chapter Thirteen. However, there are four different types of nominative-locative verbs:

1　simple **verbs of existence** (such as ཡོད་, *exist*) where the locative qualifier is optional;

2  **verbs of living**, that is, continuing existence, (such as གནས་, *stay, live*)—where the place where or time during which existence continues is in the locative case;

3  **verbs of dependence** (such as རྟེན་, *depend on*)—in which that upon which there is dependence is marked by a locative case particle;

4  **attitude verbs**—verbs that express mental attitudes taken about something (where the *about* translates a referential locative) such as འཇིགས་ (*fear, be afraid of*) and ཆགས་ (*be attached to*), as well as verbs such as མཁས་ (*be skilled in*).

Verbs of living are also quite simple, with a syntax similar to that of verbs of existence, except that the qualifier is no longer an optional element. Of course, although the qualifier is required, it need not be explicitly stated.

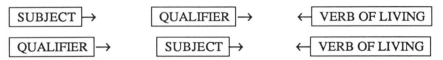

The qualifier of a verb of living is a place or a length of time. The qualifier of a verb of dependence is that thing or person upon which the subject of the sentence depends.

**Verbs of living**—taken literally—are similar to verbs of existence.[120] Saying *The monks live in a monastery* (གྲྭ་པ་དགོན་པ་ལ་བཞུགས།) is not too far from saying *The monks exist in a monastery*. Verbs of living translate into English as *live*, *dwell*, *stay*, *exist [in a place]*, and *remain*. They indicate not just existence but *continued* existence.[121]

**Verbs of dependence** and verbs of living are similar in that both verbs refer not just to their subjects but to something else as well. Just as the subject of a verb of living lives *somewhere* or remains *in something*, the subject of a verb of dependence is dependent *on something else*, something separate from that subject: འབྲས་བུ་རྒྱུ་ལ་རྟེན, *Effects depend on causes*.

> A verb of living indicates continued existence for a time or in place; the qualifier in sentences ending in such a verb is a place or a length of time.
>
> A verb of dependence also requires a qualifier—something or someone upon which the subject of the sentence depends.

## Nominative-Locative Verbs
### *Verbs of Living*

Verbs of living indicate a state of continuing to exist in a place. Their most basic use, therefore, is for persons living or dwelling somewhere; some can also mean *sit*. Verbs of living are also used to indicate not continued existence in a specific place, but continued existence in general—that is, existence that endures over time (as in ཁོང་ལོ་བརྒྱ་རུ་སྡོད། [ *He lived/remained for one hundred years*]).

Verbs of living may be thought of as verbs of existence that always require a reference to a place or a length of time. Three commonly seen verbs of living are the following.

| | | |
|---|---|---|
| བཞུགས་[122] | **<u>s</u>huk** | *live, remain, sit* |
| གནས་ | **ñë>** | *live, stay, continue* |
| སྡོད་ | **dö'** | *dwell, remain, sit* |

The word གནས་ is also used as a noun meaning mainly *place*, *abode*, or *location*, but also *situation*, *source*, *object*, *topic*, *basis*, and many other things. The noun གནས་ should not be confused with the verbal noun གནས་པ་ (*dwelling/remaining*, *one who dwells/remains*).

### *Living in a Place*

This is the basic use of verbs of living. Here is an example of the use of a common *honorific* verb of living; it is taken from the Tibetan translation of the *Diamond Cutter Sutra* (རྡོ་རྗེ་གཅོད་པ་—in Sanskrit, the *Vajracchedika*):[123]

བཅོམ་ལྡན་འདས་ མཉན་ཡོད་ན་ བཞུགས་སོ།

**J̱om-dën-dë>    n̄yën-yö'-na    s̱huk-s̱o**

*The Transcendent Victor stayed at Shravasti.*

བཅོམ་ལྡན་འདས་ has already been discussed; here it is not a vocative, however, but the nominative subject with which you are well acquainted. མཉན་ཡོད་ is the name of a city in northern India—Shravasti (*Śrāvastī*). ན་ is a case marking particle (marking nouns in the second, fourth, and seventh declensions). བཞུགས་ is an honorific verb meaning *stay* or *live* or *sit*.

One reason verbs of living are similar to verbs of existence is that their syntax is the same, SUBJECT + QUALIFIER + VERB:

SUBJECT $\rightarrow$     PLACE $\rightarrow$     $\leftarrow$ VERB OF LIVING

Remember that, like any other Tibetan sentence, one or two of these elements may be be implied without needing to be stated.

In the present example, a Tenglish reading would be:

VICTOR-TRANSCENDENT  SHRAVASTI-IN   STAYED.

Note that the verb བཞུགས་ is written and pronounced in the same way whether it refers to living, staying, or sitting in the past, present, or future. Here you know from context—the fact that the subject is Shakyamuni Buddha—that བཞུགས་ should be translated into English in the past tense. (In fact, given its place in the scene-setting material at the beginning of the sutra, it is often translated *was staying*, since it denotes a continued activity in the past.)

The sentence diagrams as follows.

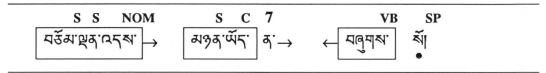

The ན་ in མཚན་ཡོད་ན་ is a locative case marker (specifically, the locative showing a place of existence or living).[124] The སོ་ is a terminator (a type of syntactic particle) such as we have seen before.

## *Verbs Indicating Duration*

Verbs of living not only indicate continued existence in a specific place, but are frequently used to indicate continued existence enduring over a certain period of time. The syntax is the same, SUBJECT + QUALIFIER + VERB, and the qualifier is still in the locative case. However, the locative is not a locative indicating place, but one indicating time.

> Recall that, unlike the locatives of place, locatives of time may occur with any verb.

| | | | |
|---|---|---|---|
| ལོ་ | བརྒྱ་རུ་ | སྡོད་པ་ | *living for a hundred years* |
| ལོ་ | བརྒྱ་རུ་ | བསྡད | *[He] lived for a hundred years.* |

The first example is not a sentence ending in a terminal verb but, rather, a clause ending in a verbal.

> Verbals are open forms of verbs that function as nouns and adjectives; they are constructed from verbs by adding a lexical particle (པ་ or བ་) to the verb.

The second example is a sentence ending in a verb. Where the verbal སྡོད་པ་ in the first example is built from the present tense of the verb སྡོད་, the verb བསྡད in the second example is the past tense of that verb.

> Many Tibetan verbs—including action verbs (whether agentive or nominative), verbs of motion, verbs of living, and verbs of dependence—may occur in different forms to indicate past, present, and future tenses, and to indicate the imperative.

The verb སྡོད་ is a two-form verb: སྡོད་ is the present tense and the imperative; བསྡད་ indicates the past and the future tenses.[125] What this means is that when you see སྡོད་, you know that it refers either to living in the present or to a command:

*I / We / You / He / She / They live* (or *lives* or *are living*).

*Live!*

When you see བསྡད་, you know that it means either future living or a state of having lived:

*I / We / You / He / She / They will live.*

*I / We / You / He / She / They lived* (or *have lived*).

The tense of a verb will typically be further clarified through the use of auxiliary verbs, continuative markers, and the like.

The verbs བཞུགས་ and གནས་ may also be used to indicate past, present, and future events, but since they are single-form verbs the various tenses are known only through the auxiliary verbs following them or other contextual clues (for example, the use of adverbs like སྔོན་ལ་, *formerly*).

Here is an example of the use of both types of qualifiers with a verb of living, the first qualifier indicating place, the second duration.

---

ཆོས་འདི་ འཛིག་རྟེན་དུ་ ཡུན་རིང་དུ་ གནས་ན...

*If this doctrine remained in the world for a long time ...*

---

The word ཡུན་རིང་ means *a long time*—ཡུན་ means *duration* and རིང་ is an abbreviated form of རིང་པོ་, an adjective meaning *long*. The དུ་ particles after the place and the time are locative case markers.

This example is not a sentence; it is a clause ending in a conditional particle, ན་. You have just seen ན་ used as a locative *case* particle after a noun, but it is often used as a syntactic particle (that is, a syntactic particle other than a case marking particle) as it is here. It is frequently used in this way after verbs, indicating that the clause it ends is stated as a condition:

*if* something is the case or *given that* something is the case.

ན་ is a rhetorical particle implying that there is more to come—if this is the case, or were to be the case, then something else would follow. In the present example, the clause *If this [Buddhist] doctrine [were to] remain in the world for a long time* is typically followed by a conclusion such as *it would be fitting*.[126]

This clause diagrams as follows. Note that the concluding ན་ links the entire clause to what follows it.

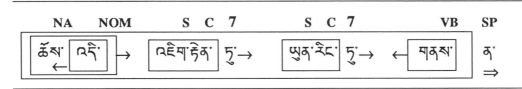

## Drill 15.1

Translate the following into Tibetan.

1 The monks stay in a monastery.

2 The Tathāgata Shakyamuni did not live in Lhasa.

3 We live in Dzang.

4 Hell-beings live for a long time.

5 They lived for six years in China.

## Drill 15.2

Identify the dots in the following and translate. Diagram the first and fourth.

1 སངས་རྒྱས་ཀྱི་ལོངས་སྐུ་དག་ཞིང་ལ་བཞུགས།

2 བདེ་བར་གཤེགས་པ་ལྷ་ར་ན་སི་ལ་བཞུགས།

3 ལྷ་དེ་དག་རེ་རབ་ལྷུན་པོར་གནས།

4 རྒྱ་གར་ལ་ལོ་མང་པོར་བསྡད་ན།

5 ཡུལ་དབུས་སུ་གནས་པ་

## Special Uses of Verbs of Living

In addition to literal uses of verbs of living—someone living for so many years or someone staying in a particular area—there are two other significant areas in which verbs of living are used:

1   on the title page of books, at the end of the title;

2   in writing about philosophy and meditation, where in many cases verbs of living are used metaphorically (as, for example, when saying *Bodhisattvas dwell in emptiness*).

## *Book Titles*

A frequently seen occurrence of བཞུགས་ is on the title pages of books. Although in the West book titles are merely labels on their covers and title pages, in Tibetan a book's title is stated in a sentence on the first page. Traditionally, Tibetan books are printed on pages that are much wider than they are long (for example, eighteen inches wide and only three inches tall), and the title is the only information on the front side of the first page.   Here, for example, is the title page—slightly simplified[127]—of the collected works of Tsong-kha-pa, founder of the Gélukba order:

ཙོང་ཁ་པ་ཆེན་པོའི་ གསུང་འབུམ་ བཞུགས་སོ།

*[Here] abide the collected works of the great Tsong-kha-pa.*

The phrase marked by the connective particle འི་ is comprised of a noun (ཙོང་ཁ་པ་) followed by an adjective (ཆེན་པོ་, *great*).  Since a great many connectives translate as *of*, a good rule of thumb is to tentatively translate this phrase as *of the great Tsong-kha-pa.*

---

Although most case particles show how a noun relates to a verb  following it, a connective particle relates a noun or pronoun to another noun or pronoun following it, not to a verb.

---

The noun གསུང་འབུམ་ (whose roots are in གསུང་ *discourse* and འབུམ་ *one-hundred-thousand*) means *collected works*. In this example, གསུང་འབུམ་ is the only word following the connective particle but yet in front of the verb.

> A noun, pronoun, or adjective in the connective case cannot relate to a word outside of the sentence in which it is found. This is a corollary of the rule that all elements of a sentence must precede the verb of that sentence.

Since གསུང་འབུམ་ is a noun and has no case ending, it must be in either the nominative or vocative case; here, clearly, it is the nominative subject of the verb. There is no qualifying PLACE OF LIVING in this sentence; a book title assumes it to be obvious that where that book exists is in the pages following the title page.

This sentence diagrams as a noun phrase in the connective case, a nominative subject, and a verb:

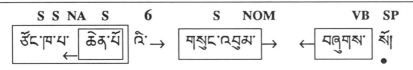

Observe the way in which the noun-adjective phrase ཚོང་ཁ་པ་ཆེན་པོ་ is diagrammed. The boxed adjective ཆེན་པོ་ modifies the noun to its left, creating the basic phrase, which is itself boxed. This *entire phrase* is marked by a connective case particle (འི་) which connects it (the phrase, not just the word ཆེན་པོ་) to a noun or pronoun to its right. This means that when diagramming such a noun phrase—a *declined* phrase—the case particle should be placed *outside* of the box, since it goes with the entire boxed phrase. Much of the time this means drawing the box in front of a case marking particle such as ལ་ or ནས་ or ཀྱི་ when it connects a boxed phrase to the rest of the sentence. Sometimes, as in the above example, it means drawing the box down the middle of a syllable.

> Syllables such as པའི་, པར་ and པས་ are examples of concluding, suffixless པ་ syllables marked, respectively, by connective, objective, and agentive particles.

Books are sometimes feminine.  Tsong-kha-pa's *Great Exposition of the Stages of the Path [to Enlightenment]* is his ལམ་རིམ་ཆེན་མོ་.

---

The word-ending syllables མ་ and མོ་ are feminine endings.

---

On the other hand, sutras do not have feminine titles.  The full name of the *Heart Sūtra* is བཅོམ་ལྡན་འདས་མ་ཤེས་རབ་ཀྱི་ཕ་རོལ་ཏུ་ཕྱིན་པའི་སྙིང་པོ་, *The Heart of the Perfection of Wisdom, Lady of Transcendent Victory*.[128]  While བཅོམ་ལྡན་འདས་མ་ *is* a feminine noun, it stands in apposition with ཤེས་རབ་ཀྱི་ཕ་རོལ་ཏུ་ཕྱིན་པ་; it is the perfection of wisdom that is feminine, not the name of the sutra.[129]

It should be noted also that the title pages of sutras (and tantras) refer to them as འཕགས་པ་ or *superior*.

---

| | |
|---|---|
| འཕགས་པ་ཤེས་རབ་ཀྱི་ཕ་རོལ་ཏུ་ཕྱིན་པའི་སྙིང་པོ་ | *The Superior Heart of the Perfection of Wisdom* |
| འཕགས་པ་ཤེས་རབ་ཀྱི་ཕ་རོལ་ཏུ་ཕྱིན་པ་ རྡོ་རྗེ་གཅོད་པ་ཞེས་བྱ་བ་ཐེག་པ་ཆེན་པོའི་མདོ་ | *The Superior Mahāyāna Sūtra on the Perfection of Wisdom Called 'Diamond Cutter'* |

---

| འཕགས་པ་ | ཤེས་རབ་ཀྱི་ཕ་རོལ་ཏུ་ཕྱིན་པ་ | རྡོ་རྗེ་གཅོད་པ་ཞེས་བྱ་བ་ | ཐེག་པ་ཆེན་པོ་ | འི་ མདོ་ |

---

The word ཕ་རོལ་ཏུ་ཕྱིན་པ་ may be further analyzed (since it ends in a verbal derived from a verb of motion), but for the moment it should be understood merely as a word meaning *perfection* (literally, *that gone to the other side* or *transcendent*).

The construction ཞེས་བྱ་བ་ means *so-called* or *called '[…]'*.  Thus, བུམ་པ་ཞེས་བྱ་བ་ means *that called 'pot'* and ཙོང་ཁ་པ་ཞེས་བྱ་བ་ means *the one called 'Tsong-kha-pa'*.  The ཞེས་ in ཞེས་བྱ་བ་ is one of the three syntactic particles that close quotations; in this case, the quotation is a word or name (similiar to the English use of apostrophes around words).  The བྱ་བ་ in ཞེས་བྱ་བ་ is a verbal noun constructed from the future tense form of the verb བྱེད་.

In general, verbal nouns indicating **agency** are constructed from the present tense form of a verb while verbal nouns that refer to **objects** are based on the future tense form.

This is discussed more fully in Chapter Eighteen. Here, merely note that བྱ་བ་ is based on the future form of the verb བྱེད་ in its attributive sense. བྱེད་ is sometimes used in the sense of *say* or *call* (that is, *designate a name to something*). Thus, the verbal བྱ་བ་ means *object of designation* and ཞེས་བྱ་བ་ may be translated *so called* or *called "..."*.

## *Verbs of Living in Philosophy and Meditation*

Tibetan books on philosophy and meditation utilize a special vocabulary and, in some cases, special sentence constructions. Verbs of living are used in such works in the ways already seen, but they are also used in a metaphorical sense indicating absorption in a state of being or in meditation.

The following example illustrates the more direct, more literal use; it concerns the disintegration of impermanent phenomena.

*Impermanent phenomena do not remain a second moment.*[130]

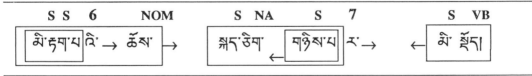

There are three main boxes in this diagram.

1   The first box surrounds the nominative subject of the sentence.

2   The second box surrounds the modifier, here one that defines duration. Note that the ར suffix on the adjective གཉིས་པ་—a locative case particle— has been isolated and placed after this box (despite the fact that it is not a separate syllable) to indicate the way in which it serves to connect the entire boxed phrase to the verb.

3    The third box surrounds the verb, which is in the present tense and has
      been negated by the lexical particle མི་.

Verbs of living are also used metaphorically, indicating absorption or involvement
in a state of being or a meditative state.  The first example below is a sentence,
whereas the second is a conditional clause;  both have "understood" (that is, not
explicitly stated) subjects.  བཏང་སྙོམས་ means *equanimity*.

---

*[He] stays in equanimity.*

---

བཏང་སྙོམས་སུ་སྡོད།

---

*If [the mind] remains in equanimity ...*

---

བཏང་སྙོམས་སུ་གནས་ན་

---

The next two examples are not of a mind staying in a particular state, but rather
of a mind continuing to perceive an object.  In the first example, the term ཡུལ་ is used
to mean *object*, although it can also mean *area* or *country*.  Thus, the sentence ཁོང་
ཡུལ་དེ་ལ་གནས། could easily mean *He remains / remained in that area*.  རང་གི་ here
means *its own*, but must be translated according to the context in which it is found.
རང་ is the basic Tibetan reflexive pronoun and is ambiguous as to number, person,
and gender.  It can mean *one, it, her, his, me,* or *you*.

---

*That mind stays on its own object.*

---

སེམས་དེ་    རང་གི་ཡུལ་ལ་    གནས།

---

In the following example, the noun དོན་ means *object*.  In other contexts དོན་ means
*meaning* and *purpose*.

---

*staying single-pointedly on an object*

---

དོན་ལ་    རྩེ་གཅིག་ཏུ་    གནས་པ་

---

དོན་ is in the locative case, marking the "place" where the mind stays.  The next
phrase— རྩེ་གཅིག་ཏུ་ —which might seem to be in the locative case, is actually an
adverb.

> **Adverbial identity** is a special—and very common—usage of the objective case. It is most often marked by སུ་, ར་, ཟ་, ད་, or ཏུ་ (and not as often by ན་ or ལ་).

ཟ་ means *point* or *peak*; ཟ་གཅིག་ thus means *a single point* or *one point*. Although you have seen many locatives used with verbs of living to indicate places, in this example ཟ་གཅིག་ཏུ་ means not *on a single point* (which would answer the question "Where?") but rather *one-pointedly*, answering the question "How?" The question "Where?" is answered in this example by དོན་ལ་.

> Adverbs answer the question "How?" Some Tibetan words are always adverbs, requiring no particles; in other instances particles of the *la*-group mark adverbs.

## Drill 15.3

Translate the following into Tibetan.

1  Foe Destroyers remain in nirvana.
2  [title page of a book entitled] *Sūtra on Renunciation*
3  Buddhas abide in ultimate truths.
4  The cities of humans do not last many years.
5  We abide in virtue.

## Drill 15.4

Translate the following. Diagram the second and third, marking their dots.

1  སེམས་དེ་བདེ་བ་ལ་གནས།

2  དགེ་བའི་སེམས་ཡུན་རིང་པོར་མི་སྡོད་

3  རྣལ་འབྱོར་པ་བདག་མེད་དུ་ཟ་གཅིག་ཏུ་གནས།

4  བྱང་ཆུབ་སེམས་དཔའ་རྣམས་སྙིང་རྗེ་ལ་གནས།

## Case Marking Particles
### *Agentive Means and Reasons*

Agentive case marking particles were introduced in Chapter Thirteen, where their main usage—to mark the subjects of agentive verbs (those verbs expressing actions done by an agent on an object separate from that agent)—was presented. However, they have other significant uses as well, indicating the means by which something is done (*by*, *through*, or *by means of*) and indicating reasons (*because of*).

### *Agentive Means*

Even verbs that do not require an agentive case subject may use the agentive case marking particles to indicate instrumentality—the means used to accomplish something or the means due to which something happens.

The following is an example of a sentence with both an agentive subject and an agentive case instrument.

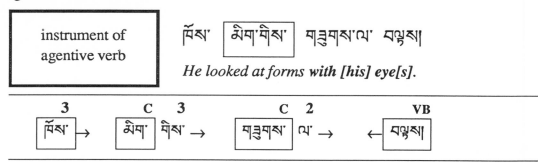

The *eyes* (མིག་) are the instrument by means of which *he looked*.

Recall that the verb ལྟ་ takes not a nominative object, but an object followed by the case marking particle ལ་. It is a Class VI, agentive-objective verb.

### *Agentives Marking Reasons*

In Tibetan, it is common (but not required) to indicate reasons with agentive case marking particles. This usage of the agentive is quite close to the previous one, since reasons, after all, are merely logical instruments.

| agentive reason | སྒྲ་མི་རྟག་པ་ཡིན་པས་ | རྟག་པ་མ་ཡིན། |

***Because sound is impermanent,** [it] is not permanent.*

The noun marked by the agentive particle here is a clause based on the sentence སྒྲ་མི་ རྟག་པ་ཡིན།.

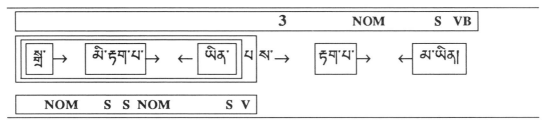

Recall from Chapter Eleven that the **V** dot follows the open form of a verb. In this case, the open form is a verbal noun, and *is only identified as such in diagramming the clause it ends.* As a component of the sentence, it functions not as an open verb, but as the noun it is. It is for this reason that the dot following it is marked as a **3**-dot, indicating that in the sentence as a whole, it is a noun in the agentive case.

## Case Marking Particles
### *Originative Case Means and Reasons*

The fifth case particle is also used to show the means through which something is done. This, in a sense, is a different sort of source (one neither physical nor verbal).

| instrumental originative | རྩོལ་བ་ལས་ | ཐོབ་པ་ |

*achieved **through effort***

Although in Tibetan it is more common to use the agentive to mark a reason, the originative case may also be used.

| originative reason | ┌─────────────────┐ དུ་བ་མཐོང་བ་ལས་ │ མེ་ཡོད་པར་ཤེས། |
|---|---|

*[One] understands, **due to seeing smoke**, that fire exists.*

This usage is seen predominantly in texts translated from Sanskrit where the fifth case is commonly used to show reasons.[131]

The clause མེ་ཡོད་པར་ is the objective case complement of the verb ཤེས་, an agentive-nominative verb. Instead of a nominative object, ཤེས་ here has a second case complement. What is known? That fire exists.

---

## Personal Pronouns
### *First Person Reflexive Pronouns*

---

The overview of pronouns continues with the first person reflexive pronouns and second person personal pronouns (in English, *you*) and third person personal pronouns (*he, she, they*).

┌──────────────────────────────────────────────────────────────────┐
│ Remember that, unlike verbs, Tibetan pronouns differ according to person. │
└──────────────────────────────────────────────────────────────────┘

Thus, within the personal pronouns, there are first, second, and third person pronouns. These are the most common:

1   ང་ and བདག་ mean *I* and are first person pronouns;

2   ཁྱོད་ means *you* and is a second person pronoun;

3   ཁོ་ and ཁོང་ mean *he* or *she* or *it* and are third person pronouns.

┌──────────────────────────────────────────────────────────────────┐
│ In Tibetan little distinction is made between between masculine and feminine. │
└──────────────────────────────────────────────────────────────────┘

You will also see the pronoun ཁྱོད་ (in its ordinary usage, *you*) used in formal debate (both written and oral) not as a second person pronoun, but as an impersonal pronoun referring to the subject under discussion. Thus, it is there an *it* rather than a *you*.

In English, words such as *myself* and *itself* are reflexive pronouns. In Tibetan, reflexive pronouns are formed by adding the syllable རང་ to ordinary personal pronouns. རང་ is a very adaptable word; in its most general sense it means *-self*.[132] It is placed at the end of nouns (as an appositive—see Chapter Eleven) or is added to pronouns as a concluding syllable.

རང་ added to ང་ gives us ང་རང་, a reflexive pronoun that may be translated *I myself* or *myself* or more often just *I* or *me*, depending on context. རང་ by itself, in contexts that refer to the first person, may also be translated *I* or *me*. It frequently occurs in the plural (meaning *we* or *our*) as རང་ཅག་ or, with the redundant addition of the pluralizer རྣམས་, as རང་ཅག་རྣམས་.

| S | C | 6 | S | |
|---|---|---|---|---|
| རང་ཅག་ | | གི་ | སྟོན་པ་ | *our teacher* |

In this phrase, which refers to Shakyamuni Buddha, the གི་ is a connective case particle. Where རང་ཅག་ means *we* or *us*, རང་ཅག་གི་ means *our*.

> There are no possessive pronouns (*my*, *his*) as such in Tibetan. The Tibetan words that translate into English as possessive pronouns are pronouns in the connective case such as ངའི་ (*mine*), ཁོང་གི་ (*hers*, *his*), and ཁྱེད་ཀྱི་ (*yours*).

རང་ཅག་རྣམས་ མི་ ཡིན། *We are humans.*

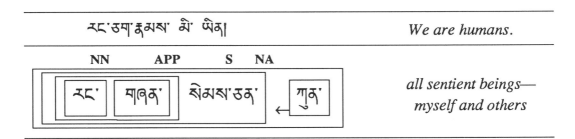

*all sentient beings— myself and others*

Note the རང་གཞན་ construction. གཞན་ means *other(s)* and is frequently seen used as a pronoun in much the same way that the adjective དེ་ may be used as a pronoun. རང་ གཞན་ and བདག་གཞན་ are both commonly used (in the sense seen here of *self and others*) in discussions of compassion and altruism and in meditation texts.

The word རང་རེ་ is also commonly used to mean *our*, even though རང་ means *own* and རེ་ means *each*. (The possessive construction—that pronoun with a connective case marker— is རང་རེའི་.) རང་རེ་ is also used in the third person sense of *each itself*.

## *Second Person Pronouns*

The second person pronouns in English are *you* and *your*. In the southern United States, where I live, we also say *you all*, which expresses the plural. What we do not have in English—or for that matter, in modern Western languages—are **honorifics**, special words that one uses to refer to others of higher status than oneself. Tibetan has many such words; many verbs, nouns, and pronouns have both honorific and non-honorific forms. The higher status involved may be social status, and this is very important in speaking to and about Tibetans. However, for our purposes in this book, honorifics are important because they are the words used when speaking about buddhas, bodhisattvas, gurus, and other persons who have a high spiritual status. Since honorifics are used to speak about *others* of higher status than the speaker, a discussion of them begins not with the first but with the second person—one does not use an honorific to speak about oneself.[133]

Whereas the ordinary (non-honorific) second person pronoun is ཁྱོད་ (*you*), the pronoun ཁྱེད་ is a more respectful or reverent form. Notice, however, in the third example below, that ཁྱོད་ may also be used in speaking of buddhas and gurus. As before, either can be explicitly pluralized by the addition of either ཅག་, ཚོ་, or རྣམས་ and reflexive pronouns may be created through the addition of the syllable རང་.

| S  S NOM S  S     S NOM VB | |
|---|---|
| ཁྱེད་ཅག་རྣམས་ དེ་བཞིན་གཤེགས་པ་ ཡིན། | *You are Tathāgatas.* |

| NOM  S NOM    VB | |
|---|---|
| ཁྱོད་ ཁྱོད་རང་ ཡིན། | *It is itself.* |

| NOM SP  NOM    NOM SP    NOM | |
|---|---|
| ཁྱོད་ ནི་ བླ་མ་    ཁྱོད་ ནི་ ཡི་དམ། | *You [are] the guru; you [are] the meditational deity.* |

The second example illustrates a use of the second person pronoun ཁྱོད་ peculiar to syllogistic presentations of philosophy. There, ཁྱོད་ most frequently means *it* rather than *you* and refers to the logical subject, that is, the topic under discussion. The last example is actually two short phrases, each of which has an understood verb: ཁྱོད་ནི་ནོ་མ་ཡིན། ཁྱོད་ནི་ཡི་དམ་ཡིན།. This example is taken from a line in verse[134] where the two understood ཡིན་ verbs were left out for metric considerations.

## Rhetorical Tools
### *Consequences*

The Rhetorical Tools section of Chapter Fourteen ended with the following syllogism.

*The subject, a pot, is impermanent because of being a product.*

བུམ་པ་ཆོས་ཅན་ མི་རྟག་པ་ཡིན་ཏེ་ བྱས་པ་ཡིན་པའི་ཕྱིར།

Seen even more frequently than the syllogism in Tibetan textbook literature is the *consequence* (ཐལ་འགྱུར་ **thën-gyur** or **thël-gyur**—Skt. *prasaṅga*). Consequences and syllogisms share the same three-part structure, SUBJECT + PREDICATE + REASON or, combining the subject and the predicate, the two-part structure THESIS + REASON. Here is the above stated syllogism restated as a consequence.

*It follows that the subject, a pot, is impermanent because of being a product.*

བུམ་པ་ཆོས་ཅན། མི་རྟག་པ་ཡིན་པར་ཐལ། བྱས་པ་ཡིན་པའི་ཕྱིར།

The formal (that is, lexical and syntactic) difference between a syllogism and a consequence is the consequence's replacement of the syntactic particle following the thesis with a verb, ཐལ་, meaning—in this context—*logically follows.*

The following diagram illustrates the syntactic dimension of this consequence.

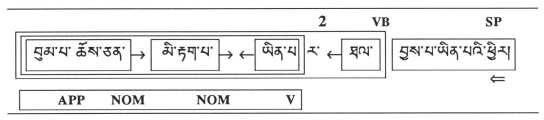

Since their syntax does not differ from that already seen in Chapter Fourteen, the subject and reason of this consequence have not been fully diagrammed.

---

Whereas some verbs take objects (*Buddha taught **the doctrine***), others take complements (*Buddhists assert **that there is no self***).  The rhetorical verb ཐལ་ is of the second sort.

---

Rhetorical verbs, along with verbs of motion and nominative action verbs, are Class III (nominative-objective) verbs.  As is seen in the case of the verb ཐལ་, rhetorical verbs often have tacit generic subjects (leading to translations such as *[It] follows* …).

---

Diagrammed below are two possible analyses of the syntactic structure of a consequence.  In the first analysis, the entire thesis (བུམ་པ་མི་རྟག་པ་ཡིན་པ་) is the objective case complement of the verb ཐལ་.

---

The rule of thumb translation of objective complements is *that* … or *to* ….  In the current example, this gives us *That pots are impermanent follows*.

---

Technically speaking—in terms of the *doctrinal* dimensions of the term—consequences do not have theses, since many are statements of unacceptably absurd consequences following from a certain position.  However, *syntactically*, it is possible to say that in the present example, for instance, བུམ་པ་མི་རྟག་པ་ཡིན་པ་ is a thesis.

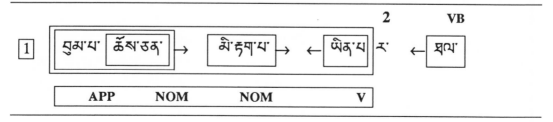

In the second possible analysis of the syntax of consequences, the subject (བུམ་པ་ཆོས་ཅན་) is the grammatical subject of ཐལ་, and the clause མི་རྟག་པ་ཡིན་པ་ is its complement.

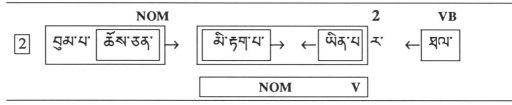

The first way of looking at this sentence, besides being simpler, is closer to the way one would want to translate it into English. However, the second analysis reflects important aspects of the doctrinal dimension of consequences and the syntactic dimension of the verb ཐལ་.

Consequences differ doctrinally from syllogisms in that whereas stating a syllogism entails acceptance of its content, stating a consequence does not necessarily imply that the stater accepts what the consequence says. Central to the Tibetan textbook literature is the concept of the *unwanted consequence* (མི་འདོད་པའི་ཐལ་འགྱུར་). Writers (or, in spoken philosophical analysis, debaters) often state consequences based on positions they are attacking, not positions they hold. In these cases, the reason is one that is acceptable in the context of the position being attacked, but the thesis is one that, to the opponent in question, is an undesired consequence.

Concerning consequences, see Perdue, *Debate in Tibetan Buddhism*, pp. 54-60.

To take as an example a well known elementary exercise in consequence manipulation found in many basic Tibetan doctrinal primers, let us suppose that there is someone who believes that whatever is a color is necessarily the color red.

Statements of the form, *whatever is a color is necessarily red*, are called **pervasions** (ཁྱབ་པ་, Skt. *vyāpti*). (See Chapter Sixteen.)

One may say to such a person that the color of something white must actually be red, since that color *is* a color, and whatever is a color, so it is claimed, is red. The traditional subject for this consequence is ཆོས་དུང་དཀར་པོའི་ཁ་དོག—*the color of a white religious conch.*

*[It] follows that the subject, the color of a white religious conch,*
*is red because of being a color.*

ཆོས་དུང་དཀར་པོའི་ཁ་དོག་ཆོས་ཅན། དམར་པོ་ཨིན་པར་ཐལ། ཁ་དོག་ཨིན་པའི་ཕྱིར

When you read and translate such a consequence, you should not jump to the conclusion that the author agrees with the point being made. The purpose in stating it may be Socratic—seeking to cause the reader to reflect on the faults inherent in the position that all colors are red—instead of stating the author's own position.

This aspect of consequences—stating a contradictory, and undesired entailment—reflects a basic meaning of the verb ཐལ་ when it is used outside of Buddhist doctrine: *go*, *pass beyond*, and *go too far*. Thus, when the color of a white conch is held to be red, it has gone beyond what it should; the subject, the color of a white religious conch, has—in the mind of the person who thinks all colors are red—gone beyond what it really is. It misses the mark. Thus it is that, following the second way of analyzing the syntax of consequences, the complement—*being red*—is a clause with an understood subject.

> For a detailed examination of this consequence and the ways it may be manipulated, see Perdue, *Debate in Tibetan Buddhism*, pp. 99ff.

# Drill 15.5

Translate the following. Diagram the first and identify its dots.

1. ཀ་བུམ་གཉིས་ཆོས་ཅན། ཡོད་པ་ཨིན་པར་ཐལ། དངོས་པོ་ཨིན་པའི་ཕྱིར

2. རྟ་དཀར་པོ་ཆོས་ཅན། དཀར་པོ་མ་ཨིན་པར་ཐལ། ཁ་དོག་མ་ཨིན་པའི་ཕྱིར

3. རྟ་དཀར་པོ་ཆོས་ཅན། ཁ་དོག་མ་ཨིན་པར་ཐལ། གང་ཟག་ཨིན་པའི་ཕྱིར

4. མིག་ཤེས་ཆོས་ཅན། ཡིད་ཤེས་མ་ཨིན་པར་ཐལ། དབང་ཤེས་ཨིན་པའི་ཕྱིར

# Doctrinal Vocabulary and Grammar
## *The Four Truths: Cessations*

Where the first of the four truths is the symptom of the illness of cyclic existence and the second is its source, the third—the cessation of suffering (འགོག་པའི་བདེན་པ་, abbreviated འགོག་བདེན་)—refers to the state of being cured. འགོག་བདེན་ are the absences of sufferings (the first truth) and their causes (the second truth). Thus, nirvana as a final goal is the sum total of the cessation of each of various sorts of attachment, aversion, and ignorance.

> Concerning nirvana, see Paul Williams, *Mahāyāna Buddhism*, pp. 67-69 and Sopa and Hopkins, *Cutting Through Appearances*, pp. 317-319.

Whereas the phenomena included in the other three truths are all impermanent, these cessations are permanent phenomena. འགོག་པའི་བདེན་པ་ are not cessations in the sense of being the actions involved in bringing the afflictions to cessation—such actions are the paths that make up the fourth truth and they are impermanent. A འགོག་བདེན་ is, rather, the state of some individual's having eliminated a certain type of affliction. Thus, like the absence of an elephant in a specific room, འགོག་བདེན་ are absences.

There are, technically, two types of cessations.

- སོ་སོར་བརྟགས་པའི་འགོག་པ་ (so-sor-dak-bë gok-ba—Sanskrit *pratisaṃkhyā-nirodha*), *analytical cessations*, are the type included in the third truth. They are cessations (of afflictions) in some particular individual's mind brought about through that individual's having analyzed (སོ་སོར་བརྟགས་པ་) the nature of things.

- སོ་སོར་བརྟགས་མིན་གྱི་འགོག་པ་ (so-sor-dak-min-gyi gok-ba—Sanskrit *aprati-saṃkhyānirodha*), *non-analytical cessations*, are cessations (that is, absences) that come about just because there are, temporarily, no conditions causing the presence of what is absent. That there is no elephant in the room in which I am writing is due not to it being impossible for an elephant to be there, but to the fact that no elephant has been brought into the room.

Unlike the second type of cessation, the first type is not a temporary absence. The metaphor used to exemplify the difference is that of a robber being thrown out of a house. If the door is then locked, the situation is like that in which a སོ་སོར་བརྟགས་འགོག་ (the abbreviated form, pronounced **so-sor-dang-go**) is found. If the robber is thrown out but the door is not then locked to prevent his return, that is like a སོ་སོར་ བརྟགས་མིན་གྱི་འགོག་པ་.

> See Jeffrey Hopkins, *Meditation on Emptiness*, p. 218.

Note that enlightenment as a positive phenomenon—including the compassion and wisdom of a buddha's or arhat's mind—cannot technically be included here among the true cessations. True cessations refer specifically to absences of afflictions and are found only in the *continuums* (རྒྱུད་ **gyü'**—Sanskrit *saṃtāna*) of hearers, solitary conquerors, bodhisattvas, and buddhas.

> རྒྱུད་ is the traditional Buddhist way of speaking about the continuation of mind and body over time. It is a term that implies continuity within the context of change.

Thus, narrowly speaking, the term *nirvana* is merely a negative way of talking about enlightenment, saying not so much what *is* there, but what is no longer there.

## Conceptual Dimension: Emptiness

A selflessness (བདག་མེད་), or emptiness (སྟོང་པ་ཉིད་ **dong-ba-nyí'**—Sanskrit *śūnyatā*), is metaphorically a nirvana. (And, for that matter, the analytic cessations just discussed are also called emptinesses.)[135] However, as the term is usually used, an emptiness is an absence of an imagined type of existence.

> The principle upon which the attainment of nirvana is based is that direct, meditative perception of emptiness destroys afflictions (and especially ignorance) in a way that prevents their return.

Thus, emptiness is really a topic for the discussion of paths, where it is one of the main objects upon which Buddhists meditate. However, given that an emptiness is—like a cessation—both an absence and a permanent phenomenon, an introduction at least to the terminology is not inappropriate at this time.

> The assertion that seeing emptiness directly destroys an individual's afflictions forever is based on the principle that phenomena do not exist in the manner in which they seem to exist. Thus, when Buddhists speak about reality, they mean not what we all agree that we see, but what Buddhas see and what we would see if our minds worked properly.

In Buddhism, the main term for reality is selflessness. In the Buddhism of Tibet, selflessness and emptiness are, for the most part, equivalents. Thus, to say that a table is selfless (བདག་མེད་པ་ **dak-mé'-ba**—Sanskrit *nairātmya, anātmaka*) is the same as saying the table is empty (སྟོང་པ་ **dong-ba**—Sanskrit *śūnya*), and they both mean that the table does not exist in some specific way or ways in which it is imagined to exist.

*Selflessness* (བདག་མེད་) and *emptiness* (སྟོང་པ་ཉིད་ **dong-ba-nyí'**) both refer to the absence of something. In the case of བདག་མེད་, what is absent, obviously, is བདག་, but there are many different sorts of བདག་. Distinctions are made between different sorts of selflessnesses both on the basis of what lacks self (for example, someone's mind) as well as on the basis of what sort of self is lacking. (One example of self that would be absent in a mind is self-sufficiency, another is permanence.) Thus, a སྟོང་པ་ཉིད་ is an absence of some imagined existence, not just a vague emptiness or void.

The following is a partial list of types of existence of which persons and things are empty according to the Consequentialist Middle Way school.

| | |
|---|---|
| *natural existence* | [literally] *established by way of its own characteristic nature* |
| རང་གི་མཚན་ཉིད་ཀྱིས་གྲུབ་པ་ | |
| *inherent existence* | [literally] *established inherently* |
| རང་བཞིན་གྱིས་གྲུབ་པ་ | |

| *objective existence* | [literally] *established from its own side* |
| --- | --- |
| རང་གི་ངོས་ནས་གྲུབ་པ་ | |

| *truly established* | *truly existent* |
| --- | --- |
| བདེན་པར་གྲུབ་པ་ | བདེན་པར་ཡོད་པ་ |

In philosophical writings, གྲུབ་ is often equivalent to ཡོད་. Although the verbal adjective གྲུབ་པ་ literally means *established* or *proven*, here it may be translated as *existent* (or, as a noun, *existence*).

The ཀྱིས་ in the first example, the གྱིས་ in the second, and the ནས་ in the third may be thought of either as case marking particles or as adverb marking syntactic particles. As case marking particles, the ཀྱིས་ and the གྱིས་ would both be instances of the instrumental usage of the agentive case and the ནས་ would be either a fifth case instrument or a fifth case source. However, given that all three particles indicate the way in which something is *established* (གྲུབ་པ་), it could be argued that they are non-case-marking usages of what are normally case marking particles.

The ར་ in བདེན་པར་གྲུབ་པ་ and བདེན་པར་ཡོད་པ་ are instances of the adverbial identity construction, a special usage of the objective case.

At any rate, when speaking of the emptinesses of these three types of imaginary existence, the agentive case marking particles *are* used in a non-case-marking way, as syntactic particles.

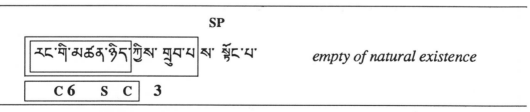

SP

| རང་གི་མཚན་ཉིད་ཀྱིས་ གྲུབ་པ ས་ སྟོང་པ་ | *empty of natural existence* |
| --- | --- |

C 6    S    C    3

Concerning the the types of existence of which things are empty, see Hopkins, *Meditation on Emptiness*, pp. 35-41 and Wilson, *Chandrakirti's Sevenfold Reasoning*, pp. 16-36.

Although སྟོང་པ་ཉིད་ itself is a negative term, it has positive synonyms. Here are some frequently used terms that are positive equivalents of *emptiness*.

| དེ་བཞིན་ཉིད་ | **té-shîn-nyí'** | *suchness, thusness* [Skt. *tathatā*] |
|---|---|---|
| དེ་ཁོ་ན་ཉིད་ | **té-kho-na-nyí'** | *suchness, thusness* [Skt. *tattva*] |
| ཆོས་ཀྱི་དབྱིངས་ | **chö>-ḡyí-yíng** | *sphere of truth, expanse of reality* [Skt. *dharmadhātu*] |
| ཆོས་ཉིད་ | **chö>-nyí'** | *nature, reality* [Skt. *dharmatā*] |

## The Four Truths: Paths

The fourth of the Four Noble Truths is where the practice of Buddhism is found. Its most basic division is into what are called the *three trainings* (བསླབ་པ་གསུམ་): ethics, meditation, and wisdom.

| བསླབ་པ་ | **lab-ba** | *training, practice* |
|---|---|---|
| ཚུལ་ཁྲིམས་ | **tshül-ṭhím** | *ethics* [Skt. *śīla*] |
| ཏིང་ངེ་འཛིན་ | **ḍíng-ngé-dzîn** | *concentration* [Skt. *samādhi*] |
| ཤེས་རབ་ | **shé>-rap** | *wisdom* [Skt. *prajñā*] |

Ethics is held to be the basis of concentration, and concentration the basis of wisdom.    In terms of karmic cause and effect, the result of training in ethics is rebirth in a pleasant migration in the Desire Realm (for example, as a human being), the result of training in concentration is rebirth in one of the two higher realms (that is, the Form and Formless Realms), and the result of training in wisdom is *liberation* (ཐར་ པ་ **thar-ba**).[136]

## Ethics

There are a number of ways of categorizing actions that are ethically significant (see Chapter Fourteen), the main of which is into *virtuous* or *positive* (དགེ་བ་) and *nonvirtuous* or *negative* (མི་དགེ་བ་) actions.  Buddhist ethics is minimally a matter of avoid-

ing negative actions and, as a result, tends to be discussed in terms of vows to refrain from negative behavior of body, speech, and mind.

The word སྡོམ་པ་ (*vow*) literally means *restraint*.

There are three main types of vows—termed the སྡོམ་པ་གསུམ་ (*three vows*).
Discussions of vows belong, generically, to *vinaya* (འདུལ་བ་).

| | | |
|---|---|---|
| སོ་སོར་ཐར་པའི་སྡོམ་པ་ | s̄o-s̄or-thar-b̈ë dom-b̄a | *vows of individual emancipation* |
| བྱང་ཆུབ་སེམས་དཔའི་སྡོམ་པ་ | c̱hang-chup-s̄êm-b̈ë dom-b̄a | *bodhisattvas' vows* |
| གསང་སྔགས་ཀྱི་སྡོམ་པ་ | s̄ang-n̄gak-ḡyí dom-b̄a | *vows of secret mantra* |

The vows of individual emancipation include monks' and nuns' vows as well as the
basic vows of lay Buddhists and are common to all forms of Buddhism (both
Hearers' Vehicle and Great Vehicle Buddhism). The latter two types of vows are
found exclusively in Mahāyāna Buddhism. Secret Mantra is the system of Buddhist
practice based on the tantras. It is also called Vajrayāna. Both sutras and tantras are
held by Tibetans to be Buddha's word.

| | | |
|---|---|---|
| གསང་བ་ | s̄ang-wa | *secret* |
| སྔགས་ | n̄gak | *mantra* |
| རྒྱུད་ | gyü' | *continuum, tantra* |
| རྡོ་རྗེ་ཐེག་པ་ | dor-jé thék-b̄a | *Vajrayāna* |
| སངས་རྒྱས་ཀྱི་བཀའ་ | s̄ang-gyë> ḡyí ḡa | *Buddha's word* |

In general, being a Buddhist means going for refuge to the three jewels: Buddha,
the Buddhist doctrine, and the Buddhist community.

| | | |
|---|---|---|
| སྐྱབས་འགྲོ་ | ḡyam-ḍo | *going for refuge* |

| སྐྱབས་ | ğyap | refuge |
| དཀོན་མཆོག་གསུམ་ | ğön-chok šum | three jewels |
| སངས་རྒྱས་ | šang-gyë> | Buddha |
| ཆོས་ | chö> | doctrine |
| དགེ་འདུན་ | gén-dün | spiritual community |

དཀོན་མཆོག (translated as *jewel*) literally means *best* (མཆོག) of *rarities* (དཀོན). དགེ་འདུན་ (translated *spiritual community*) means those who *aspire* (འདུན) to *virtue* (དགེ).

> On refuge in the three jewels, see *Essence of Refined Gold*, pp. 76-82, Khetsun Sangpo, *Tantric Practice in Nying-ma*, pp. 113-124, *Liberation in Our Hands*, pp. 148-160, and H. H. Tenzin Gyatso, *The Dalai Lama at Harvard*, pp. 15-18.

One of the ways of distinguishing between different sorts of Buddhists is to speak of the vows that they have assumed—that is, the specific ethics that they have promised to maintain. From the point of view of the vows of individual emancipation, there are four basic sorts of Buddhists.

| དགེ་སློང་ | gé-long | monks |
| དགེ་སློང་མ་ | gé-long-ma | nuns |
| དགེ་བསྙེན་ | gé-ñyên | laymen |
| དགེ་བསྙེན་མ་ | ge-ñyên-ma | laywomen |

Actually, there are seven classes of vows of individual emancipation, three for men and four for women. In addition to the four listed above, there are three more for novices or probationers.

| དགེ་ཚུལ་ | gé-tshül | *novice monks* |
| དགེ་ཚུལ་མ་ | gé-tshül-ma | *novice nuns* |
| དགེ་སློབ་མ་ | gé-lop-ma | *probationary nuns* |

## Concentration

*Concentration* (ཏིང་ངེ་འཛིན་) refers to the practice of meditation. There are a number of terms that, in their most general senses, are more or less equivalent.

| སྒོམ་པ་ | gom-ba | *meditation* [Skt. *bhāvanā*] |
| བསམ་གཏན་ | sam-dën | *concentration* [Skt. *dhyāna*] |
| མཉམ་པར་བཞག་པ་ | ñyam-bar-shak-ba | *meditative equipoise* [Skt. *samādhi*] |
| སྙོམས་པར་འཇུག་པ་ | ñyom-bar-juk-ba | *meditative absorption* [Skt. *samāpatti*] |

There are many ways of speaking about different types of meditation and there are various ways in which the word *meditation* is used. Moreover, potential meditation objects in Tibetan Buddhism are so numerous as to make a list of representative objects beyond this general introduction.[137]

For a traditional scholastic presentation of meditation objects, see Lati Rinbochay et al, *Meditative States in Tibetan Buddhism*, pp. 80-91.[138]

However, according to the *Perfection Vehicle* (པར་ཕྱིན་གྱི་ཐེག་པ་—the non-Tantric or sutra system presentation), two advanced types of meditation stand out as absolutely necessary for the attainment of enlightenment. In calm abiding (or quiescence meditation), the mind remains focussed on its object in a clear and steady way. In special insight—which is built upon calm abiding—the mind penetrates to the nature of things.

| ཞི་གནས་ | **s̱hí-n̄ë>** | *calm abiding* [Skt. *śamatha*] |
|---|---|---|
| ལྷག་མཐོང་ | **hlak-thong** | *special insight* [Skt. *vipaśyanā*] |

The first, ཞི་གནས་, is the development of single-pointed focus which is stable and clear. The second, ལྷག་མཐོང་, is the development of meditative wisdom. The first is technique; the second, meditative wisdom.[139]

| རྩེ་གཅིག་པ་ | **d̄zé ǰík-b̄a** | *single-pointed* |
|---|---|---|
| ཐབས་ | **thap** | *means, technique* [Skt. *upāya*] |
| ཤེས་རབ་ | **s̄hé>-rap** | *wisdom* [Skt. *prajñā*] |

There are also four social-ethical attitudes central to all types of Buddhism—the *four immeasurables* (ཚད་མེད་བཞི་)—that are to be cultivated in meditation. They are listed here in the order in which they occur in Mahāyāna meditation practice.

| ཚད་མེད་ | **tshë'-mé'** | *without measure, immeasurable* |
|---|---|---|
| བཏང་སྙོམས་ | **d̄ang-nyom** | *equanimity* |
| བྱམས་པ་ | **c̱ham-b̄a** | *love* |
| སྙིང་རྗེ་ | **n̄yíng-jé** | *compassion* |
| དགའ་བ་ | **ga-wa** | *joy* |

See Khetsun Sangpo, *Tantric Practice in Nyingma*, pages 125-140.

## Wisdom

There are various sorts of wisdom, the most commonly seen division being into those derived from *study* (ཐོས་པ་—literally, *hearing*), *reflection* (བསམ་པ་—literally, *thinking*), and meditation (བསྒོམ་པ་ or སྒོམ་པ་).

| ཐོས་པ་ལས་བྱུང་བའི་ཤེས་རབ་ | thö>-b̄a-lë> c̱hung-wë s̄hé>-rap | *the wisdom arising from hearing* |
| བསམ་པ་ལས་བྱུང་བའི་ཤེས་རབ་ | s̄am-b̄a-lë> c̱hung-wë s̄hé>-rap | *the wisdom arising from thinking* |
| བསྒོམ་པ་ལས་བྱུང་བའི་ཤེས་རབ་ | gom-b̄a-lë> c̱hung-wë s̄hé>-rap | *the wisdom arising from meditation* |

བྱུང་བ་ is a verbal made from the nominative verb བྱུང་. The usage of the fifth case marking particle, ལས་, is an example of its simplest use, that marking a source or origin.

ཐོས་པ་ (*hearing*) as the initial stage from which liberating wisdom is derived underscores the importance in Buddhism of oral transmission. The closest analogue in Western education is the initial study of a topic in which its essentials are learnt.

# Vocabulary

Memorize the spelling and pronunciation of these words; practice speaking them.

## Nouns and Adjectives

| སྐྱབས་འགྲོ་ | ḡyam-d̤o | going for refuge |
| སྐྱབས་ | ḡyap | refuge |
| དཀོན་མཆོག་གསུམ་ | ḡön-chok s̄um | three jewels |
| ཁང་པ་ | khang-b̄a | house, building |
| ཁམས་ | kham | Kam [in eastern Tibet] |
| གྲོང་ཁྱེར་ | t̤ong-kyér | city |

| དགེ་བསྙེན་ | **gé-ñyên** | laymen |
|---|---|---|
| དགེ་བསྙེན་མ་ | **gé-ñyên-ma** | laywomen |
| དགེ་འདུན་ | **gén-dün** | spiritual community |
| དགེ་ཚུལ་ | **gé-tshül** | novice monks |
| དགེ་ཚུལ་མ་ | **gé-tshül-ma** | novice nuns |
| དགེ་སློང་ | **gé-l̄ong** | monks |
| དགེ་སློང་མ་ | **gé-l̄ong-ma** | nuns |
| དགེ་སློབ་མ་ | **gé-l̄op-ma** | probationary nuns |
| རྒྱུད་ | **gyü'** | continuum, tantra |
| སྒོམ་པ་ | **gom-b̄a** | meditation [Skt. *bhāvanā*] |
| བསྒོམ་པ་ | **gom-b̄a** | meditation |
| ངོས་ | **ngö>** | side, surface |
| སྔགས་ | **ñgak** | mantra |
| ཆོས་ཀྱི་དབྱིངས་ | **chö>-ḡyí-yíng** | sphere of truth, expanse of reality [Skt. *dharmadhātu*] |
| ཆོས་ཉིད་ | **chö>-nyí'** | nature, reality [Skt. *dharmatā*] |
| མཉན་ཡོད་ | **ñyen-yö'** | Shravasti [*Śrāvastī*] |
| མཉམ་པར་བཞག་པ་ | **ñyam-b̄ar-s̲hak-b̄a** | meditative equipoise [Skt. *samādhi*] |
| སྙིང་རྗེ་ | **ñyíng-jé** | compassion |
| སྙོམས་པར་འཇུག་པ་ | **ñyom-b̄ar-juk-b̄a** | meditative absorption [Skt. *samāpatti*] |
| ཏིང་ངེ་འཛིན་ | **d̄ing-ngé-dzîn** | concentration (*samādhi*) |

| | | |
|---|---|---|
| བདང་སྙོམས་ | d̄ang-nyom | equanimity |
| སྟོང་པ་ཉིད་ | d̄ong-b̄a-nyi' | emptiness |
| ཐབས་ | thap | means, method, technique [*upāya*] |
| ཐལ་འགྱུར་ | thën-gyur | consequence |
| ཐལ་བ་ | thël-wa | consequence |
| ཐོས་པ་ | thö>-b̄a | hearing |
| དག་ཞིང་ | tak-s̱híng | pure land |
| དུ་བ་ | tu-wa | smoke |
| སྡོམ་པ་ | dom-b̄a | vow |
| ཕ་རོལ་དུ་ཕྱིན་པ་ | pha-röl-d̄u-chîn-b̄a | perfection, transcendence |
| བྱང་ཆུབ་སེམས་དཔའ་ | c̱hang-chup-sêm-b̄a | bodhisattva |
| བྱམས་པ་ | c̱ham-b̄a | love |
| དབུས་ | ü̱ | U [central Tibet] |
| དབྱིངས་ | yíng | sphere, expanse |
| གཙང་ | d̄zang | Dzang [west central Tibet] |
| རྗེ་ | d̄zé | point |
| རྩོལ་བ་ | d̄zöl-wa | effort |
| ཚད་མ་ | tshë'-ma | prime cognition, valid cognition |
| ཚད་མེད་ | tshë'-mé' | without measure, immeasurable |
| ཚུལ་ཁྲིམས་ | tshul-ṭhim | ethics (*śīla*) |
| ཞི་གནས་ | s̱hí-n̄ë> | calm abiding [Skt. *śamatha*] |

| ཝ་ར་ན་སི་ | **wa-ra-na-si** | Vāraṇāsi [city in India] |
|---|---|---|
| ཡུན་རིང་ | **yün-ring** | long time |
| ཡུལ་ | **yül** | object [Skt. *viṣaya*] |
| ཡུལ་ | **yül** | place, area, country [Skt. *deśa*] |
| རང་བཞིན་ | **rang-zhîn** | nature, inherent nature |
| ཤེས་རབ་ | **s̄hé>-rap** | wisdom (Skt. *prajñā*) |
| སོ་སོར་ཐར་པ་ | **s̄o-s̄or-thar-b̄a** | individual emancipation |
| བསམ་གཏན་ | **s̄am-d̄ën** | concentration [Skt. *dhyāna*] |
| བསམ་པ་ | **s̄am-b̄a** | thought, thinking, reflection |
| བསླབ་པ་ | **l̄ab-b̄a** | training |
| ལྷག་མཐོང་ | **hlak-thong** | special insight [Skt. *vipaśyanā*] |

## Verbs

Verbs are marked by the Roman numeral indicating the class to which they belong—that is, the syntax they require.

| | | | |
|---|---|---|---|
| I | nominative-nominative | V | agentive-nominative |
| II | nominative-locative | VI | agentive-objective |
| III | nominative-objective | VII | purposive-nominative |
| IV | nominative-syntactic | VIII | locative-nominative |

The first part of the name of each class identifies the case of the subject and the second, that of the object, complement, or principal qualifier.

| མཁས་ | **khë>** | is skilled in **II** |
|---|---|---|
| གྲུབ་ | **ṭup** | is established, is proven **III** |
| ཆགས་ | **chak** | is attached to **II** |
| འཇིགས་ | **jík** | is afraid of **II** |

| ཐལ་ | thal | logically follow **III**, go too far **III** |
|---|---|---|
| ཐོབ་ | thop | is obtained, is attained **III** |
| མཐོང་ | thong | see **V** |
| སྡོད་ | dö' | dwell, remain, sit **II** |
| བསྡད་ | dë' | [past and future of སྡོད་] **II** |
| གནས་ | n̄ë> | live, stay, continue **II** |
| བྱུང་ | c̲hung | arise, occur **III** |
| བཞུགས་ | s̲huk | live, remain, sit **II** [HON] |

## Pronouns

| ཁྱོད་ | khyö' | you |
|---|---|---|
| ཁྱོད་ཚོ་ | khyö'-tsho | you [plural] |
| ཁྱོད་རྣམས་ | khyö'-ñam | you [plural] |
| ཁྱོད་རང་ | khyö'-rang | you, you yourself |
| ཁྱེད་ | khyé' | you [HON] |
| ཁྱེད་ཅག་ | khyé'-j̄ak | you [HON] |

## Adjectives

| དཀོན་པོ་ | ḡön-b̄o | rare |
|---|---|---|
| མཆོག་ | chok | best |
| སྟོང་པ་ | d̄ong-b̄a | empty |
| བདེན་པར་གྲུབ་པ་ | dên-b̄ar-ḍup-b̄a | truly established |

| བདེན་པར་ཡོད་པ་ | dên-b̄ar-yö'-b̄a | truly existent |
| འདོད་པ་ | dö'-b̄a | desired, accepted |
| མི་འདོད་པ་ | mín-dö'-b̄a | undesired, unaccepted, unwanted |
| རིང་པོ་ | ríng-b̄o | long |
| གསང་བ་ | s̄ang-wa | secret |

## Syntactic and Case Marking Particles

| གང་ཞིག་ | kang-s̲hík | [punctuational syntactic particle] |
| ཅིང་ | j̄íng | [continuative syntactic particle] |
| ཅེས་ | j̄é> | [close quote (syntactic particle)] |
| ཏེ་ | d̄é | [continuative syntactic particle] |
| དུར་ | d̄ar | [adverb marking syntactic particle] |
| སྟེ་ | d̄é | [continuative syntactic particle] |
| དེ་ | dé | [continuative syntactic particle] |
| ནས་ | në> | [continuative syntactic particle] |
| ཞིང་ | s̲híng | [continuative syntactic particle] |
| ཞེས་ | s̲hé> | [close quote (syntactic particle)] |
| ལས་ | lë> | [fifth case marking particle] |
| ཤིང་ | s̄híng | [continuative syntactic particle] |
| ཤེས་ | s̄hé> | [close quote (syntactic particle)] |

# Chapter 16

*Syntactic Elements*
*Verbs of Dependence*
*Third Person and Reflexive Pronouns*
*Variety in the Doctrinal Dimension:  Tenet Systems*

## Patterns in Tibetan Language
### *Syntactic Elements*

A Tibetan clause or sentence is constructed of the following five syntactic elements:

1  a verb,

2  a subject,

3  an object,

4  a complement,

5  one or more qualifiers—including adverbs.

The five are listed in order of importance.  The verb is the governing element of a clause or sentence;  it is what must be found and analyzed first.  Not all verbs require all five elements, and some verbs (for example, verbs of existence) do not allow all elements.  The qualifier is optional and, for those verbs that allow both objects and complements, the complement may be optional.

Thus the generic syntax of a Tibetan sentence is the following, with two qualifications: (1) some verbs require only a subject and a verb and (2) a sentence may have multiple qualifiers.

[ QUALIFIER ] → | SUBJECT | → | OBJECT | → | COMPLEMENT | → ← | VERB |

Listed below are the classes of verbs and the basic syntax seen in each. (Although all eight classes have been introduced, not all have been examined in detail.)

**I    NOMINATIVE-NOMINATIVE VERBS** (linking verbs)

བུམ་པ་མི་རྟག་པ་ཡིན།            *Pots are impermanent.*

nominative                nominative
[ SUBJECT ] →        [ COMPLEMENT ] →        ← [ VERB ]

**II    NOMINATIVE-LOCATIVE VERBS** (such as verbs of existence)

བོད་ལ་རི་ཡོད།              *There are mountains in Tibet.*

locative                  nominative
[ QUALIFIER ] →        [ SUBJECT ] →            ← [ VERB ]

**III    NOMINATIVE-OBJECTIVE VERBS** (such as nominative action verbs)

འོད་ཟེར་རང་ལ་ཐིམ།          *Light rays dissolve into us.*

nominative                objective
[ SUBJECT ] →        [ QUALIFIER ] →            ← [ VERB ]

**IV    NOMINATIVE-SYNTACTIC VERBS** (such as verbs of absence)

གཟུགས་རང་བཞིན་གྱིས་སྟོང་པ་    *form being empty of inherent existence*

nominative              (syntactic particle or fifth case)
[ SUBJECT ] →            [ QUALIFIER ] →        ← [ VERB ]

**V    AGENTIVE-NOMINATIVE VERBS**

སངས་རྒྱས་ཀྱིས་ཆོས་བསྟན།    *Buddha taught the doctrine.*

agentive              nominative          optional objective
[ SUBJECT ] →        [ OBJECT ] →        [ COMPLEMENT ] →        ← [ VERB ]

**VI    AGENTIVE-OBJECTIVE VERBS**

ཁོས་གཟུགས་ལ་ལྟ།            *He sees a form.*

agentive              objective          optional objective
[ SUBJECT ] →        [ OBJECT ] →        [ COMPLEMENT ] →        ← [ VERB ]

**VII PURPOSIVE-NOMINATIVE VERBS** (such as verbs of necessity)

སྱུ་གུ་ལ་ཆུ་དགོས།       *Sprouts need water.*

| purposive | nominative | |
|---|---|---|
| SUBJECT → | OBJECT → | ← VERB |

**VIII LOCATIVE-NOMINATIVE VERBS** (such as verbs of possession)

ང་ལ་བུམ་པ་ཡོད།       *I have a pot.*

| locative | nominative | |
|---|---|---|
| SUBJECT → | OBJECT → | ← VERB |

> You should by now be familiar with the patterns seen in clauses and
> sentences ending in Class I, II, VII, and VIII verbs.
> Memorize the patterns for Classes V and VI as preparation for work
> with these verbs in the next chapters.

## Clauses as Syntactic Elements

Tibetan is a language in which there are more verbals than verbs. Beyond the level of books written for beginning students, most sentences are made up of several clauses, and the clauses themselves often employ not just simple single-word subjects, qualifiers, and objects but rather have phrases or clauses as their subjects, objects, and qualifiers. The philosophy underlying the book you are now reading is that Tibetan can be easily understood if it is first broken up into the phrases and clauses that make it up.

Here are some examples of noun phrases ending in verbals. Any of them could serve as a subject, object, or qualifier in a clause or sentence.

| | |
|---|---|
| ཡུལ་དེར་བཞུགས་པ་རྣམས་ | *those [who] live in that area* |
| བོད་ལ་གནས་པ་རྣམས་ | *those who remain / live in Tibet* |

| ཉོན་མོངས་མ་ཡིན་པ་དེ་ | *those/that [which] are not afflictions* |
| འདོད་ཁམས་ལ་མེད་པ | *[something] not existing in the desire realm* |
| རི་ལ་སྡོད་པ་དེ་དག་ | *those [who] dwell in the mountains* |

Note the addition of the words *who*, *which*, and *something* in the translations. These words are in brackets because they are not actually present in the Tibetan; they serve only to make the translation read more easily.

Each of these phrases can be broken up and analyzed. The first gives us the following, taken step by step.

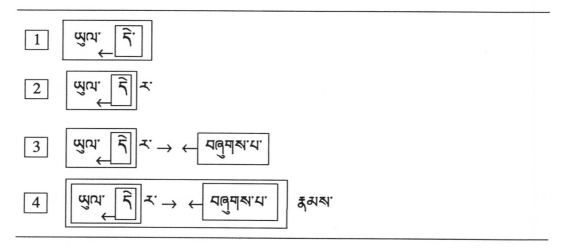

- Step 1 is the simplest noun phrase possible, NOUN + ADJECTIVE: *that place*. A noun phrase should be thought of as a noun taking the form of a phrase.

- Step 2 declines that noun by adding the locative case ending ར to the དེ: *in that place*. The case ending has been isolated outside the box here to emphasize its function of connecting the boxed phrase to a verb (or verbal) following it.

- Step 3 shows the verbal which the noun phrase qualifies. Does what in that place? *Lives in that place.* This follows the typical verb of living syntax we have just been examining. The phrase formed in Step 3 is a bit more complex than the basic noun-adjective phrase; we now have a verbal phrase whose syntax is QUALIFIER + VERBAL.

- Step 4 adds the pluralizing particle རྣམས་ to the verbal phrase: *those who live in that place.* When you see the རྣམས་, you know that the immediately preceding phrase refers to persons or things (more often persons). It serves to terminate the phrase, acting as a clue that what precedes it is in fact a unit that then relates as a whole to what comes later in the sentence.

Any of the noun phrases given above as examples may then serve as the subject, object, complement, or qualifier of a sentence or clause. For example, one could say ཡུལ་དེར་བཞུགས་པ་རྣམས་མང་པོ་མེད།—*There are not many who live in that area.*

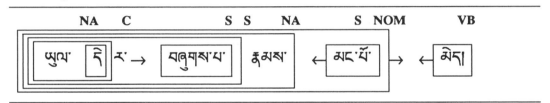

The literal translation of this sentence would be *Many [who] live in that area do not exist*, but that is not very good English.

Here are some other examples of verbal phrases attached to other elements of a sentence. Note the use in all three of the connective case particle འི་ to join the verbal phrase to a noun following it. This is very common in Tibetan.

| | |
|---|---|
| སངས་རྒྱས་ཀྱི་ཆོས་གནས་པའི་ཡུལ་དེར་ | *in that area [where] Buddha's doctrine remains* |
| དགེ་འདུན་གནས་པའི་དུས་ | *a time [when] the Spiritual Community remains* |
| གཟུགས་ཁམས་ལ་ཡོད་པའི་ཉོན་མོངས་ | *afflictions [which] exist in the Form Realm* |

## Drill 16.1

Translate the following into Tibetan.

1. the monks who live in that monastery
2. water existing in the pot
3. There are no Foe Destroyers without [i.e., who have no] love.
4. the effects which depend on that cause
5. the humans who live in the south
6. sentient beings who are animals
7. those who dwell at the stage of a Buddha

## Drill 16.2

Identify the dots in the following and translate. Diagram the second and third. Check the vocabulary at the end of the chapter for unknown words.

1. སྟོང་ཕྱིར་ལ་གནས་པའི་སྐྱེས་བུ་

2. སྣད་ཅིག་གཅིས་པར་མི་སྟོད་པའི་ཆོས་དེ་དག་མི་རྟག་པ་ཡིན།

3. འདོད་ཆགས་དང་ཞེ་སྡང་མེད་པའི་བསམ་པ་

4. སྐྱེ་མི་རྟག་པ་ཡིན་པ་

5. ཡུལ་དབུས་སུ་གནས་པ་རྣམས་

## Nominative-Locative Verbs
### *Verbs of Dependence*

Similar to verbs of existence and verbs of living, verbs of dependence have nominative subjects. Similar to verbs of living, they require a qualifier to make a complete sentence. Similar to verbs of existence, their subjects necessarily exist.[140] Three commonly seen verbs of dependence are the following.

| ཏེན་ | dên | *depend on* |
|---|---|---|
| རག་ལས་ | rak-lë> | *depend on, rely on* |
| ལྟོས་[141] | dö> | *depend on, relate to, be contingent on* |

Verbs of dependence, like verbs of living, may take different forms to indicate the three tenses and the imperative.

> Action verbs and verbs of motion, living, and dependence may occur in as many as four forms—past, present, future, and imperative.

ཏེན་ is a four-form verb. When you see ཏེན་, you know that it should be translated in the present tense, *depend(s) on*. And in a dictionary or glossary, this is where you will find a verb—listed alphabetically by its present tense form. In this book, the forms of a verb are listed from the past, through the present, to the future, and finally the imperative.[142] In the glossary, however, as in Tibetan-English dictionaries, the main entry of a verb is its present tense.[143]

| past: བརྟེནད་ | present: ཏེན་ | future: བརྟེན་ | imperative: ཏེནད་ |
|---|---|---|---|

Note that although བརྟེནད་ is the past tense root, the secondary suffix ད is rarely seen outside of a presentation such as the present one. Thus, what you will see in print for the past tense is བརྟེན་. Since བརྟེན་ is also the future root, this means that you will have to seek other clues to differentiate བརྟེན་ as *will depend* from བརྟེན་ as *have depended*. Fortunately these clues are common.[144] ཏེནད་ is the imperative root; you should expect to see it as ཏེན་.

རག་ལས་, on the other hand, is a single-form verb. It does not change form from past to present to future.

## Syntax of Verbs of Dependence

Verbs of dependence are often used to show a cause and effect relationship.

AN EFFECT ⊢→    ON A CAUSE ⊢→    ←⊣ DEPENDS

This is the syntax seen before with verbs of living—SUBJECT + QUALIFIER + VERB—the difference being that the qualifier indicates not a place of living, but the "place of dependence," the thing upon which the subject depends.

| NOMINATIVE SUBJECT |→| LOCATIVE PLACE OF DEPENDENCE |→ ←| VERB |

The strictly literal use of a verb of dependence to show causality is illustrated by the following sentence which also formulates the concept of causation in its most abstract sense.

| འབྲས་བུ་རྒྱུ་ལ་རྟེན། | **ḏë-bu gyu-la ḏēn** | *Effects depend on causes.* |

This could also mean *An effect depends on a cause.* The ལ་ is a seventh case particle marking རྒྱུ་ as a modifying object. The subject (འབྲས་བུ་, *effect*) is in the nominative case. The sentence can serve as a paradigm for the diagramming of sentences and clauses ending in verbs of dependence.

S NOM     C    7            VB

| འབྲས་བུ་ |→| རྒྱུ་ | ལ་ |→| ←| རྟེན། |

Another causal use of a verb of dependence may be seen in the following example. བྱང་ཆུབ་ཀྱི་སེམས་ is *bodhicitta*, the *mind of enlightenment*, meaning the bodhisattva's attitude whereby enlightenment is sought not for one's own sake, but that of others. སྙིང་རྗེ་ means *compassion*.

*The mind of enlightenment depends on great compassion.*

བྱང་ཆུབ་ཀྱི་སེམས་སྙིང་རྗེ་ཆེན་པོ་ལ་རག་ལས།

In this example it is implied, although not explicitly stated, that great compassion is the cause of the mind of enlightenment.

The next example is of a type frequently seen in བློ་རིག་ literature.

> བློ་རིག་ literally means *minds [and] awarenesses* and deals with types of cognition, correct and incorrect perception, and types of inference. See Lati Rinboché et al, *Mind in Tibetan Buddhism.*

A sense consciousness comes into existence based on three things:

1  a particular sort of object (a visual object such as a color or a shape, an odor, a sound, and so on),

2  a sense power (such as that found in the eye),

3  a previous moment of awareness.

In this case, an *eye consciousness* (མིག་གི་ཤེས་པ་ or མིག་ཤེས་ **mík-shé>**) depends on an *eye sense power* (མིག་དབང་ **mík-w̄ang** is an abbreviation for མིག་གི་དབང་པོ་). མིག་ (**mík**) means *eye*, but མིག་གི་ may often be translated *visual*.

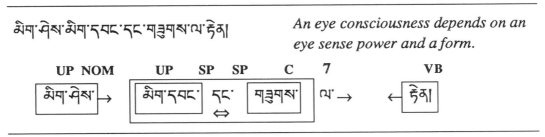

| An eye consciousness depends on an eye sense power and a form. | | | | | | |

Verbs of dependence are also used in situations where a cause and effect relationship cannot be seen as clearly as in the examples seen above. In most of these examples, the case for a causal relationship could still be made, however the dependence is more a case of establishing a motivation or context than of direct cause and effect.

| ཤིང་རྟ་ རང་གི་ཡན་ལག་ལ་ རྟེན། | *A chariot depends on its parts.* |
|---|---|
| བླ་མའི་མཐུ་ལ་བརྟེན་ན་ | *if one depends on the power of the guru …* |

ཡན་ལག་ means *branch* or *part*.  མཐུ་ means *power* or *ability*.

Both examples are loosely cases of cause and effect. In the first example, the cause would be the perception of the parts of the chariot and the effect would be the recognition of a chariot or the use of the word *chariot*. Alternatively, the cause would be the assembled parts of the chariot and the effect would be the ability of that assemblage of parts to perform the expected function of being a chariot. In the second example, the verb of dependence ends a conditional *clause*—marked by the conditional syntactic particle ན་. Something, we may assume, will take place if one depends on the power of the guru. The past tense form (in this case, བརྟེན་) is regularly used to indicate a conditional action, one that is a condition of something else occurring.

In the next example, the past form བརྟེན་ is again used, but this time with the syntactic particle ནས་ indicating that it is not a terminal verb but rather a participle—not *depended*, but *having depended*.

---

*Having depended on the three trainings, liberation is attained.*

བསླབ་པ་གསུམ་ལ་བརྟེན་ནས་ཐར་པ་ཐོབ།

---

Verbs of dependence typically do not have persons as subjects. It would be a mistake to suppose that the understood subject of the བརྟེན་ in this sentence is *one* or *we*. Insofar as the verb བརྟེན་ even needs a subject here, it would be *liberation* (ཐར་པ་) or, better, the *attainment of liberation* (ཐར་པ་ཐོབ་པ་). But remember, this is an *understood subject*—the actual subject of a verb is never *stated* after that verb.

> A verb *ends* a sentence. A verbal or a syntactic particle *ends* a clause. The subjects, objects, and qualifiers of verbs and verbals always precede the verb or verbal.

The verb ཐོབ་ (at the end of the sentence) is a nominative verb. Its subject is stated in the nominative case: ཐར་པ་.

The circumstance of the verb ལྟོས་ is a special one. Although clearly a verb used frequently in the context of dependence, it is equally clearly related to the verb ལྟ་, an agentive-objective verb meaning *look at*. Here are the two verbs compared—with the agentive verb ལྟ་ above and the verb of dependence ལྟོས་ below.

---

| past: བལྟས་ | present: ལྟ་ | future: བལྟ་ | imperative: ལྟོས་ |
|---|---|---|---|
| past: བལྟོས་ | present: ལྟོས་ | future: ? | imperative: ? |

---

There may have been, at some point in the evolution of the Tibetan language to its present form, a metamorphosis of the imperative root of ལྟ་. In those cases where

སློས་ was used to mean that something should be *considered* or *looked at* in a certain light, it may have been taken to be a separate verb meaning *contingent on* or *being in the context of*.[145] In many contexts, moreover, སློས་ is clearly used as a synonym of རྟེན་.[146]

The implications of this for a grammatical analysis of Tibetan are as follows.

● In some cases སློས་ is used to show dependence or contingency.

● In other cases སློས་ is used (seemingly ungrammatically) as a past or present form of the verb ལྟ་.[147]

● In yet other cases སློས་ is used ambiguously.[148]

The following are two sentences that seem to be unambiguous examples of the use of སློས་ as a verb of dependence.[149]

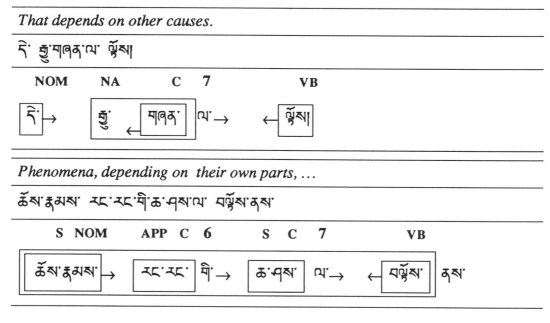

*That depends on other causes.*

དེ་ རྒྱུ་གཞན་ལ་ ལྟོས།

| NOM | NA | C | 7 | VB |
|---|---|---|---|---|
| དེ་ → | རྒྱུ་ | ← གཞན་ | ལ་ → | ← ལྟོས། |

*Phenomena, depending on their own parts, ...*

ཆོས་རྣམས་ རང་རང་གི་ཆ་ཤས་ལ་ བལྟོས་ནས་

| S NOM | APP C 6 | S C 7 | VB |
|---|---|---|---|
| ཆོས་རྣམས་ → | རང་རང་ གི་ → | ཆ་ཤས་ ལ་ → | ← བལྟོས་ ནས་ |

# Drill 16.3

Translate the following into Tibetan.

1 Attachment depends on ignorance.

2 A consciousness depends on a sense power.

3  A consciousness depends on its object.

4  A sentient being depends on mind and body.

5  Compassion is contingent on renunciation.

## Drill 16.4

Identify the dots in the following and translate. Diagram the first and third.

1  ཏིང་ངེ་འཛིན་ལ་བརྟེན་ནས་ཤེས་རབ་ཐོབ།

2  མི་དྲུག་པའི་ཆོས་ལ་མ་བསྟོས་པ།

3  དེ་དག་ཀྱུ་གཞན་ལ་རག་མ་ལས།

4  ཤེས་རབ་ཚུལ་ཁྲིམས་དང་ཏིང་ངེ་འཛིན་ལ་རྟེན།

5  ཏིང་ངེ་འཛིན་ཚུལ་ཁྲིམས་ལ་བརྟེན།

## Multi-syllable Verbs

Most verbs are single-syllable words. Thus, verbs with more than a single syllable like རག་ལས་ are an exception.[150] Multi-syllable verbs include **phrasal verbs** (that is, verbs whose basic form is a phrase) such as the following.

| | | |
|---|---|---|
| དོན་དུ་གཉེར་ | **tön-du-ñyér** | *seek* |
| ཁས་ལེན་ | **khë>-lên** | *assert* [literally, MOUTH-BY HOLD] |
| ཞལ་བཞེས་ | **s̲hël-s̲hé>** | [honorific of ཁས་ལེན་] |
| ཁྱད་དུ་གསད་ | **khyë'-du-s̲ë'** | *disparage* |
| ཁོང་དུ་ཆུད་ | **khong-du-chü'** | *understand* |
| ཉམས་སུ་ལེན་ | **nyam-s̲u-lên** | *practice* [lit. EXPERIENCE-IN HOLD] |
| ཡིད་ལ་བྱེད་ | **yí'-la-c̲hé'** | *attend to* [lit. MIND-IN DO] |

Verbs such as མངོན་པར་རྟོགས་ (*realize*) are **multi-syllable** but not phrasal. Such verbs often incorporate literal translations of Sanskrit prefix syllables. མངོན་པར་རྟོགས་, for example, translates the Sanskrit verb *abhisami*, where the root of the verb is *i* and *abhi* and *sam* are prefix syllables. མངོན་པར་ is the standard Tibetan translation of *abhi-*, leaving the *i* to be translated as རྟོགས་. **Multi-syllable phrasal verbs** are formed from what in other contexts would be brief phrases. The verb ཁས་ལེན་, for instance, a verb quite common in philosophical writing, is built out of other words, ཁ་ (*mouth*) and ལེན་ (*grasp*). Translated overly literally, ཁས་ལེན་ means *grasped by the mouth* (since ཁས་ is the agentive form of ཁ་). ཁས་ལེན་, however, is not a phrase; it is a word. The dot between the two syllables is not a C dot but rather an S dot.

Verbs with two or more syllables function in most ways as do other verbs. However, when they change forms to show the different tenses, they do not change completely, but only in the last syllable—that is, only in their core syllable. Thus, ཉམས་སུ་ལེན་ changes form in the following way—from past, through present and future tenses, ending in the imperative.

| | | | |
|---|---|---|---|
| ཉམས་སུ་བླངས་ | ཉམས་སུ་ལེན་ | ཉམས་སུ་བླང་ | ཉམས་སུ་ལེནད་ |

རག་ལས་ is a single-form verb; it does not change form to indicate past, present, and future.

All multi-syllable verbs, however, are negated in the same way.

> Multi-syllable verbs are negated by negating their final syllables. Some verbs require the use of the negative particle མ་; others require the use of མི་.

| | | |
|---|---|---|
| རག་མ་ལས་ | **rak-ma-lë>** | *does not depend* |
| ཁས་མི་ལེན་ | **khë>-mí-lên** | *does not assert* |
| ཡིད་ལ་མི་བྱེད་ | **yí'-la-mí-<u>ch</u>é'** | *does not pay attention [to]* |

# Pronouns
## *Third Person Pronouns*

Third person pronouns in English include *he*, *she*, and *it*. We are already familiar with the most common *impersonal* third person pronoun in Tibetan: དེ. The most common *personal* form of the third person pronoun is ཁོ—it most often means *he* but can also mean *she* or *it*. The word མོ can be used to specify the feminine gender, but is not felt to be polite usage. The honorific third person pronoun is ཁོང.

As before, these may be pluralized by the addition of the usual particles.

---

Recall that Tibetan sentences do not have to be complete in the sense of stating subject, predicate, and verb. This means that pronouns need not be used repeatedly when they are understood through context.

---

The following are examples of the use of third person pronouns.

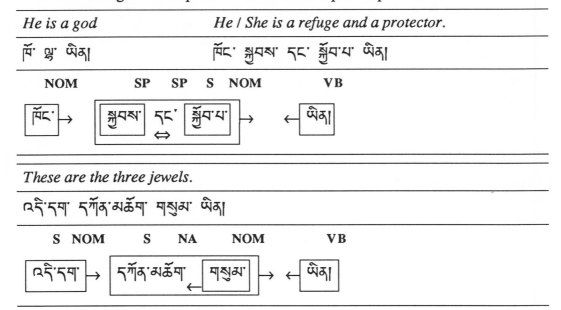

The pronoun འདི་དག in this example is an illustration of the use of the pluralizing particle དག; such pluralization is also seen in དེ་དག (*those*).

## *Reflexive Pronouns*

In the last chapter, you saw that the pronoun རང་ (*own, self*) could be used for the first person. This is explicit in ང་རང་ (*myself, I*) and is also seen in the first person plural pronoun རང་ཅག (*our*). The pronoun ཁྱོད་རང་ (*yourself* or *itself*) used in the sentence ཁྱོད་ཁྱོད་རང་ཨིན། is a reflexive pronoun. However, the syllable རང་ by itself is ambiguous—it may refer to any of the three persons.

You will see རང་ used in apposition to a noun to emphasize that noun. In the following sentence, the sense is that a Transcendent Victor is really a Buddha.

| S | S NOM | S APP NOM | VB | |
|---|---|---|---|---|
| ཤཱཀྱ་ཐུབ་པ་ | སངས་རྒྱས་ | རང་ | ཨིན། | *Shakyamuni is Buddha himself.*[151] |

You will also frequently see རང་ used in the connective case (རང་གི་). This may have either a personal or an impersonal sense, depending on context.

| རང་གི་དོན་ | *one's own aims*—as opposed to གཞན་གྱི་དོན་ (*others' aims*) |
| རང་གི་འབྲས་བུ་ | *one's / its own effect* |
| རང་གི་སྲོག་ | *one's own life* |
| རང་གི་ལུགས་ | *our own system* or *their own system* |
| རང་གི་ངོ་བོ་ | *own entity* |

There are other instances of རང་ that, while appearing to be used in phrases such as those seen above ('OWN' + CONNECTIVE-CASE + NOUN), are rather the first syllables of multiple syllable *words*.[152]

| རང་སྡེ་ | *one's / our own group* |
| རང་རྒྱལ་ | *solitary victor* (Skt. *pratyekabuddha*—'Solitary Realizer') |
| རང་དབང་ | *independence* |
| རང་བཞིན་ | *nature* (Skt. *svabhāva*) |
| རང་རྒྱུད་ | *autonomy*—literally, *its / one's own continuum* (*svatantra*) |

Finally, རང་ itself may be modified by a limiting adjective, as in རང་ཁོ་ནའི་དོན་. ཁོ་ན་ is an adjective meaning *only* and ཁོ་ནའི་ is the form it takes when marked by the case particle འི་. Whereas རང་གི་དོན་ means *one's/our own aims*, རང་ཁོ་ནའི་དོན་ means *the aims of one alone*.

Pronouns may be duplicated to show that they refer to each one of a group—*each of you, each of us, each of them*. (You will also see numbers duplicated in the same way: གཉིས་གཉིས་ [*each of the two*].)[153]

---

| NN C 6    C (7) | |
|---|---|
| རང་ རང་གི་ ལུགས་ལ་ | *according to each of their own systems* |

---

The case particle ལ་ marks the objective, beneficial, and locative cases. In the specific context seen here, especially if this phrase seemed not to relate to the next verbal or verb, it would most likely be a topical locative or objective place of activity. The topical locative is like a title or subtitle in English. As an objective place of activity, on the other hand, the phrase would be used with a verb meaning *assert* or *say*—indicating in whose philosophy something is asserted.

## Pronouns with Emphasizing Particles

Tibetan has a number of lexical particles serving to emphasize the words to which they are affixed. (See Chapter Eleven.) With the addition of the emphasizing particle ཉིད་, རང་ becomes རང་ཉིད་ and may mean *I, we, you, he, she, it, they*, or *one*. (The S dots in the first example have not been marked.)

---

| APP   NOM   NOM   VB | |
|---|---|
| བླ་མ་ རང་ཉིད་ རྒྱལ་བ་ ཡིན། | *The guru himself is a Conqueror [Buddha].* |
| རང་ཉིད་ སངས་རྒྱས་ ཡིན། | *He himself is a Buddha.* |
| རང་ཉིད་ མི་ ཡིན། | *We ourselves are humans.* |

---

Whether རང་ཉིད་ is first, second, or third person depends on the context in which it is used.

## *Abbreviations*

In the proper contexts, the term རང་ may be used as an abbreviation for a word beginning with རང་. These are *not* pronouns.[154] Here are some examples.

- In the term ཉན་རང་, རང་ abbreviates རང་རྒྱལ་ (*pratyekabuddha*, 'solitary realizer'). The syllable ཉན་ abbreviates ཉན་ཐོས་ (*śrāvaka*, 'hearer'). Of course, if you see ཉན་རང་གཉིས་, you will know that there are two people or things being discussed, one of which is a ཉན་ and the other a རང་. However, be prepared to see the abbreviation used without the appositive གཉིས་. Hearers and solitary realizers are the practitioners of the first two of the three Buddhist *vehicles* (ཐེག་པ་, *yāna*); the third vehicle is that of the bodhisattvas.

- In the term ཐལ་རང་ (or, more explicitly, ཐལ་རང་གཉིས་), རང་ abbreviates རང་ རྒྱུད་པ་ (*Svātantrika*) and ཐལ་ abbreviates ཐལ་འགྱུར་བ་ (*Prāsaṅgika*). These are the two main philosophical systems within the Mādhyamika or *Middle Way School* (དབུ་མ་པ་) of Buddhist philosophy. The རང་རྒྱུད་པ་ school was founded in India by Bhāvaviveka and the ཐལ་འགྱུར་བ་ by Candrakīrti. Candrakīrti's interpretation of Mādhyamika is held by many in Tibet to be the best philosophical system.

- In another school of Buddhist philosophy—the Sautrāntika—impermanent phenomena are also known as *specifically characterized phenomena* (རང་མཚན་) and permanent phenomena may be called *generally characterized phenomena* (སྤྱི་མཚན་). In contexts related to this philosophy, you may see the term རང་སྤྱི་ used to abbreviate རང་མཚན་དང་སྤྱི་ མཚན་.

Most of the time the use of these abbreviations will be obvious, *provided that you are aware that such abbreviations exist*. This is more evidence for the contention that Tibetan texts are not written to be read by any literate reader. Rather, literacy in Tibetan means knowing not just the language, but also the technical terminology of a specific field of study.

## Drill 16.5

Translate the following into Tibetan.

1. They live in a city.
2. You yourself exist.
3. He is a human, not a god.
4. The pot itself is impermanent.
5. They are Foe Destroyers.

## Drill 16.6

Identify the dots in the following and translate.

1. ཉིན་རང་ལ་དགྲ་བཅོམ་པ་ཡོད།

2. འདི་དག་བཅོམ་ལྡན་འདས་མ་ཨིན།

3. ཁོང་དགྲ་བཅོམ་པ་རང་ལགས།

4. བདེ་བར་གཤེགས་པ་རང་ཉིད་མཉན་ཡོད་ན་བཞུགས།

## Rhetorical Tools
### *Analysis of Permutations*

The analysis of **permutations** (མུ་ *mu*) is the most basic sort of analysis in Buddhist logic as it is used in Tibet. No, this is not the same *mu* as seen in Japanese—the response in the koan which asks whether or not a dog has Buddha-nature. It is, however, possible to use this Indo-Tibetan[155] analysis of མུ་ to think about whether or not a dog has Buddha-nature.

Analysis of permutations is built on the premise that any two different things[156] must be related in one of four ways, and in no more than one of those four ways.[157] In an analysis of permutations, two things are either:

- སུ་གསུམ་ (**mu sum**)—*[things which have] three permutations*;
- སུ་བཞི་ (**mu shí**)—*[things which have] four permutations*;
- འགལ་བ་ (**gël-wa**)—*mutually exclusive*;
- དོན་གཅིག (**tön-jík**)—*equivalent*.

It is easiest to think about these relationships using a spatial model. Think of any two things, A and B. If you imagine that all things that are A make up one circle and all things that are B make up another, the four possible relationships look like the four sets of circles on the following two pages, where the set of things that are A is symbolized by horizontal lines and the set of things that are B is symbolized by vertical lines.

## Mutual Exclusion

If the two circles overlap nowhere, then A and B are mutually exclusive—there is nothing anywhere that is both A and B. This would be the case if A were apples and B were bananas, or if A was matter and B was consciousness.

## Equivalence

If the two circles exactly correspond—that is, if *everything* in the A circle is in the B circle and vice versa—then A and B are equivalent. This is the case where A is existents and B is phenomena.

## Three Permutations

If everything in the A circle is in the B circle, but there is at least one thing in the B circle that is not in the A circle, then A and B have three permutations. There need be *only one* B that is not A for the two to have three permutations. (This is also true if the opposite is the case—when everything in the B circle is in the A circle, but there is at least *one* thing in the A circle that is not in the B circle.)

This is the case where (using the model on the left) A is pots and B is matter (གཟུགས་—*material form*) and where A is impermanent phenomena and B is phenomena. In these examples, B is the broader group and A is a subset of that group.

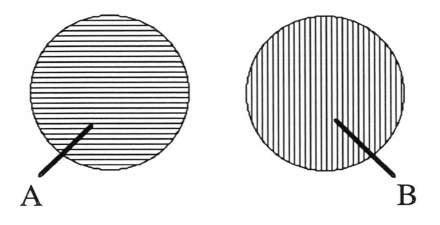

Mutual Exclusion

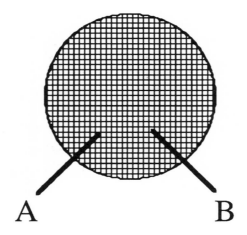

Equivalence

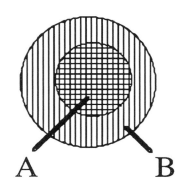 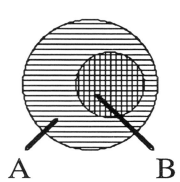

Three Permutations

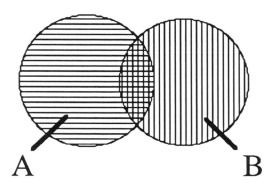

Four Permutations

The three permutations here are: (1) things that are both A and B; (2) things that are B but not A; and (3) things that are neither B nor A. The third group includes everything outside both circles.

## *Four Permutations*

If some, but not all things in the A circle are in the B circle, and some, but not all things in the B circle are in the A circle, then A and B have four permutations. This differs from equivalence in that there is at least one A that is not also B and at least one B that is not also A.

The color blue and the color of a pot are two things that have four permutations. If A is the color blue and B is the color of a pot, then the group in the middle—things both A and B—includes such things as the color of a large blue pot. Things that are A and not B are things like the color of a blue car; things that are B but not A are exemplified by the color of a red pot. Finally, there is a vast group of things that are neither the color blue nor the color of a pot; an example would be this piece of paper.

## Analysis of Permutations
### *Equivalence*

For two things to be *equivalent* (དོན་གཅིག), two criteria must be met.

● They must be *different* (ཐ་དད).

● All eight modes of pervasion between the two must be present.

To be equivalent is to be mutually inclusive but not to be *identical* (གཅིག). As understood in the doctrinal primers, the only things that are identical are things such as pot and pot, or existent and existent. Even pot and བུམ་པ are mutually inclusive, but not identical. Using དངོས་པོ and མི་རྟག་པ as examples, here are the two requisite criteria for equivalence stated as a syllogism.

*The subject, the two, functioning thing and impermanent, are equivalent because of (1) being different and (2) the eight modes of pervasion being complete.*

དངོས་པོ་དང་མི་རྟག་པ་གཉིས་ཆོས་ཅན། དོན་གཅིག་ཡིན་ཏེ། ཐ་དད་ཡིན་པ་གང་ཞིག་ཁྱབ་པ་སྒོ་བརྒྱད་ཚང་བའི་ཕྱིར།

Note that the second part of the reason ends not in ཡིན་པ་ but in the verbal ཚང་ བ་, a nominative-objective verb meaning *is complete* and *is present*.

---

When a thesis or reason ends in a verbal noun or adjective, the verb ཡིན་ is often replaced by that verb.

---

For example, instead of གཞི་གྲུབ་ཡིན་པའི་ཕྱིར། (*because of being a basic phenomenon*), one will often see གཞི་གྲུབ་པའི་ཕྱིར། (which may be translated in the same way).

The eight modes of pervasion (ཁྱབ་པ་སྒོ་བརྒྱད་—literally, *eight doors* [or *approaches*] *of pervasion*) are the following eight relationships.
- Whatever is A must also be B.
- Whatever is B must also be A.
- Whatever is not A must also not be B.
- Whatever is not B must also not be A.
- If A exists, B must also exist.
- If B exists, A must also exist.
- If A does not exist, B must also not exist.
- If B does not exist, A must also not exist.

Or, to condense these eight to four:
- whatever is the one must be the other;
- whatever is not the one must also not be the other;
- if the one exists, so must the other;
- if the one does not exist, neither must the other.

The spatial metaphor here is that of two circles which include the same areas exactly, but which are not *exactly* the same because they have different names.

An example of two things that are equivalent is the two, our sun and our nearest star. These two different names refer to the same thing. Whatever is our sun must also be our nearest star; whatever is our nearest star must also be our sun; whatever is not our sun must also not be our nearest star (and vice versa); if our sun exists, so does our nearest star (and vice versa); and if our sun does not exist, neither does our nearest star (and vice versa). *Our sun* and *our nearest star* are words for the same thing; they are different ways of talking about the same thing.

Stated in Tibetan using དངོས་པོ་ (*functioning thing*) and མི་རྟག་པ་ (*impermanent*) as the example of equivalence, the eight modes of pervasion read as follows.

- དངོས་པོ་ཡིན་ན་མི་རྟག་པ་ཡིན་པས་ཁྱབ།
- མི་རྟག་པ་ཡིན་ན་དངོས་པོ་ཡིན་པས་ཁྱབ།
- དངོས་པོ་མ་ཡིན་ན་མི་རྟག་པ་མ་ཡིན་པས་ཁྱབ།
- མི་རྟག་པ་མ་ཡིན་ན་དངོས་པོ་མ་ཡིན་པས་ཁྱབ།
- དངོས་པོ་ཡོད་ན་མི་རྟག་པ་ཡོད་པས་ཁྱབ།
- མི་རྟག་པ་ཡོད་ན་དངོས་པོ་ཡོད་པས་ཁྱབ།
- དངོས་པོ་མེད་ན་མི་རྟག་པ་མེད་པས་ཁྱབ།
- མི་རྟག་པ་མེད་ན་དངོས་པོ་མེད་པས་ཁྱབ།

*Pervasion* (ཁྱབ་པ་ **khyap-ba**, Skt. *vyāpti*) is a concept basic to Buddhist logic. The verb ཁྱབ་ in its complete syntax will be examined as part of the analysis of agentive-objective verbs. For the time being, only the formal statement of a ཁྱབ་པ་ in its rhetorical dimension will be analyzed.

---

Like syllogisms and consequences, philosophical pervasions are stated in a fixed, formal style that is not grammatically regular.

---

*Whatever is a functioning thing is necessarily impermanent.*

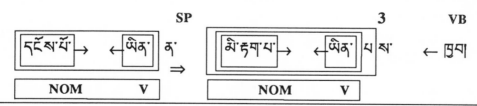

The pervasion དངོས་པོ་ཡིན་ན་མི་རྟག་པ་ཡིན་པས་ཁྱབ། literally means *If [it] is a functioning thing, [it] is pervaded by being impermanent.* དངོས་པོ་ཡིན་ན་ is a conditional clause ending in the syntactic particle ན་. མི་རྟག་པ་ཡིན་པས་ (*being impermanent*) is the agent of the verb ཁྱབ་. As is often the case in Tibetan, part of the sentence (here, the object—དངོས་པོ་) must be inferred from what has gone before (དངོས་པོ་ཡིན་ན་).

Any verb may replace the two ཡིན་ in the above example.  Thus, དངོས་པོ་མེད་ན་མི་རྟག་པ་མེད་པས་ཁྱབ། literally means *If functioning things do not exist, then the impermanent necessarily does not exist.*


Some equivalents have already been introduced, for example སེམས་, ཡིད་, and རྣམ་པར་ཤེས་པ་.  Here are some others.

---

*Object of knowledge, existent, object of comprehension,*
  *and basic existent are equivalent.*

---

ཤེས་བྱ། ཡོད་པ། གཞལ་བྱ། གཞི་གྲུབ་རྣམས་ དོན་གཅིག་ ཡིན།

---

Both ཤེས་བྱ་ and གཞལ་བྱ་ are **object verbals**—that is, they are verbal nouns created from the future tense form of the verb plus the strong future auxiliary.  Thus ཤེས་པར་བྱ་ (*will* or *should know*) becomes ཤེས་པར་བྱ་བ་ as an object verbal, and is abbreviated ཤེས་བྱ་.  Object verbals such as ཤེས་བྱ་ do not refer to a future activity, but to the object of an activity, here, *that which is known*, or *object of knowledge.*

---

*Functioning thing, impermanent, product, compound phenomena,*
  *cause, and effect are equivalent.*

---

དངོས་པོ་ མི་རྟག་པ་ བྱས་པ་ འདུས་བྱས་ རྒྱུ་ འབྲས་བུ་རྣམས་ དོན་གཅིག་ ཡིན།

---

*Mind, awareness, and knowledge are equivalent.*

---

བློ་ རིག་པ་ ཤེས་པ་རྣམས་ དོན་གཅིག་ ཡིན།

---

Note the way in which each set of equivalents ends in the pluralizing particle རྣམས་, often a clue that a noun phrase has ended.

For more on equivalence (or mutual inclusion), see Perdue, *Debate in Tibetan Buddhism*, pp. 138-142.

In terms of the permutations just introduced, **equivalence** is a case in which A pervades B and B pervades A, while **three permutations** is a case in which either A pervades B or B pervades A, but not both.

Pervasion means one of two things:

the two groups have the same membership, and so each can be said to include the other within it;

one group of things is larger than the other, and includes all of the smaller group within it.

## Doctrinal Vocabulary and Grammar
### *Variety within the Doctrinal Dimension: Systems of Tenets*

One of the attractions of Tibetan Buddhism (both for the practitioner and the scholar) is that it is so systematic; this is also one of its drawbacks. In building systems, Tibetan writers tend to gloss over some of the differences between individual philosophers and texts, and pigeonhole them into categories—the so-called 'tenet systems.' Whether one, as a reader of Tibetan or a translator of Tibetan texts, chooses to attempt to go beyond this sort of taxonomy or to retain it, what remains the case is that Tibetan texts cannot be translated or even read without understanding that these categories are built into them (if they are written by Tibetans) and, at any rate, are the ones used by Tibetan readers to understand both Indian and indigenous Tibetan texts.

### *Tenet Systems*

As noted in Chapters Seven and Eight, the doctrinal dimension of a word's meaning differs from its lexical dimension in that a number of doctrinal interpretations are possible for a single lexical meaning.

For example, the noun ཡོད་པ་, as you know, means *existence* or *existent*. Lexically, the meaning of the word is simple—to exist means to be somewhere, either physically or mentally. One of the central questions in Buddhism, however, is "How do things exist?" Some Buddhist philosophers say that whatever exists does so truly (བདེན་པར་ཡོད་པ་), others say that impermanent phenomena such as pots exist truly but that some permanent phenomena (for example, space) only inherently exist (རང་བཞིན་གྱིས་གྲུབ་པ་—where གྲུབ་པ་ means ཡོད་པ་) and do not truly exist. Other Buddhist philosophers say that nothing anywhere, whether permanent or impermanent, truly exists. Yet others say that nothing exists either truly or inherently.[158]

This sort of analysis of existence is done in Buddhism as an attempt to develop a terminology that describes the way people actually see things to exist. The principle is that ordinary perceptions and thoughts are pathologically flawed (that is, controlled by ignorance [མ་རིག་པ་]), and that in order to attain enlightenment (བྱང་ཆུབ་), one has to determine the way that things really do exist and then actually see them in that way.

When speaking about the conflicting assertions seen in various texts, it is not very clear to say, as I have done just above, that "some Buddhists" say this, "others" say that, and "yet others" say something else. This *is* done in Tibetan books, using indefinite pronouns such as ཁ་ཅིག་ and ལ་ལ་, both of which may be translated as *someone*. The most precise way to speak about someone's doctrinal position, of course, is to identify the writer and the text(s) in which that writer asserts or implies the position in question. However, Tibetan writers generally take a position midway between these two, avoiding both ambiguity and precision. Instead of saying, for example, that the denial of true existence is seen in such and such a book written by Candrakīrti (ཟླ་བ་གྲགས་པ་), they will say that it is an assertion of the Consequentialist Middle Way school (the system "founded" by Candrakīrti).

Thus, it is necessary to become familiar first with the names of these systems of assertions, or tenet systems (གྲུབ་མཐའ་, **dup-tha** or **dum-tha**—Sanskrit *siddhānta*), and then with the Indian Buddhist philosophers associated with these systems.

## *Buddhist and Non-Buddhist Doctrines*

The Sanskrit term that translates into English as Buddhism or Buddhist is *Bauddha* (in Tibetan, སངས་རྒྱས་པ་). However, Buddhists tend more often to speak of Buddhism as the middle way or as the *dharma* (ཆོས་—truth, doctrine). When ཆོས་ refers in this manner to an entire way of life—as the middle way between hedonism and asceticism, between distraction and withdrawal, and between ontological exaggeration and nihilism—it is probably better to translate it as *worldview* rather than *religion* or to translate it more literally, as *doctrine*. Thus སངས་རྒྱས་ཀྱི་ཆོས་ means *Buddha's doctrine* and སངས་རྒྱས་པའི་ཆོས་, *Buddhist doctrine*.

Only when it is necessary to separate the Buddhist worldview from non-Buddhist views is ཆོས་ qualified as ནང་པའི་ཆོས་—*insiders' doctrine* (where ནང་པ་, *insider,* is from ནང་, *in*), distinguishing it from ཕྱི་རོལ་པའི་ཆོས་ (*outsiders' doctrines*). What distinguishes ནང་པ་ from ཕྱི་རོལ་པ་ is 'going for refuge' (སྐྱབས་འགྲོ་, abbreviating སྐྱབས་སུ་འགྲོ་བ་)—where Buddhists are those who go for refuge to Buddha, the Buddhist doctrine, and the Buddhist community (see Chapter Fifteen).[159]

---

> The པ་ in ནང་པ་ and སངས་རྒྱས་པ་ is a subjective suffix syllable, a type of lexical particle introduced in Chapter Eleven.

---

What distinguishes Buddhist tenet systems (a category narrower than Buddhist doctrine) from non-Buddhist systems is acceptance of the 'four seals' (ཕྱག་རྒྱ་བཞི་ **cha-gya shí**), four propositions that are characteristically Buddhist:[160]

1 འདུས་བྱས་ཐམས་ཅད་མི་རྟག་པ།     *all composed phenomena*
                                  *[are] impermanent;*

2 ཟག་བཅས་ཐམས་ཅད་སྡུག་བསྔལ་བ།     *all contaminated phenomena*
                                  *[are] unsatisfactory;*

3 ཆོས་ཐམས་ཅད་བདག་མེད་པ།        *all phenomena [are] without a self;*

4 མྱ་ངན་ལས་འདས་པ་ཞི་བ།         *nirvana [is] pacification.*

Asserting these four makes a philosopher a proponent of Buddhist tenets.

---

> Note that, in the forms stated above, these four are examples of sentences ending in understood linking verbs.

---

## The Four Buddhist Tenet Systems

There are four main Indian schools of Buddhist tenets as seen from Tibet. The order traditionally given is from "highest" to "lowest." The highest doctrines are those held to be most correct, whereas the lowest are those seen as most naive or farthest from how a Buddha perceives things and, thus, the least adequate explanations of what Buddha taught.

The four main tenet systems are the following.

| Mādhyamika | (*mādhyamika*, དབུ་མ་པ་) | Middle Way School |
| Cittamātra | (*cittamātra*, སེམས་ཙམ་པ་) | Mind-Only School |
| Sautrāntika | (*sautrāntika*, མདོ་སྡེ་པ་) | Sutra School |
| Vaibhāṣhika | (*vaibhāṣika*, བྱེ་བྲག་སྨྲ་བ་) | *Great Exposition* School |

The *Great Exposition* School is named after the བྱེ་བྲག་བཤད་མཚོ་ཆེན་མོ་ (*Great Exposition of Distinctions*) or *Mahāvibhāṣā*, a Sanskrit abhidharma text not extant in Tibetan.[161]

Note that whereas དབུ་མ་ means *middle* or *middle way*, the word དབུ་མ་པ་ means *Middle Way School*.

> This is the same process seen above in ནང་པ་ and སངས་རྒྱས་པ་. The principle involved is that adding a final syllable (པ་, བ་, པོ་, བོ་, མ་, or མོ་) to a word ('X') that is already a noun creates a word that means *having to do with X*.[162]

The སེམས་ཙམ་པ་ school is also known as the རྣལ་འབྱོར་སྤྱོད་པ་ (**ñën-jor-jö'-ba**—Sanskrit *yogācāra*) or Yogic Practice School.

The Sutra, Mind-Only, and Middle Way Schools are also divided into subschools:

| | | | |
|---|---|---|---|
| Middle Way School | དབུ་མ་པ་ | ཐལ་འགྱུར་བ་<br>**thën-gyur-wa** | Prāsaṅgika<br>*Consequentialists* |
| | | རང་རྒྱུད་པ་<br>**rang-gyü'-ba** | Svātantrika<br>*Autonomists* |
| Mind-Only School | སེམས་ཙམ་པ་ | རིགས་པའི་རྗེས་འབྲང་ | *Epistemologists* |
| | | ལུང་གི་རྗེས་འབྲང་ | *Scripturalists* |

Sutra School   མདོ་སྡེ་པ་ {
 རིགས་པའི་རྗེས་འབྲང་   *Epistemologists*

ལུང་གི་རྗེས་འབྲང་   *Scripturalists*

ལུང་གི་རྗེས་འབྲང་ (**lung-gí-jé>n-ḍang**) literally means *follower of scripture* and རིགས་པའི་ རྗེས་འབྲང་ (**rík-b̄ë-jé>n-ḍang**) means *follower of reasoning*.

> Note the pronunciation of རྗེས་འབྲང་. The ཨ prefix letter beginning the syllable འབྲང་ causes the previous syllable to end in a nasal: **jé>n-ḍang**.

Like the terms *Sutra School* and *Yogic Practice School*, these terms are not meant to imply a monopoly. All Buddhists are in one way or another both followers of scripture and followers of reasoning, just as all Buddhists—not only the Sutra School—are followers of Buddha's sutras and all—not only the Yogic Practice School—are practitioners of yoga (that is, meditation).

These tenet systems may be grouped in two ways. The most common grouping is in terms of 'vehicle.'

- དབུ་མ་པ་ and སེམས་ཙམ་པ་ are both Mahāyāna (ཐེག་ཆེན་) systems.
- མདོ་སྡེ་པ་ and བྱེ་བྲག་སྨྲ་བ་ are the Hīnayāna (ཐེག་དམན་) systems.

The present Dalai Lama has suggested that, instead of speaking of Mahāyāna and Hīnayāna, translators use the equivalent terms *Bodhisattvayāna* (བྱང་སེམས་ཀྱི་ཐེག་པ་) and *Śrāvakayāna* (ཉན་ཐོས་ཀྱི་ཐེག་པ་)—in English, the *Bodhisattva Vehicle* and the *Hearers' Vehicle*.[163]

Another, less common way to categorize the four tenet systems is in terms of the types of existence they accept and reject, that is, in terms of the kind of selflessness they assert to be most profound. Buddhist tenet systems are in this way grouped first into two categories, those that accept and those that reject true existence (བདེན་ པར་གྲུབ་པ་—Sanskrit *satyasiddha*).[164]

> Recall that, as in the term གཞི་གྲུབ་ (*basic existent*), the nominative verb གྲུབ་ (*is established*) may mean *exist*. Thus, བདེན་པར་གྲུབ་པ་ means བདེན་པར་ཡོད་པ་.

Proponents of True Existence (དངོས་པོར་སྨྲ་བ་ n̄gö>-b̄or-m̄a-wa) include the *Great Exposition* School, the Sutra School, and the Mind-Only School.[165] Proponents of No Intrinsic Identity (ངོ་བོ་ཉིད་མེད་པར་སྨྲ་བ་ **ngo-wo-nyí'-mé'-b̄ar-m̄a-wa**—Sanskrit *Niḥsvabhāvavadins*), that is, rejectors of true existence, are the Middle Way School, including both རང་རྒྱུད་པ་ and ཐལ་འགྱུར་བ་.

| | | |
|---|---|---|
| དངོས་པོར་སྨྲ་བ་ | **n̄gö>-b̄or-m̄a-wa** | *Proponent of True Existence* |
| ངོ་བོ་ཉིད་མེད་པར་སྨྲ་བ་ | **ngo-wo-nyí'-mé'-b̄ar-m̄a-wa** | *Proponent of No Intrinsic Identity* [Skt. *Niḥsvabhāvavadin*] |

(Note that the དངོས་པོ་ in དངོས་པོར་སྨྲ་བ་ means བདེན་པར་གྲུབ་པའི་དངོས་པོ་—*truly established things*.)

The syntax in བདེན་པར་གྲུབ་པ་ (*established truly*) is that of ADVERBIAL IDENTITY + VERBAL. The syntax in དངོས་པོར་སྨྲ་བ་ (*propounding [phenomena] to be truly existent*) is OBJECTIVE COMPLEMENT + VERBAL.

The first group, the Proponents of True Existence—who assert that at least some phenomena are truly existent—may be further divided into two subgroups.[166]

1    Proponents of [External] Objects (དོན་སྨྲ་བ་ **t̄ön-m̄a-wa**) assert truly existent external objects and include the *Great Exposition* School and the Sutra School.

2    Proponents of Mind-Only (སེམས་ཙམ་པ་) assert that minds are truly existent but that objects which are different entities from the minds perceiving them are not; that is, they reject truly existent external objects.

The དོན་ in དོན་སྨྲ་བ་ is used in a narrow, specialized way here, one peculiar to the Mind-Only School. Normally དོན་ means *goal, aim,* and *purpose,* but it can mean *object* (that is, ཡུལ་, an object of consciousness). Here, it is used in that restricted sense, further narrowed to mean ཕྱི་རོལ་གྱི་དོན་—*external object.*

Listed below are some important Indian writers and the tenet systems with which they are associated.

| | | |
|---|---|---|
| ཀླུ་སྒྲུབ་ | Nāgārjuna | Middle Way School |

| | | |
|---|---|---|
| འཕགས་པ་ལྷ་ | Āryadeva | Middle Way School |
| ཐོགས་མེད་ | Asaṅga | Scripturalist Mind-Only School |
| དབྱིག་གཉེན་ | Vasubandhu | Scripturalist Sutra & Mind-Only |
| ཕྱོགས་ཀྱི་གླང་པོ་ | Dignāga | Epistemologist Sutra & Mind-Only |
| ཆོས་ཀྱི་གྲགས་པ་ | Dharmakīrti | Epistemologist Sutra & Mind-Only |
| ཟླ་བ་གྲགས་པ་ | Candrakīrti | Consequentialist Middle Way School |
| ཞི་བ་ལྷ་ | Śāntideva | Consequentialist Middle Way School |
| ཞི་བ་འཚོ་ | Śāntarakṣita | Autonomist Middle Way School |

The historical Buddha, Śākyamuni (ཤཱཀྱ་ཐུབ་པ་ *sha-gya-thup-ba*), is generally agreed by Western scholars to have been born in 563 B.C.E. (B.C.E. for 'Before the Common Era'), to have lived for eighty years, and to have died in 483 B.C.E. However, according to the noted Japanese scholar, Nakamura Hajime, he lived a century later, from 463-383 B.C.E.[167] Nakamura's dating of the Indian Buddhist doctrinalists listed above is somewhat less controversial, although not all of the following dates agree with the Tibetan historical tradition.[168]

| | | |
|---|---|---|
| ཀླུ་སྒྲུབ་ | Nāgārjuna | 150-250 C.E. |
| འཕགས་པ་ལྷ་ | Āryadeva | 170-270 C.E. |
| ཐོགས་མེད་ | Asaṅga | 310-390 C.E. |
| དབྱིག་གཉེན་ | Vasubandhu | 320-400 C.E. |
| ཕྱོགས་ཀྱི་གླང་པོ་ | Dignāga | 400-485 C.E. |
| ཆོས་ཀྱི་གྲགས་པ་ | Dharmakīrti | about 650 C.E. |
| ཟླ་བ་གྲགས་པ་ | Candrakīrti | about 650 C.E. |
| ཞི་བ་ལྷ་ | Śāntideva | 650-750 C.E. |
| ཞི་བ་འཚོ་ | Śāntarakṣita | 680-740 C.E. |

Tibetan historians, for example, hold that Dignāga was a student of Vasubandhu. If that is indeed the case, then Nakamura's dates for those two scholars need revision.

# *Vocabulary*

Memorize the four seals, the names of the four Buddhist tenet systems and their subdivisions, and the names of the important Indian writers listed in the Doctrinal Vocabulary section.

## *Nouns*

| ཁྱབ་པ་ | **khyap-b̄a** | pervasion |
|---|---|---|
| གྲུབ་མཐའ་ | **ṭup-tha** | tenet(s) |
| གྲོང་ཁྱེར་ | **ṭong-khyér** | city |
| འགལ་བ་ | **gël-wa** | mutual exclusion, exclusive |
| ངོ་བོ་ | **ngo-wo** | entity, nature |
| གཅིག་ | **j̄ík** | one |
| ཆ་ | **cha** | part, factor |
| ཆ་ཤས་ | **cha-s̄hë>** | part |
| ཉན་ཐོས་ | **nyën-thö>** | hearer, audiant |
| ཉན་རང་ | **nyën-rang** | hearers and solitary conquerors |
| ཐར་པ་ | **thar-b̄a** | liberation |
| ཐལ་འགྱུར་བ་ | **thël-gyur-wa /** <br> **thën-gyur-wa** | Consequentialist (Prāsaṅgika) |
| ཐལ་རང་ | **thël-rang** | Prāsaṅgika and Svātantrika |

| | | |
|---|---|---|
| མཐུ་ | **thu** | power |
| དོན་ | **tön** | goal, aim, purpose, object, meaning |
| དོན་གཅིག་ | **tön-jík** | equivalent |
| ཕྱི་རོལ་ | **chí-röl** | outside, external |
| བློ་རིག་ | **lo-rík** | minds and awarenesses |
| མུ་ | **mu** | boundary, permutation, possibility |
| གཞལ་བྱ་ | **shël-ja** | object of comprehension |
| གཞི་གྲུབ་ | **shi-ḍup** | established base |
| ཡན་ལག་ | **yën-lak** | branch, limb, part |
| རང་རྒྱལ་ | **rang-gyël** | solitary conqueror |
| རང་རྒྱུད་ | **rang-gyü'** | autonomy |
| རང་རྒྱུད་པ་ | **rang-gyü'-ba** | Autonomists (Svātantrika) |
| རང་སྡེ་ | **rang-dé** | own group |
| རང་དབང་ | **rang-wang** | independence ('self-power') |
| རང་བཞིན་ | **rang-shîn** | nature, natural existence |
| རིག་པ་ | **rík-ba** | knowledge, awareness |
| རིགས་པ་ | **rík-ba** | reasoning |
| ལུགས་ | **luk** | system, mode, [doctrinal] positions |
| ལུང་ | **lung** | scripture, tradition |
| བསླབ་པ་ | **lab-ba** | training |
| ཤིང་རྟ་ | **shing-da** | chariot |

| ཤེས་པ་ | **s̄hé>-b̄a** | consciousness, knowledge |
| ཤེས་བྱ་ | **s̄hé>-ja** | object of knowledge |
| སྲོག་ | **s̄ok** | life [being alive] |
| གསེར་ | **s̄ér** | gold |
| བསམ་པ་ | **s̄am-b̄a** | thinking, reflection |

## Verbs

Verbs are marked by the Roman numeral indicating the class to which they belong—that is, the syntax they require.

| | | | |
|---|---|---|---|
| **I** | nominative-nominative | **V** | agentive-nominative |
| **II** | nominative-locative | **VI** | agentive-objective |
| **III** | nominative-objective | **VII** | purposive-nominative |
| **IV** | nominative-syntactic | **VIII** | locative-nominative |

The first part of the name of each class identifies the case of the subject and the second, that of the object, complement, or principal qualifier.

| ཁས་བླང་ | **khë>-lang** | [future of ཁས་ལེན་] |
| ཁས་བླངས་ | **khë>-lang** | [past of ཁས་ལེན་] |
| ཁས་ལེན་ | **khë>-lên** | assert **V** |
| ཁོང་དུ་ཆུད་ | **khong-du-chü'** | understand **V** |
| ཁྱད་དུ་གསད་ | **khyë'-du-s̄ë'** | disparage, despise **V** |
| གྲུབ་ | **ṭup** | is established, is proven **III** |
| ཉམས་སུ་བླང་ | **nyam-s̄u-lang** | [future of ཉམས་སུ་ལེན་] |
| ཉམས་སུ་བླངས་ | **nyam-s̄u-lang** | [past of ཉམས་སུ་ལེན་] |
| ཉམས་སུ་ལེན་ | **nyam-s̄u-lên** | practice **V** |

| ཇེན་ | dēn | depend on, rely on **II** |
| ཇེནད་ | dēn | [imperative of ཇེན་] |
| ལྟ་ | da | look at **VI** |
| བློས་ | dö> | relates to, is contingent on **II** |
| བཇེན་ | dēn | [future and past of ཇེན་] |
| བཇེནད་ | dēn | [past of ཇེན་] |
| བལྟ་ | da | [future of ལྟ་ (*look at*)] |
| བལྟས་ | dë> | [past of ལྟ་] |
| བློས་ | dö> | [past of བློས་] depends on |
| ཐོབ་ | thop | [past of འཐོབ་] |
| འཐོབ་ | thop | is obtained, is reached **III** |
| དོན་དུ་གཉེར་ | tön-du-nyér | seek **V** |
| ལྟང་ | lang | [future of ལེན་] |
| ལྟངས་ | lang | [past of ལེན་] |
| ཚང་ | tshang | is complete **III** |
| ཞལ་བཞེས་ | shël-shé> | HONORIFIC of ཁས་ལེན་ |
| ཡིད་ལ་བྱེད་ | yí-la-ché' | attends to **V** |
| རག་ལས་ | rak-lë> | depend on, rely on |
| ལེན་ | lên | take **V** |

## Pronouns

| | | |
|---|---|---|
| ཁོ་ | **kho** | he, she |
| ཁོ་རང་ | **kho-rang** | he, he himself, itself |
| ཁོང་ | **khong** | he, she  [HON] |
| ཁོང་ཚོ་ | **khong-tsho** | they  [HON] |
| དེ་དག་ | **té-dak** | those |
| འདི་དག་ | **di-dak** | these |
| མོ་ | **mo** | she |
| རང་ | **rang** | self, own |
| རང་ཉིད་ | **rang-nyí'** | oneself |
| རང་རང་ | **rang rang** | each their own, each of them |

## Adjectives

| | | |
|---|---|---|
| གཅིག་ | **j̄ík** | one, identical |
| གཅིག་པ་ | **j̄ík-b̄a** | similar |
| ཐ་དད་ | **tha-dë'** | different |
| དོན་གཅིག་པ་ | **tön-j̄ík-b̄a** | equivalent |

# Chapter 17

*Action Verbs*
*Agentive-Nominative Verbs*
*Originative Case: Separation, Comparison, Inclusion*
*Interrogative Pronouns*
*Definitions: Basic Existents*

## Patterns in Tibetan Language
### Action Verbs

At the beginning of Chapter Sixteen, the three categories and eight classes of verbs were reviewed. This classification is based on the principal that the syntax of a clause or sentence is determined by the verb that terminates it. Of those eight classes, linking verbs and verbs indicating existence, possession, necessity, and dependence have already been examined and it is now time to move on to more complex verbs, those indicating actions rather than states of being.

In order to show the similarities between the various classes of action verbs, it will be useful to turn briefly to the alternate system of classifying verbs that was introduced in Chapter Twelve. In the alternate classification, there are two basic types of verbs:

1  **existential verbs** such as ཡིན་, ཡོད་, གནས་, and དགོས་;
2  **action verbs** such as བྱེད་, སྟོན་, འགྲུབ་, and སྐྱེ་.

The existential verbs include most of the nominative verbs and all of the specialized verbs.

Existential verbs include the following types:
all Class I (linking) verbs;
all four types of Class II (nominative-locative) verbs—verbs of existence,
   verbs of living, verbs of dependence, and attitude verbs;
the rhetorical verbs in Class III;
all Class IV (nominative-syntactic) verbs (such as སྤེལ་ and སྐྱེང་);
all the specialized verbs of Classes VII and VIII.

The action verbs include two types of nominative verbs and all agentive verbs.

Action verbs include the following types:
nominative action verbs and verbs of motion
   —both found in Class III (nominative-objective verbs);
all Class V agentive-nominative verbs;
all Class VI agentive-objective verbs.

There are, thus, two subtypes of action verbs—those that require nominative subjects and those that normally take agentive subjects.

● Action verbs that do not speak of objects distinct from their agents require a nominative subject.

● Verbs expressing the action of an agent on something other than itself, as in *The woodsman fells the tree* and *Buddha taught the doctrine*, require an agentive subject.

The first of these two groups include verbs of motion and nominative action verbs (two of the three types of Class III, or nominative-objective, verbs). As in འཁོར་ལོ་ འཁོར། (*The wheel turns*), they express actions without making reference to agents or objects. The subject and object of the verb འཁོར་ are identical—here, འཁོར་ལོ་.

   The second group is made up of Class V and VI agentive verbs. As in སངས་རྒྱས་ ཀྱིས་ཆོས་བསྟན། (*Buddha taught the doctrine*), they express actions done by an agent on an object. The subject སངས་རྒྱས་ and the object ཆོས་ are distinct. In a sense, the agentive case marking particle separates the subject from the object.

Here is a list of a few of the more commonly used action verbs, shown in their present tense forms. Following the convention used in the chapter vocabularies, Roman numerals are used to indicate the class to which they belong—thus, **III** means nominative-objective; **V** means agentive-nominative; and **VI** means agentive-objective.

| | | |
|---|---|---|
| སྒྲུབ་ | ḍup | *establish, achieve, accomplish, prove, complete* **V** |
| གྲུབ་ | ṭup | *is established, is accomplished, is achieved, exists* **III** |
| སྐྱེད་ | ḡyé' | *create, generate, give birth to* **V** |
| སྐྱེ་ | ḡyé | *arise, is born, is created* **III** |
| ཤེས་ | s̄hé> | *know, realize, understand* **V** |
| འཛིན་ | dẑîn | *hold, apprehend, grasp, conceive* **V** |
| སྒོམ་ | gom | *meditate, cultivate* **V** |
| སྟོན་ | d̄ön | *teach, demonstrate, show* **V** |
| འཐོབ་ | thop | *is attained, obtained, reached* **III** |
| ལེན་ | lên | *take, obtain, grasp, seize* **V** |
| ཁྱབ་ | khyap | *pervade, spread* **VI** |
| ལྟ་ | d̄a | *look at, view* **VI** |
| འབད་ | bë' | *strive to, make effort in* **VI** |

Notice with གྲུབ་ and སྒྲུབ་, on the one hand, and སྐྱེ་ and སྐྱེད་, on the other, that there are sometimes pairs of related nominative and agentive verbs.

Although both agentive and nominative verbs have grammatical subjects, the relations these subjects have to their verbs—that is, the function the subjects perform in the sentence—differ.[169]

> The subject of an agentive verb is an agent, and accordingly is marked by an agentive case particle. The subject of a nominative verb is not an agent and is in the nominative case.

There are five agentive case particles. གིས་ is used after nouns, pronouns, and adjectives whose final syllable ends in ག and ང. ཀྱིས་ is used after words whose final syllable ends in ད, བ, and ས. གྱིས་ is used after words whose final syllable ends in ན, མ, ར, and ལ. འིས་ and ཡིས་ are used after words whose final syllable ends in འ or has no suffix.

## Agentive Verbs

All agentive verbs are action verbs. They all express an action done by an agent on something other than itself. A complete agentive sentence requires three basic elements:

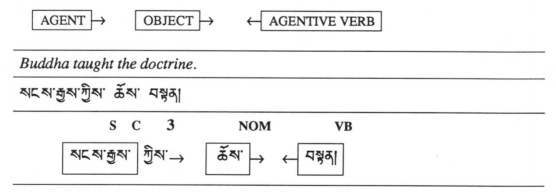

Buddha taught the doctrine.

Not all agentive verbs take direct objects in the nominative case. There are two classes of agentive verbs:

  agentive-nominative verbs (Class V);
  agentive-objective verbs (Class VI).

Most agentive-objective verbs take a second case direct object, but one common agentive-objective verb—ཕན་ (**phën**, *help, aid, benefit*)—takes a fourth case direct object.

## Nominative Action Verbs

Unlike agentive verbs, nominative verbs make no reference to objects separate from their subjects. The subject of a nominative verb is not an agent, but merely a person or thing which takes part in the action expressed by the verb. For example, in the nominative verb construction *The wheel turns* (འཁོར་ལོ་འཁོར་རོ།), the wheel is what is turning—but not what is *causing* the turning. In the nominative verb phrase *The reason is proven* (རྟགས་གྲུབ་), the reason spoken of takes part in the action (in that it is proven), but it is *not* what does the proving.

Reasons, of course, are stated in order to prove something. The statement, རྟགས་གྲུབ་, however, is used to indicate that the reason that has just been stated has already itself been proven. Thus, the reason spoken of in the phrase རྟགས་གྲུབ་ has itself been proven by *another* reason.

Thus, a complete sentence ending in a nominative verb needs only two elements, not the three required in agentive sentences:[170]

```
SUBJECT ⊢→    ←⊣ NOMINATIVE VERB
```

*The wheel turns.*

འཁོར་ལོ་ འཁོར་རོ།

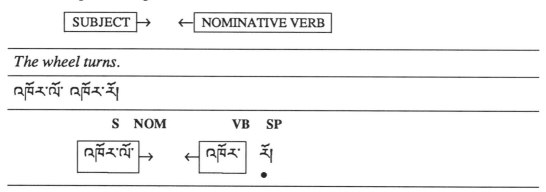

Although nominative action verbs have no separate objects, they often have complements or qualifiers in the objective case:

It is for this reason that they are included among the Class III (nominative-objective verbs).  The example below illustrates the use of the verb སྣང་ (*appear, shine, is perceived*) with two second case qualifiers.

*The snow mountain appears blue to the visual consciousness.*

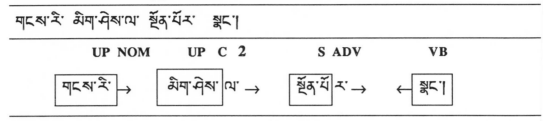

The first qualifier in the sentence above—མིག་ཤེས་ལ་—shows *where* the action of appearing takes place and is thus in the second case.  The second qualifier indicates *how* the snow mountain appears, an adverbial usage of the second case.

Both གངས་རི་ and མིག་ཤེས་ are contractions of noun-noun phrases in which there are connective case marking particles between the two nouns.

> Although the second case is called the objective case, its most common uses are to mark the place where an activity is done, the destination of motion, complements of verbs, and identity.

Adverbial identity—seen in གངས་རི་སྔོན་པོར་སྣང་།—is one type of identity.  Because the *blue* and the *appearance* are not separate entities, their relationship is termed 'identity.'

Identity here does not refer to the philosophical concept of identity, but merely to sameness of entity.  In the above example, although blue and the activity of appearing are not identical, they are only conceptually differentiable and, thus, are not separate entities.  The appearance itself is blue.

## Action Verb Forms

Like the verbs of living and dependence you have seen, agentive verbs and nominative verbs may occur in different forms to indicate past, present, future, and imperative.  In most cases, the likeness between the different tenses of a verb is clear, even in the case of four-form verbs. The most common agentive verb, བྱེད་ (*do, perform, act, make; act as, serve as; say, refer to*) is a four-form verb.[171]

| past: བྱས་ | present: བྱེད་ | future: བྱ་ | imperative: བྱོས་ |
|---|---|---|---|

The honorific of བྱེད་ is མཛད་, a two-form verb.

| past: མཛད་ | present: མཛད་ | future: མཛད་ | imperative: མཛོད་ |
|---|---|---|---|

> The past, present, and future forms of verbs are encountered much more frequently than their imperative forms.

The most common nominative action verb is འགྱུར་ (*become*), a two-form verb in which the present and future occur in one form and the past and imperative take another.

| past: གྱུར་ | present: འགྱུར་ | future: འགྱུར་ | imperative: གྱུར་ |
|---|---|---|---|

While བྱེད་ and འགྱུར་ are the most commonly seen action verbs, some of their forms occur as often as **auxiliary verbs** as they do on their own. Auxiliaries include the present and future forms of བྱེད་ and the past and future forms of འགྱུར་. For example, where ཤེས་ is an agentive verb (in its basic form) meaning *know*, ཤེས་པར་བྱ་ and ཤེས་ པར་འགྱུར་ mean *will know* (as well as having other meanings).

# Agentive Verbs
## *Agentive-Nominative Verbs*

The two classes of agentive verbs—agentive-nominative verbs and agentive-objective verbs—are differentiated by their objects. However, translators should avoid the temptation to translate the agentive and objective case particles "literally," that is, as *by* and *to*, respectively.

> Case marking particles have no unambiguous meanings in themselves. They serve merely to relate words, clauses, and phrases to one another.

Thus, even though it is sometimes the case that an agentive case particle clearly ought to be translated *by* or *by means of* (especially in its instrumental usage), in many instances, it will not be rendered as a separate word in English.

The paradigm agentive-nominative construction, སངས་རྒྱས་ཀྱིས་ཆོས་བསྟན།, may be translated either *Buddha taught the doctrine* or *The doctrine was taught by Buddha*, depending on the context in which the sentence is found—that is, depending on whether the subject being discussed is Buddha or doctrine. The *by Buddha* in the second translation is dictated not by the Tibetan particle ཀྱིས་, but by the word order required in the English construction.

In English, word order determines the meaning of a sentence. For example, the sentences *The farmer sees the yak* and *The yak sees the farmer* are identical except for the position of the nouns *farmer* and *yak*. In Tibetan, on the other hand, word order is not as significant. Rather, it is case marking particles (or their absence) that determine which word is the subject and which is the object. Using the agentive-nominative verb མཐོང་ (*see*), there are two ways to say *The farmer sees the yak* and two ways to say *The yak sees the farmer*.

---

ཞིང་པས་ གཡག་ མཐོང་།    གཡག་ ཞིང་པས་ མཐོང་།

*The farmer sees the yak.*

---

གཡག་གིས་ ཞིང་པ་ མཐོང་།    ཞིང་པ་ གཡག་གིས་ མཐོང་།

*The yak sees the farmer.*

---

In all four examples, it is not the word order that determines the meaning, but rather the case marking particles—the subject is marked by an agentive case marker and the object, in the nominative case, by the lack of a case marking particle.

Thus, while the subject of a Tibetan sentence is *often* the first element in the sentence, it is not *necessarily* the first element in the sentence.

| SUBJECT + OBJECT + VERB |
|---|

སངས་རྒྱས་ཀྱིས་ ཆོས་ བསྟན།

*Buddha taught the doctrine.*

| OBJECT + SUBJECT + VERB | ཆོས་ སངས་རྒྱས་ཀྱིས་ བསྟན། |
|---|---|

*Buddha taught the doctrine.*

The English speaker is tempted, when translating the second example, to use the passive—*The doctrine was taught by Buddha*—thus making *doctrine* the subject acted on by the verb *was taught*. And, in fact, where the Tibetan emphasizes ཆོས་ and not སངས་རྒྱས་, that is an acceptable translation. Nonetheless, however one chooses to translate, it must be remembered that the active-passive options present in English are not found in Tibetan. Whereas in English the passive is considered weak and the stronger active construction is preferred to it, in Tibetan all agentive verbs are equally active (or, if you prefer, equally passive—although in *Translating Buddhism from Tibetan* they are considered active). སངས་རྒྱས་ཀྱིས་ཆོས་བསྟན། and ཆོས་ སངས་རྒྱས་ཀྱིས་བསྟན། are grammatically equivalent. Both sentences end in the agentive-nominative verb བསྟན་.

In the following example, the subject of discussion—Buddhist doctrinalists who are not of the Consequentialist Middle Way School—is the object of the verb (གཞལ་, *measure*), but comes first in the clause.

---

*When those of our own school who are Autonomists and below are measured by the Consequentialists ...*[172]

---

རང་རྒྱུད་པ་མན་ཆད་ཀྱི་རང་སྡེ་འདི་དག་ ཐལ་འགྱུར་བས་ གཞལ་ན་

---

When a sentence or clause has a component as complex as the object of this one, it is useful to reduce it first to its basic structure, plugging the complex element back into it once the core syntax has been analyzed. In the present case, the complex object རང་རྒྱུད་པ་མན་ཆད་ཀྱི་རང་སྡེ་འདི་དག་ may be reduced to འདི་དག་, *they*.

---

*When they are measured by the Consequentialists ...*

---

| NOM | 3 | V SP |
|---|---|---|
| འདི་དག་→ | ཐལ་འགྱུར་བས་ → | ←གཞལ་ ན་ |

Note the standard nominative object and agentive subject syntax.

The verb གཞལ་ is the future form of འཇལ་, a Class V verb meaning *measure* and, by extension, *assess* and *comprehend*.

| past: བཅལ་ | present: འཇལ་ | future: གཞལ་ | imperative: འཇལད་ |
|---|---|---|---|

The object of this clause, extended to its full complexity, may be diagrammed as follows.

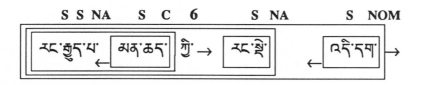

The word མན་ཆད་ (*that and below*) is often used as a syntactic particle which, placed at the end of a phrase, acts as an adverb marker. Here it is obviously not a syntactic particle, since it is declined with the case marking particle ཀྱི་. The best reading of it is as an adjective.

The noun-adjective phrase རང་རྒྱུད་པ་མན་ཆད་ is in an appositive relationship with the noun རང་སྡེ་ (OWN-GROUP—that is, *our own school[s]*). Which of our own schools? Autonomists and below. The adjective འདི་དག་ then modifies that entire construction.

In the next example, the complex construction is the agentive-nominative clause itself, which then functions as the nominative object of another agentive-nominative verb.

*Having practiced the doctrine taught by that virtuous spiritual friend, …*[173]

དགེ་བའི་བཤེས་གཉེན་དེས་ ཆོས་བསྟན་པ་ ཉམས་སུ་བླངས་ནས་

The clause དགེ་བའི་བཤེས་གཉེན་དེས་ཆོས་བསྟན་པ་ is the nominative object of the verb ཉམས་སུ་བླངས་ (the past form of the verb ཉམས་སུ་ལེན་—*practice*). Its structure is the same as that seen in སངས་རྒྱས་ཀྱིས་ཆོས་བསྟན།, but with དགེ་བའི་བཤེས་གཉེན་དེས་ as the agentive subject.

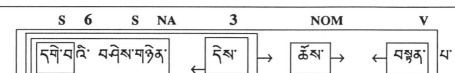

Actually, the adjective-noun phrase དགེ་བའི་བཤེས་གཉེན་ is used so often as a unit that it should probably be considered a word in its own right. Translating the Sanskrit *kalyāṇamitra*, it refers to a religious teacher.

The next example illustrates the same agentive-nominative verb with both direct and indirect objects.

---

*Therefore, the gurus taught us the means to liberation*
*from the three bad migrations.*

---

དེས་ན་བླ་མ་རྣམས་ཀྱིས་བདག་ཅག་ལ། ངན་སོང་གསུམ་ལས་ཐར་པའི་ཐབས་བསྟན་ཏེ།

---

As before, the first step in reading such a sentence is to isolate its basic structure. Even if you were not already familiar with the verb བསྟན་, its proximity to a closing | and the fact that the continuative syntactic particle ཏེ་ follows it suggest that it is a verb. Recognizing བསྟན་ as a verb and looking for case marking and syntactic particles will enable you to identify seven elements in this sentence.

1  དེས་ན་ is an introductory syntactic particle meaning *therefore*.

2  བླ་མ་རྣམས་ཀྱིས་ is clearly a noun with the pluralizing lexical particle རྣམས་ marked by the agentive particle ཀྱིས་.

3  བདག་ཅག་ལ་ is the pronoun བདག་ (*I*), followed by the pluralizer ཅག་ and marked by ལ་ which, as a case marking particle, indicates the second, fourth, and seventh cases.

4  Seeing the number གསུམ་ in ངན་སོང་གསུམ་ལས་ suggests a noun-adjective phrase ending in the adjective *three* and marked by an originative case marking particle.

5  ཐར་པའི་ is a noun ending in a connective case marking particle.

6  ཐབས་, as a noun without a case marker immediately before a verb, must be a noun in the nominative case.

7    བསྟན་དེ་ is the past tense of the agentive-nominative verb སྟོན་ followed by the continuative syntactic particle དེ་, indicating that there is more to come on the subject just expressed.

The second, third, and fourth elements illustrate an important rule of thumb.

---

Pluralizing lexical particles and numbers used as adjectives are good clues that a noun or noun phrase has ended.

---

Simplifying the complex nominative object here—reducing ངན་སོང་གསུམ་ལས་ཐར་པའི་ ཐབས་ to its core noun ཐབས་—allows the following analysis.

| S SP | S S | C | 3 | S C | 4 | NOM | V SP |
|---|---|---|---|---|---|---|---|
| དེས་ན་ ⇒ | བླ་མ་རྣམས་ | ཀྱིས་ → | | བདག་ཅག་ | ལ་ → | ཐབས་ → | ← བསྟན་ དེ། ⇒ |

It is *for us* or *to us* that the gurus teach a liberating method. This gives us the following syntax.

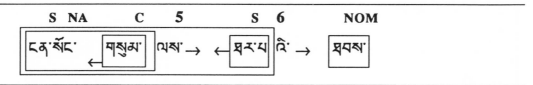

The nominative object of བསྟན་ is an appositive phrase incorporating the Class IV (nominative-syntactic) verb ཐར་ (*is liberated, is freed*), a verb whose qualifier is marked by a fifth case marker. Liberated from what? From the three bad rebirths.

| S NA | C | 5 | S | 6 | NOM |
|---|---|---|---|---|---|
| ངན་སོང་ ← གསུམ་ | ལས་ → | ← ཐར་པ | དེ་ → | | ཐབས་ |

The connective between ངན་སོང་གསུམ་ལས་ཐར་པ་ and ཐབས་ is a clause connective, a very common construction in Tibetan.

---

A noun following a clause ending in a verbal noun or adjective, and connected to it by a connective case marking particle, is often the *understood* subject, object, qualifier, or complement of that clause.

---

This is the typical way in which one element of a clause is singled out for connection to the remainder of a sentence. The connective marker between the clause—here, དེ་སྲོང་གསུམ་ལས་ཐར་པ་—and the noun ཐབས་ is a **clause connective**. (See Appendix Five, section 6.6 for more examples.)

In the present example, ཐབས་—if it were a part of the clause that precedes it—would be the means through which liberation occurs. It would be an agentive case instrument and, syntactically, would be a qualifier. Since, however, it does not precede the verbal ཐར་པ་, it is merely an *understood* qualifier. Isolated in its position following the clause, it becomes the focus of the construction and may be a subject, object, qualifier, or complement of the sentence that surrounds it.

It is often the case in Tibetan that the subject of a clause or sentence is understood, not explicitly stated. Here are some examples of agentive-nominative constructions without stated subjects.

---

*Although seeking objects of desire, [one] does not find [them] ...*

འདོད་པའི་ དོངས་པོ་ བཙལ་ཀྱང་ མི་རྙེད་

---

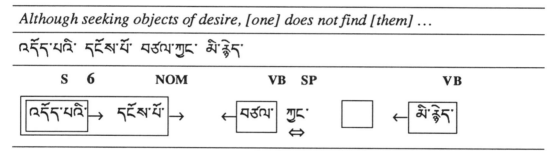

| S | 6 | | NOM | | VB | SP | | | VB |
|---|---|---|---|---|---|---|---|---|---|

---

The second verb, རྙེད་, is negated with the lexical particle མི་. The empty box before it symbolizes its understood object—འདོད་པའི་དོངས་པོ་.

The following example is a more complex illustration of a sentence with an implicit subject.

---

*[Buddha] turned the wheel of the doctrine of the four truths at Varanasi for the meritorious group of five.*

ཡུལ་བཱ་རཱ་ཎ་སཱི་ར་ ལྔ་སྡེ་བཟང་པོ་ལ་ བདེན་པ་བཞིའི་ཆོས་ཀྱི་འཁོར་ལོ་ བསྐོར།

---

Note the small འ under the བ, ར, ས in བཱ་རཱ་ཎ་སཱི་. They are used to transliterate the Sanskrit long vowels. Thus, བཱ་ is *vā*, རཱ་ is *rā*, and སཱི་ is *sī*. The ཎ་—a backwards ན་—represents the Sanskrit *ṇa*.

This sentence has four elements.

1 ཁྱལ་ལྷུ་རྫ་ཏ་སྩེར་ indicates the place where Buddha taught the four truths. The ending ར་ marks the objective case, here showing a place of activity.

2 ལྔ་སྡེ་བཟང་པོ་ལ་, a noun-adjective phrase marked by one of the *la* group of particles, is the indirect object, *the meritorious group of five* to whom Buddha first taught—his five former ascetic companions.

3 བདེན་པ་བཞིའི་ཆོས་ཀྱི་འཁོར་ལོ་ is the nominative object. ཆོས་ཀྱི་འཁོར་ལོ་ (*wheel of doctrine*—Skt. *dharmacakra*) is the traditional metaphor for a buddha's teaching.

4 བསྐོར་ is an agentive-nominative verb meaning *turned*.

བསྐོར་ is an example of an agentive verb with a closely related nominative verb cognate. The agentive-nominative སྐོར་ is a four-form verb, whereas the nominative-objective འཁོར་ is a two-form verb. Both may be translated *turn*, reflecting the ambiguity of the English term.

| past: བསྐོརད་ | present: སྐོར་ | future: བསྐོར་ | imperative: སྐོརད་ |
|---|---|---|---|
| past: འཁོརད་ | present: འཁོར་ | future: འཁོར་ | imperative: འཁོརད་ |

In neither case is the secondary suffix ད་ normally spelled out, although it does determine which particles may follow those forms that have it (even when it is not written). Thus, the usually written forms of these two verbs look like the following.

| past: བསྐོར་ | present: སྐོར་ | future: བསྐོར་ | imperative: སྐོར་ |
|---|---|---|---|
| past: འཁོར་ | present: འཁོར་ | future: འཁོར་ | imperative: འཁོར་ |

Thus, སྐོར་ has the appearance of a two-form verb and འཁོར་ appears to be a single-form verb.

## Instrumental Qualifiers

Not all agentives in clauses and sentences ending in agentive verbs are necessarily subjects. In the following example, the agentive ཐོ་བས་ indicates the instrument used (a hammer), not the subject.

*When a clay pot is broken with a hammer …*[174]

 རྫ་བུམ་ ཐོ་བས་ བཅོམ་པ་ ན་

| UP NOM | | S 3 | | S C 7 | |
|---|---|---|---|---|---|
| རྫ་ བུམ་ → | | ཐོ་བ ས་ → | | ← བཅོམ་ པ་ | ན་ |

རྫ་བུམ་ literally means *pot [of] clay*. The UP dot marks an omitted connective case particle. The ན་ at the end is not a conditional syntactic particle, but a seventh case marker indicating the time when the breaking is done.

In the following example, both the agentive subject and the agentive instrument are present.

*This mother of mine sustained me in the womb with love.*[175]

བདག་གི་ མ་ འདིས་ མངལ་དུ་ བརྩེ་བས་ བསྐྱངས།

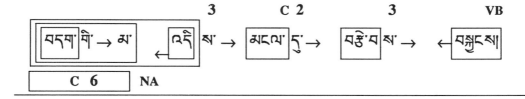

# Drill 17.1

Translate the following into Tibetan.

1. I have committed evil[s].
2. Bodhisattvas generate love and compassion towards hell-beings.
3. The reverend Maitreya taught the perfection of wisdom to [his] retinue.

## Drill 17.2

Translate the following, diagramming the second, fourth, and fifth and marking their dots.  Take care with the agentive-nominative clause in number five.  The phrase མིའི་ རྟེན་ means *a human [physical] support*—that is, a lifetime in which a human rebirth has been achieved.

1  ཁོ་བོས་ཆོས་དང་མཐོང་།

2  སློན་པས་སྐྱེས་བུ་གསུམ་གྱི་ལམ་བཤད།

3  དེ་དག་གིས་ཐར་པ་དོན་དུ་གཉེར།

4  བྱིས་པ་རྣམས་ལ་བསྟན་པ་བཤད།  རྒྱལ་འགྱུར་པ་ལ་སྒྲུབ་མཐའ་བཤད།

5  མིའི་རྟེན་ལ་བདག་གི་མ་མ་བྱས་པ་གཅིག་ཀྱང་མེད།

## *Negation of Agentive-Nominative Verbs*

The following example illustrates the negation of an agentive-nominative verb.  It takes place in the same way as that of other verbs.

---

*[one whose] mind has not been transformed by tenets*

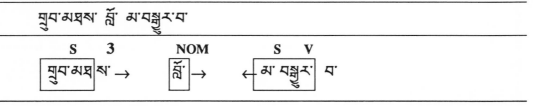

---

བསྒྱུར་ is the past tense of སྒྱུར་, the agentive cognate of the nominative verb འགྱུར་.

## Constructions with Auxiliary Verbs

Although tense is sometimes clearly indicated by the form of a verb, in many cases verbs do not have four distinct forms, but only two or three, or, sometimes, only one. There have been a number of examples using the verb བསྟན་, ambiguously both the past and future form of the verb སྟོན་.

---

past: བསྟན་    present: སྟོན་    future: བསྟན་    imperative: སྟོན་

---

Given that the quoted examples ending in བསྟན་ have referred to the activities of Shakyamuni Buddha, the context defines the tense as the past tense.

However, this is not always the case. The verb སྒྲོལ་, for example, is an agentive-nominative verb meaning *liberate*.

---

past: བསྒྲལ་    present: སྒྲོལ་    future: བསྒྲལ་    imperative: སྒྲོལ་

---

སྒྲོལ་ is ambiguously either the present or the imperative form. However, used with an auxiliary verb of definite future tense, even the present tense form may be used for the future, as in the following example.

---

*More than that, I will liberate all beings!*

---

དེ་བས་ འགྲོ་ཀུན་ བདག་གིས་ སྒྲོལ་བར་བྱ།

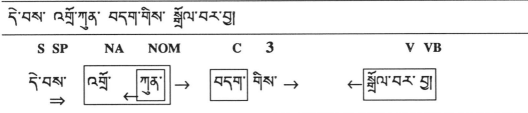

དེ་བས་ is an introductory syntactic particle with a comparative meaning—*more than that* or *beyond that*. The syllable བས་—as an added syllable (here, added to the pronoun དེ་)—conveys this normally fifth case meaning.

Note that སྒྲོལ་བར་ is marked with a **V** dot, the dot indicating an open verb. In this example སྒྲོལ་བར་ is the verbal infinitive form of སྒྲོལ་.

> Verbal infinitives are used (as in the present example) in auxiliary verb constructions and in some compound verb constructions (for example, སྒྲོལ་བར་ནུས་, *able to liberate*). They do not translate into English infinitives (such as *to liberate*) when used with auxiliaries, but they may in other situations.

In སྒྲོལ་བར་བྱ་, the verb བྱ་ (future of བྱེད་) is the strong future auxiliary verb in Tibetan, indicating that an effort will be—or should be—made to do something.

> There are two auxiliary verbs in Tibetan: བྱེད་ and its future form (བྱ་) are the strong auxiliaries, while the past (གྱུར་) and future (འགྱུར་) of འགྱུར་ are the weak auxiliaries.

The weak auxiliary future indicates either that something will happen or that something might be the case contingent on something else happening.

Here is another example of an agentive-nominative verb used with an auxiliary verb, but this time in the present tense.

*[He] seeks merely the happiness of this lifetime.*

ཚེ་འདིའི་ བདེ་བ་ཙམ་ དོན་དུ་གཉེར་བར་བྱེད།

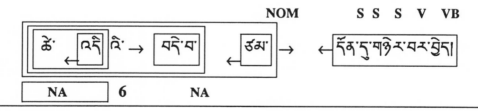

Note the nesting of adjectives and qualifiers in the phrase ཚེ་འདིའི་བདེ་བ་ཙམ་.
   What life? ཚེ་འདི་—*this life.*
   What happiness? ཚེ་འདིའི་བདེ་བ་—*the happiness of this life.*
   What about the happiness of this life? *Merely* that happiness.

Remember that དོན་དུ་གཉེར་ is a phrasal verb. It is seen here in its verbal infinitive form, དོན་དུ་གཉེར་བར་.

## Drill 17.3

Translate the following into Tibetan using auxiliary constructions.

1 Our Teacher set forth the doctrines of impermanence and emptiness.
2 One will realize the intention of the Conqueror.
3 One stops hating and meditates.   (Ceasing hatred, [one] meditates.)

## Drill 17.4

Identify the dots in the following and translate.  Diagram the first and the fourth.

1 སྙིང་རྗེ་སྐྱོམ་པའི་ཚུལ་ནི་ཡིག་ཏུ་འཆད་པར་འགྱུར་རོ།

2 གཞི་ལམ་འབྲས་གསུམ་གྱི་རྣམ་བཞག་སྨྲ་བར་བྱེད།

3 ངས་སེམས་ཅན་གྱི་དོན་དུ་སངས་རྒྱས་ཐོབ་པར་འགྱུར།

4 སངས་རྒྱས་ཀྱིས་ཆོས་འཁོར་བསྐོར་བར་མ་གྱུར་ན་

5 ཆེ་འདོད་སྙིང་པོ་ལྡན་པའི་ཚུལ་ཤེས་པར་བྱ།

## Case Marking Particles
### *Fifth Case Separation and Inclusion*

Originative case particles were introduced in Chapter Fifteen, where two of their usages—those indicating means and reasons—were introduced.  These two usages are seen more frequently in texts translated from Sanskrit than in indigenous Tibetan writings.  The following four uses of the fifth case, on the other hand, are quite frequently seen.

## *Originatives Indicating Separation*

Where some one thing or a group of things are set apart *from* a larger group, the originative particle is used.  Separation in the sense of **isolation**—that is, singling out some one item to discuss—is very common.

| originative isolation | གསུམ་ལས་ | དང་པོ་ ནི། |

*Among the three*, *the first [is] as follows.*

In the following example, the originative particle is attached to the postposition ནང་.

---

*Out of all the systems*, *that is the best.*

---

| ལུགས་ཐམས་ཅད་ཀྱི་ནང་ནས་ | དེ་ མཆོག་ཏུ་གྱུར་པ |

---

The clause མཆོག་ཏུ་གྱུར་ illustrates a quasi-linking usage of the verb གྱུར་. It does not mean *that which has become the best*, but merely *that which is the best*. The case marking particle ཏུ་ marks objective identity.

Separation in the sense of removal (or going *out of* a situation) is not as frequently seen as isolation, but is a regular usage.

| originative removal | འཁོར་བ་ལས་ | གྲོལ་བ་ |

*liberation from cyclic existence*

The verb གྲོལ་ is an example of a nominative-syntactic verb, the qualifier here marked not by a syntactic particle, but by the fifth case marker ལས་.

In the following example, the verb སྒྲོབ་ takes an agentive subject and a nominative object and, thus, is not a nominative-syntactic verb.

---

*providing refuge from suffering*

---

| སྡུག་བསྔལ་ལས་ | སྐྱོབ་པ |

---

As is not infrequently the case with nominative verbs, གྲོལ་ has an agentive cognate, སྒྲོལ་, which, like སྐྱོབ་, takes a fifth case qualifier but is not a syntactic verb.

## *Originatives Indicating Comparison*

Any sentence may include comparative elements. The standard means of indicating a comparison is with the originative case.

| originative comparison | དེ་ལས་ ཆེ་བ་ |
|---|---|

*greater than that*

*Cho-mo-lang-ma [is] higher than all mountains.*

ཇོ་མོ་གླང་མ་ རི་བོ་ཀུན་ལས་ མཐོ་

*[That] red silk [is] redder than fire.*

དར་དམར་པོ་ མེ་ལས་ དམར་

The syntactic particles བས་ and པས་—when they are syllables added to a word—also show comparison.

The example seen earlier in this chapter was དེ་བས་འགྲོ་ཀུན་བདག་གིས་སྒྲོལ་བར་བྱ། (*More than that, I will liberate all beings*).

## *Originatives Indicating Inclusion*

The beginning of a sequence, a distance travelled, or a period of time elapsed is marked by the originative particle ནས་ (but not by ལས་).

| originative beginning (sequence) | གཅིག་ནས་ བཅུའི་བར་ |
|---|---|

*from one through ten*

*from the beginning to the conclusion*

མགོ་ནས་ མཇུག་གི་བར་

In the following example, the past tense form of the verb འཛིན་ is used in the sense of beginning with something, a common construction.

---

*beginning **with the first stage***

---

ས་དང་པོ་ནས་ བཟུང་སྟེ་

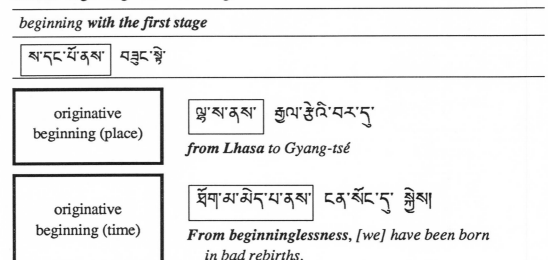

originative beginning (place)

ལྷ་ས་ནས་ རྒྱལ་རྩེའི་བར་དུ་

*from Lhasa to Gyang-tsé*

originative beginning (time)

ཐོག་མ་མེད་པ་ནས་ ངན་སོང་དུ་ སྐྱེས།

***From beginninglessness, [we] have been born in bad rebirths.***

The above example alludes to the assertion that cyclic existence has no beginning.

---

*[She] lived there **from the first [lunar] month** through the sixth month.*

---

ཟླ་བ་དང་པོ་ནས་ ཟླ་བ་དྲུག་པའི་བར་དུ་དེར་བཞུགད།

---

The syntactic particle དེ་ནས་ (*then*) has its origins in this usage (དེ་ནས་ literally meaning *after that*).


## Interrogative Pronouns

In Chapters Fourteen through Sixteen the most straightforward sort of pronouns were examined, the personal pronouns meaning *I, me, you, she*, and so forth. You also saw the use of adjectives such as དེ་ and དེ་དག་ as pronouns.

In this chapter the pronouns used to make declarative sentences into questions will be introduced. The most basic **interrogative pronouns** are the following four:

1   གང་   — *what, which, who*;

2   ཅི་   — *what* (also sometimes seen as ཇི་);

3  སུ་     — *who*;

4  ཇི་ལྟར་  — literally *like what* (that is, *how*), but also *what*.

གང་, like its declarative counterpart དེ་, may refer either to a person or a thing. All four (གང་, ཅེ་ [or ཇི་], ཇི་ལྟར་, and སུ་) also function as relative pronouns (as in, for example, *the Buddha who taught*). The fourth "pronoun" is an adverbial pronoun. Its use should be considered to be an instance of adverbial identity.

The ordinary position in which interrogative pronouns are found is next to the verb.

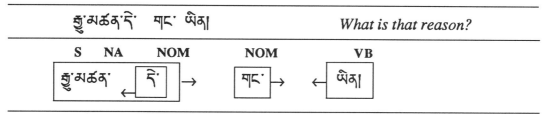

Notice that whereas in English we place the interrogative pronoun first ("*What* is that reason?"), in Tibetan the word order is just the opposite.

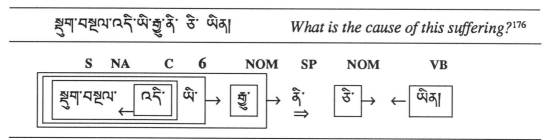

The same syntax may be observed in the above example as well:

| SUBJECT → | INTERROGATIVE PRONOUN → | ← VERB |

The subject here consists of two brief phrases: a NOUN + ADJECTIVE phrase (སྡུག་ བསྔལ་འདི་) which is itself the first noun within a NOUN + CONNECTIVE-PARTICLE + NOUN (སྡུག་བསྔལ་འདི་ཡི་རྒྱུ་) phrase. To make it clear where the subject ends, the syntactic particle ནི་ has been placed at its end.

The interrogative pronouns listed above occur not just as nominatives but in inflected forms, that is, with case particles affixed to them: གང་ན་ (*in what, where*), གང་ ལ་ or ཅི་ལ་ (*to what, for what*), གང་གིས་ or ཅིས་ (*by what, because of what*), ཅི་ལས་ or ཅི་

ནས་ (*than what, from what*), གང་གི་ or ཅིའི་ (*of what*).  These need not be learnt separately since they reflect the normal uses of the various cases.

---

*On what does compassion depend?*

---

སྙིང་རྗེ་ གང་ལ་ བརྟེན།

---

*Where is something greater than that?*[177]

---

འདི་ལས་ཆེ་བ་ གང་ན་ ཡོད།

---

ཆེ་བ་ is the comparative form of the adjective ཆེན་པོ་, and means *larger* or *greater*.

In both examples the pronoun གང་ is in the locative case.  In the first example it is the locative place of dependence; in the second it is the locative place of existence.

ཅི་ and གང་ may stand free, acting as subject or qualifier as they do in the above examples, or they may follow a noun, standing in apposition to it.

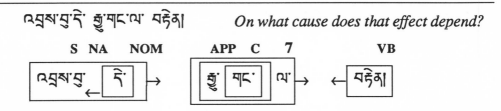

འབྲས་བུ་དེ་ རྒྱུ་གང་ལ་ བརྟེན།                    *On what cause does that effect depend?*

| S NA | NOM | APP | C | 7 | VB |
|------|-----|-----|---|---|-----|
| འབྲས་བུ་ | དེ་ | རྒྱུ་ | གང་ | ལ་ | བརྟེན། |

You will sometimes see ཅི་ with a postposition or a syntactic particle (for example, ཅིའི་ཕྱིར་—WHAT + OF + BECAUSE, *because of what* or *why*) or used as part of an adverb construction (ཅི་ལྟར་ *how*, ཅི་ཙམ་ *how much*).  The word ཇི་ལྟར་ listed at the beginning of this section is also an adverb.

གང་ and ཅི་ are used not only in the impersonal sense of *what*, but also in the personal sense of *who* and *whom*.  In order to specify a person rather than a place or thing, it is necessary to use the pronoun སུ་.  The following are examples of interrogative pronouns used to ask questions about persons.

---

*Where is / Who has such fault(s)?*

---

ཉེས་སྐྱོན་ དེ་འདྲ་ ཅི་ལ་ མངའ།

---

ཉེས་སྐྱོན་ means *fault*; དེ་འདྲ་ is a variant on the pronoun དེ་, meaning *such* (literally, *like that*). འདྲ་ derives from a nominative-syntactic verb meaning *is like* and *is similar*. Thus, the syllable འདྲ་ in དེ་འདྲ་ is a verbal.

*In whom is there great compassion?* OR *Who has great compassion?*

སྙིང་རྗེ་ཆེན་པོ་ སུ་ལ་ ཡོད།

The verbs ཡོད་ and མངའ་ are used here as verbs of possession. The case particle ལ་ in these examples marks the pronouns as locative subjects of ཡོད་ and མངའ་. The best translation into English would involve the use of the verb *have*. Thus, the preferable translation of the second example would be *Who has great compassion?*

Here are some other examples of the use of སུ་.

*Who lives for a hundred years?*

ལོ་བརྒྱ་རུ་ སུ་ སྡོད།

*Who is Samantabhadra?*

ཀུན་ཏུ་བཟང་པོ་ སུ་ ཡིན།

> Recall that སུ་ is also a case particle, used to mark the second, fourth, and seventh cases.

As mentioned above, ཇི་ལྟར་ (based on the pronoun ཇི་) is an adverbial pronoun—a category not seen in English. However, it is sometimes used in a sense that is very much like the interrogatives seen above. The sentence རྒྱུ་མཚན་ཇི་ལྟར་ཡིན།, for example, literally means REASON WHAT-LIKE IS, or *How is the reason?* Unfortunately, this is not reasonable English. རྒྱུ་མཚན་ཇི་ལྟར་ཡིན། should be translated *What is the reason?* or *The reason is of what sort?*

## Rhetorical Questions

Tibetan writing is full of rhetorical questions, most of which ought not to be translated literally as questions. In Tibetan it is good style to pepper a book with sentences that literally begin *If one were to ask, what is* ... or *If one were to ask, why* ... and so on, and then to answer those questions. This is not the case in English writing.

The Tibetan construction, which is common enough to be considered a syntactic particle in its own right, occurs at the end of complete interrogative sentences. It occurs in three forms: ཅེ་ན, ཞེ་ན, and སེ་ན. Which one is used is contingent on the suffix letter of the last word in the sentence.

---

If the last letter of the last syllable is ག་, ད་, བ་, or the secondary suffix ད་, then one uses ཅེ་ན. If the last letter of the last syllable is ང་, ན་, མ་, འ་, ར་, ལ་, or if that syllable has no suffix, then one uses ཞེ་ན. If the last letter of the last syllable is ས་, then one uses སེ་ན.

---

Here are a few examples of very simple constructions using this particle.

| C 7 VB SP<br>གང་ལ་ཡོད་ཅེ་ན། | *Where is [it]? Where are [they]?* |
|---|---|
| སུ་ལ་མཆིས་སེ་ན། | *Who has [that]?* |
| དོན་གང་ཞེ་ན། | *What is the meaning?*<br>*What is the purpose?* |
| གང་ལས་གྲོལ་ཅེ་ན། | *From what is [one] liberated?* |
| སུས་བསྟན་ཞེ་ན། | *Who taught [that]?* |

● The first three examples are straightforward. The first two end in verbs of existence and the third ends in an understood linking verb. Note in the dot analysis of the first example that even though an **SP** dot is a dot before or after a syntactic particle, it is a very weak dot and thus the dot after the verb takes precedence.

● The fourth example—གང་ལས་གྲར་ཅི་ན།—uses the nominative-syntactic verb གྲར་ (*free* or *liberate*). Its qualifier is in the fifth case, here indicating separation (which may be roughly translated as *from*): *From what is [one] liberated?*

● The fifth example—སུས་བསྟན་ཞེ་ན།—uses the agentive verb བསྟན་ (*taught, demonstrated*). Here as well the subject is in the third or agentive case: སུ་, *who*, with the agentive ending -ས་.

The fifth example may be diagrammed in the following way if an object is added to yield the sentence *Who taught the doctrine?*

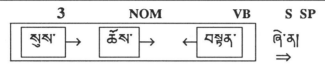

The construction ཅི་ན་ is an open-ended one. The particle ན་, typically a rhetorical syntactic particle meaning *if* (or *when*), shows that it is not a termination but leads to more discussion. This is shown in the diagram by a double arrow pointing to the right, in the direction of words yet to be said. When reading and translating Tibetan, however, a sentence ending in a particle such as ཅི་ན་ should be translated as a rhetorical question leading to an answer.

Although ཅེ་, ཞེ་, and ཤེ་ are not actually verbs,[178] they act as if they were once constructed from or were related to a verb meaning something such as *say* or *call*. In support of this, modern Tibetan dictionaries tend to define the ཅི་ན་ construction as *if it is said that*....[179]

Three similar syntactic particles are ཅེས་, ཞེས་, and ཤེས་. They follow quotations and act as close quote markers (").

---

# Drill 17.5

Translate the following into Tibetan.

[1] What is there in the ocean?

[2] Who are they?

3 One might ask, "What is a Tathāgata?"

4 Where is Nepal?

5 Of what is that the color?

---

## Drill 17.6

Identify the dots in the following and translate. Diagram the first and fifth.

1 འདི་ཡི་རྒྱུ་ནི་ཅི་ཞི་ན།

2 དེ་འདྲའི་ཤེས་རབ་སུ་ལ་ཡོད་ཅེ་ན།

3 ངས་པར་འབྱུང་བ་གང་ལ་རག་ལས།

4 འཁོར་བའི་རྒྱུ་ནི་གང་ལ་ཡོད།

5 མི་རྟག་པའི་མཚན་ཉིད་གང་ཡིན་ཞི་ན།

6 སྟོན་པ་གང་གིས་ཆོས་གང་བསྟན།

---

## Rhetorical Tools
### *Critical Analysis*

Many Tibetan philosophical commentaries are written in the མཐའ་དཔྱོད་ (*critical analysis*) style. In this genre, individual topics are treated in three part style:

1 གཞན་ལུགས་དགག་པ་ (s̲hën-luk gak-b̄a)—*refutation of others' positions* or འཁྲུལ་བ་དགག་པ་ (t̪hül-wa gak-b̄a)—*refutation of mistaken [positions]*;[180]

2 རང་ལུགས་བཞག་པ་ (rang-luk s̲hak-b̄a)—*presentation of our own position* or of *one's own position*;

3 རྩོད་པ་སྤོང་བ་ (d̄zö'-b̄a b̄ong-wa)—*elimination of objections.*

> Concerning this tripartite structure, see Perdue, *Debate in Tibetan Buddhism*, pp. 171-172.

 རྩོད་པ་ means *argument, debate,* or *objection.* དགག་, བཞག་, and སྤོང་ are common, Class V (agentive-nominative) verbs.

| | | |
|---|---|---|
| དགག་ | **gak** | *refute, stop, cease* |
| བཞག་ | **s̲hak** | *put, posit, present* |
| སྤོང་ | **b̄ong** | *eliminate, abandon* |

All three are four-form verbs.

| | | | |
|---|---|---|---|
| past: བཀག་ | present: འགོག་ | future: དགག་ | imperative: ཁོགས་ |
| past: བཞག་ | present: འཇོག་ | future: གཞག་ | imperative: ཞོག་ |
| past: སྤངས་ | present: སྤོང་ | future: སྤང་ | imperative: སྤོངས་ |

The first and third sections of a དགག་བཞག་སྤོང་ sequence are composed of a series of rhetorical sequences. The individual sequences, or debates, are sometimes logically connected with one another but are sometimes merely a series of relevant, but not logically sequential treatments of subtopics. Each rhetorical sequence is set up as a debate between two positions and is itself constructed of a series of consequences.

The most basic subject matter and the simplest rhetorical sequences are to be found in the doctrinal primers (བསྡུས་གྲྭ) used at the elementary school level of monastic education as an introduction to the study of Buddhist doctrine in general, and to epistemology and logic (ཚད་མ་) in particular. These primers typically begin with debates about colors (generically termed ཁ་དོག་དཀར་དམར་—*the colors white and red*) as a technique for teaching debating methods and the principles of logic. It is in this section as well that the basic *abhidharma* (ཆོས་མངོན་པ་ *higher knowledge*) analysis of the physical world (types of colors, shapes, sounds, odors, and so forth) is introduced.

Some of this material has already been introduced in Chapter Thirteen's discussion of the five aggregates. An extensive presentation and analysis of ཁ་དོག་དཀར་དམར་ is to be found in Perdue, *Debate in Tibetan Buddhism,* pp. 185-266.

In *Translating Buddhism from Tibetan*, however, the analysis of rhetorical sequences will focus not on ཁ་དོག་དཀར་དམར་ but on the rhetorical analysis of basic existents (གཞི་གྲུབ་).

## The Structure of Tibetan Books

Tibetan texts are written in outline form. The "Presentation of Basic Existents" is the second chapter of the first volume of the doctrinal primer written by Pur-bu-jok Cham-ba-gya-tso (ཕུར་བུ་ལྕོག་བྱམས་པ་རྒྱ་མཚོ་, **Phur-bu-jok C͟ham-b̄a-gya-tsho**), a work divided into three volumes. The title page of the book alludes to this.

ཚད་མའི་གཞུང་དོན་འབྱེད་པའི་བསྟུས་གྲུབའི་རྣམ་བཤག་རིགས་ལམ་འཕྲུལ་གྱི་ལྡེ་མིག་ཅེས་བྱ་བ་ལས་ རིགས་ལམ་ཆུང་དུའི་རྣམ་པར་བཤད་པ་བཞུགས་སོ།

This is literally a sentence ending in the verb of living བཞུགས་. ཚད་མའི་གཞུང་དོན་འབྱེད་པའི་ བསྟུས་གྲུབའི་རྣམ་བཤག་ and རིགས་ལམ་འཕྲུལ་གྱི་ལྡེ་མིག་ཅེས་བྱ་བ་ are noun phrases in apposition. Together, marked by the originative case marker ལས་, they act as a qualifier in the sentence. A literal translation might read something like the following.

*[Here] Abides an Explanation of the Lesser Path of Reasoning—from "The Magical Key to the Path of Reasoning," A Presentation [which is] a Doctrinal Primer Revealing the Meaning of the Texts on Valid Cognition*

The following two translations illustrate the way in which a translator might move from the above literal rendition to something more typical of an English title page. The first of the two represent an intermediate step and the second (in which some words are not translated and others are added), a more finished product.

*An Explanation of the Introductory Path of Reasoning*
*[Part One of] "The Magical Key to the Path of Reasoning,"*
*A Doctrinal Primer Revealing the Meaning of the Texts of Logic & Epistemology*

# The Magical Key to the Path of Reasoning
*A Doctrinal Primer Revealing the Meaning of the Texts of Logic & Epistemology*

## Part One
*An Explanation of the Introductory Path of Reasoning*

The first page of the book (actually, following the Tibetan convention, page two—since page one is the title page) begins with a line of homage to Manjushri.

*[I] bow down to the guru and protector Manjughosha.*

བླ་མ་དང་མགོན་པོ་ འཇམ་དཔལ་དབྱངས་ལ་ ཕྱག་འཚལ་ལོ།

བླ་མ་དང་མགོན་པོ་ and འཇམ་དཔལ་དབྱངས་ are nouns in apposition; together they are the indirect object of the verb ཕྱག་འཚལ་.

> An indirect object to which no obvious benefit is done is not in the fourth case, but in the second. Bowing down to or paying homage to Manjushri is done in order to collect merit and, thus, benefits not Manjushri but the person paying homage or bowing down.

The homage to Manjushri is followed by a verse of respect to previous Indian and Tibetan epistemologists and logicians, ending as follows.

*Homage to the scholars and adepts of India and Tibet who have gone before.*

སྔོན་བྱོན་འཕགས་བོད་མཁས་གྲུབ་རྣམས་ལ་འདུད།

As before, this is a sentence with the understood subject *I*. The words that are present in this line are—typical of Tibetan verse—seen in abbreviated forms. སྔོན་བྱོན་ is a brief, verbal adjective clause that may be expanded to སྔོན་དུ་བྱོན་པ་ (BEFORE + COME). འཕགས་བོད་ means འཕགས་པའི་ཡུལ་དང་བོད་ (*the land of the superiors and Tibet*). India is the land of superiors (Skt. *āryadeśa*). མཁས་གྲུབ་ are *scholars* (མཁས་པ་) and *adepts* (གྲུབ་ཐོབ་) or, alternately, *scholarly practitioners*.[181]

The first section in Pur-bu-jok's doctrinal primer is that on ཁ་དོག་དཀར་དམར་, but we will skip ahead to the beginning of the "Presentation of Basic Existents" chapter.

> This is translated and discussed in Perdue, *Debate in Tibetan Buddhism*, pp. 267ff.

The basic existents section begins with a sentence whose first word is གཉིས་པ་, telling you that you have arrived at the second section or subsection (or sub-subsection) of the text.

---

*The second [section], the presentation of basic existents ...*

གཉིས་པ་ གཞི་གྲུབ་ཀྱི་ རྣམ་བཞག་བཤད་པ་

---

རྣམ་བཞག་ is the nominative object of བཤད་, the past form of the agentive-nominative verb འཆད་ (*explain, set forth*).

Here the topic of the second section—གཞི་གྲུབ་ཀྱི་རྣམ་བཞག་བཤད་པ་—is stated as an appositive of གཉིས་པ་.

A numeric section heading is part of a ས་བཅད་ (**sap-jë'**), the topic outline of a text. It is more the rule than not that Tibetan books are written around such outlines. However, it is often the case—especially as one gets down to the sub-subtopics—that only the number and not the name of the topic is given.

---

Study or translation of a Tibetan text should often be preceded by the creation of a Western-style table of contents made by copying out the ས་བཅད་ in a line-by-line format and noting the page and line number on which each section begins.

---

In context, the section heading looks like this.

---

*The second [section], the presentation of basic existents [has] three [parts]: refutation, presentation, and elimination. Among [them], the first [is as follows].*

གཉིས་པ་ གཞི་གྲུབ་ཀྱི་ རྣམ་བཞག་ བཤད་པ་ལ། དགག་ བཞག་ སྤོང་ གསུམ་ལས། དང་པོ་ལ།

---

Recall that དགག་བཞག་སྤོང་གསུམ་ means གཞན་ལུགས་དགག་པ་, རང་ལུགས་བཞག་པ་, and རྩོད་པ་ སྤོང་བ་.

This is the typical format in which a section is divided into parts. There is an understood Class VIII verb of possession after དགག་བཞག་སྤོང་གསུམ་, which is then the nominative object of that verb. གཅིས་པ་གཞི་གྲུབ་ཀྱི་རྣམ་བཞག་བཤད་པ་ལ་ is the locative case subject of the understood ཡོད་.

དགག་བཞག་སྤོང་གསུམ་ is then repeated in the fifth case not as a qualifier within a sentence but as a **block language** construction, དགག་བཞག་སྤོང་གསུམ་ལས་ དང་པོ་ལ. The fifth case is used here to indicate separation—from among these three, the first. དང་པོ་ལ་ is a locative construction, that special locative which does not connect a noun to a later verb but rather connects it to the entire following section of the text: the **topical locative**.

> There are also topical nominatives. If used here, a topical nominative would look something like དགག་བཞག་སྤོང་གསུམ་ལས་དང་པོ་ནི. The topical nominative and locative are similar in that neither marks a relationship with a specific phrase, clause, or sentence.

The rule of thumb "literal" translation for block language is *That is as follows*, where *that* is the word marked by the topical nominative or locative and *is as follows* is added to fulfill the English requirement for complete sentences.

---

The best translation for block language is often as a topic heading on its own line.

---

In the present case, that gives us the following.

---

## II Presentation of Basic Existents
*This section has three parts: refutation [of others' positions], presentation [of our own position], and elimination [of objections].*

## Refutation of Others' Positions
*[Whatever text came next would begin here.]*

---

The text that actually does come next in Pur-bu-jok's doctrinal primer is an extended rhetorical sequence that will be examined in Chapters Eighteen and Nineteen.

> A consequence or syllogism is a rhetorical statement. A series of such statements bound together logically is a rhetorical sequence.

## Rhetorical Tools
### *Analysis of Permutations:  Mutual Exclusion*

Indo-Tibetan Buddhism classifies the differences possible between two things into four types:

1    three permutations (སྐྱ་གསུམ་);

2    four permutations (སྐྱ་བཞི་);

3    mutually exclusive (འགལ་བ་);

4    equivalent (དོན་གཅིག་).

If two things—A and B—are **mutually exclusive** (or **contraries**), they must meet two criteria.

1    They must be different.

2    There must be nothing which is both of them.[182]

Thus, one definition of mutual exclusion reads as follows.

*different and not having a common locus*

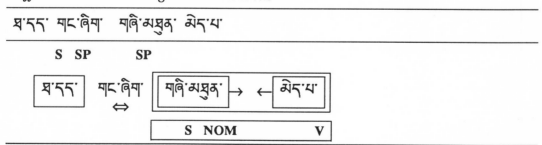

The syntactic particle གང་ཞིག་ here separates the two parts of the definition, both of which are necessary for mutual exclusion.

A *common locus* (གཞི་མཐུན་ shí-thün or shín-thün) of two things is something which is both of them.  A common locus of A and B is something which *is* (ཡིན་) A and is B.  For example, this page is a common locus of impermanent thing and material thing.

Although mutually exclusive things have no common loci, all of the other relationships have at least some.  For example, a red pot is a common locus of impermanent phenomenon and momentary phenomenon (two things that are equivalent). It is also a common locus of pot and impermanent phenomenon (two things that have three permutations), as well as being a common locus of red thing and pot (two things with four permutations).

A more complex definition of mutual exclusion is the following. It features the use of the pronoun ཁྱོད་ in the sense not of *you* but as a generic *it*, and—as in the present instance—in the plural as *they* or *those two*.

Technically, this is not the definition of *mutual exclusion*; rather, it is the definition of *their being mutually exclusive*—ཁྱོད་འགལ་བ་ཡིན་པའི་མཚན་ཉིད་.

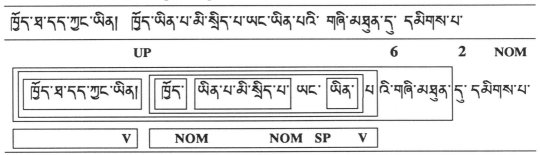

The first clause—ཁྱོད་ས་དད་གྱང་ཡིན་—is an example of a verbal noun (here, a noun phrase ending in a verbal) which does not end in a generic suffix syllable (that is, it is not ཁྱོད་ས་དད་གྱང་ཡིན་པ་).

The two items that are mutually exclusive are *seen* (དམིགས་པ་) to be a common locus of two things—that is, they meet two criteria: (1) they are different and (2) their *occurrence* (ཡིན་པ་) is *not possible* (མི་སྲིད་པ་). The second criterion merely means that there can be nothing which is both. The UP dot between the two clauses indicates that there is an understood conjunctive syntactic particle linking the two.

This latter characteristic—that there be nothing that is both A and B—is the more important. As stated in the simpler definition, if two things, A and B, are mutually exclusive, there must be *no* common locus of those two things. There is nothing about which you could say, "It is A and it is also B." For example, there is nothing about which you can say, "This is a cobra and also a mongoose." There is nothing about which you can say, "This is mind and also form."

Another example would be the two, permanent and impermanent (རྟག་པ་དང་མི་རྟག་པ་). Permanent and impermanent are mutually exclusive because:

1   they are different—that is, they are not identical;

2   there is nothing that is both permanent and impermanent.

The first criterion is intuitive; thus, the way to determine whether two things are mutually exclusive is based on the second criterion. And the best way to determine that there is nothing that is both permanent and impermanent is to search for a contradictory example—some one thing that *is* both. If cobras and mongeese are mutually exclusive, there can be nothing anywhere that has the two qualities of (1) being a cobra and (2) being a mongoose. Likewise, if permanent and impermanent are mutually exclusive, you will be unable to find anything that has these two qualities: being permanent and being impermanent. Whatever you can think of that is impermanent will necessarily not be permanent and vice-versa.

Cobras and mongeese are mutually exclusive—they are contraries—but are not a **dichotomy**. It is not the case that whatever exists must be either a cobra or a mongoose. Similarly, red and blue are mutually exclusive but are not a dichotomy. Permanent and impermanent, on the other hand, are mutually exclusive and, within that category, are also a dichotomy.[183]

Contrary examples—things that are not mutually exclusive—would be any two things that are equivalent, any two things that have three permutations, or any two things that have four permutations.[184]

●   Existent and phenomenon are equivalent; so are mind and consciousness. Whatever is the one is the other. Any existent thing is a common locus of the first; any mental phenomenon is a common locus of the second.

●   Existent and permanent have three permutations; so do apple and red apple. (1) All red apples are apples; however (2) not all apples are red apples and (3) there are things such as cows that are neither apples nor red apples. A large red apple is a common locus of apple and red apple.

● Apple and red fruit have four permutations. (1) Red apples are both. (2) Green apples are apples but are not red, whereas (3) pomegranates are red but not apples. (4) There are things such as brooms that are neither red fruits nor apples.

The common loci in the last two examples are called the གཉིས་ཀ་ཡིན་པའི་སྒོ་ (*the permutation that is both*). The connective after གཉིས་ཀ་ཡིན་པ་ is a clause connective. In this instance, the word སྒོ་ is the understood subject of ཡིན་.

---

*This permutation is both.*

སྒོ་འདི་ གཉིས་ཀ་ ཡིན།

---

Placing སྒོ་ outside of the clause allows it to be the focus of the construction.

## Doctrinal Vocabulary and Grammar
### *Basic Existents*

As set forth earlier (in Chapter Seven), the analysis of doctrinal terminology seen in Tibetan commentarial literature revolves around four basic categories: མཚན་ཉིད་ (*definitions*); དོན་གཅིག (*equivalents*); མཚན་གཞི་ (*illustrations*, that is, examples); and དབྱེ་བ་ (*divisions*, that is, categories and subcategories).

---

A particular མཚན་ཉིད་ is a *definition* of a particular མཚོན་བྱ་ — *that which is defined*. Thus, where མི་རྟག་པ་ is a མཚོན་བྱ་, སྐད་ཅིག་མ་ is its མཚན་ཉིད་.

---

A traditional formal way of stating the equivalents of གཞི་གྲུབ་ is the following.

---

*Phenomena equivalent to basic phenomenon exist*
*because object of knowledge, existent, phenomenon, object of comprehension, object, and hidden [phenomenon] are that.*

གཞི་གྲུབ་དང་དོན་གཅིག་པའི་ཆོས་ཡོད་དེ།
ཤེས་བྱ་ ཡོད་པ་ ཆོས་ གཞལ་བྱ་ ཡུལ་ དང་ལྐོག་གྱུར་ དེ་ཡིན་པའི་ཕྱིར།

---

| | | |
|---|---|---|
| ཤེས་བྱ་ | **shé>-ja** | *object of knowledge* |
| གཞལ་བྱ་ | **shël-ja** | *object of comprehension* |

| ཤོག་གྱུར་ | **g̱ok-gyur** | *hidden [phenomenon]* |

The thesis—གཞི་གྲུབ་དང་དོན་གཅིག་པའི་ཚོས་ཡོད་—makes use of the construction of the word དོན་གཅིག་ from དོན་ (*meaning*) and གཅིག་ (*one*). Like ཕ་དང་, གཅིག་ is used with the syntactic particle དང་.

| བུམ་པ་དང་གཅིག་ | *one with pot* |

| བུམ་པ་དང་ཐ་དད་ | *different from pot* |

In the phrase, གཞི་གྲུབ་དང་དོན་གཅིག་པའི་ཚོས་, the noun དོན་གཅིག་ becomes an adjective, དོན་གཅིག་པ་.

> For a list and brief discussion of the phenomena equivalent to basic existent, see Perdue, *Debate in Tibetan Buddhism*, pp. 269-272, and Hopkins, *Meditation on Emptiness*, pp. 214-215.

The རང་ལུགས་ (*our own positions*) section of Pur-bu-jok's basic existents chapter provides definitions and divisions for these terms.

*There is a definition of basic existent*
   *because established by valid cognition is that [definition].*

གཞི་གྲུབ་ཀྱི་མཚན་ཉིད་ཡོད་དེ། ཚད་མས་གྲུབ་པ་དེ་ དེ་ཡིན་པའི་ཕྱིར།

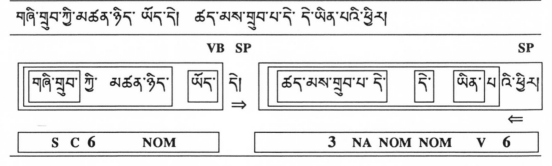

- The thesis—གཞི་གྲུབ་ཀྱི་མཚན་ཉིད་ཡོད་—follows the standard syntax of a verb of existence.

- The reason—ཚད་མས་གྲུབ་པ་དེ་དེ་ཡིན་པ་—is a linking verb clause with a syntactic particle (ཕྱིར་) attached.

● Within the reason, the definition itself—ཚད་མས་གྲུབ་པ—is a clause ending in a nominative action verb. Thus, the agentive ཚད་མས་ is not the subject of that clause (which would be in the nominative), but an instrumental agentive, *by means of valid cognition*. The understood subject of གྲུབ་ is any basic existent; it is basic existents that are established by valid cognition.

---

*When basic existents are divided, there are two*
*because the two, permanent [phenomenon] and functioning thing, exist.*

---

གཞི་གྲུབ་ལ་དབྱེ་ན་ གཉིས་ཡོད་དེ། རྟག་པ་དང་དངོས་པོ་གཉིས་ ཡོད་པའི་ཕྱིར།

---

Here the thesis is a very simple sentence ending in a verb of existence with a conditional qualifier.

---

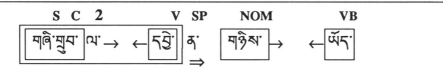

---

The verb དབྱེ་ is a commonly used Class VI (agentive-objective) verb. It is most frequently seen as it is here, with an understood generic subject (*we*, *you*, or *one*).

---

*There is a definition of permanent [phenomenon]*
*because the common locus of [being] a phenomenon and*
*not being momentary is the definition of permanent [phenomenon].*

---

རྟག་པའི་མཚན་ཉིད་ཡོད་དེ།
ཆོས་དང་སྐད་ཅིག་མ་མ་ཡིན་པའི་གཞི་མཐུན་པ་དེ། རྟག་པའི་མཚན་ཉིད་ཡིན་པའི་ཕྱིར།

---

A common locus of ཆོས་ and སྐད་ཅིག་མ་མ་ཡིན་པ is something about which it is correct to say both དེ་ཆོས་ཡིན། (*It is a phenomenon*) and དེ་སྐད་ཅིག་མ་མ་ཡིན། (*It is not momentary*).

Defining རྟག་པ merely as སྐད་ཅིག་མ་མ་ཡིན་པ (*non-momentary*) incurs the fault that non-existents would be permanent, since they also are not momentary. Remember that ཡིན་ does not imply ཡོད་.

Concerning permanent phenomena, see Perdue, *Debate in Tibetan Buddhism*, pp. 279-283, and Hopkins, *Meditation on Emptiness*, pp. 215-219.

# *Vocabulary*

## *Nouns*

| | | |
|---|---|---|
| སྐྱེས་བུ་ | ḡyé>-bu | being, person |
| སྐྱོབ་པ་ | ḡyop-b̄a | protector, refuge |
| འཁྲུལ་བ་ | ṭhul-wa | mistake, error |
| གྲོལ་བ་ | ṭöl-wa | liberation |
| དགེ་བའི་བཤེས་གཉེན་ | gé-wë-s̄hé>-nyén | spiritual friend |
| དགོངས་པ་ | gong-b̄a | thought, intention [HON] |
| མགོ་ | go | beginning |
| ལྔ་སྡེ་ | n̄ga-dé | group of five |
| མངལ་ | n̄gël | womb |
| མཇུག་ | juk | end, conclusion [of text] |
| རྗེ་བཙུན་ | jé-d̄zün | revered one |
| ཉེས་སྐྱོན་ | nyé>-ḡyön | fault |
| ཉེས་པ་ | nyé>-b̄a | fault |
| སྙིང་པོ་ | ñyíng-b̄o | heart, essence, pith |
| རྟེན་ | d̄ên | basis, support, [bodily] support |

| ཐབས་ | thap | means, method, technique |
| ཐོ་བ་ | tho-wa | hammer |
| ཐོག་མ་ | thok-ma | beginning |
| དར་ | tar | silk |
| ལྡེ་མིག་ | dé-mík | key |
| སྡིག་པ་ | dík-b̄a | evil |
| བསྡུས་གྲྭ་ | dü>-ḍa | doctrinal primer |
| དཔེ་ | b̄é | example |
| འཕྲུལ་ | ṭhül | magic |
| བལ་ཡུལ་ | pë-yül | Nepal |
| བྱིས་པ་ | <u>ch</u>í>-b̄a | child, immature person |
| མ་ | ma | mother |
| བརྩེ་བ་ | d̄zé-wa | love |
| མཚན་གཞི་ | tshën-<u>sh</u>í | illustration, instance |
| མཚོན་བྱ་ | tshön-ja | that which is defined |
| རྫ་ | <u>dz</u>a | clay |
| ཞིང་པ་ | <u>sh</u>íng-b̄a | farmer |
| གཞུང་ | <u>sh</u>ung | text, classic |
| ཟླ་བ་ | da-wa | moon, month |
| གཡག་ | yak | yak |

## *Verbs*

Verbs are marked by the Roman numeral indicating the class to which they belong—that is, the syntax they require.

| | | | |
|---|---|---|---|
| **I** | nominative-nominative | **V** | agentive-nominative |
| **II** | nominative-locative | **VI** | agentive-objective |
| **III** | nominative-objective | **VII** | purposive-nominative |
| **IV** | nominative-syntactic | **VIII** | locative-nominative |

The first part of the name of each class identifies the case of the subject and the second, that of the object, complement, or principal qualifier.

| | | |
|---|---|---|
| བགག་ | g̱ak | [past of དགག་] |
| སྐོར་ | g̱or | turn **v** |
| བསྐོར་ | g̱or | [future of སྐོར་] |
| བསྐོརད་ | g̱or | [past of སྐོར་] |
| སྐྱེ་ | g̱yé | arise, is born, is created **III** |
| སྐྱེད་ | g̱yé' | create, generate, give birth to **V** |
| སྐྱོང་ | g̱yong | nurture, sustain **V** |
| སྐྱབ་ | g̱yop | provide refuge **V** |
| བསྐྱངས་ | g̱yang | [past of སྐྱོང་] |
| ཁོགས་ | khok | [imperative of དགག་] |
| ཁྱབ་ | khyap | pervade, cover **VI** |
| འཁོར་ | khor | turn **VI** [present & future] |
| འཁོརད་ | khor | [past and imperative of འཁོར་] |
| གྲུབ་ | ṭup | is established, is accomplished, is achieved, exists **III** |
| དགག་ | gak | refute, stop, cease **V** |

| འགོག་ | gok | [future of དགག་] |
|---|---|---|
| སྒོམ་ | gom | meditate, cultivate **V** |
| སྒྱུར་ | gyur | transform, change **V** |
| སྒྲུབ་ | ḍup | establish, achieve, accomplish, prove, complete **V** |
| སྒྲོལ་ | ḍöl | liberate **V** |
| བསྒྱུར་ | gyur | [past and future of སྒྱུར་] |
| བསྒྲལ་ | ḍël | [past and future of སྒྲོལ་] |
| བཅལ་ | jël | [past of འཇལ་] |
| བཅོམ་ | jom | [past of འཇོམས་] |
| འཇལ་ | jël | measure, assess, comprehend **V** |
| འཇལད་ | jël | imperative of འཇལ་ |
| འཇོག་ | jok | put, posit, present **V** |
| འཇོམས་ | jom | destroy, conqueror **V** |
| ཐར་ | thar | is liberated, is freed **IV** |
| སྟོན་ | dön | teach, indicate, demonstrate **V** |
| བསྟན་ | dën | [past and future of སྟོན་] |
| འདུད་ | dü' | pay homage **V** |
| འདོད་ | dö' | wish, assert **V** |
| སྤང་ | bang | [future of སྤོང་] |
| སྤངས་ | bang | [past of སྤོང་] |
| སྤོང་ | bong | eliminate, abandon **V** |

| | | |
|---|---|---|
| སློངས་ | b̄ong | [imperative of སློང་] |
| ཕྱག་འཚལ་ | chak-tshël | bow down |
| བྱ་ | c̱ha | [future of བྱེད་] |
| བྱས་ | c̱hë> | [past of བྱེད་] |
| བྱེད་ | c̱hé' | do, make, perform, serve as V |
| བྱོས་ | c̱hö> | [imperative of བྱེད་] |
| དབྱེ་ | yé | divide VI |
| འབད་ | bë' | strive to, make effort in VI |
| འབྱེད་ | jé' | separate, open, reveal V |
| བཙལ་ | d̄zël | [past and future of འཚོལ་] |
| འཚོལ་ | tshöl | seek, search for V |
| མཛད་ | ḏzë' | do, make, perform V [HON] |
| མཛོད་ | ḏzö' | [imperative of མཛད་] |
| ཞོག་ | s̱ho | [imperative of འཇོག་] |
| གཞག་ | s̱hak | [future of འཇོག་] |
| གཞལ་ | s̱hël | [future of འཇལ་] |
| བཞག་ | s̱hak | [past of འཇོག་] |
| ཤེས་ | s̄hé> | know, realize, understand V |
| གསུང་ | s̄ung | say V [HON] [present and future] |
| གསུངས་ | s̄ung | [past and imperative of གསུང་] |

## Pronouns

| གང་ | kang | what, which, that which, who |
|---|---|---|
| ཅི་ | j̄í | what, which |
| ཇི་ལྟར་ | jí-d̄ar | how, what sort, what |
| སུ་ | s̄u | who, whom |

## Adjectives

| སྐོག་པ་ | ḡok-b̄a | hidden |
| ཆེ་བ་ | ché-wa | great, greater |
| མཆོག་ | chok | highest, best |
| མཐོ་ | tho | high, higher |
| དེ་འདྲ་ | té-ḍa | such, 'like that' |
| མན་ཆད་ | mën-chë' | that and below |
| བཟང་པོ་ | s̱ang-b̄o | good, auspicious, meritorious |

## Adverbs

| ད་ལྟ་ | tan-d̄a | now |
| མན་ཆད་ | mën-chë' | that and below |
| * ནས་བཟུང་སྟེ་ | në>-s̱ung-d̄é | beginning with * |

## Postpositions

| ནང་ | nang | inside, within, among |
| བར་ | par | up to, through |

## *Syntactic Particles*

| ཅེ་ན་ | jé-na | [question marker] if one says |
|---|---|---|
| དེ་བས་ | té-wë> | more than that, beyond that |
| དེས་ན་ | té>-na | therefore |
| * བས་ | wë> | more than *, rather than * |
| ཞེ་ན་ | s̲hé-na | [question marker] if one says |
| ཤེ་ན་ | s̄hé-na | [question marker] if one says |

# *Chapter 18*

*Agentive-Objective Verbs*
*Objective Complements*
*Nominative-Objective Verbs*
  *Verbs of Motion • Nominative Action Verbs*
*The Objective Case*
*Definitions: Impermanent Phenomena*

---

## Patterns in Tibetan Language
### *Transitive and Intransitive Verbs*

---

A secondary method of distinguishing between verbs was reviewed in Chapter Seventeen, one based on the relationship between a verb's subject (or agent) and its complement (or object). In this alternate classification, there are three types of verbs:

1   **existential verbs,** including linking verbs such as ཡིན་, verbs of existence and possession such as ཡོད་, and rhetorical verbs like རུང་ and ཐལ་;

2   **intransitive action verbs** including verbs of motion (such as འགྲོ་) and nominative action verbs (such as སྐྱེང་) in which agent and object do not differ;

3   **transitive action verbs** such as སྟོན་, in which agent and object do differ.

**Intransitive action verbs** are verbs such as སྐྱེ་ (*arise*) and གྲུབ་ (*is established*) that take their subjects in the nominative case and denote actions without reference to agents or objects.

| ངེས་འབྱུང་སྐྱེས་པ | *renunciation having arisen* |
| ཏགས་གྲུབ | *The reason is proven.* |

This group also includes verbs of motion.

| རང་ཉིད་གཅིག་པུ་འཇིག་རྟེན་ཕ་རོལ་ཏུ་འགྲོ | *One goes alone to the other world.* |

**Transitive action verbs** are verbs whose subjects are in the agentive case, verbs such as བྱེད་ (*do, make*), སྐྱེད་ (*produce*), and སྒྲུབ་ (*prove, establish*); they denote an action performed by an agent on an object separate from itself.

| རྣལ་འབྱོར་པས་ སྙིང་རྗེ་ བསྐྱེད | *The yogi generated compassion.* |
| ངས་དེ་བསྒྲུབས | *I accomplished that.* |

There are, thus, two ways to speak about actions in Tibetan. In one way, one merely states the occurrence of an action (as in འཁོར་ལོ་འཁོར་རོ, *The wheel turns*), without explicit reference to an agent. Such a statement makes use of a nominative action verb. Verbs of motion, although they have agents in the sense of those who do the going, do not have agents that are separate from the action of going. Agentive verbs, on the other hand, allow reference to agents and objects—the paradigm agentive construction being སངས་རྒྱས་ཀྱིས་ཆོས་བསྟན (*Buddha taught the doctrine*).

In the present chapter, agentive-objective verbs are examined, with particular emphasis on the verb བྱ་. Among the Class III (nominative-objective) verbs, verbs of motion and nominative action verbs are also discussed. The other Class III verbs—the rhetorical verbs—will be examined in Chapter Nineteen.

# Verbs and Verb Syntax
## *Agentive-Objective Verbs*

This class includes those agentive verbs whose *direct* objects are in the second case.

> *Indirect* objects in Tibetan—those to whom an action is directed, that is, those who receive benefit from it—are typically in the fourth case, the beneficial-purposive. In the sentence, *He gave medicine to the poor*, the direct object is *medicine* and the indirect object is *the poor*.

Common agentive-objective verbs include the following.

| | | |
|---|---|---|
| ལྟ་ | **ḏa** | *look at* |
| ཁྱབ་ | **khyap** | *pervade, cover, spread* |
| འབད་ | **ḇë'** | *make effort* |
| གནོད་ | **ṉö'** | *harm* |
| དབྱེ་ | **yé** | *divide* |
| དགོངས་ | **gong** | *consider, think about* [HON] |

There are, in addition, verbs such as དམིགས་ (**mík**, *observe, visualize*) which are sometimes used as agentive-objective verbs and at other times as nominative verbs.

There is at least one verb—ཕན་ (**phën**, *help, aid, benefit*)—whose direct object, the person or thing benefitted, is traditionally considered a fourth case object (because of the *benefit* done to it).[185]

The basic syntax of a clause or sentence ending in an agentive-objective verb is the following:

agentive          objective

SUBJECT →     OBJECT →       ← VERB

The paradigm of agentive-objective syntax is the sentence ཁོས་གཟུགས་ལ་བལྟས, *He looked at forms*, which has been diagrammed a number of times already. The following example uses the same verb in an adverbial clause, but without an explicit subject.

---

*without having looked even at her own life ...*[186]

[in more fluent English] *without consideration of her own life ...*

---

རང་སྲོག་ལ་འང་ མ་བལྟས་པར་

---

The syntactic particle འང་ sometimes shows conjunction or inclusion (*also* and *even*) and sometimes disjunction (*but*).

---

ཀྱང་, ཡང་, and འང་ are equivalent. ཀྱང་ is used after words or particles ending in the suffixes ག་, ད་, བ་, and ས་. ཡང་ follows the suffixes ང་, ན་, མ་, འ་, ར་, and ལ་, as well as suffixless words and particles. འང་ follows only suffixless words and particles.

---

The same syntax is seen here in slightly more complex form.

---

*Therefore, [one] makes effort in the means for realizing dependent arising.*[187]

དེ་ཕྱིར་རྟེན་འབྲེལ་རྟོགས་པའི་ཐབས་ལ་འབད།

---

དེ་ཕྱིར་ is a syntactic particle meaning *therefore*. རྟེན་འབྲེལ་ abbreviates རྟེན་ཅིང་ འབྲེལ་བར་འབྱུང་བ་ (literally, *arising in dependence and in relation*), the Tibetan translation of the Sanskrit *pratītyasamutpāda*.

The second case object of the verb འབད་ is the noun phrase རྟེན་འབྲེལ་རྟོགས་པའི་ཐབས་ (*the means for realizing dependent arising*). རྟེན་འབྲེལ་རྟོགས་པ་ is a verbal noun clause connected to the noun ཐབས་ with a clause connective.

---

The connective case marking particle in the construction CLAUSE + CONNECTIVE + NOUN is often a clause connective. A noun following a clause ending in a verbal noun or adjective, and connected to it by a connective case marking particle, is often the *understood* subject, object, qualifier, or complement of that clause.

As introduced in Chapter Seventeen, this is the typical way in which one element of a clause is singled out for connection to the remainder of a sentence. Here, པབས་ is the understood agentive qualifier of the clause it follows.

## Agentive-Objective Verbs with Qualifiers

As with the other classes of verbs already examined, the syntax seen in simple clauses or sentences ending in agentive-objective verbs may be made more complex with qualifiers of various sorts.

In the following example, there is an instrumental qualifier (in the agentive case).

---

*This mother of mine looked at me with loving eyes.*

---

བདག་གི་ མ་འདིས་ བྱམས་པའི་མིག་གིས་ བལྟས།

---

The following two examples have understood subjects and objective complements.

---

*Having looked upon [self] cherishing as an enemy ...*[188]

---

གཅེས་འཛིན་ལ་ དགྲར་ བལྟས་ཏེ་

---

The term གཅེས་འཛིན་ abbreviates the རང་གཅེས་འཛིན་ (or བདག་གཅེས་འཛིན་—*holding self to be dear*) that you have already seen.

---

*visualizing the body itself in the aspect* (or *form*) *of a deity*

---

ལུས་ཉིད་ལ་ ལྷའི་རྣམ་པར་ དམིགས་པ་

---

Although རྣམ་པར་ is a possible lexical prefix, here it is a noun (རྣམ་པ་) in the objective case.

A qualifier may be an entire clause. In the following example, the verb—ལྟ་བར་བྱ་ (*should look*), terminated by the syntactic particle ོ་—is qualified by a conditional clause.

---

*If one wishes to understand these [ideas] in detail, one should look in [texts] such as the Ra-dö [primer on] minds and awarenesses.*[189]

---

འདི་དག་ ཞིབ་ཏུ་ ཤེས་པར་འདོད་ན་ རྭ་སྟོད་བློ་རིག་སོགས་ལ་ ལྟ་བར་བྱའོ།།

There are two constructions here.  The second is the core sentence.

---

*One should look in [texts]*
  *such as the Ra-dö [primer on] minds and awarenesses.*

---

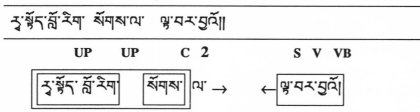

---

The word སོགས་ is a contraction for the frequent ལ་སོགས་པ་ (*and so forth, et cetera*) construction.  This construction may be treated either as the last member of a list of nouns—with the syntactic particle ལ་ acting, as it sometimes does, as an *and*—or as a lexical particle akin to the pluralizing syllable རྣམས་ (which may also end a list of nouns or a phrase).

In the present example of such a construction—ར་སྟོད་བློ་རིག་སོགས་ (that is, ར་སྟོད་བློ་རིག་ལ་ སོགས་པ་)—ར་སྟོད་བློ་རིག་ is the first member of an implicit list of nouns.

> Given the frequency with which lists—especially commonly known lists—are
> abbreviated by the phrase ལ་སོགས་པ་, translating it as *and so forth* will quickly
> become cumbersome.  In some situations, the phrase *such as* is a useful
> translation.

Thus, གཟུགས་ལ་སོགས་པ་དབང་ཤེས་ཀྱི་ཡུལ་ could yield the translation, *objects of the sense consciousnesses such as forms.*

The initial construction in the sentence above is a conditional clause.

---

*If one wishes to understand these [ideas] in detail ...*

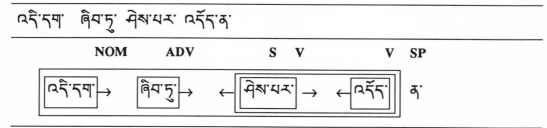

---

The verb here is a compound verb, ཤེས་པར་འདོད་ (*desire to know*).

> In compound verb phrases, the syntax of the sentence is not governed by the ending verb, but by the first verb.

This is parallel to the situation seen in auxiliary verb phrases. A sentence ending in the verb phrase རྟོགས་པར་འགྱུར་ (meaning either *will realize* or *would realize*) is governed by the syntax of the verb རྟོགས་, not that of the verb འགྱུར་. Likewise, in the present example, the main verb of the clause is ཤེས་ and not འདོད་.

The following example illustrates a negative usage of the verb གནོད་ (*harm, damage*),

*If one has meditated on an empti[ness] other than that,*
  *[it] will not harm at all the conception of self.*

དེ་ལས་གཞན་པའི་སྟོང་པ་ བསྒོམས་ན་ནི་ བདག་འཛིན་ལ་ ཅི་ཡང་ མི་གནོད་དོ།།

The phrase ཅི་ཡང་ (literally, *even what*) is an adverb meaning *at all* or *in any way*. The syntactic particles ཀྱང་, ཡང་, and འང་ may sometimes make a word or phrase into an adverb.

The following sentence uses both གནོད་ and ཕན་. Although the constructions ending in them seem syntactically identical, following the conventions of Tibetan grammar, the direct object of གནོད་ is second case and that of ཕན་ is fourth case.

*For example, if one uses a medicine for hot [diseases],*
  *it will be of benefit to hot [diseases], but will be harmful for cold [diseases].*[190]

དཔེར་ན་ ཚ་བའི་སྨན་ བསྟེན་ན་ ཚ་བ་ལ་ཕན་ཀྱང་ གྲང་བ་ལ་གནོད།

དཔེར་ན་ (literally, *if as an example*) is an introductory syntactic particle meaning *for example* or *for instance*.

The following uses another compound verb. As before, the main verb of the sentence is འབད་ and not དགོས་.

*[One] must make effort in the means for realizing emptiness.*[191]

སྟོང་ཉིད་ རྟོགས་པའི་ཐབས་ལ་ འབད་ དགོས་སོ།།

# Drill 18.1

Translate the following into Tibetan.

1. observing the body
2. One should make effort in the generation of the mind of enlightenment.
3. energetic in the purposes of others
4. cherishing others

---

# Drill 18.2

Translate the following. Diagram the first clause and identify its dots.

1. གཞན་གྱི་སྡུག་བསྔལ་གྱིས་བདག་ལ་མི་གནོད་པ་

2. སྐྱོན་གྱིས་ནད་པ་ལ་ཁན།

3. སྙིང་པ་ལ་ཁན་ཡོན་དུ་བསྒྱུ།

4. བཅོམ་ལྡན་འདས་ཀྱིས་ཅི་ལ་དགོངས་ནས།

---

# Agentive-Objective Verbs
## The Verb ཁྱབ་

The concept of pervasion (ཁྱབ་པ་ **khyap-b̄a**, Skt. *vyāpti*) is at the heart of the syllogisms and consequences examined in earlier chapters, as well as being central to the analysis of permutations.

ཁྱབ་པ་ is a verbal noun created from the agentive-objective verb ཁྱབ་, whose basic meanings are *spread*, *cover*, and *pervade*.

| | | |
|---|---|---|
| ཁྱབ་པ་ | **khyap-b̄a** | *pervasion* (Skt. *vyāpti*) |
| སྦྱོར་བ་ | **jor-wa** | *syllogism* [literally] *application [of a reason]* |
| ཐལ་བ་ | **thël-wa** | *consequence* |

The verb ཁྱབ་ in its complete syntax has an agentive subject and an objective case object. Although you have seen the agentive-objective verb ཁྱབ་ used only in formal, rhetorical constructions, it is used non-technically as well.

---

*moonlight pervading the autumn sky*

---

སྟོན་དུས་ཀྱི་ ནམ་མཁའ་ལ་ ཟླ་འོད་ཀྱིས་ ཁྱབ་པ་

---

སྟོན་དུས་—a contraction of སྟོན་ཀའི་དུས་—is the *time of autumn*. ནམ་མཁའ་ here means not *space*, but *sky*.

---

*where space pervades*

---

ནམ་མཁའ་ གང་ར་ ཁྱབ་པ་

---

|  | S | 3 | 2 | V |
|---|---|---|---|---|
|  | ནམ་མཁ ས་ → | | ག ར་ → | ← ཁྱབ་པ་ |

---

གང་ར་ is the relative pronoun ག་ (equivalent to གང་) with the case marking particle ར་, here serving as the second case object of the verb.

The following example reports an assertion of the *Great Exposition* School that is not accepted as normative in Tibetan Buddhism.

---

*True existence pervades functioning things.*

---

དངོས་པོ་ལ་ བདེན་གྲུབ་ཀྱིས་ ཁྱབ།

---

|  | S | C | 2 |  | OM | C | 3 |  | VB |
|---|---|---|---|---|---|---|---|---|---|
|  | དངོས་པོ་ | ལ་→ | | | བདེན་གྲུབ་ | ཀྱིས་ → | | | ← ཁྱབ་ |

---

Cited below is the full context in which the above sentence is found (as a clause). It illustrates the typical nesting of clauses seen in Tibetan.[192]

---

*This system asserts that functioning things are pervaded by true existence.*

---

ལུགས་འདིས་ དངོས་པོ་ལ་ བདེན་གྲུབ་ཀྱིས་ ཁྱབ་པ་ ཁས་ལེན།

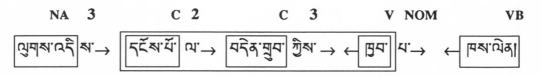

The noun-adjective phrase ལྱགས་འདི་ས་ is the agentive subject of the agentive-nominative verb ཁས་ལེན། (*assert*), a phrasal verb. Its object, in the nominative case, is the clause དངོས་པོ་ལ་བདེན་གྲུབ་ཀྱིས་ཁྱབ་པ་.

A more natural English rendering would be, *In this system it is asserted that functioning things are necessarily truly established.*

> The rule of thumb translation of a pervasion statement of the form *A pervades B*, where A is in the agentive case and B is in the objective case, is *B are necessarily A.*

The claim, *A pervades B*, is the claim that every instance of B is an instance of A—with the possibility that there are some A that are not B. Technically, A is the ཁྱབ་བྱེད་ (**khyap-jé'**, *pervader*) and B is the ཁྱབ་བྱ་ (**khyap-ja**, *that which is pervaded* or *object of pervasion*). ཁྱབ་བྱེད་ and ཁྱབ་བྱ་ are, respectively, examples of agent and object verbals.

> **Object verbals** are built from the future tense form of a verb and the future auxiliary བྱ་. **Agent verbals** are built from the present tense form and the auxiliary བྱེད་.

When logical pervasion is spoken of, as it often is, in the formal language used in rhetorical sequences, the syntax employed is not the one seen above. In place of the second case object of pervasion, a conditional phrase is used. Thus, starting with a doctrinally acceptable pervasion—དངོས་པོ་ལ་མི་རྟག་པས་ཁྱབ་—the following is a more typical statement of pervasion following the conventions of logical analysis.

*Whatever is a functioning thing is necessarily impermanent.*

དངོས་པོ་ཡིན་ན་    མི་རྟག་པ་ཡིན་པས་    ཁྱབ།

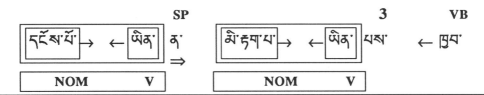

Both the conditional clause and the agentive clause have understood subjects. You will sometimes see this written—still quite formally—with the subjects of the བྱ་བྱེད་ and བྱ་བ་ clauses explicitly stated.

*If it is a functioning thing, then it is necessarily impermanent.*

ཁྱོད་དངོས་པོ་ཡིན་ན་ ཁྱོད་མི་རྟག་པ་ཡིན་པས་ཁྱབ།

Both ཁྱོད་ are examples of the impersonal use of that pronoun, giving us *If it is a functioning thing, [it] is pervaded by its being impermanent.*

Here is an illustration of the use of both syntaxes in the same sentence.

*Although whatever is a superior's path is necessarily uncontaminated, being uncontaminated does not pervade paths in the continuums of superiors.[193]*

འཕགས་ལམ་ཡིན་ན་ ཟག་མེད་ཡིན་པས་ཁྱབ་ཀྱང་།
འཕགས་རྒྱུད་ཀྱི་ལམ་ལ་ ཟག་མེད་ཡིན་པས་མ་ཁྱབ་སྟེ།

Note the negative མ་ཁྱབ་སྟེ། in the second clause. Recall that ཡིན་པས་མ་ཁྱབ་ is not equivalent to མ་ཡིན་པས་ཁྱབ་.

The following is a more complex example of the negative construction.

*That being the case, I think that whatever is a mind is not necessarily one or another of the seven minds and awarenesses.[194]*

དེ་ལྟར་ན་ བློ་ཡིན་ན་ བློ་རིག་བདུན་པོ་གང་རུང་ཡིན་པས་ མ་ཁྱབ་པར་ སེམས་ཏེ།

དེ་ལྟར་ན་ is a very brief conditional statement qualifying the verb སེམས་. The clause, བློ་ཨིན་ན་བློ་རིག་བདུན་པོ་གང་རུང་ཨིན་པས་མ་ཁྱབ་པར་, is the objective complement of སེམས་.

སེམས་ is a four-form agentive verb meaning *think about*, *reflect on*, and *consider*.

| | | | |
|---|---|---|---|
| past: བསམས་ | present: སེམས་ | future: བསམ་ | imperative: སོམས་ |

གང་རུང་ is an indefinite pronoun meaning *either*. Used with a negative verb, as it is here, it means *neither*. Since *either* and *neither* are words that refer only to two things, in situations such as the above a different translation must be used—*any among* or, in the negative, *none of*.

Closely related to གང་རུང་ is the pronoun གང་ཡང་, meaning *any*, or, with a negative verb, *none*. The following is an example of its use.

*Clearly visualizing in front [of oneself] a sentient being*
*who is neutral [in the sense] of having done no help or harm [to one]* ...[195]

ཕན་གནོད་གང་ཡང་མ་བྱས་པའི་བར་མའི་སེམས་ཅན་ཞིག་མདུན་དུ་གསལ་བར་དམིགས་ནས།

The connective case marking particle between ཕན་གནོད་གང་ཡང་མ་བྱས་པ་ and བར་མ་ is an appositive connective. It indicates that བར་མ་ (*neutral*) is being used in the sense of ཕན་གནོད་གང་ཡང་མ་བྱས་པ་ (*[a person who] has done no help or harm [to one]*).

---

## Drill 18.3

Translate the following into Tibetan.

1. If it is a white horse, it is necessarily a person.
2. Whatever is a person is necessarily neither matter nor consciousness.
3. There are no hell beings in the Formless Realm.
4. Sentient beings are pervaded by living in cyclic existence.
5. Whatever is a consciousness is necessarily either a sense or a mental consciousness.

# Drill 18.4

Translate the following.

1. ཀློ་ཨིན་ན་བེམ་པོ་མ་ཨིན་པས་ཁྱབ།

2. ཀློ་ཨིན་ན་དབང་ཤེས་ཨིན་པས་མ་ཁྱབ།

3. གཞི་མ་གྲུབ་ན་ཡོད་པ་མ་ཨིན་པས་ཁྱབ།

4. དངོས་པོ་ཨིན་ན་བེམ་ཤེས་སྟུན་མིན་འདུ་བྱེད་གང་རུང་ཨིན་པས་ཁྱབ།

## *Agentive Verbs with Objective Complements*

Recall from Chapter Sixteen that the generic syntax of a Tibetan sentence is the following, with two qualifications—(1) some verbs require only a subject and a verb and (2) a sentence may have multiple qualifiers:

[ QUALIFIER ]→ SUBJECT → OBJECT → COMPLEMENT→ ←VERB

> Complements of agentive verbs say something additional about the *object* of the verb.

Here is an example of an agentive-nominative verb (འདོད་—*desire, assert*) with an objective case complement.

*Someone asserts mind to be the illustration of the person.*

ཁ་ཅིག་གིས་ སེམས་ གང་ཟག་གི་མཚན་གཞིར་ འདོད་དོ།

| C 3 | NOM | C 6 | 2 | VB SP |
|------|------|------|------|------|
| ཁ་ཅིག་གིས་ → | སེམས་ → | གང་ཟག་གི་ → མཚན་གཞི ར་→ | | ←འདོད་ དོ། |

Also possible is the translation, *Someone asserts mind to be the illustration of the person* (or, depending on context, *an illustration of the person*).

The object in this sentence is *mind*. The complement, *illustration of the person*, says something about *mind*.

The syntax of the following example is the same, but the subject is understood.

---

*The three—forms, consciousness, and non-associated compositional factors—
are asserted to be impermanent functioning things.*

གཟུགས་ཤེས་ཕྲན་མིན་འདུ་བྱེད་གསུམ་ མི་རྟག་པའི་དངོས་པོར་ འདོད་དོ།

---

Note the termination of the object, a noun phrase, by the number གསུམ.

The syntax seen in the next example—NOMINATIVE OBJECT + OBJECTIVE COMPLEMENT linked together by a verb such as འདོད་ or གསུངས་—provides a means for reporting someone's speech or thought without the use of quotation.

---

*[Buddha] said in the sutras that all phenomena lack identity.*

མདོ་རྣམས་ལས་ ཆོས་ཐམས་ཅད་ ངོ་བོ་ཉིད་མེད་པར་ གསུངས།

---

Here the pattern is fifth case qualifier, nominative object, and objective complement.

Another agentive-nominative verb which commonly uses this syntax is འཛིན་ (*hold, grasp*—and, by extension, *apprehend, conceive*). འཛིན་ is a four-form verb.

---

past: བཟུང་        present: འཛིན་        future: གཟུང་        imperative: ཟུངས།

---

Using the verb འཛིན་, the concept of selfishness may be be expressed in Tibetan in the following way.

---

*holding oneself as dear* OR (less literally) *cherishing oneself*

རང་ཉིད་གཅེས་པར་འཛིན་པ་

---

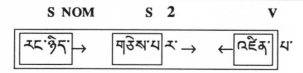

---

རང་ཉིད་, of course, may mean *oneself, himself, herself, yourself,* or *myself,* depending on context.

In the following example, the nominative object is the indefinite pronoun རེས་འགའ་ set off by the syntactic particle ནི་.

---

*having held some [people] as intimates*

---

རེས་འགའ་ནི་ ཉེ་བར་ བཟུང་ནས་

---

ཉེ་བ literally means *near*. རེས་འགའ་ is an indefinite pronoun meaning *some*.

---

*this [one] now conceived to be an enemy*

---

ད་ལྟ་ དགྲར་ བཟུང་བ་འདི་

---

ད་ལྟ་ is an adverb meaning *now* and serves as a qualifier here. Both subject and object are understood elements in this construction.

Although གཙོ་བོར་ (གཙོ་བོ, *principal*, in the second case) is often an adverb (meaning *principally*), in the following it is an objective complement.

---

*Those of intelligence, having held only altruism to be chief, ...*

---

བློ་གྲོས་དང་ལྡན་པ་རྣམས་ཀྱིས་ གཞན་ཕན་འབའ་ཞིག་ གཙོ་བོར་ བཟུང་ནས་

---

གཞན་ཕན་ means *helping others*, thus *altruism*. འབའ་ཞིག་ is an adjective meaning *only*. A more understandable English translation would be *those of intelligence, holding altruism alone to be the principal [attitude]*.

---

*the delusion that conceives whatever appears to be true*

---

སྣང་ཚད་ བདེན་པར་ འཛིན་པའི་ གཏི་མུག

---

ཚད་ means *measure* and *size*. Affixed to the core form of a verb, A, it creates a verbal noun meaning *whatever is A or however many things are A*. Thus, སྣང་ཚད་ means *everything that appears*.

བདེན་པ་ here means *tru[ly existent]*—བདེན་པར་གྲུབ་པ་.

The verb འཛིན་ is a useful example of another facet of the Tibetan language that is common enough to be a rule of thumb.

> Tibetan is a natural and not a planned language. Be prepared to find verbs used in ways other than their regular syntactic patterns.

In the following two examples འཛིན་ appears not as an agentive-nominative verb, but an agentive-objective verb. Agentive-objective verbs may also have objective complements.

---

*apprehending persons and [other] phenomena to be a self*

གང་ཟག་དང་ཆོས་ལ་ བདག་ཏུ་ འཛིན་པ་

---

*having apprehended the selfless to be a self*

བདག་མེད་པ་ལ་ བདག་ཏུ་ བཟུང་བ་

---

Conversely, where the verb དབྱེ་ is often seen as an agentive-objective verb, it sometimes acts as if it were an agentive-nominative verb. In the clause བློ་རིག་བདུན་དུ་ དབྱེ་བ་—*dividing minds and awarenesses into seven* (that is, *a sevenfold division of minds and awarenesses*)—བློ་རིག་ is the nominative object and བདུན་དུ་ is the objective complement.

---

## Drill 18.5

Translate the following into Tibetan.

1. Having seen these sentient beings to be one's own friends, ...
2. the ignorance that conceives the momentary to be permanent
3. understanding sentient beings to be [one's] mothers
4. The master Vasubandhu said that all phenomena were of the nature of mind alone.
5. The Teacher taught mind to be the chief among functioning things.

## Drill 18.6

Identify the dots in the following and translate. Diagram the first clause.

1. གང་ཟག་དུག་གཅིག་རང་དབང་ཅན་དུ་འཛིན་པ་

2. ལུགས་འདིས་བདེན་པར་འཛིན་པ་ཅིན་མོངས་ཅན་གྱི་སྒྲིབ་པར་ཁས་ལེན།

3. ལུས་མེ་གཅོང་བར་བསྐོམ་པ་

## Verbs and Verb Syntax
### *Nominative-Objective Verbs*

Class III (nominative-objective verbs) include three types: verbs of motion, nominative action verbs, and rhetorical verbs. These verbs take their subjects in the nominative but require—for a full expression of meaning—a qualifier in the second or objective case.

- Sentences and clauses ending in **verbs of motion** (such as འགྲོ་) either state or imply a destination—one marked by a second case particle.

- **Nominative action verbs** are verbs that have nominative subjects but express actions (such as *appearing,* སྣང་) done in a certain place (which, in Tibetan, is marked by the second case).

- **Rhetorical verbs** (such as རུང་, *is admissible,* རིགས་, *is correct,* and ཐལ་, *logically follows*) are like verbs of existence in that the syntax NOMINATIVE SUBJECT + VERB is often a complete thought. However, they are unlike verbs of existence in that most may occur in the syntax OBJECTIVE-CASE COMPLEMENT + VERB, in the sense *To ... is correct.* Often, when they have qualifiers, those qualifiers are marked by an objective case marker showing existential identity.

Verbs of motion and nominative action verbs are examined in the present chapter. Rhetorical verbs will be examined in Chapter Nineteen.

# Nominative-Objective Verbs
## *Verbs of Motion*

Common verbs of motion include the following.

| | | |
|---|---|---|
| འགྲོ་ | ḍo | *go* |
| འོང་ | ong | *come* |
| སླེབ་ | lép | *arrive* |
| འཁྱམ་ | khyam | *wander* |
| ལྷུང་ | ḍung | *fall* |
| ཕྱིན་ | chön | *come, arrive* |

འཇུག་ is also, in many instances, a verb of motion meaning *enter*.

The basic syntax of a clause or sentence ending in a verb of motion is the following.

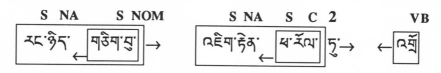

The paradigm construction ending in a verb of motion is the following.

*One alone goes to the next world.*[196]

རང་ཉིད་གཅིག་པུ་ འཇིག་རྟེན་ཕ་རོལ་ཏུ་ འགྲོ

| S NA | S NOM | | S NA | S C 2 | | VB |
|---|---|---|---|---|---|---|
| རང་ཉིད་ | གཅིག་པུ་ → | | འཇིག་རྟེན་ | ཕ་རོལ་ | ཏུ་ → | འགྲོ |

In English we would be more likely to say, *One goes alone to the next world.* It is often the case with words meaning *only* in Tibetan that they translate more clearly if treated as if they were adverbs.

The phrase རང་ཉིད་གཅིག་པུ་ is the nominative subject. The phrase འཇིག་རྟེན་ཕ་རོལ་ is the qualifier, stating the destination of the motion.

འགྲོ is by far the most frequently seen verb of motion. Its basic meaning is *goes*, but it is often used metaphorically in the sense of *serves as* and *becomes*. It is a three-form verb, but with variant past forms.

| | | | |
|---|---|---|---|
| past: སོང་ or ཕྱིན་ | present: འགྲོ | future: འགྲོ་ | imperative: སོང་ |

འགྲོ and its forms make a multitude of verbal nouns. Here are some that are commonly used in the doctrinal context.

| | | |
|---|---|---|
| འགྲོ་བ་ | ḍo-wa | *going, migration [rebirth], migrator [sentient being]* |
| དུད་འགྲོ | tün-ḍo | *animal* [literally, *bent goer*] |
| སྔོན་འགྲོ | ṅgön-ḍo | *preliminary, preparation* |
| ཕ་རོལ་ཏུ་ཕྱིན་པ་ | pha-röl-du-chîn-b̄a | *perfection, transcendence* |
| ངན་སོང་ | ngën-song | *bad migration* |

མཆི་ is a more elegant form of འགྲོ.

| | | | |
|---|---|---|---|
| past: མཆིས་ | present: མཆི་ | future: མཆི་ | imperative: མཆིས་ |

Note that this verb has the same forms as the Class II verb of existence མཆི་. Only context will serve to distinguish them.

As seen in Chapter Fifteen, a Buddhist is defined as someone who goes for refuge to the three jewels—Buddha, doctrine, and spiritual community. Thus, going for refuge is the basis of all Buddhist practice and of all Buddhist liturgy. Although going for refuge is called སྐྱབས་འགྲོ་ (ḡyam-ḍo), the expression of refuge typically uses the verb མཆི་.

In Tibetan Buddhism, refuge is taken first in the gurus—an individual's own spiritual teachers and the lineage of those teachers back to Buddha.

*I go for refuge to the guru[s]. I go for refuge to the buddha[s].*
*I go for refuge to the doctrine. I go for refuge to the spiritual community.*

བླ་མ་ལ་སྐྱབས་སུ་མཆིའོ།    སངས་རྒྱས་ལ་སྐྱབས་སུ་མཆིའོ།

ཆོས་ལ་སྐྱབས་སུ་མཆིའོ།    དགེ་འདུན་ལ་སྐྱབས་སུ་མཆིའོ།

| C 2 | C 4 | VB SP |
|---|---|---|
| ཆོས་ ལ་ → | སྐྱབས་ སུ་ → | ← མཆིའོ། |

Note that when the verb མཆི་ is terminated, the termination merges into the suffixless syllable. Thus, the word མཆིའོ་ is actually a combination of core verb and syntactic particle. When doing dot analysis, the **VB** dot always takes precedence over the **SP** dot in such a conflict situation.

As is often the case, the subject is not explicitly stated; it can be taken as a generic *I* or *we*, depending on context and on the intentions of the person reciting the refuge formula. These four statements of refuge are examples of a more complex syntax than that seen before:

nominative            objective
| SUBJECT | → | DESTINATION | → | [ QUALIFIER ] → | ← | VERB OF MOTION |

In general, the qualifier of a verb of motion could be an adverbial phrase, a locative time of activity, an agentive of means or reason, or—as in the present instance—a fourth case statement of purpose or benefit. One goes where? To the gurus, buddhas, doctrine, and spiritual community. And for what purpose? For the sake of refuge (from *the frights of cyclic existence*—འཁོར་བའི་འཇིགས་པ་).

The following are examples of clauses ending in verbs of motion. The first two invoke the metaphor of falling to the abyss of lower rebirths (rebirth as a hell-being, hungry ghost, or animal).

*Were [one] to fall into an abyss ...*[197]

གཡང་སར་ ལྷུང་གྱུར་ ན་

In expanded form, this would read གཡང་སར་ལྷུང་བར་གྱུར་ན་, with ལྷུང་བར་གྱུར་ being the conditional use (*were*) of the past form of the auxiliary འགྱུར་.

*because of falling into an evil migration*[198]

ངན་འགྲོར་ལྷུང་ཕྱིར་

ལྷུང་ is a common verb of motion meaning *fall*.

past: ལྷུང་　　　present: ལྷུང་　　　future: ལྷུང་　　　imperative: ལྷུངས་

The verb འཁྱམ—seen below in its past tense form—is often used to indicate uncontrolled rebirth in cyclic existence.

*migrators who have wandered in cyclic existence*[199]

སྲིད་པར་ འཁྱམས་པའི་ འགྲོ་བ་

སྲིད་པ་ is often used as a synonym of འཁོར་བ་ (*cyclic existence*).

*One will subsequently wander in boundless evil migrations.*[200]

ཕྱི་མར་ངན་སོང་མུ་མཐའ་མེད་པར་འཁྱམ།

མུ་མཐའ་མེད་པ་ (*without bounds or ends*) is an adjective modifying ངན་སོང་. ཕྱི་མ་ is an adjective meaning *subsequent*, here used adverbially through the addition of a particle marking the second case.

*[Those] like us, wandering in cyclic existence*
　　*because [we] have been bound by actions and afflictions, …*[201]

རང་ཚོ་འདྲ་མོ་ལས་ཉོན་གྱིས་བཅིངས་པས་འཁོར་བར་འཁྱམས་བཞིན་པ།

| NA NOM | OM | 3 | 3 | 2 | V SP |
|---|---|---|---|---|---|
| རང་ཚོ་འདྲ་མོ་ → | ལས་ཉོན་གྱིས་བཅིངས་པ ས་ → | | འཁོར་བ ར་→ | ←འཁྱམས་བཞིན་ | པ། |

རང་ཚོ་འདྲ་མོ་ is a noun-adjective phrase, where འདྲ་མོ་ is an adjective meaning *like*. ལས་ཉོན་ abbreviates ལས་དང་ཉོན་མོངས་, and ལས་ཉོན་གྱིས་བཅིངས་པས་ is a clause ending in an agentive-nominative verbal.

Both ལས་ཉོན་གྱིས་བཅིངས་པས་ and འཁོར་བར་ are qualifiers, the one explaining why we have wandered, the other, where. The syntactic particle བཞིན་ added to the core form of a verb expresses continuing or habitual action in the present. Here the entire sentence has been made into a clause with the addition of the lexical particle པ་, leaving us with a construction focussed on the verbal noun, *those wandering.*

The following is a verbal noun based on the past tense form of འགྲོ་.

---

*those [who] have gone thus for refuge*[202]

དེ་ལྟར་ སྐྱབས་སུ་སོང་བ་

---

The verb འགྲོ་ is often used metaphorically—that is, *goes* is used in the sense of *turns into* or *becomes.* In the following sentence it means *becomes.*

---

*Although emptiness, if [one] has meditated on [it],*
  *becomes an antidote to the conception of self, ...*

སྟོང་ཉིད་ བསྒོམས་ན།   བདག་འཛིན་གྱི་གཉེན་པོར་འགྲོ་བ་ ཡིན་གྱི་

---

གྱི་, which you have seen as a connective case marker, here follows a verb and not a noun, functioning as a disjunctive syntactic particle meaning *although.*

There are two ways to construe this sentence. It is often the case in philosophical literature that sentences ending in ཡིན་ and མིན་ mean, respectively, *It is the case that ...* and *It is not the case that ....* This suggests a reading in which སྟོང་ཉིད་བསྒོམས་ན། is a conditional qualifier of འགྲོ་ and བདག་འཛིན་གྱི་གཉེན་པོར་ is its second case destination, with the subject being supplied by context. This might be translated, *Although it is the case that if [one] has meditated on emptiness, [something] becomes an antidote to the conception of self, ...* The translation given first, on the other hand, is based on construing སྟོང་ཉིད་ as both the object of བསྒོམས་ and the subject of the verb ཡིན་. Read in that way, it is emptiness that is a བདག་འཛིན་གྱི་གཉེན་པོར་འགྲོ་བ་ (*something which goes as an antidote to the conception of self*).

Here is another metaphoric use of a verb of motion, stated in the negative (མི་འགྲོ་ being the negative of འགྲོ་བ་). The phrase དབང་དུ་མི་འགྲོ་, although literally meaning *not going to the power,* actually means *not coming under the power.*

---

*not coming under the power of evil companions*[203]

---

སྟེག་པའི་གྲོགས་པོའི་དབང་དུ་མི་འགྲོ་བ་

---

A more fluent English translation would be *not coming under the influence of evil companions*. The clause could also mean *one who does not come under the influence of evil companions*.

In the following example, the main verb—the one at the end—is actually a nominative action verb (སྐྱེས—*arose, was produced*) ending a clause in which verbs of motion are embedded.

---

*Once compassion has been produced towards all the sentient beings who,*
*by the power of bad actions, have fallen or will fall into the hells[s], ...*[204]

---

ལས་ངན་པའི་དབང་གིས་དམྱལ་བར་ལྷུང་བ་དང་ལྷུང་བར་འགྱུར་བའི་
སེམས་ཅན་ཐམས་ཅད་ལ་  སྙིང་རྗེ་  སྐྱེས་ནས།

---

The long clause ending in སེམས་ཅན་ཐམས་ཅད་ལ་ is not the objective case qualifier with which you have become familiar—*all sentient beings* are not the place where compassion has arisen. Traditional Tibetan grammar would probably want to assign this construction to the fourth case because the sentient beings are *benefitted* by the compassion. However, it is more meaningful syntactically to call this a **referential locative**.

---

| The rule of thumb translation of a referential locative is *about* or *with regard to*. |

---

ལས་ངན་པའི་དབང་གིས་ literally means *by the power of bad actions*, but could be translated *under the power of bad actions* and is an instrumental agentive.

The connective case marking particle ending the clause ལས་ངན་པའི་དབང་གིས་དམྱལ་བར་ ལྷུང་བ་དང་ལྷུང་བར་འགྱུར་བ་ is a clause connective. སེམས་ཅན་ is the understood subject of both ལྷུང་བ་ and ལྷུང་བར་འགྱུར་. With the subject interpolated into it, the verb of motion clause in the sentence reads as follows.

---

*Sentient beings, by the power of bad actions,*
*have fallen or will fall into the hells[s].*

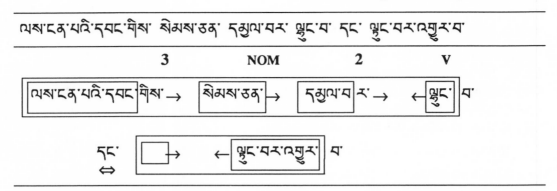

The empty box indicates that the previous subject, qualifier, and destination—ལས་ངན་ པའི་དབང་གིས་ སེམས་ཅན་ དཀྱལ་བར་—are understood as relating to the second verb as well. ལྱུང་བར་འགྱུར་ is ལྱུང་ with a future auxiliary verb.

Although འཇུག་ often means *engage in* or *refers to*, it is also used as a verb of motion.

---

*Followers of Reasoning assert that Hīnayāna arhats*
*[later] enter into the path of the Mahāyāna.*

---

རིགས་པའི་རྗེས་འབྲང་རྣམས་ཀྱིས་ ཐེག་དམན་དགྲ་བཅོམ་པ་ཐེག་ཆེན་ལམ་དུ་འཇུག་པར་ འདོད་དོ།

---

Here the verb of motion ends a clause—ཐེག་དམན་དགྲ་བཅོམ་པ་ཐེག་ཆེན་ལམ་དུ་འཇུག་པར་—which is the objective complement of the construction རིགས་པའི་རྗེས་འབྲང་རྣམས་ཀྱིས་འདོད་དོ།.

An objective case complement may serve as the object of a sentence, even when the object of the verb ending that sentence is normally in the nominative case.

The verb of motion portion of this sentence is the following.

---

*Hīnayāna arhats [later] enter into the path of the Mahāyāna.*

---

ཐེག་དམན་དགྲ་བཅོམ་པ་ ཐེག་ཆེན་ལམ་དུ་ འཇུག

---

ཐེག་དམན་དགྲ་བཅོམ་པ་ is the nominative subject (with an understood sixth case particle between the two nouns) and ཐེག་ཆེན་ལམ་དུ་ is the objective case destination.

## Drill 18.7

Translate the following into Tibetan.

1. All sentient beings, from [time] without beginning, have wandered in cyclic existence.
2. Although arhats enter into peace, ...
3. If [one] accumulates evil [actions, one] will fall to a bad rebirth.
4. The Buddha came to Varanasi.
5. When the gods came to earth (*Jambudvīpa*) ...

## Drill 18.8

Translate the following. Diagram the second and third, marking their dots.

1. འཁོར་བར་ཉུགས་པ་

2. སེམས་ཅན་མོངས་ཅན་དུ་སོང་ན་

3. གང་ཟག་དེ་དག་ནི་ཆོས་སྟོར་བཅུག་ན།

4. དེ་དག་འཛམ་བུའི་གླིང་དུ་གཤེགས་ཏེ།

## Nominative-Objective Verbs
### *Nominative Action Verbs*

The second of the three types of Class III (nominative-objective verbs) are the nominative action verbs. Common nominative action verbs include the following.

| | | |
|---|---|---|
| སྐྱེ་ | **gyé** | *is born, arises, is created* |
| འགྱུར་ | **gyur** | *becomes, changes, is* |
| འགྲུབ་ | **dup** | *is established, is proven, exists* |

| སྣང་ | **ñang** | *appears, is perceived* |
|---|---|---|
| རྒྱས་ | **gyë>** | *extends, expands* |
| འཆར་ | **char** | *appears, rises* |
| འབྱུང་ | **jung** | *occurs, arises* |
| འཁོར་ | **khor** | *turns* |

The basic syntax of a clause or sentence ending in a nominative action verb is the following.

nominative
| SUBJECT |→          ←| NOMINATIVE ACTION VERB |

The paradigm of this is the sentence འཁོར་ལོ་འཁོར།, *The wheel turns*, which has been diagrammed a number of times already.

A more complex syntax is the following, incorporating a qualifier.

nominative          objective
| SUBJECT |→     | QUALIFIER |→          ←| NOMINATIVE ACTION VERB |

*Rays of light dissolve into us.*

འོད་ཟེར་    རང་ལ་    ཐིམ།

The qualifier in this sentence—རང་ལ་—is an objective place of activity.

*From his / her body, rays of light spread in the ten directions.*[205]

རང་གི་སྐུ་ལས་    འོད་ཟེར་    ཕྱོགས་བཅུར་    འཕྲོས།

Here རང་གི་སྐུ་ལས་, which can only be translated in context (since རང་ is not specific as to person, gender, or number), is the fifth case qualifier. འོད་ཟེར་ is the nominative subject and ཕྱོགས་བཅུར་ (*in the ten directions*) is another qualifier, declined in the second case since it is a place of activity.

སྐྱེ་ is one of the more frequently encountered nominative action verbs.

*In particular, all three vows are generated in this [physical] support.*[206]

ཁྱད་པར་རྟེན་འདི་ལ་སྡོམ་པ་གསུམ་ག་སྐྱེ་ཞིང་།

ཁྱད་པར་ is a word with many meanings. It is unusual in that it is a word whose last syllable (པར་) ends in the suffix ར་—that is, the ར་ is not a case marking particle. As a noun, it means *attribute, feature, quality*, or *difference*. Here, however, it is an adverb meaning *especially* or *in particular*.

A རྟེན་ is a *basis* or *support*, in this context a *physical support*—the particular sort of body acquired in a certain rebirth. The context of this statement is that when one achieves a human rebirth, it is possible to receive and maintain all three vows (individual emancipation, bodhisattva, and secret mantra).

གསུམ་ག་ means *all three*. Similarly, གཉིས་ཀ་ means *both*.

ཞིང་ is one of three continuative syntactic particles that follow either adjectives or core verbs. Here, it suggests that something more will be said (about either རྟེན་འདི་ or སྡོམ་པ་གསུམ་, depending on context).

The examples of nominative action verbs seen so far have illustrated a simple syntax, NOMINATIVE SUBJECT + QUALIFIER + VERB. Adding an objective complement creates the following, more complex syntax:

| nominative | objective | objective | |
|---|---|---|---|
| SUBJECT $\rightarrow$ | QUALIFIER $\rightarrow$ | COMPLEMENT $\rightarrow$ | $\leftarrow$ VERB |

You have already seen an example of this (in Chapter Seventeen), repeated here below.

*The snow mountain appears blue to the visual consciousness.*

གངས་རི་ མིག་ཤེས་ལ་ སྔོན་པོར་ སྣང་།

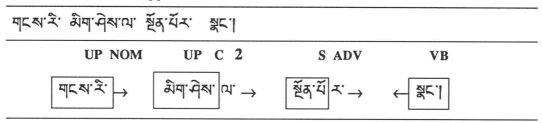

The phrase གངས་རི་ (snow + mountain) is the nominative subject of the verb སྣང་. The phrase མིག་ཤེས་ལ་ (abbreviating མིག་གི་ཤེས་པ་ལ་) is an objective case qualifier, stating the place of activity. སྔོན་པོར་ is another second case element, an adverbial identity construction functioning as the complement of སྣང་.

> Complements of nominative verbs differ from their qualifiers in that a complement says something about the subject of the verb either in the sense that the subject *is* the complement or in the sense that it is *believed* or *perceived to be* the complement.

In the present example, while the གངས་རི་ (*snow mountain*) is not, in fact, སྔོན་པོ་ (*blue*), it is *perceived to be* སྔོན་པོ་.

> Whereas the objective complements of agentive verbs say something about their *objects*, the objective complements of nominative verbs say something about their *subjects*.

འགྱུར་ is by far the most frequently seen nominative action verb. Its basic meanings are *becomes* and *changes*, but it is often used lexically as if it were a linking verb meaning *is*, but with a nominative action syntax. It is a two-form verb in which the present and future occur in one form and the past and imperative take another.

---

past: གྱུར་        present: འགྱུར་        future: འགྱུར་        imperative: གྱུར་

---

The following is an example of the simplest sort of clause ending in འགྱུར་.

---

*because friends become enemies …*[207]

---

གཉེན་དགྲར་འགྱུར་བས་

| NOM | 2 | V | 3 |
|---|---|---|---|
| གཉེན་→ | དགྲ་ར་ → | ←འགྱུར་ | བ ས་ |

---

Such a syntax may be expanded with the addition of a qualifier—in the example below, a conditional clause.

---

*Renunciation, if there is no conjunction with generation of the attitude*
*[aspiring to become a buddha], will not become a cause*
*of the consummate bliss of highest awakening.*[208]

---

ངེས་འབྱུང་ སེམས་བསྐྱེད་ ཀྱིས་ ཟིན་ པ་མེད་ ན་ བླ་ མེད་ བྱང་ ཆུབ་ ཀྱི་ ཕུན་ ཚོགས་བདེ་ བའི་ རྒྱུ་ ར་ མི་ འགྱུར།

The core sentence here is ངེས་འབྱུང་བདེ་བའི་རྒྱུ་ར་མི་འགྱུར།—*Renunciation will not become a cause of bliss.*

སེམས་བསྐྱེད་, *generation of the attitude*, is the standard way of referring to the bodhisattva's attitude of seeking to attain enlightenment as a buddha for the sake of others. སེམས་བསྐྱེད་ abbreviates བྱང་ཆུབ་ཏུ་སེམས་བསྐྱེད་པ་ and བྱང་ཆུབ་ཀྱི་སེམས་བསྐྱེད་པ་. བླ་མེད་ abbreviates བླ་ན་མེད་པ་ (*nothing higher*).

The expression, *A is conjoined with B*, when used with states of mind, means that attitude or realization A is mixed with attitude or realization B.

Here is a more complex example, incorporating a number of syntactic particles, in which the nominative action clause is the subject of a verb of existence (སྲིད་—*is possible*). The doctrinal context is the possibility of an arhat falling from that position and having to again achieve nirvana. In the example below, it is suggested that an arhat of the Hearer's Vehicle may fall back to the status of stream enterer (རྒྱུན་ ཞུགས་), the position attained when emptiness is seen for the first time.

---

*Because it is possible that even arhats of the lesser [vehicle], having fallen from their eliminations and realizations, may become stream enterers …*[209]

---

དགྲ་བཅོམ་པའི་དགྲ་བཅོམ་པ་ ཡང་

རང་གི་སྤངས་རྟོགས་ལས་ ཉམས་ནས་ རྒྱུན་ཞུགས་སུ་ འགྱུར་བ་ སྲིད་པས་

---

There are a number of elements in this sentence, including three noun phrases and three verbs.

1   The nominative subject is the phrase དམན་པའི་དགྲ་བཅོམ་པ་ (*arhats of the lesser [vehicle]*) followed by a syntactic particle—ཡང་ (*even*). ཡང་ sometimes shows conjunction or inclusion (*also* and *even*) and sometimes disjunction (*but*). A syntactic particle such as ཡང་ may follow a noun phrase or clause, setting it off from other words in the sentence.

2   དམན་པའི་དགྲ་བཅོམ་པ་ serves as the nominative subject of two verbs: ཉམས་ and འགྱུར་. ཉམས་, translated here as *fall*, literally means *deteriorate*, *degenerate*, and *weaken*.

3   རང་གི་སྤངས་རྟོགས་ལས་ is a qualifier in which, although it appears to be a core verb, རྟོགས་ is part of the abbreviated noun phrase སྤངས་པ་དང་རྟོགས་པ་ (*eliminations and realizations*—referring to the elimination of the afflictions and the realization of emptiness). One clue that སྤངས་ and རྟོགས་ are not used as verbs here is that they are preceded by the connective case marking particle གི་ and followed by the fifth case marker ལས་. Although the other fifth case marker—ནས་—appears frequently after verbs as a continuative syntactic particle, ལས་ may not be so used.

4   The ནས་ following the verb ཉམས་ is just such a continuative syntactic particle, indicating a sequence of action, *falling from* and then *becoming* (འགྱུར་).

5   རྒྱུན་ཞུགས་སུ་ is the objective identity complement of the verb འགྱུར་. *Will become* what? A *stream enterer*.

6   The entire construction up to that point—the complex verbal noun, དམན་པའི་དགྲ་བཅོམ་པ་ཡང་རང་གི་སྤངས་རྟོགས་ལས་ཉམས་ནས་རྒྱུན་ཞུགས་སུ་འགྱུར་བ་—is the nominative subject of the verb of existence སྲིད་.

སྲིད་ has a more restricted meaning than ཡོད་. It means not just to exist, but to be possible. There are things that do exist, but are not possible. ཀ་བུམ་གཉིས་—*the two, pillar and pot*—for example, exist, but they are not possible. There are pillars and there are pots, but there is nothing that is both a pillar and a pot.

The core of the above clause is the following.

---

*because an arhat becoming a stream enterer is possible ...*

---

དགྲ་བཅོམ་པ་རྒྱུན་ཞུགས་སུ་འགྱུར་བ་སྲིད་པས་

It may be diagrammed in the following way.

*because an arhat becoming a stream enterer is possible ...*

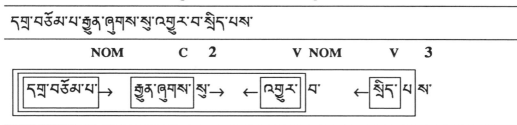

The following example has འགྱུར་ as its main verb, but is qualified by the clause མྠུ་ཅན་དུ་གྱུར་ནས་, which in its own turn is qualified by the clause, བག་ཆགས་བཞག་ནས་.

*A latency having been deposited, [it] becomes potent.*
*[That] having [taken place, one then] is established in a bad rebirth.*[210]

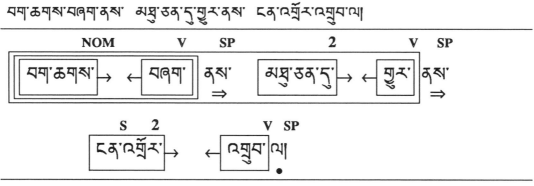

བག་ཆགས་བཞག་ནས་ is a clause ending in a past tense agentive-nominative verb and མྠུ་ཅན་དུ་གྱུར་ནས་ is a clause ending in another past tense verb. The syntactic particle ནས་ in both clauses shows sequence: *having done something, something else happens.*

The past tense form of འགྱུར་ also occurs in situations where it retains its nominative-objective syntax but acts lexically (that is, in terms of its meaning) as if it were an existential verb. The clearest illustration of this is in the name of one of the two types of tangible objects (རེག་བྱ་).

---

*tangible object that is an element*

---

འབྱུང་བར་གྱུར་པའི་རེག་བྱ་

---

འབྱུང་བ་ means *element* and refers to the traditional four elements of Indian natural science—earth, water, fire, and air (ས་ཆུ་མེ་རླུང་). If གྱུར་པ་ were used here with its normal meaning, the reading would be *a tangible object which has become an element*. However, these objects *are* elements, the basic building blocks out of which the physical universe is composed. It is, thus, hard to imagine what could *become* an element.

---

# Drill 18.9

Translate the following into Tibetan.

1. a visual consciousness to which a white conch appears yellow
2. All appearances arise as buddha and doctrine.
3. A long lifetime occurs through having eliminated killing.

---

# Drill 18.10

Translate the following. The དེ་ particles at the ends of the fourth and fifth sentences are continuative syntactic particles, indicating that something more is to come.

1. ཀྱི་མ་འགྲོ་བ་འདི་དག་ཐམས་ཅད་ནི་ཕན་ཚུན་པ་མ་རུ་གྱུར་ཀྱང་

2. རྒྱུ་དེ་ལས་འབྲས་བུ་འདི་འབྱུང་བར་འགྱུར།

3. རང་རྒྱུད་ལ་ངེས་འབྱུང་སྐྱེས་པ་ན་

4. ཐོག་མ་མེད་པ་ནས་ཁམས་གསུམ་གྱི་འཁོར་བར་རང་དབང་མེད་པར་འཁོར་ཏེ།

5. ཚེས་ཀུན་བདེན་པ་གཉིས་ཀྱི་རང་བཞིན་དུ་འདུས་ཏེ།

# Case Marking Particles
## *Objective Case*

The second or *objective* (ལས་སུ་བྱ་བ་) case is marked by the *la* group of particles: སུ་, རུ་, ཏུ་, དུ་, ན་, ར་, and ལ་. It has six main uses.

1   The place in which an activity is done is marked by the second case.

2   Those agentive verbs whose objects are not in the nominative case—the agentive-objective verbs—take second case objects.

3   Destinations of verbs of motion are in the objective and not the locative case.

4   Complements—of either Category One (nominative) or Category Two (agentive) verbs—are in the objective case.

5   The indirect objects of verbs, that or those to whom an action is directed, are usually in the fourth case. However, following traditional Tibetan grammar, where there is no benefit, or where benefit is not obvious, indirect objects are in the second and not the fourth case.

6   Identity constructions—adverbial, existential, or transformed—are expressed in the second case.

The first five uses are examined here. Identity constructions will be examined in Chapter Nineteen.

## *Objective Place of Activity*

The place where something is done is not in the locative but in the objective case.

| | |
|---|---|
| objective place of activity | སངས་རྒྱས་ཀྱིས་ ⟨རྒྱ་གར་ལ་⟩ ཆོས་བསྟན། |

*Buddha taught the doctrine **in India**.*

This usage occurs with both Category One verbs (verbs with nominative subjects) and Category Two verbs (verbs with agentive case subjects).

## *Objective Object*

Agentive-objective verbs regularly take their objects not in the nominative but in the objective case.

| object of agentive-objective verb | ཁོས་ མིག་གིས་ | གཟུགས་ལ་ | བལྟས། |
|---|---|---|---|

*He looked **at forms** with [his] eye[s].*

དཔྱེ་ is a verb that often—but not invariably—takes a second case object.

---

*When **that** is divided ...*

---

| དེ་ལ་ | དཔྱེ་ན་ |
|---|---|

## *Objectives with Verbs of Motion*

Verbs of motion belong among Class III (nominative-objective) verbs—verbs not associated with a separate agent. Grammatically, they have neither agents nor objects *per se*, merely subjects which are in a sense both their agents and their objects and are in the nominative case. However, verbs of motion are distinguished from other nominative-objective verbs in that they have destinations. These destinations are marked not by locative but by objective case particles.

| objective destination of a verb of motion | རང་ཉིད་གཅིག་པུ་ | འཇིག་རྟེན་ཕ་རོལ་དུ་ | འགྲོ |
|---|---|---|---|

*One goes alone **to the next world**.*

Destination is often metaphoric. For example, although the most basic literal meaning of the verb ཞུགས་ (present tense འཇུག་) is *entered*—seen earlier in this chapter in the term རྒྱུན་ཞུགས་, *stream enterer*—it is used frequently, still with a nominative subject, in the sense of *being involved in* or *engaging in* something. In the following example of a metaphorical destination, *others' aims* is the place into which bodhisattvas have entered.

| objective destination | ང་རྒྱུབ་སེམས་དཔའ་ | གཞན་དོན་ལ་ | ཞུགས་པ་རྣམས་ |

*Bodhisattvas who are involved in others' aims ...*

## Objective Complements

Although Class VI (agentive-objective) verbs take second case objects, many other types of verbs seem also to have objective objects. Many Class II (nominative-locative) verbs, all Class III (nominative-objective), Class V (agentive-nominative), Class VI (agentive-objective) verbs, and the attributive verbs of Class VIII seem sometimes to have objects marked by particles from the *la*-group. Such constructions are often objective complements, and the rule of thumb for translating them is to use a phrase beginning with the word *that* (on the order of *knows that ...*, *It is correct that ..., It follows that ...*), or as an infinitive phrase such as *It is correct to ....*

An objective complement shows what a verb is doing with its object—for example, how it is being thought of or what it is being said to be.

| objective complement of an agentive verb | སེམས་ཅན་ ཐམས་ཅད་ | མར་ | ཤེས། |

*[They] understand all beings to be [their] mothers.*

Objective complements are often used to report what someone says or thinks.

*[Buddha] said in the sutras that all phenomena lack identity.*

མདོ་རྣམས་ལས་ | ཆོས་ཐམས་ཅད་དོ་བོ་ཉིད་མེད་པར་ | གསུངས།

They may, thus, also be used to report doctrinal positions.

*[Some] assert mind to be the illustration of the person.*

ཁ་ཅིག་གིས་ སེམས་ | གང་ཟག་གི་མཚན་གཞིར་ | འདོད་དོ།

Objective complements are used frequently to indicate how something is perceived or thought of. This may be seen both with agentive-nominative verbs (as in the example below) and with verbs expressing attitudes.

---

*Once one has seen those sentient beings **to be one's friends** ...*

སེམས་ཅན་དེ་རྣམས་ རང་གི་གཉེན་དུ་ མཐོང་ནས་

---

Moreover, the objective complement often occurs with nominative verbs (especially rhetorical verbs) in place of a nominative subject. It is helpful to think of these constructions as having **tacit generic subjects** (as in *It is correct* and *It follows*).

| objective complement of a nominative verb | གཉེན་ཤོགས་ལ་ ཆགས་པར་ མི་རིགས་པའོ། |
|---|---|

*It is not correct **to be attached to friends and so forth**.*

Notice the form the verb takes in this construction. The best analysis of རིགས་པའོ་ is as a verbal noun (རིགས་པ་) made into a verb with the terminating syntactic particle འོ་. The literal translation then becomes, *[It is the case that] it is incorrect.*

The verb ཆགས་ is a Class II (nominative-locative) attitude verb. The clause གཉེན་ཤོགས་ལ་ཆགས་པ་ has a locative object, but leaves the subject unstated. Here it may be assumed to be a generic *one* or *you*.

You have seen this usage of the objective case in rhetorical statements such as the following.

---

*It follows **that sound is impermanent**.*

སྒྲ་ མི་རྟག་པ་ ཡིན་པར་ ཐལ།

---

## Indirect Objects

The recipient of an action (that is, the **indirect object** of a Category Two, agentive verb) is in the fourth (purposive-beneficial) case if there is benefit done to it; if there is no obvious benefit, the indirect object is in the objective case. (If there is obvious harm, the indirect object is also objective, but the construction is syntactically parallel to the fourth case usage in which benefit is obvious.)

| objective<br>indirect object | སངས་རྒྱས་ལ་ | མཆོད་པ་ ཕུལ། |

*[They] offer worship **to the Buddhas**.*

## Rhetorical Tools
### *Rhetorical Sequences*

In Chapter Seventeen, we arrived at the beginning of the second chapter of Pur-bu-jok's doctrinal primer, the "Presentation of Basic Existents." Since the first section of a chapter in a *critical analysis*—མཐའ་དཔྱོད་—is a section refuting others' positions, you are now confronted with a position that will be shown to be flawed in some way or another.

*Should someone say, "Whatever is a basic existent is necessarily permanent," …*

ཁ་ཅིག་ན་རེ། གཞི་གྲུབ་ན་ དུག་པ་ཡིན་པས་ ཁྱབ་ ཟེར་ན།

| ཁ་ཅིག་ | **kha-jík** | *a certain person, someone* |
| ན་རེ་ | **na-ré** | *according to* [syntactic particle] |
| ཟེར་ | **s̲ér** | *says, is called* |

The construction here is quite formal and stylized, and—although it appears to be an open-ended conditional construction which leads to a conclusion (*If … then …*)—is actually a complete thought. The sense of the statement is: suppose someone were to say *Whatever is a basic existent is necessarily permanent*, then to that person I would make the following answer.

When an understood personal subject occurs in a book associated with the positions held by a particular lineage, monastery, or monastic college, it is just as correct to say *we* as it is to say *I*. A Tibetan or Indian writer is much more *self-consciously* part of a tradition of understanding and interpretation than a Western author. As a result of the value they attach to tradition, Tibetan and Indian writers do not value novelty as much as do modern Western authors.

The syntactic particle ནི་རེ་ serves to mark the subject of indirect discourse; thus, ཁ་ཅིག་ནི་རེ་ would translate as *according to a certain [position]*. Indirect statements of others' positions may also be introduced with other syntactic phrases.

| | |
|---|---|
| གཞན་དག་ནི་རེ་ | *according to others ...* |
| ཁོ་ན་རེ་ | *according to him ...*<br>*according to that [position] ...* |
| བྱས་པ་ལ་ཁོ་ན་རེ་ | *according to him—[in response] to [what has just] been said—...* |

In the third example the verbal བྱས་པ་ means *what has been said*—following the attributive usage of that verb (*say, call [something by a certain name]*).

The particle ནི་རེ་ is not always used in this situation. In many cases, the format seen is ཁ་ཅིག ...ཟེར་ན། or even ཁ་ཅིག ...ཟེར། , with no difference in meaning.

A flawed position having been stated, Pur-bu-jok is now ready to attack it using a series of consequences that he does not accept himself, and that he hopes will be unacceptable to the person who holds the position that གཞི་གྲུབ་ན་རྟག་པ་ཡིན་པས་ཁྱབ་ .

> Recall that stating a *consequence* does not entail accepting it. Consequences are often stated in order to highlight contradictions in an opponent's position.

The first rhetorical move that Pur-bu-jok makes is determined by his opponent's position.

Concerning the procedure followed in rhetorical sequences, see Perdue, *Debate in Tibetan Buddhism*, pp. 99-130.

In order to discredit the flawed position, it is necessary to find something that is a basic existent but is not permanent.

*It follows that the subject, a pot, is permanent because of being a basic existent.*

བུམ་པ་ཆོས་ཅན། རྟག་པ་ཡིན་པར་ཐལ། གཞི་གྲུབ་པའི་ཕྱིར།

Any rhetorical statement, if it is to express something correct, must meet three criteria. Using as an example a correct syllogism—སྒྲ་ཆོས་ཅན། མི་རྟག་པ་ཡིན་ཏེ། བྱས་པ་ཡིན་པའི་ཕྱིར། (*The subject, sound, is impermanent because of being a product*)—the three are the following.

1 The subject is the reason: སྒྲ་བྱས་པ་ཡིན། —*sound is a product*.

2 The reason is pervaded by the predicate of the thesis: བྱས་པ་ཡིན་ན་མི་རྟག་པ་ཡིན་ པས་ཁྱབ། —*whatever is a product is necessarily impermanent*.

3 The opposite of the predicate of the thesis is pervaded by the opposite of the reason: མི་རྟག་པ་མ་ཡིན་ན་བྱས་པ་མ་ཡིན་པས་ཁྱབ། —*whatever is **not** impermanent is necessarily **not** a product*.

མི་རྟག་པ་མ་ཡིན་ན་བྱས་པ་མ་ཡིན་པས་ཁྱབ། (the third criterion) is not the same as མི་རྟག་པ་མ་ ཡིན་ན་བྱས་པ་ཡིན་པས་མ་ཁྱབ། (*whatever is not impermanent is not necessarily a product*). Whereas the former excludes all non-impermanent phenomena from being products, the latter does not. The latter merely says that pervasion is lacking; the former says that there is a pervasion.

For a detailed presentation of correct syllogisms, see Perdue, *Debate in Tibetan Buddhism*, pp. 33-60.

Using the consequence just stated by Pur-bu-jok as an example—བུམ་པ་ཆོས་ཅན། རྟག་པ་ ཡིན་པར་ཐལ། གཞི་གྲུབ་པའི་ཕྱིར། —the three criteria would be the following.

1 བུམ་པ་གཞི་གྲུབ་ཡིན། —*a pot must be a basic existent*.

2 གཞི་གྲུབ་ཡིན་ན་རྟག་པ་ཡིན་པས་ཁྱབ། —*whatever is a basic existent must necessarily be permanent*.

3 རྟག་པ་མ་ཡིན་ན་གཞི་གྲུབ་མ་ཡིན་པས་ཁྱབ། —*whatever is not permanent must necessarily not be a basic existent*.

Note that the second criterion is the pervasion with which this rhetorical sequence began. Thus, Pur-bu-jok next reminds his opponent of that.

*[You] have asserted the pervasion.*

ཁྱབ་པ་ཁས།

ཁྱབ་པ་ཁས། is an abbreviated way of saying ཁྱབ་པ་ཁས་བླངས།, *[You] have asserted the pervasion* (in colloquial Tibetan, ཁྱབ་པ་ཁས་བླངས་པ་རེད།).
In oral debate, there are three possible responses to the statement of a consequence:

1   མ་ཁྱབ་—*there is no pervasion* (literally, *not pervaded*);

2   རྟགས་མ་གྲུབ་—*the reason is not established*;

3   འདོད་—*[I] accept [the thesis].*

Pur-bu-jok anticipates that his opponent is unwilling to accept either the reason or the thesis (that a pot is permanent), and replies to the second of the three possible responses.

*If [you respond, saying, "The reason] is not established," [then I will say the following]. It follows that the subject, that, is that because of being established by valid cognition.*

མ་གྲུབ་ན། དེ་ཆོས་ཅན། དེར་ཐལ། ཚད་མས་གྲུབ་པ་ཡིན་པའི་ཕྱིར།

Whereas the first consequence stated an internal contradiction in the opponent's position and was unacceptable either to Pur-bu-jok or the opponent, the present consequence is one acceptable to Pur-bu-jok.

The construction དེ་ཆོས་ཅན། དེར་ཐལ། continues the abbreviated language characteristic of the critical analysis literature. དེ་ཆོས་ཅན། refers to the subject previously stated, བུམ་པ་. དེ་ཆོས་ཅན། དེར་ཐལ། means *it follows that [the previous] subject, [a pot], is that [previous reason, being a basic existent].* Replacing the pronouns with their referents yields the following, showing that all that has been added here is a new reason, one proving that the subject is the old reason.

*If [you respond, saying, "The reason] is not established," [then I will say the following]. It follows that the subject, a pot, is a basic existent because of being established by valid cognition.*

མ་གྲུབ་ན། བུམ་པ་ཆོས་ཅན། གཞི་གྲུབ་ཡིན་པར་ཐལ། ཚད་མས་གྲུབ་པ་ཡིན་པའི་ཕྱིར།

## Rhetorical Tools
### *Analysis of Permutations: Three Permutations*

Some of the principles of Buddhist logic discussed in the last section are easier to conceptualize if, instead of speaking in terms of equivalent things such as གཞི་གྲུབ་ and ཚད་མས་གྲུབ་པ་, phenomena that are not equivalent are examined. In particular, it is easier to understand the pervasions inherent in correct rhetorical statements in the context of two things whose relationship is one of three permutations.

### *Three Permutations*

There are only two relationships where pervasion exists, those of equivalence and three permutations (སུམ་གསུམ་).

> Mutual exclusion is a case of two separate sets of things, with no overlap.
> In the case of four permutations there is an overlap between the two sets,
> but not one in which one group entirely covers the other.

In fact, a relationship of pervasion does exist between the two phenomena, གཞི་གྲུབ་ and རྟག་པ་, but the other way around: རྟག་པ་ཡིན་ན་གཞི་གྲུབ་པས་ཁྱབ་—*Whatever is permanent is necessarily a basic existent.* The two have three permutations.

> Recall that the spatial metaphor to be used in thinking about this type of relationship is that of two circles, one of which is smaller than the other but completely contained within it.

There are many examples of sets of two things that have three permutations; here are a few:

1  ཡོད་པ་དང་མི་རྟག་པ་,
2  གཟུགས་དང་ཁྲམ་པ་,
3  ཁ་དོག་དང་དམར་པོ་,
4  སེམས་ཅན་དང་རྟ་.

All horses are sentient beings, but not all sentient beings are horses. Of course, there are a multitude of sentient beings that are not horses, but in order for horses and sentient beings to qualify as two things that have three permutations, there must be at least *one thing* that is a sentient being but is not a horse.

Or, alternatively, there must be at least one thing that is a horse but is not a sentient being. In fact, there is nothing that is a horse but not a sentient being.

Clearly there are many sentient beings that are not horses, but you have only to find one thing that is a sentient being but not a horse. The three permutations (སུ་གསུམ་) in this relationship are:

1    all stallions are both sentient beings and horses (all A is B);

2    an ox is a sentient being, but not a horse (A but not B);

3    a pot is neither a sentient being nor a horse (neither A nor B).

A more traditional example, the first lesson in many of the doctrinal primers, is color and red:

1    whatever is the color of the *Buddha Amitāyus* (སངས་རྒྱས་ཚེ་དཔག་མེད་) is necessarily red—it is both a color and red;

2    the color of a white *religious conch* (ཆོས་དུང་) is a color but is not red;

3    the horns of a hare (རི་བོང་རྭ་—a famous non-existent, since hares have no horns) are neither a color nor red.

---

The principle here is that if two things, A and B, have three permutations, then one can posit three possibilities:
1  something which is both A and B;
2  something which is A but is not B;
3  something which is neither A nor B.

---

The third possibility—something which is neither (གཅིས་ཀ་མ་ཡིན་པའི་མུ་)—may not exist.

---

Remember that ཡིན་ (*being something*) does not imply ཡོད་ (*existing*).

---

Applying what has been said to the example of color and the color white, we have:

1 the color of a white conch is both (A) a color and (B) the color white;

2 the color of the Buddha Amitāyus is (A) a color but not (B) the color white;

3 a barren woman's son is neither (A) a color nor (B) the color white.

The third possibility here is, in fact, something that does not exist.

## *Forward and Reverse Pervasion*

Recall, from earlier in this chapter, that three criteria must be met in order for a rhetorical statement to be valid.

1 The subject must be the reason.

2 The reason must be pervaded by the predicate of the thesis.

3 The opposite of the predicate of the thesis must be pervaded by the opposite of the reason.

Let us now examine this using a rhetorical statement that embodies the three permutations relationship existing between གཞི་གྲུབ་ and རྟག་པ་.

*The subject, non-product space, is a basic existent because [it] is permanent.*

འདུས་མ་བྱས་ཀྱི་ནམ་མཁའ་ཆོས་ཅན། གཞི་གྲུབ་ཡིན་ཏེ། རྟག་པ་ཡིན་པའི་ཕྱིར།

འདུས་མ་བྱས་ཀྱི་ནམ་མཁའ་ (*the non-product space*) is the most commonly used illustration of a permanent phenomenon. Grammatically, འདུས་མ་བྱས་ and ནམ་མཁའ་ are in apposition; the connective case marking particle is an appositive connective.

This syllogism is valid only if the following three statements are true.

1 འདུས་མ་བྱས་ཀྱི་ནམ་མཁའ་རྟག་པ་ཡིན།—the non-product space is permanent.

2 རྟག་པ་ཡིན་ན་གཞི་གྲུབ་ཡིན་པས་ཁྱབ།—whatever is permanent is necessarily a basic existent (literally: *if [something] is permanent, then [that thing] is pervaded by being a basic existent*).

3 གཞི་གྲུབ་མ་ཡིན་ན་རྟག་པ་མ་ཡིན་པས་ཁྱབ།—whatever is not a basic existent is necessarily not permanent (literally: *if [something] is not a basic existent, then [that thing] is pervaded by not being permanent*).

The second and third statements are true only if གཞི་གྲུབ་ and རྟག་པ་ are either equivalent or have three permutations. However, if they were equivalent, then གཞི་གྲུབ་ཡིན་ན་རྟག་པ་ ཡིན་པས་ཁྱབ། would also be correct, and it is not.

The second and third statements are seen as different ways of saying the same thing and are called the *forward* and *reverse pervasions*.

| རྗེས་ཁྱབ་ | **jé>-khyap** | *positive pervasion, forward pervasion* |
|---|---|---|
| ལྡོག་ཁྱབ་ | **dok-khyap** | *counter-pervasion, reverse pervasion* |

See Perdue, *Debate in Tibetan Buddhism*, pp. 41-49.

Despite the fact that there are three elements in a correct rhetorical statement, there are only two possible avenues that a rhetorical sequence may take once a syllogism or consequence has been stated:

1   proving that the subject is the reason;

2   proving the positive pervasion.

There is no need to prove the counter-pervasion separately. Once either the positive or counter-pervasion is proven, then so is the other. Proving—as in the immediately preceding syllogism—that གཞི་གྲུབ་ pervades རྟག་པ་ proves, by implication, that རྟག་པ་མ་ ཡིན་པ་ pervades གཞི་གྲུབ་མ་ཡིན་པ་.

# Doctrinal Vocabulary and Grammar
## *Impermanent Phenomena*

Basic existents are divided into two types: permanent and impermanent phenomena. Permanent phenomena are existents that do not disintegrate moment by moment.

*A definition of functioning thing exists because able to perform a function is that.*

དངོས་པོའི་མཚན་ཉིད་ཡོད་དེ། དོན་བྱེད་ནུས་པ་དེ་ དེ་ཡིན་པའི་ཕྱིར།

The principal function a functioning thing performs is to produce an effect. In the phrase དོན་བྱེད་ནུས་པ་, the main verb is བྱེད་, its object is དོན་, and ནུས་ is a verb commonly used in compound verb constructions.

*When functioning things are divided, there are three. For, there are the three, matter, consciousness, and non-associated compositional factors.*

དངོས་པོ་ལ་དབྱེ་ན་གསུམ་ཡོད་དེ། གཟུགས་ཤེས་ལྡན་མིན་འདུ་བྱེད་གསུམ་ ཡོད་པའི་ཕྱིར།

གཟུགས་ is short for གཟུགས་པོ་ and is equivalent to the broader use of the term གཟུགས་ introduced in Chapter Thirteen, the sense in which གཟུགས་ means not just color and shape, but also sounds, odors, tastes, and tangible objects.

*There is a definition of matter because established atomically is that.*

གཟུགས་པོའི་མཚན་ཉིད་ཡོད་དེ། རྡུལ་དུ་གྲུབ་པ་དེ་ དེ་ཡིན་པའི་ཕྱིར།

The རྡུལ་དུ་ in རྡུལ་དུ་གྲུབ་པ་ is an existential identity construction. *Established* (that is, existent) as what? *As atoms.*

*When matter is divided, there are two. For, there are the two, external matter and internal matter.*

གཟུགས་པོ་ལ་དབྱེ་ན་ གཉིས་ཡོད་དེ། ཕྱིའི་གཟུགས་པོ་དང་ནང་གི་གཟུགས་པོ་གཉིས་ ཡོད་པའི་ཕྱིར།

This is not a qualitative difference, since the difference between the two is merely from the viewpoint of whether or not the matter in question is part of the body-mind aggregates making up a person or not.

*There is a definition of external matter because that established atomically which is not included within the continuum of a being is that.*

ཕྱིའི་གཟུགས་པོའི་མཚན་ཉིད་ཡོད་དེ།

སྐྱེས་བུའི་རྒྱུད་ཀྱིས་མ་བསྡུས་པའི་རྡུལ་དུ་གྲུབ་པ་དེ་ དེ་ཡིན་པའི་ཕྱིར།

The phrase སྐྱེས་བུའི་རྒྱུད་ཀྱིས་མ་བསྡུས་པ་ is a straightforward agentive-nominative verb clause with an understood གཟུགས་པོ་ as its object.

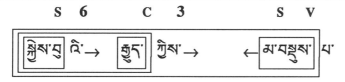

Where in English one says that this type of matter is *not included **within a being's continuum***, in Tibetan one says that *a being's continuum does not include* (or *gather*) it.

བསྡུས་ is the past tense form of the agentive-nominative verb སྡུད་, a four-form verb.

| past: བསྡུས་ | present: སྡུད་ | future: བསྡུ་ | imperative: སྡུས་ |
|---|---|---|---|

Although the past tense form is used here, it does not convey the past any more than the generic use of གྱུར་ to mean *is* conveys a sense of a past action.

The nominative-objective cognate of སྡུད་ is འདུ་ (*is gathered, is included*), a three-form verb.

| past: འདུས་ | present: འདུད་ | future: འདུ་ | imperative: འདུས་ |
|---|---|---|---|

The following is an illustration of the nominative-objective form.

*All the rivers gather in the ocean.*

ཆུ་བོ་ཐམས་ཅད་ རྒྱ་མཚོར་ འདུ།

Continuing with the analysis of matter, Pur-bu-jok lists some illustrations.

*There are illustrations [of external matter] because pot, pillar, and the four—earth, water, fire, and wind—are that.*

མཚན་གཞི་ཡོད་དེ། བུམ་པ། ཀ་བ། ས་ཆུ་མེ་རླུང་བཞི་པོ་དེ་ དེ་ཡིན་པའི་ཕྱིར།

The other two categories of functioning things are consciousness and non-associated compositional factors.

*There is a definition of consciousness because clear and aware is that.*

ཤེས་པའི་མཚན་ཉིད་ཡོད་དེ། གསལ་ཞིང་རིག་པ་དེ་ དེ་ཡིན་པའི་ཕྱིར།

*There is a definition of non-associated compositional factor because a compositional factor which is neither matter nor consciousness is that.*

ཕྱན་མིན་འདུ་བྱེད་ཀྱི་མཚན་ཉིད་ ཡོད་དེ།

བེམ་ཤེས་གང་རུང་མ་ཡིན་པའི་འདུ་བྱེད་དེ་དེ་ཡིན་པའི་ཕྱིར།

གང་རུང་ is an indefinite pronoun meaning *either*. Used with a negative verb, as it is here, it means *neither*.

---

*There are illustrations [of non-associated compositional factors]*
  *because functioning things, impermanent things,*
  *and persons such as horses and oxen are that.*

---

མཚན་གཞི་ཡོད་དེ།

དངོས་པོ་དང་། མི་རྟག་པ་དང་། རྟ་དང་བ་གླང་སོགས་གང་ཟག་རྣམས་ དེ་ཡིན་པའི་ཕྱིར།

As before, རྟ་དང་བ་གླང་སོགས་ is an abbreviated form of རྟ་དང་བ་གླང་ལ་སོགས་པ་, where the ལ་ is a conjunctive syntactic particle meaning *and* and the སོགས་པ་ should be considered the last in a list of nouns.

དངོས་པོ་ and མི་རྟག་པ་ are non-associated compositional factors because, while they are definitely impermanent, they are themselves neither matter nor consciousness. Persons are non-associated compositional factors for the reason that they are merely designations for certain aggregations of body and mind.

# *Vocabulary*

## *Nouns*

| | | |
|---|---|---|
| ཀ་བ་ | **ḡa-wa** | pillar |
| ཁྱད་པར་ | **khyë'-b̄ar** | attribute, feature, and quality |
| ཁྱབ་བྱ་ | **khyap-ja** | that pervaded, object pervaded |
| ཁྱབ་བྱེད་ | **khyab-jé'** | pervader |
| གྲང་བ་ | **ṭang-wa** | cold |
| དགྲ་ | **ḍa** | enemy |
| འགྲོ་བ་ | **ḍo-wa** | going, migration [rebirth], migrator [sentient being] |
| རྒྱུན་ཞུགས་ | **gyün-s̱huk** | stream enterer |
| ངོ་བོ་ཉིད་ | **ngo-wo-nyí'** | identity, entity |
| སྔོན་འགྲོ་ | **n̄gön-ḍo** | preliminary, preparation |
| མཆོད་པ་ | **chö'-b̄a** | worship |
| གཉེན་ | **n̄yén** | friend, relative |
| གཉེན་པོ་ | **n̄yén-b̄o** | antidote |
| རྗེས་ཁྱབ་ | **jé>-khyap** | positive pervasion |
| གཏི་མུག་ | **dí-muk** | delusion, obscuration |
| རྟེན་ཅིང་འབྲེལ་བར་འབྱུང་བ་ | **ḍên-jíng-ḍél-war-jung-wa** | dependent arising |
| རྟེན་འབྲེལ་ | **ḍên-ḍél** | dependent arising |

| ཚོགས་པ་ | dok-b̄a | realization |
|---|---|---|
| སྟོན་ཀ་ | d̄ön-ḡa | autumn |
| མཐའ་ | tha | end, extreme |
| དུད་འགྲོ་ | tün-ḍo | animal [literally, 'bent goer'] |
| རྡུལ་ | dül | atom |
| ལྡོག་ཁྱབ་ | dok-khyap | counter-pervasion |
| ནམ་མཁའ་ | nam-kha | space |
| གནོད་པ་ | n̄ö'-b̄a | harm, refutation |
| རྣམ་པ་ | n̄am-b̄a | aspect, type, form |
| སྤང་བ་ | b̄ang-b̄a | elimination |
| ཕན་པ་ | phën-b̄a | help, assistance |
| ཕན་ཡོན་ | phën-yön | benefit |
| བེམ་པོ་ | pém-b̄o | matter |
| སྦྱོར་བ་ | jor-wa | syllogism |
| མ་ | ma | mother |
| ཚ་བ་ | tsha-wa | heat |
| ཚད་ | tshë' | measure, extent |
| གཞན་ཕན་ | s̱hën-phën | altruism |
| གཡང་ས་ | yang-s̄a | abyss |
| ར་སྟོད་ | ra-d̄ö' | [name of monastery] |
| སོགས་པ་ | s̄ok-b̄a | so forth, so on [only in * ལ་སོགས་པ་] |

## *Verbs*

Verbs are marked by the Roman numeral indicating the class to which they belong—that is, the syntax they require.

| | | | | |
|---|---|---|---|---|
| I | nominative-nominative | V | agentive-nominative |
| II | nominative-locative | VI | agentive-objective |
| III | nominative-objective | VII | purposive-nominative |
| IV | nominative-syntactic | VIII | locative-nominative |

The first part of the name of each class identifies the case of the subject and the second, that of the object, complement, or principal qualifier.

|  |  |  |
|---|---|---|
| སྐྱེ་ | ḡyé> | is born, arises, is created III |
| ཁྱབ་ | khyap | pervade, cover, spread VI |
| འཁྱམ་ | khyam | wander III |
| དགོངས་ | gong | consider, think about [HON] VI |
| གྱུར་ | gyur | [past and imperative of འགྱུར་] |
| འགྱུར་ | gyur | becomes, changes, is III [present & future] |
| འགྲུབ་ | ḍup | is established, is proven, exists III |
| འགྲོ་ | ḍo | go III [present and future] |
| རྒྱས་ | gyë> | extends, expands III |
| སྒྱུར་ | gyur | change, transform, translate V |
| སྒོམ་ | gom | meditate, cultivate V |
| བསྒོམས་ | gom | [past of སྒོམ་] |
| བསྒྱུར་ | gyur | [past and future of སྒྱུར་] |
| བཅིངས་ | jíng | [past of འཆིངས་] |

| ཆགས་ | chak | is attached to **II** |
|---|---|---|
| མཆི་ | chí | go **III** [present and future] |
| མཆིས་ | chí> | [past and imperative of མཆི་] |
| འཆར་ | char | appears, rises **III** |
| འཆིངས་ | chíng | tie, bind **V** |
| འཇུག་ | juk | enter **III** |
| ཉམས་ | nyam | degenerate, fall from **III** |
| ལྷུང་ | d̄ung | fall **III** [present and future] |
| བསྟེན་ | d̄ên | use [medicine], serve [a guru] |
| འཐད་ | thë' | is correct **III** |
| འདུ་ | du | [future of འདུད་] |
| འདུད་ | dü' | is gathered, is included **III** |
| འདུས་ | dü> | [past and imperative of འདུད་] |
| སྡུད་ | dü' | include, gather **V** |
| བསྡུ་ | du | [future of སྡུད་] |
| བསྡུས་ | dü> | [past of སྡུད་] |
| གནོད་ | n̄ö' | harm **VI** |
| སྣང་ | n̄ang | appears, is perceived **III** |
| ཕན་ | phën | help, aid, benefit **VI** |
| ཕྱིན་ | chîn | [past of འགྲོ་] |
| འཕྲོས། | ṭhö> | spreads **III** |

| ཕྱིན་ | <u>ch</u>ön | come, arrive **III** |
|---|---|---|
| དབྱེ་ | yé | divide **VI** |
| འབད་ | b̄ë' | make effort **VI** |
| འབྱུང་ | jung | occurs, arises **III** |
| དམིགས་ | mík | observe, visualize |
| བརྩོན་ | d̄zön | makes effort, is energetic **VI** |
| འཛིན་ | <u>dz</u>în | hold, apprehend, grasp, conceive **V** |
| ཉེན་ | <u>s</u>în | conjoins **V** |
| ཟུངས་ | <u>s</u>ung | [imperative of འཛིན་] |
| ཟེར་ | <u>s</u>ér | says **V**, is called **VIII** |
| གཟུང་ | <u>s</u>ung | [future of འཛིན་] |
| བཟུང་ | <u>s</u>ung | [past of འཛིན་] |
| ཆོང་ | ong | come **III** |
| གཤེགས་ | s̄hék | go, come [HON] **III** |
| སེམས་ | s̄êm | think about, reflect on, consider **VI** |
| སོམས་ | s̄om | [imperative of སེམས་] |
| སོང་ | s̄ong | [past and imperative of འགྲོ་] |
| སྲིད་ | s̄í' | is possible **II** |
| སླེབ་ | lép | arrive **III** |
| བསམ་ | s̄am | [future of སེམས་] |
| བསམས་ | s̄am | [past of སེམས་] |

| ཤུང་ | **hlung** | [past of ཤུང་] |
| ཤུངས་ | **hlung** | [imperative of ཤུང་] |

## Pronouns

| ཁ་ཅིག | **kha-jík** | someone, a certain person |
| ག་ | **ka** | what, which |
| གང་ཡང་ | **kang-yang** | any |
| གང་རུང་ | **kang-rung** | either |
| དེ་ལྟར་ | **té-dar** | thus [adverbial pronoun] |
| རེས་འགའ་ | **rén-ga** | some people |

## Adjectives

| གཅེས་པ་ | **jé>-ba** | dear, cherished |
| ཉེ་བ་ | **nyé-wa** | near |
| གཉིས་ཀ | **ńyí>-ga** | both |
| མཐུ་ཅན་ | **thu-jën** | potent |
| འདྲ་མོ་ | **da-mo** | like |
| ཕ་རོལ་ | **pha-röl** | other, far |
| ཕྱི་མ | **chí-ma** | subsequent |
| འབའ་ཞིག་ | **ba-shík** | only |
| གསུམ་ག་ | **sum-ga** | all three |

## *Adverbs*

| | | |
|---|---|---|
| ཁྱད་པར་ | **khyë'-b̄ar** | in particular |
| ཅི་ཡང་ | **j̄i-yang** | at all, in any way |
| ཞིབ་ཏུ་ | **shíp-d̄u** | in detail |

## *Syntactic Particles*

| | | |
|---|---|---|
| ཀྱང་ | **ḡyang** | even, also, but |
| གྱི་ | **gyí** | although, but [disjunctive—following verb] |
| དེ་ཕྱིར་ | **té-chír** | therefore |
| * ན་རེ་ | **na-ré** | according to * |
| བཞིན་ | **s̲hîn** | [marks continuing present after verbs] |
| འང་ | **ang** | even, also, but |
| ཡང་ | **yang** | even, also, but |

# *Chapter 19*

*Rhetorical Verbs • Attitude Verbs*
*Nominative-Syntactic Verbs*
*Objective Case Identity*
*Classes and Types of Verbs*

## Patterns in Tibetan Language

The focus of *Translating Buddhism from Tibetan* has moved from the pronunciation of letters and syllables to the construction of words out of syllables and lexical particles, and then from the types and functions of words to the construction of complex phrases, clauses, and sentences out of words, case marking particles, and syntactic particles. These changes in focus have brought with them a move from explaining Tibetan in terms of its nouns, pronouns, and objects to an explanation in terms of verbs.

Reading the complex Tibetan used in Buddhist literature, in which even the subject or object of a sentence may be a complex clause or phrase involving a number of verbal nouns or adjectives, requires a facility with verbs and their syntax. It is for this reason that—since Chapter Twelve—this book has spoken principally of verbs and their types.

The student should always remember, however, that the classification of verbs in *Translating Buddhism from Tibetan* is merely a heuristic device. Unlike English and Sanskrit—languages which have normative literary forms—Tibetan syntactic patterns vary considerably. Thus, the patterns presented with each class of verbs are best considered to be rules of thumb.

> Expedient techniques have a long history in Buddhism, Buddha having presented his own teaching as a raft to be set aside once used (see Sangharakshita, *Survey of Buddhism*, pp. 228-229).[211]

Likewise, while the grammatical and syntactic analyses presented in *Translating Buddhism from Tibetan* are not liberative techniques, they also should be applied in a way appropriate to the situation.

> Learning and applying the syntactic patterns presented in this book are a useful beginning to an understanding of Tibetan. If they are applied mechanically and inflexibly, however, they may become a hindrance to translation.

In the present chapter, the remaining types of verbs—the rhetorical verbs of Class III, the attitude verbs of Class II, and Class IV (nominative-syntactic) verbs—will be examined. The chapter ends with a review of all the various classes of verbs and their subdivisions.

# Nominative-Objective Verbs
## *Rhetorical Verbs*

The third of the three types of Class III (nominative-objective verbs) is that of rhetorical verbs, verbs that act like verbs of existence, but are more complex syntactically and lexically. Common rhetorical verbs include the following.

| | | |
|---|---|---|
| རུང་ | **rung** | *is suitable, is admissible, is correct* |
| རིགས་ | **rík** | *is correct* |
| འཐད་ | **thë'** | *is correct* |
| ཐལ་ | **thël** | *logically follows* |

All four are single-form verbs.

The basic syntax of a clause or sentence ending in a rhetorical verb is the following:

nominative
SUBJECT ⊢→          ←⊢ RHETORICAL VERB

That syntax may be seen in the following simple sentence.

*Both of those as well are incorrect.*

དེ་གཉིས་ཀ་ཡང་མི་རིགས་སོ།

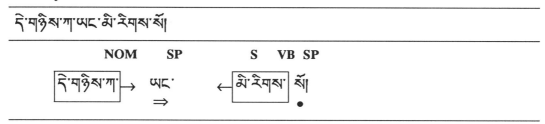

More complex—and more representative of rhetorical usage in general—is the following syntax:

nominative              objective
SUBJECT ⊢→          COMPLEMENT ⊢→          ←⊢ VERB

The following sentence exemplifies this syntax. Its sense is that it is not correct to say that a sense power, which is a physical and not a mental phenomenon, is a type of valid cognition.

*Valid cognition* is an interpretive translation for ཚད་མ་. Neither ཚད་མ་ nor its Sanskrit original, *pramāṇa*, necessarily designate only mental phenomena.

*A physical sense power is not admissible as a valid cognition.*[212]

དབང་པོ་གཟུགས་ཅན་པ་ ཚད་མར་ མི་རུང་།

དབང་པོ་གཟུགས་ཅན་པ་ ([SENSE]-POWER + FORM-POSSESSING) is a noun-adjective phrase which serves as the subject of the negative verb phrase མི་རུང་།. Its complement, ཚད་ མར་, is in the second case, an example of an existential identity construction.

The following sentence illustrates the same syntax. Its meaning is that if one talks about a person as a construction dependent on a certain body and mind (the aggregates), it is not logical to say that this imputed person is part of the mind and body to which it is designated.

---

*The person imputed in dependence on the aggregates
    is not admissible as an aggregate.*[213]

---

ཕུང་པོ་ལ་བརྟེན་ནས་བཏགས་པའི་གང་ཟག་ཕུང་པོར་མི་རུང་།

---

བཏགས་ is the past tense form of the verb འདོགས་ (*designates, imputes*).

---

past: བཏགས་          present: འདོགས་          future: གདགས་          imperative: ཐོགས་

---

In the above example— whose essential form is གང་ཟག་ཕུང་པོར་མི་རུང་།—the subject of the verb is the noun གང་ཟག་. གང་ཟག་ is qualified by the adjective phrase ཕུང་པོ་ལ་བརྟེན་ནས་ བཏགས་པ་ which is connected to it with a sixth case particle. This is another example of the very common clause connective construction.

---

A noun following a clause connective is often the understood subject, object, qualifier, or complement of the preceding clause.

---

   The clause that modifies གང་ཟག་ is actually quite complex, including within it another clause—ཕུང་པོ་ལ་བརྟེན་ནས་ (*depending on the aggregates*). Although a past tense verb followed by the continuative syntactic particle ནས་ usually indicates a sequence of action, here the sense is almost adverbial. How is the imputation done? Having depended on the aggregates—that is, *in dependence on the aggregates.*

   An alternate way of conceptualizing the syntax of a clause or sentence ending in a rhetorical verb is the following, seen earlier as the syntax of the verb ཐལ་ in statements of logical consequence:

unstated            objective
| SUBJECT | →     | COMPLEMENT | →     ← | RHETORICAL VERB |

As in the following example, the unstated subject—a tacit generic subject— translates into English as a generic pronoun (such as *it*).

---

*Otherwise, it would not be correct* **to say that lack of identity is an ultimate.**[214]

---

གཞན་དུ་ན་ངོ་བོ་ཉིད་མེད་པ་དོན་དམ་མོ་ཞེས་སྨྲ་བར་མི་རིགས་ཏེ།

---

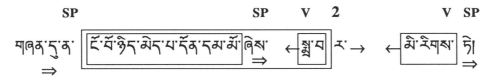

The terminator མོ་ serves as an understood linking verb in the sentence ངོ་བོ་ ཉིད་མེད་པ་དོན་དམ་མོ་.

The core of this construction is a very simple sentence, in which the lack of any specific nominative subject is apparent.

*It is not correct to say.*

སྐྱ་བར་ མི་རིགས་ ཏེ།

The objective construction—ངོ་བོ་ཉིད་མེད་པ་དོན་དམ་མོ་ཞེས་སྐྱ་བར་ in the full sentence—functions as if it were a subject and may be thought of as what in English would be an infinitive phrase: *to say that lack of identity is an ultimate.* Although the ཞེས་ is the syntactic particle that closes quotations, here it is translated *that*.

Remember that, as in English, quoted material has no syntactic connection to the sentence or clause that surrounds it.

## Case Marking Particles
### *Objective Case Identity Constructions*

The identity marking particle (usually སུ་, རུ་, དུ་, ད་, or ར་ and, some would argue, never ན་ or ལ་) is a species of the second case.

There are three sorts of identity: adverbial, existential, and transformative. The Tibetan term descriptive of this usage is དེ་ཉིད་ (*just that*) and indicates sameness of entity (not, technically, identity) between the action and whatever is described in the identity construction.

| | |
|---|---|
| adverbial identity | གསལ་བར་ བཤད་ |

*[She] explains clearly.*

In this example, the *explaining* and *clearly* are not different things.  In the following example, *existing* and *truly* are the same.  How does it *exist*? *Truly*.

---

**truly existent**

| བདེན་པར་ | ཡོད་པ་ |

---

Not all identity constructions are adverbial, however.  It makes more sense to think of the following clause as an example of existential identity, since བུམ་པའི་རྒྱུར་གྱུར་པ means *that which is a cause of a pot*.

| existential identity | བུམ་པའི་ རྒྱུར་ | གྱུར་པའི་ དངོས་པོ་ |

*the thing which is **pot's cause***

This is an illustration of the existential use of the verb འགྱུར.  If the basic nominative-objective usage of འགྱུར were applied here, the meaning would be *that which has **become** pot's cause*.  Instead, here གྱུར means *is*.

Existential identity is common with rhetorical verbs.

---

*That path is not admissible **as a cause of liberation***.

ལམ་དེ་ནི་ | ཐར་པའི་རྒྱུར་ | མི་རུང་སྟེ།

---

| transformed identity | སངས་རྒྱས་ཀྱི་ མདོ་ | བོད་སྐད་དུ་ | བསྒྱུར། |

*Buddha's sutras were translated **into Tibetan***.

This usage is neither existential nor adverbial, but indicates the end result of a process of transformation.  These constructions are, nonetheless, traditionally classified as instances of དེ་ཉིད.

---

*transmuting iron **into gold***

ལྕགས་ | གསེར་དུ་ | སྒྱུར་བ་

## Drill 19.1

Translate the following into Tibetan.

1. a being who is [one of the] causes of a pot
2. the appropriateness [suitability] of meditating on compassion
3. In the Sutra School, lack of identity is not admissible as an ultimate.
4. It follows that the color of the buddha Amitayus is not white.
5. fearful [literally: *suitable to be feared*]

## Drill 19.2

Identify the dots in the following and translate. Diagram the first.

1. འདུས་མ་བྱས་ཡིན་པས་ཀུན་ནས་ཉོན་མོངས་པའི་ཆོས་སུ་མི་རུང་ངོ་།

2. སྐྱེ་འགག་གནས་གསུམ་མི་རུང་བའི་ཆོས་

3. ཕན་པ་མི་བྱེད་པ་མི་རིགས་སོ།

4. ཆད་མར་གྱུར་པའི་སྐྱེས་བུ་

5. གཞན་སྟེ་ལ་རང་གི་སྟོན་པའི་ལུང་གིས་འགོག་ཏུ་མི་རུང་བས།

## Verbs and Verb Syntax
### *Attitude Verbs*

Attitude verbs—verbs expressing mental attitudes such as ཁྲོ་ (*is angry*), འཁྲུལ་ (*is mistaken*), and ཆགས་ (*is attached*)—are the only Class II (nominative-locative) verbs yet to be examined.

The other Class II verbs are the verbs of existence, verbs of living, and verbs of dependence.

Not all verbs expressing attitudes or states of mind are included in this type, only those with nominative subjects. For example, the verbs ཤེས་, རྟོགས་, འཛིན་, and དམིགས་ express cognitive processes but are agentive verbs and, thus, cannot be included here. The designation, 'attitude verb,' alludes to the fact that most verbs of this type do refer to attitudes, feelings, or cognitive states. An exception to that general rule is the verb མཁས་ (*is skilled in*) which belongs to this group syntactically, but not in terms of its meaning.

Common attitude verbs include the following.

| | | |
|---|---|---|
| ཆགས་ | **chak** | *is attached* |
| ཞེན་ | **s͟hên** | *clings, determines, conceives* |
| གུས་ | **kü>** | *trusts* |
| མོས་ | **mö>** | *is interested, believes, imagines* |
| འཁྲུལ་ | **ṭhül** | *is mistaken* |
| སྐྱོ་ | **ḡyo** | *is disheartened* |
| མཁས་ | **khë>** | *is skilled, is learned* |

With the exception of ཞེན་ and འཁྲུལ་, all the above are single-form verbs. The past and imperative of ཞེན་ have a ད་ secondary suffix (ཞེནད་), as do the past and imperative of འཁྲུལ་.

The basic syntax of a clause or sentence ending in an attitude verb is the following:

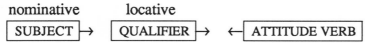

That syntax may be seen in the following example.

*The Teacher [Buddha] is skilled in the means [to liberation].*

སློབ་དཔོན་ ཐབས་ལ་ མཁས་

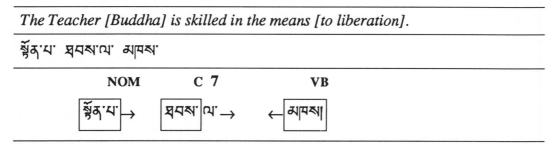

However, even more than in other syntactic patterns, the subjects of phrases, clauses, and sentences ending in attitude verbs are not explicitly stated. This is perhaps because these verbs are most frequently used in their verbal noun forms at the end of short clauses expressing generic attitudes or mental processes—not in statements of specific actions done by specific persons at specified times. Here are some examples.

---

*attachment to a self*

---

བདག་ལ་ཆགས་པ་

---

བདག་ལ་ is the locative qualifier of the verb ཆགས་. The locative qualifiers of attitude verbs are examples of the **referential locative**, whose rule of thumb translation is *about* or *towards*.

As with rules of thumb in general, the procedure is first to apply the rule and then tailor the translation to the specific situation in such a way that it reads as English and not Tenglish—an English that makes sense only to those who know Tibetan.

---

*being attached to some sentient beings and feeling aversion towards others*

---

སེམས་ཅན་ཁ་ཅིག་ལ་ ཆགས་ཤིང་ ཁ་ཅིག་ལ་ སྡང་བ་

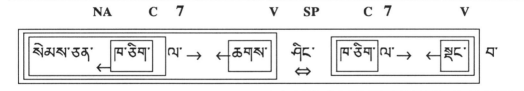

Here the entire phrase is a complex verbal noun. The lexical particle བ་ at the end serves not merely to nominalize the verb སྡང་, but attaches to the entire construction. The double arrow under the syntactic particle ཤིང་ marks its conjunctive use, bringing together what comes before it and what follows it.

In the next example, ལས་འབྲས་ is actually an abbreviated noun phrase. As is sometimes the case with abbreviations, this one may be read in more than one way, as either ལས་ཀྱི་འབྲས་བུ་ (*the effects of actions*) or ལས་དང་དེའི་འབྲས་བུ་ (*actions and their effects*).

*confused about the effects [of] actions*
  OR *confused about actions [and their] effects*

ལས་འབྲས་ལ་ རྨོངས་ཤིང་

The following two phrases employ appositive connectives tying attitude verb clauses to the nouns ཤེས་པ་ (*consciousness*) and སེམས་ (*mind*), making their reference to attitudes explicit.

*a consciousness that is mistaken about the natures of [phenomena] like that*
  OR *a consciousness that is mistaken about such natures*

དེ་ལྟ་བུའི་རང་བཞིན་ལ་ འཁྲུལ་པའི་ ཤེས་པ་

*a mind that fears suffering*

སྡུག་བསྔལ་ལ་ འཇིགས་པའི་ སེམས་

Attitude verbs also express positive attitudes.

*interest in the Mahāyāna*                *trust in the three jewels*

ཐེག་པ་ཆེན་པོ་ལ་ མོས་པ་          དཀོན་མཆོག་གསུམ་ལ་ དད་པ་

The next example literally reads, *About what is who, due to what, mistaken?*

*Who is mistaken?  About what?  [And] due to what?*

གང་ལ་གང་ཞིག་གང་གིས་འཁྲུལ་

Here, གང་ལ་ is the seventh case qualifier: *about what* (or, *about whom*). གང་ཞིག་, seen before as a syntactic particle, is here (in its more obvious usage) a pronoun, the nominative subject of the sentence. གང་གིས་ (*by what*) is another qualifier, indicating either the reason, the means, or possibly (in a non-case-marking syntactic usage) the way in which there is a mistake.

*not being patient towards the occurrence of one's own suffering*

རང་གི་སྡུག་བསྔལ་ བྱུང་བ་ལ་ མི་བཟོད་པ་

A better translation might be *not being patient towards one's own suffering* or *not being patient when suffering happens to one*, since the nominative verb འབྱུང་ is used for things that happen to a person.

Attitude verbs are also used with auxiliary verbs.

*Do not, for even an instant, be attached to one's own aims.*

རང་གི་དོན་ལ་ སྐད་ཅིག་ཙམ་ ཆགས་པར་མི་བྱ།

རང་གི་དོན་—*one's own aims* or *one's own purposes*—are opposed to གཞན་དོན་, *others' purposes*. In English, the opposition would be between *selfishness* and *altruism*.

Note the way in which the phrase སྐད་ཅིག་ཙམ་ is used as an adverb, *for even an instant*.

The following are also examples of sentences ending in auxiliary verb phrases.

*Do not be disheartened about cyclic existence.*

འཁོར་བ་ལ་ སྐྱོ་བར་མི་བྱ།

*[One] should become skilled in accomplishing positive [actions].*

དགེ་བ་ བསྒྲུབ་པ་ལ་ མཁས་པར་བྱ།

The qualifier, དགེ་བ་བསྒྲུབ་པ་ལ་, is itself a clause ending in an agentive-nominative verbal noun.

## The Referential Locative

The locative case is used to mark some subjects and many sorts of qualifiers:

● qualifiers stating that upon which something else depends,

● qualifiers stating the place where something or someone lives or exists,

● qualifiers stating the category within which something exists,

● the subject who possesses something,

● qualifiers stating the time when something is done,

- general topics which are neither subjects nor qualifiers,
- the general context or reference of an action or a state of mind.

> The topical locative introduced in Chapter Seventeen differs from the referential locative in that whereas a referential locative has a grammatical relationship to the phrase, clause, or sentence in which it is found, a topical locative does not.

The rule of thumb translations for referential locatives include *about*, *with regard to*, *towards*, and *in the context of*. Thus, the locatives in many of the above attitude verb clauses may be translated as *about \** or *towards \**.

The paradigmatic referential locative construction is the following sentence.

| referential<br>locative | སྨན་ལ་ | མཁས་པ་ |
|---|---|---|

*skilled **in medicine***

The rule of thumb translation here would be, *[he] is skilled about medicine*. The next example illustrates the same simple syntax.

---
*patience **towards suffering***
---
| སྡུག་བསྔལ་ལ་ | བཟོད་པ་ |
|---|---|
---

The following is a less intuitive usage of the referential locative.

---
*A child was born **to her**.*
---

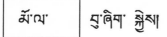

| མོ་ལ་ | བུ་ཞིག་ སྐྱེས། |
|---|---|

Although the sentence ends in a nominative-objective verb, མོ་ལ་ is not the objective case place of activity—the baby was not born *in her*.

The rule of thumb translation here would be, *As regards her, a child was born*.

## Drill 19.3

Translate the following into Tibetan.

1. fear of being born in the three bad migrations
2. aversion towards sentient beings who have harmed one
3. It is not correct to be attached to [people] such as friends.
4. adherence [clinging] to a personal self

## Drill 19.4

Translate the following.  Diagram the second and identify its dots.

1. འཁོར་བར་ལྷགས་པ་ལ་མི་དགའ་བ་

2. བདེ་སྤྱུག་གི་ཐབས་ལ་ཚོངས་ཤིང་

3. རང་གི་སྐྱང་བའི་ཡུལ་ལ་མ་འཁྲུལ་བའི་རིག་པ་

## Verbs and Verb Syntax
### *Nominative-Syntactic Verbs*

Like some of the other names for classes or types of verbs (for example, 'agentive-objective'), the name 'nominative-syntactic,' while it applies to most verbs of this class, does not fit all of them.  Thus, whereas most nominative-syntactic verbs have qualifiers marked by syntactic particles, some of them have fifth case qualifiers.

Common nominative-syntactic verbs include the following.

| | | |
|---|---|---|
| གྲོལ་ | ḍöl | *is freed [from], is liberated [from]* |
| ཐར་ | thar | *is liberated [from]* |
| འདའ་ | da | *is beyond, transcends* |
| སྟོང་ | ḍong | *is empty [of]* |

| འབྲེལ་ | ḍêl | is connected [with], is related [to] |
| ཕྲད་ | ṭhë' | meets [with] |
| བྲལ་ | ṭël | is devoid [of], is separated [from] |

The basic syntax of clauses or sentences ending in nominative-syntactic verbs is the following, where the 'syntactic particle' is sometimes the fifth case marker ལས་:

nominative       syntactic particle

| SUBJECT | → | QUALIFIER | → | ← | ATTITUDE VERB |

This syntax is seen in the following example.

*If we meet with the unpleasant ...*

ང་རང་ མི་སྡུག་པ་དང་ ཕྲད་ ན་

|  | NOM |  | SP | SP |  | V | SP |
|--|-----|--|----|----|--|---|----|
|  | ང་རང་ → |  | མི་སྡུག་པ་ | དང་ → | ← | ཕྲད་ | ན་ |

The qualifier in this construction is མི་སྡུག་པ་དང་ and the syntactic particle that marks it is the conjunction དང་.

The other qualifier-marking syntactic particles used with this class of verbs are the five particles that usually mark the agentive case—གིས་, གྱིས་, གྱིས་, འིས་, and ཡིས་—and the originative particle ལས་.

---

Many of the case marking particles also have non-case-marking syntactic uses. The use of གིས་, གྱིས་, གྱིས་, འིས་, and ཡིས་ to mark the qualifier of a nominative-syntactic verb is an example.

---

However, the use of the originative particle ལས་ with nominative-syntactic verbs is a case-marking use.

Any given verb requires a specific type of qualifier marking particle. There are four types of nominative-syntactic verbs, classified not solely in terms of the type of particle marking the qualifier, but also in terms of the lexical dimension of the verb.

- **Separative verbs** such as ཐར་ and འདའ་ require a fifth case marker (usually ལས་, but sometimes ནས་), yielding a sense of *liberation from* something or *passing beyond* something.

- The qualifiers of **verbs of absence** such as སྟོང་ and དབེན་ (*is isolated*) are marked by syntactic particles otherwise used to mark the agentive case. The qualifier of such verbs states that which is absent and, thus, gives the sense of being *empty of* something or *isolated from* something.

- **Conjunctive verbs** such as ཕྲད་ and འཕྲིལ་ require qualifiers marked by the syntactic particle དང་ (in the sense of *with—meeting with* something or *related to* something).

- **Disjunctive verbs** such as བྲལ་ and འགལ་ also require qualifiers marked by དང་, in the sense of *separation from* something or being *contradictory with* something.

## *Separative Verbs*

The following exemplify the use of separative nominative-syntactic verbs.

*They themselves are free from cyclic existence.*

རང་ཉིད་ འཁོར་བ་ལས་ ཐར་

The qualifier here is འཁོར་བ་ལས་, *from cyclic existence*. This is an actual fifth case usage and, thus, ལས་ is not technically a syntactic particle.

There are also agentive verbs that commonly take fifth case qualifiers—for example, སྐྱབ་ (*provide refuge*) and སྲུང་ (*guard, protect*).

The verb འདའ་ (འདས་ in the past tense) has the sense of *pass beyond* and *transcend*. The noun མྱ་ངན་ལས་འདས་པ་—literally meaning *passed beyond suffering*—derives in part from this verb. འདའ་ is also used in the sense of *going beyond* what one should, as in the following example.

*the dangers of transgressing the precepts*

བསླབ་པ་ལས་ འདས་པའི་ ཉེས་དམིགས་

In the following example, the nominative-syntactic clause acts as the objective complement of the verb འདོད་.

---

*a mind desiring liberation from those*

---

དེ་དག་ནས་ ཐར་པར་ འདོད་པའི་ བློ་

---

## Verbs of Absence

Verbs of absence include སྟོང་ (*is empty*), དབེན་ (*is isolated from, is free of*), དབུལ་ (*lacks, is devoid of*), and ཡོངས་ (*destitute, devoid of*).

There is also a verb འབུལ་ (*gives, offers*) of which དབུལ་ is the future tense form. The དབུལ་ that means *lacks* is a different verb.

For a full expression of their meaning, these verbs require qualifiers—stating what is absent—marked by the syntactic particles otherwise used to mark the agentive case: གིས་, ཀྱིས་, གྱིས་, འིས་, and ཡིས་.

The first two examples illustrate the basic syntax used with this type of verb.

---

*Forests **are isolated** from commotion.*

---

ནགས་ཚལ་ འདུ་འཛིས་ དབེན་ ཞིང་

---

ནགས་ཚལ་ is the nominative subject and འདུ་འཛིས་ (the noun འདུ་འཛི་ marked by the syntactic particle ས་) is the qualifier.

The next example isolates བྱེ་ཐང་—the subject (technically, the understood subject) of the verb དབེན་—using a clause connective.

---

*a desert **devoid** of water*

---

ཆུས་ དབེན་པའི་ བྱེ་ཐང་

---

ཆུས་ is ཆུ་ followed by the syntactic particle ས་. བྱེ་ཐང་ abbreviates བྱེ་མའི་ཐང་ (*a plain of sand*).

In the next example, the qualifier is the clause རང་བཞིན་གྱིས་ཡོད་པས་, which itself incorporates a qualifier—རང་བཞིན་གྱིས་ (*inherently*)—marked by the same sort of syntactic particle.

*All phenomena **are empty** of inherent existence.*

ཆོས་ཐམས་ཅད་ རང་བཞིན་གྱིས་ཡོད་པས་ སྟོང་ ངོ་

ཆོས་ཐམས་ཅད་ is the subject of སྟོང་. རང་བཞིན་གྱིས་ཡོད་པ་ (*inherently existing*) is an existential verb clause in which the noun རང་བཞིན་ is given an adverbial sense by the syntactic particle གྱིས་.

## *Conjunctive Verbs*

These verbs have qualifiers marked by the syntactic particle དང་ (where the qualifier states that to which the verb relates the subject). Conjunctive verbs include འབྲེལ་ (*is related*), ཕྲད་ (*meets*), བཅས་ (*possesses*), and མཐུན་ (*accords, is in harmony*).

Of these four verbs, འབྲེལ་, བཅས་, and མཐུན་ are most commonly used in clause connective situations such as the following.

*phenomena related to positive actions*

དགེ་བའི་ལས་དང་འབྲེལ་བའི་ཆོས་

དགེ་བའི་ལས་དང་ is the qualifier of the nominative-syntactic verb འབྲེལ་. The lexical particle བ་ makes it a verbal adjective, connected using the case marking particle འི་ to the noun ཆོས་. Were ཆོས་ to precede the verbal, it would be the nominative subject of འབྲེལ་.

The following is an example of the same syntax.

*a nonconceptual mind not connected with any appearing object*

སྣང་ཡུལ་ གང་དང་ཡང་ མ་འབྲེལ་བའི་ རྟོག་མེད་

The pronoun གང་ཡང་ modifies the noun སྣང་ཡུལ་ (སྣང་བའི་ཡུལ་, *appearing object*): སྣང་ཡུལ་གང་ཡང་ (*any appearing object*).

Note the way in which the pronoun is broken by the syntactic particle དང་, forming གང་དང་ཡང་. Where གང་ཡང་ by itself means *any*, with a negative it means *none*.

In the following example, the syntactic particle is not explicitly stated.

*If one does not have the wisdom realizing the mode of abiding ...*[215]

གནས་ལུགས་ རྟོགས་པའི་ ཤེས་རབ་ མི་ལྡན་ན།

Thus, ཤེས་རབ་མི་ལྡན་ན། means ཤེས་རབ་དང་མི་ལྡན་ན།.

There are also *agentive* verbs (such as སྦྱོར་) which express the joining of things or people that may take a qualifier marked by the syntactic particle དང་. They are not included in this type of nominative verb.

## Disjunctive Verbs

Disjunctive verbs have qualifiers marked by the syntactic particle དང་ (where the qualifier states that from which the verb separates the subject). བྲལ་ (*is free of*) and འགལ་ (*is contradictory, contradicts, is mutually exclusive*) are disjunctive verbs.

*Such a mind is free of attachment.*

བློ་དེ་འདྲ་ ཆགས་པ་དང་ བྲལ།

A frequently cited definition of direct perception (མངོན་སུམ་) utilizes this synatx in a clause connective construction.

*knowledge which is free of conceptuality and unmistaken*

རྟོག་པ་དང་བྲལ་ཞིང་ མ་འཁྲུལ་བའི་ རིག་པ་

The clause is a compound construction—རྟོག་པ་དང་བྲལ་ཞིང་མ་འཁྲུལ་བ་. རྟོག་པ་དང་བྲལ་ and མ་འཁྲུལ་བ་ are joined by the conjunctive syntactic particle ཞིང་.

# Drill 19.5

Translate the following into Tibetan.

1. That lacking arising and cessation is a non-product.
2. Such a mind is bereft of happiness.
3. It follows that the subject, a red pot, is mutually exclusive with a red pillar.

## Drill 19.6

Translate the following.

1 ཚིན་མོངས་དང་བྲལ་བར་བྱའོ།

2 རང་གི་ངོ་བོས་དབེན་པ།

3 ལྷ་མའི་བཀའ་དང་འགལ་བ།

4 འཁོར་བའི་ཕུན་སུམ་ཚོགས་པ་དང་ཕུད་ན་

5 ང་རང་གྲོགས་དང་ཕུད་ནས་དགའ།

## Case Marking and Syntactic Particles
### *Particles Used as Both Case Marking and Syntactic Particles*

Tibetan has nineteen case marking particles. Some of them are usually used as case marking particles, whereas others are more commonly used as syntactic particles. For example, the particle ནས་ is used more frequently after core verbs to indicate continuation or sequence than it is as a case marking particle.

*The Teacher, having turned the wheel of the doctrine, ...*

སྟོན་པས་ ཆོས་ཀྱི་འཁོར་ལོ་ བསྐོར་ནས།

On the other hand, the particles གི་, ཀྱི་, གྱི་, འི་, and ཡི་—while they may be used after verbs as syntactic particles indicating disjunction (*but, even though*)—are much more commonly seen as connective case markers.

The agentive case marking particles—གིས་, ཀྱིས་, གྱིས་, འིས་, and ཡིས་—have various non-case-marking usages. As syntactic particles after verbs they indicate disjunction, but, more often than that, they are seen after nouns and adjectives in an adverbial sense.

*naturally existent    [established by way of its own characteristic nature]*

རང་གི་མཚན་ཉིད་ཀྱིས་གྲུབ་པ།

The particle ལ་ is used both disjunctively and conjunctively—usually, but not invariably, after verbs. The first of the following two examples illustrates the use of the syntactic particle ལ་ after a verb; the second show its use after a noun.

---

*the permutation that is impermanent **but** is not a color*

མི་རྟག་པ་ཡིན་ལ་ཁ་དོག་མ་ཡིན་པའི་མུ་

---

*white **and** so forth*

དཀར་པོ་ལ་སོགས་པ་

---

However, ལ་ is used more often as a second, fourth, or seventh case marking particle.

ན་ may be used to mark the second, fourth, or seventh cases, but more often is seen marking the seventh case place or time. However, its most common usage is as a conditional syntactic particle.

---

*If [one] does not realize emptiness,*
   *one will not become liberated from cyclic existence.*

སྟོང་ཉིད་ མ་རྟོགས་ན་ འཁོར་བ་ལས་ འགྲོལ་བར་མི་འགྱུར་

---

The other particles in the *la* group (that is, སུ་, ར་, རུ་, ཏུ་, and དུ་) are used as verb modifying syntactic particles (creating, for instance, infinitives such as the བསྒོམ་པར་ in བསྒོམ་པར་བྱ་—*one will cultivate*).

Nine of the nineteen case marking particles also occur as common words.

- ●  ལས་ also means *action* (that is, *karma*).
- ●  སུ་ also means *who.*
- ●  རུ་ also means *section* or *[animal] horn.*
- ●  དུ་ is a common contraction of དུ་མ་ (*many*).
- ●  ན་ is also a verb meaning *is ill.*
- ●  ར་ also means *goat.*
- ●  ལ་ also means *[mountain] pass.*

- བྱས་ is also the imperative form of the verb བགྱི་ (*do*).
- ནས་ also means *barley*.


# Rhetorical Tools
## *Rhetorical Sequences*

The rhetorical sequence in Chapter Eighteen ended in the following consequence.

---

*It follows that the subject, a pot, is a basic existent
    because of being established by valid cognition.*

བུམ་པ་ཆོས་ཅན། གཞི་གྲུབ་ཡིན་པར་ཐལ། ཚད་མས་གྲུབ་པ་ཡིན་པའི་ཕྱིར།

---

If the reason—ཚད་མས་གྲུབ་པ་—is to prove བུམ་པ་གཞི་གྲུབ་ཡིན་པ་ (*pot's being a basic existent*), three criteria must be met.

1  བུམ་པ་ཚད་མས་གྲུབ་པ་ཡིན།—a pot must be established by prime cognition.
2  ཚད་མས་གྲུབ་པ་ཡིན་ན་གཞི་གྲུབ་ཡིན་པས་ཁྱབ།—whatever is established by prime cognition must necessarily be a basic existent.
3  གཞི་གྲུབ་མ་ཡིན་ན་ཚད་མས་གྲུབ་པ་མ་ཡིན་པས་ཁྱབ།—whatever is not a basic existent must necessarily not be established by prime cognition.

Thus, once the claim བུམ་པ་ཆོས་ཅན། གཞི་གྲུབ་ཡིན་པར་ཐལ། ཚད་མས་གྲུབ་པ་ཡིན་པའི་ཕྱིར། has been made, two things must be established: (1) the reason (ཚད་མས་གྲུབ་པ་) must be proven to be a quality of the subject (བུམ་པ་) and (2) it must be demonstrated that whatever is the reason is necessarily also the predicate (གཞི་གྲུབ་) of the consequence statement (བུམ་པ་གཞི་གྲུབ་ཡིན་པ་). Proving the latter establishes both the second and third criteria listed above.

There are, therefore, two possible avenues that a rhetorical sequence may take once a consequence or syllogism is stated:

1  proving that the subject is the reason—here, proving བུམ་པ་ཚད་མས་གྲུབ་པ་ཡིན།;
2  proving that whatever is the reason must necessarily be the predicate of the thesis (or, in a consequence, the predicate of the ཐལ་ statement)—here, proving ཚད་མས་གྲུབ་པ་ཡིན་ན་གཞི་གྲུབ་ཡིན་པས་ཁྱབ།.

In a critical analysis text, the sign that the first avenue is being taken is the statement མ་གྲུབ་ན་—that is, རྟགས་མ་གྲུབ་ན་ (*if [you say] the reason is not proven*). However, this need not be explicitly stated. The second avenue follows the statement ཁྱབ་སྟེ། or མ་ཁྱབ་ ན།  ཁྱབ་པ་ཡོད་པར་ཐལ། (*If [you say], no pervasion, then [I say that] it follows the pervasion exists*).

In the rhetorical sequence now under examination, Pur-bu-jok takes the second avenue, introducing it with the statement ཁྱབ་སྟེ།, which in this instance means the following.

---

*Being a basic existent pervades being established by prime cognition.*
    OR *Whatever is established by prime cognition is necessarily a basic existent.*

---

ཆད་མས་གྲུབ་པ་ཡིན་ན་ གཞི་གྲུབ་ཡིན་པས་ ཁྱབ་སྟེ།

---

Saying ཁྱབ་སྟེ། is Pur-bu-jok's response to his hypothetical opponent's saying མ་ཁྱབ།, a statement that implies the opponent's acceptance of the reason that Pur-bu-jok has just stated. In other words, it means, *I accept that the subject is the reason, but it does not prove what you say it does.* Thus, here, the pervasion statement given by Pur-bu-jok in response means, *Given that you have accepted that a pot (the subject) is established by prime cognition, you have to accept that it is a basic existent.*

Thus, Pur-bu-jok says the following.

---

*[Being a basic existent] pervades [being established by prime cognition] because established by prime cognition is the definition of basic existent.*

---

ཁྱབ་སྟེ།   ཆད་མས་གྲུབ་པ། གཞི་གྲུབ་ཀྱི་མཚན་ཉིད་ཡིན་པའི་ཕྱིར།

---

Expanded to its full form and translated in a syntax more natural to English, this syllogism reads as follows.

---

*Whatever is established by prime cognition is necessarily a basic existent because established by prime cognition is the definition of basic existent.*

---

ཆད་མས་གྲུབ་པ་ཡིན་ན་ གཞི་གྲུབ་ཡིན་པས་ཁྱབ་སྟེ།
    ཆད་མས་གྲུབ་པ། གཞི་གྲུབ་ཀྱི་མཚན་ཉིད་ཡིན་པའི་ཕྱིར།

---

As seen in Chapter Seventeen, ཆད་མས་གྲུབ་པ་ is the definition of གཞི་གྲུབ་. A definition and what it defines are—according to the definition of definition—equivalent. Thus, whatever is a thing's definition is also that thing, and vice versa.

This statement marks the *first* conclusion of the rhetorical sequence under examination.

> A rhetorical sequence often has two conclusions. The first occurs at the end of a route that begins with a proof of the reason in the first consequence. The second occurs at the end of a route that begins by demonstrating how the first consequence is, in fact, a contradiction in terms.

In the present rhetorical sequence, the first consequence was the following.

---

*It follows that the subject, a pot, is permanent because of being a basic existent.*

བུམ་པ་ཆོས་ཅན། རྟག་པ་ཡིན་པར་ཐལ། གཞི་གྲུབ་པའི་ཕྱིར།

---

Thus, in this rhetorical sequence, the second route occurs when the hypothetical opponent accepts the initial statement, བུམ་པ་ཆོས་ཅན། རྟག་པ་ཡིན་པར་ཐལ།. This is marked in the critical analysis style by the following statement.

---

*If [one] accepts the root [consequence—that pots are permanent], ...*

རྩ་བར་འདོད་ན།

---

Pur-bu-jok then proves that a pot cannot be permanent.

---

*If [one] accepts the root [consequence], then it follows that a pot, the subject, is not permanent because of being impermanent.*

རྩ་བར་འདོད་ན། བུམ་པ་ཆོས་ཅན། རྟག་པ་མ་ཡིན་པར་ཐལ། མི་རྟག་པ་ཡིན་པའི་ཕྱིར།

---

Why is a pot impermanent?

---

*If [one says that] it is not established [that a pot is impermanent], then it follows that [a pot], the subject, is [impermanent] because of being momentary.*

མ་གྲུབ་ན། དེ་ཆོས་ཅན། དེར་ཐལ། སྐད་ཅིག་མ་ཡིན་པའི་ཕྱིར།

---

Why does being momentary prove being impermanent? Because being momentary is the definition of impermanent, and definitions and what they define are mutually pervasive.

---

*[Being impermanent] pervades [being momentary]*
*because momentary is the definition of impermanent.*

---

ཁྱབ་སྟེ། སྐད་ཅིག་མ་ མི་རྟག་པའི་མཚན་ཉིད་ ཡིན་པའི་ཕྱིར།

---

This is the conclusion of the second route of this rhetorical sequence. The only reason to go further would be to prove that སྐད་ཅིག་མ་ is, in fact, the definition of མི་རྟག་ པ་, a move Pur-bu-jok does not choose to make here. Such a proof, were it attempted, might well involve the quotation of *tradition* (ལུང་—Skt. *āgama*), perhaps making use of a sutra passage or, more likely in the present circumstance, a citation of one of the Indian Sutra School thinkers such as Dharmakīrti.

## Rhetorical Tools
### *Four Permutations*

A commonplace example of two things with four permutations is the pair consisting of (A) the color blue (ཁ་དོག་སྔོན་པོ་) and (B) the color of a pot (བུམ་པའི་ཁ་དོག་).

- The color of a blue pot is both (A) and (B)—both the color blue and the color of a pot.

- The color of a blue lake is (A) but not (B)—it is the color blue but is not the color of a pot.

- The color of a red pot is (B) but not (A)—it is the color of a pot but not the color blue.

- There are many things that are neither (A) nor (B)—neither the color blue nor the color of a pot; some examples are the pot itself, a horse, an eye consciousness perceiving blue, and the non-product space (which is a permanent phenomenon).

A skillful analysis of permutations attempts to produce examples that would seem not to meet particular criteria, but actually do. Thus—as regards the fourth permutation in this case—whereas a horse is certainly neither the color blue nor the color of a pot, it is not a particularly clever illustration of this permutation.

> The principle here is that if two things, A and B, have four permutations, then one must be able to posit:
> 1 something that is both A and B;
> 2 something that is A but is not B;
> 3 something that is B but is not A;
> 4 something that is neither A nor B.

# Patterns in Tibetan Language
## *An Overview of the Classes and Types of Verbs*

Here, first in outline form and then with examples, are the three categories and eight classes of verbs, with their subdivisions.

**CATEGORY ONE**  (verbs with nominative subjects)

Class I — nominative-nominative verbs, also called **linking verbs** (such as ཡིན་)

Class II — nominative-locative verbs

    2.1  simple **verbs of existence** (such as ཡོད་)

    2.2  **verbs of living** (such as གནས་)

    2.3  **verbs of dependence** (such as རྟེན་)

    2.4  **verbs expressing attitudes** (such as ཆགས་)

Class III — nominative-objective verbs

    3.1  **verbs of motion** (such as འགྲོ་)

    3.2  **nominative action verbs** (such as སྐྱེ་)

    3.3  **rhetorical verbs** (such as རུང་ and ཐལ་)

Class IV — nominative-syntactic verbs

    4.1  **separative verbs** (such as སྒྲོལ་) whose qualifiers are marked by the case marking particles ལས་ and ནས་

    4.2  **verbs of absence** (such as སྟོང་) whose qualifiers are marked by the syntactic particles ཀྱིས་, གིས་, གྱིས་, འིས་, and ཡིས་

    4.3  **conjunctive verbs** (such as འབྲེལ་) whose qualifiers are marked by the syntactic particle དང་

    4.4  **disjunctive verbs** (such as བྲལ་) whose qualifiers are marked by the syntactic particle དང་

**CATEGORY TWO**  (verbs with agentive subjects)

Class V — agentive-nominative verbs (such as སྟོན་)

Class VI — agentive-objective verbs (such as བྱ་)

**CATEGORY THREE**  (verbs in specialized usages)

Class VII — purposive-nominative verb of necessity (དགོས་)

Class VIII — locative-nominative verbs

    8.1  **verbs of possession** — a specialized usage of verbs of existence such as ཡོད་

    8.2  **attributive usage** — a specialized usage of agentive verbs such as ཟེར་ and བྱེད་

---

## *1 Nominative-Nominative Verbs*

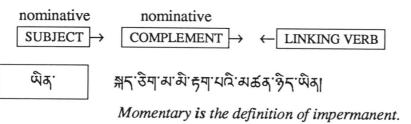

*Momentary is the definition of impermanent.*

## 2.1 *Verbs of Existence*

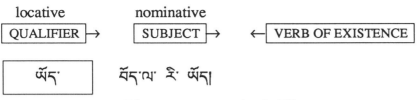

**There are** *mountains in Tibet.*

## 2.2 *Verbs of Living*

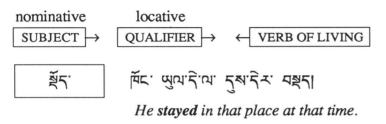

*He* **stayed** *in that place at that time.*

## 2.3 *Verbs of Dependence*

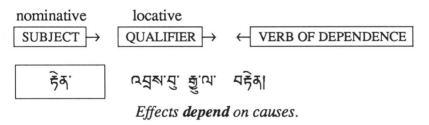

*Effects* **depend** *on causes.*

## 2.4 *Attitude Verbs*

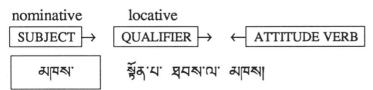

*The Teacher [Buddha]* **is skilled** *in techniques [of liberation].*

## 3.1 Verbs of Motion

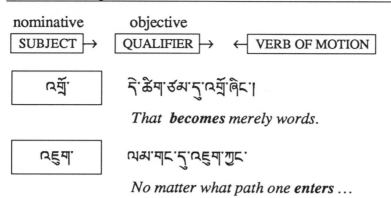

| nominative | objective | |
|---|---|---|
| SUBJECT → | QUALIFIER → | ← VERB OF MOTION |

འགྲོ་

དེ་ཚིག་ཙམ་དུ་འགྲོ་ཞིང་།

*That **becomes** merely words.*

འཇུག་

ལམ་གང་དུ་འཇུག་ཀྱང་

*No matter what path one **enters** …*

## 3.2 Nominative Action Verbs

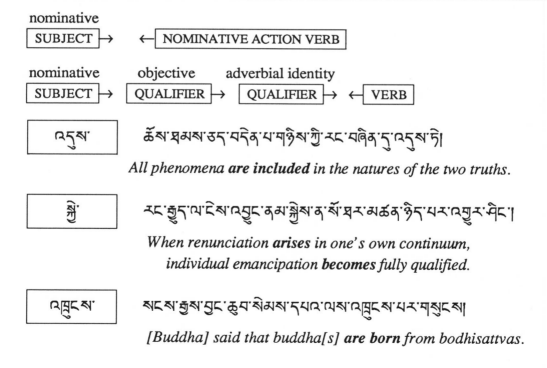

| nominative | |
|---|---|
| SUBJECT → | ← NOMINATIVE ACTION VERB |

| nominative | objective | adverbial identity | |
|---|---|---|---|
| SUBJECT → | QUALIFIER → | QUALIFIER → | ← VERB |

འདུས་

ཆོས་ཐམས་ཅད་བདེན་པ་གཉིས་ཀྱི་རང་བཞིན་དུ་འདུས་ཏེ།

*All phenomena **are included** in the natures of the two truths.*

སྐྱེ་

རང་རྒྱུད་ལ་ངེས་འབྱུང་རྣམ་སྐྱེས་ན་སོ་ཐར་མཚན་ཉིད་པར་འགྱུར་ཞིང་།

*When renunciation **arises** in one's own continuum,*
    *individual emancipation **becomes** fully qualified.*

འབྱུང་

སངས་རྒྱས་བྱང་ཆུབ་སེམས་དཔའ་ལས་འབྱུང་བར་གསུངས།

*[Buddha] said that buddha[s] **are born** from bodhisattvas.*

## *3.3 Rhetorical Verbs*

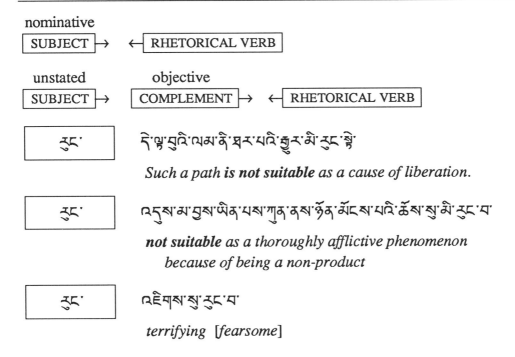

nominative

| SUBJECT |→    ←| RHETORICAL VERB |

unstated                        objective

| SUBJECT |→    | COMPLEMENT |→    ←| RHETORICAL VERB |

| རུང་ |    དེ་ལྟ་བུའི་ལམ་ནི་ཐར་པའི་རྒྱུར་མི་རུང་སྟེ།

*Such a path is **not suitable** as a cause of liberation.*

| རུང་ |    འདུས་མ་བྱས་ཡིན་པས་ཀུན་ནས་ཉོན་མོངས་པའི་ཆོས་སུ་མི་རུང་བ

**not suitable** *as a thoroughly afflictive phenomenon*
*because of being a non-product*

| རུང་ |    འཇིགས་སུ་རུང་བ

*terrifying  [fearsome]*

## *4 Nominative-Syntactic Verbs*

Since the nominative-syntactic verbs were examined in this chapter, they are not reviewed individually here.

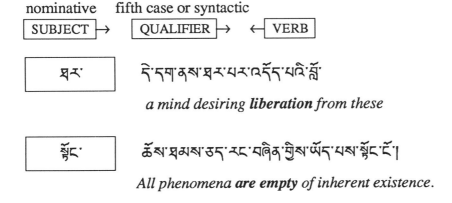

nominative        fifth case or syntactic

| SUBJECT |→    | QUALIFIER |→    ←| VERB |

| ཐར་ |    དེ་དག་ནས་ཐར་པར་འདོད་པའི་བློ་

*a mind desiring **liberation** from these*

| སྟོང་ |    ཆོས་ཐམས་ཅད་རང་བཞིན་གྱིས་ཡོད་པས་སྟོང་ངོ་།

*All phenomena **are empty** of inherent existence.*

## 5 Agentive-Nominative Verbs

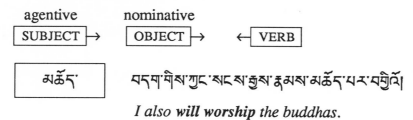

*I also* **will worship** *the buddhas.*

## 6 Agentive-Objective Verbs

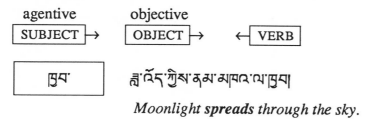

*Moonlight* **spreads** *through the sky.*

## 7 Purposive-Nominative Verbs

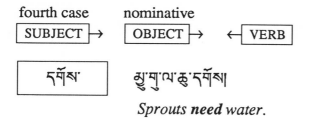

*Sprouts* **need** *water.*

## 8.1 Verbs of Possession

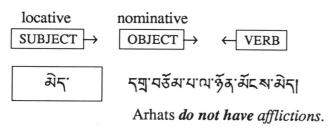

Arhats ***do not have*** *afflictions.*

## 8.2 Attributive Syntax

The verbs བྱེད་, འཆད་, and གསུང་ are used to indicate that something is being *spoken of* in a certain way, *characterized* in a certain way, or something is being *called* a certain name or *referred to* in a certain way. Although these verbs are regularly agentive-nominative verbs, in the above instances, they act sometimes like locative-nominative verbs and sometimes like nominative-locative verbs. The specialized attributive syntax is the following.

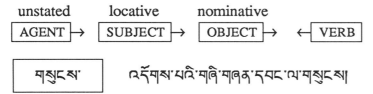

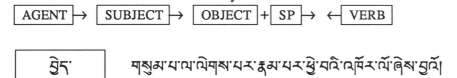

*Dependent phenomena **are called** the basis of imputation.*

An alternate syntax replaces the nominative object with a phrase ending in a quotation marking syntactic particle.

unstated | locative | syntactic
AGENT ⊢→ | SUBJECT ⊢→ | OBJECT + SP ⊢→ | ← VERB

| བྱེད་ | | གསུམ་པ་ལ་ལེགས་པར་རྣམ་པར་ཕྱེ་བའི་འཁོར་ལོ་ཞེས་བྱའོ། |

*To the third **is given** [the name] "wheel of good differentiation."*[216]
OR *The third **is called** "wheel of good differentiation."*

# *Vocabulary*

## *Nouns*

| བཀའ· | ḡa | speech, words [HON] |
|---|---|---|
| གྲོགས· | ṭok | friend, companion |
| ལྕགས· | jak | iron |
| ཉེས·དམིགས· | nyé>-m̄ík | danger |
| ཐང· | thang | plain [geographical] |
| ཐབས· | thap | means, technique, method |
| དེ·ཉིད· | té-nyí' | that itself, reality, adverbial identity [grammar] |
| འདུ·འཛི· | du-<u>dz</u>í | commotion |
| ནགས·ཚལ· | nak-tshël | forest |
| ནམ·མཁའ· | nam-kha | space |
| གནས·ལུགས· | n̄ë>-luk | mode of abiding, reality |
| ཕུན·སུམ·ཚོགས·པ· | phün-s̄um-tshok-b̄a | marvel |
| བོད·སྐད· | pö'-ḡë' | Tibetan language |
| བྱེ·ཐང· | <u>ch</u>é-thang | desert |
| བྱེ·མ· | <u>ch</u>é-ma | sand |
| སྨན· | m̄ën | medicine |
| ར·བ· | <u>dz</u>a-wa | root [consequence] |

| གསེར་ | **s̄ér** | gold |
| ཡེ་ཤེས་ | **ye-s̄hé>** | knowledge, wisdom |
| བསམ་གཏན་ | **s̄am-d̄ën** | concentration |
| བསླབ་པ་ | **l̄ab-ba** | training, precept |

## Verbs

Verbs are marked by the Roman numeral indicating the class to which they belong—that is, the syntax they require.

|   |   |   |   |
|---|---|---|---|
| I | nominative-nominative | V | agentive-nominative |
| II | nominative-locative | VI | agentive-objective |
| III | nominative-objective | VII | purposive-nominative |
| IV | nominative-syntactic | VIII | locative-nominative |

The first part of the name of each class identifies the case of the subject and the second, that of the object, complement, or principal qualifier.

| སྐྱོ་ | **ḡyo** | is sad, depressed, disheartened II |
| ཁྲོ་ | **ṭho** | is angry II |
| མཁས་ | **khë>** | is skilled, is learned II |
| འཁྲུལ་ | **ṭhül** | is mistaken II |
| གུས་ | **kü>** | trusts, respects II |
| གྱུར་ | **gyur** | [past and imperative of འགྱུར་] |
| གྲོལ་ | **ṭöl** | is free IV |
| དགའ་ | **ga** | delight in, enjoy II |
| འགལ་ | **gël** | contradicts IV |
| འགྱུར་ | **gyur** | becomes, changes, is III [present & future] |

| | | |
|---|---|---|
| སྒྱུར་ | **gyur** | change, transform, transmute **V** |
| བཅས་ | **j̄ë>** | possesses, is together with **IV** |
| ཆགས་ | **chak** | is attached to **II** |
| འཆད་ | **chë’** | says, presents, proclaims **V** |
| འཇིགས་ | **jík** | fears **II** |
| སྟོང་ | **d̄ong** | is empty of, lacks |
| བཏགས་ | **d̄ak** | [past of འདོགས་] |
| ཐར་ | **thar** | is liberated **IV** |
| ཐལ་ | **thël** | logically follows **III** |
| ཐོགས་ | **thok** | [imperative of འདོགས་] |
| མཐུན་ | **thün** | accords, is in harmony **IV** |
| འཐད་ | **thë’** | is correct **III** |
| དད་ | **të’** | trusts **II** |
| གདགས་ | **dak** | [future of འདོགས་] |
| འདའ་ | **da** | is beyond, transcends **IV** |
| འདོགས་ | **dok** | designates, imputes **V** |
| ལྡན་ | **dën** | possesses **IV** |
| སྡང་ | **dang** | hates, is averse to **II** |
| ཕོངས་ | **phong** | is destitute, is devoid of **IV** |
| ཕྲད་ | **ṭë’** | meets **IV** |
| བྱུང་ | **c̲hung** | [past of འབྱུང་] |

| | | |
|---|---|---|
| སྒྲུབ་ | ṭël | is free of **IV** |
| དབེན་ | én / wén | is isolated from, lacks **IV** |
| དབུལ་ | ül | lacks, is devoid of **IV** |
| འབྱུང་ | jung | occurs, arises **III** [present & future of འབྱུང་] |
| འབྲེལ་ | ḍél | is related **IV** |
| མོས་ | mö> | is interested **II** |
| རྨོངས་ | m̄ong | is confused **II** |
| སྨྲ་ | m̄a | says, propounds, claims **VI** |
| ཞེན་ | shên | clings, determines, conceives **II** |
| བཟོད་ | sö' | is patient, bears **II** |
| རིགས་ | rík | is correct **III** |
| རུང་ | rung | is suitable, is admissible, is correct **III** |
| ཤོད་ | s̄hö' | [imperative of འཆད་] |
| བཤད་ | s̄hë' | [past and future of འཆད་] |

## Pronouns

| | | |
|---|---|---|
| གང་ཞིག་ | kang-s̲hík | what, which |
| གང་ཡང་ | kang-yang | none [with negative] |
| དེ་འདྲ་ | té-ḍa | such |

## *Adjectives*

| | | |
|---|---|---|
| ཀུན་ནས་ཉོན་མོངས་པ་ | ḡün-në>-nyön-mong-b̄a | thoroughly afflicted |
| གཉིས་ཀ་ | ñyí>-ḡa | both |
| དམ་པ་ | tam -b̄a | holy, superior, ultimate |
| དུ་མ་ | tu-ma | many |
| དེ་ལྟ་བུ་ | té-d̄a-bu | such |
| འདྲ་མོ་ | ḍa-mo | like |
| ཕུན་སུམ་ཚོགས་པ་ | phün-s̄um-tshok-b̄a | marvelous, consummate |
| མི་སྡུག་པ་ | mí-duk-b̄a | unpleasant |
| གསལ་བ་ | s̄ël-wa | clear, bright |
| གསུམ་ག་ | s̄um-ḡa | all three |

## *Adverbs*

| | | |
|---|---|---|
| ངང་གིས་ | ngang-gí> | naturally |

## *Syntactic Particles*

| | | |
|---|---|---|
| གཞན་དུ་ན་ | s̲hën-du-na | otherwise |

# Appendices

# Appendix One
# The Phonemic Dimension

*Pronunciation Rules and Exceptions*
*Transliteration*
*Dictionary Order*

## Phonemics, Phonetics, and Transliteration

Appendix One provides summaries of three topics:

1  rules for the pronunciation of Tibetan syllables;
2  transliteration (writing Tibetan words using the letters of non-Tibetan alphabets—here, the Roman letters of the English alphabet);
3  rules for determining Tibetan dictionary order.

*Translating Buddhism from Tibetan* does not attempt a phonetic analysis of Tibetan, nor does it attempt to record and classify regional variants in pronunciation. The phonemic "equivalents" given throughout this book are based on the pronunciation of Buddhist Tibetan by those for whom Lhasa Tibetan was a cradle language. Tibetans who have been raised in Kham or Amdo, Mongolians, Ladakhis, and expatriate Tibetans who have been raised in India, Europe, or North America pronounce Tibetan differently. Some of the differences are minor, some—especially in the Kham-ba, Am-do-wa, and Ladakhi dialects—are significant.

The Tibetan alphabet is presented in systematic chart form on the next page, with the basic pronunciation of each letter indicated. Note that **tha, pha**, and **tsha** are pronounced as harder forms of **ta, pa**, and **tsa**, respectively, and not as in English.

|         | Column 1 | Column 2 | Column 3 | Column 4 |
|---------|----------|----------|----------|----------|
| Row 1 | ग྄ $\bar{\text{g}}$a | ख྄ kha | ग྄ ka | ང྄ n̲ga |
| Row 2 | ཙ྄ $\bar{\text{j}}$a | ཚ྄ cha[217] | ཇ྄ c̲ha | ཉ྄ n̲ya |
| Row 3 | ད྄ $\bar{\text{d}}$a | ཐ྄ tha | ཏ྄ ta | ན྄ n̲a |
| Row 4 | བ྄ $\bar{\text{b}}$a | ཕ྄ pha | པ྄ pa | མ྄ m̲a |
| Row 5 | ཛ྄ $\bar{\text{d}}$za | ཆ྄ tsha | ཇ྄ d̲za | ཥ྄ wa |
| Row 6 | ཞ྄ s̲ha | ཟ྄ s̲a | འ྄ a | ཡ྄ ya |
| Row 7 | ར྄ ra | ལ྄ la | ཤ྄ $\bar{\text{s}}$ha | ས྄ $\bar{\text{s}}$a |
| Row 8 | ཧ྄ ha | ཨ྄ a |          |          |
| Vowels | ཨ྄ི í | ཨ྄ུ u | ཨ྄ེ é | ཨ྄ོ o |

The Tibetan Alphabet
Phonemic Dimension

Because there are, among native speakers of Tibetan, variant pronunciations of many letters and words, and because so many Tibetan syllables are homophones, Western writers on Buddhism and Tibet have generally not presented their readers with the pronounced forms of Tibetan words, but have transliterated Tibetan—replacing Tibetan letters with "equivalent" Roman letters from Western alphabets. Writing Tibetan using the Roman alphabet is called **transliteration** or **romanization**. Several transliteration schemes are outlined later in this appendix.

One unfortunate side-effect of transliteration has been to instill in speakers of Western languages the idea that Tibetan root letters are pronounced as they are transliterated. Since a ཀ is transliterated as *ka*, English speakers tend to pronounce this letter **ka**, whereas it is pronounced **ḡa** by most Tibetan speakers. Both Western scholars and young Tibetans raised in exile exhibit a tendency to pronounce Tibetan consonants the way they are transliterated into English.

## The Phonemic Dimension of Tibetan

The Tibetan alphabet is called **ḡa-ka** (ཀ་ཁ་), after its first two letters, or **a-lí-ḡa-lí** (ཨ་ལི་ཀ་ལི་—*the vowels and consonants*). It has thirty consonants and four vowels which are combined into syllables as short as one letter and as long as seven letters (if vowel markers are counted as letters). In terms of spelling, a letter in a syllable is either:

1 a root letter

2 a vowel marker

3 a prefix

4 a superscribed letter

5 a subscribed letter

6 a suffix

7 a secondary suffix.

Prefixes, superscripts, subscripts, suffixes, and secondary suffixes are all consonants. The only component of a Tibetan syllable that is pronounced with a vowel is the root letter. (Suffixes are often pronounced, but they *follow* the vowel.)

1   All thirty consonants are potential root letters.

2   Apart from the inherent **a** sound of all Tibetan root letters, there are four vowel markers: ཨི་, ཨུ་, ཨེ་, and ཨོ་ (shown on the letter ཨ་).

3   The letters ག་, ད་, བ་, མ་, and འ་ are the five possible prefixes.

4   The letters ར་, ལ་, and ས་ may be superscribed to some (but not all) root letters.

5   The letters ཡ་, ར་, ལ་, and ཝ་ are the letters that may be subscribed.

6   The letters ག་, ང་, ད་, ན་, བ་, མ་, འ་, ར་, ལ་, and ས་ are the ten suffixes.

7   Only ད་ and ས་ may function as secondary suffixes.

The root letter is the main letter of a Tibetan syllable and is the letter under which a syllable or word is alphabetized in a dictionary or lexicon.

●   The root letter is almost always sounded first.  Prefixes and superscribed letters, although written prior to a root letter, are never themselves pronounced.

●   The root letter carries the vowel—either the ཨ་ (**a**) sound inherent in a Tibetan consonant or one of the four vowels (i, u, e, and o—pronounced **í, u, é,** and **o**).

●   If there is a subscript in the syllable, it can only be subscribed to the root letter.

●   If there is a superscript in the syllable, it is superscribed to the root letter.

Despite the number of consonants that may be piled up in a Tibetan syllable, it is more often than not the case that most are not pronounced with their own full value. Most Tibetan words are like the English word *knight*, in which only the *n, i,* and *t* are pronounced.  Thus, in terms of its *pronunciation* a typical Tibetan syllable has only three parts:

1   an initial consonant sound (provided by the root letter);

2   one vowel sound (carried by the root letter);

3   an optional closing consonant (the suffix).

## *Vowels*

The basic vowel sound inherent in every Tibetan consonant and, thus, in every Tibetan syllable is an **a**—the sound of the 'a' in the English word *farther* and the 'o' in the American pronunciation of *opt*. The other four Tibetan vowels are indicated by markers written either above or below the Tibetan root letter.

The non-**a** vowels are transliterated as 'i,' 'u,' 'e,' and 'o'. If the 'i' and the 'e' are pronounced as English speakers would intuitively pronounce them, the result will not be recognizably Tibetan. Their pronunciations are closer to the French pronunciations of these letters than to standard English pronunciation.

- The Tibetan ཨི་—'i'—is pronounced like the 'ee' in *keep*.
- The Tibetan ཨུ་—'u'—is pronounced like the 'u' in *tune*.
- The Tibetan ཨེ་—'e'—is usually pronounced like the 'a' in *fade*.
- The Tibetan ཨོ་—'o'—is pronounced like the 'o' in *bone*.

The pronunciation of vowels is also affected by suffix letters. A more complete list of Tibetan vowel sounds is the following.

**a**     the vowel sound in the first syllable of *farther*, corresponding to the Tibetan ཨ་;

**ĕ**     the vowel sound in *edge*, as heard in ངན་ and ལས་;

**é**     the vowel sound in *say*, corresponding to the Tibetan ཨེ་;

**ê**     a sound between the vowels in *same* and *set*, as in སེམས་;

**í**     the vowel sound in *keep*, corresponding to the Tibetan ཨི་;

**î**     the vowel sound in *bin*, heard in the Tibetan ཡིན་;

**o**     the vowel sound in *boat*, corresponding to the Tibetan ཨོ་;

**ö**     like the vowel sound in the first syllable of *surprise* pronounced with pursed lips—as heard in དོན་;

**u**     the vowel sound in *tune*, corresponding to the Tibetan ཨུ་;

**ü**     like the vowel sound in *push* pronounced with pursed lips—as heard in ཚུལ་.

## *Consonants*

As seen above (in the four column, eight row chart of the alphabet), there are regular phonemic patterns in at least some of the rows of consonants. In each of the first five rows, there is a repeated pattern of aspiration and tone. (The exception is the ཝ [**wa**] at the end of Row 5.)

- The first consonant in each or these rows is high in tone and lacks aspiration.
- The second is of middle tone and is strongly aspirated.
- The third consonant is low in tone and, by itself, is semi-aspirate—with the exception of the Row 5 letter ཇ which, in the dialect presented in this book, is not aspirated; it is pronounced **dza**.
- The fourth is a nasal and low in tone.

The phonemic transcriptions of the second column consonants is potentially confusing. The second column **cha** is technically a **chha**, a fully aspirated and middle tone version of what is a low tone, partially aspirated sound in the third column. The Tibetan **tha** is a hard 't', not the **th** in the English word 'the' but the **t** in 'tight'. The Tibetan **pha** is a hard 'ph', not the **ph** in the English word 'phone' but the **p** in 'pop'.

The following are phonemic transcriptions of Tibetan consonants where differences in tone are potentially confusing.

- Whereas **b̄a** is pronounced with a high tone, **ba** has a low tone.
- Whereas **cha** is pronounced with a middle tone, **c̱ha** has a low tone.
- Whereas **d̄a** is pronounced with a high tone, **da** has a low tone.
- Whereas **ḡa** is pronounced with a high tone, **ga** has a low tone.
- Whereas **j̄a** is pronounced with a high tone, **ja** has a low tone.
- The sound represented by **ka** is pronounced with a low tone.
- The sound represented by **kha** is pronounced with a middle tone.
- The sound represented by **pa** is pronounced with a low tone.
- The sound represented by **pha** is pronounced with a middle tone and is not the English 'ph' in *phone*.

- Whereas s̄a is pronounced with a high tone, <u>s</u>a has a low tone.
- Whereas s̄ha is pronounced with a high tone, <u>sh</u>a has a low tone.
- The sound represented by **ta** is pronounced with a low tone.
- The sound represented by **tha** is pronounced with a middle tone and is not the 'th' in the English *the*.

In summary, when **b, d, g, j, k, p,** and **t** are seen with no diacritical marks, they are to be pronounced with a low tone. When the nasals—**ng, ny, n,** and **m**—are seen with no diacritics, they are pronounced with a low tone.

## Suffixes

The letters that may follow the root letter—the four subscribed letters (ཡ', ར', ལ', and ཝ'), the ten suffixes (ག', ང', ད', ན', བ', མ', འ', ར', ལ', and ས'), and the two secondary suffixes (ད' and ས')—are more important for pronunciation than the ones that precede the root letter. Whereas the letters that precede the root letter—the prefixes and superscripts—are almost never pronounced themselves, but do affect the aspiration or tone of the root letter, the letters that follow the root letter—the subscribed letters and suffixes—are usually pronounced with something of their own values.

- Where ཏ' is **ta**, ཏག' is pronounced **tak**.
- Where ཀ' is **ka**, ཀང' is pronounced **kang**.
- Where ཚ' is **tsha**, ཚབ' is pronounced **tshap̣**.
- Where ར' is **ra**, རམ' is pronounced **ram**.
- Where བ' is **b̄a**, དཔའ' is pronounced **b̄a**.
- Where ཕ' is **pha**, ཕར' is pronounced **phar** (that is, a hard **par**).

Other suffix letters are never pronounced with their own value, but do change the pronunciation of some vowels.

- Where ཏ' is **ta**, ཏད' is pronounced **të'** (with the apostrophe symbolizing an abrupt cutting off of the vowel sound).
- Where ན' is **na**, ནས' is pronounced **në>** (with the > symbolizing a falling tone).

Yet other suffix letters both give something of their natural value to a syllable and change the pronunciation of that syllable's vowel.

- Where པ་ is **pha**, པན་ is pronounced **phën**.
- Where ང་ is **nga**, ངལ་ is pronounced **ngël**.

## Prefixes and Superscribed Letters

Although the prefixes and superscripts are almost never pronounced themselves, they *do* alter the aspiration or tone of eight root letters. Found after a prefix or beneath a superscript, the pronunciations of the following root letters change.

- ཀ་ which by itself is pronounced **ka** becomes **ga**.
- ཅ་ which by itself is pronounced **cha** becomes **ja**.
- ཏ་ which by itself is pronounced **ta** becomes **da**.
- པ་ which by itself is pronounced **pa** becomes **ba**.
- ང་ which by itself is low tone becomes high tone—n̄ga.
- ཉ་ which by itself is low tone becomes high tone—n̄ya.
- ན་ which by itself is low tone becomes high tone—n̄a.
- མ་ which by itself is low tone becomes high tone—m̄a.

In summary, when preceded by a prefix or superscribed letter, the first four low tone semi-aspirates (ཀ་, ཅ་, ཏ་, and པ་) lose their aspiration but retain their low tone, while the four nasals (ང་, ཉ་, ན་, and མ་) become high tone.

## Subscribed Letters

Subscribed consonants radically alter the pronunciation of the root letters to which they are affixed.

ཡ་ is subscribed (in the form ྱ) to only seven letters.

- ཀྱ་ is pronounced **ḡya**.
- ཁྱ་ is pronounced **khya**.
- གྱ་ is pronounced **kya** or (with a prefix or superscript) **gya**.

- ● ཡ་ is pronounced not **b̄ya** but **j̄a**—as if it were found in the second row.
- ● ཡ་ is pronounced not **pya** but **cha**.
- ● ཡ་ is pronounced not **pya** but **c̲ha** or (after a prefix or superscript) **ja**.
- ● ཡ་ is pronounced not **mya** but **nya**.

ར་ is subscribed (in the form ྲ ) to thirteen letters.

- ● In Column 1, ཀྲ་, ཏྲ་, and པྲ་ are all an unaspirated, high tone **ḍa**.
- ● In Column 2, ཁྲ་, ཐྲ་, and ཕྲ་ are all a fully aspirated **ṭha**.
- ● In Column 3, གྲ་, དྲ་, and བྲ་ are all a semi-aspirated and low tone **ṭa**.
- ● Three other letters—མྲ་, སྲ་, and ཧྲ་—are pronounced with no change (that is, as **ma**, **s̄a**, and **s̄ha**).
- ● The letter ཧྲ་ is pronounced **hra**.

The dot under the phonemic equivalents *ḍ*, *ṭ*, and *ṭh* indicates a **retroflex** letter. These are similar to the dentals like ཏ་ (**ta**), but, instead of touching the back of the upper front teeth, the tongue is turned backwards on the roof of the mouth, a little behind the upper front teeth.

ལ་ is subscribed to six letters only and does not undergo any change of shape when it is subscribed. In the cases of five of the letters, the root letters become completely silent and only the ལ་ is sounded, but high, as **l̄a**.

- ● ཀླ་, གླ་, བླ་, རླ་, and སླ་ are all pronounced **l̄a**.
- ● When ཟ་ takes this subscription—as ཟླ་—it becomes a low tone **da**.

## Exceptions to the Pronunciation Rules

1   ལ་ superscribed to ཧ་— ལྷ་ —is pronounced **hla**. This is the only case in which a superscribed letter is pronounced. Note that the pronunciation is not **l** followed by **h**, but **hla**—**h** followed by **l**. ལྷ་ means *god* or *deity*.

2   མ་ is pronounced **ma** and not *ṭa*. ས་ is normally pronounced **s̄a**; only sometimes is it pronounced **ḍa**. This follows no discernible pattern.

3   ཧྲ་ is pronounced as it is spelt—**hra**. (It is pronounced neither ṭa, following the general rule, nor **ha**, following the model of ཧ་ being pronounced s̄a. ཧྲིལ་པོ་ is an adjective meaning *complete* and *round*.

4   ཟླ་ is pronounced **da** and not l̄a. The word ཟླ་བ་ (**da-wa**) means *moon*.

5   ད་ as a prefix to the root letter བ་ causes the pronunciation of the བ་ to change in a regular way. The root letter བ་ becomes a high tone w̄a only when it has a ད་ prefix *and has no subscript*. It becomes a high tone ȳa only in those cases in which it has a ད་ prefix and a subscribed ཡ་. Thus, དབང་པོ་ is pronounced w̄ang-b̄o (or āng-b̄o) and དབྱིབས་ is ȳíp.

6   When the generic suffix syllable བ་ is the concluding *syllable* of a word, it is pronounced **wa**; པོ་ in the same situation is pronounced **wo**.

7   Syllables that do not end in suffixes—such as པ་, པོ་, བ་, and བོ་—are declined in the agentive and connective cases by adding, respectively, ས་ and འི་ to the syllables themselves. པ་ becomes པས་ in the agentive case and is pronounced b̄ë>, with a falling tone; པོ་ in the agentive case—པོས་—is b̄ö>. པ་ becomes པའི་ in the connective case, and is pronounced b̄ë, with a flat high tone; in the connective case, པོ་ becomes པོའི་ and is pronounced b̄ö.

8   The letters ཀ་, ཅ་, ད་, and བ་ often lose their aspiration when they are the root letters of the unstressed (second, third, or fourth) syllables of words.

9   Sometimes an འ་ prefix beginning a syllable causes the suffix of the previous syllable to be pronounced as a nasal, as in རྣལ་འབྱོར་ (**ñen-jor**).

## Transliteration

Phonemic equivalents should not be confused with the *transliteration* of Tibetan, a one-to-one substitution of English letters for Tibetan in which each Tibetan letter—whether it is pronounced or not—is represented by a letter of the Roman alphabet.

|  | Column 1 | Column 2 | Column 3 | Column 4 |
|---|---|---|---|---|
| Row 1 | ཀ་ ka | ཁ་ kha | ག་ ga | ང་ nga |
| Row 2 | ཙ་ ca | ཚ་ cha | ཇ་ ja | ཉ་ nya |
| Row 3 | ཏ་ ta | ཐ་ tha | ད་ da | ན་ na |
| Row 4 | པ་ pa | ཕ་ pha | བ་ ba | མ་ ma |
| Row 5 | ཙ་ tsa | ཚ་ tsha | ཛ་ dza | ཝ་ wa |
| Row 6 | ཞ་ zha | ཟ་ za | འ་ 'a | ཡ་ ya |
| Row 7 | ར་ ra | ལ་ la | ཤ་ sha | ས་ sa |
| Row 8 | ཧ་ ha | ཨ་ a |  |  |
| Vowels | ི i | ུ u | ེ e | ོ o |

Turrell Wylie's Standardized
Transliteration System[218]

| | Column 1 | Column 2 | Column 3 | Column 4 |
|---|---|---|---|---|
| Row 1 | ཀ ka | ཁ kha | ག ga | ང ṅa |
| Row 2 | ཙ ca | ཚ cha | ཛ ja | ཉ ña |
| Row 3 | ཏ ta | ཐ tha | ད da | ན na |
| Row 4 | པ pa | ཕ pha | བ ba | མ ma |
| Row 5 | ཙ tsa | ཚ tsha | ཛ dza | ཝ wa |
| Row 6 | ཞ źa | ཟ za | འ 'a | ཡ ya |
| Row 7 | ར ra | ལ la | ཤ śa | ས sa |
| Row 8 | ཧ ha | ཨ a | | |
| Vowels | ི i | ུ u | ེ e | ོ o |

Library of Congress
Tibetan Transliteration

Very few Western studies of Buddhism print Tibetan words in Tibetan letters. Nor, with the exception of the names of places, people, and lineages, is Tibetan cited as it is pronounced. Instead, various conventional transcriptions of Tibetan letters into the Roman alphabet have been devised. The most commonly used **transliteration system** at the current time is the one used by René de Nebesky-Wojkowitz in *Oracles and Demons of Tibet* and by Turrell Wylie of the University of Washington in slightly modified form.[219] (Wylie's modification was to abandon the capitalization of the root letters of words as is seen, for example, in the transcription *rDzogs-chen*.) In the preceding pages, first Wylie's standardized system, then the one used by the United States Library of Congress are presented. Many Western scholars use the Wylie system, although some use the Library of Congress transliteration.[220]

Most of the transliteration equivalents are the same in both systems. The differences lie in the first two nasals—ང and ཉ—and in the letters ཝ and ཧ. The great merit of Wylie's system, in addition to its widespread acceptance, is that no diacritical marks are needed.

## Dictionary Order

The order in which words are listed in a Tibetan dictionary is, first of all, the order in which the consonants are found in the alphabet—ཀ, ཁ, ག, ང, ཅ, ཆ, ཇ, ཉ and so forth—and then, within each letter, the order of the vowels. (Using ཀ as an example, the order of the vowels is: ཀ, ཀི, ཀུ, ཀེ, ཀོ—that is, a, i, u, e, o).

The following is a description of the order used in the *New Compilation Lexicon* for the root letter ཀ.[221] Words and particles are always listed with their root letters, never by their prefixes or superscriptions, although these other letters do occur first in spelling.

1   First, the bare root letter—that is, one with neither superscript nor subscript—is followed by the suffixes, in alphabetical order (ག, ང, ད, ན, བ, མ, འ, ར, ལ, ས):

    ཀ ཀག ཀང་ ཀན་ ཀར.

2    Once that list is finished, the next vowel—i—is then added to the bare
     root letter (making ཀི་), to which the suffixes are then added in order.
     These words and particles are then followed by the ཀུ་s, ཀེ་s, and ཀོ་s:

     ཀི་ ཀིན་ ཀུ་ ཀུག་ ཀུམ་ ཀེ་ ཀེག་ ཀོ་ ཀོག་ ཀོལ་.

     Within each LETTER + SUFFIX combination, syllables with secondary
     suffixes immediately follow syllables with the same primary suffix:

     ཀུ་ ཀུག་ ཀུགས་ ཀུམ་ ཀུམས་.

3    Once all the combinations of bare root letters, vowels, and suffixes have
     been listed, the various subscriptions are then added to the bare root
     letter, and the entire sequence seen in steps 1 and 2 is then repeated—for
     each subscript. The first subscript is ྭ་, which is fairly rare. Following
     the ཀྭ་ words are the ཀྱ་ words and particles, then the ཀྲ་s and the ཀླ་s.
     Here—in dictionary order—are some representative ཀྱ་ syllables:

     ཀྱུ་ ཀྱུག་ ཀྱུལ་ ཀྱེ་ ཀྱེས་ ཀྱུ་ ཀྱུག་ ཀྱུར་ ཀྱེ་ ཀྱོ་.

     As before, within each LETTER + SUFFIX combination, syllables with
     secondary suffixes immediately follow syllables with the same primary
     suffix:

     ཀློ་ ཀློག་ ཀློགས་ ཀློང་ ཀློད་.

4    Once all the combinations of root letter, subscripts, vowels, and suffixes
     have been listed, the prefix letters—in the order ག་, ད་, བ་, མ་, འ་ —are then
     added to the bare root letter, and the sequence seen in steps 1 through 3
     is recapitulated *for each prefix*:

     དགག་ དགའ་ དགུ་ དགོར་  དགུར་ དགྱིལ་ དགྱུག་ དགྱུགས་ དགྲབ་ དགྲེ་ དགྲོགས་

     བགག་ བགད་ བགུ་ བགུམས་ བགོལ་ བགུགས་ བགྱིག་ བགྱུན་ བགྲ་ བགླག་.

5    Once all combinations of root letters, vowels, consonants, with prefixes
     and subscripts have been listed, one then begins all over again with the
     bare root letter and the superscribed ར་:

     རྐ་ རྐང་ རྐུ་ རྐུན་ རྐེ་ རྐོ་ རྐོས་.

6 The various subscriptions are then added to the root letter and super-scribed ར་, as in steps 1 through 3:

ཀྲུ་ ཀྲུང་ ཀྲུན་ ཀྲུང་ ཀྲུངས་ ཀྲུལ་.

These would be followed by ཀོ་ with subscribed ར་, if such a combination existed.

7 Then—prior to adding the various prefix letters steps 5 and 6 are reca-pitulated for each superscribed letter:

ཤག་ ཤ་ ཤུ་ ཤྲུ་.

8 Step 4 is then recapitulated—that is, once all the combinations of super-scribed root letters with the various subscripts, vowels, and suffixes have been listed, the various prefix letters are then added to them, and the sequence seen in steps 1 through 3 is recapitulated for each prefix:

བཀལ་ བཀལས་ བཀུང་

བཀྲ་ བཀྲང་ བཀྲངས་ བཀྲུ་ བཀྲེ་ བཀྲེལ་ བཀྲུད་ བཀྲོགས་.

Most Tibetan words have more than one syllable, of course, and this is handled as it is in English dictionary order. Words are alphabetized first by their initial syllable. All words with the same first syllable are alphabetized within that based on their second syllables. If a conflict remains, later syllables are examined until the two words can be differentiated.

What follows on the next page is a representative alphabetical listing of words whose first syllables center on the root letter ག་.[222] Individual words are separated by bullets (•) and alphabetical order is to be seen by reading from left to right.

ག་ • གཁལ་ • གག་ • གག་ཚལ་ • གཔེ་མོ་ • གབོན་ • གཆད་ • གན་ •

གན་མེད་ • གནང་ • གཔར་ • གཙམ་ • གཞ་ • གརེ་ • གཱུ་ • གཀག་པ་ •

གང་བ་ • གརཔོ་ • གིགུ་ • གུགུལ་ • གུསྲ་ • གུང་ • གོ་ • གོཁི་ • གོང་ •

གུགུ་ • གུདག་ • གུགཔ་ • གྱེནཔ་ • གྱེས་ • གྱོགས་ •

གྲ་ ・ གྲམ་ ・ གྲུ་ ・ གྲགཔ་ ・ གྲགས་ ・ གྲང་བ་ ・ གྲངས་ ・

གླ་ ・ གླིང་ཆེན་ ・ གླུད་ ・ གླིང་ ・

དཀག་པ་ ・ དཀང་བ་ ・ དཀའ་བ་ ・ དཀའ་ཕྱུན་ ・ དཀར་བ་ ・ དཀུ་ ・ དཀུ་པ་ ・

དཀུང་ ・ དཀུད་ ・ དགེ་སྣོན་ ・ དགེ་ཚུལ་ ・ དགེ་བཤེས་ ・ དགོ་བ་ ・ དགོས་པ་ ・

དགྱེ་བ་ ・ དགྲ་ ・ དགྲོལ་བ་ ・

བཀད་པ་ ・ བཀོ་ ・ བཀོམ་བྱུ་ ・ བགྲད་པ་ ・ བགྲོད་ལམ་ ・

མཁལ་བ་ ・ མཁུ་ ・ མཁྱེན་པ་ ・ འཁོ་བ་ ・ འཁོག་པ་ ・ འཁོགས་ ・ འཁྲོས་ ・

ང་ ・ ངང་ ・ ངད་པོ་ ・ ངན་པ་ ・ ངུ་ ・ ངུན་ ・ ངོ་ ・ རྒྱ་ ・ རྒྱ་གར་ ・

རྒྱགས་པ་ ・ རྒྱལ་ཆབ་ ・ རྒྱལ་སྲས་ ・ རྒྱུ་ ・ རྒྱུད་ ・ རྒྱོ་ ・

ཁ་ ・ ཁར་ ・ ཁོ་ ・ ཁོ་བསྟན་ ・ ཁོམ་པ་ ・ སྐ་གཅན་ ・ སྐྱལ་མ་ ・

བཀལ་ ・ བཀྱུ་ ・ བཀྱིངས་པ་ ・ བཀྱར་པ་ ・ བཀྱལ་བ་

# Appendix Two
# The Structure of Tibetan

*Parts of Speech*
*The Science of the Dots*

## Words and Particles

In the lexical and syntactic dimensions of Tibetan (see Chapter Eight), there are four principal categories of linguistic units (introduced and defined in Chapter Nine):

- words (such as སྨན་པ་ and ཡིན་);

- lexical particles (such as པ་, རྣམས་, and རྣམ་པར་);

- case marking particles (such as གྱིས་ and ལ་);

- syntactic particles (such as སྟེ་ and དང་).

A word is a part of speech that has its own meaning and does not serve merely to relate other parts of speech to one another. Words are either nouns, verbs, pronouns, adjectives, adverbs, or postpositions.

| words | སྨན་པ|ས་ | ནད་པ|ལ་ | སྨན་ | སྟེ|ར |

*A doctor gives medicine to the ill.*

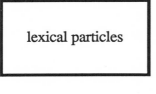

སྨན་པ་ས་ ནད་པ་ རྣམས་ ལ་ སྨན་ སྟེར། 

*A doctor gives medicine to the ill.*

རྣམ་པར་ཤེས་ པ་ དང་གཟུགས་ དག་ འགལ་ བ་ ཡིན་ནོ། 

*Consciousness and form are mutually exclusive.*

Lexical particles are merely parts of words, functioning only in the lexical dimension.  Words, case marking particles, and syntactic particles function at the next higher level, in the syntactic dimension.

case marking particles

སྨན་པ་ས་ ནད་པ་ ལ་ སྨན་ སྟེར། 

*A doctor gives medicine to the ill.*

syntactic particles

རྣམ་པར་ཤེས་པ་ དང་ གཟུགས་ ནི་ འགལ་བ་ཡིན་ ནོ། 

*Consciousness and form are mutually exclusive.*

ཡོད་པ་ལ་དབྱེ་ ན་ རྟག་པ་ དང་ མི་རྟག་པ་གཉིས་ ཡོད། 

*If existents are divided, there are two,*
                              *permanent and impermanent.*

## Phrases, Clauses, and Sentences

Lexical, case marking, and syntactic particles—unlike words—cannot stand by themselves.  While lexical particles are found only as parts of words, case marking and syntactic particles serve only to relate words, phrases, and clauses to one another.

- A **phrase** is a group of words that forms a meaningful unit but is not a clause. There are both verb phrases (for example, compound verbs and verbs with auxiliary verbs) and noun phrases (see Appendix Three).

- A **clause** is a meaningful group of words that ends either in a verbal (such as ཡོད་པ་, བྱས་པ་, or སྟོན་པ་), a verb followed by a continuative particle such as ནས་, or a verb followed by a rhetorical syntactic particle such as ན་. In general, a clause is similar to a sentence, the difference being that a Tibetan sentence is a complete thought, whereas clauses either act as units within larger clauses or sentences, or indicate (through the use of a continuative particle) that there is more to come.

- A **sentence** is a meaningful group of words, phrases, and clauses ending in a terminal verb. Sentences may end either in verbs in their simple core forms, in verbs followed by a terminating syntactic particle, or in verb phrases formed of verbs followed by an auxiliary phrase. Tibetan sentences may be quite long, much longer than English sentences.

| phrases | སེམས་ཡིད་རྣམ་པར་ཤེས་པ་ |
|---|---|

*mind, mentality, and consciousness*

གཞན་ལའང་ མར་ ཤེས་པར་བྱས་ ལ་

*[One] has understood others also as [one's] mother.*[223]

| clauses | སྒྲ་རྟག་པར་འཛིན་པའི་ རྟོག་པ་ |
|---|---|

*thought apprehending sound as permanent*

དེ་སྟོན་པས་གཟིགས་ནས། ཀུན་དགའ་བ་ལ་དྲིས་

*The Teacher having seen that, [he] asked Ananda …*[224]

ཡོད་པ་ལ་དབྱེ་ན།   རྟག་པ་དང་མི་རྟག་པ་གཉིས་ཡོད།

*If existents are divided, there are two,*
*permanent and impermanent.*

| sentences | སྨན་པས་  ནད་པ་ལ་  སྨན་  སྦྱིན།  |
|---|---|

*A doctor gives medicine to the ill.*

ཡོད་པ་ལ་དབྱེ་ན་རྟག་པ་དང་མི་རྟག་པ་གཉིས་ཡོད།

*If existents are divided, there are two,*
*permanent and impermanent.*

There is a fourth category that does not fit neatly either among phrases, clauses, or sentences—direct quotations (in English, the quoted material in *Buddha said, "All caused things are impermanent."*).

- A **direct quotation** is a syntactic unit that is more than a clause, but less than a sentence. A direct quotation may be a single word, but, equally, it may embody pages of material and many complete sentences from the quoted text. The end of a direct quotation is typically marked by one of the quotation-marking syntactic particles (ཅེས་, ཞེས་, and ཤེས་).

A clause acts as a mini-sentence that is grammatically connected to a larger clause or to a sentence. A sentence ends in a terminal verb and is not grammatically connected to other clauses and sentences. However, a direct quotation is often a sentence, or even a group of sentences, each with their own terminal verb that are nonetheless found within a longer clause or sentence. In the following example, the quoted text is རྒྱུ་ལས་བྱུང་བ་དེ་དག་མི་རྟག་པ་ཡིན་ནོ་. The syntactic particle ཞེས་ marks the end of the direct quotation.

| direct quotation | རྒྱལ་བས་ ༎རྒྱུ་ལས་བྱུང་བ་དེ་དག་མི་རྟག་པ་ཡིན་ནོ་ཞེས་༎གསུངས་སོ། |
|---|---|

*Buddha said, "What arises from causes is impermanent."*

The quotation functions as a self-contained unit with its own grammar. The closing syntactic particle ཞེས་ relates this unit to the sentence that encloses it— རྒྱལ་བས་གསུངས། This relationship is both an objective and an adverbial one, in that while the quoted material is, in a sense, the object of the verb གསུངས་ (and, thus, akin to a nominative object), it also states *in what way* Buddha taught this idea.[225]

Tibetan, like English, allows indirect quotation as well (*Buddha said that all caused things are impermanent.*). Indirect quotation is typically in the objective case. (In the example below, རྒྱལ་ས་བྱུང་བ་དེ་དག་ is the nominative object and མི་རྟག་པར་ is the objective complement, stating what Buddha said about the nominative object.)

| indirect quotation | རྒྱལ་བས་ | རྒྱ་ལས་བྱུང་བ་དེ་དག་མི་རྟག་པར་ གསུངས། |
|---|---|---|

*Buddha said that what arises from causes is impermanent.*

Indirect quotation with only an objective complement and no object is also common.

| indirect quotation | མདོ་རྣམས་ལས་ | ཕུང་པོ་ལ་བདག་མེད་པར་ གསུངས། |
|---|---|---|

*In the sutras, [Buddha] said that among the aggregates there is no self.*

## Types of Words

The six types of Tibetan words may be divided into four groups.

- The most basic sorts of words are **verbs** and **nouns**.

- **Pronouns** are words that stand for other words.

- **Adjectives** and **adverbs** are words that modify other words.

- **Postpositions** are words—showing, for example, time, place, and purpose—that in English would be prepositions, but in Tibetan occur *after* the words or phrases to which they are attached.

The core of a Tibetan clause or sentence is the verb standing at its end, after the other words—subjects, objects, and qualifiers—are stated. Nouns, pronouns, ad-

jectives, and postpositions are **declined**—by means of affixing case marking particles—to show their relation to other words and phrases following them. Verbs,
while they are not declined, may be modified through the use of auxiliary verbs or
syntactic particles (both of which follow the verb). A verb may occur in as many as
four related forms, three indicating tense (past, present, and future), and one
indicating imperative.

---

**Declension** is what distinguishes postpositions from lexical and syntactic particles. Neither lexical particles nor syntactic particles are declined.
The other types of words differ from lexical and syntactic particles in that they
are not merely parts of other words (as are lexical particles) nor do they merely
mark relationships between words (as do syntactic particles).

---

## Word Usage Paradigms

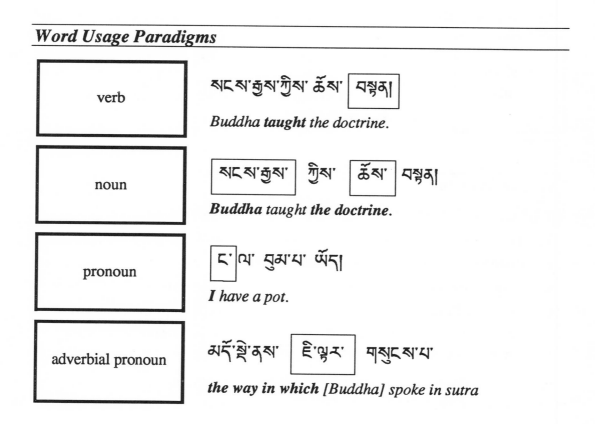

| verb | སངས་རྒྱས་ཀྱིས་ ཆོས་ བསྟན། |
|---|---|
| | *Buddha **taught** the doctrine.* |

| noun | སངས་རྒྱས་ ཀྱིས་ ཆོས་ བསྟན། |
|---|---|
| | ***Buddha** taught **the doctrine**.* |

| pronoun | ང་ ལ་ བུམ་པ་ ཡོད། |
|---|---|
| | ***I** have a pot.* |

| adverbial pronoun | མདོ་སྡེ་ནས་ ཇི་ལྟར་ གསུངས་པ་ |
|---|---|
| | ***the way in which** [Buddha] spoke in sutra* |

| | |
|---|---|
| adjective | ཆོས་དུང་ དཀར་པོ་ |

*a **white** religious conch*

| | |
|---|---|
| adverb | འགྲོ་བ་འདི་དག་ ཕན་ཚུན་ ཕ་མ་རུ་གྱུར། |

*These beings have **mutually** been father and mother.*
[English syntax] ... *have been **each others'** parents*

| | |
|---|---|
| postposition | རང་གི་ མདུན་ དུ་ |

*in **front** of one*

Adjectives may also sometimes be used independently, as subject or predicate adjectives.

| | |
|---|---|
| subject adjective | དེ་ མི་རྟག་པ་ ཡིན། |

***That** is impermanent.*

| | |
|---|---|
| predicate adjective | བུམ་པ་ མི་རྟག་པ་ ཡིན། |

*Pots are **impermanent**.*

Verbs are often made into verbals through the addition of generic suffix syllables. Verbals may stand alone as nouns or may be used as adjectives. Since a verbal is formed from a verb which may have a subject, complement, qualifier, and object, verbals are often not merely single words but entire phrases.

| | |
|---|---|
| verbal noun | གངས་རི་ སྔོན་པོར་ སྣང་བ་ |

*the appearance of a snow mountain as blue*

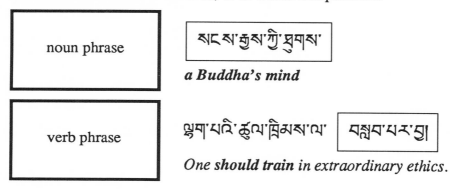

| verbal adjective | སངས་རྒྱས་ཀྱིས་ གསུངས་པའི་ ཆོས་ |

*the doctrine **spoken by Buddha***

Both verbs and nouns occur in simple forms—as single words—and as phrases, made of a combination of words, or of words and particles.

| noun phrase | སངས་རྒྱས་ཀྱི་ཐུགས་ |

*a **Buddha's** mind*

| verb phrase | ལྷག་པའི་ཚུལ་ཁྲིམས་ལ་ བསླབ་པར་བྱ |

*One **should train** in extraordinary ethics.*

## The Dots between Words and Syllables

In English, the division of a word into syllables is not indicated in writing except in cases where a word is hyphenated at the end of a line. English *words*, however, are either separated from other words by a space or followed immediately by punctuation. In Tibetan, on the other hand, *syllables* are separated from one another by terminating dots (ཚེག་ **tsék**), but so are words and even phrases and clauses. The difficulty for beginners lies in determining where one word ends and another begins.

The "functions" of the dots separating syllables and words in Tibetan were introduced in Chapter Eleven. The principle underlying dot analysis is the identification of each dot in a Tibetan sentence in terms of either

1    the type of syllable it follows or
2    the relationship between the syllable it follows and the rest of the sentence.

> Dots actually perform no other function than to separate syllables or to end words. The "functions" of dots, therefore, are merely metaphors for the relationships among the syllables, particles, and words that precede and follow the dots.

The main purpose in identifying the functions of the dots is to facilitate the reading of complex sentences by providing a structure for analysis of the possible relationships between words.

The following is a list of the "functions" of dots. Preceding the description of the context in which a dot occurs is its abbreviation, used in the analysis of phrases, clauses, and sentences.

| | |
|---|---|
| S | between syllables within words, particles, and verb phrases |
| OM | indicating an omitted syllable in a contraction or abbreviation |
| NA | between a noun and an adjective modifying that noun |
| NN | between nouns in a list |
| APP | between two words or phrases in an appositional relationship |
| VB | after a final verb (either a simple verb or a verb phrase) |
| V | after an open verb (infinitives, verbals at the ends of clauses, etc.) |
| ADV | after an adverb or after a particle marking adverbial identity |
| NOM | after a noun in the nominative case |
| VOC | after a noun in the vocative case or an interjection |
| C | before or after a case marking particle |
| UP | indicating an understood particle (case or syntactic particle) |
| SP | before or after a non-case-marking syntactic particle |

The **C** dot occurring after a case marking particle may be clarified through the substitution of a number indicating the case being marked. Thus a **3** dot would follow an agentive case particle. (An **SP** dot, on the other hand, would mark the particle གྱིས་ when it is used as a disjunctive syntactic particle after a verb.)

## Lexical Dots

The first group of dots—**S** and **OM** dots—are found only within words and particles, in the lexical dimension of Tibetan. The remaining dots are syntactic—they follow (or precede) particles and words and are named after the ways in which those particles and words relate to other words in phrases, clauses, and sentences.

In these examples, the labels of the dots being illustrated are underlined.

<table>
<tr><td>
S<br>between syllables
</td><td>
<u>S</u>    <u>S</u>  <u>S</u><br>
བུམ་པ་ མི་རྟག་པ་ ཡིན།<br>
↑     ↑ ↑<br>
Pots are impermanent.
</td></tr>
<tr><td>
OM<br>omitted syllable
</td><td>
<u>OM</u>     S  S<br>
རྣམ་ཤེས་ མི་རྟག་པ་ ཡིན།<br>
↑<br>
Consciousness is impermanent.
</td></tr>
</table>

## Dots within Noun Phrases

The second group of dots—**NA**, **NN**, and **APP** dots—occur within certain types of noun phrases.

<table>
<tr><td>
NA<br>between a noun and<br>an adjective
</td><td>
<u>NA</u>   S<br>
རྟ་ དཀར་པོ་<br>
↑<br>
white horse
</td></tr>
</table>

The first dot in རྟ་དཀར་པོ་ is an **NA** (Noun-Adjective) dot, one between a noun and an adjective. The second dot is an **S** (Syllable) dot.

| NN | | |
|---|---|---|
| between nouns in a list | | |

NN  NN  NN

ས་ ཆུ་ མེ་ རླུང་

↑  ↑  ↑

*earth, water, fire, wind*

The first three dots in ས་ཆུ་མེ་རླུང་ are NN dots, separating nouns in a list (that is, a Noun and a Noun).

| APP | |
|---|---|
| between appositives | |

APP

ཁ་དོག་དམར་པོ་ ནི་ རྩ་བའི་ཁ་དོག་ ཨིན།

↑

*The color red is a basic color.*

## Dots Used with Verbs and Adverbs

The third, fourth, and fifth groups of dots are true syntactic dots. They help show how words relate to one another in clauses and sentences.

The third group of dots occurs after verbs, within verb phrases, or after adverbs. The VB (VerB) dot is found after complete verbs—that is, final verbs such as ཤེས། and terminal verb phrases such as ཤེས་པར་འགྱུར.. The V (open Verb) dot is found within verb phrases, that is, after the first verb in a compound verb phrase, after infinitives such as ཤེས་པར་ and ཤེས་སུ་, after verbs preceding continuative particles (as seen in དགོས་ཏེ།), and—when diagramming clauses—after the verbal ending the clause.

| VB | |
|---|---|
| after a final verb | |

           NOM                S  V  VB  SP

རྒྱལ་བའི་དགོངས་པ་ བདེ་བླག་ཏུ་ རྟོགས་པར་འགྱུར་ རོ།

                                               ↑

*[One] will easily understand the Conqueror's thought.*

|  | NA | 2 | V | <u>VB</u> |
|---|---|---|---|---|

ཐེག་པ་གསུམ་གྱི་ལམ་ལ་ བསླབ་ དགོས།

↑

*[One] must train in the paths of the three vehicles.*

---

| V<br>between compound<br>verbs and before<br>continuative particles |
|---|

|  | NA | 2 | <u>V</u> | <u>V</u> SP |
|---|---|---|---|---|

ཐེག་པ་གསུམ་གྱི་ལམ་ལ་ བསླབ་ དགོས་ཏེ།

↑     ↑

*[One] must train in the paths of the three vehicles.*

---

| V<br>after a clause-ending<br>verbal |
|---|

|  | NOM | NOM | VB |
|---|---|---|---|

སངས་རྒྱས་ཀྱིས་ བསྟན་པ་ ནི་ ཆོས་ ཡིན།

↑

| S | C | 3 | <u>V</u> |
|---|---|---|---|

*That taught by Buddha is the doctrine.*

---

| V<br>after verbal<br>infinitives |
|---|

| S | <u>V</u> | VB | | S | NOM | S | <u>V</u> | VB |
|---|---|---|---|---|---|---|---|---|

བསྒྲུབས་པར་ནུས།།          སྟོང་ཉིད་ རྟོགས་པར་བྱ།།

↑                    ↑

*able to have been accomplished*

*Emptiness should be realized.*

---

| V<br>after a simple<br>infinitive |
|---|

| C | 2 | S | 3 | SP | <u>V</u> | VB |
|---|---|---|---|---|---|---|

བདག་ལ་བརྩེ་བས་དགོངས་སུ་གསོལ།

↑

*[I] entreat [you] to consider me with love.*[226]

ADV (**AD**Verb) dots occur both after words that are always adverbs and after nouns and adjectives declined in the adverbial objective case.

| | |
|---|---|
| **ADV** after adverbs; before and after adverbial particles | **6    NOM    ADV    S    V    VB    SP**<br><br>རྒྱལ་བའི་དགོངས་པ་ བདེ་བླག་ཏུ་ རྟོགས་པར་འགྱུར་ རོ།<br>                    ↑ ↑ |

*[One] will easily understand the Conqueror's thought.*

## Dots and Declension

The fourth group—the **NOM, VOC, C,** and **UP** dots—are used when nouns, pronouns, and adjectives are declined. **NOM** and **VOC** dots follow nouns in the nominative and vocative cases, respectively. These are the two cases that are identified by the fact that no case particle is used to mark them.

Thus, the second and fifth dots in the sentence ཐུབ་པ་མི་རྟག་པ་ཡིན། are **NOM**inative dots.

The cases other than the nominative and vocative are marked by syntactic particles, and the dots before and after these Case particles are **C** dots. Sometimes case particles are dropped, and in those instances, the dot where the case-marking particle would normally have been seen is an Understood Case dot.

| | |
|---|---|
| **NOM** noun in nominative case | **3    NOM    VB**<br><br>སངས་རྒྱས་ ཀྱིས་ ཆོས་ བསྟན།<br>            ↑ |

*Buddha taught the doctrine.*

| | |
|---|---|
| **VOC** after vocative noun or interjection | **VOC  VOC            VOC**<br><br>ཀྱི་མ་ ཀྱི་ཧུད་ སྐལ་ལྡན་རིགས་ཀྱི་བུ།<br>↑        ↑            ↑ |

*Alas, alack, o fortunate son of [good] family …*

**VOC**

ཧཱུྃ༔ ཨོ་རྒྱན་ཡུལ་གྱི་ནུབ་བྱང་མཚམས༔

↑

*Hūṃ. [On] the northwest border of the land of Odiyana …*

---

| C |
|---|
| before or after a case marking particle |

**C    3    NOM   VB**

སངས་རྒྱས་ ཀྱིས་ ཆོས་ བསྟན།

↑    ↑

*Buddha taught the doctrine.*

---

| UP |
|---|
| understood particle |

**UP   7     V SP**

བཏང་སྙོམས་དང་དུ་ གནས་ན་ ཅི་མ་རུང་།

↑

*Would it not be suitable were [one] to remain
in a state of equanimity.*

**UP UP**

ལས་ཉོན་དབང་གིས་སྐྱེ་བ་བླངས།

↑ ↑

*[We] have taken birth by the power
of actions and afflictions.*

The understood case particle in the first illustration is a sixth case particle connecting the nouns བཏང་སྙོམས་ and དང་—བཏང་སྙོམས་ཀྱི་དང་ (*state of equanimity*). A more revealing alternative to the **UP** dot is to identify the case relation that is understood in parentheses, in this example **(6)**.

The second example in uncontracted form is ལས་དང་ཉོན་མོངས་ཀྱི་དབང་གིས་སྐྱེ་བ་བླངས།. In the abbreviated form there are two understood particles; the first is the syntactic particle དང་ and the second is the connective case marking particle གྱི་. The alternative identification of the first is **(SP)** and the second, **(6)**.

## *Dots Used with Syntactic Particles*

The fifth group of dots is actually only one type—the dots found before and after Syntactic Particles.

| SP before or after syntactic particles |
| --- |

V SP         V SP   V SP   VB

མིག་མེད་ན་ གཟུགས་མི་མཐོང་ཞིང་ ཡོད་ན་ མཐོང།

↑             ↑    ↑

*[Those who] have no eyes do not see [visible] forms,*
*but those who have, do.*

The example shows the particle ན་, often used as a case marking particle (especially with the locative case), in its non-case-marking usage as a conditional syntactic particle. Although ཞིང་ does occur as a noun (meaning *field*), it is more often seen—as it is here—as a conjunctive syntactic particle.

# *Appendix Three*

*Nouns, Pronouns, and Adjectives*

## Nouns

Nouns may occur as simple nouns or as noun phrases. An example of a simple noun is the word ཕུམ་པ་. There are five types of noun phrases:

- noun-adjective phrases:
- lists of nouns;
- nouns modified by nouns or pronouns preceding them (connected to them by connective case particles);
- nouns modified by adjectives preceding them (connected to them by connective case particles);
- appositive phrases.

| noun-adjective phrase | ཕུམ་པ་དམར་པོ་ *red pot* <br> NOUN + ADJECTIVE |
|---|---|

The noun-adjective phrase is the way in which most adjectives modify nouns and noun phrases.

| list phrase | ས་དང་ཆུ་ *earth and water* <br> NOUN + CONJUNCTION + NOUN |
|---|---|

ས་ཆུ་མེ་རླུང་ *earth, water, fire, and wind*

NOUN + NOUN + NOUN + NOUN ...

Conjunctions are a type of syntactic particle. Note in the second example (ས་ཆུ་མེ་རླུང་) that Tibetan does not *require* a conjunction in a list of nouns (as English does).

| noun-noun phrase |
|---|

སངས་རྒྱས་ཀྱི་ཐུགས་ *Buddha's mind*

NOUN (or PRONOUN) + CONNECTIVE + NOUN

There are similar PRONOUN + NOUN phrases (for example, རང་གི་སེམས་—*one's mind*).

| adjective-noun phrase |
|---|

དམ་པའི་ཆོས་      *holy doctrine*

ADJECTIVE + CONNECTIVE + NOUN

This translates the Sanskrit *saddharma*. Adjectives usually follow the nouns they modify (as in the first example in this section, ཐུབ་པ་དམར་པོ་). In those instances when they do precede their nouns, they must be connected to them with a connective case particle.

| appositive phrase |
|---|

སངས་རྒྱས་ཚེ་དཔག་མེད་ *the Buddha Amitāyus*

NOUN followed by a NOUN in apposition to it

In an appositive phrase, the second noun qualifies the first—that is, among the many Buddhas, here Amitāyus is being discussed.

Nouns are used within these phrases, but the phrases themselves—as single units—are also nouns. It is for the second reason that they are called noun phrases—they function as nouns in the larger patterns of which *they* form a part.

A noun phrase is a unit that connects only at its end to the remainder of the larger phrase, clause, or sentence in which it is found.

Tibetan has many nouns that are formed from verbs and that, in some ways, still act like verbs—the verbal nouns. There are also many nouns that are just nouns—for example, བུམ་པ་ (*pot*), མི་ (*human*), and བོད་ (*Tibet*).

The declension of nouns is presented, with paradigmatic examples, in Appendix Five.

## Pronouns

Tibetan has a variety of pronouns similar to those found in English. The following list of types is based on the types of English pronouns.

| personal pronouns | ང་ ཁྱོད་ ཁོ་ |
|---|---|
| | *I, you, he* |

| reflexive pronouns | རང་ ང་རང་ |
|---|---|
| | *itself, myself* |

| relative pronouns | སུ་ གང་ ནམ་ |
|---|---|
| | *who, which, when* |

| indefinite and general relative pronouns | གང་ཡང་ ཅི་ཡང་ སུ་ཡང་ ནམ་ཡང་ |
|---|---|
| | *whatever / any, whomever, whenever* |

འགའ་ཞིག་ ཁ་ཅིག་ ལ་ལ་

*someone, certain one, some*

| interrogative pronouns | སུ་ | གང་ | ཅི་ | ཇི་ | ཇི་ལྟ་བུ་ | ཅི་ལྟ་བུ་ |
|---|---|---|---|---|---|---|
| | *who,* | | *what / which,* | | *of what sort* | |

|  | ཅི་ཙམ་ | ཅིའི་ཕྱིར་ |
|---|---|---|
| | *how much,* | *why* |

| limiting adjectives used as pronouns | དེ་ | འདི་ | ཐམས་ཅད་ |
|---|---|---|---|
| | *that one,* | *this one,* | *all* |

|  | མང་པོ་ | ཆང་མ་ | གཞན་ | གཉིས་ཀ |
|---|---|---|---|---|
| | *many,* | *all,* | *other / another,* | *both* |

|  | གཅིག་པོ་ | འདི་འདྲ་ | སོ་སོ་བ་ | རེ་རེ་ | རེ་ |
|---|---|---|---|---|---|
| | *alone,* | *such,* | *individuals,* | *each* | |

## Adverbial Pronouns

These words are adverbial because they answer questions such as how, how much, to what extent, and why. However, they are classified here as a type of relative pronoun because, by using them, the phrase, clause, or sentence in which they are found is related to something that has already been or that will be said. Adverbial pronouns may also be used in an indefinite sense—using, for example, ཇི་ཙམ་ to mean *however much*, with no specific connection made to anything outside the phrase, clause, or sentence in which it is found.

Note that all members of this group of pronouns are declined—either through affixing a ར་ case marking ending to a suffixless syllable or through the addition of the དུ་ case marking particle. These typically serve as objective case particles in the sense of adverbial identity.

ཇི་ལྟར་     *the way in which, as ...*
This is formed from ཇི་ལྟ་, which also forms the noun ཇི་ལྟ་བ་. Therefore, one can say that ཇི་ལྟར་ (as well as དེ་ལྟར་ and འདི་ལྟར་) are "frozen" adverbial constructions. They may be said to be frozen because, although ཇི་ལྟར་ and so forth are quite common, one never sees ཇི་ལྟ་ marked by any other case marking particle.

དེ་ལྟར་     *such, thus ...*

འདི་ལྟར་     *such, thus ...*

ཇི་སྐད་དུ་     *as ...*    [used with citation of discourse]

འདི་སྐད་དུ་     *thus ...*    [used with citation of discourse]

དེ་སྐད་དུ་     *thus ...*    [used with citation of discourse]

ཇི་བཞིན་དུ་     *just as ...*

དེ་བཞིན་དུ་     *thus, so, in that way ...*

ཇི་ཙམ་དུ་     *how much, to the extent that ...*

དེ་ཙམ་དུ་     *that much, to that extent ...*
As with all of these particles, ཇི་ཙམ་དུ་ and དེ་ཙམ་དུ་ may occur without case marking, as ཇི་ཙམ་ and དེ་ཙམ་ — as, for example, in ལམ་ཇི་ཙམ་གཏོད་པ་དེ་ཙམ་ནི་.[227]

ཇི་སྲིད་དུ་     *as long as ...*

དེ་སྲིད་དུ་     *for that long ...*

ཇི་སྙེད་དུ་     *as many as ...*

དེ་སྙེད་དུ་     *that many ...*

## Adjectives

Adjectives modify nouns.  Most adjectives follow the nouns they modify, creating noun-adjective phrases such ཕུམ་པ་དམར་པོ་ (*red pot*), སེམས་ཅན་ཀུན་ (*all sentient beings*), and མི་བདུན་ (**mí dün**, *seven humans*).

| | |
|---|---|
| noun-adjective phrase | སེམས་ཅན་ཀུན་  *all sentient beings*<br><br>NOUN followed by an ADJECTIVE |

Some adjectives, however, typically *precede* the nouns they modify, connected to them by connective case markers.  Examples are དགེ་བའི་སེམས་ (**gé-wë sêm**, *virtuous mind[s]*) and དམ་པའི་ཆོས་ (**tam-bë chö>**, *holy doctrine*).

| | |
|---|---|
| adjective-noun phrase | དམ་པའི་ཆོས་  *holy doctrine*<br><br>ADJECTIVE connected to a NOUN |

In both of those instances, the noun-and-adjective combination creates a noun phrase—that is, a phrase that is itself a noun.  Like any noun, this noun phrase may then be modified by an adjective.

| | |
|---|---|
| complex noun-adjective phrase | ཕུམ་པ་དམར་པོ་ཀུན་  *all the red pots*<br><br>NOUN-ADJECTIVE PHRASE followed by an ADJECTIVE |

# *Appendix Four*
# *Verbs and Verb Syntax*

*Classes of Verbs*
*Forms of Verbs*
*Verb Marking Particles*

## Verb Syntax

The Tibetan verb always occurs at the end of a clause or sentence. This simple looking statement has many implications. First, a **sentence** is defined by the fact that a verb ends it.

> A sentence ends in a verb.
> A clause ends in a verbal noun or adjective or in a syntactic particle such as ནས་,
>    ཅིང་, or ན་. A clause—taken as a whole—acts as a unit within a sentence.

**Verbs** in their most basic forms look like ཡིན་ (*is*) and བྱེད་ (*do, make, perform*); only in exceptional circumstances do they end in པ་ or བ་.[228] **Verbal nouns** and **verbal adjectives** (collectively known as **verbals**), on the other hand, usually do end in པ་ or བ་, although they need not (especially in verse).

   Any verb may be made into a verbal noun or adjective; the verbals formed from the two finite verbs ཡིན་ and བྱེད་ are ཡིན་པ་ and བྱེད་པ་. Much that is true about verbs is true about verbals as well—for example, they may have, depending on the type of verb from which they were made, subjects, complements, objects, and qualifiers.

Besides a terminal verb, a Tibetan sentence has a subject, usually either a complement or an object, and often a qualifier (or a group of qualifiers).  The same holds true for clauses, with the exception that they often end in verbal nouns or adjectives.

The **subject** of a verb or verbal is, in most instances, its agent, the thing or person that performs the action indicated by the verb—going somewhere or doing something—or, in the case of the existential verbs, the thing or person that is something, that exists, that has something, or that needs something.

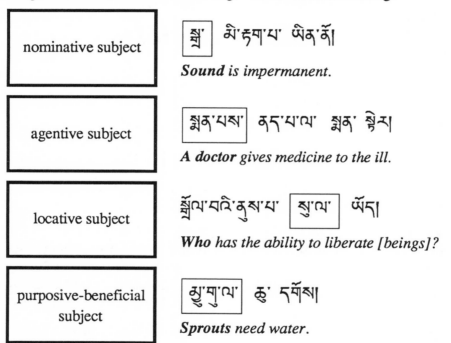

| | |
|---|---|
| nominative subject | སྒྲ་ མི་རྟག་པ་ ཡིན་ནོ། |
| | *Sound is impermanent.* |
| agentive subject | སྨན་པས་ ནད་པ་ལ་ སྨན་ སྟེར། |
| | *A doctor gives medicine to the ill.* |
| locative subject | སྒྲོལ་བའི་ནུས་པ་ སུ་ལ་ ཡོད། |
| | *Who has the ability to liberate [beings]?* |
| purposive-beneficial subject | མྱུ་གུ་ལ་ ཆུ་ དགོས། |
| | *Sprouts need water.* |

The primary classification of verbs in *Translating Buddhism from Tibetan* is in terms of their subjects.  Thus, nominative verbs usually have nominative subjects, agentive verbs, agentive subjects, while specialized verbs include those whose subjects (from the viewpoint of an English speaking reader) are in the locative or purposive-beneficial cases).

Most Tibetan clauses and sentences have either objects, or complements, or both, depending on what sort of verb ends them.  Whereas action verbs have **objects**—

the *tree* that is felled, the *doctrine* that is taught—linking verbs have **complements**, for example, the word *impermanent* in *Sound is impermanent.*

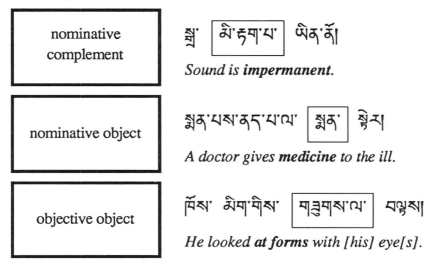

nominative complement

སྒྲ་ | མི་རྟག་པ་ | ཡིན་ནོ།

*Sound is **impermanent**.*

nominative object

སྨན་པས་ནད་པ་ལ་ | སྨན་ | སྟེར།

*A doctor gives **medicine** to the ill.*

objective object

ཁོས་ མིག་གིས་ | གཟུགས་ལ་ | བལྟས།

*He looked **at forms** with [his] eye[s].*

Complements are not found only with linking verbs. The following example illustrates the way in which agentive verbs may have complements as well objects. The object of འདོད་ is སེམས་; its complement is གང་ཟག་གི་མཚན་གཞི་.

objective complement

ཁ་ཅིག་གིས་ སེམས་ | གང་ཟག་གི་མཚན་གཞིར་ | འདོད་དོ།

*Some assert mind **as the illustration of the person**.*

Most clauses and sentences have **qualifiers**, and some require them; the destination of a verb of motion is a qualifier, as is the thing on which something depends. Some qualifers are adverbs, but many are not. Qualifiers include words, clauses, and phrases showing reasons, origins, comparison, the place where or time when an activity is done, the means by which something is done, how it is done, the purpose for which it is done, and the person for whom it is done.

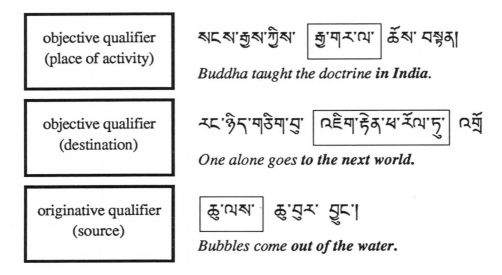

| objective qualifier (place of activity) | སངས་རྒྱས་ཀྱིས་ རྒྱ་གར་ལ་ ཆོས་ བསྟན། |
| --- |

*Buddha taught the doctrine **in India**.*

| objective qualifier (destination) | རང་ཉིད་གཅིག་པུ་ འཇིག་རྟེན་ཕ་རོལ་དུ་ འགྲོ |
| --- |

*One alone goes **to the next world**.*

| originative qualifier (source) | ཆུ་ལས་ ཆུ་བུར་ བྱུང་། |
| --- |

*Bubbles come **out of the water**.*

That Tibetan verbs always occur at the end of sentences means that verbs function grammatically to end the sentences in which they are found. Nothing that comes after the verb is a part of the sentence terminated by that verb.

> The subjects, complements, and objects of verbs must precede the verbs that terminate their sentence or clause.

This, as mentioned throughout *Translating Buddhism from Tibetan*, is a basic principle of Tibetan.

Any phrases that qualify the action expressed by the verb—where it is done, how it is done, why it is done—all of these must precede the verb. There are some exceptions to this, but they are well-defined and not numerous.[229] Stated another way, the principle is that whereas the other elements of the sentence (such as the subject, the object, and the modifying words or phrases) lead to subsequent parts of the sentence, the verb relates to those elements coming before it.

> Like verbs, adjectives relate to the word(s) to their left rather than to the ones that follow them. However, they do it on a much smaller scale than verbs, since an adjective relates backwards only to a noun in front of it.

Thus, the verb is the main element of the sentence in Tibetan, determining the structure of the sentence and the way in which nouns are used. In *Translating Buddhism from Tibetan*, verbs are classified according to the structure of the sentences and clauses that they terminate.

## Types of Verbs

In English, word order determines the meaning of a sentence. For example, the sentences *The farmer sees the yak* and *The yak sees the farmer* are identical except for the position of the nouns *farmer* and *yak*.

In Tibetan, on the other hand, word order is not as significant. Rather, it is case marking particles (or their absence) that determine which word is the subject and which is the object. Using the verb མཐོང་ (*see*), there are two ways to say *The farmer sees the yak* and two ways to say *The yak sees the farmer*.

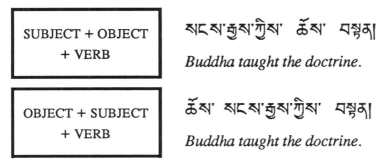

ཞིང་པས་ གཡག་ མཐོང་།    གཡག་ ཞིང་པས་ མཐོང་།

*The farmer sees the yak.*

གཡག་གིས་ ཞིང་པ་ མཐོང་།    ཞིང་པ་ གཡག་གིས་ མཐོང་།

*The yak sees the farmer.*

In all four examples, it is not the word order that determines the meaning, but rather the case marking particles. The subject is marked by an agentive case marker and the object, in the nominative case, by the lack of a case marking particle.

Thus, while the subject of a Tibetan sentence is *often* the first element in the sentence, it is not *necessarily* the first element in the sentence.

| SUBJECT + OBJECT<br>+ VERB | སངས་རྒྱས་ཀྱིས་ ཆོས་ བསྟན།<br>*Buddha taught the doctrine.* |
|---|---|
| OBJECT + SUBJECT<br>+ VERB | ཆོས་ སངས་རྒྱས་ཀྱིས་ བསྟན།<br>*Buddha taught the doctrine.* |

The English speaker is tempted, when translating the second example, to use the passive—*The doctrine was taught by Buddha*—thus making *doctrine* the subject acted on by the verb *was taught*. And, in fact, where the context suggests an emphasis on ཆོས་ and not སངས་རྒྱས་, that is an acceptable translation. Nonetheless, however one chooses to translate, it must be remembered that the active-passive options present in English are not found in Tibetan. Whereas in English the passive is considered weak and the stronger active construction is preferred to it, in Tibetan all agentive verbs are equally active (or, if you prefer, equally passive—although in *Translating Buddhism from Tibetan* they are considered active). སངས་རྒྱས་ཀྱིས་ཆོས་བསྟན། and ཆོས་སངས་རྒྱས་ཀྱིས་བསྟན། are grammatically equivalent. Both sentences end in the agentive-nominative verb བསྟན་.

In this way the case in which a noun, pronoun, or adjective is found is what determines whether or not it may be the subject of a particular verb. Subjects, in Tibetan, occur in only three such syntactic configurations:

1    as a word followed by no case marking particle,
2    as a word marked by one of the five agentive particles,
3    as a word marked by one of the *la*-group of particles.

It is thus possible to speak of three basic **categories of verbs** in Tibetan:

1    verbs whose subjects are in the nominative case—**nominative verbs**,
2    verbs whose subjects are in the agentive case—**agentive verbs**,
3    verbs whose subjects are in the locative or purposive cases—**specialized verbs**.

The third category is called "specialized" because it includes only one verb— དགོས་—that does not in most situations have an agentive or a nominative subject. When these verbs have fourth or seventh case subjects, they are being used in specialized ways. For example, the verb ཡོད་ (*exist, is*)—a Category One, nominative verb—is also used to show possession (*have, has*). Whereas who or what exists— the subject in the ordinary usage—is in the nominative case, who or what has something—the subject in the specialized usage—is in the locative case.

Many, but not all, verbs in the first category (nominative verbs) are verbs in which no action takes place—for example, linking verbs such as ཡིན་, verbs of existence such as ཡོད་, and verbs of dependence such as རྟེན་. Category Two, agentive verbs, includes only action verbs—but not all action verbs, since certain action verbs (for instance, verbs of motion) have nominative subjects and are thus included in the first category. Category Three verbs include verbs of possession (one usage of ཡོད་), necessity (དགོས་), and attribution (such as ཟེར་ when it means *be called* or *named*).

There is an important exception to the general rule that any given verb regularly takes only a nominative, only an agentive, or only a *la*-particle marked subject.

> Many verbs whose subjects are theoretically agentive occur at least occasionally with nominative subjects.

This is especially the case with agentive verbs such as འདོད་ and གསུང་. Although they are technically of a class which distinguishes the subject of the verb from its object by the use of a third case particle, འདོད་ and གསུང་ are sometimes seen with nominative subjects. (See the material on irregular subjects below.) Likewise, it is possible for a nominative action verb to take an agentive subject (as in ངས་སངས་རྒྱས་ འགྲུབ་པར་ཤོག). 

Within these three categories, there are **eight classes** of verbs. While the three categories are determined by the case in which the subject of the verb is found, the classes within a category are distinguished from one another in terms of whether their objects (or complements) are marked by nominative, objective, or locative case marking particles, or by syntactic particles that are not case markers. The eight classes of verbs will be discussed with examples later in this appendix.

## *Alternate Classifications of Verbs*

There are, in fact, a number of different ways to classify Tibetan verbs, none of them absolutely correct to the exclusion of all others. One popular modern Tibetan dictionary, the དག་ཡིག་གསར་བསྒྲིགས། (*New Compilation Lexicon*), classifies verbs—which it calls ལས་ཚིག, *action words*—into three types. The first two types follow the traditional Tibetan grammarians, whereas the third is a means of speaking of words such as ཡིན་ and ཡོད་ that are not traditionally accorded the status of verbs:

1   verbs associated with agents which are separate from their objects (ཕྱི་འབྲེལ་ལས་ཚིག),

2   verbs lacking agents separate from objects (ཕྱི་མེད་ལས་ཚིག),

3   similitudes of verbs (ལས་ཚིག་རྗེས་མཐུན་པ).[230]

Another modern dictionary, the བོད་རྒྱ་ཚིག་མཛོད་ཆེན་མོ (*Great Tibetan-Chinese Dictionary*) classifies verbs into two types, corresponding to the *New Compilation Lexicon's* first two types:

1   those whose agents and objects are different (བྱ་བྱེད་ཐ་དད་པ—for example, སྐོར་ and སྒྲུབ་),

2   those whose agents and objects are not different (བྱ་བྱེད་ཐ་མི་དད་པ—for example, འཁོར་ and འགྲུབ་).[231]

Using the traditional terminology of Latin and English grammars, the first type in these two classifications would be transitive verbs and the second, intransitive action verbs.

---

Transitive verbs—such as the English *teach* and *do*—are verbs that take direct objects—that is, verbs in which an agent acts on an object separate from it. Intransitive verbs—like *were* and *stand*—are verbs that have no direct objects.

---

The paradigm transitive construction is *The woodsman fells the tree with an ax*, where the agent, *woodsman*, and the object, *tree*, are clearly different entities. Intransitive constructions, on the other hand, do not allow a differentiation of agent and object. Thus, in *A blue pot appears to a visual consciousness*, the blue pot is both the appearer (the agent) and that which appears (the object). In *Rays of light dissolve into one's body*, the rays of light are both the dissolver (the agent) and that which dissolves (the object).

While these classifications are not followed in *Translating Buddhism from Tibetan*, they are useful. Thus, a secondary method of distinguishing between verbs is employed here, one based on the relationship between a verb's subject (or agent) and its complement (or object):

1    **existential verbs** such as ཡིན་ (*is*), ཡོད་ (*exists*), རུང་ (*is suitable, is admissible*), and འཐད་ (*is correct*),

2    **intransitive action verbs** such as འགྲོ་ (*goes*), and ཤར་ (*appears*) in which agent and object do not differ,

3    **transitive action verbs** such as སྟོན་ (*teaches, demonstrates*) and བྱེད་ (*do, make, perform*) in which agent and object do differ.

The first type, the existential verbs, are found only among Category One nominative-subject verbs and Category Three locative- or purposive-subject verbs. The second type—in which the action happens without reference to agents acting on objects—are also found among the Category One and Three verbs. The third type—in which an action is performed on something by an agent separate from it—is coextensive with Category Two agentive verbs.

## *Nominative Verbs*

Classes of verbs are differentiated from each other in this book mainly in terms of the syntax used in the clauses and sentences that they terminate. Thus, a nominative-locative verb is one whose subject is in the nominative case and whose principal qualifier or object—if explicitly stated—is in the locative case.

> Recall that Tibetan sentences may have *implicit* subjects, complements, or objects, implicit in that they are not stated in the printed or spoken sentence.

There are four classes of verbs whose subjects are regularly in the nominative case:

I    nominative-nominative verbs—also called linking verbs—are existential verbs with nominative subjects and nominative complements (the paradigm being ཡིན་);

II    nominative-locative verbs, of which there are four types:
    (a)  simple verbs of existence (such as ཡོད་),
    (b)  verbs of living (such as གནས་),
    (c)  verbs of dependence (such as རྟེན་),
    (d)  verbs expressing attitudes (such as ཆགས་);

III   nominative-objective verbs, of which there are three types:
  (a)  verbs of motion (such as འགྲོ་),
  (b)  nominative action verbs (such as སྐྱེང་),
  (c)  rhetorical verbs (such as ཟེང་ and རིགས་);

IV   nominative-syntactic verbs, of which there are four types:
  (a)  separative verbs (such as གྲོལ་) whose qualifiers are marked by the case marking particles ལས་ and ནས་,
  (b)  verbs of absence (such as སྟོང་) whose qualifiers are marked by the syntactic particles ཀྱིས་, གིས་, གྱིས་, འིས་, and ཡིས་,
  (c)  conjunctive verbs (such as འབྲེལ་) whose qualifiers are marked by the syntactic particle དང་,
  (d)  disjunctive verbs (such as བྲལ་) whose qualifiers are marked by the syntactic particle དང་.

All Category One verbs are—according to the grammars of languages such as English and Latin—intransitive verbs, verbs that cannot take direct objects. These verbs, even when they do express actions, do not express actions in which an agent acts on an object separate from that agent.

## *Irregular Nominative Subjects*

Most verbs are members of only one of the eight classes of verbs. Some verbs, however, occur sometimes in one syntactic pattern, sometimes in another. The verb འདོད་ is an example of a verb that is used in a number of variant constructions under a single meaning, *assert*. It sometimes has an agentive subject and sometimes a nominative subject.[232] In this way འདོད་ is an example of a verb that is fairly regularly irregular.

The following is an example of འདོད་ with an irregular nominative subject.

NOMINATIVE SUBJECT + [NON-CASE] OBJECT

| མདོ་སྡེ་པ་དག་ | འདུས་བྱས་རྣམས་ སྐད་ཅིག་གིས་འཇིག་པ་ཞེས་ འདོད་དོ། |

**Sautrāntika**s *assert that compounded things disintegrate momentarily.*

Note that the phrase ending in the quote-marking syntactic particle ཞེས་ acts as the complement of the verb—explaining what it is that Sautrāntikas assert.

The next example shows འདོད་ with an agentive subject and an objective case complement.

---

AGENTIVE SUBJECT + NOMINATIVE OBJECT + OBJECTIVE COMPLEMENT

རིགས་པའི་རྗེས་འབྲང་རྣམས་ཀྱིས་ ཐེག་དམན་དྒྲ་བཅོམ་པ་ཐེག་ཆེན་ལམ་དུ་འཇུག་པར་འདོད་དོ།

***Followers of Reasoning*** *assert that Hīnayāna arhats [later] enter into the path of the Mahāyāna.*

---

It would seem that any agentive verb may be *occasionally* seen with nominative subjects; in these cases, the nominative subject should be thought of as an irregular subject of what remains an agentive verb. The following is an example of such a construction.

---

NOMINATIVE SUBJECT + NOMINATIVE OBJECT + VERB

བདག་ཅག ཀྱང་ སྲོག་གཅོད་ སྤོང་ངོ་ ཞེས་ དམ་བཅས་པས།

*Through [their] promising, "We give up killing," ...*[233]

---

## Agentive Verbs

There are two classes of verbs whose subjects are in the third or agentive case:

V    agentive-nominative verbs (such as སྟོན་, *teaches*)

VI   agentive-objective verbs (such as ལྟ་, *looks at, views*)

Action verbs express various types of activities: giving, doing, making, speaking, helping, seeing, meditating, and going are merely a few examples. Some action verbs signify actions done by an agent on an object; others express actions without making reference to agents or objects. In order to speak of agents acting on objects, Tibetan requires the use of these Category Two verbs. When there is no need to separate agents and objects (or when it is not possible), Category One verbs are used.

> All actions have agents in the sense of a subject that does something. When nominative action verbs are used, the agent is in the nominative case. When agentive verbs are used, the agent is separated from the object and placed in the agentive case.

## Specialized Verbs

There is one class of verbs whose subjects are in the seventh or locative case, and one whose subject is in the fourth case:

VII   the purposive-nominative verb of necessity (དགོས་) has a fourth case (purposive-beneficial) subject;

VIII  locative-nominative verbs (including verbs of possession) have locative subjects.

Since the particles that mark the seventh and fourth cases (the *la*-group of particles) are the same, both classes are structurally similar.

Verbs of necessity—following traditional Tibetan grammar— require fourth case subjects, since the fact of needing something shows purpose (དགོས་པ་) or potential benefit. They are, therefore, purposive-nominative verbs. The following is an example of such a verb.

---

*Sprouts **need** water.*

མྱུ་གུ་ལ་ ཆུ་ ⟨དགོས།⟩

---

The syntactic pattern seen in clauses and sentences ending in verbs of possession (Class VIII) appears to be identical to that seen with verbs of necessity. The subject is marked by one of the *la*-group of particles and the object is nominative.

*Arhats **have no** afflictions*

དགྲ་བཅོམ་པ་ལ་ ཉོན་མོངས་ མེད།

In fact, however, verbs of possession—based on the examples seen in traditional Tibetan grammars—require seventh case subjects. Possession and existence in a place are expressed in the same way in Tibetan. Verbs of possession and verbs of existence are both locative-nominative verbs.

The other type of specialized verbs—the attributive verbs (verbs that attribute a meaning to a word or phrase)—are somewhat more complex. They are normally agentive verbs (such as ཟེར་ and བྱེད་) which are being used in a specialized way, translating into English as *is called*, *refers to*, or *is taken to mean*. Such a usage of verbs belongs to Class VIII.

*The experienced object of feeling **is called** a fruition.*

ཚོར་བའི་མྱོང་བྱ་ལ་ རྣམ་པར་སྨིན་པ་ ཟེར།

As in sentences ending in verbs of possession, so here as well the actual syntax is somewhat farther away from English than the LOCATIVE + NOMINATIVE + VERB being used here.[234] A more literal translation would read: *[We] say 'fruition' about experienced objects of feeling*—in Tenglish:

| [WE] | FEELING-OF | OBJECT-OF-EXPERIENCE-ABOUT | FRUITION | SAY. |

That these verbs have subjects marked by a *la*-particle reflects the orientation of the grammatical analysis in *Translating Buddhism from Tibetan*. In English, the verb of possession, *have*, is distinct from the verbs of existence, *is* and *exist*. In Tibetan, posession and simple existence are shown with the same verb— ཡོད་. As a matter of convenience to those who think in English, the locative qualifier of ཡོད་ as *exist* becomes the locative subject of ཡོད་ as *have*.

## Category One:  Nominative Verbs

The four classes of nominative verbs are:

    I    nominative-nominative verbs—that is, linking verbs,

    II   nominative-locative verbs,

    III  nominative-objective verbs,

    IV  nominative-syntactic verbs.

## Class I: *Nominative-Nominative Verbs*

There is only one type of verb within this class—linking verbs—although there are many *irregular* instances in which a normally agentive-nominative verb occurs as a nominative-nominative verb.

## *Linking Verbs*

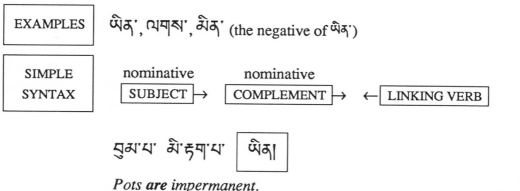

Pots *are* impermanent.

## Class II: *Nominative-Locative Verbs*

Nominative-locative verbs take their subjects in the nominative but require—for a full expression of meaning—an object or qualifier in the seventh or locative case. There are four types of Class II verbs:

    1    simple **verbs of existence** (such as 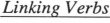);

2   **verbs of living**, that is, continuing existence, (such as གནས་)—where the place where or time during which such existence takes place is in the locative case;

3   **verbs of dependence** (such as རྟེན་)—in which that upon which there is dependence is marked by a locative case particle;

4   **attitude verbs**—verbs that express mental attitudes taken about something (where the *about* translates a referential locative) such as འཇིགས་ (*fear, is afraid*) and བཟོད་ (*bear, is patient*);

---

## *Verbs of Existence*

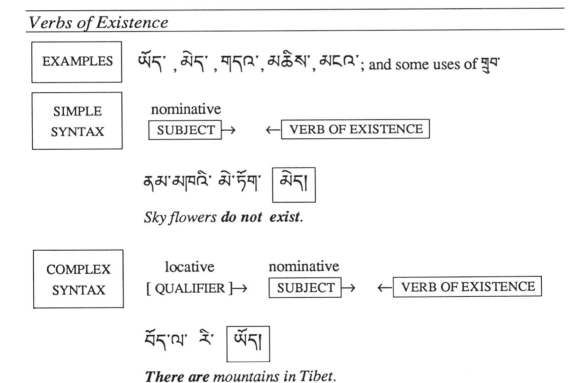

EXAMPLES    ཡོད་ , མེད་ , གདའ་ , མཆིས་ , མངའ་; and some uses of གྱུར་

SIMPLE SYNTAX

nominative
SUBJECT ⊢→     ←⊣ VERB OF EXISTENCE

ནམ་མཁའི་ མེ་ཏོག་  མེད།

*Sky flowers **do not exist**.*

COMPLEX SYNTAX

locative                nominative
[ QUALIFIER ] ⊢→     SUBJECT ⊢→     ←⊣ VERB OF EXISTENCE

བོད་ལ་ རི་  ཡོད།

***There are** mountains in Tibet.*

> The **box** around the subject indicates that it is an obligatory part of a clause or sentence ending in this type of verb. It may not be explicitly stated, but, if not, it may be inferred. The **brackets** around the qualifier indicate that not all clauses and sentences ending in this type of verb require a qualifier.

The verb གྲུབ་ is sometimes used in a way *lexically* and (to a certain extent) *syntactically* equivalent to the verb ཡོད་. The difference is that it typically has an adverbial and not a locative qualifier. (Adverbial qualifiers may be marked either by objective case marking particles or by particles such as གིས་, normally third case markers, but in these constructions used as non-case-marking syntactic particles.)

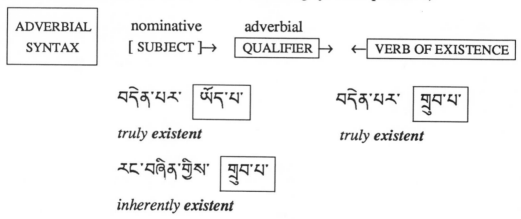

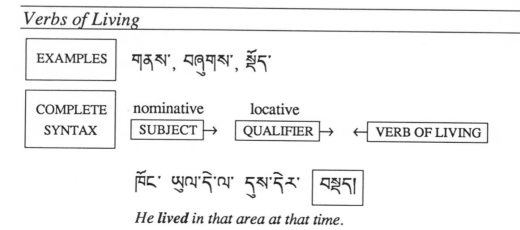

## Verbs of Living

He **lived** in that area at that time.

## *Verbs of Dependence*

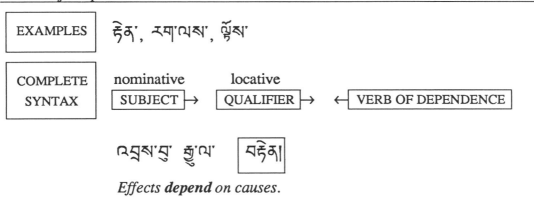

*Effects* **depend** *on causes.*

## *Attitude Verbs*

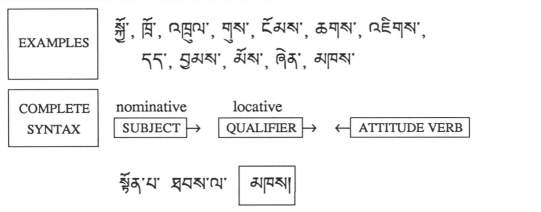

*The Teacher [Buddha]* **is skilled** *in methods [of liberation].*

## Class III: *Nominative-Objective Verbs*

Nominative-objective verbs take their subjects in the nominative but require—for a full expression of meaning—a qualifier in the second or objective case. There are three types of Class III verbs.

1   Sentences and clauses ending in **verbs of motion** (such as འགྲོ་) either state or imply a destination—one marked by a second case particle.

2   **Nominative action verbs** are verbs that have nominative subjects but, unlike attitude verbs, express actions (such as *appearing*, སྣང་) done in a certain place (which, in Tibetan, is marked by the second case).

3   **Rhetorical verbs** (such as རུང་, *be admissible*, and རིགས་, *be correct*) are like verbs of existence in that the syntax NOMINATIVE SUBJECT + VERB is often a complete thought. They are unlike verbs of existence in that most may occur in the syntax OBJECTIVE-CASE INFINITIVE PHRASE + VERB, in the sense *To … is correct*. Often, when they have qualifiers, those qualifiers are marked by an objective case marker showing existential identity. This type of qualification is the reason for including the quasi-existential use of the verb གྱུར་ among the rhetorical verbs.

---

## *Verbs of Motion*

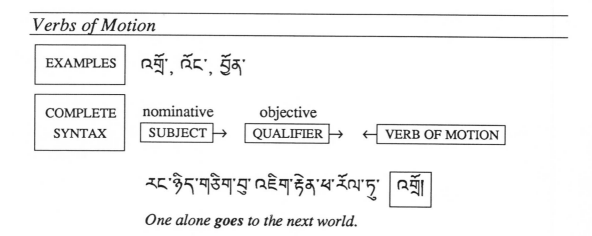

One alone **goes** to the next world.

---

## *Nominative Action Verbs*

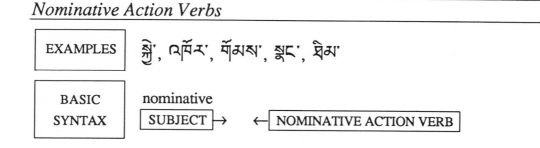

*The wheel **turns**.*

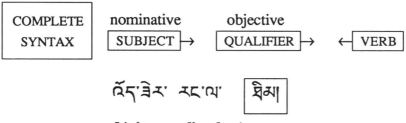

*Light rays **dissolve** into us.*

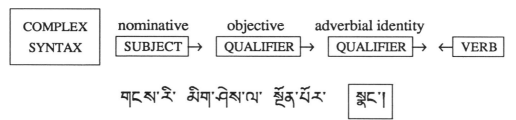

*The snow mountain **appears** blue to the visual consciousness.*

The verb གྱུར་ often functions in a way *lexically* equivalent to the verb ཨིན་ but *syntactically* similar to the verb ཡོད་. It is typically used in this way as a verbal adjective ending a clause. The objective case qualifier is an instance of existential identity. (See Appendix Five.)

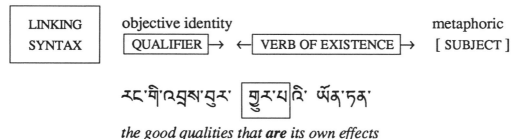

*the good qualities that **are** its own effects*

## Rhetorical Verbs

These verbs act like verbs of existence, but are more complex syntactically and lexically.

| EXAMPLES | རུང་, རིགས་, འཐད་, ཐལ་ |
|----------|------------------------|

| BASIC SYNTAX | nominative<br>SUBJECT →   ← VERB |
|--------------|---------------------------------------------|

དེ་གཉིས་ཀ་ ཡང་ མི་རིགས་ སོ།

*Both of these **are** also **incorrect**.*

| COMPLETE SYNTAX | nominative<br>SUBJECT → | objective<br>COMPLEMENT →   ← VERB |
|-----------------|--------------------------|-----------------------------------------------|

ཕུང་པོ་ལ་ བརྟེན་ནས་ བཏགས་པའི་ གང་ཟག་ ཕུང་པོར་ མི་རུང་།

*The person imputed in dependence on the aggregates
**is not admissible** as an aggregate.*[235]

དབང་པོ་ གཟུགས་ཅན་པ་ ཚད་མར་ མི་རུང་།

*A physical sense power **is not admissible** as a prime cognition.*[236]

| ALTERNATE SYNTAX | unstated<br>SUBJECT → | objective<br>COMPLEMENT →   ← RHETORICAL VERB |
|------------------|------------------------|---------------------------------------------------------|

གཞན་དུ་ན་ ངོ་བོ་ཉིད་མེད་པ་ དོན་དམ་མོ་ ཞིས་སྨྲ་བར་ མི་རིགས་ ཏེ།

*Otherwise, it **would not be correct** to say that lack of identity is an ultimate.*[237]

## Class IV: *Nominative-Syntactic Verbs*

Nominative-syntactic verbs take their subjects in the nominative but require—in clauses and sentences that fully express their meaning—a qualifier marked by a particle that is not one of the *la*-group of particles. The first type is marked by fifth-case particles, but all the rest are marked by non-case-marking syntactic particles. There are four types of Class IV verbs.

1   **Separative verbs** (such as གྲོལ་) indicate separation or protection from something (or someone); the fifth case particles are used to mark that from which the subject is separated or protected.

2   **Verbs of absence** (such as སྟོང་) indicate a lack of something—marked by the syntactic particles otherwise used to mark the agentive case.

3   **Conjunctive verbs** (such as འབྲེལ་) indicate a relationship to something which is marked by the syntactic particle དང་.

4   **Disjunctive verbs** (such as བྲལ་) indicate an absence of something which is marked by the syntactic particle དང་.

---

## *Separative Verbs*

These verbs have fifth case qualifiers (where the qualifier states that from which the verb separates the subject).

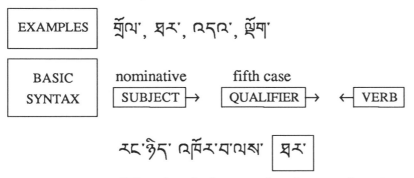

| EXAMPLES | གྲོལ་, ཐར་, འདའ་, ཕྱུག་ |

| BASIC SYNTAX | nominative  SUBJECT →  fifth case  QUALIFIER →  ← VERB |

རང་ཉིད་ འཁོར་བ་ལས་ ཐར་

*[They them]selves **are free** from cyclic existence.*

Note that there are also agentive verbs that take fifth case qualifiers—for example, ${\text{སློབ}}$ and ${\text{སྲུང}}$. They are not included in this class of nominative verbs.

---

## Verbs of Absence

These verbs have qualifiers marked by the syntactic particles otherwise used to mark the agentive case (where the qualifier states that which is absent).

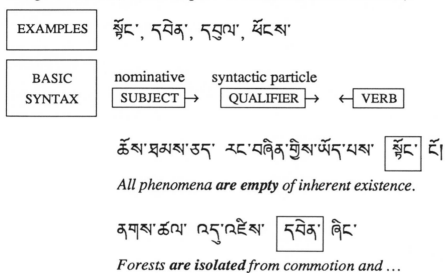

| EXAMPLES | སྟོང་, དབེན་, དབྲལ་, ཕོངས་ |

BASIC SYNTAX

nominative | syntactic particle
SUBJECT → | QUALIFIER → | ← VERB

ཆོས་ཐམས་ཅད་ རང་བཞིན་གྱིས་ཡོད་པས་ སྟོང་ ངོ།

*All phenomena **are empty** of inherent existence.*

ནགས་ཚལ་ འདུ་འཛིས་ དབེན་ ཞིང་

*Forests **are isolated** from commotion and ...*

---

## Conjunctive Verbs

These verbs have qualifiers marked by the syntactic particle དང་ (where the qualifier states that to which the verb relates the subject).

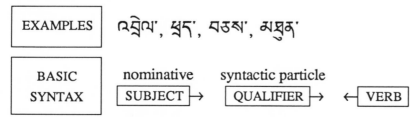

| EXAMPLES | འབྲེལ་, ཕྲད་, བཅས་, མཐུན་ |

BASIC SYNTAX

nominative | syntactic particle
SUBJECT → | QUALIFIER → | ← VERB

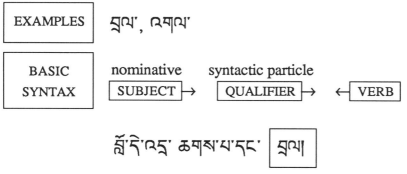

ང་རང་ མི་སྡུག་པ་དང་ ཕྲད་ ན།

*If we meet with the unpleasant, ...*

There are also agentive verbs (such as སྦྱོར་) which express the joining of things or people that may take a qualifier marked by the syntactic particle དང་. They are not included in this type of nominative verb.

## Disjunctive Verbs

These verbs have qualifiers marked by the syntactic particle དང་ (where the qualifier states that from which the verb separates the subject).

| EXAMPLES | གྲོལ་, འགའལ་ |
| --- | --- |

| BASIC SYNTAX | nominative  SUBJECT → | syntactic particle  QUALIFIER → | ← VERB |

བློ་དེ་འདྲ་ ཆགས་པ་དང་ གྲོལ།

*Such a mind is free of attachment.*

## Category Two:  Agentive Verbs

Most Tibetan action verbs take subjects in the third or agentive case.  Such verbs also have objects—in English, direct objects.  Some take these objects in the objective or beneficial cases, but most take them in the nominative case.  There are two classes of verbs whose subjects are in the third or agentive case:

V  agentive-nominative verbs,

VI  agentive-objective verbs.

Class VI includes the very few verbs that take a direct object in the fourth case (although there are many that take indirect fourth case objects).

> In the sentence, *He gave medicine to the poor*, the direct object is *medicine* and the indirect object is *the poor*.

The one common verb that takes a fourth case direct object is ཕན་ (*help, aid, benefit*), although in fact ཕན་ usually occurs not as a free-standing verb, but as the first part of the phrasal verb ཕན་འདོགས་ (which also means *help, aid, benefit*).

Some agentive-nominative verbs are used—as Class VIII verbs—to show attribution as well. Calling something by a certain name or speaking about something may be expressed using normally agentive-nominative verbs in an unusual syntax (sometimes nominative-locative, sometimes locative-nominative).

## Agentive-Nominative Verbs

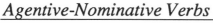

| EXAMPLES | བསྟན་, བྱེད་, འཛིན་ |

SIMPLE SYNTAX

agentive SUBJECT →    nominative OBJECT →    ← VERB

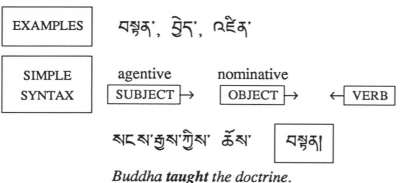

སངས་རྒྱས་ཀྱིས་ ཆོས་ བསྟན། 

*Buddha **taught** the doctrine.*

## Agentive-Objective Verbs

| EXAMPLES | ལྟ་, སྟོད་, ཁྲབ་ |

SIMPLE SYNTAX

agentive SUBJECT →    objective OBJECT →    ← VERB

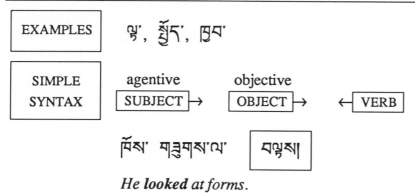

ཁོས་ གཟུགས་ལ་ བལྟས། 

*He **looked** at forms.*

## *Irregular Agentive-Nominative Syntax*
## Irregular Subjects

The syntactic particle ནི་ following a noun or pronoun distinguishes it as the subject of a clause or sentence reporting discourse or opinion. It thus acts like an agentive case particle, since the verbs ending such constructions are typically agentive-nominative verbs.

Nouns or pronouns (including noun phrases and clauses) ending in the pluralizing syntactic particles རྣམས་ or དག་, especially when they are followed by the punctuational syntactic particle ནི་, are often the subjects of the clauses and sentences in which they are found—even when those clauses and sentences end in agentive verbs.

Any of the agentive-nominative verbs may be seen, it would seem, with nominative subjects. This is especially to be expected with reports of discourse or opinion. The attributive verbs of Class VIII—verbs that attribute a meaning to a word or phrase—sometimes seem to function as locative-nominative verbs and at other times as nominative-locative verbs. In the first instance, a literal translation would read something like *That* [locative subject] *is called that* [nominative], and the nominative object is actually marked by a non-case, syntactic particle (such as ཞེས་). In the second instance, one might say *That* [nominative subject] *refers to that* [locative].

Note that the attributive verb བྱེད་, although it does not vary in form from the even more common agentive-nominative action verb བྱེད་, is used very differently. If it ever occurred with an agent—someone who attributed the meaning to the word or phrase—that agent would be in the agentive case. However, when བྱེད་ is used as an attributive verb, it is used without this agentive case agent, in the same manner as ཟེར་—another verb which, in its meaning of *speak* or *discuss*, is an agentive-nominative verb, but in its meaning of *be called*, is a locative-nominative verb.[238]

The attributive verbs are not easy to classify. Whereas བྱེད་ probably ought to be considered a transitive verb even here, at least one lexicographer distinguishes the two senses of ཟེར་ (related immediately above) as transitive and intransitive, respectively.[239]

Thus, in *Translating Buddhism from Tibetan*, the attributive syntax has been assigned to Class VIII—the locative nominative verbs.

## *Irregular Agentive-Nominative Syntax*
## Irregular Objects

There are certain syntactic particles that act as if they were case marking particles indicating subjects or objects. The syntactic particles ཅེས་, ཞེས་, and ཤེས་ following a word, phrase, clause, or sentence serve the function of an English end-of-quotation marker ( " ). They cause the word, phrase, clause, or sentence they follow to act syntactically as a noun phrase in the nominative case. This nominative phrase is then to be construed as the object of the agentive-nominative verb terminating the clause or sentence in which is is found.

| EXAMPLES | ཟེར་, འདོད་ |
| --- | --- |

| SIMPLE SYNTAX | nominative SUBJECT → nominative OBJECT + SP → ← VERB |

མདོ་སྡེ་པ་དག་ འདུས་བྱས་རྣམས་ སྐད་ཅིག་གིས་འཇིག་པ་ ཞེས་ | འདོད་ | དོ།

*Sautrāntikas **assert**, "Compound phenomena are momentarily disintegrating."*

## Category Three:  Specialized Verbs

There are two classes of specialized verbs—verbs whose subjects as we understand them in English are marked by one or another of the *la*-group of particles:

  VII  purposive-nominative verbs;

  VIII  locative-nominative verbs.

## *Purposive-Nominative Verbs*

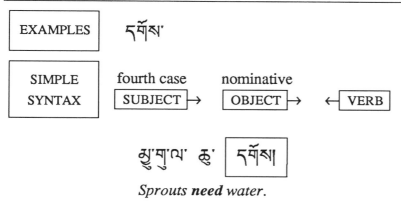

Sprouts **need** water.

## *Locative-Nominative Verbs*

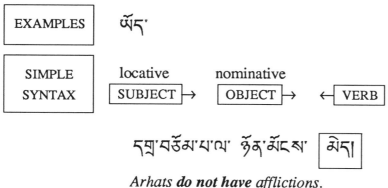

Arhats **do not have** afflictions.

## *Attributive Syntax*

EXAMPLES བྱེད་, གསུང་

The verbs བྱེད་, འཆད་, and གསུང་ are used in Tibetan in situations where something is being *spoken of* in a certain way, *characterized* in a certain way, or something is being *called* a certain name or *referred to* in a certain way.

Although these verbs are regularly agentive-nominative verbs, they act sometimes like locative-nominative verbs and sometimes like nominative-locative verbs.

The following example illustrates the use of a locative qualifier—གཞན་དབང་ལ་—which here translates as *about dependent phenomena* or *in the context of dependent phenomena*. The sentence thus tells us that Buddha *spoke of* (གསུངས་) bases of imputation in the context of speaking about *dependent phenomena* (གཞན་དབང་).

རྫོགས་པོ་དང་ཁྱད་པར་དུ་འདོགས་པའི་གཞི་ གཞན་དབང་ལ་  གསུངས།

[Literally] *Buddha **spoke of** the bases of imputing entities and particulars about dependent phenomena.*[240]

[English syntax] *[Buddha] **called** dependent phenomena the basis of imputing entities and particulars.*

The irregular, attributive syntax of these normally agentive verbs is the following.

| ATTRIBUTIVE SYNTAX | unstated AGENT → | locative SUBJECT → | nominative OBJECT → | ← VERB |
|---|---|---|---|---|

The following two examples are common patterns seen where the verb བྱེད་ means not *do*, but *call* or *refer to*. In the first example, the word order suggests translating the sentence as if the syntax were NOMINATIVE SUBJECT + LOCATIVE OBJECT + VERB.

དམ་པ་ནི་ ཟག་མེད་ཀྱི་མཉམ་གཞག་གི་ཡེ་ཤེས་ལ་  བྱས་  ནས་

*[The term] ultimate **referring** to uncontaminated meditative wisdom.*[241]

However, བྱེད་ may also be translated as *is called*, as if the syntax were LOCATIVE SUBJECT + NOMINATIVE OBJECT + VERB.

An alternate syntax replaces the nominative object with a phrase ending in a quotation-marking syntactic particle.

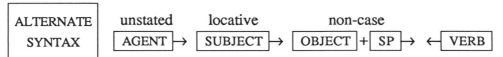

| ALTERNATE SYNTAX | unstated AGENT → | locative SUBJECT → | non-case OBJECT + SP → | ← VERB |

གསུམ་པ་ལ་ ལེགས་པར་རྣམ་པར་ཕྱེ་བའི་འཁོར་ལོ་ ཞེས་ བྱའོ།

*To the third **is given** [the name] "wheel of good differentiation."* [242]

*The third **is called** "wheel of good differentiation."*

## Understood Linking Verbs

Many Tibetan clauses and sentences end in an implicit ཡིན་. Thus, where the syntax of a clause or sentence does not seem proper, this option should not be overlooked in favor of a conclusion that the syntax is irregular.

For example, the best way to understand གཞན་དབང་ནི་ in the following sentence is not as an irregular *object* of the nominative verb བྱ་ (*refer to*—which takes a locative object), but rather as a regular nominative subject of an understood linking ཡིན་, whose complement is then དོན་དམ་པ་ངོ་བོ་ཉིད་མེད་པ་ཞེས་བྱ་. In that latter phrase, ཞེས་བྱ་ should be read as the object verbal it very commonly is (giving the literal translation, *the so-called "lack of an identity [which is] an ultimate"*).

གཞན་དབང་ནི་ དོན་དམ་པ་ངོ་བོ་ཉིད་མེད་པ་ ཞེས་ བྱ་ སྟེ།

*Dependent phenomena **are termed** "lacking an identity [which is] an ultimate."* [243]

## Verb Forms

There are three fundamental structures that form the basis for Tibetan verb constructions:

1 the **basic** verb (as seen in བྱེད་, ཐོགས་, དགོས་, ཡིན་, and རན་);

2 the **simple infinitive** (such as རན་དུ་ and ཐོགས་སུ་);

3　the **verbal infinitive** (such as དྲན་པར་, རྟོགས་པར་, and ཡིན་པར་).

The basic verb acts as the basis for the two infinitives. Whereas basic verbs end sentences—with or without the addition of a second, modifying verb (as in རྟོགས་ དགོས་), infinitives may not. Tibetan infinitives sometimes translate into their English counterparts (that is, as infinitives such as *to remember* and *to realize*), but often do not. For example, the verb phrase བསྒོམ་པར་བྱ་ —from the basic verb བསྒོམ་, the future tense of སྒོམ་ (*meditate*)—means *should meditate* or *will meditate*, depending on context. It does not mean *will perform* (བྱ་) *to meditate* (བསྒོམ་པར་), despite the fact that the future tense construction བསྒོམ་པར་བྱ་ is based on what is technically an infinitive.

---

In English, there are three non-finite verb constructions: the infinitive (*to finish*), the *ing*-participle (*finishing*), and the *ed*-participle (*finished*). However, neither Tibetan participles (called verbals in this book) nor infinitives function in the same ways as they do in English. They are similar in that they are not complete verbs.

---

## *Basic Verbs*

The basic verb is the verb with no added syntactic particles. Basic verbs are most often single-syllable, or **core verbs**—such as བྱེད་ (*do, make, perform*) or དྲན་ (*remember, be mindful of*). However, some Tibetan verbs have more than one syllable. Multisyllable verbs include **phrasal verbs** (that is, verbs whose basic form is a phrase) such as the following.

| | | |
|---|---|---|
| དོན་དུ་གཉེར་ | **tön-du-ñyér** | *seek* |
| ཁས་ལེན་ | **khë>-lên** | *assert* [literally, MOUTH-BY HOLD] |
| ཞལ་བཞེས་ | **shël-shé'** | [honorific of ཁས་ལེན་] |
| ཁྱད་དུ་གསད་ | **khyë'-du-s̄ë'** | *disparage* |
| ཁོང་དུ་ཆུད་ | **khong-du-chü'** | *understand* |

| ཉམས་སུ་ལེན་ | **nyam-su-lên** | *practice* [lit. EXPERIENCE-IN HOLD] |
| ཡིད་ལ་བྱེད་ | **yí'-la-<u>ch</u>é'** | *attend to* [MIND-IN DO] |

Verbs such as མངོན་པར་རྟོགས་ (*realize*) are **multisyllable** but not phrasal. Such verbs often incorporate literal translations of Sanskrit prefix syllables: མངོན་པར་རྟོགས་, for example, translates the Sanskrit verb *abhisami*, where the root of the verb is *i* and *abhi* and *sam* are prefix syllables. མངོན་པར་ is the standard Tibetan translation of *abhi-*, leaving the *i* to be translated as རྟོགས་. The Sanskrit prefix *sam* is not translated in the Tibetan མངོན་པར་རྟོགས་.

**Multisyllable phrasal verbs** are formed from what in other contexts would be brief phrases. The verb ཁས་ལེན་, for instance, a verb quite common in philosophical writing, is built out of other words, ཁ་ (*mouth*) and ལེན་ (*grasp*). Translated overly literally, ཁས་ལེན་ means *grasped by the mouth* (since ཁས་ is the agentive form of ཁ་). ཁས་ལེན་, however, is not a phrase; it is a word. The dot between the two syllables is not a C dot but rather an S dot.

Two (or more) syllabled verbs function in most ways as do other verbs. However, when they change forms to show the different tenses, they do not change completely, but only in the last syllable—that is, only in their core syllable. Thus, ཉམས་སུ་ལེན་ changes form in the following way—from past, through present and future tenses, ending in the imperative.

| ཉམས་སུ་བླངས་ | ཉམས་སུ་ལེན་ | ཉམས་སུ་བླང་ | ཉམས་སུ་ལེནད་ |

རག་ལས་ is a single-form verb; it does not change form to indicate past, present, and future.

All multisyllable verbs, however, are negated in the same way.

> Multi-syllable verbs are negated by negating their final syllables. Some verbs require the use of the negative particle མ་; others require the use of མི་.

| རག་མ་ལས་ | **rak-ma-lë>** | *does not depend [on]* |

| ཁས་མི་ལེན་ | **khë>-mí-lên** | *does not assert* |
| ཡིད་ལ་མི་བྱེད་ | **yí'-la-mí-<u>ch</u>é'** | *does not pay attention [to]* |

## Simple Infinitives

The **simple infinitive** is used in constructions such as that expressing activity caused by an outside force, the **causative** verb phrase. (An example is དྲན་དུ་བཅུག—*made to remember*—where the simple infinitive form of དྲན་ is དྲན་དུ་, དུ་ in this instance being not a case marking particle but a syntactic particle.) Simple infinitives are also used in **entreaty** constructions (such as དགོངས་སུ་གསོལ་—*please consider*). The dot before the syntactic particle is an **SP** dot, but the dot at the end of the simple infinitive is an open verb, **V** dot.

## Verbal Infinitives

The **verbal infinitive** requires the core verb (for example, དྲན་) first to be made into a verbal (དྲན་པ་) and then into an infinitive (དྲན་པར་). Verbal infinitives are used in many verb phrases. In some cases, they carry a meaning akin to the English infinitive (*to remember, to meditate, to say*), but in most instances merely the form of the verbal infinitive is present (as in བསྒོམ་པར་བྱ་, which means *will meditate* and *should meditate*).

The infinitive-making particle—here, ར་—is a verb modifying syntactic particle. However, the dot after it—that is, the dot after the བསྒོམ་པར་ in བསྒོམ་པར་བྱ་—is a **V** dot, since an infinitive is an open verb.

## Verbs in Context

There are thus five basic contexts in which a verb may occur.

● A simple or core form of a verb (such as རྟོགས་ or བསྒོམ་) is marked by a **VB** dot.

- A core verb as a member of a compound verb construction (such as ཪྟོགས་ དགོས་, *must realize*) is marked by the open verb, **V** dot. (The entire construction is followed by a **VB** dot.)

- A core verb followed by a continuative syntactic particle (as seen in ཪྟོགས་ ནས་, *having realized*) is marked by a **V** dot (and the syntactic particle is followed by an **SP** dot).

- A core verb followed by a sentence-terminating syntactic particle is followed by a **VB** dot. Examples include ༠བྱེད་དོ། (*[He] makes ...*) and མ་ འཇིགས་ཤིག (*Do not fear!*).

- Verbs in their infinitive forms are used in verb phrases indicating, for example, tense (such as the བསྒོམ་པར་ in བསྒོམ་པར་བྱ་, *will meditate* or *should meditate*). The infinitive is followed by a **V** dot, but the phrase as a whole is followed by a **VB** dot.

Core verbs may have up to four forms, with different forms for the past tense, present tense, future tense, and imperative. There are also three-form, two-form, and single-form verbs. The very common verb བྱེད་ (*do, make, perform*) is a four-form verb.

---

| past: བྱས་ | present: བྱེད་ | future: བྱ་ | imperative: བྱོས་ |

---

Verbs are often used in their core forms—as simple verbs at the end of clauses and sentences, as verbs in compound verb constructions, and when followed by syntactic particles.

| core verb | སངས་རྒྱས་ཀྱིས་ ཆོས་ བསྟན། |

*Buddha **taught** the doctrine.*

| compound verb | བདེ་བའི་རྒྱུ་ བསྒྲུབ་དགོས། |

*[One] **must accomplish** the causes of happiness.*

| verb followed by syntactic particle | བག་ཆགས་ | བཞག་ནས། | མཐུ་ཅན་དུ་ | གྱུར་ནས། |

*a latency **is deposited** and, **having become** powerful ...*

Verbs are also used in their core form when followed by syntactic particles marking imperatives, completed action, and permission.

| verb followed by imperative particle | བརྩོན་འགྲུས་ | རྩོམས་ཤིག |

***Make effort!***[244]

In some compound forms (as with ནུས་), the verb must first be made into its verbal infinitive form in order to be connected to the second verb.

| infinitive compounds | བསྒྲུབས་པར་ནུས། | རྙེད་པར་དཀའ། |

***able to have achieved***        ***difficult to obtain***

སྐུའི་བཀོད་པ་དུ་མ་ཅིག་ཅར་ཉིད་དུ་ སྟོན་པར་ནུས།

*[A Buddha] is **able to display** many bodies at once.*[245]

It should be noted that the actual verbs of these phrases and sentences—the verbs governing their syntax—are the ones occurring first (བསྒྲུབས་, རྙེད་, and སྟོན་) and not the ནུས་ or the དཀའ་.

   The verbal infinitive form is also used in all constructions employing the auxiliary verbs བྱེད་ (usually in the present བྱེད་ or future བྱ་, but also sometimes as བྱས་) and འགྱུར་ (as either the past གྱུར་ or future འགྱུར་).

| auxiliary construction | ལྷག་པའི་ཚུལ་ཁྲིམས་ལ་ | བསླབ་པར་བྱ། |

*One should train in extraordinary ethics.*

Of course these verb phrases often appear in abbreviated form, especially in verse, where meter dictates a fixed number of syllables. In that case, the middle པར་ or བར་ is omitted as in ཉེད་གྱུར་ and གོམས་བྱས་.

In some forms, such as causative constructions, the simple infinitive (the core verb + སུ་, ར་, རུ་, དུ་, or ཏུ་) is used.

| causative | གཞན་གྱིས་བསགས་པའི་ལས་ཀྱི་འབྲས་བུ་ | མྱོང་དུ་བཅུག་པ་ | མིན་པ་ |

*It is not the case that [one] **has been made to experience** the effects of actions accumulated by others.*[246]

Adding འཇུག་ or one of its other forms to a simple infinitive conveys a strong causative sense. འཇུག་ is a four-form verb.

| past: བཅུག་ | present: འཇུག་ | future: གཞུག་ | imperative: ཆུགས་ |

Used as a causative, the འཇུག་ then governs the syntax of the sentence, something auxiliary verbs do not do.

*It is suitable [in either case]: whether [one] remembers onself or has been caused to remember by someone else.*[247]

རང་གིས་དྲན་པའམ་གཞན་གྱིས་དྲན་དུ་བཅུག་ཀྱང་རུང་སྟེ།

## Auxiliary Verbs

Tibetan has a number of different auxiliary verbs, verbs that are used on a regular basis following other verbs to convey the following ideas.

- ཤ་ indicates that one will do or ought to do something or that one will cause something to happen.

- བྱེད་ indicates that one does something or one causes something to happen.

- འགྱུར་ conveys the sense that something will happen or that something would happen or would be the case contingent on something else happening or being the case.

- གྱུར་ (the past tense form) is used in conditional statements in the sense of *if something were the case*, then something else would come to be (འགྱུར་) the case. It may also to be used to mark past actions.

- ཟིན་ indicates that an action has been completed in the past.

- A verbal infinitive followed by བོག་ conveys an optative sense—*hoping* that something is the case or will come to pass.

Constructions ending in a simple infinitive followed by གསོལ་ and those ending in a core verb followed by ཚག་ are not auxiliary constructions, but rather compound verb phrases. Core verbs or simple infinitives followed by ནུས་ and core verbs followed by རུང་ are also compound verb constructions.

The auxiliary verbs ཤ་, བྱེད་, འགྱུར་, and གྱུར་ follow the verbal infinitive form.

| strong present auxiliary | ཚེ་འདིའི་བདེ་བ་ཙམ་དོན་དུ་གཉེར་བར་ བྱེད་ པ་ |
|---|---|

*seeking merely the bliss of this lifetime ...*[248]

---

*Therefore, a profound doctrine such as this has been taught by the gurus and disciples listen.*[249]

---

དེས་ན་འདི་ལྟ་བུའི་ཆོས་ཟབ་མོ་སྔ་མས་བསྟན། སློབ་མས་ཉན་པར་ བྱེད །

| strong future auxiliary | དགེ་བ་ཀུན་ལ་བདག་གིས་བརྩོན་པས་བསླབ་པར་ བྱ། |
|---|---|

*I will train with effort in all positive [attitudes].*[250]

The more elegant equivalent form of བྱེད་ — བགྱི་ (in its past བགྱིས་, present བགྱིད་, and future བགྱི་)—and the honorific མཛད་ may also be used as strong auxiliary verbs.

| elegant strong auxiliary | མི་དགེ་བ་སྙིང་ནས་བཤགས་ཤིང་སྡོམ་པར་ བགྱི། |
|---|---|

*I will confess negative [attitudes] and refrain from [them] from [my] heart.*[251]

| honorific strong auxiliary | རྒྱལ་བའི་བསྟན་པ་ཉིན་མོ་ལྟར་གསལ་བར་མཛད་དེ། |
|---|---|

*[He] illuminated like the day the teaching of the Conqueror.*[252]

## Strong Auxiliaries with Nominative Verbs

The auxiliaries བྱ་ and བྱེད་, and even the past form བྱས་, when used with nominative verbs introduce an almost causative sense.

| strong past auxiliary | གོམས་པར་བྱས་ཀྱང་ |
|---|---|

*Although one has familiarized …*[253]

Thus, the meaning of the above example is that familiarity has been made to happen. The following sentence shows the way in which the phrase བར་བར་བྱས་ཏེ་ shows sequence (*First I will liberate and then I will …*) and also brings an agentive sense to the nominative verb བར་.

*I [will] liberate this sentient being from suffering [and], having done that,*
  *I alone will bear this suffering of hell.*[254]

སེམས་ཅན་འདི་ སྡུག་བསྔལ་ལས་ ཐར་བར་བྱས་ཏེ་
དམྱལ་བའི་སྡུག་བསྔལ་འདི་ ང་གཅིག་པུས་ བཟོད་པར་བྱའོ།

An alternate interpretation of constructions such as ཐར་བར་བྱས་ and གོམས་པར་བྱས་ is that བྱས་ is not an actual auxiliary, but the main verb of the clause or sentence. This is easily seen in the following example.

*No matter how many pleasures of cyclic existence [one] has enjoyed,*
  *[they] bring about an increase in craving.*[255]

འཁོར་བའི་བདེ་བ་ལ་ཇི་ཙམ་སྤྱད་ཀྱང་སྲེད་པ་རྒྱས་པར་བྱས་ཏེ་

Thus, in the above example, instead of བྱས་པར་ being a verbal infinitive, it may be understood as a verbal noun, བྱས་པ་, marked in the second case as an objective complement.

## Weak Auxiliaries

Forms of the past and the future that are less forceful are made using the nominative verb འགྱུར་ as an auxiliary. The future form is much more common than the past and, in fact, the past tense གྱུར་ is used most frequently in the first part of a conditional *if ... then ...* sequence, meaning *were*. The subsequent *then ...* clause may then end in the auxiliary འགྱུར་, although it often ends in a simple core verb.

*If sound were permanent, [it] would be causeless.*

སྒྲ་རྟག་པ་ཡིན་པར་གྱུར་ན། རྒྱུ་མེད་ཡིན་པར་འགྱུར།

| weak past auxiliary | ཆོས་འདིའི་གཏིང་རྟོགས་དཀའ་བར་མཐིན་གྱུར་ནས།། |
|---|---|
| | *Having come to realize that the depths*<br>  *of this doctrine are difficult to understand ...*[256] |

| weak future auxiliary | རྡོ་རྗེ་འཆང་གི་གོ་འཕང་ཚེ་འདི་ཉིད་ལ་ཐོབ་པར་འགྱུར། |
|---|---|

*[One] will achieve the status of a Vajradhara
in this very lifetime.*

The auxiliary ཤོག creates an optative construction, one that indicates a hope that something will be the case.

| optative auxiliary | འགྲོ་ཀུན་སྒྲོལ་བར་ཤོག |
|---|---|

*May [I] liberate all beings!*[257]

The auxiliary ཟིན་ follows the past form of a core verb to show an action completed in the past.

| completed action auxiliary | དལ་འབྱོར་ཐོབ་པའི་རྒྱུ་བསྒྲུབས་ཟིན་ཡང་། |
|---|---|

*Even though [one] has achieved the causes
for obtaining leisure and opportunity, ...*[258]

# *Appendix Five*
# *Usages of the Declensions*

## The Eight Cases and Nineteen Case Marking Particles

The English words 'case' and 'declension' translate the Tibetan རྣམ་པར་དབྱེ་བ.
Although the system of describing Tibetan grammar used in this book is not rigidly
based on traditional Tibetan grammars, an attempt has been made to incorporate
traditional terminology and categories where useful. Tibetan tradition dictates that
the ways in which nouns, pronouns, and adjectives are used in phrases, clauses, and
sentences is described—at least in part—by the eight cases. The terms that are used
in this book are the ones in the middle column of the following table, closely following the names used in Tibetan. The terms more often seen in English-language
books on Tibetan grammar follow the Sanskritist's convention of using Latinate
terms; these terms are listed in the right-hand column immediately below.

| | | | |
|---|---|---|---|
| 1 | first case | **nominative** | (nominative) |
| 2 | second case | **objective** | (accusative) |
| 3 | third case | **agentive** | (instrumental) |
| 4 | fourth case | **beneficial & purposive** | (dative) |
| 5 | fifth case | **originative** | (ablative) |
| 6 | sixth case | **connective** | (genitive) |
| 7 | seventh case | **locative** | (locative) |
| 8 | eighth case | **vocative** | (vocative) |

Actually, the cases are known *either* by numbers (*first* and so forth) or by names (*nominative* and so forth). In this book, the fourth case will be identified sometimes as beneficial and sometimes as purposive, depending on how it is being used at the time.

The chart below gives the Tibetan numbers and the less frequently used names of the case marking particles.

| 1 | རྣམ་དབྱེ་དང་པོ་ | nominative | མིང་ཚམ་ |
| 2 | རྣམ་དབྱེ་གཉིས་པ་ | objective | ལས་སུ་བྱ་བའི་སྒྲ་ |
| 3 | རྣམ་དབྱེ་གསུམ་པ་ | agentive | བྱེད་སྒྲ་ |
| 4 | རྣམ་དབྱེ་བཞི་པ་ | beneficial & purposive | དགོས་ཆེད་ཀྱི་སྒྲ་ |
| 5 | རྣམ་དབྱེ་ལྔ་པ་ | originative | འབྱུང་ཁུངས་ཀྱི་སྒྲ་ |
| 6 | རྣམ་དབྱེ་དྲུག་པ་ | connective | འབྲེལ་སྒྲ་ |
| 7 | རྣམ་དབྱེ་བདུན་པ་ | locative | རྟེན་གནས་ཀྱི་སྒྲ་ |
| 8 | རྣམ་དབྱེ་བརྒྱད་པ་ | vocative | བོད་སྒྲ་ |

The following chart lists the **case marking particles** according to the declensions they mark.

1 first or nominative — marked by no particle
2 second or objective — either སུ་, ར་, ཏུ་, དུ་, ན་, ར་, or ལ་
3 third or agentive — either གིས་, ཀྱིས་, གྱིས་, འིས་, or ཡིས་
4 fourth or beneficial & purposive — either སུ་, ར་, ཏུ་, དུ་, ན་, ར་, or ལ་
5 fifth or originative — either ནས་ or ལས་
6 sixth or connective — either གི་, ཀྱི་, གྱི་, འི་, or ཡི་
7 seventh or locative — either སུ་, ར་, ཏུ་, དུ་, ན་, ར་, or ལ་
8 eighth or vocative — marked by no particle

Two particles are listed by grammarians as particles denoting the eighth case; they are ཀྱེ་, and ཀྭ་ཡེ་. In English these would be called interjections.

## Non-Case-Marking Usages of the Case Marking Particles

All nineteen case marking particles are also sometimes used as syntactic particles (that is, as particles that do not mark declension). Many of the *la* group of particles, for instance, are also used with verbs to create infinitives. (For a more complete explanation, see Appendix Seven.)

Of the nineteen case marking particles, nine also occur as common words.

| *la*-group of particles | སུ་ also means *who*. |
|---|---|
| | ར་ also means *section* or *[animal] horn*. |
| | དུ་ is a common contraction of དུ་མ་ (*many*). |
| | ན་ is also a verb meaning *is ill*. |
| | ར་ also means *goat*. |
| | ལ་ also means *[mountain] pass*. |
| third case particles | གྱིས་ is also the imperative form of the verb བགྱི་ (*do*). |
| fifth case particles | ནས་ also means *barley*. |
| | ལས་ also means *action* (that is, *karma*). |

Many of the case marking particles also occur as syllables within words. As such, they are merely syllables and are not to be diagrammed as case markers.

| དོན་དུ་གཉེར་ | **tön-du-ñyér** | seek [AG-NOM verb] |
|---|---|---|
| རྗེས་སུ་ཡི་རང་བ་ | **jé>-su-yi-rang-wa** | admiration |
| ཉམས་སུ་ལེན་ | **nyam-su-lên** | practice [AG-NOM verb] |

In the second example—རྗེས་སུ་ཡི་རང་བ་—the སུ་ is part of the lexical particle རྗེས་སུ་ and, thus, derives from the objective/locative particle སུ་, however the ཡི་ is merely a syllable within the word and has no relation to the connective case.

## *A Modern Tibetan Grammarian on the Eight Cases*

Each of the eight cases indicates a number of actual usages, some of which do not completely accord with the names of the cases in which they are found. (For example, a common usage of the objective case is to indicate not the object of a verb but the place in which an activity is done.) Before these different usages are enumerated in detail, let us briefly examine how one modern Tibetan grammarian and lexicographer, Mugé Samden, writing in 1980,[259] summarizes the syntactic functions indicated by the eight cases in a way that attempts to preserve the meaning of the traditional terminology.

Samden bases his explanation on a literal rendering of the term རྣམ་པར་དབྱེ་བ་, *distinguishing*. Case-marking particles are thus seen as enabling one to distinguish between actors, actions, objects of actions, places in which actions are done, and so on. The **first case** is relatively straightforward, merely distinguishing things themselves from each other. The **second case** distinguishes the place in which an action is done (or at which an action is directed) from the action. Mugé Samden further distinguishes three types of relations between the *action* (བྱ་), the *object* of the action (ལས་), and the *place* where the action is done (ཡུལ་):[260]

- where the action and its object are substantially the same, but the object and the place the action is done are different—as in *seeing a form in a mirror* (མེ་ལོང་ནང་དུ་གཟུགས་མཐོང་);

- where the action and its object are substantially different, but the object and the place the action is done are substantially the same—as in *looking at a form* (གཟུགས་ལ་ལྟ་);

- where the action, its object, and the place the action is done are all different (for which no example is given).

In the first situation, the second case particle indicates the place in which the action is done; in the second, it indicates the object of the action.

The **third case** particle separates the *agent* (བྱེད་པ་པོ་) and the *action* (བྱ་བ་) performed by that agent. The **fourth case** distinguishes the *place* (གནས་ཡུལ་) where (or for whom)[261] a purpose is accomplished from that *purpose* (དགོས་པ་). The **fifth case** separates the *basis* (གཞི་) from which something originates from the phenomenon originating from it. The **sixth case** particle separates the place to which there is a connection from the phenomenon connected to it. The **seventh case** distinguishes the place where something (or someone) is located from the phenomenon located there.[262] As has been noted, the **eighth case**—the vocative—is a fairly artificial case in Tibetan; Mugé Samden, seemingly in reference to the interjectory particles, says the eighth case distinguishes the simple noun from nouns qualified with the vocative.

Samden goes on to consider three further uses of the case-marking particles otherwise used to mark the second, fourth, and seventh cases (སུ་, ར་, རུ་, དུ་, ན་, ར་, and ལ་ —the so-called *la*-equivalents). These are the *temporal* (ཆེ་སྐབས་), *identity* (དེ་ཉིད་), and *'foundational'* (གཞི་འཛིན་པའི་) uses. (It is possible to include the temporal and foundational functions in the seventh case and the identity function in the second case, and that has been done in the system used throughout this book. That notwithstanding, the identity and foundational [in this book's terminology—referential] usages have been treated as special instances of those cases.)

The identity-marking particle is used, according to Mugé Samden, in situations where the dynamic verbal action or static verbal statement is not substantially different from that to which the particle is applied.[263] Thus, *existing truly* (བདེན་པར་གྲུབ་པ་) is a phrase in which the existence and the truly are not different. Likewise, the significance of the sentence *Among trees, there are sandalwoods* (ཤིང་ལ་ཙན་དན་ཡོད།) is that there are sandalwoods which are of the nature of trees—that is, sandalwoods *are* trees. (This is distinct from the syntax of a sentence such as *Trees have leaves* [ཤིང་ལ་ལོ་མ་ཡོད།], despite the structural identity of the Tibetan. In *Trees have leaves*, ཤིང་ལ་ is a locative; leaves are not themselves trees but, rather, are dependent on trees.[264] I have not followed Mugé Samden's system in this book. My analysis is syntactic and structural, and this differentiates it from traditional Tibetan grammars which are, at least in part, grounded in philosophical analyses such as whether a subject and a predicate are substantially the same or different.)

The 'foundational particle'—called here **referential**—is ubiquitous in Tibetan. Mugé Samden lists a multitude of examples, all of which in some way or another present the use of *la*-equivalent particles in ways that do not fit into the traditional definitions of the second, fourth, and seventh cases. Examples include *I am afraid of that* (ང་དེ་ལ་སྐྲག), *I need that book* (དཔེ་ཆ་དེ་ང་ལ་དགོས), and *[He] is skilled in* *medicine* (སྨན་ལ་གཏགས།).²⁶⁵ In many instances the words marked with the *la* appear to be objects or aims of words which are not technically verbs. (Again, this illustrates the difference between a traditional Tibetan grammar and one which seeks to describe the language to English speakers. In the present book words such as ཡོད་ and དགོས་ are called verbs, although traditionally, since they are not words referring to actions [བྱ་ཚིག], they are not verbs. I am thus able to rescue many of Mugé Samden's examples of 'foundational' particles and reclassify them as second, fourth, or seventh case.)

## The Eight Cases

The remainder of Appendix Five is a list of the various usages of the eight Tibetan cases, with examples.

## First Case: Nominative          མིང་ཚམ

Endings: none.

## *Nominatives with Linking Verbs*

Nominatives in sentences or clauses ending in linking verbs are typically either the subject or the predicate.

| | |
|---|---|
| 1.1.1 subject of a linking verb | བུམ་པ་ མི་རྟག་པ་ ཡིན། <br> *Pots are impermanent.* |

| | |
|---|---|
| 1.1.2 complement of a linking verb | བུམ་པ་ མི་རྟག་པ་ ཡིན། <br> *Pots are **impermanent**.* |

## Nominatives with Verbs of Existence, Living, and Dependence

Verbs of existence, living, and dependence require a subject (respectively, that which exists, lives, or depends) in the nominative.

| | |
|---|---|
| **1.2.1** <br> subject of a verb of existence | བུམ་པ་ ཡོད། <br> *Pots exist.* <br><br> བོད་ལ་ རི་ ཡོད། <br> *There are **mountains** in Tibet.* |
| **1.2.2** <br> subject of a verb of living | ཆོས་ འཇིག་རྟེན་དུ་ གནས། <br> ***The doctrine** remains in the world.* |
| **1.2.3** <br> subject of a verb of dependence | འབྲས་བུ་ རྒྱུ་ལ་ རྟེན་ནོ། <br> ***Effects** depend on causes.* |

## Nominative Subjects of Action Verbs

Nominative verbs and verbs of motion have subjects in the nominative case. Nominative verbs and verbs of motion are intransitive action verbs, verbs not associated with separate agents, that is, verbs whose agents and objects are not separate entities.

| | |
|---|---|
| **1.3.1** <br> subject of a nominative verb | འཁོར་ལོ་ འཁོར་རོ། <br> ***The wheel** turns.* |

| 1.3.2<br>nominative agent of a<br>verb of motion | རང་ཉིད་གཅིག་པུ་ | འཇིག་རྟེན་ཕ་རོལ་ཏུ་ འགྲོ |

*One alone* goes to the next world.

| སངས་རྒྱས་ | འཇིག་རྟེན་དུ་ འབྱོན། |

*A Buddha* comes / will come into the world.

## Nominative Subject of Agentive Verbs

In addition, it is possible for the agent of verbs such as ཉེད་ and མཐོང་, regularly seen in the agentive case, to appear in the nominative.

| 1.3.3<br>irregular subject of<br>an agentive verb | འཕགས་པ་རྣམས་ | ནི་ བདག་མེད་ མངོན་སུམ་དུ་ མཐོང། |

*Superiors* see emptiness directly.

This happens with enough frequency in the case of the verb འདོད་ —both those con-structions in which འདོད་ means *desire* and those in which it means *assert*—to sug-gest the possibility that འདོད་ functions regularly either as a nominative verb or as an agentive verb.

---

*All these migrating beings always desire only pleasure.*

---

འགྲོ་བ་འདི་དག་ཐམས་ཅད་ནི་ རྟག་ཏུ་ བདེ་བ་འབའ་ཞིག་ འདོད།

---

---

*Sautrāntikas assert that composed phenomena disintegrate momentarily [moment by moment].*[266]

---

མདོ་སྡེ་པ་དག་ འདུས་བྱས་རྣམས་ སྐད་ཅིག་གིས་འཇིག་པ་ཞེས་ འདོད་དོ།

---

## Nominative Objects

Agentive-nominative verbs have nominative objects.

| | |
|---|---|
| **1.4.1**<br>object of an agentive-<br>nominative verb | སངས་རྒྱས་ཀྱིས་ ☐ཆོས་☐ བསྟན། <br> *Buddha taught **the doctrine**.* |

ལུགས་འདིས་ ☐ཕྱི་དོན་☐ འདོད། 

*This system asserts **external objects**.*

Verbs of possession and verbs of necessity have subjects (respectively, the possessor and the one who needs) in the locative case but their objects (what is possessed or needed) are in the nominative case.

| | |
|---|---|
| **1.4.2**<br>object of a verb of<br>possession | ང་ལ་ ☐བུམ་པ་☐ ཡོད། <br> *I have **a pot**.* |

| | |
|---|---|
| **1.4.3**<br>object of a verb of<br>necessity | མྱུ་གུ་ལ་ ☐ཆུ་☐ དགོས། <br> *Sprouts need **water**.* |

## Topical Nominatives

A nominative standing alone at the beginning of a sentence or as a separate unit may be grammatically unrelated to the sentence, serving as a title or section heading. This corresponds to the **block language** of English grammar.[267]

| | |
|---|---|
| **1.5**<br>topical nominative | གཞི་ལམ་འབྲས་གསུམ་ལས། ☐དང་པོ་☐ ནི། <br> *From among the three—bases, paths, and fruits—* <br> ***the first** is as follows.* |

The nominative དང་པོ་ is not related grammatically to what follows it (in this case, ལུགས་འདིས་བྱེ་དོན་འདོད་ཅིང་').[268] In a polished translation, this would either be translated in outline format or simply as a section heading: *Section One: Bases*. Or, in fuller form, one could say *[This section has] three [parts]: bases, paths, and fruits* and then on the next line place a section heading (*Bases*).

## Second Case: Objective   ལས་སུ་བྱ་བའི་སྐ་

Endings: སུ་  ར་  ཏུ་  དུ་  ན་  ར་  ལ་

## *Objectives with Action Verbs*

The place where something is done (either by an agent or without reference to a separate agent) is not in the locative but in the objective case.

| 2.1<br>place of activity | སངས་རྒྱས་ཀྱིས་ $\boxed{\text{རྒྱ་གར་ལ་}}$ ཆོས་ བསྟན། |
|---|---|

*Buddha taught the doctrine **in India**.*

Some agentive action verbs regularly take their object not in the nominative (as above in case 1.4) but in the objective case. These are the agentive-objective verbs.

| 2.2<br>object of agentive-<br>objective verbs | ཁོས་ མིག་གིས་ $\boxed{\text{གཟུགས་ལ་}}$ བལྟས། |
|---|---|

*He looked **at forms** with [his] eye[s].*

$\boxed{\text{དེ་ལ་}}$ དབྱེ་ན་

*When **that** is divided ...*

Given the name of the second case—ལས་སུ་བྱ་བ་ or *objective*—the syntax just exemplified would seem to be the normal manner in which verbs operate. Nevertheless, they do not. Many—if not most—agentive verbs take nominative, and not objective objects.

## Objectives with Verbs of Motion

Verbs of motion are technically of the class of nominative verbs—that is, verbs not associated with a separate agent. Thus, they make no distinction between agent and object. This means that grammatically they have neither agents nor objects *per se*, merely subjects which are in a sense both their agents and their objects. The subjects of verbs of motion are here termed agents and are in the nominative case.

However, verbs of motion are distinguished from other verbs of the nominative class in that they have destinations. These destinations are marked not by locative but by objective case particles.

| | |
|---|---|
| **2.3.1**<br>destination of a verb<br>of motion | རང་ཉིད་གཅིག་པུ་ འཇིག་རྟེན་ཕ་རོལ་ཏུ་ འགྲོ<br>*One alone goes **to the next world**.* |

There are a number of Tibetan verbs that, in their most basic meanings, are verbs of motion, but that are used metaphorically on many occassions. For example, although the most basic literal meaning of the verb ཞུགས་ (present tense འཇུག་) is *entered*, it is used frequently, still with a nominative subject, in the sense of *being involved in* or *engaging in* something. Thus, in the following example of a metaphorical destination, *others' aims* is the place into which Bodhisattvas have entered.

| | |
|---|---|
| **2.3.2**<br>metaphorical<br>destination | བྱང་ཆུབ་སེམས་དཔའ་ གཞན་དོན་ལ་ ཞུགས་པ་རྣམས་<br>*Bodhisattvas who are involved **in others' aims** ...* |

## Objective Complements

Many agentive verbs that normally take an object in the nominative case, along with some nominative verbs (verbs that do not take objects *per se*), seem sometimes to have objects marked by particles from the *la*-group. The rule of thumb translation for such a construction is as a phrase beginning with the word *that* (on the order of *knows that ..., It is correct that ..., It follows that ...*), or as an infinitive phrase such as *It is correct to ....*

In the case of nominative verbs, however, the objective case complement often occurs in place of a nominative subject. (Alternatively, one can think of the subject as being an unstated one.) The number of examples given for these usages reflects the frequency with which they are seen in Tibetan.

| 2.4 complement of a nominative verb | གཉེན་བཤེས་ལ་ ཆགས་པར་ མི་རིགས་པའོ། |
|---|---|

*It is not correct **to be attached to friends and so forth**.*

སྒྲ་ མི་རྟག་པ་ ཡིན་པར་ ཐལ།

*It follows **that sound is impermanent**.*

In the case of agentive verbs, the object remains in the nominative case, with the objective case complement showing what the verb is doing with that object—for example, how it is being thought of, or what it is being said to be.

| 2.5 complement of an agentive verb | སེམས་ཅན་ ཐམས་ཅད་ མར་ ཤེས། |
|---|---|

*[They] understand all beings **to be [their] mothers**.*

མདོ་རྣམས་ལས་ ཆོས་ཐམས་ཅད་དོ་བོ་ཉིད་མེད་པར་ གསུངས།

*[Buddha] said in sutras **that all phenomena lack identity**.*

སེམས་ཅན་དེ་རྣམས་ རང་གི་གཉེན་དུ་ མཐོང་ནས་

*Once [one] has seen those sentient beings **to be ones friends** ...*

ཁ་ཅིག་གིས་ སེམས་ གང་ཟག་གི་མཚན་གཞིར་ འདོད་དོ།

*Some assert mind **to be the illustration of the person**.*

## *Indirect Objects*

The recipient of an action (that is, the **indirect object** of an agentive verb) is in the fourth (purposive) case if there is benefit done to it; if there is no obvious benefit, the indirect object is in the objective case. (If there is obvious harm, the indirect object is also objective, but the construction is syntactically parallel to the fourth case usage in which benefit is obvious.)

| 2.6 recipient of an action where benefit is not obvious | སངས་རྒྱས་ལ་ | མཆོད་པ་ ཕུལ། |
|---|---|---|

*[They] offer worship to the Buddhas.*

## *Special Use of the Objective: Identity*

The identity marking particle (usually ཤ, ར, ཏ, ད, or ར and, some would argue, never ན or ལ) is a species of the second case, but, because of its great importance, deserves to be treated separately.

| adverbial identity | གསལ་བར་ | བཤད་ |
|---|---|---|

*[He] explains clearly.*

| | བདེན་པར་ | ཡོད་པ་ |
|---|---|---|

*truly existent*

| existential identity | བུམ་པའི་ རྒྱུར་ | གྱུར་པའི་ དངོས་པོ་ |
|---|---|---|

*the thing which is pot's cause*

ལམ་དེ་ནི་ ཐར་པའི་རྒྱུར་ མི་རུང་སྟེ་

*that path is not admissible **as a cause of liberation***

transformed<br>identity

སངས་རྒྱས་ཀྱི་ མདོ་ བོད་སྐད་དུ་ བསྒྱུར

*Buddha's sutras were translated **into Tibetan**.*

ལྕགས་ གསེར་དུ་ སྒྱུར་བ

*transmuting iron **into gold***

---

## Non-case usage of objective particles

The endings that mark the objective, purposive, and locative cases are also some-times used in other ways—that is, as syntactic particles. They may act as conjunctions; they may show a condition or an infinitive.

---

## Third Case: Agentive          བྱེད་པའི་སྒྲ་

Endings: གིས་ ཀྱིས་ གྱིས་ འིས་ ཡིས་

---

## Agentive Agent

One of the most common constructions in Tibetan is seen with agentive verbs, where the agent (or subject) is in the agentive case and the object is in either the nominative case or the objective case (depending on the verb).

3.1.1<br>subject of agentive-<br>nominative verb

སངས་རྒྱས་ཀྱིས་ ཆོས་ བསྟན།

***Buddha** taught the doctrine.*

Not all such Tibetan agents translate smoothly into English agents, as seen in the following very common construction.

འཁོར་འདས་ཀྱིས་ | བསྡུས་པའི་ཆོས་ཐམས་ཅད་

*all phenomena included*
**within cyclic existence and nirvana**

| 3.1.2<br>subject of an<br>agentive-objective<br>verb | ཁོས་ མིག་གིས་ གཟུགས་ལ་ བལྟས། |
|---|---|

*He looked at forms with [his] eye[s].*

## Agentive Instrument

Action verbs may have a secondary agent—not the agent doing the action but the means by which it is done. This secondary agent is also marked by an agentive particle.

| 3.2.1<br>instrument of an<br>agentive-nominative<br>verb | བྱང་ཆུབ་སེམས་དཔས་ བརྩོན་གྲུས་ཀྱིས་ ལམ་ སྒྲུབ། |
|---|---|

*The Bodhisattva accomplishes the path* **through effort.**

| 3.2.2<br>instrument of an<br>agentive-objective<br>verb | ཁོས་ མིག་གིས་ གཟུགས་ལ་ བལྟས། |
|---|---|

*He looked at forms* **with [his] eye[s].**

## *Agentive Reason*

Any sentence or clause may include a reason; one of the ways of marking a word or clause that gives a reason is with the agentive case particles.

<table>
<tr>
<td>

3.3<br>
reason

</td>
<td>

ཚིག་མང་ས་སུ་དོགས་པས། མ་བྲིས་སོ།

**Fearing too many words, [I] did not write [on this].**

</td>
</tr>
</table>

མི་ཤེས་པས་ ནེ་ འགྲོ་བ་ འཁྱམས་པར་གྱུར་

*Beings have wandered because they do not understand.*

ཆོས་ཐམས་ཅད་ཐ་སྙད་དུ་ཡོད་པས་ ཆད་མཐའ་ལས་གྲོལ།

**Because all phenomena conventionally exist, there is**
**freedom from the extreme of nihilism.**[269]

Such an agentive construction may be seen with any verb. It serves as a qualifier marking a word, phrase, or clause as the reason that logically entails what is being said in the clause or sentence following it.

## *Non-case usage of agentive particles*

The particles that usually mark the third case are also used in non-case ways, as syntactic particles. As syntactic particles, they may mark adverbs; they are used with some verbs (for example, སྟོང་, *is empty*) to mark the object absent; and like the connective particles, they may function as conjunctions.

## Fourth Case: Beneficial and Purposive  དགོས་ཆེད་ཀྱི་སྒྲ་

Endings: སུ་  རུ་  ཏུ་  དུ་  ན་  ར་  ལ་

---

### *Indirect Objects  (Benefit)*

---

The indirect object of a dynamic verb which clearly receives benefit is in the fourth case.

| |
|---|
| 4.1<br>beneficiary |

སྨན་པས་ ནད་པ་ལ་ སྨན་ སྟེར

*A doctor gives medicine **to the ill**.*

ཤིང་ལ་ ཆུ་ འདྲེན་

*bringing water **to the trees** [irrigating the trees]*

---

### *Purpose*

---

Any sentence may include a word or clause which indicates the purpose or aim of an action or state of being;  these words or clauses are marked by fourth case particles.

| |
|---|
| 4.2<br>purpose |

སངས་རྒྱས་ཐོབ་པ་ལ་ ལམ་ སྒྲུབ་དགོས།

**To become a Buddha**, *one must practice the path.*

ཤིང་གཅོད་དུ་ སྟ་རེ་ དགོས།

*An axe is needed **to cut trees**.*[270]

Note the irregular form of the verbal noun—གཅོད་ and not གཅོད་པ་.

དགེ་འདུན་ལ་ སྐྱབས་སུ་ མཆིའོ།

*[We] go **for refuge** to the spiritual community.*

## *Subject of Verb of Necessity*

Verbs of necessity take their subjects in the fourth case.[271]

| | |
|---|---|
| **4.3**<br>subject of a verb of<br>necessity | མྱུ་གུ་ལ་ ཆུ་ དགོས། <br> ***Sprouts*** *need water*. |

## Fifth Case: Originative   འབྱུང་ཁུངས་ཀྱི་སྒྲ་

Endings: ལས་   ནས་

## *Source of Things and Actions*

The originative case may indicate the actual source of something or, less directly, the
means that cause something to come about.

| | |
|---|---|
| **5.1.1**<br>source<br>(place or substance) | ཆུ་ལས་ ཆུ་བུར་ བྱུང་། <br> *Bubbles come* ***out of the water***. |

གནམ་ནས་ ཆར་ བབས།

*Rain falls* ***from the sky***.

ཤར་ཕྱོགས་ནས་ ཉི་མ་ ཤར།

*The sun rises* ***out of the east***.

| 5.1.2<br>source (speech) | ཙུ་ཚིག་ལས་ ··· ཞེས་ གསུངས་པ་ ལྟར། |

*As is said **in the basic text**, ...*

བདག་ཉིད་ཆེན་པོའི་ཞལ་ནས། ···

[literally] ***Out of the mouth of the Great Being*** *...*
[in English syntax] ***According to the Great Being*** *...*

| བཅོམ་ལྡན་འདས་ཀྱི་ཞལ་ནས་ | གསུངས་པ་ |

*spoken **by the Transcendent Victor***

| བླ་མ་ལས་ | གཞུང་ལ་ གསན། |

*[They] listened to the texts **from the guru.**[272]*
*[English syntax] [They] studied the texts **with the guru.***

## Instrumental Originative

The fifth case particle is also used to show the means through which something is done. This, in a sense, is a different sort of source (one neither physical nor verbal).

| 5.2<br>instrumental<br>originative | རྩོལ་བ་ལས་ | ཐོབ་པ་ |

achieved *through effort*

## Separation

Where some one thing or a group of things are set apart *from* a larger group, the originative particle is used. Separation in the sense of isolation—that is, singling out some one item to discuss—is very common. Separation in the sense of removal (or going *out of* a situation) is not as frequently seen, but is a regular usage.

| 5.3<br>isolation | གསུམ་ལས་ | དང་པོ་ནི། |

*Among the three, the first [is] as follows.*

| ལུགས་ཐམས་ཅད་ཀྱི་ནང་ནས་ | དེ་ མཆོག་ཏུ་གྱུར་པ |

*Out of all the systems, that is the best.*

| 5.4<br>removal | འཁོར་བ་ལས་ | གྲོལ་བ |

*liberation from cyclic existence*

| སྡུག་བསྔལ་ལས་ | སྐྱོབ་པ |

*providing refuge from suffering*

---

## Comparison

Any sentence may include comparative elements. The standard means of indicating a comparison is with the originative case (e.g., 'greater *than* that').

| 5.5<br>comparison | དེ་ལས་ | ཆེ་བ |

greater *than that*

ཇོ་མོ་གླང་མ་ རི་བོ་ཀུན་ལས་ མཐོ

Cho-mo-lang-ma is higher *than all mountains*.

དར་དམར་པོ་ མེ་ལས་ དམར་

[That] red silk [is] redder *than fire*.

The syntactic particles བས་ and པས་ also mark that to which a comparision is made.

## *Inclusion*

The beginning of a sequence, a distance, or a period of time is marked by the originative particle ནས་ (not ལས་).  The syntactic particle དེ་ནས་ (*then*) has its origins in this usage (དེ་ནས་ literally meaning *after that*).

| | |
|---|---|
| **5.6.1**<br>beginning of a<br>sequence | གཅིག་ནས་ བཅུའི་བར་<br><br>*from one* through ten |
| | ས་དང་པོ་ནས་ བཟུང་སྟེ་<br><br>beginning *with the first stage* |
| | མགོ་ནས་ མཇུག་གི་བར་<br><br>*from the beginning* until the conclusion |
| **5.6.2**<br>beginning (place) | ལྷ་ས་ནས་ རྒྱལ་རྩེའི་བར་དུ་<br><br>*from Lhasa to Gyangtsé* |
| **5.6.3**<br>beginning (time) | ཐོག་མ་མེད་པ་ནས་ འཁོར་བོང་དུ་ སྐྱེས།<br><br>*From beginninglessness,* we have been born<br>in cyclic existence. |
| | ཟླ་བ་དང་པོ་ནས་ ཟླ་བ་དྲུག་པའི་བར་དུ་དེར་བཞུགས།<br><br>*[She] lived there from the first [lunar] month*<br>*through the sixth month.* |

## *Logical Sequence*

Although in Tibetan it is more common to use the agentive to mark a reason, the originative case may also be used.

| | |
|---|---|
| 5.7<br>originative reason | དུ་བ་མཐོང་བ་ལས་ མེ་ཡོད་པར་ཤེས། |

*One understands, **due to seeing smoke**, that fire exists.*

This usage is seen predominantly in texts translated from Sanskrit where the fifth case is commonly used to show reasons.[273]

## *Non-case usage of originative particles*

The particles that mark the fifth case are often used in other, non-case ways. They may mark adverbs, past or present participles, and disjunction—*except for*, *other than*.

## Sixth Case: Connective  འབྲེལ་བའི་སྒྲ་

Endings: གི་    ཀྱི་    གྱི་    འི་    ཡི་

Except for the topical nominative, the topical locative, and the separative and comparative uses of the originative case, all the case usages listed elsewhere are ways of indicating how nouns and pronouns relate to *verbs*. Connective case particles, on the other hand, are used to link nouns, pronouns, and sometimes adjectives not with verbs but with other nouns and pronouns.

## *Connectives Linking Nouns or Pronouns with Nouns*

The first group of connectives are similar in that they indicate either actual or metaphoric possession. The type connective is very broad and covers probably the greatest part of overall connective use. Note that it translates into many different English prepositions, depending on context.

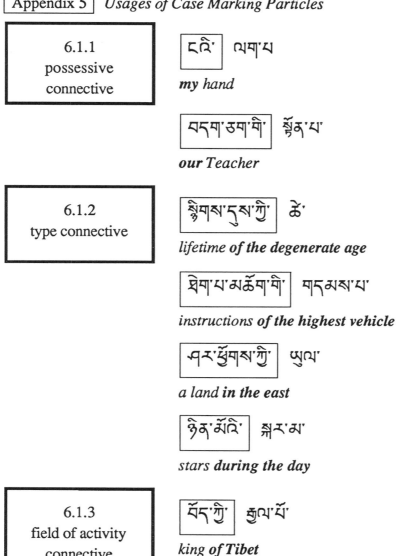

| | |
|---|---|
| 6.1.1<br>possessive<br>connective | ངའི་ ལག་པ་<br>*my hand*<br><br>བདག་ཅག་གི་ སྟོན་པ་<br>*our Teacher* |
| 6.1.2<br>type connective | སྙིགས་དུས་ཀྱི་ ཚེ་<br>*lifetime of the degenerate age*<br><br>ཐེག་པ་མཆོག་གི་ གདམས་པ་<br>*instructions of the highest vehicle*<br><br>ཤར་ཕྱོགས་ཀྱི་ ཡུལ་<br>*a land in the east*<br><br>ཉིན་མོའི་ སྐར་མ་<br>*stars during the day* |
| 6.1.3<br>field of activity<br>connective | བོད་ཀྱི་ རྒྱལ་པོ་<br>*king of Tibet* |

## *Apposition and Composition*

The next three connectives are associated because they link two nouns that are similar. They indicate that two nouns, or a pronoun and a noun, are appositives, or that the second is made up of the first, or that the second is a metaphor for the first.

| | |
|---|---|
| **6.2.1**<br>**appositional**<br>**connective** | དུད་འགྲོ་ལ་སོགས་པའི་ ངན་འགྲོ་<br>*bad migrations **such as** animals*<br><br>ཡིད་ཆེས་ཀྱི་ དད་པ་<br>*faith **of** conviction* |
| **6.2.2**<br>**compositional**<br>**connective** | འཕགས་པའི་ དགེ་འདུན་<br>*spiritual community **of** superiors (āryas)*<br><br>མདོའི་ དཔེ་ཆ་<br>*a book **of** sutras* |
| **6.2.3**<br>**metaphorical**<br>**connective** | སྙིང་རྗེའི་ ཆུ་<br>*water **of** compassion* |

---

## Postpositional Connectives

In this group, the connective particle follows a noun or pronoun, connecting it to Tibetan postpositions. (The postpositions themselves generally translate into English as prepositions such as *because of, in order to, in front of, before,* and so on.)

| | |
|---|---|
| **6.3**<br>**postpositional**<br>**connective** | རང་གི་ མདུན་དུ་<br>*in front **of** one* |

མི་རྟག་པ་ ཡིན་པའི་ ཕྱིར

*because of being impermanent*

## Connectives Imitating Other Case Endings

These connectives are used where the two words linked could in other syntaxes be (1) agent and object, (2) object and agent, (3) group and separated member of the group, or (4) origin and result.

Some connectives mark words that—if they were in a phrase or sentence with a verb—would be agents bringing about or acting on the objects or actions indicated by the words following them.

| 6.4.1<br>agentive connective | སངས་རྒྱས་ཀྱི་ བསྟན་པ་ |
|---|---|

*teaching of [that is, taught by] **Buddha***

མི་དགེ་བའི་ལས་ཀྱི་ འབྲས་བུ་

*effects of [that is, produced by] **nonvirtuous actions***

The 'agent' here is the word prior to the connective particle, the word that the particle marks. It is for this reason called an agentive connective.

Some connectives mark words that—in a phrase or sentence—would be objects of verbs whose agents are indicated by the words following them.

| 6.4.2<br>objective connective | བདེ་འགྲོའི་ རྒྱུ་ |
|---|---|

*the causes of **pleasant rebirths***

སྔོན་འཛིན་མིག་ཤེས་ཀྱི་ དམིགས་རྐྱེན་

*the observed-object condition of [that is, giving rise to]*
***a visual consciousness apprehending blue***

Other connectives mark words that are destinations and would be in the objective case were the connective phrase made into a sentence with a verb.

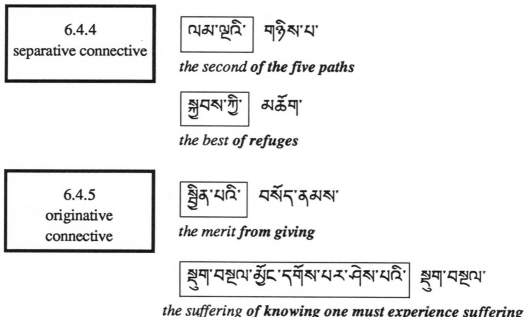

| 6.4.3 destination connective | བྱང་ཆུབ་ཀྱི་ ལམ་ |
| --- | --- |

*path to awakening*

Other connectives indicate separative and originative functions that are, in more complete phrases or clauses, performed by the originative case.

| 6.4.4 separative connective | ལམ་ལྔའི་ གཉིས་པ་ |
| --- | --- |

*the second of the five paths*

 སྐྱབས་ཀྱི་ མཆོག་

*the best of refuges*

| 6.4.5 originative connective | སྦྱིན་པའི་ བསོད་ནམས་ |
| --- | --- |

*the merit from giving*

སྡུག་བསྔལ་མྱོང་དགོས་པར་ཤེས་པའི་ སྡུག་བསྔལ་

*the suffering of knowing one must experience suffering*

## *Connectives Linking Adjectives to Nouns*

It is possible to link adjectives to nouns following them through the use of the connective case. (The verbal adjectives spoken of in the next section [clause connectives] are technically examples of this. However, the adjectives spoken of in the present section are not the verbal adjectives ending phrases and clauses but rather non-verbal words which are adjectives such as དམ་པ་.)

| 6.5<br>adjectival connective | དམ་པའི་ ཆོས་<br><br>***holy*** *doctrine* |
| --- | --- |
| | མི་དགེ་བའི་ བསམ་པ་<br><br>***nonvirtuous*** *attitude* |

## *Clause Connectives: Verbal Adjectives*

Very often an entire phrase or clause will be connected to a following noun (or phrase or clause) by means of a connective case particle. Such usage of the connective case is very important in Tibetan; it is the dominant way of modifying a noun adjectivally with a phrase or clause.

It is useful when analyzing clauses and sentences to name these connectives after the grammatical function the nouns that follow them would play *were they to appear in the clause that precedes them*. Thus, verbals may be followed by different sorts of clause connectives:

1    those connecting the verbal to a noun that would be its agent were it to be found within the clause (and, thus, *before* the verbal),

2    those connecting the verbal to a noun that would be its object,

3    those connecting the verbal to a noun that would in some way be its qualifier,

4    those connecting the verbal to a noun that would be its complement.

In the following two examples, ཤེས་རབ་ and སངས་རྒྱས་ are not the actual subjects of རྟོགས་ and བསྐྱེན་; they are, rather, metaphoric subjects. The actual subject of a verb occurs before it, to its left, not after it. The same holds true for the remainder of the "subjects," as well as for the "objects," "qualifiers," and "complements."

| 6.6.1<br>connecting clause to<br>"subject" | སྟོང་ཉིད་རྟོགས་པའི་ ཤེས་རབ་<br><br>*wisdom* ***which realizes emptiness*** |
| --- | --- |

ཆོས་བསྟན་པའི།  སངས་རྒྱས་

*the Buddha **who taught the doctrine***

སྣང་བའི།  ཡུལ་

***appearing** object [that is, object **which appears**]*

བྱང་ཆུབ་ཀྱི་ ལམ་ལ་ བགྲོད་པའི།  གང་ཟག

*a person **who is travelling the path to awakening***

རྒྱུ་དགེ་བ་ལ་ བརྟེན་པའི།  བདེ་འགྲོའི་ བདེ་བ་

*the happiness of pleasant rebirths **that depends
on virtue [as its] cause***

བསམ་གཏན་དང་པོ་ལ་ གནས་པའི།  འཕགས་པ་

*a Superior **who remains in the first concentration***

ཡི་དྭགས་ནི་ ཟས་དང་ཆུ་དགོས་པའི།  སེམས་ཅན་ཡིན།

*Hungry ghosts are sentient beings **who need food
and water.***

| | |
|---|---|
| **6.6.2**<br>connecting clause to<br>"object" | སངས་རྒྱས་ཀྱིས་ བསྟན་པའི།  ཆོས་<br><br>*the doctrine **which was taught by Buddha***<br><br>རང་ཅག་རྣམས་ཀྱིས་ཐོབ་པའི།  དལ་འབྱོར་<br><br>*leisure and opportunity **which we have achieved*** |

| | |
|---|---|
| **6.6.3**<br>connecting clause to<br>"qualifier" | སངས་རྒྱས་ཀྱིས་ ཆོས་བསྟན་པའི་ ཡུལ་ |

*the place **where Buddha taught the doctrine***

དགེ་བ་ བསགས་པའི་ མིའི་ལུས་རྟེན་

*the human physical support **[on which]** virtue
is accumulated.*

བུམ་པ་ མི་རྟག་པ་ ཡིན་པའི་ རྒྱུ་མཚན་

*the reason **why pots are impermanent***

མི་ མེད་པའི་ ས་

*a place **where there are no human beings***

གངས་རི་ སྔོན་པོར་ སྣང་བའི་ མིག་ཤེས་

*a visual consciousness **to which a snow mountain
appears blue***

གང་ལ་ འགྲོ་བའི་ གྲོང་ཁྱེར་

*the city **to which [we] are going***

| | |
|---|---|
| **6.6.4**<br>connecting clause to<br>"complement" | མི་རྟག་པ་ ཡིན་པའི་ ཆོས་ |

*phenomena **which are impermanent***

## Non-case usage of the connective particle

The connective particles are also used as conjunctions following verbs.

## Seventh Case: Locative    རྟེན་གནས་ཀྱི་སྒྲ་

Endings: སུ་   ར་   ཏུ་   དུ་   ན་   ར་   ལ་

### *Locatives with Verbs of Dependence*

The qualifiers in clauses and sentences ending in verbs of dependence are in the locative case.

<table>
<tr>
<td>

**7.1**

place of dependence

</td>
<td>

འབྲས་བུ་ ⟨རྒྱུ་ལ་⟩ བརྟེན་ནོ།

*Effects depend **on causes**.*

</td>
</tr>
</table>

བསླབ་པ་གསུམ་ལ་ བརྟེན་ནས་ ཐར་པ་ ཐོབ།

*Liberation is achieved in reliance **on the three trainings**.*

ཆོས་རྣམས་ རང་རང་གི་ ཆ་ཤས་ལ་ བལྟོས།

*Phenomena depend **on their own parts**.*

### *Locatives with Verbs of Existence*

The first usage of the locative with verbs of existence—in which the locative particle marks the place where someone or something exists or lives or remains—is a locative according to the traditional grammarians. The second type may not be; Mugé Samden invokes it as an example of the identity-marking particle and, thus, not a case usage (see above). However, structurally it is identical to the locative place of existing or living and, thus, has been included here.

<table>
<tr>
<td>

**7.2.1**

place of existing or living

</td>
<td>

བོད་ལ་ རི་མང་པོ་ ཡོད།

*There are many mountains **in Tibet**.*

</td>
</tr>
</table>

བཅོམ་ལྡན་འདས་ | མཉན་ཡོད་ན་ | བཞུགས་སོ།

*The Transcendent Victor stayed **at Shravasti**.*

| 7.2.2 locative of inclusion | བོད་མི་ལ་ མཁས་པ་མང་པོ་ ཡོད། |
|---|---|

***Among the Tibetans** there are many scholars.*

གཞི་གྲུབ་ལ་ དག་པ་དང་མི་དག་པ་ གཉིས་ ཡོད།

[literal] ***Among established bases** there are two [types], permanent and impermanent.*

[English syntax] *There are two [types of] basic phenomena, the permanent and the impermanent.*

## Locatives with Verbs of Possession

Verbs of possession have locative subjects—that is, the possessor is stated in the locative case.

| 7.3 subject of verb of possession | དགྲ་བཅོམ་པ་ལ་ ཉོན་མོངས་མེད། |
|---|---|

***Arhats** do not have afflictions.*

སྒྲོལ་བའི་ནུས་པ་ | སུ་ལ་ | ཡོད།

***Who** has the ability to liberate [beings]?*

## Locatives Used with Any Verbs

Unlike the locative place of existence or living—which is used only with those two types of verbs—the locative of time may be used with any verb.

| 7.4<br>locative of time | ཚེ་ གཅིག་ཉིད་ལ་ ཐོགས་པ |
|---|---|

*complete [the path]* ***in a single lifetime***

ཆོས་འདི་ འཇིག་རྟེན་དུ་ ཡུན་རིང་དུ་ གནས་ན་

*If this doctrine remains in the world **for a long time*** ...

ཉི་མ་ཤར་བ་ན་ ཆོས་ བསྟན།

*[He] taught the doctrine **when the sun rose**.*

The topical locative is like the topical nominative. It indicates block language—a word or phrase that is not connected grammatically to the material following it.

| 7.5<br>topical locative | དང་པོ་ལ་ |
|---|---|

***The first [is as follows].***

དང་པོ་རང་ལུགས་བཞག་པ་ལ།

***1 A Presentation of Our Own Position***

## Special Use of the Locative:  Referential Particles

The referential particle is usually a ལ་ and, as a rough approximation, translates into English as *about, with regard to,* or *in the context of.* It differs from the topical locative in that it does indicate a connection, albeit a general one, to the verb or verbal ending the phrase, clause, or sentence in which it is found.

| referential locative | མོ་ལ་ བུ་ཞིག་ སྐྱེས། |
|---|---|

*A child was born **to her**.*

| སྨན་ལ་ | མཁས་པ་ |
|---|---|

*skilled **in medicine***

| སྡུག་བསྔལ་ལ་ | བཟོད་པ་ |
|---|---|

*patience **towards suffering***

## Eighth Case: Vocative བོད་སྒྲ་

Endings: none.

The vocative case is indistinguishable, except contextually, from the nominative case, unless an interjection such as ཀྱེ་ or ཀྭ་ཡེ་ also appears in the phrase or sentence. These interjections are traditionally called vocative particles.

| 8 vocative | ཀྱེ་ | ལྷའི་ལྷ། |
|---|---|---|

***Oh, god of gods!***

| བཅོམ་ལྡན་འདས་ | ངོ་མཚར་ ལགས་སོ། |
|---|---|

***O Transcendent Victor**, it is amazing!*

# *Appendix Six*
# *Adverbs and Postpositions*

## Types of Words:  Adverbs

Like adjectives, adverbs are modifiers, modifying adjectives, verbs, and other adverbs.  Tibetan adverbs answer the questions how, how much, to what extent, and why.  Although English adverbs also answer the questions where and when, in Tibetan time is shown in the seventh case and location is shown in the seventh and sometimes the second cases.  (See Appendix Five.)

Before presenting common adverbs, it must be noted that many, if not most, Tibetan "adverbs" are instances of a noun or an adjective marked by one of the *la*-group of particles as instances of objective case adverbial identity.

---

*clearly explained*

གསལ་བར་བཤད་པ་

---

*newly incontrovertible*

གསར་དུ་མི་སླུ་བ་

---

These words are not themselves adverbs, but have been made into adverbs through the addition of case marking particles.  However, in grammatical analysis both natural adverbs and these adverbial constructions are to be marked with the ADV dot, since their syntactic functions are the same.

| S ADV S | C ADV S S |
|---|---|
| གསལ་བར་ བཏད་པ་ | གསར་དུ་    མེ་སྐྱེ་བ་ |

Note that the dot prior to the objective adverbial marker is not an **ADV** dot but a **C** dot, since it precedes a case marking particle.

There are, apart from these ad hoc adverbial constructions, some words that are actually full-time adverbs. Many of them are, in traditional Tibetan grammar, called ཚིག་ཕྲད་ (*particles*). Moreover, not all would be adverbs in English, since many Tibetan adverbial constructions translate into English prepositional phrases.

> Adverbs differ from syntactic particles in that they do more than merely relate other words, phrases, clauses, or sentences to one another. They themselves bring some new meaning to an adjective or a verb.

| adverb |
|---|

འགྲོ་བ་འདི་དག་ ཕན་ཚུན་ ཕ་མ་རུ་གྱུར་ཀྱང་

*although these beings have **mutually** been*
*father and mother*

A more fluid English translation is *although these beings have been **each others'** parents.*

## Simple Adverbs

The following list of common Tibetan adverbs are all words in their own right, and not just relational particles. However, unlike the other non-verb words (nouns, pronouns, adjectives, and postpositions), they are not declined. In dot analysis, they are adventified with an **ADV** dot.

ཕན་ཚུན་    — *mutually*
རེས་འགའ་    — *sometimes, occasionally*
རེ་ཞིག་     — *temporarily*
ཤ་ཅང་      — *greatly, much, very*

ཞི་དྲག་    — *greatly, much, very*

ཅུང་ཟད་    — *a little*

ཆེས་    — *very*

ཇེ་ indicates increase. The construction ཇེ་ + ADJECTIVE + OBJECTIVE CASE MARKER is an adverbial construction, where the ཇེ་ is an adverb modifying the adjective that follows it.

---

*The conception of self becomes **more extensive**.*[274]

| UP | NOM | ADV | ADV | VB | SP |
|---|---|---|---|---|---|
| བདག་འཛིན་ | | ཇེ་འཕེལ་དུ་ | འགྲོ་ | ལ། | |

---

*ascertainment becoming **smaller** ...*

| NOM | ADV | ADV | V |
|---|---|---|---|
| ངེས་པ་ | | ཇེ་ཆུང་དུ་ | འགྲོ་བ་ |

---

## *Adverbial Phrase Markers*

The following syntactic particles immediately follow nouns or adjectives, making the word, clause, or phrase preceding them an adverbial construction. Thus, although the dots preceding them are SP dots, the dots immediately following them are ADV dots. While most are similar to postpositions, they differ in that they do not take declension nor are they preceded by connective case particles.

ཞིག་    (also an indefinite pronoun meaning *a* or *an*) may make an adjective into an adverb, as in དུས་ལན་གཅིག་ཙམ་ཞིག་རྙེད། (*found only one time*), where the phrase དུས་ལན་གཅིག་ཙམ་ (*only one time*) comes to be an adverbial modifier;

ཕྱིན་ཆད་    *subsequent to, since, henceforth* — follows word, clause, or phrase;

མན་ཆད་    *that and below, then and before* — follows word, clause, or phrase;

ཡན་ཆད་    *above, subsequent to* — follows word, clause, or phrase;

ཕན་ཆད་    *beyond, from here on, subsequent to* — follows word, clause, or phrase;

མ་གཏོགས་    *except for, other than* — follows word, clause, or phrase;

བཞིན་    *like, as, in accordance with* — follows word, clause, or phrase; this also occurs in declined form (adverbial identity) as བཞིན་དུ་;

ལྟར་    *like, as, in accordance with* — follows word, clause, or phrase; this also occurs in adverbial pronouns such as དེ་ལྟར་.

## Types of Words: Postpositions

This category of words is something of a grab-bag, and many postpositions are, in fact, something like syntactic particles. However, syntactic particles cannot be declined, and postpositions are declined—typically in the second or seventh cases (showing time or location). Moreover, postpositions are connected to the word or phrase that precedes them with a connective case particle.

The most common postpositions are listed here, classified in terms of their meaning. They are shown without the *la*-particles that follow them.

| space | རྒྱབ་ | *behind, in back of* |
|---|---|---|
| | མདུན་ | *in front of* |
| | འོག | *below* |
| | སྟེང་ | *above* |
| time | སྔོན་ | *before* |
| | རྗེས་ | *after* |
| | བར་ | *between, until* |
| | གོང་ | NEGATIVE VERB + གོང་ (*before*) |
| intention | ཆེད་ | *for the sake of, for the purpose of* |
| | སླད་ | *for the sake of* |
| | ཕྱིར་ | *for the sake of, for the purpose of* — when used with the particle དུ་ |
| [other] | ཀུལ་ | *in place of* |
| | བློ་ནས་ | *from the viewpoint of* — declined in the fifth case |

# *Appendix Seven*
# *Particles*

## *Lexical and Syntactic Particles*

---

## Particles

The concept of the particle is more complex than that of the word. Moreover, Tibetan grammarians tend to include so many different sorts of items among particles (ཚིག་ཕྲད་ **tshík-ṭhë'**) as to make the traditional category not very useful for the English speaker. Thus, in this book particles are defined somewhat more narrowly. In *Translating Buddhism from Tibetan*, there are three classes of **particles**:

- lexical particles,
- case marking particles,
- syntactic particles.

Unlike words, the meanings that particles bring to a phrase, clause, or sentence are either ambivalent or general. For example, some particles merely show plurality, while others are conjunctions indicating relations such as *and* or *but*. They gain fuller, more specific meanings only when they are used in specific contexts.

Case marking and syntactic particles need to be used with words to make sense. They are similar to the symbols called operators used in mathematics: + - =. These mathematical symbols mean nothing by themselves but, like particles, show how other things are related to one another. Thus, although particles may have lexical or dictionary meanings, those meanings are minimal. ལ་ and ལས་, for example, have no more concrete meaning than their English counterparts, *in* and *from*.

Note that ལ་ may also occur as a word meaning *[mountain] pass*, but it is much more frequently a case marking particle. ལས་, on the other hand, is frequently seen as a word meaning *action* (Sanskrit *karma*).

## Lexical Particles

Lexical particles are so called because they do *not* function, as do the other two sorts of particles, to show how words in phrases, clauses, and sentences are related to one another. They operate merely at the lexical level, serving as constituents of words and particles. They do not function independently of words.

There are five classes of lexical particles.

1   Prefix particles such as the རྣམ་པར་ in རྣམ་པར་ཤེས་པ་ (*consciousness*) are parts of some verbs (and, thus, some verbal nouns and adjectives).

2   Negative prefix syllables—the མ་ in མ་ཡིན་ (*is not*) and the མི་ in མི་དམིགས་པ་ (*not observed*)—may be used to negate verbs (as well as verbal nouns and adjectives). Some negative verbals have fixed lexical meanings (for example, མ་རིག་པ་) and will be found in a dictionary. Others are created as needed as clause-ending verbals.

3   Final syllables are of five types:

    3.1   generic suffix syllables (པ་, པོ་, བ་, བོ་, མ་, or མོ་);

    3.2   subjective suffix syllables (པ་, པོ་, བོ་, ཅན་, and མཁན་);

    3.3   restrictive suffix syllables (such as ཉིད་);

    3.4   possessive suffixes (དང་བཅས་པ་ and དང་ལྡན་པ་);

    3.5   separative suffixes (དང་བྲལ་བ་).

4   Optional syllables are of two types. Words ending in these syllables will not be found in a dictionary. Such syllables, rather, are used as needed with nouns, pronouns, and noun phrases:

    4.1   pluralizing syllables (རྣམས་, དག་, and ཚོ་—where དག་ may also show the dual [two of something]);

    4.2   generalizing syllables (ལ་སོགས་པ་, *and so forth, etc.*).

5  Negative verbal particles—མེད་པ་ and མ་ཡིན་པ་—follow nouns and adjectives. While they do occur as parts of fixed words, they also may be used to create words or phrases meaning, respectively, *without ...* and *not being ....*

Types 3.4 (དང་བཅས་པ་ and དང་ལྡན་པ་), 3.5 (དང་བྲལ་བ་), and 5 (མེད་པ་ and མ་ཡིན་པ་) are technically themselves verbals, making the 'words' they terminate actually brief phrases.

## Syntactic Particles

Like lexical particles, and unlike words, syntactic and case marking particles do not have their own distinct lexical meanings. Unlike lexical particles, however, they do not normally become parts of words. Rather, they are used to connect words, and even phrases and clauses, to one another.

> **Syntactic particles** (or **grammatical particles**) are units of one or two syllables that have only a grammatical function. Although, unlike lexical particles, they are not parts of words, they too cannot function independently of words, but must be used with words in phrases, clauses, and sentences.[275]

- A word is a part of speech whose meaning stands by itself. Words are either nouns, verbs, pronouns, adjectives, adverbs, or postpositions.

- A phrase is a group of words that forms a meaningful unit but is not a clause. There are both verb phrases and noun phrases.

- A clause is a group of words that ends either in a verbal or in a verb followed by a syntactic particle such as ནས་ or ན་. Clauses either act as units within larger clauses or sentences, or indicate (through the use of a continuational particle) that there is more to come.

- A sentence is a group of words, phrases, and clauses ending in a terminal verb—either in its simple core form, followed by a terminating syntactic particle, or in a verb phrase with an auxiliary verb.

Case marking particles are *technically* also syntactic particles. There are thus—theoretically—two main types of syntactic particles: case marking particles and syntactic particles other than case marking particles. However, in *Translating Buddhism from Tibetan*, the term 'syntactic particle' is consistently used to mean 'a syntactic particle that is not a case marking particle.'

Excluding case marking particles, then, there are eight main types of syntactic particles:

1   **introductory particles** serve to begin phrases, clauses, and sentences;

2   **terminating particles** serve as definite periods or exclamation marks in a Tibetan sentence and are, thus, in many instances redundant;

3   **rhetorical particles** are used in conditional and logical constructions and translate words such as *because* or *given that*;

4   **punctuational particles** serve to show where a quote ends, or to set off a word or a phrase, functions that in English would be performed by punctuation marks;

5   **conjunctive** and **disjunctive particles** also act to tie together phrases, clauses, and sentences, but are also used with individual words—sometimes conjunctively in the sense of *and*, sometimes disjunctively in the sense of *but* or *although*;

6   **verb modifying particles** occur within verb phrases, connecting verbs in either their core or verbal forms to auxiliary verbs following them;

7   **continuational particles** tie phrases, clauses, and sentences together, sometimes by showing sequence in verbal action, sometimes by leading to a reason or a further elaboration of what has gone before;

8   **adverbial particles**, when placed after a word, clause, or phrase make that word, clause, or phrase into an adverb.

Adverbial particles differ from the others in that only the dot preceding them is marked as an SP dot. The dot after them, symbolizing the role played by the unit they terminate, is an ADV dot. Thus, they are not treated here, but in Appendix Six with the adverbs.

## *Particles Used as Both Case Marking and Syntactic Particles*

All nineteen Tibetan case marking particles are also sometimes used as syntactic particles (that is, as particles that do not mark declension). Some—like དས—are used as syntactic particles more frequently than they are used as case marking particles. Others, for example the གི, ཀྱི, གྱི, འི, ཡི group, are used as syntactic particles indicating disjunction (*but, even though*), but are much more commonly connective case markers. The གིས, ཀྱིས, གྱིས, འིས, ཡིས group have various non-case-marking usages. As syntactic particles after verbs they indicate disjunction, but they are often seen after nouns and adjectives in an adverbial sense (for example, རང་བཞིན་གྱིས—*naturally*). Where ལ is also used disjunctively after verbs and ན is most frequently a conditional syntactic particle, the other particles in the *la* group (that is, སུ, ར, རུ, ཏུ, and དུ) are used as verb modifying syntactic particles (creating, for instance, infinitives such as the བསྒོམ་པར in བསྒོམ་པར་དུ [*will meditate* or *should meditate*]).

Of the nineteen case marking particles, nine also occur as common words. (See Appendix Five.)

## Type One: *Introductory Particles*

These particles introduce phrases, clauses, and sentences. They imply a relationship in meaning to what has been stated immediately before, but do not tie two sentences together *grammatically*, as do, for example, the sequential particles discussed later.

| | |
|---|---|
| དེས་ན | *therefore* |
| དེ་ཕྱིར | *therefore* |
| དེའི་ཕྱིར | *therefore* |
| དེ་ཡང | *further* |
| གཞན་ཡང | *moreover* |
| དེ་ཚེ | *then, at that time* |
| དེར་མ་ཟད | *not only that* |
| དེ་བས | *beyond that, rather than that* |
| དེ་བས་ན | *therefore* |
| གལ་ཏེ | *if* |
| འོ་ན | *well then* |

| ཕན་ཀྱང་ | *however* |
| ཡང་ | *further* |
| ཡང་ན་ | *on the other hand* |

## Type Two:  *Terminating Particles*

Terminating particles bring sentences to a definite end, as well as in some instances making sentences out of phrases.  They include the following groups of syntactic particles:

- གོ་, ངོ་, དོ་, ནོ་, བོ་, མོ་, འོ་, རོ་, ལོ་, སོ་, and ཏོ་—the eleven terminators;
- the eleven disjunctive syntactic particles གམ་, ངམ་, དམ་, ནམ་, བམ་, མམ་, འམ་, རམ་, ལམ་, སམ་, and ཏམ་ when they are used at the end of a sentence to indicate doubt or to ask a rhetorical question;
- the imperative markers ཅིག་, ཞིག་, and ཤིག་.

## *Terminators*

Terminators are simply a duplication of the suffix letter that ends the final syllable of a core verb, a verb and auxiliary phrase, or—not infrequently—any word or particle. The duplicated suffix letter then becomes the root letter of its own syllable, and the vowel **o**—that is, a ན་རོ་—is added to it.  The terminators ངོ་, དོ་, ནོ་, བོ་, མོ་, འོ་, རོ་, ལོ་, and སོ་ follow, respectively, words ending in the suffix letters ང་, ད་, ན་, བ་, མ་, འ་, ར་, ལ་, and ས་.  The terminator ཏོ་ follows the secondary suffix ད་ and the secondary suffix ས་ is followed by the terminator སོ་.   In this way ཡིན་ is terminated as ཡིན་ནོ་ and ཞིངད་ (*was attached to*) is terminated ཞིངད་དོ་, although—since secondary suffixes are rarely written—it appears as ཞིན་ཏོ་.  Words that do not end in a suffix may be terminated with the particle འོ་.  Thus, གིས་པ་, for instance, is terminated as གིས་པའོ་.

The simplest usage of a terminator follows a core verb.

---

*From this, this arises.*[276]

---

འདི་ལས་འདི་འབྱུང་ | ངོ། |

Terminators may also be added to nouns and adjectives, producing an effect akin to adding a linking verb and then terminating the sentence.

*This is the nature of phenomena.*

འདི་ནི་ཆོས་རྣམས་ཀྱི་ཆོས་ཉིད་ དོ། 

Terminators may even be added to syntactic particles. As when they follow words other than verbs, the construction acts as if there were a sentence ending in a linking verb.

*[That is] by the way of making the potential powerful.[277]*

ནུས་པ་མཐུ་ཅན་དུ་བྱས་པའི་ཚུལ་གྱིས་ སོ། 

## Interrogative Markers

The interrogative marking particles—གམ་, ངམ་, དམ་, ནམ་, བམ་, མམ་, འམ་, རམ་, ལམ་, སམ་, and ཏམ་—are used in a way similar to the terminators in that they duplicate the suffix letter of the syllables they follow. When used at the end of a sentence, they transform a declarative statement into an interrogative.

*Well then, is there—in the mental continuum of a buddha superior—*
   *an attitude of going for refuge?[278]*

འོ་ན་སངས་རྒྱས་འཕགས་པའི་རྒྱུས་རྒྱུད་ན་སྐྱབས་སུ་འགྲོ་བའི་བློ་ཡོད་ དམ་ ཞེ་ན་

The construction ཞེ་ན་ is technically a conditional one, traditionally thought of as meaning *if it is said that...* or *if one asks ...* However, unlike most conditional clauses, the construction ending in ཅེ་ན་, ཞེ་ན་, or ཤེ་ན་ is an open-ended one. Like the topical locative, it serves to initiate an explanation of the topic it introduces but needs not be grammatically connected to what follows it.

The primary meaning of the particles གམ་, ངམ་, དམ་, ནམ་, བམ་, མམ་, འམ་, རམ་, ལམ་, སམ་, and ཏམ་, however, would seem to be their use as disjunctive syntactic particles meaning *or.*

*Is it **or** is it not allowed to explain tantra*
  *to one who has not received empowerment?*[279]

དབང་མ་ཐོབ་པ་ལ་རྒྱུད་བཤད་ཆོག་ གམ་ མི་ཆོག

Questions ending in interrogative particles are thus similar to English sentences ending in *or [what]?* In the following example, for instance, one could consider the sentence སྒྲ་ཐལ་ཆེར་མི་རྟག་གམ་ to mean literally *sound probably [is] impermanent or ....*

*doubt which thinks, "Sound probably is impermanent"*[280]

སྒྲ་ཐལ་ཆེར་མི་རྟག་ གམ་ སྙམ་པའི་ཐེ་ཚོམ་

སྙམ་ is a verb meaning *thinks*.

## Imperative Markers

There are three imperative marking syntactic particles.

- ཅིག་ follows verbs ending in the suffixes ག་, ད་, བ་, and the secondary suffix ད་.
- ཞིག་ follows verbs ending in the suffixes ང་, ན་, མ་, འ་, ར་, and ལ་, as well as syllables without suffixes.
- ཤིག་ follows verbs ending in the suffix ས་ or the secondary suffix ས་.

Imperative markers often follow the core form of a verb.

*Come here through [your] love, by the power of [your] magic!*

རྡུ་འཕུལ་སྟོབས་ཀྱིས་བརྩེ་བས་འདིར་གཤེགས་ ཤིག

They may also follow auxiliary verb phrases.

*May [they] come to have happiness!*

བདེ་བ་དང་ལྡན་པར་གྱུར་ ཅིག

In the above example, the particle ཅིག་ follows the secondary suffix ད་ (གྱུར་ད་).

## Type Three: *Rhetorical Particles*

Rhetorical syntactic particles link phrases, clauses, and sentences with other phrases, clauses, and sentences at the rhetorical level of Tibetan.

- ན་, in addition to being a case marking particle, is used as a syntactic particle terminating a conditional clause.
- ཕྱིར་—used without declension at the end of a phrase or clause—marks that phrase or clause as a reason. (Declined as a postposition, however, it indicates purpose.)
- The particles also used to mark the agentive case may be used—with the addition of the particle ན་—to indicate logical sequence. དེ་, for example, becomes དེས་ན་ and means *therefore.*
- There are a number of syntactic particles (syntactic phrases, really) such as ཅི་མ་རུང་ (*how nice*—literally, *what would not be suitable*) and ལྟ་ཅི་སྨོས་ (*how much more so*) that occur at the end of a clauses or sentences.

## *Conditional Syntactic Particles*

The use of the particle ན་ as a syntactic particle following verbs or verb phrases and marking them as conditional statements is quite common.

*This [physical] support is difficult to find and, **if** found, [is] of great value.*

རྟེན་འདི་རྙེད་པར་དཀའ་ཞིང་། རྙེད་ [ན་] དོན་ཆེ་བ་

*an action done not being wasted **if** [it] does not meet with a hindrance.*

གེགས་བྱེད་དང་མ་ཕྲད་ [ན་] ལས་བྱས་པ་ཆུད་མི་ཟ་བ་

*Thinking [that] **if** such a doctrine were to stay a long time in the world, it would be good ...*[281]

ཆོས་འདི་ལྟ་བུ་འཇིག་རྟེན་དུ་ཡུན་རིང་དུ་གནས་ [ན་] ཅི་མ་རུང་སྙམ་ནས།

## *Logical Syntactic Particles*

Constructions showing reasons or logical sequence may end in agentive case particles but are often marked by syntactic particles such as ཕྱིར or one or another of the following five particles: ཀྱིས་ན, གིས་ན, གྱིས་ན, ཡིས་ན and ས་ན.

---

***because [it] was spoken of in a scripture [taught by] Buddha***[282]

---

སངས་རྒྱས་ཀྱི་ལུང་ལས་གསུངས་པའི་ ཕྱིར

---

It is not the case that all instances of phrases or clauses ending in ཕྱིར are examples of the use of the syntactic particle ཕྱིར. The *postposition* ཕྱིར (*for the sake of*) sometimes occurs with an *understood* case marking particle as seen in the following clause.

---

*an explanation of the source for the lineage of gurus*
    ***in order to*** *generate certainty about [their] instructions.*[283]

---

གདམས་ངག་ལ་ངེས་པ་བསྐྱེད་པའི་ཕྱིར་བླ་མ་བརྒྱུད་པའི་ཁུངས་བཤད་པ

---

Here, the ཕྱིར is not a syntactic particle but the postposition which, in its complete form, is ཕྱིར་དུ.

---

The syntactic particles * ཀྱིས་ན, * གིས་ན, * གྱིས་ན, * ཡིས་ན and * ས་ན are used to show logical sequence. (The asterisks indicate that they follow what they mark to be a reason.)

---

*[It] is called 'opportunity'* ***because*** *the outer and inner concordant conditions*
    *for the practice of the doctrine are complete.*[284]

---

ཆོས་སྒྲུབ་པའི་ཕྱི་ནང་གི་མཐུན་རྐྱེན་ཚང་བ་ ས་ན འབྱོར་བ་ཞེས་བྱ་ལ

# Type Four: *Punctuational Particles*

Punctuational particles mark quotations or set certain parts of a clause or sentence off from the remainder of that clause or sentence.

- ནི་ sets off a word or noun phrase, but does not change the declension of the word or phrase before it.

- གང་ཞིག་ is most naturally a pronoun, but may be used as a syntactic particle to separate major parts of a phrase or clause.

- ན་རེ་ marks a subject which is the source of an opinion or a statement.

- ཞེས་, ཅེས་, and གེས་ follow reportage of speech or thought. They may act adverbially and they are sometimes made into nouns and declined.

- ཏེ་, སྟེ་, and དེ་ are often continuative syntactic particles but may also function (after words or phrases) as appositive markers.

In the following example, the syntactic particle ནི་ sets the nominative case object off from the rest of the sentence.

*Buddha taught the stages of the profound path to the revered Manjushri.*[285]

ཟབ་མོའི་ལམ་གྱི་རིམ་པ་ $\boxed{\text{ནི་}}$ སངས་རྒྱས་ཀྱིས་རྗེ་བཙུན་འཇམ་པའི་དབྱངས་ལ་གསུངས།

In this sentence the particle ནི་ sets off the nominative subject.

*Because one must go alone to the next world, there is no confidence about friends.*[286]

རང་ཉིད་གཅིག་པུ་འཇིག་རྟེན་ཕ་རོལ་ཏུ་འགྲོ་དགོས་པས་གྲོགས་ལ་ཡིད་བརྟན་ $\boxed{\text{ནི་}}$ མེད།

ནི་ may follow any syntactic element in a sentence. In the following two examples it follows locative qualifiers.

*To whom should one be attached? Whom should one hate?*[287]

གང་ལ་ $\boxed{\text{ནི་}}$ ཆགས་པར་བྱ། གང་ལ་ $\boxed{\text{ནི་}}$ ཁྲོ་བར་བྱ།

*Because a thousand buddhas come in this aeon,*
   *[it] is called the 'Auspicious Aeon.'*[288]

བསྐལ་པ་འདི་ལ་ནི་སངས་རྒྱས་སྟོང་འབྱོན་པ་ ས་ན་ བསྐལ་པ་བཟང་པོ་ཞེས་བཟོད་པ་ཡིན་ཏེ།

## Quotations

As seen in Appendix Two, the closing syntactic particle ཞེས་ relates a quotation, as a self-contained unit, to the sentence that encloses it—in the following example, རྒྱལ་ བས་གསུངས། .

*Buddha said, "What arises from causes is impermanent."*

རྒྱལ་བས་ རྒྱུ་ལས་བྱུང་བ་དེ་དག་མི་རྟག་པ་ཡིན་ནོ་ཞེས་ གསུངས།

These particles may also be nominalized and then declined.

*The term 'tenet' is not my own creation.*[289]

གྲུབ་མཐའ་ ཞེས་ པའི་ཐ་སྙད་རང་བཟོ་མ་ཡིན་ཏེ།

## Appositive Markers

དེ་, སྟེ་, and ཏེ་, as appositive markers, follow a noun or noun phrase and are followed by a noun or noun phrase in apposition with the first.

- དེ་ follows words ending in the suffixes ན་, ར་, ལ་, and ས་.
- སྟེ་ follows words ending in the suffixes ག་, ང་, བ་, མ་, འ་, as well as words ending in syllables without suffixes.
- ཏེ་ follows words ending in the suffix ད་.

*the buddha jewel, [that is,] the Sugatas of the three times*[290]

དུས་གསུམ་གྱི་བདེ་བར་གཤེགས་པ་ སྟེ་ སངས་རྒྱས་དཀོན་མཆོག

*With the weapon of the three poisons—attachment, hatred, and bewilderment—*
*one takes one's own life.*[291]

ཆགས་པ་ཞེ་སྡང་གཏི་མུག ། སྟེ ། དུག་གསུམ་གྱི་མཚོན་གྱིས་རང་སྲོག་རང་གིས་གཅོད།

## Type Five: *Conjunctive and Disjunctive Particles*

Conjunctive and disjunctive particles include the following:

* The particle དང་ (*and*, sometimes *or*) connects nouns or adjectives;
* གྱང་, ཡང་, and འང་ (*also, even, but*) are used after nouns, pronouns, adjectives, and verbs.
* གམ་, ངམ་, དམ་, ནམ་, བམ་, མམ་, འམ་, རམ་, ལམ་, སམ་, and ཏམ་ mean *or*.
* The particle ལ་ may be used as a syntactic particle after verbs.
* The particles ཀྱི་, གི་, གྱི་, ཡི་, and འི་ are also seen after verbs as syntactic particles.

The syntactic particle དང་ is most often a simple conjunction meaning *and*.

*conceptual **and** nonconceptual minds*

རྟོག་བཅས་ དང་ རྟོག་མེད་ཀྱི་བློ་

However, དང་ is also used to mark the qualifiers of a variety of nominative-syntactic verbs.

*when a latency [created by] a positive [action] does not meet **with** hindrance ...*

དགེ་བའི་བག་ཆགས་གེགས་བྱེད་ དང་ མ་ཕྲད་ན་

*free **of** conceptuality*

རྟོག་པ་ དང་ བྲལ་བ་

དང་ is used with some adjectives in the same sort of way it is used with nominative-syntactic verbs.

| *one* **with** *functioning thing* | *different* **from** *pot* |
| --- | --- |
| དངོས་པོ་ དང་ གཅིག | བུམ་པ་ དང་ ཐ་དད་ |

དངོས་པོ་དང་གཅིག does not mean *functioning thing and one*, nor does བུམ་པ་དང་ཐ་ དད་ mean *pot and different*. If adjectives had qualifiers, the phrase དངོས་པོ་དང་ would be a qualifier. How is it *one*? It is *one with functioning thing*.

དང་ also occurs as a conjunction in syntactically irregular but frequently seen constructions such as the following, where it connects two syntactic particles which are then adverbialized with the particle དུ.

| *because [one] must again **and** again give up [one's body]* |
| --- |
| ཡང་ དང་ ཡང་དུ་འདོར་དགོས་པས་ |

The syntactic particles གམ་, ངམ་, དམ་, ནམ་, བམ་, མམ་, འམ་, རམ་, ལམ་, སམ་, and ཏམ་ are most often used as conjunctions meaning *or*.

| *If there is no illumination such as a lamp **or** the sun, …*[292] |
| --- |
| སྒྲོན་མེ་ འམ་ ཉི་མ་ལྟ་བུའི་སྣང་བ་མེད་ན་ |

The particles ཀྱང་, ཡང་, and འང་ may be used after any sort of word or particle, sometimes conjunctively in the sense of *also* or *even*, sometimes disjunctively in the sense of *but* or *although*.

- ཀྱང་ follows words and particles ending in the suffixes ག, ད, བ, and ས.
- ཡང་ follows words and particles ending in the suffixes ང, ན, མ, འ, ར, and ལ, as well as syllables without suffixes.
- འང་ follows words and particles ending in syllables without suffixes.

These particles sometimes follow simple nouns or adjectives in the nominative case.

---

*There is not **even** one [sentient being] who has not been born here.*

འདིར་མ་སྐྱེས་པ་གཅིག་ གྱང་ མེད།

---

*[Among the three jewels], the doctrine jewel may **also** be posited.*[293]

ཆོས་དཀོན་མཆོག་ གྱང་ བཞག་ཏུ་ཡོད་དེ།

---

*Having practiced giving, ethics, and patience **as well**
    with this [physical] support ...*[294]

སྦྱིན་པ་ཚུལ་ཁྲིམས་བཟོད་པ་ གྱང་ རྟེན་འདིས་སྒྲུབ་ནས།

---

However, གྱང་, ཡང་, and འང་ follow declined nouns and adjectives as well.

*These **also** serve as hindrances to the attainment of leisure and opportunity.*[295]

དེ་དག་གིས་ གྱང་ དལ་འབྱོར་ཐོབ་པའི་གེགས་བྱེད་ཅིང་

---

These particles are frequently used after verbs and verb phrases.

***Although** its object appears clearly,
    [it] cannot induce ascertainment of that [object].*

རང་གི་ཡུལ་གསལ་བར་སྣང་ ཡང་ དེ་ལ་ངེས་པ་འདྲེན་མི་ནུས།

---

Literally: ***Even** if except for a few, negative [actions] are not done,
    there will occur extremely great suffering [as their] effect.*[296]

མི་དགེ་བ་ཆུང་ངུ་ལས་མ་སྤྱད་ གྱང་། འབྲས་བུ་སྡུག་བསྔལ་ཤིན་ཏུ་ཆེ་བ་འབྱུང་།

---

A more fluid translation begins ***even** if only a few negative actions are done.*

Relative pronouns, when followed by these particles, act as indefinite pronouns (*any, whichever*), or, when they are part of constructions ending in negative verbs, as universally negative pronouns or qualifiers (*none at all, no matter what, no one*).

---

*a mind which thinks that sound is impermanent with **no reason at all**[297]*

རྒྱུ་མཚན་ གང་ཡང་ མེད་པར་སྒྲ་མི་རྟག་སྙམ་པའི་བློ་

---

*[I] will attain the status of buddha **no matter what**!*

སངས་རྒྱས་ཀྱི་གོ་འཕང་ཞིག་ ཅི་ནས་ཀྱང་ ཐོབ་པར་བྱའོ།

---

*How nice it would be if [they] were **never** separated from happiness.[298]*

ནམ་ཡང་ བྲལ་མ་གྱུར་ན་ཅི་མ་རུང་།

---

Where ནམ་ means *when*, ནམ་ཡང་ means *ever*—negatively, *never*.

*If one does not commit the two causes—positive [actions] and evil—
there will not be an experience of **any** effects—happiness and suffering.[299]*

རྒྱུ་དགེ་སྡིག་གཉིས་མ་སྤྱད་ན། འབྲས་བུ་བདེ་སྡུག་ གང་ཡང་ མྱོང་བ་མེད།

---

*a difficult point which **no** scholars **at all** have been able to understand[300]*

མཁས་པ་ སུས་ཀྱང་ རྟོགས་པར་མི་ནུས་པའི་དཀའ་བའི་གནད་

---

## Conjunctive and Disjunctive Uses of Case Marking Particles

Particles that are also used to decline nouns, pronouns, and adjectives are sometimes used—usually after verbs—to show disjunction or conjunction. These are not actually special usages of case marking particles, since these particles are not inherently either case marking or syntactic particles.

In the following examples, the particle གྱི་—more frequently used to mark the sixth case—is used as a disjunctive syntactic particle.

***Although*** *it is not asserted that [means] such as giving are unnecessary …*[301]

སྦྱིན་པ་ལ་སོགས་པ་མི་དགོས་པར་མི་འདོད་ཀྱི།

***Although*** *these sufferings are just the effects of the actions that [one] has oneself accumulated …*[302]

སྡུག་བསྔལ་དེ་དག་རང་ཉིད་ཀྱིས་བསགས་པའི་ལས་ཀྱི་འབྲས་བུ་ཉིད་ཡིན་ཀྱི།

As a syntactic particle, ལ་ may be used either disjunctively as in the first of the next two examples, or conjunctively, as in the second.

*the permutation which is an existent **but** is not impermanent*

ཡོད་པ་ཡིན་ ལ་ མི་རྟག་པ་མ་ཡིན་པའི་མུ་

*the bad rebirths, animals **and** so forth*

ངན་འགྲོ་ ལ་ སོགས་པའི་དན་འགྲོ་

The most frequent non-case-marking use of ལ་, however, is disjunctive.

*a mind [to which an object] appears **but** is not ascertained*

སྣང་ ལ་ མ་ངེས་པའི་བློ་

*For example, if [one] has no eyes, [one] will not see anything, **however**, if [one] has eyes, [one] will see …*[303]

དཔེར་ན་མིག་མེད་ན་དངོས་པོ་གང་ཡང་མི་མཐོང་ ལ་ མིག་ཡོད་ན་མཐོང་བ་བཞིན་དུ་

## Type Six: *Verb Modifying Syntactic Particles*

There are many syntactic particles that are used with verbs—for example, the conditional particles discussed earlier and the continuative particles discussed in the next section. However, the only true verb *modifying* particles are the syntactic particles སུ་, ར་, རུ་, དུ་, and ཏུ་ used to create the infinitives used within verb phrases.

As explained in Appendix Four, there are two sorts of Tibetan infinitives. Simple infinitives are used in causative verb phrases such as དྲན་དུ་བཅུག (*made to remember*) and entreaty constructions such as དགོངས་སུ་གསོལ་ (*please consider*).

> *It is suitable whether [one] remembers onself*
> *or has been caused to remember by someone else.*[304]

རང་གིས་དྲན་པའམ་གཞན་གྱིས་དྲན་ | དུ་ | བཅུག་ཀྱང་རུང་སྟེ།

Verbal infinitives require the core verb first to be made into a verbal and then into an infinitive. Thus, དྲན་ becomes དྲན་པ་ and then དྲན་པར་. The infinitive-making particle—here, ར་—is a verb modifying syntactic particle. The auxiliary verbs བྱ་, བྱེད་, འགྱུར་, and གྱུར་ then follow the verbal infinitive form.

> *I will train with effort in all positive [phenomena].*[305]

དགེ་བ་ཀུན་ལ་བདག་གིས་བརྩོན་པས་བསླབ་པ | ར་ | བྱ།

## Type Seven: *Continuative Particles*

Continuative particles are syntactic particles that follow verbs in their core forms, less frequently follow auxiliary verb phrases, and never follow infinitive forms.

- The syntactic particle ནས་ frequently indicates sequence. It follows a verb whose action has been completed and leads to another clause or sentence which describes something happening after that.

- The particles སྟེ་, ཏེ་, and དེ་ are used to show sequence and, in a more general way, to indicate that something relevant follows.

- The particles ཅིང་, ཞིང་, and ཤིང་ are used conjunctively after verbs.

The syntactic particle ནས་—used in other contexts as a particle marking the fifth case—follows verbs in their core forms. It most frequently indicates a sequence of actions following the pattern "having done something, [he then did something else]." In the initial example, first *a latency is deposited* (in the mind) and then it *becomes powerful.*

---

*a latency is deposited and, having become powerful ...*

བག་ཆགས་བཞག་ ནས།  མཐུ་ཅན་དུ་གྱུར་ནས།

---

*Clearly visualizing an attractive sentient being in front [of one],*
    *[one] cultivates even-mindedness.*[306]

ཡིད་དུ་འོང་བའི་སེམས་ཅན་ཞིག་མདུན་དུ་གསལ་བར་དམིགས་ ནས་ སེམས་སྙོམས་པ་སྒོམ་པར་བྱེད།

---

The continuational particles སྟེ་, ཏེ་, and དེ་ follow core verbs and auxiliary verb phrases.

- ཏེ་ follows words ending in the suffixes ན་, ར་, ལ་, and ས་.
- སྟེ་ follows words ending in the suffixes ག་, ང་, བ་, མ་, འ་, as well as words ending in syllables without suffixes.
- དེ་ follows words ending in the suffix ད་.

These particles are also used to show apposition. They are then punctuational syntactic particles and not continuatives.

---

*No matter how many of the pleasures of cyclic existence [one] has enjoyed,*
    *not only is there no limit [at which one is] satisfied, [they] bring about*
    *an increase in craving and induce many intolerable sufferings.*[307]

འཁོར་བའི་བདེ་བ་ལ་ཇི་ཙམ་སྤྱད་ཀྱང་ངོམས་པའི་མཐའ་མེད་པར་མ་ཟད།

སྲིད་པ་རྒྱས་པར་བྱས་ དེ་ སྡུག་བསྔལ་མི་བཟད་པ་དུ་མ་ནི་འདྲེན་པར་བྱེད།

---

མ་ཟད་ is an adverb marking syntactic particle. (See Appendix Six.)

*Having become completely and perfectly enlightened,*
*[Buddha] turned the three wheels of the doctrine.*[308]

མངོན་པར་རྫོགས་པར་སངས་རྒྱས་ ཏེ་ ཆོས་འཁོར་གསུམ་བསྐོར་བ།

*Contemplating the way in which that very [body] is cast aside, without remaining*
*for a long time, [he] turned from the appearances of this lifetime ...*[309]

དེ་ཉིད་རིང་དུ་མི་གནས་པར་འདོར་བའི་ཚུལ་བསམ་ སྟེ་ ཚེ་འདིའི་སྣང་ཤས་ལོག་ནས།

Note that this clause ends in the syntactic particle ནས་, indicating that there is something more of relevance to come.

*Having eliminated the afflictive obstructions,*
*[he] actualized the effect [of that elimination, the status of] arhat.*[310]

ཉོན་མོངས་ཅན་གྱི་སྒྲིབ་པ་སྤངས་ ཏེ་ དགྲ་བཅོམ་པའི་འབྲས་བུ་མངོན་དུ་བྱེད་དོ།

These particles are also used extensively in rhetorical constructions, leading from the statement of the thesis to the statement of the reason.

*Sound is impermanent because [it] is a product.*

སྒྲ་མི་རྟག་པ་ཡིན་ ཏེ། བྱས་པ་ཡིན་པའི་ཕྱིར།

The particles ཅིང་, ཞིང་, and ཤིང་ are used after both verbs and adjectives.

- ཅིང་ follows words ending in the suffixes ག་, ད་, བ་, and the secondary suffix ད་.
- ཞིང་ follows words ending in the suffixes ང་, ན་, མ་, འ་, ར་, and ལ་, as well as syllables without suffixes.
- ཤིང་ follows words ending in the suffix ས་ or the secondary suffix ས་.

Care should be taken to distinguish the use of ཞིང་ as a syntactic particle from its use as a noun meaning *field*. Likewise, ཤིང་ as a word means *wood*.

These three syntactic particles usually follow verbs, as in the following example.

---

*All three vows [may be] produced*
*    and the status of a perfect buddha may be achieved.*[311]

---

སྡོམ་པ་གསུམ་ག་སྐྱེ་ ཞིང་། ཇོགས་པའི་སངས་རྒྱས་ཀྱི་གོ་འཕང་སྒྲུབ་ནུས་སོ།

---

In the following example the particle ཞིང་ is used after an adjective.

---

*Clear and aware [is] the definition of consciousness.*

---

གསལ་ ཞིང་ རིག་པ་ཤེས་པའི་མཚན་ཉིད།

# Answers to Drills

## Drill 5

| | | | | | | | |
|---|---|---|---|---|---|---|---|
| 1 | དག་ tak | དོག་ tok | ཞུགས་ s̲huk | རིག་ rîk |
| 2 | དང་ tang | དུང་ tung | སོང་ s̄ong |
| 3 | དུད་ tü' | ཆེད་ ché' | རེད་ ré' | ཟད་ s̲ë' |
| 4 | ཆུད་ chü' | སིད་ s̄í' | ཁོར་ khor |
| 5 | མན་ mën | མིན་ mîn | སུན་ s̄ün |
| | ཐོམ་ thom | ལེན་ lên | པོན་ pön |
| 6 | ཟབ་ s̲ap | རིབ་ ríp | ཧོབ་ hop | ཐུན་ thün |
| 7 | དམ་ tam | དོམ་ tom | དུམ་ ngum | འབའ་ ba | འབད་ bë' |
| 8 | ཚར་ tshar | ཚོར་ tshor | ཁུར་ khur | ཁོལ་ khöl |
| 9 | དུལ་ tül | ཁིལ་ khíl | དུལ་ dül | ཕེལ་ phél | གོལ་ köl |
| 10 | རས་ rë> | གིས་ ḡí> | གིས་ gí> |
| | དུས་ tü> | ཆེས་ ché> | ཆོས་ chö> |
| 11 | ཆ་ cha | ཆད་ chë' | ཆན་ chën | ཆལ་ chël | ཆས་ chë> |

| | | | | | | | | | |
|---|---|---|---|---|---|---|---|---|---|
| 12 | ད་ tu | དད་ tü' | དན་ tün | དལ་ tül | དས་ tü> |
| 13 | གོ་ go | གོད་ gö' | གོན་ gön | གོལ་ göl | གོས་ gö> |
| 14 | རེ་ ré | རེད་ ré' | རེན་ rén | རེལ་ rél | རེས་ ré> |

## Drill 6

| | | | | |
|---|---|---|---|---|
| 7 | གོ་ ko | སྒོ་ go | མགོ་ go | ཁོ་ kho |
| 8 | མཁོ་ kho | དགེ་ gé | བསྒོ་ go | ག་ ga |
| 9 | ཏ་ d̄a | ཊ་ d̄a | བརྗེ་ jé | ཇེ་ chí |
| 10 | ང་ n̄ga | སྔ་ n̄ga | ཉེ་ n̄ya | ཉ་ n̄ga |
| 11 | རྩ་ d̄za | ཇ་ j̄a | ཙ་ d̲za | ཙ་ d̄za |
| 12 | ཟ་ ba | སྦ་ ba | ཌ་ da | ལྷ་ hla |
| 13 | ཟེ་ dé | ལ་ da | སྙ་ n̄ya | |
| 14 | དབུ་ ū | དཔང་ b̄ang | དབང་ w̄ang | དཔེ་ b̄é |
| 15 | དཔལ་ b̄el | འབའ་ ba | དབུ་ u | དབང་ w̄ang |
| 16 | དཔག་ b̄ak | དབུལ་ ül | དབུས་ ü> | དཔའ་ b̄a |

## Drill 7.1

| | | | | | | |
|---|---|---|---|---|---|---|
| 2 | ག་ ḡa | གྱ་ ḡya | ཁ་ kha | ཁྱ་ khya | ག་ ka | གྱ་ kya |
| 3 | ཁ་ kha | ཁྱ་ khya | ཁུ་ khu | ཁྱུ་ khyu | | |
| | | འཁྱུ་ khyu | ཀྱུ་ ḡya | ཀྱུ་ ḡya | | |
| 4 | ག་ ka | གྱ་ kya | ཀྱུ་ ḡya | འགྱེ་ gyé | | |

| 5 | གུ་ ḡya | རྒྱུ་ gya | རྒྱུ་ ḡya | ཀྱ་ kya | ཁྱ་ khya |
|---|---|---|---|---|---|

| 6 | བ་ b̄a | ཇ་ j̄a | ཕ་ pha | ཆ་ cha | པ་ pa | ཅ་ c̱ha |
|---|---|---|---|---|---|---|

| 7 | བ་ b̄a | ཇ་ j̄a | དཇ་ j̄a | རྗ་ j̄a |
|---|---|---|---|---|

| | ཕ་ pha | ཆ་ cha | འཆ་ cha |
|---|---|---|---|

| 8 | བ་ ba | ཅ་ c̱ha | འཇི་ j̄í | འཇེ་ j̄é | ཉ་ nya | ཉོ་ ñyo |
|---|---|---|---|---|---|---|

---

## Drill 7.4

| 5 | ལ་ l̄a | ལུ་ l̄u | ལིང་ l̄íng | |
|---|---|---|---|---|
| 6 | ལ་ l̄a | ལོ་ l̄o | ལང་ l̄ang | ལུ་ l̄u |
| 7 | ལ་ l̄a | ལང་ l̄ang | ལོ་ l̄o | |
| 8 | ལ་ l̄a | ལག་ l̄ak | ལམ་ l̄am | ལུང་ l̄ung |
| 9 | ལ་ l̄a | ལེ་ l̄é | ལོང་ l̄ong | ལོབ་ l̄op |
| 10 | ད་ da | དོག་ dok | དུམ་ dum | |
| 11 | ཁ་ kha | ཀ་ ka | ཏང་ tang | ཚ་ tsha |

---

## Drill 7.5

| 1 | དག་ད tak | 2 | ཐིག་ད dík | 3 | འདིལ་ད d̠îl |
|---|---|---|---|---|---|
| 4 | ཊག་ད ṭak | 5 | ཐུད་ད dü' | 6 | པ་པ ḍa |
| 7 | ཐག་བ ḍak | 8 | གད་ག kë' | 9 | ཋ་ག ḍa |
| 10 | ཀོམ་ག gom | 11 | འབྱུར་བ jor | 12 | ཀྱུར་བ jor |
| 13 | དབྱར་བ ȳar | 14 | དམར་མ m̄ar | 15 | རྣལ་ན ñël |

| | | | | | |
|---|---|---|---|---|---|
| 16 | ཚོས་ ཚ chö> | 17 | ཟད་ ཟ s̲ë' | 18 | སད་ ས s̲ë' |
| 19 | བཤད་ ཤ s̲hë' | 20 | བཞིད་ ཞ s̲hé' | 21 | སྒྲུབ་ ག ḍup |
| 22 | དངར་ ང n̄gar | 23 | དང་ ད tang | 24 | དམངས་ མ m̄ang |
| 25 | དངས་ ད tang | 26 | གྲུབ་ ག ṭup | | |

---

## Drill 8.2

Boxes are drawn here only around words.  The first line of each answer is a
**Tenglish** translation—English vocabulary written in Tibetan syntax.  The second
line of each answer is an English translation.

[1]  MATTER   CONSCIOUSNESS  NON-ASSOCIATED-COMPOSITIONAL-FACTOR
    THREE

*the three—matter, consciousness, and non-associated compositional factors*

| བེམ་པོ་ | ཤེས་པ་ | ལྡན་མིན་འདུ་བྱེད་ | གསུམ་ |
|---|---|---|---|

[2]  EXISTENT  NON-EXISTENT  TWO

*the two, existents and non-existents*

| ཡོད་པ་ | མེད་པ་ | གཉིས། |
|---|---|---|

[3]  MATERIAL-FORM  MIND  CONTRADICTORY

*material form [and] mind being contradictory*

| གཟུགས་ | སེམས་ | འགལ་བ་ |
|---|---|---|

4 CYCLIC-EXISTENCE  NIRVANA

*cyclic existence and nirvana*

| འཁོར་བ་ | མྱ་ངན་ལས་འདས་པ་ |

5 POT  THAT  IMPERMANENCE  IS

*That pot is impermanent.*

| བུམ་པ་ | དི་ | མི་རྟག་པ་ | ཡིན། |

6 BUDDHA-IN  IGNORANCE  NOT-EXIST

*Buddhas have no ignorance..*

| སངས་རྒྱས་ | ལ་ | མ་རིག་པ་ | མེད། |

7 CYCLIC-EXISTENCE-FROM  LIBERATION  EXISTS

*There is liberation from cyclic existence.*

| འཁོར་བ་ | ལས་ | སྒྲོལ་བ་ | ཡོད། |

8 ACTION  POSITIVE  AND  NEGATIVE

*positive and negative actions*

| ལས་ | དགེ་བ་ | དང་ | མི་དགེ་བ་ |

9 WISDOM  IGNORANCE  CONCEPTUALITY  OBJECT-POSSESSOR  IS

*Wisdom, ignorance, and conceptuality are subjects.*

| ཡེ་ཤེས་ | མ་རིག་པ་ | རྣམ་པར་རྟོག་པ་ | ཡུལ་ཅན་ | ཡིན། |

[10]  MIND  MENTALITY  CONSCIOUSNESS  EQUIVALENT  ARE

*Mind, mentality, and consciousness are equivalent..*

| སེམས་ | ཡིད་ | རྣམ་པར་ཤེས་པ་ | དོན་གཅིག | ཡིན། |

---

# Drill 9.1

[1] MOUNTAINS  EXIST is correct.

[2] THERE  ARE  MOUNTAINS should read MOUNTAINS  EXIST.

[3] BUDDHA  TURNED  WHEEL-OF DOCTRINE is corrected in number (4).

[4] BUDDHA  DOCTRINE-OF  WHEEL  TURNED is correct.

[5] ATISHA  TRAVELLED  TO  TIBET should read ATISHA TIBET-TO TRAVELLED.

[6] ATISHA  TRAVELLED  TIBET-TO should read ATISHA  TIBET-TO  TRAVELLED.

[7] RED  IS  COLOR should read RED COLOR IS.

[8] IS  RED  COLOR should read RED COLOR IS.

[9] RED  COLOR  IS is correct.

[10] FROM-EMPTINESS  BODY-OF  BUDDHA  ARISES is corrected in number (11).

[11] EMPTINESS-FROM  BUDDHA-OF  BODY  ARISES is correct.

[12] FROM-EMPTINESS  BODY-OF  BUDDHA  ARISES is corrected in number (11).

---

# Drill 9.2

Verbs—both final and open forms—are boxed.  The first line of each answer is Tenglish and the second line is an English translation.

[1] I-BY  EVIL  DID

*I have done evil.*

བདག་གིས་  སྡིག་པ་  བྱས།

2  IMPERMANENCE  REALIZE  SHOULD-BE

*One should realize impermanence.*

མི་རྟག་པ་ རྟོགས་པར་ བྱ།

3  BUDDHA-BY  TAUGHT :  DOCTRINE  IS

*That taught by Buddha is the doctrine..*

སངས་རྒྱས་ཀྱིས་ བསྟན་པ་ ནི་ ཆོས་ ཡིན།

4  BUDDHA  TEACHER  IS

*A buddha is a teacher.*

སངས་རྒྱས་ སྟོན་པ་ ཡིན།

5  ARHAT-BY  PEACE  FOUND

*An arhat has found peace.*

དགྲ་བཅོམ་པ་ས་ ཞི་བ་ བརྙེས།

---

# Drill 9.3

1  old [i.e., earlier] textbook  (རྙིང་པ་ in the sense of *older version*)
2  great intelligence
3  white conch shell
4  five energy winds
5  holy *guru*

1  འཕྲུལ་བུ་དང་པོ་

2  ཤོད་དམར་པོ་

3  ཊ་དཀར་པོ་

[4] མི་དགེ་བའི་སེམས་

[5] དྲག་པའི་ཚོས་

---

## Drill 11.1

[1] འདི་དུང་དཀར་པོ་ཨིན།

[2] རྟ་དཀར་པོ་འདི་

[3] ཚོས་མང་པོ་

[4] ཉ་ཐམས་ཅད་སེམས་ཅན་ཨིན།

---

## Drill 11.2

[1] *Mind is an impermanent phenomenon.*

སེམས་ མི་རྟག་པའི་ཚོས་ ཨིན།

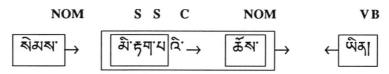

[2] *There are many buddhas.*

སངས་རྒྱས་མང་པོ་ཡོད།

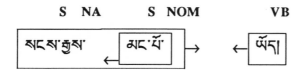

3 *All sentient beings are impermanent.*

སེམས་ཅན་ཐམས་ཅད་མི་རྟག་པ་ཡིན།

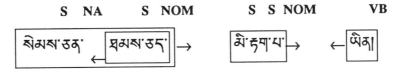

4 *There are five chapters.*

      **NA NOM   VB**

    བཞིའི་  ལྔ་  ཡོད།

5 *This is a white horse.*

    **NOM  NA    S NOM VB**

    འདི་  རྟ་ དཀར་པོ་  ཡིན།

---

# Drill 11.3

1 *white, blue, red, [and] yellow*

     **S NN    S NN    S NN    S**

  དཀར་པོ་  སྔོན་པོ་  དམར་པོ་  སེར་པོ་

2 *buddhas and meditational deities*

      **S  SP   SP    S**

   སངས་རྒྱས་   དང་   ཡི་དམ་

3 *the two, humans and horses*

     **NN  APP**

    མི་  རྟ་  གཉིས་

4  *the three—forms, sense powers, and consciousnesses*

         NN       S NN     OM  APP

      ལུལ་    དབང་པོ་    རྣམ་ཤེས་   གསུམ་

---

# Drill 12.1

Where possible, the translation of the connective case marking particle is in italics.

1    obstructions *which are* actions
2    offspring *of* the Buddhas
3    definition *of* shape
4    actions *which are* misdeeds
5    the phenomena *of* cyclic existence and nirvana
6    path *of* the great vehicle
7    radiance *of* the moon
8    Mind Only system
9    afflictions *in* the continuums *of* immature beings
10   the head *of* a pig,  a pig'*s* head
11   protector deities' room
12   the connection *between* energy-winds and minds

---

# Drill 12.2

1   ཨེ་ཤེས་ཀྱི་

2   ཁ་དོག་གི་

3   སྲིད་པའི་

4   གྲུབ་ཐོབ་ཀྱི་

5   ཇ་པོའི་

6   གུན་མཐིན་གྱི་

7   ཨེ་དམ་གྱི་

8   འོད་ཟེར་གྱི་

9   སྒྲའི་

10   གངས་ཀྱི་

11   ཨིད་ཀྱི་

12   དེའི་

---

# Drill 12.3

1   *Blue is a color.*

    སྔོན་པོ་ཁ་དོག་ཨིན།

| S NOM | S NOM | VB |
|---|---|---|

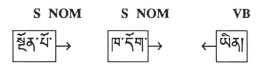

2   *I am a person.*

| NOM | S NOM | VB |
|---|---|---|
| ང་ | གང་ཟག | ཨིན། |

3   *Minds are impermanent.*

| NOM | S | S NOM | VB |
|---|---|---|---|
| སེམས་ | | མི་རྟག་པ་ | ཨིན། |

4   *That is tea.*

| NOM | NOM | VB |
|---|---|---|
| དེ་ | ཇ་ | ཨིན། |

5   *Oceans are water.*

| S NOM | NOM | VB |
|---|---|---|
| རྒྱ་མཚོ་ | ཆུ་ | ཨིན། |

6 *Shapes are phenomena.*

|NOM|NOM|VB|
|---|---|---|
|དབྱིབས་|ཆོས་|ཡིན།|

7 *Red is impermanent.*

|S NOM|S S NOM|VB|
|---|---|---|
|དམར་པོ་|མི་རྟག་པ་|ཡིན།|

8 *Pots are existents.*

བུམ་པ་ཡོད་པ་ཡིན།

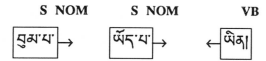

---

## Drill 12.4

1 སེམས་དང་གཟུགས་འགལ་བ་ཡིན།

2 ཆོས་མང་པོ་ཁ་དོག་མ་ཡིན།

3 མི་རྟ་མ་ཡིན།

4 སེམས་ཅན་ཐམས་ཅད་མི་མ་ཡིན།

5 བུམ་པ་ལྟ་སྟོན་པོ་ཡིན། གཉིས་སེར་པོ་ཡིན།

---

## Drill 12.5

1 *Horses and humans are sentient beings.*

རྟ་དང་མི་སེམས་ཅན་ཡིན།

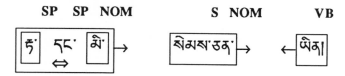

2  *Many pots are yellow.*

3  *Non-associated compositional factors are not minds.*

4  *A white religious conch is not the color red.*

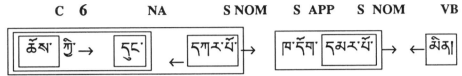

5  *All functioning things are impermanent.*

6  *Great compassion is a mind.*

## Drill 12.6

1  *[That] is not the buddha Amitāyus.*

2  *[The three poisons] are the three—attachment, hatred, and obscuration.*

3  *[The four truths] are the contaminated and uncontaminated phenomena of cyclic existence and nirvana.*

4  *[A buddha] knows all objects of knowledge.*

5  *You taught [the path to enlightenment].*

## Drill 13.1

These sentences have been constructed using words from the vocabularies of previous chapters. Practice reading and speaking them. Identify their dots and translate them. Diagram the third and fourth with boxes and arrows.

1  *There are buddhas.*

    **S NOM    VB**

    སངས་རྒྱས་  ཡོད།

2  *There are humans and horses.*

    **SP   SP   NOM   VB**

    མི་   དང་   རྟ་   ཡོད།

[3]   *There are three—buddhas, arhats, and bodhisattvas.*

སངས་རྒྱས་དང་དགྲ་བཅོམ་པ་བྱང་ཆུབ་སེམས་དཔའ་གསུམ་ཡོད།

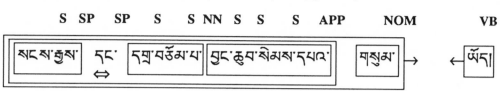

| S SP | SP | S | S NN S S | S | APP | NOM | | VB |
|------|-----|---|----------|---|-----|-----|---|----|
| སངས་རྒྱས་ | དང་ ⟺ | དགྲ་བཅོམ་པ་ | བྱང་ཆུབ་སེམས་དཔའ་ | | | གསུམ་ → | | ←ཡོད། |

[4]   *There are conceptual and nonconceptual minds.*

རྟོག་བཅས་དང་རྟོག་མེད་ཀྱི་བློ་ཡོད།

| OM SP | SP | OM | C 6 | NOM | | VB |
|-------|-----|-----|-----|-----|---|----|
| རྟོག་བཅས་ | དང་ ⟺ | རྟོག་མེད་ | ཀྱི་ → | བློ་ → | | ←ཡོད། |

[5]   *Earth, water, fire, and wind exist.*

| NN | NN | NN | NOM | VB |
|----|----|----|-----|-----|
| ས་ | ཆུ་ | མེ་ | རླུང་ | ཡོད། |

---

## Drill 13.2

[1]   གཟུགས་མེད་ཁམས་ལ་མི་མེད།

[2]   ནུབ་ཕྱོགས་ལ་སྐྱང་པོ་ཆེ་མང་པོ་མེད།

[3]   དག་ཞིང་ལ་ཨི་དྭགས་མེད།

## Drill 13.3

[1] *There are no snow mountains in the north.*

བྱང་ཕྱོགས་ལ་གངས་རི་མེད།

| UP | C | 7 | | UP NOM | VB |
|---|---|---|---|---|---|

བྱང་ཕྱོགས་ལ་ →    གངས་རི་ →    ←མེད།

[2] There are no contaminated minds among the wisdoms of a superior.

[3] Complete enjoyment bodies have no defilements.

[4] Great compassion is not present in the continuum of an ordinary being.

## Drill 13.4

[1] འཇམ་དཔའི་སྙིང་ལ་རྒྱ་མཚོ་དང་རི་འདུག

[2] བོད་ལ་རྒྱ་པོ་ཆེན་པོ་འདུག

[3] དགྲ་མའི་ལམ་ཡོད།

[4] སངས་རྒྱས་ཀྱི་ཆོས་སྐུ་ལ་ཉིན་མོངས་མེད།

## Drill 13.5

[1] *The two—positive and negative actions—exist.*
OR *Both positive and negative actions exist.*

| NA | SP | SP | APP | NOM | VB |
|---|---|---|---|---|---|

ལས་ དགེ་བ་ དང་ མི་དགེ་བ་ གཉིས་ ཡོད།

2. *There are no oceans in Nepal.*

S   C 7      NOM   S    VB

བལ་ཡུལ་ལ་    རྒྱ་མཚོ་    མ་མཆིས།

3. *There are no great rivers in India.* [an incorrect statement]

S   NA    NOM          C 7          S    VB

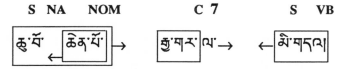

4. *Among functioning things there are many causes and effects.*

C 7    SP   SP     NA    NOM    VB

དངོས་པོ་ལ་    རྒྱུ་   དང་   འབྲས་བུ་   མང་པོ་   ཡོད།

5. *Great compassion is not present in Hearers [but] is in Bodhisattvas.*
[a statement open to debate]

NA     NOM     C 7     VB               C 7     VB

སྙིང་རྗེ་ ཆེན་པོ་ ཉན་ཐོས་ལ་ མེད། བྱང་ཆུབ་སེམས་དཔའ་ལ་ ཡོད།

---

## Drill 14.1

1. དགྲ་བཅོམ་པ་ལ་དགེ་བའི་ཆོས་མང་པོ་ཡོད།

2. དེ་དག་ལ་ཕྱུག་པ་མེར་པོ་ཡོད།

3. སངས་རྒྱས་རྣམས་ལ་ཕུགས་པ་དང་སྙིང་རྗེ་ཡོད།

4. དགེ་སློང་དེ་རྣམས་ལ་ཁ་ལག་མེད།

5. ཁྱོད་ལ་སྐྱང་པོ་ཆེ་མེད།

## Drill 14.2

1 *Arhats do not have all of the virtues of buddhas.*

S    S C 7    S C 6   S NA  S NOM  VB

དགྲ་བཅོམ་པ་ལ་ སངས་རྒྱས་ཀྱི་ ཡོན་ཏན་ ཐམས་ཅད་ མེད།

2 *There are, among those, colors and shapes.*

S  S 7      SP   SP S NOM  VB

དེ་དག་ལ་ དབྱིབས་ དང་ ཁ་དོག་ ཡོད།

3 *People who are in cyclic existence have no independence.*

འཁོར་བ་ལ་ཡོད་པའི་གང་ཟག་ལ་རང་དབང་མ་མཆིས།

     S C 7       V  6    S C 7        S NOM      S  VB

| འཁོར་བ་ལ་ → | ←ཡོད་པ་ འི་ → | གང་ཟག་ ལ་ → | རང་དབང་→ | ←མ་མཆིས། |

4 *Oneself and others have bodies and resources.*

NN    C 7   SP   SP    S NOM   VB

བདག་ གཞན་ལ་ ལུས་ དང་ ལོངས་སྤྱོད་ མཆིས།

5 *A bodhisattva has many positive [virtuous] phenomena.*
OR *Bodhisattvas have many positive phenomena.*

S    S    S    C 7   S 6   NA  S NOM  VB

བྱང་ཆུབ་སེམས་དཔའ་ལ་ དགེ་བའི་ ཆོས་ མང་པོ་ ཡོད།

---

## Drill 14.3

1 *Among pots there are the two, golden pots and copper pots.*
OR *Pots include both golden pots and copper pots.*

2  *Among [visible] forms there are two, shape and color.*
   Taking the locative to be a referential locative gives the following:
   *As regards [visible] forms, there are two, shape and color.*

3  *Among enlightenments, there are three.*
   OR  *As regards enlightenments, there are three.*

4  *Among truths are the two, conventional truths and ultimate truths.*
   OR  *As regards the truths, there are two, conventional truths and ultimate truths.*

5  *Among impermanent things there are causes and effects.*

---

# Drill 14.4

1  བདག་ཅག་སངས་རྒྱས་མ་ཡིན།

2  ང་རྟ་མ་ཡིན།

3  བདག་ཅག་རྣམས་ཡོད།

4  བདག་དང་གཞན་འཛམ་བུའི་གླིང་ལ་ཡོད།

5  བདག་དེ་བཞིན་གཤེགས་པ་ཡིན།

---

# Drill 14.5

1  *We are not horses.*
2  *I am an arhat.*
3  *The four of us are not humans, nor are we gods.*
4  *There are many monks in India.*
5  *We are not teachers [who are] Conquerors [i.e., buddhas].*

---

# Drill 14.6

1  མོ་གཤམ་གྱི་བུ་ཚོས་ཙན། མི་རྟག་པ་མ་ཡིན་ཏེ། ཡོད་པ་མ་ཡིན་པའི་ཕྱིར།

2  ཏ་དགར་པོ་ཆོས་ཅན། ཁྱན་མིན་འདུ་བྱེད་ཡིན་ཏེ།  གང་ཟག་ཡིན་པའི་ཕྱིར།

3  ཏ་དགར་པོའི་ཁ་དོག་ཆོས་ཅན།  གཟུགས་ཡིན་ཏེ།  ཁ་དོག་ཡིན་པའི་ཕྱིར།

4  དོག་པ་ཆོས་ཅན།  ཡིད་ཤེས་ཡིན་ཏེ།  ཤེས་པ་ཡིན་ཕ་གང་ཞིག
   དབང་ཤེས་མ་ཡིན་པའི་ཕྱིར།

---

## Drill 14.7

1  *A visual consciousness is a sense consciousness because of being a consciousness but not being a mental consciousness.*

      6    NOM   NOM  VB SP   NOM   V    SP   NOM    V 6 SP

མིག་གི་རྣམ་ཤེས་ དབང་ཤེས་ ཡིན་ཏེ་ ཤེས་པ་ཡིན་པ་ གང་ཞིག་ ཡིད་ཤེས་མ་ཡིན་པའི་ཕྱིར།

2  *The subject, material form, is a basic existent because of being impermanent.*

       APP    NOM    NOM  VB SP    NOM    V 6   SP

གཟུགས་ ཆོས་ཅན་ གཞི་གྲུབ་ ཡིན་ཏེ་ མི་རྟག་པ་ ཡིན་པའི་ཕྱིར།

3  *The subject, consciousness, is not permanent, because of not being an existent which is not impermanent.*

4  *The subject, a fish, is a migrating being because of living in cyclic existence.*

---

## Drill 15.1

1  དགེ་སློང་རྣམས་དགོན་པ་ན་བཞུགས།

2  དེ་བཞིན་གཤེགས་པ་ཤཀྱ་ཐུབ་པ་ལྷ་ས་ར་མ་བཞུགས།

3  ང་ཙག་གཙང་ལ་སྐྱོད།

4  དམྱལ་བ་པ་ཡུན་རིང་པོར་གནས།

5  རྒྱ་ནག་ལ་ལོ་ལྔག་བསྡད།

## Drill 15.2

1. *A Buddha's complete enjoyment body remains in [that Buddha's] pure land.*

         C 6    OM NOM    C 7      VB

སངས་རྒྱས་ཀྱི་ ལོངས་སྐུ་ དག་ཞིང་ལ་ བཞུགས།

2. *The Sugata stayed in Varanasi.*

            NOM        C 7      VB

བདེ་བར་གཤེགས་པ་ ཝཱ་ར་ཎ་སཱི་ལ་ བཞུགས།

3. *Those gods live on Mount Meru.*

    NA   NOM    APP     7      VB

ལྷ་ དེ་དག་ རི་རབ་ ཕྱུན་པོར་ གནས།

4. *If one were to stay in India for many years …*

       C 7  NA    7    V SP

རྒྱ་གར་ལ་ ལོ་ མང་པོར་ བསྡད་ན།

5. *[those who] live in the central region [Magadha]*

      APP   C 7    V

ཡུལ་ དབུས་སུ་ གནས་པ་

## Drill 15.3

1. དགྲ་བཅོམ་པ་ཀླུ་ངན་ལས་འདས་པར་གནས།

2. འཕགས་པ་ཇིས་འབྱུང་གི་མདོ་བཞུགས་སོ།

3. སངས་རྒྱས་རྣམས་དོན་དམ་བདེན་པ་ལ་གནས། །

4. མིའི་གྲོང་ཁྱེར་ནི་ལོ་མང་པོར་མི་སྟོད།

5. བདག་ཅག་དགེ་བ་ལ་གནས

## Drill 15.4

1. *That mind abides in bliss.*

2. *Positive minds do not remain long.*

|  | 6 | NOM | NA | 7 |  | VB |
|---|---|---|---|---|---|---|
|  | དགེ་བའི་ | སེམས་ | ཡུན་ | རིང་པོར་ | | མི་སྡོད། |

3. *A yogi remains one-pointedly in selflessless.*

|  | NOM |  | 7 | ADV | VB |
|---|---|---|---|---|---|
|  | རྣལ་འབྱོར་པ་ | བདག་མེད་དུ་ | | རྩེ་གཅིག་ཏུ་ | གནས། |

4. *Bodhisattvas abide in compassion.*

---

## Drill 15.5

1. *It follows that the subjects—a pillar and a pot—are existent because [they] are functioning things.*

ཀ་བུམ་གཉིས་ཆོས་ཅན། ཡོད་པ་ཨིན་པར་ཐལ། དངོས་པོ་ཨིན་པའི་ཕྱིར།

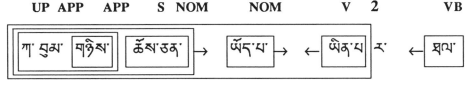

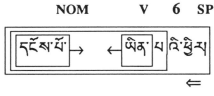

2. *It follows that the subject, a white horse, is not white because of not being a color.*

3. *It follows that the subject, a white horse, is not a color because of being a person.*

4   *It follows that the subject, a visual consciousness, is not a mental consciousness because of being a sense consciousness.*

---

## Drill 16.1

1   དགོན་པ་དེ་ལ་བཞུགས་པའི་དགེ་སློང་རྣམས་

2   ཕྱུག་པ་ན་ཡོད་པའི་ཆུ་

3   བྱམས་པ་མེད་པའི་དགྲ་བཅོམ་པ་མེད།

4   རྒྱུ་དེ་ལ་བརྟེན་པའི་འབྲས་བུ་

5   བློ་ཕྱུགས་སུ་གནས་པའི་མི་

6   དུད་འགྲོ་ཡིན་པའི་སེམས་ཅན་

7   སངས་རྒྱས་ཀྱི་ས་ལ་གནས་པ་རྣམས་

---

## Drill 16.2

1   *beings who live in cities*

      S C7      S 6      S

    གྲོང་ཁྱེར་ལ་ གནས་པའི་ སྐྱེས་བུ་

2   *Those phenomena that do not last for a second moment are impermanent.*

          NA       7        6    NA NOM    NOM     VB

   སྐད་ཅིག་ གཉིས་པར་ མི་སྡོད་པའི་ ཆོས་ དེ་དག་ མི་རྟག་པ་ ཡིན།

3   *an attitude without attachment or aversion*

       S    SP   SP   NOM     6

   འདོད་ཆགས་ དང་ ཞེ་སྡང་ མེད་པའི་ བསམ་པ་

4 *sound's being impermanent*

      NOM   NOM   V

སྒྲ་ མི་རྟག་པ་ ཡིན་པ་

5 *those who live in the central region*

      APP     7     V S

ཡུལ་ དབུས་སུ་ གནས་པ་རྣམས་

---

## Drill 16.3

1 འདོད་ཆགས་མ་རིག་པ་ལ་རག་ལས།

2 རྣམ་པར་ཤེས་པ་དབང་ཤེས་ལ་ཏེན།

3 རྣམ་པར་ཤེས་པ་ནི་རང་གི་ཡུལ་ལ་ཏེན།

4 སེམས་ཅན་ནི་ལུས་དང་སེམས་ལ་ཏེན།

5 སྐྱིང་རྗེ་ངེས་འབྱུང་ལ་རག་ལས།

---

## Drill 16.4

1 *Wisdom is attained in dependence on concentration.*

          7    V SP     NOM VB

ཏིང་ངེ་འཛིན་ལ་ བརྟེན་ནས་ ཤེས་རབ་ ཐོབ།

2 *not depending on impermanent phenomena*
   ALSO: *not in the context of impermanent phenomena*

        6       7     V

མི་རྟག་པའི་ ཆོས་ལ་ མ་བསྟོས་པ་

3    *Those do not depend on other causes.*

        NOM  NA      7       S S  VB

        དེ་དག་ རྒྱུ་ གཞན་ལ་ རག་མ་ལས།

4    *Wisdom depends on ethics and concentration.*

         NN         SP  SP           7   VB

        ཤེས་རབ་ ཚུལ་ཁྲིམས་ དང་ ཏིང་ངེ་འཛིན་ལ་ རྟེན།

5    *Concentration depends on ethics.*

         NOM         C 7   VB

        ཏིང་ངེ་འཛིན་ ཚུལ་ཁྲིམས་ལ་ རྟེན།

---

## Drill 16.5

1    དེ་རྣམས་གྱོང་ཁྲིར་ལ་སྟེད།

2    ཁྱོད་རང་ཡོད།

3    ཁོང་མི་ཨིན། བླ་མ་ཨིན།

4    ཕྱམ་པ་རང་མི་དྲག་པ་ཨིན།

5    ཁོང་དགྲ་བཙམ་པ་ཨིན།

---

## Drill 16.6

1    *There are arhats among Hearers and Solitary Conquerors.*

        OM  C 7       NOM   VB

        ཉན་ རང་ལ་ དགྲ་བཙམ་པ་ ཡོད།

2  *These are not Transcendent Victors.*

       **NOM**       **NOM**   **VB**

འདི་དག་ བཅོམ་ལྡན་འདས་ མ་ཡིན།

3  *He is a real arhat.* [The རང་ shows emphasis.]

    **NOM**      **APP**  **NOM**  **VB**

ཁོང་ དགྲ་བཅོམ་པ་ རང་ ལགས།

4  *The Sugata himself stayed in Shravasti.*

              **APP**    **NOM**         **7**       **VB**

བདེ་བར་གཤེགས་པ་ རང་ཉིད་ མཉན་ཡོད་ན་ བཞུགས།

---

# Drill 17.1

1  བདག་གིས་སྟེག་པ་བུས།

2  བྱང་ཆུབ་སེམས་དཔས་དམྱལ་བ་པ་ལ་བྱམས་པ་དང་སྙིང་རྗེ་སྐྱེད།

3  རྗེ་བཙུན་བྱམས་པས་འཁོར་རྣམས་ལ་ཕར་ཕྱིན་བསྟན།

---

# Drill 17.2

1  *I / We  see / saw a religious conch.*

  **S**  **3**    **UP** **NOM**   **VB**

ཁོ་བོས་ ཆོས་ དུང་ མཐོང་།

2  *The Teacher [Buddha] spoke of the paths of the three [types of] beings.*

      **3**      **NA**     **6**    **NOM**  **VB**

སྟོན་པས་ སྐྱེས་བུ་ གསུམ་གྱི་ ལམ་ བཤད།

3    *They are seeking liberation.*

         **3**     **NOM**      **VB**

དེ་དག་གིས་ ཐར་པ་ དོན་དུ་གཉེར།

4    *[I] explained the teaching to those [who are] immature [or foolish]. To yogis, [I] explained tenets.*

            **4**      **NOM**   **VB**        **4**      **NOM**    **VB**

བྱིས་པ་རྣམས་ལ་ བསྟན་པ་ བཤད། རྣལ་འབྱོར་པ་ལ་ གྲུབ་མཐའ་ བཤད།

5    *There is not even one [being who] has not acted as my mother in a human [life-]support [that is, in a human body].*

         **2**        **6 NOM**    **V NA**   **NOM SP**    **VB**

མིའི་རྟེན་ལ་ བདག་གི་མ་ མ་བྱས་པ་ གཅིག་ ཀྱང་ མེད།

---

# Drill 17.3

1    བདག་ཅག་གི་སྟན་པས་མི་དག་པ་དང་སྟོང་པ་ཉིད་ཀྱི་ཆོས་བཤད་པར་གྱུར།

2    རྒྱལ་བའི་དགོངས་པ་རྟོགས་པར་འགྱུར།

3    ཞི་སྟང་བཀག་ནས་སློམ་པར་བྱེད།

---

# Drill 17.4

1    *The way [in which to] meditate compassion will be explained below.*

     **NOM**       **6 NOM SP**    **2**        **S**    **V**   **VB SP**

སྙིང་རྗེ་ སྒོམ་པའི་ཚུལ་ ནི་ འོག་ཏུ་ འཆད་པར་འགྱུར་རོ།

2  *[This book] propounds a presentation of the three, bases, paths, and [their] fruits.*

NN    NN    APP     6       NOM     V VB

གཞི་ ལམ་ འབྲས་ གསུམ་གྱི་ རྣམ་བཞག་ སྟ་བར་བྱེད།

3  *I will attain [the position of] a buddha for the sake of sentient beings.*

3         6      4      NOM     V    VB

ངས་ སེམས་ཅན་གྱི་ དོན་དུ་ སངས་རྒྱས་ ཐོབ་པར་འགྱུར།

4  *Had Buddha not turned the wheel [of] the doctrine, ...*

3       UP   NOM       V    V   SP

སངས་རྒྱས་ཀྱིས་ ཆོས་ འཁོར་ བསྐོར་བར་མ་གྱུར་ ན་

5  *[One] should understand the way [in which] to take the essence of this life.*

6     NOM        NOM     V VB

ཚེ་འདིའི་ སྙིང་པོ་ ལེན་པའི་ཚུལ་ ཤེས་པར་བྱ།

---

## Drill 17.5

1  རྒྱ་མཚོ་ལ་གང་ཡོད།

2  དེ་དག་སུ་ཡིན།

3  དེ་བཞིན་གཤེགས་པ་གང་ཡིན་ཞེ་ན།

4  བལ་ཡུལ་གང་ལ་ཡོད།

5  དེ་གང་གི་ཁ་དོག་ཡིན།

## Drill 17.6

1. *What is the cause of this?*

   6 NOM SP NOM   SP

   འདི་ཡི་ རྒྱུ་ ནི་ ཅི་ ཞིག

2. *Who has such wisdom?*

   6       NOM   7 VB SP

   དེ་འདྲའི་ ཤེས་རབ་ སུ་ལ་ ཡོད་ ཅེ་ན

3. *Upon what is renunciation dependent?*

   NOM          7          VB

   ངེས་པར་འབྱུང་བ་ གང་ལ་ རག་ལས

4. *Where are the causes of cyclic existence?*
   OR *Among what are the causes of cyclic existence?*

   NOM SP       7      VB

   འཁོར་བའི་རྒྱུ་ ནི་ གང་ལ་ ཡོད

5. *What is the definition of impermanent?*

   6        NOM NOM VB    SP

   མི་རྟག་པའི་ མཚན་ཉིད་ གང་ ཡིན་ ཞིག་ན

6. *What teacher taught which doctrine?*
   OR *Which doctrine was taught [and] by what teacher?*

   APP    3    APP NOM   VB

   སྟོན་པ་ གང་གིས་ ཆོས་ གང་ བསྟན

# Drill 18.1

[1] ལུས་ལ་དམིགས་པ་

[2] བྱང་ཆུབ་ཏུ་སེམས་བསྐྱེད་པ་ལ་འབད་པར་བྱ།

[3] གཞན་གི་དོན་ལ་བརྩོན་པ་

[4] གཞན་གཅེས་པར་འཛིན་པ་

---

# Drill 18.2

[1] *the suffering of others not harming me*

གཞན་གྱི་སྡུག་བསྔལ་གྱིས་བདག་ལ་མི་གནོད་པ་

| **6** | | **C** | **3** | | **C** | **7** | | **V** | |
|---|---|---|---|---|---|---|---|---|---|
| གཞན་གྱི་སྡུག་བསྔལ་ | གྱིས་ → | | བདག་ | ལ་ → | | ← མི་གནོད་ | པ་ | | |

[2] *Medicine is beneficial for illness.*

[3] *One will view [cyclic] existence as of benefit.*

[4] *The Transcendent Victor, intending what, [taught] ...*
   [that is, *What was Buddha thinking of when he taught ...*]

---

# Drill 18.3

[1] ཁྱོད་ཏུ་དགར་པོ་ཡིན་ན་ཁྱོད་གང་ཟག་ཡིན་པས་བྱུག

[2] གང་ཟག་ཡིན་ན་ཞིམ་ཤེས་གང་རུང་མ་ཡིན་པས་ཁྱབ

[3] གཟུགས་མེད་ཁམས་ལ་དཀྱིལ་བ་པ་མེད།

[4] སེམས་ཅན་ལ་འཁོར་བ་ལ་གནས་པས་བྱུག

[5] ཤེས་པ་ཡིན་ན་དབང་ཤེས་དང་ཡིད་ཤེས་གང་རུང་ཡིན་པས་བྱུག

## Drill 18.4

1. *Whatever is mind is necessarily not matter.*
2. *Whatever is an awareness is not necessarily a sense consciousness.*
3. *If [something] is not an established base [it] is necessarily not an existent.*
4. *Whatever is a functioning thing is necessarily either matter, consciousness, or a non-associated compositional factor.*

## Drill 18.5

1. སེམས་ཅན་དེ་རྣམས་རང་གི་གཉེན་དུ་མཐོང་ནས།

2. སྐྱེད་ཚིག་མ་ལ་རྟག་ཏུ་འཛིན་པའི་མ་རིག་པ

3. སེམས་ཅན་ལ་མར་ཤེས་པ

4. སློབ་དཔོན་དཔྱིག་གཉེན་གྱིས་ཆོས་ཐམས་ཅད་སེམས་ཙམ་གྱི་བདག་ཉིད་དུ་བཤད་ལ།

5. སློན་པས་སེམས་དངོས་པོའི་གཙོ་བོར་བསྟན།

## Drill 18.6

1. *conceiving a person to be permanent, unitary, and independent*

གང་ཟག་     རྟག་ གཅིག་ རང་དབང་ཅན་དུ་     འཛིན་པ

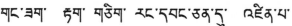

NOM        NN    NN            C    2                    V

2 *This system asserts that the conception of true existence* [literally, *conceiving (things) to be true*] *is an afflictive obstruction.*

NA 3    2    NOM    6    2    VB

ལུགས་འདིས་ བདེན་པར་ འཛིན་པ་ ཉོན་མོངས་ཅན་གྱི་ སྒྲིབ་པར་ ཁས་ལེན།

3 *meditating on the body as unclean* [a meditation in which one's body is perceived to be unclean]

NOM    2    V

ལུས་ མི་གཙང་བར་ བསྒོམ་པ་

---

## Drill 18.7

1 སེམས་ཅན་ཀུན་ཕྱོག་མ་མེད་པ་ནས་འཁོར་བར་འཁྱམས།

2 དགྲ་བཅོམ་པ་ཞི་བར་འཇུག་གུང་

3 ཕྱིག་པ་བསགས་ན་ངན་འགྲོར་འཁྱམ།

4 རང་རྒྱུས་ལྷ་ར་ན་སེར་གཤེགས་ཏེ།

5 ཀླུ་རྣམས་འཛམ་བུའི་གླིང་དུ་འོངས་པའི་ཚེ་

---

## Drill 18.8

1 *[those who have] entered into cyclic existence*
OR *[those] involved in cyclic existence*

S    2

འཁོར་བར་ ཞུགས་པ་

2 *if the mind becomes afflicted …*

NOM    2    V    SP

སེམས་ ཉོན་མོངས་ཅན་དུ་ སོང་ ན་

③ *Had these people entered into the door [of] the doctrine ...*

|  | NA | NOM | SP | UP | 2 |  | VB | SP |

གང་ཟག་ དེ་དག་ ནི་ ཆོས་ སྒོར་ བཅུག་ ན།

④ *They came to Jambu Isle [this world].*

|  | NOM |  | 2 |  | V | SP |

དེ་དག་ འཛམ་བུའི་གླིང་དུ་ གཤེགས་ ཏེ།

---

## Drill 18.9

① དུང་དཀར་པོ་མེར་པོར་སྣང་བའི་མིག་ཤེས།

② སྣང་བ་མཐའ་དག་སངས་རྒྱས་དང་ཆོས་སུ་ཤར།

③ ཚེ་རིང་པོར་གནས་པ་ནི་སྔོག་གཅོད་པ་སྲངས་པ་ལས་བྱུང་ངོ༌།

---

## Drill 18.10

① Alas, although all these migrating beings have been each other's parents, ...

② This effect arises from that cause.

③ When renunciation has arisen in one's continuum ...

④ From beginningless time [we have] cycled without independence in the cyclic existence of the three realms.

⑤ All phenomena are included in the natures of the two truths.

---

## Drill 19.1

① བུམ་པའི་རྒྱར་གྱུར་པའི་སྐྱེས་བུ་

② སྲིད་རྗེ་བསྒོམ་པར་རིགས་པ་

③ མདོ་སྡེ་པའི་ལུགས་ལ་ཌོ་པོ་ཉིད་མེད་པ་དོན་དམ་པར་མི་རུང་ངོ༌།

4 སངས་རྒྱས་ཆོས་དཔག་མེད་ཀྱི་ཁ་དོག་དཀར་པོ་མ་ཡིན་པར་ཐལ།

5 འཇིགས་སུ་རུང་བ

---

# Drill 19.2

1 *Because [it] is an uncompounded phenomenon,
[it] may not be a thoroughly afflictive phenomenon.*

འདུས་མ་བྱས་ཡིན་པས་ཀུན་ནས་ཉོན་མོངས་པའི་ཆོས་སུ་མི་རུང་ངོ་།

|  | NOM V 3 |  | 6 | C 2 |  | VB |
|---|---|---|---|---|---|---|
| འདུས་མ་བྱས་ཡིན་པ ས་ → | | ཀུན་ནས་ཉོན་མོངས་པའི་ → | ཆོས་ སུ་ → | | ← མི་རུང་ངོ་། | |

2 *a phenomenon [whose] arising, cessation, and abiding are inadmissible
[that is, logically impossible]*

3 *Not helping [literallly, not making help] is not proper.*

4 *a being who is a valid [source of knowledge]*

5 *Because a scriptural passage from our own Teacher is not suitable for
refuting [those of] other schools, ...*

---

# Drill 19.3

1 ངན་སོང་གསུམ་དུ་སྐྱེ་བ་ལ་འཇིགས་པ

2 རང་ལ་གནོད་པ་བྱས་པའི་སེམས་ཅན་ལ་སྟང་བ

3 གཉེན་སོགས་ལ་ཆགས་པར་མི་རིགས་སོ།

4 གང་ཟག་གི་བདག་ཏུ་ཞེན་པ

## Drill 19.4

1. *being unhappy about having entered into cyclic existence*

        **2**             **7**         **V**

   འཁོར་བར་   ཞུགས་པ་ལ་   མི་དགའ་བ

2. *[They are] confused about the methods [for bringing about] happiness and suffering*

   བདེ་སྡུག་གི་ཐབས་ལ་རྨོངས་ཤིང་

              **6**               **7**          **VB**  **SP**

   བདེ་སྡུག་གི་→   ཐབས་ ལ་→  ←རྨོངས་   ཤིང་

3. *an awareness which is not mistaken about its own appearing object*

          **6**       **6**       **7**       **V 6**

   རང་གི་   སྣང་བའི་   ཡུལ་ལ་   མ་འཁྲུལ་བའི་   རིག་པ

## Drill 19.5

1. སྐྱེ་འགག་དང་བྲལ་བ་ནི་འདུས་མ་བྱས་ཡིན།

2. སེམས་དེ་བདེ་བས་ཕོངས་སོ།

3. བྱམ་པ་དམར་པོ་ཚོས་ཅན།   ཀ་བ་དམར་པོ་དང་འགལ་བ་ཡིན་པར་ཐལ།

## Drill 19.6

1. *One should become free of the afflictions.*
2. *devoid of an identity of its own*
3. *contrary to the guru's word [or, pronouncements]*
4. *If one meets with the marvels of cyclic existence …*
5. *Meeting with a friend, [I] am happy.*

# *Notes*

1  This latter (**a-lí-g̱a-lí**) is the term used in the classical Tibetan grammars. See, for example, S̄i-d̄u Paṇ-chen's (*si tu paṇ chen*) *Commentary on (Tön-mi Sambhota's) "Thirty Stanzas" and "Application of Grammatical Marks"* (སུམ་ཅུ་པ་དང་རྟགས་ཀྱི་འཇུག་པའི་འགྲེལ་པ་), edited in Tibetan in Sarat Chandra Das, *An Introduction to the Grammar of the Tibetan Language* (originally published in 1915, reprinted in 1972 by Motilal Banarsidass, Delhi), Book II, p. 7.

Various formats are used by Western writers when they refer in notes to Tibetan texts. Some use the Tibetan title, written not as it is above, but in transliterated form. Thus, the book cited in this note, the སུམ་ཅུ་པ་དང་རྟགས་ཀྱི་འཇུག་ པའི་འགྲེལ་པ་, becomes—using the Wylie transliteration system described in Appendix One—*Sum cu pa dang rtags kyi 'jug pa'i 'grel pa.* Others create an abbreviation based on the first letters in the principal words of the title. Here, one might use the abbreviation STG (*Sum cu pa dang rTags kyi 'jug pa'i 'Grel pa*). A few writers use English translations of the Tibetan titles.

The convention followed in *Translating Buddhism from Tibetan* will be to cite the author in Wylie transliteration (and, in the first citation, in phonemic form as well) and to cite the title in Wylie transliteration (and, in the first citation, also in English translation). Subsequent citations of the same work will use shortened forms of both the author's name and the book's title. See note 38.

2  The vowels are called **ȳang-yík** (དབྱངས་ཡིག་) or, as a group, **a-lí** (ཨ་ལི་). The consonants are **s̄el-c̱hé** (གསལ་བྱེད་) or, as a group, **g̱a-lí** (ཀ་ལི་).

3  An English word may begin with the two-consonant combinations **ch, cl,** and **cr.**

4  Pronunciation is indicated in this book in bold face: **a-lí-ga-lí.** Note that both **a**'s in this example are actually pronounced as the **a** is in *farther*. The system of phonemics used in this book is different from those you will see in Tibetan-English dictionaries (or in English dictionaries, for that matter). Words (singly or in sentences) are discussed using italics: "the word *cat*;" "the best translation is *He went to Lhasa*."

5  The second column **cha** is technically a **chha**, a fully aspirated and middle tone version of what is a low tone, partially aspirated sound in column 3.

6  The Tibetan **tha** is a hard 't,' not the **th** in the English word *the* but the sound of the first **t** in *tight*.

7  The Tibetan **pha** is a hard 'ph,' not the **ph** in the English word *phone* but the **p** in *pop*.

8  This arrangement goes back to Tönmi Sambhota, the father of Tibetan grammar, who put it this way in his *Thirty Stanzas*:
     "The consonants—with seven and a half sets           ཀ་ལི་ཕྱི་དང་བཅུད་སྟེ་ནི།
     Are divided into [sets of] four each."                        བཞི་བཞི་དག་ཏུ་ཕྱེ་བ་ལས།

See Sarat Chandra Das, *An Introduction to the Grammar of the Tibetan Language*, Book II (hereafter cited as Das, *Grammar*), p. 8.

9  In Tibetan, this row is called **ḡa-dé** (ཀ་སི་), the **ḡa** group. For a phonemic analysis of spoken Tibetan, see Melvyn C. Goldstein and Ngawangthondup Narkyid, *English-Tibetan Dictionary of Modern Tibetan* (Berkeley: University of California Press, 1984), pp. xx-xxiii. Goldstein and Narkyid use a pronunciation scheme differing from the one presented in this book.

10 The example *canyon* is from Andrew Bloomfield and Yanki Tshering, *Tibetan Phrasebook* (Ithaca: Snow Lion, 1987), p. 9.

11 The example *grits* is from Bloomfield and Tshering, *Tibetan Phrasebook*, p. 9.

12 See Das, *Grammar,* p. 11.

13 See Das, *Grammar,* p. 1, note.

14 The consonant ཤ (and some others—see Chapter Five) change the pronunciation of an **o** immediately preceding them to **ö**.

15 Regarding the difference between copulas ("A is B") and verbs of existence ("A exists"), see Chapters 6 and 7.

16 René de Nebesky-Wojkowitz, *Oracles and Demons of Tibet* — reprint edition (Graz/Austria: Akademische Druck-u.Verlagsanstalt, 1975), first published, 1956, p. xv.

17 Turrell Wylie, "A Standard System of Tibetan Transcription," *Harvard Journal of Asiatic Studies*, Vol. 22 (1959), pp. 261-267.

18 Jeffrey Hopkins, *Meditation on Emptiness* (London: Wisdom Publications, 1983), pp. 19-21.

19 There are several different schemes of transliteration, as noted above. See Appendix One for a table of the Wylie system.

20 The examples of the sequence of strokes in writing **ū-jen** letters are adapted from Lhasawa Losang Thonden, *Modern Tibetan Language* (Dharamsala: Library of Tibetan Works and Archives, 1980), p. 4

21 ཆོས་དུང་དགར་པོའི་ཁ་དོག་ (**chö-tung ḡar-bö kha-dok**).

22 ཟླ་ is a contraction of ཟླ་བ་ (**da-wa**).

23 *Theology* is a word that covers much of what I mean by *religious philosophy* or Buddhist *philosophy and religion*. Nevertheless, the word is so weighted with theistic—and in particular, monotheistic—overtones, that I will not use it here.

24 In the case of philosophical texts, as opposed to, for example, devotional texts, the most readily available dictionaries (Das and Jäschke) are not adequate. The Das dictionary is: Sarat Chandra Das, *A Tibetan-English Dictionary with Sanskrit Synonyms*, revised and edited by Graham Sandberg and A. William Heyde (Calcutta: Bengal Secretariat Book Depot, 1902)—reprinted in a compact edition (Kyoto, Japan: Rinsen Book Company, 1977). The Jäschke dictionary is: H. A. Jäschke, *A Tibetan-English Dictionary, with special reference to the prevailing dialects* (London: Routledge & Kegan Paul, 1968—first published in 1881).

25 The མ་ in ཕུམ་ is a suffix. It is pronounced as written.

26 In addition, the prefixes མ་ and འ་ sometimes cause the *previous* syllable to end in a nasal.

27 Actually, the suffix ན་ nasalizes the vowels, in addition to changing their vowel pronunciations.

28 The traditional distinction is between ཆོས་ in the sense of scripture or tradition (ལུང་) and ཆོས་ as what has been or is to be internalized (རྟོགས་པ་). The Indian source for this distinction is Vasubandhu's *Treasury of Advanced Knowledge* (*Abhidharmakośa*—in Tibetan, ཆོས་མངོན་པ་མཛོད་), Chapter Eight, verse 39, in Sanskrit: *saddharmo dvividhaḥ śātur āgamādhigamātmakaḥ / dhātāras tasya vaktāraḥ pratipattāra eva ca //.*

29 One does see constructions such as རྣམ་པར་བཞག་པ་ (ñam-b̄ar-shak-b̄a, *presentation*) in which the རྣམ་པར་ is merely an internal part of the word (technically, a lexical particle). Moreover, many verbal constructions contain internal elements (for example, the ཡིན་པར་ in ཡིན་པར་འགྱུར་) which might be mistaken for nouns, but are actually better considered otherwise. See Appendices Four and Seven.

30 ཡིན་ means *be* and is a linking verb—that is, it means *be [something]* (e.g., "Lhasa is a city."). ཡོད་, on the other hand, means *exist* and may not be used as a linking verb; you cannot use ཡོད་ to say *A is B*.

31 Although prefixes and superscripts are almost never pronounced themselves and usually affect only the aspiration or tone of the root letter, the prefixes མ་ and འ་ sometimes cause the *previous* syllable to end in a nasal.

32 The first group of superscript combinations are the ར་མགོ་བཅུ་གཉིས་ (**ra-go j̄u-ñyi** — **ra** + *head* + *twelve*: "the twelve with **ra** superscribed").

33 The second group of superscript combinations are the ལ་མགོ་བཅུ་ (**la-go j̄u** — where བཅུ་ means *ten*).

34 The third group of superscript combinations are the ས་མགོ་བཅུ་གཅིག (**s̄a-go j̄u-jik** — where བཅུ་གཅིག means *eleven*).

35 Sounds are not ideas; that is, they are neither mental events nor are they naturally inextricably linked to mental events. However, they are—in human

languages—generated by mental events (the intention to make such a sound, and so on) and, when heard by humans, they give rise to other mental events. This is a complex subject and one that is relevant at this point, but not necessary to the understanding of Tibetan. See Anne Klein, *Knowledge and Liberation* (Ithaca: Snow Lion, 1986), especially pp. 115-205.

36 Grammarians distinguish between lexical meaning and grammatical meaning. While this is not quite what is meant here by the lexical dimension of meaning, it is related in that the lexical meaning of a word is the meaning of the base before it is inflected (as opposed to the meaning of one or another inflection). Similarly, the lexical dimension of meaning is prior to the syntactic dimension, since it is in the syntactic dimension that a word is inflected to show its relation to other words in a sentence.

37 It should be noted that I am defining the lexical dimension rather narrowly. As understood in this book, it comprises the basic dictionary meanings of terms without distinguishing between greater and lesser degrees of education or literacy. The lexical meaning of a word corresponds to Tzvetan Todorov's concept of linguistic encoding (Oswald Ducrot and Tzvetan Todorov, *Encyclopedic Dictionary of the Sciences of Language* [Baltimore and London: John Hopkins University Press, 1979], p. 254): "the linguistic meaning of a word is present in every use of the word and constitutes its very definition." The lexical dimension of a word is its meaning according to the general lexicon of a language and not as defined in the specialized lexicons of professional groups or subcultures. The technical use of terms by the various schools of Buddhist doctrine and within specialized areas of doctrine (epistemology, monastic discipline, and so on) is the province of the conceptual dimension of meaning.

38 The lexical dimension of བུམ་པ་ is its meaning *pot*, conveying the idea of something that is (following *Webster's Ninth New Collegiate Dictionary* [Springfield, Massachusetts: Merriam-Webster, 1989]) "a usually rounded metal or earthen container used chiefly for domestic purposes (as in cooking or for holding liquids or for growing plants)," or (following Tibetan epistemologists), "a flat-based, bulbous thing able to hold fluids." See Anne Klein, *Knowledge and Liberation*, pp. 121-122ff., and Daniel Perdue, *Debate in Tibetan Buddhism* (Ithaca: Snow Lion, 1991), p. 274. See also lCang skya rol

pa'i rdo rje (Jang-ḡya Röl-b̄ë-dor-jé—1717-86), *Grub mtha'i rnam par bzhag pa gsal bar bshad pa thub bstan lhun po'i dmzes rgyan* (*Clear Exposition of the Presentations of Tenets, Beautiful Ornament for the Meru of the Subduer's Teaching* [Sarnath: Lama Guru Deva, 1970])—cited hereafter as lCang skya, *Grub mtha'*—p. 101.

39  The rules for finding a root letter were formulated in the literary Tibetan classes at the University of Virginia beginning in 1976. A somewhat more complex, but similar, set of rules may be seen in Lhasawa Losang Thonden's *Modern Tibetan Language*, Volume I (Dharamsala: Library of Tibetan Works and Archives, 1980), pp. 37-39.

40  Of course, if a root letter has a superscript or a subscript *and* a vowel marker, then, strictly speaking, the superscript and/or subscript will have a vowel marker either above it or below it depending on the vowel. Thus, strictly speaking, the first condition should read: "there is a vowel marker either above or below it and it is neither a subscript nor a superscript."

41  Just as *dharma* has many meanings in Sanskrit, so ཆོས་ has many meanings in Tibetan. བུ་སྟོན་ (**Pu-d̄ön**) following the Indian scholar Vasubandhu, lists ten, and notes that there are in fact more (E. Obermiller, *History of Buddhism (Chos-hbyung) by Bu-ston* [Heidelberg: O. Harrassowitz., 1931], p. 18): (1) phenomenon; (2) path (that is, accurate view of reality); (3) *dharma* as object of the Buddhist statement of faith, "I go for refuge to the *dharma*"; (4) an object of the mental consciousness (as opposed to the objects peculiar to each sense consciousness); (5) virtue; (6) concerns—as in *worldly concerns*; (7) doctrine—that taught by Buddha; (8) attribute; (9) religious vow; and (10) custom. Pu-d̄ön identifies the third with *nirvāṇa*; however one very frequently seen gloss of this usage of ཆོས་ includes both the teachings of Buddha and the individual's practice of those teachings;

42  Statements of proof follow a standardized syntax of the form, *The subject X is Y because of being Z.* According to the rules of Buddhist logic, such a basic logical statement means also that *All Z are Y* and *All non-Y are non-Z.* See Chapters Fourteen and Fifteen.

43 The association of the idea of loyalty or the concept of 'man's best friend' with *dog* is common among English speakers, but is not to be found in the dictionary definition of *dog* (and thus is not part of *dog*'s lexical dimension). That it would not easily appear to the mind of someone raised in traditional India is suggestive of the way in which it is tied to a particular culture. However, this dimension of the word *dog* is relevant to the way in which the word is understood; it is not usually articulated, but it is tacitly present.

44 Some forms of Buddhism—for example, Nyingma and Zen—emphasize non-conceptual meditative knowledge from the very beginning and stress the dangers of conceptuality, whereas others (such as Géluk) suggest that conceptual analytic knowledge aids in the development of nonconceptual wisdom.

45 Melvyn Goldstein (in his *Tibetan-English Dictionary of Modern Tibetan* [Kathmandu: Ratna Pustak Bhandar, 1975], p. 659) lists two meanings of རྣམ་ རྟོག, *superstition* and *complete understanding*. The *Dag yig gsar bsgrigs* (*New Compilation Lexicon*) of Comrade Samden (*bLo mthun bSam gtan*)—Mtsho sngon [Kokonor, Tibet]: Mtsho sngon Mi rigs dpe skrun khang, 1979—p. 443, lists three: (1) thought or awareness that does not accord with the way things really are; (2) indecisive thought; and (3) analytic thought.

46 Prefixes and superscripts may alter the pronunciation of the root letter *in their own syllable*. However, as noted in Exception Nine, sometimes a prefix letter will change the pronunciation of the *end of the previous syllable*. Thus, they do not in those cases alter the pronunciation of the previous root letter; they affect the previous suffix.

47 The Latin names for the cases have not been used here; rather, I have translated their Tibetan names. Most Western-language grammars of Tibetan, however, follow the convention already followed by Sanskritists and do use the Latin nomenclature, calling the third declension not agentive but instrumental, and the sixth not connective but genitive. See Appendix Five.

48 སྐྱེ་བ་འཇིག is a technical term in Buddhist epistemology, referring to the way in which all impermanent aspects of an object appear to direct perception. For an explanation, see Anne Klein, *Knowledge and Liberation*, pp. 91ff.

49 G. Tucci, *Religions of Tibet*, p. 41.

50 མངོན་པར་རྟོགས་པར་སངས་རྒྱས་པ་ translates *abhisambuddha* and མངོན་པར་རྟོགས་པར་སངས་ རྒྱས་པར་འགྱུར་ translates *abhisambhotsyate* (Lokesh Chandra, *Tibetan-Sanskrit Dictionary* [Kyoto: Rinsen Book Company, 1976—reprint of the 1959 New Delhi edition] p. 632). See the section on prefix particles in Chapter Ten.

51 Randolph Quirk, Sidney Greenbaum, Geoffrey Leech, Jan Svartik, *A Grammar of Contemporary English* (New York: Seminar Press, 1972), pp. 44-45.

52 Likewise, a clause is defined by the fact that it is ended either by a verbal noun or adjective, or a verb followed by a continuative syntactic particle. We will, in later chapters, see how verbals act as nouns (or adjectives) to their right (that is, they are declined and lead to or connect with what follows them), but act as verbs to their left (they have subjects and predicates, or agents and objects, among the nouns preceding them).

53 It is possible for a sentence to end in ཡིན་པའོ། instead of ཡིན། or ཡིན་ནོ།; similarly, a sentence may end in བྱེད་པའོ། instead of བྱེད། or བྱེད་དོ།. However, the typical finite or closing verb looks like ཡིན། or བྱེད།. Tibetan does not require a special punctuation mark (such as a period or semicolon) to end a complete sentence, nor does it require the use of terminating particles such as are seen in the constructions བྱེད་པའོ།, བྱེད་དོ།, and so on.

54 The exceptions to this rule are sentences and clauses ending in verbs of existence like ཡོད་ and those ending in nominative verbs like གྲུབ་ (*is established*) and སྐྱེ་ (*arises*). Such verbs have no objects and thus the sentences they terminate have no predicates.

55 There is a verb—བོད་ or འབོད་—which means *call*, *cry out*, and *invite*. Some scholars have suggested that this verb and the name བོད་ are related linguistically to the verb བོན་, meaning *recite* or *mutter [prayers]*. This kind of recitation calling on the gods gave its name to the pre-Buddhist, indigenous religion of Tibet. (See, for example, Giuseppe Tucci, *The Religions of Tibet* [Bombay: Allied Publishers, 1980], p. 213 and p. 271, n. 2). Whatever may be the origin of the place name བོད་, the point I am making here is that it is not now directly linked to any verb. As we will see, many Tibetan nouns have an intimate con-

nection—etymologically, semantically, and in terms of their significance—with verbs.

56 Nouns are མིང་ཚིག་, literally *name words*. The *Dag yig gsar bsgrigs* (q.v.) identifies words such as དེ་, ང་, གང་, and ཅེ་—the main pronouns—as ཚབ་ཚིག་, *substitution words*.

57 As will be seen, the pronoun ཁྱོད་ is used in formal debate as an impersonal pronoun meaning *the subject which is under discussion*. Thus, it is there more an *it* than a *you*.

58 Technically, these are limiting adjectives used as pronouns. Other examples include ཐམས་ཅད་ (*all*), ཀུན་ (*all*), and མང་པོ་ (*many*).

59 The other four traditional key doctrines of Buddhist philosophy are the unsatisfactory nature of mind and the world as we know it, impermanence, and the peace of nirvana (see Chapter Sixteen).

60 See, for example, Geshe Lhundup Sopa and Jeffrey Hopkins, *Cutting Through Appearances* (Ithaca: Snow Lion, 1989), p. 224.

61 See, for example, gSer tog bLo bzang tshul khrims rgya mtsho (Sér dok lo sang tshül thrím gya tsho, b. 1845), *Sum-chu-pa and Rtags-kyi-hjug-pa (A Wonder Key to the Tibetan Grammar)* (Kathmandu: Guru Deva Lama, 1962), pp. 257-270. This is a codex printing of the *Bod kyi brda' sprod pa sum ju ba dang rtags kyi 'jug pa'i mchan 'grel mdor bsdus te brjod pa ngo mtshar 'phrul gyi lde mig* (བོད་ཀྱི་བརྡ་སྤྲོད་པ་སུམ་ཅུ་པ་དང་རྟགས་ཀྱི་འཇུག་པའི་མཆན་འགྲེལ་མདོར་བསྡུས་ཏེ་བརྗོད་པའི་མཆར་འཕྲུལ་གྱི་ལྡེ་མིག་)—cited hereafter as gSer tog, *Sum rtags mchan 'grel*.

62 བཅས་པ་ is actually a verbal noun (or adjective) made from the core verb བཅས་. It takes its "object"—that which is possessed—not in the nominative case or the objective case, but using the conjunction དང་ (a syntactic particle). For this reason, བཅས་ is a syntactic verb, and བཅས་པ་ is a syntactic verbal noun whose qualifier is marked by a syntactic particle.

63 Almost all prefix particles have two syllables. The exception is ཡང་དག་པར་, which has three. See Chapter Twelve.

64  Many examples of the ways in which verbals end clauses (and thus have subjects and objects and qualifiers as do verbs) may be seen in Appendix Five, in the section on clause connectives.

65  In certain cases grammatical particles combine with suffixless syllables at the ends of words and thus do become parts of words. Examples of particles combining in this way with the word མདོ are མདོས (dö>, *by the sutra*), མདོར (dor, *in the sutra*) and མདོའི (dö, *of the sutra*). Although these particles never become part of the **lexical word** མདོ, they do form parts of what may be termed the **grammatical word**—in this instance, the word མདོ marked for use in a phrase, clause, or sentence as, for example, མདོའི.

66  The construction ཕྱིར་དུ does occur, but this is a postposition used to indicate purpose.

67  Case marking particles are *technically* a type of syntactic particle, but are used only with nouns, pronouns, and adjectives and show how these words are to be read as part of a phrase, clause, or sentence. In *Translating Buddhism from Tibetan*, the term 'syntactic particle' will always refer to syntactic particles that are not case marking particles.

68  The term 'science of the dots' was coined, to the best of my knowledge, by Jeffrey Hopkins at the University of Virginia. The system presented in this book, although based on Hopkins' original insights, has been modified and expanded.

69  In the unlikely event that one would classify the dot following a noun without considering its use in a sentence, I suppose that the final dot could be called an **IN** dot—**IN** abbreviating "indeterminate."

70  Postpositions are also declined. They were introduced in Chapter Nine. See also Appendices Two and Six.

71  See Candrakīrti's *Madhyamakāvatārabhāṣya*, on Chapter One, verse 4 of the root verses (pp. 9-10 in *Dbu ma la 'jug pa rang 'grel* [Dharamsala: Council of Cultural and Religious Affairs, 1968]). See also Jeffrey Hopkins, *Compassion in Tibetan Buddhism* (London: Rider and Company, 1980), pp. 120-125.

72  See Nebesky-Wojkowitz, *Oracles and Demons of Tibet*, p. 3.

73  མ་དམིགས་པ་ is used in logic. There are three types of correct reasons (རྟགས་ཡང་དག་
    —literally, *correct sign*); མ་དམིགས་པའི་རྟགས་ཡང་དག་ is one of them.

74  For more information on Buddhist cosmology according to Géluk literature,
    see Lati Rinbochay, Denma Lochö Rinbochay, and Leah Zahler, with Jeffrey
    Hopkins, *Meditative States in Tibetan Buddhism* (London: Wisdom Press,
    1983).

75  There is a term, ཡང་སྲིད་པ་ (AGAIN + CYCLIC EXISTENCE) that is sometimes seen,
    but it is not common.  According to Lokesh Chandra's *Tibetan-Sanskrit
    Dictionary*, it translates the Sanskrit *punarbhava*.

76  མཛད་པ་དང་སྦྱར་ (*activities + with + associate*) means *associate with activities*. དེ་
    དང་བྲལ་བ་ (*that + from + separated*) means *separated from that*.  And the very
    common construction of the form དེ་དང་ལྡན་པ་ simply means *possessing that* or
    *having that*—the དང་ not being translated with its ordinary value at all.

77  In Sanskrit, every noun that is not part of a compound word must be declined.
    Thus, in Sanskrit both nouns would be in the nominative case, as well as any
    adjectives modifying them.  Jeffrey Hopkins points out (written communica-
    tion, 1990) that the fact of this not being the case in Tibetan reflects its true na-
    ture of being a language without inflection.  The so-called Tibetan case endings
    are actually separate syllables added not to the end of every individual word,
    but to units as large as phrases and clauses.  Thus, the case particles are actu-
    ally postpositions and Tibetan is actually an agglutinative language.

78  In an actual sentence, however, the lack of a case ending could indicate any of
    the following dots: **NOM, APP, NA, NN, UP,** or **NC**.

79  Appositives can be equivalent.  I have two sons, Jason and Gareth.  Thus, if I
    say, *my two sons, Jason and Gareth*, the phrases *my-two-sons* and *Jason-and-
    Gareth* are equivalent.

80  Examples of phrases, clauses, and sentences using ཙམ་, ཁོ་ན་, and ཉིད་ as adjec-
    tives include the following:
    ཕྱུང་པོ་གྲུབ་ཙམ་ནས་, སྐད་ཅིག་ཙམ་ཡང་, དེ་གཉིས་ཙམ་གྱིས་, ཆོས་དྲུལ་ཙམ་ཡང་, མཚོག་གསུམ་ཉིད་ལས་,
    སྐྱོན་བྲལ་སྐྱོན་ལྡན་ཉིད་དུ་མཐོང་, སེམས་བསྐྱེད་ཉིད་ཡིན་ཏེ།, and ཟད་པར་གྱུར་པ་ཉིད་ཡིན་ལ།.

81  Apte, *Practical Sanskrit-English Dictionary* (Delhi: Motilal Banarsidass, 1975 [fourth revised and enlarged edition]), q.v.

82  རྟོགས་ most often translates the verb *adhigam* and its derivatives.

83  See *Bod rgya tshig mdzod chen mo* (*Great Tibetan-Chinese Dictionary* [Beijing: Mi rigs dPe skrun khang, 1986]), p. 1868. The term ཁོང་དུ་ཆུབ་པ་ seems an artificial paraphrase of the common term ཁོང་དུ་ཆུད་པ་ (*internalize, understand*).

84  See *Bod rgya tshig mdzod chen mo*, p. 2916. Given that the term འཚང་རྒྱ་ is used in verb constructions with the sense of the action involved in becoming a Buddha, one would think that the term སངས་རྒྱས་ derives from it, as a sort of past tense meaning 'one who has become a Buddha.' However, this is not the case. སངས་ is, in fact, not the past tense form of the verb འཚང་; the two are not related, even in terms of meaning (འཚང་ meaning *complete* or *insert* and སངས་ meaning *wake up* and *be purified*).

85  The first etymology is seen in the very early work on Sanskrit-to-Tibetan translation, the *sGra sbyor bam po gnyis pa* (སྒྲ་སྦྱོར་བམ་པོ་གཉིས་པ་)— p. 8 in the Leh, Ladakh edition of Sonam Angdu [*Tibeto-Sanskrit Lexicographical Materials* (Leh: Basgo Tongspon, 1973)].

86  The cases are treated more thoroughly in Appendix Five. Recall that the names used here are translations of the Tibetan names and thus do not correspond to the traditional *Western* use of Latin case names: nominative, accusative, instrumental, dative, ablative, genitive, locative, and vocative.

87  Although ཀྱེ་ and ཀ་ཡེ་ are called case particles here, their English equivalents— words such as *oh* —are interjections.

88  Quirk et al, *A Grammar of Contemporary English*, pp. 414-15.

89  ཡིན་ is technically not a verb in traditional Tibetan grammar, as it does not refer to an action. The Tibetan word for verb is བྱ་ཚིག་, *word [expressing an] action*. The English term *verb* has a wider meaning than this, including verbs such as *be* which do not express actions. The principle in this book's analysis is to use the English grammatical sense to describe Tibetan grammar, and not the traditional Tibetan analysis.

90 According to traditional grammar, the མ་ is a non-case particle, and is thus technically separate from the verb ཡིན་.

91 མ་ also means *mother*. However, when it is used as a non-case negative particle it has no meaning unless it is prefixed to a verb or verbal noun. མ་ by itself does not mean *no*. To say *no*, you have to negate a specific verb and say something like མ་ཡིན་ (*is not*).

92 The Sanskrit is given in paragraph 2, on line 2 in the modern Sarnath edition of the sutra (*Vajracchedikā Prajñāpāramitāsūtra* [Sarnath, India: Central Institute of Higher Tibetan Studies, 1978] p. 29): *āścaryaṃ bhagavan*.

93 Donald Lopez, *The Heart Sūtra Explained: Indian and Tibetan Commentaries* (Albany: State University of New York Press, 1988), p. 196 (note 46). There is much for discussion here. Although Buddhism has traditionally held that sentient beings liberate *themselves* through relying on what Buddha taught, not all Buddhists agree. This is most clearly apparent in the Pure Land Buddhisms of East Asia, but it may be seen in Tibet as well. The aspirational prayers (སྨོན་ ལམ་) and techniques for actualizing (སྒྲུབ་ཐབས་) the cognitive and physical powers of Buddhas used in Vajrayāna Buddhism present practices that rely heavily on empowering blessings from Buddhas, Bodhisattvas, ḍākinīs and others. Thus, there is a reliance on awakened beings for more than teaching.

Notwithstanding this theistic strand in Vajrayāna, the term བཅོམ་ལྡན་འདས་ or *bhagavan*—used in Buddhist texts from the earliest times—clearly does not imply that Buddhahood is attained through the efforts of others.

94 Lopez, ibid. See also Lokesh Chandra, *Tibetan-Sanskrit Dictionary*, p. 2321, where the Tibetan ལེགས་ལྡན་ (*fortunate*) translates the Sanskrit *bhagavan*.

95 Thus, the Tibetan བཅོམ་ལྡན་འདས་ justifies neither the translation *Blessed One* nor *Fortunate One*. བཅོམ་ means *conquered*; ལྡན་ means *possessing*; འདས་ means *beyond*. Lopez (*Heart Sūtra*, pp. 28-29) reports a contemporary explanation of the term: "An oral commentary states that *bcom* [བཅོམ་] means the destruction of the two obstructions and indicates the Buddha's marvelous abandonment; *ldan* [ལྡན་] means that the Buddha is endowed with the Wisdom Truth Body (*jñānadharmakāya*), the omniscient consciousness, and indicates the Buddha's

marvelous realization; and *'das* [འདས་] means that the Buddha has passed beyond the extremes of mundane existence and solitary peace."

96   Lopez, p. 196.

97   རེད་ is the second and third person declarative copula in modern spoken
     Tibetan.  As noted before, ཡིན་ is used only for the first person in modern spo-
     ken Tibetan.

98   The *Dag yig gsar bsgrigs* (p. 444) suggests intensification as a general func-
     tion of the prefix particle རྣམ་པར་.

99   The Sanskrit prefix *vi* becomes *vy* before vowels.

100  The case could be made that in all instances of the prefix particle and verb (or
     verbal) combination, the prefix particle is actually an adverb in that it modifies
     the meaning of the verb.  It seems easier and clearer to accept these combina-
     tions as words and have one less element to analyze in phrases, clauses, and
     sentences.

101  It would be somewhat clearer to say, *A square circle would be a strange
     shape*.

102  An example of a complete sentence with a conditional qualifier is སྒྲ་རྟག་པ་ཡིན་ན་
     འདུས་བྱས་མ་ཡིན་པར་འགྱུར་ —*If sound were permanent, it would not be a com-
     pounded phenomenon*.

103  The syntax of SUBJECT + OBJECT + VERB + ADVERB is sometimes seen in
     colloquial Tibetan, as an idiomatic way of emphasizing the adverb.  Other ele-
     ments may also occur after the verb for emphasis in the colloquial language.

104  See *Grammar Summary Materials Developed for Use at the University of
     Virginia Tibetan I*, compiled and edited by Elizabeth Napper (Charlottesville:
     n.d.), pp. 12-13.  This list appears in a somewhat different form in Appendix
     Five of the present work.  Napper's list and the present list share a common
     ancestor.

105  See *Lam rim bde lam* (p. 1.4): ཡིད་མཐུན་གྱི་གནས་སུ་བདེ་བའི་སྟན་ལ་ལུས་འདུག་ལུགས་བརྒྱད་དམ་
     སྤྱོད་ལམ་གང་བདེར་གནས་ནས། (*remaining in an agreeable place [and either] in the
     eight manners of sitting or in whatever posture is comfortable*).

106 Some dictionaries list མཆིས་ as the past tense root of མཆི་ (which is the present and future root); others say that མཆིས་ is a single-rooted verb. The *Dag yig gsar bsgrigs* lists མཆིས་ as the past tense root of མཆི་. The *Bod rgya tshig mdzod chen mo* cites མཆིས་ as both the past root of མཆི་ and as a verb meaning to exist; however, it cites only the usage of མཆི་ as a verb of motion (meaning *go*). The *Bod brda'i tshig mdzod* of Brag g'yab blo ldan shes rab (Ḍa-yap Lo-den-shé-rap) (Dharamsala: Library of Tibetan Works and Archives, 1989) agrees, defining མཆི་ as *go* and མཆིས་ as *exist*.

107 See *Dag yig gsar bsgrigs*, pp. 217 and 409. All three—བཅས་, ལྡན་, and བྲལ་— are (using the terminology of *Translating Buddhism from Tibetan*) nominative prepositional verbs. Examples of such usage is seen in the following phrases: ཤེས་རབ་དང་མི་ལྡན་ན་, རང་འགྱུར་དུ་ལྡན་པ་, རྟོག་པ་དང་བྲལ་ཞིང་, འཇིག་རྟེན་ལྷ་མིར་བཅས་པ་. Note in the latter example that the object possessed is marked not with a དང་, but with the syntactic particle ར་.

108 མེན་ and མེད་ are included here among the lexical particles as much because they are traditionally grouped with མ་ and མི་ as for any other reason. It is interesting to see that the examples given by gSer tog in his *Sum rtags mchan 'grel* (*Wonder Key to the Tibetan Grammar*) are really phrases or sentences and not words at all. (The examples listed on page 259 are: སྲིད་ཞིན་ཆེ་བ་མེད། and ཆོས་ལ་དད་ པ་མེན།. The first is a sentence ending in a verb of existence and the second is one ending in a linking verb.)

109 See Jeffrey Hopkins, *Meditation on Emptiness*, pp. 289-90.

110 Attributive verbs sometimes seem to function as locative-nominative verbs and at other times as nominative-locative verbs.

111 Note that the attributive verb བྱེད་, although it does not vary in form from the even more common agentive-nominative action verb བྱེད་, is used very differently. If it ever occurred with an agent—someone who attributed the meaning to the word or phrase—that agent would be in the agentive case. However, when བྱེད་ is used as an attributive verb, it is used without this agentive case agent, in the same manner as ཟེར་—a verb which, in its meaning of *speak* or *discuss*, is an agentive-nominative verb, but in its meaning of *be called*, is a locative-nominative verb. (See *Dag yig gsar bsgrigs* under ཟེར་.)

112 Most Western analysts of Tibetan assert that the person who does the possessing is marked by the fourth or "dative" case (really, following Tibetan nomenclature, the purposive-beneficial case). The implication would seem to be that when person A has thing B, thing B exists *for* that person A.

113 See dMu dge bsam gtan (Mu-gé Sam-den), *brDa sprod blo gsal dga' ston* (Kan-su'u Mi-dmangs-dpe-skrun-khang, 1980), p. 48. This contemporary Tibetan analysis of grammar will be cited hereafter as dMu dge bsam gtan, *brDa sprod*.

114 This example has been adapted and abbreviated from its original, which is in the *Lam rim chen mo* (*Great Exposition of the Stages of the Path*) of Tsong kha pa (blockprint—n.p., n.d.), 151a.5-6 (page 151, front side, lines 5 to 6): འཁོར་བ་འབྱུང་བའི་རྒྱུ་ལ་ལས་དང་ཉོན་མོངས་པ་གཉིས་དགོས་ཀྱང་། ཉོན་མོངས་པ་གཙོ་བོ་ཡིན་ཏེ།.

115 The *Dag yig gsar bsgrigs* (p. 137) cites two main usages of དགོས. The first is as the second element in a compound verb phrase and serves to indicate exhortation, as in ཞིང་ལ་ཆུ་གཏོང་དགོས། (*One must give water to the field*). The second is applied to nouns and indicates need, as in ལྱུག་ལ་ཆུ་དགོས། (*Sprouts need water*).

116 *[We] go to the spiritual community as refuge* is also grammatically possible.

117 The source for this classification scheme is George O. Curme, *English Grammar* (New York: Barnes and Noble, 1970), pp. 13ff. Curme lists eight types: personal pronouns (*I, me, it*), reflexive pronouns (*myself, itself*), reciprocal pronouns (*each other, one another*), relative pronouns having an antecedent (*who, whom, which, what*), indefinite and general relative pronouns (*who, what, whichever*), indefinite pronouns (*somebody, anybody, anything, nobody*), interrogative pronouns (*who, what*), and limiting adjectives used as pronouns (*this, that, all, any*).

118 *I* is the subject of a verb; *me* is a verbal object. *My* and *mine* in Tibetan would be in the connective case.

119 See p. 539 of the doctrinal primer (བསྡུས་གྲྭ **dü>-ḍa**) of Ngag dbang bkra shis (**Nga-wang Ḍa-shí>**), the *Tshad ma'i dgongs 'grel gyi bstan bcos chen po rnam 'grel gyi don gcig tu dril ba blo rab 'bring tha ma gsum du ston pa legs bshad chen po mkhas pa'i mgul rgyan skal bzang re ba kun skong (Necklace for the Wise, Fulfilling All Hopes for the Fortunate: An Explanation in which*

the topics of [Dharmakīrti's] Great Treatise Unravelling the Thought of Valid Cognition, [His] "Commentary on [Dignāga's] 'Compendium on Valid Cognition'," Are Brought Together and Shown to those of Best, Middling, and Least Intellect)—cited hereafter as the *sGo mang bsDus grva* (the *Go-mang Doctrinal Primer*), since it is the primer used at the Gomang College of Drebung (**dé b̄ung**) Monastery.

120 Verbs of living are also similar to nominative verbs; in fact, insofar as some of them occur in past, present, future, and imperative forms, they could properly be thought of as a type of nominative verb.

121 The close relation of verbs of being such as ཡོད་ and verbs of living such as གནས་ is supported by the *Dag yig gsar bsgrigs* which gives one meaning of མཆི་ as ཡོད་པ་དང་གནས་པ་ (*existing and abiding*).

122 བཞུགས་ is an honorific verb used in place of གནས་ and སྡོད་.

123 This is the first sentence of the sutra. In order to provide a useful example here, a great deal has been left out; the example given is merely the core of the original sentence.

124 The locative case is not the only case used to show location. A destination or place or activity is shown by the objective case (the second case). Additionally, the locative case can indicate things other than location—for instance, time.

125 The terminology of verbal *roots* is taken from Sanskrit grammar, where the conjugation of verbs is quite complex and much more specific than in Tibetan, and every verb has a "root" (*dhātu*) from which the verb as actually used in sentences is formed.

126 The source for this sentence is 15a.6 (page 15, front side, line 6) of the *dMar khrid thams cad mkhyen par bgrod pa'i myur lam bzhin khrid skyong ba la nye bar mkho ba'i zhal shes 'ga' zhig gi brjed tho* of *rGyal rong chos mdzad blo bzang thogs med* (**Gyël rong chö> d̲zë' L̲o s̲ang thok mé'**)—called, and cited hereafter as, the *sKu tshab lam rim*:

ཆོས་འདི་ཀླུ་བུ་འཇིག་རྟེན་དུ་ཡུན་རིང་དུ་གནས་ན་ཅི་མ་རུང་སྙམ་ནས།.

This text may be found in *Two Instructions on the Lam-Rim Teachings, the*

*Lam Rim Myur Lam and the Lam Rim Bde Lam, of the Bkra-Sis-Lhun-Po Tradition* (New Delhi: Ngawang Sopa, 1979).

127   The full title is *Khams gsum chos kyi rgyal po tsong kha pa chen po'i gsung 'bum* (ཁམས་གསུམ་ཆོས་ཀྱི་རྒྱལ་པོ་ཙོང་ཁ་པ་ཆེན་པོའི་གསུང་འབུམ་བཞུགས་སོ།).

128   Although the *Heart Sūtra* is often referred to with the epithet, བཅོམ་ལྡན་འདས་མ་, it is also refered to as འཕགས་པ་ཤེས་རབ་ཀྱི་ཕ་རོལ་ཏུ་ཕྱིན་པའི་སྙིང་པོ་ and not འཕགས་མ་ཤེས་རབ་ཀྱི་ཕ་རོལ་ཏུ་ཕྱིན་པའི་སྙིང་པོ་. (འཕགས་མ་ and འཕགས་པ་ both translate the Sanskrit *ārya* [Lokesh Chandra, pp. 1590-1], whereas although བཅོམ་ལྡན་འདས་ translates *bhagavat*, བཅོམ་ལྡན་འདས་མ་ translates *bhagavatī* [ibid., p. 383].)

129   See Lopez, *The Heart Sūtra Explained*, pp. 28-31.

130   The example is based on a passage in the presentation of Sautrāntika tenets by lCang skya (**Jang gya**) (*Grub mtha'* p. 107.18-19): རང་གྲུབ་དུས་ལས་དུས་གཅིས་པར་མི་སྲིད་པའི་འཇིག་པ་.

131   dMu dge bsam gtan, *brDa sprod*, p. 61, nonetheless says that although the fifth case is over-used nowadays as a substitute for the third (especially in letters, which are written *from* someone rather than *by* someone), this practice is extremely rare in older texts.

132   རང་ translates many Sanskrit words; the most common are *sva-* (as a first syllable) and *svayam.*

133   The general rule is not to use an honorific to speak about oneself. The exception—and it relates not to the first person pronouns but rather to verbs—is that when offering something to or receiving something from a person of higher status (for example, receiving teachings), an honorific form of the verb is used.

134   This is part of a line from the Tantric liturgy of the Gélukba order—specifically the *bLa ma mchod pa* (བླ་མ་མཆོད་པ་) of bLo bzang chos kyi rgyal mtshan (**Lo-sang-chö-gyí-gyël-tsën**)—pp. 61-62 in *bLa ma'i rnal 'byor dang yi dam khag gi bdag bskyed sogs zhal don gces btus* (*Selected Brief Recitation Texts: the Guru Yoga and the Self-Generations of Various Meditational Deities* [Dharamsala: Tibetan Cultural Printing Press: n.d.—codex edition].

135   See Jeffrey Hopkins, *Meditation on Emptiness*, pp. 288-89.

136   Tsong-kha-pa, *Lam rim chen mo*, 174b.3-4.

137 See *Lam rim chen mo*, 318b.2ff.

138 Lati Rinbochay, Denma Lochö Rinbochay, Leah Zahler, and Jeffrey Hopkins, *Meditative States in Tibetan Buddhism* (London: Wisdom Publications, 1983).

139 See *Lam rim chen mo*, 305b.1-306a.6 on the natures of calm abiding and special insight.

140 Similar to the subjects of verbs of existence, as opposed to those of copulas, the subjects of verbs of dependence must exist. Although it is grammatically possible to say, for example, "The nonexistent self depends on the aggregates of body and mind," what one finds in fact are phrases such as བདག་ཕུང་པོ་ལ་བརྟེན་ ནས་བཏགས་པ་ (Tsong-kha-pa, *dBu ma dgongs pa rab gsal* [Sarnath: Pleasure of Elegant Sayings Printing Press, 1973], p. 378.3-4)—*the self being imputed in dependence on the aggregates of body and mind*. Transformed into a sentence ending in a verb of dependence, this gives us, *The imputation of the self depends on the aggregates*, and in that case the subject is not the self but the imputation (བཏགས་པ་) of the self, a type of mental activity which does exist, even if the self it imagines does not. See also lCang skya, *Grub mtha'*, p. 447.12 and p. 454.11.

Care must be taken when reading about the self (བདག་). Sometimes, as in the following sentence, the term refers not to the nonexistent self of the doctrine of selflessness, but to the conventionally designated person: བདག་འདི་ནི་ཕུང་པོ་ལ་བརྟེན་ ནས་གྲུབ་པར་འགྱུར་བའོ། (Tsong-kha-pa, *dBu ma dgongs pa rab gsal*, p. 393.7-8).

141 ལྟོས་ is also the imperative root of ལྟ་, an agentive verb meaning *see* and *view*. བལྟས་ is the past tense root form of this verb, ལྟ་ is the present root, and བལྟ་ the future. Here, on the other hand, ལྟོས་ is the present tense root, བལྟོས་ is the past root, and the meaning is *depend* and *relate to*. The relation of the two verbs is discussed below.

142 There are different ways of charting Tibetan verb forms. Some lexicographers list verbal roots in the order future-present-past-imperative (for example, gSer tog, *Sum rtags mchan 'grel*, pp. 195-229). Others reverse that order and list the past tense first: past-present-future-imperative. This is done in the *Great Tibetan-Chinese Dictionary* (*Bod rgya tshig mdzod chen mo*) and by Dorje Wangchuk Kharto in his *Thumi: dGongs gTer (The Complete Tibetan Verb*

*Forms*). (This is his own title, translating the Tibetan *Dus gsum re'u mig thu mi'i dgongs gter*.) One modern day scholar who writes in Tibet, Mugé Samden (dMu dge bsam gtan), uses the unusual order present-past-future-imperative in his *brDa sprod*.

143 My custom is to cite verbs in their "finite" forms—as, for example, རྟེན་ and not རྟེན་པ་. Many lexicographers, however, will cite a verb in what I have called its **verbal** [noun] form—in this instance, རྟེན་པ་. Either system is viable, as long as consistency of description is maintained.

144 For example, the construction བརྟེན་ནས་ must be construed to mean *having depended*, since ནས་ is used after a verb (as a non-case particle) to indicate either a present or past participle, but never a future construction.

145 There are a number of cases where ཐློས་ is used in a **frozen form**, that is, as part of an expression where it seems no longer to be grammatically restricted to being an imperative root of ཐློ་: གར་ཐློས་ཀྱང་ (*in any event*) and ཐློས་མེད་ཀྱང་ (*no matter what*) are examples of this.

146 lCang skya (in his *Grub mtha'*, p. 447.7) glosses the use of the term in the context of dependent arising as a phenomenon's being what it is in dependence on, that is, in relation to, its *parts* (ཆ་ཤས་):

བལྟོས་པ་ཞེས་བྱ་བས་ནི་འདུས་བྱས་དང་འདུས་མ་བྱས་ཀྱི་ཆོས་རྣམས་རང་རང་གི་ཆ་ཤས་ལ་བལྟོས་ནས་ རང་གི་བདག་ཉིད་རྙེད་པའི་གཏན་ཚིགས་བསྟན་པ.

*[The term] 'contingent' indicates the reason which is that produced [i.e., impermanent] and unproduced [i.e., permanent] phenomena attain their natures contingent on their parts.*

Another clear example of this (also from lCang skya, p. 179) may be seen in the following, where བལྟོས་ and བརྟེན་ are used more or less synonymously: དེ་ལས་ གཞན་པ་དག་ལ་བལྟོས་ཤིང་། དེ་ལས་གཞན་པ་དག་ལ་བརྟེན་པ་—"[They] are contingent on [what is] other than them; [they] are dependent on [what is] other than them."

147 Ye shes brtson 'grus (**Yé s̄hé> dzön ḍu**—known as Kong po Ye shes brtson 'grus), *Lam rim bdud rtsi'i snying po* (*Essence of Ambrosia: Stages of the Path to Enlightenment*—known, and cited hereafter, as *Lam rim tshigs bcad ma* [*Stages of the Path in Verse*]), verse 165 (p. 11a): དམྱལ་བ་ཡི་དགས་དུད་འགྲོ་ཡི། ཁྱུངས་སུ་མཐའ་མེད་པ་ལ་བལྟོས་ན། —*If one observes the limitless number of hell-beings,*

*hungry ghosts, and animals,* ... The full title is *Byang chub lam gyi rim pa'i gtams pa zab mo rnams tshigs su bcad pa'i sgo nas nyams su len tshul dam chos bdud rtsi'i snying po.* The edition used here is a hand written copy, with the verses numbered (something not usually done in Tibetan texts, although many are written in verse). Citations are to the verse number and to the pagination of the original text (n.p., n.d.—copy in the library of the Tibetan Buddhist Learning Center).

148  Tsong-kha-pa, *Legs bshad snying po* (*Essence of the Well Explained* [codex edition—Sarnath: Pleasure of Elegant Sayings, 1973], p. 214.7): ཉིན་ལ་སྐྱེས་ཏེ་སྲོག་གཅོད་ལ་གནང་བ་མེད་—*[In Hīnayāna] there are no cases of permission to take life in consideration of circumstances.* ཉིན་ལ་སྐྱེས་ཏེ་ occurs in the proper syntax, but the verb and the syntax would lead to translation either as *considering the circumstances* (the agentive verb) or as *depending on the circumstances* (the verb of dependence).

149  The first example is a simplified version of a sentence in lCang skya, *Grub mtha'*, p. 107.13. The second is from lCang skya, p. 447.7; in its full form, it reads ཚོས་རྣམས་རང་རང་གི་ཆ་ཤས་ལ་བསྒྲས་ནས་རང་གི་བདག་ཉིད་ཉེད་པའི་གཏན་ཚིགས་བསྟན་པ.

150  Multisyllable verbs include phrasal verbs such as དོན་དུ་གཉེར་ (*seek*), ཁས་ལེན་ (and its honorific form ཞལ་བཞིན་, *assert*), ཕྱུར་དུ་གསད་ (*disparage*), ཁོང་དུ་ཆུད་ (*understand*), and ཉམས་སུ་ལེན་ (*practice*). Verbs such as མངོན་པར་རྟོགས་ (*realize*) are multisyllable but not phrasal. Such verbs include literal translations of Sanskrit prefix syllables: མངོན་པར་རྟོགས་, for example, translates the Sanskrit verb *abhisami*, where the root of the verb is *i* and *abhi* and *sam* are prefix syllables. མངོན་པར་ is the standard Tibetan translation of *abhi-*, leaving the *i* to be translated as རྟོགས་. Multisyllable phrasal verbs are formed from what in other contexts would be brief phrases. The verb ཁས་ལེན་ (*assert*), for instance, a verb quite common in philosophical writing, is built out of other words, ཁ་ (*mouth*) and ལེན་ (*grasp*). Translated overly literally, ཁས་ལེན་ means *grasped by the mouth* (since ཁས་ is the agentive form of ཁ་). ཁས་ལེན་, however, is not a phrase; it is a word. The dot between the two syllables is not a C dot but rather an S dot.

151  This translation would, in most contexts, be overly literal.

152   Some of these uses are clearly derived originally from phrases beginning in རང་ གི་; others, however, are not.  At any rate, these words have all become words, whatever their original derivation, through frequent use as such.

153   Whereas རང་རང་ (*own own*) here means *each of their own*, གཉིས་གཉིས་ (*two two*) in a similar context would mean *each of the two* or *both*.  Another way to say *each* is to use the adjective meaning *each*— རེ་རེ་ —as a pronoun.  Another way to say *both* is the adjective གཉིས་ཀ.

154   The origin of words such as རང་རྒྱལ་, of course, involves the use of the pronoun རང་.

155   *Indo-Tibetan* is like *Judaeo-Christian*—there aren't any.  That is, there is no one you can point to who is both (confessionally) a Jew and a Christian, although, from a longer term perspective, one can speak of a shared heritage.  Likewise, Indian Buddhism is Indian, and Tibetan Buddhism is Tibetan.  The term *Indo-Tibetan* is useful only to underscore the way in which Tibetans have tried to preserve as faithfully and as meaningfully as possible the Buddhism they inherited primarily from Indian gurus.

156   The word *thing* is used here in its broader sense of phenomenon.  *Thing* (དངོས་ པོ་) in some contexts refers to *impermanent* phenomena and is equivalent to མི་ རྟག་པ་ (*impermanent thing*).

157   "Any two things" is an overstatement, because it is possible to choose two things that are different but do not fit into any of the four categories here.  This will be discussed later.  For those who cannot wait, consider the case of two things that are themselves neither equivalent nor mutually exclusive, but there is nothing anywhere that that is neither the one nor the other.

158   See Hopkins, *Meditation on Emptiness*, p. 39, for a chart of these different forms of existence as seen in Géluk analyses of Indian Buddhist tenets.

159   See, for example, lCang skya, *Grub mtha'*, p. 13.  He lists གཞན་སྟེ་ (more properly, གཞན་སྟེ་བ་ **shën-dé-ba**) and མུ་སྟེགས་བྱེད་ (**mu-dék-chê'**, usually seen as མུ་ སྟེགས་པ་) as terms equivalent to ཕྱི་རོལ་པ་; he cites རང་སྟེ་ (that is, རང་སྟེ་བ་ **rang-dé-ba**) as an equivalent of སངས་རྒྱས་པ་ and ནང་པ་.

160 lCang skya, *Grub mtha'*, p. 13: ཕྱག་རྒྱ་བཞི་ actually means ལྟ་བ་བཀར་བཏགས་ཀྱི་ཕྱག་རྒྱ་བཞི་
—*the four seals that certify a view as [Buddha's] Word.* The four propositions are taken from the *Grub pa'i mtha'i rnam par bzhag pa rin po che'i*
*'phreng ba* of dKon mchog 'jigs med dbang po (Gön-chok-jík-mé-wang-
bo), p. 17. As *Presentation of Tenets: A Precious Garland*, it is translated in
the second section of Sopa and Hopkins, *Cutting Through Appearances*.
Citations are to the 1980 edition printed for Gomang College at the Drepung
Loseling Printing Press in Mundgod, India—cited hereafter as *Grub mtha' rin*
*chen 'phreng ba.*

161 See Sopa and Hopkins, *Cutting Through Appearances*, p. 180, and Paul
Griffiths, *On Being Mindless* (La Salle: Open Court, 1986), p. 189 and pp. 44-
45.

162 What can be very easily seen in the present instance is that this is the Tibetan
version of the "strengthening" (*vṛddhi*) process in Sanskrit. Where *sūtrānta*
means sutra, *sautrāntika*—formed by strengthening the Sanskrit *ū* to *au* and
adding the suffix *ika*—means *something/someone having to do with sūtras.*
The exception among the names of the Buddhist philosophies is སེམས་ཙམ་
(*cittamātra*)—the addition of a nominalizing པ་ creates the term སེམས་ཙམ་པ་, perhaps corresponding to *cittamātrin* as a Sanskrit original.

163 H. H. Tenzin Gyatso, *The Dalai Lama at Harvard* (Ithaca: Snow Lion, 1988),
p. 19.

164 Ngag dbang dpal ldan (**Ngak w̄ang b̄el den**, b. 1797—also known as dPal
ldan chos rje [**B̄en d̄en ch̄ö j̄é**]), *Grub mtha' chen mo'i mchan 'grel dka'*
*gnad mdud grol blo gsal gces nor* (*Annotations for [Jam-yang-shé-ba's]*
*'Great Exposition of Tenets', Freeing the Knots of the Difficult Points,*
*Precious Jewel of Clear Thought* [Sarnath: Pleasure of Elegant Sayings Press,
1964]), vol. *stod*, 20.4-6. This text is cited hereafter as *Grub mtha' chen mo'i*
*mchan 'grel*

165 'Jam dbyangs bzhad pa (**Jam ȳang shé b̄a**, 1648-1721), *Grub mtha'i rnam*
*bshad rang gzhan grub mtha' kun dang zab don mchog tu gsal ba kun bzang*
*zhing gi nyi ma lung rigs rgya mtsho skye dgu'i re ba kun skong* (*Great*
*Exposition of Tenets: Explanation of 'Tenets', Sun of the Land of*

*Samantabhadra Brilliantly Illuminating All of Our Own and Others' Tenets and the Meaning of the Profound [Emptiness], Ocean of Scripture and Reasoning Fulfilling All Hopes of All Beings* [Musoorie: Dalama, 1962]): 249.5.

166  *Grub mtha' chen mo'i mchan 'grel*, Vol. *stod*, 20.7.

167  Nakamura Hajime, *Indian Buddhism, A Survey with Bibliographical Notes* (Delhi: Motilal Banarsidass, 1989—first edition, Japan 1980), p. 14.

168  Beginning with Nāgārjuna's, these dates are found in Nakamura, *Indian Buddhism*, pp. 235, 244, 264, 268, 296, 301, 286, 287, 281.

169  See Randolph Quirk et al, *A Grammar of Contemporary English*, p. 352, for a clear tabular treatment of the differences between agentive and non-agentive subjects.

170  Nominative verbs are sometimes seen with agentive subjects. The most common example is a sentence of the sort often seen in devotional and liturgical works, བདག་གིས་སངས་རྒྱས་གྲུབ་པར་ཤོག—*May I achieve [the position of] a Buddha*, where གྲུབ་ has the force of *become*. Although the subject བདག་ is grammatically separate from the object སངས་རྒྱས་, it is not logically separate, since the future *I* and *Buddha* are not distinct. Thus, there is, in this sentence, no object separate from the subject.

171  The imperative form is uncommon and also appears as བྱེད་. In fact, it is given as བྱེད་ in Dorje Wangchuk Kharto's *Thumi: dGongs gTer (The Complete Tibetan Verb Forms)*. Dorje Wangchuk's compilation of verb tense forms is the standard to which the present work refers, although occasional reference is made to Sarat Chandra Das' *Tibetan-English Dictionary* (Calcutta: Bengal Secretariat Book Depot, 1902—reprinted Kyoto: Rinsen Book Company, 1977). The Das dictionary is the best published dictionary for literary Tibetan.

172  *Grub mtha' rin chen 'phreng ba*, p. 15.

173  *sKu tshab lam rim*, 3a.1.

174  *Grub mtha' rin chen 'phreng ba*, p. 19.

175  This sentence is adapted from a passage on p. 58 of the *gSung rab kun gyi snying po lam gyi gtso bo rnam pa gsum gyi khrid yig gzhan phan snying po*

*(Instructions on [Tsong-kha-pa's] 'Three Principal Aspects of the Path: Essence of All the Scriptures, Quintessence of Helping Others'*) written by the Fourth Paṇ-chen Lama, *bLo bzang dpal ldan bstan pa'i nyi ma* (**Lo sang b̄el dën d̄en b̄é nyí ma**, 1781-1852/4)—cited hereafter as *Lam gtso khrid yig*.

176    The model for this example is a passage from verse 296 (p. 21b) of the *Lam rim tshigs bcad ma*: མནར་བ་འདི་ཡི་རྒྱ་ནི་ཙེ་སྙམ་ན།.

177    The model for this example is *Lam rim tshigs bcad ma*, verse 172 (p. 11b): ལས་འདི་ལས་སྐྱོངས་པ་གང་ན་ཡོད།.

178    Neither the *Dag yig gsar bsgrigs* nor the *Bod rgya tshig mdzod chen mo* accord verb status to ཟེ་, ཞེ་, or ཤེ་. However, their usage here, as well as the related usage of ཟེས་, ཞེས་, and ཤེས་ to mark the termination of quoted material and reported discourse leads me to speculate a linguistic origin in a word meaning *say* or *be called*.

179    *Bod rgya tshig mdzod chen mo* and *Dag yig gsar bsgrigs*, q.v.

180    See Daniel Perdue, *Debate in Tibetan Buddhism*, pp. 171-172.

181    See *Bod rgya tshig mdzod chen mo*, q.v.

182    Mutually exclusive is defined as *being different and a common locus not being possible* (ས་དད་ཅིང་གཞི་མཐུན་པ་མི་སྲིད་པ་) according to p. 164 of the *sGo mang bsDus grva*.

183    The Tibetan term for dichotomy is ཕན་ཚུན་སྤངས་འགལ་གྱི་དངོས་འགལ་ (**pën-tsün-b̄ang-gël-gyi n̄gö-gël**). See *sGo mang bsDus grva*, pp. 478-479.

184    These four categories are themselves mutually exclusive. There are no cases of two things that are both mutually exclusive and have three permutations; there are no cases of two things that are both mutually exclusive and have four permutations; finally, there are no cases of two things that are both mutually exclusive and equivalent.

185    ཕན་ often occurs not as a free-standing verb, but as the first part of the phrasal verb ཕན་འདོགས་ (which means *help, aid*, and *benefit*).

186    *Lam gtso khrid yig*, p. 58

187    rMog lcog [Rin po che] (**M̄ok j̄ok R̄in b̄o ché**), *Lam gyi gtso bo rnam gsum gyi mchan 'grel* (*A Commentary of Annotations on [Tsong-kha-pa's] 'Three*

*Principal Aspects of the Path'* [n.p., n.d.]—cited hereafter as *Lam gtso mchan 'grel*): p. 6.

188  dbYangs can dga' ba'i blo gros (**Yang jën ga wé lo dö>**), also known as A kya yongs 'dzin (**A ḡya yong dzîn**), *Bar do 'phrang sgrol gyi gsol 'debs 'jigs sgrol gyi dpa' bo zhes bya ba'i 'grel pa gdams ngag gsal ba'i sgron me* (in *The Collected Works of A-kya Yongs-'dzin*, Vol. I, sides 336-363 [New Delhi: Lama Guru Deva, 1971]): 7a.1.

189  'Jam dpal bsam 'phel, dGe bshes (**Jam bël sam phêl**, d. 1975), *bLo rig gi rnam bzhag nyer mkho kun 'dus blo gsar mig 'byed* (translated in *Mind in Tibetan Buddhism* as *Presentation of Awareness and Knowledge, Composite of All the Important Points, Opener of the Eye of New Intelligence* [modern blockprint—n.p., n.d.]): p. 4b.  This is the epistemology primer used at Loseling College of Drebung Monastery;  it will be cited hereafter as *bLo gsal gling blo rig* (*Loseling Awareness and Knowledge*).

190  *sKu tshab lam rim*, p.13b.4.

191  *Lam gtso mchan 'grel*,  p. 6.

192  *Grub mtha' rin chen 'phreng ba*, p. 20.

193  *Grub mtha' rin chen 'phreng ba*, p. 21.

194  *bLo gsal gling blo rig*, p. 6a.

195  *Lam gtso khrid yig*, p. 52.

196  *Lam gtso khrid yig*, p. 47.

197  *Lam rim tshigs bcad ma*, verse 12.

198  *Lam rim tshigs bcad ma*, verse  13.

199  *Lam rim tshigs bcad ma*, verse  15.

200  *Lam rim tshigs bcad ma*, verse  110 (p. 8a).

201  *sKu tshab lam rim*, p.2b6.

202  *Lam rim tshigs bcad ma*, verse 19 (p. 3a).

203  *sKu tshab lam rim*, 12a.3-5.

204  Ye shes rgyal mtshan (**Yé ṣhé> gyël tshën**), *Lam rim bla brgyud thub bstan mdzes rgyan las ston pa'i rnam par thar pa* (Mundgod India:  Drepung

Loseling Printing Press, 1978): p.6. This text, a biography (རྣམ་ཐར་—literally, a *liberation*) of Buddha, is cited hereafter as *sTon pa'i rnam thar* (*Biography of the Teacher*).

205 *Lam rim tshigs bcad ma*, verse 26 (p. 3b).

206 *Lam gtso khrid yig*, p. 40.

207 *Lam gtso khrid yig*, p. 46.

208 *Lam gtso khrid yig*, p. 51.

209 *Grub mtha' rin chen 'phreng ba*, p. 27.

210 This example is a modification of a passage from Tsong-kha-pa, *Lam rim chen mo*, 165a.6ff.

211 For more detailed presentations of the various approaches to heuristic devices in Buddhism, see D. S. Lopez (editor), *Buddhist Hermeneutics* (Honolulu, University of Hawaii Press, 1988), and M. Pye, "Upāya" (*Encyclopedia of Religion* 15: 152-155).

212 *Grub mtha' rin chen 'phreng ba*, 37.1-2.

213 Tsong-kha-pa, *Legs bshad snying po*, Prāsaṅgika Chapter.

214 Tsong-kha-pa, *Legs bshad snying po*, p. 39.1-2.

215 *Lam gtso mchan 'grel*, p. 6.

216 *Legs bshad snying po*, p. 27.

217 The second column **cha** is technically a **chha**, a fully aspirated and middle tone version of what is a low tone, partially aspirated sound in column 3. The Tibetan **tha** is a hard 't', not the **th** in the English word 'the' but the **t** in 'tight'. The Tibetan **pha** is a hard 'ph', not the **ph** in the English word 'phone' but the **p** in 'pop'.

218 Turrell Wylie, "A Standard System of Tibetan Transcription," p. 267.

219 René de Nebesky-Wojkowitz, *Oracles and Demons of Tibet*, p. xv.

220 See, for example, Lambert Schmithausen, *Ālayavijñāna: On the Origin and Early Development of a Central Concept of Yogācāra Philosophy* (Studia Philologica Buddhica, monograph series IVa-b—Tokyo: International Institute for Buddhist Studies, 1987). David Seyfort Ruegg, in his *Buddha-nature,*

*Mind and the Problem of Gradualism in a Comparative Perspective*, (London: School of Oriental and African Studies, 1989) uses a modified form of the Library of Congress system . It differs only in the transliteration of ཤ and ཞ, which he does as **š̌a** and **ž̌a**.

221 *Dag yig gsar bsgrigs*, pp. 2-4.

222 This list was extracted by Karen Saginor, formerly a student at the University of Virginia, based on entries in the *Tibetan-English Dictionary* of Sarat Chandra Das.

223 གཞན་ལའང་མར་ཤེས་པར་བྱས་ལ་ literally reads *As for others, [they] also have been understood be to [one's] mother*. The verb ཤེས་ regularly takes its object in the nominative; thus, the མར་ is an objective complement. This is taken from Tsong-kha-pa, *Lam rim chen mo*, 196a.4.

224 According to *Lam rim chen mo*, (167b.5), this is from Vinaya.

225 Here is a passage from the beginning (p. 2) of Tsong-kha-pa's *Legs bshad snying po* illustrating this point. The nominative object of the verb གསུངས་ is ངོ་བོ་ ཉིད་མེད་པ་གཉིས་པ་ (*the second [sort of] lack of identity*). Although the quotation from the *Saṃdhinirmocana Sūtra* does answer the question, 'What did Buddha say,' it also answers the question, 'How did Buddha speak of this sort of lack of identity?'

ངོ་བོ་ཉིད་མེད་པ་གཉིས་པ་ནི་དགོངས་འགྲེལ་ལས། ཆོས་རྣམས་ཀྱི་སྐྱེ་བ་ངོ་བོ་ཉིད་མེད་པ་ཉིད་གང་ཞེ་ན། ཆོས་རྣམས་ཀྱི་གཞན་གྱི་དབང་གི་མཚན་ཉིད་གང་ཞེ་ན། ཆོས་རྣམས་ཀྱི་གཞན་གྱི་དབང་གི་མཚན་ཉིད་ གང་ཡིན་པའོ།། དེ་ཅིའི་ཕྱིར་ཞེ་ན། འདི་ལྟར་དེ་ནི་རྐྱེན་གཞན་གྱི་སྟོབས་ཀྱིས་བྱུང་བ་ཡིན་གྱི་ བདག་ཉིད་ཀྱིས་མ་ཡིན་པས་དེའི་ཕྱིར་དེ་ནི་སྐྱེ་བ་ངོ་བོ་ཉིད་མེད་པ་ཉིད་ཅེས་བྱ་ཞེས་གསུངས་སོ།།

226 *Lam rim tshigs bcad ma*, verse 36 (p. 4a).

227 Tsong-kha-pa, *Lam rim chen mo*, 226b.6.

228 It is possible for a sentence to end in ཡིན་པའོ། instead of ཡིན། or ཡིན་ནོ།; similarly, a sentence may end in བྱེད་པའོ། instead of བྱེད། or བྱེད་དོ།. However, the typical finite or closing verb looks like ཡིན། or བྱེད།. Tibetan does not require a special punctuation mark (such as a period or semicolon) to end a complete sentence, nor does it require the use of terminating particles such as are seen in the constructions བྱེད་པའོ།, བྱེད་དོ།, and so on.

229 The most common exception in more colloquial language is to place an adverb after the verb. This has the effect of dangling the adverb after the sentence and thus emphasizing it. An example of the same technique in English is the command "Come home! Quickly!"

230 According to the *Dag yig gsar bsgrigs* (pp. 2, 536-537), copulas, verbs of existence, verbs of possession, and verbs of necessity are ལས་ཚིག་རྟེས་མཐུན་པ་; nominative verbs, verbs of motion, and verbs of dependence are བྱེད་མེད་ལས་ཚིག་; agentive verbs are བྱེད་འབྲེལ་ལས་ཚིག་. See also the entries for representative examples of each class of verb where they are so designated.

231 *Bod rgya tshig mdzod chen mo*, p. 15 and pp. 1862-63.

232 Both examples are from the same text; the first is found in the *Grub mtha' rin chen 'phreng ba* on p. 16 and the second, on p. 52.

233 'Jigs med gling pa, *Yon tan rin po che'i mdzod kyi rgya cher 'grel pa bden gnyis shing rta* (in *The Collected Works of Kun-mkhyen 'Jigs-med-gling-pa* [Gangtok: Sonam T. Kazi, 1971], Vol. I—cited hereafter as *bden gnyis shing rta*): 34a.4..

234 Note that the attributive verb བྱེད་, although it does not vary in form from the even more common agentive-nominative action verb བྱེད་, is used very differently. If it ever occurred with an agent—someone who attributed the meaning to the word or phrase—that agent would be in the agentive case. However, when བྱེད་ is used as an attributive verb, it is used without this agentive case agent, in the same manner as ཟེར་—a verb which, in its meaning of *speak* or *discuss*, is an agentive-nominative verb, but in its meaning of *be called*, is a locative-nominative verb. (See *Dag yig gsar bsgrigs* under ཟེར་.)

235 Tsong-kha-pa, *Legs bshad snying po*, Prāsaṅgika chapter.

236 *Grub mtha' rin chen 'phreng ba*, p. 37.1-2.

237 Tsong-kha-pa, *Legs bshad snying po*, p. 39.1-2.

238 See *Dag yig gsar bsgrigs* under ཟེར་.

239 *Dag yig gsar bsgrigs*, p. 694.

240 *Legs bshad snying po*, p. 33.

241 Tsong-kha-pa, *Legs bshad snying po*, p. 47.

242  *Legs bshad snying po*, p. 27.

243  *Legs bshad snying po*, p. 10.

244  Tsong-kha-pa, *Lam rim chen mo*, 226a.5.

245  Adapted from *Lam rim tshigs bcad ma*, verse 351 (p. 25a).

246  Adapted from *Lam rim tshigs bcad ma*, verse 253 (p. 17b).

247  *Lam rim chen mo*, 157b.6.

248  *Grub mtha' rin chen 'phreng ba*, p. 3.

249  *sKu tshab lam rim*, 10b.4.

250  Adapted from *Lam rim tshigs bcad ma*, verse 263 (p. 18a).

251  Adapted from *Lam rim tshigs bcad ma*, verse 66 (p. 5a).

252  *sKu tshab lam rim*, 3a.4.

253  *Lam rim tshigs bcad ma*, verse 384 (p. 27a).

254  *sTon pa'i rnam thar*, p.6.

255  *Lam gtso khrid yig*, p. 46.

256  This is an abridged version of two lines from Nāgārjuna's *Mūlamadhyamakakārikā* (24.12ab):

དེ་ཕྱིར་ཞེན་པས་ཆོས་འདི་ཨི།    གཏིང་རྟོགས་དཀའ་བར་མཐྲིན་གྱུར་ནས༎.

257  *Lam rim tshigs bcad ma*, verse 96.

258  *Lam rim tshigs bcad ma*, verse 161.

259  dMu dge bsam gtan, *brDa sprod*, pp. 44-47 and 50-53.

260  dMu dge bsam gtan, pp. 50 and 52.

261  See gSer tog, *Sum rtags mchan 'grel*, p. 65.

262  gSer tog, p. 65: "[The seventh case] shows the basis or place where something depends or exists."

263  dMu dge bsam gtan, *brDa sprod*, pp. 52-53.

264  dMu dge bsam gtan, p. 53.

265  dMu dge bsam gtan, p. 71.

266 In *Grub mtha' rin chen 'phreng ba*, dKon mchog 'jigs med dbang po some-times uses the agentive with འདོད་ and, less frequently, the nominative. Here is a passage in which he describes the manner in which the four schools of tenets avoid falling to one or another of the two extremes (p. 16):

ཏེ་བྲག་སྨྲ་བ་རྣམས་འབྲས་བུ་སྐྱེ་བའི་ཚེ་རྒྱུ་འགགས་པས་ཏག་པའི་མཐའ་སྤོང་ལ། རྒྱུའི་མཇུག་ཐོགས་སུ་འབྲས་བུ་འབྱུང་བས་ཆད་པའི་མཐའ་སྤོང་ངོ་ཞེས་ཟེར་རོ། མདོ་སྡེ་པ་དག་འདུས་བྱས་རྣམས་རྒྱུན་མ་ཆད་པར་འཇུག་པས་ཆད་པའི་མཐའ་སྤོངས་ཞིང་། སྐད་ཅིག་གིས་འཇིག་པས་ཏག་པའི་མཐའ་ལས་གྲོལ་ཞེས་འདོད་དོ། སེམས་ཙམ་པ་རྣམས་ཀུན་བཏགས་བདེན་པར་མ་གྲུབ་པས་ཏག་པའི་མཐའ་སྤོང་ལ། གཞན་དབང་བདེན་པར་མ་གྲུབ་པས་ཏག་པའི་མཐའ་སྤོང་ངོ་ཞེས་སྐྲོ།ཧྲུ་མ་པ་རྣམས་ཆོས་ཐམས་ཅད་ཐ་སྙད་དུ་ཡོད་པས་མཐའ་ལས་གྲོལ་ཞིང་། དོན་དམ་དུ་མེད་པས་ཏག་པའི་མཐའ་ལས་གྲོལ་ཞེས་བཞེད་དོ།།

267 Quirk et al, pp. 414-15.

268 The full context of this passage is the following (from *Grub mtha' rin chen 'phreng ba*, p. 63): གཉིས་པ་མདོ་སྡེ་སྤྱོད་པའི་དབུ་མ་རང་རྒྱུད་པའི་ལུགས་ལ། གཞི་ལམ་འབྲས་གསུམ་ལས། དང་པོ་ནི། ལུགས་འདིས་ཏེ་དོན་འདོད་ཅིང་. The phrase ending in ལུགས་ལ། may be taken to be either a topical locative or a locative of inclusion (implying a verb of existence after གཞི་ལམ་འབྲས་གསུམ. After དང་པོ་ནི།, the sentence continues with in-formation that is topically but not grammatically related to the locative and topi-cal nominative.

269 *Lam rim bde lam*, 387.1

270 གིང་གཅོད་དུ resembles an infinitive construction (which is a syntactic and not a case marking usage). This highlights the somewhat arbitrary nature of the fourth case as traditionally understood in Tibet—indicating benefit but not harm (two syntactically parallel situations), and ascribed to situations where benefit is seen even when the syntax is not a truly nominal one.

271 See dMu dge bsam gtan, *brDa sprod*, p. 48.

272 The example is taken from *sKu tshab lam rim*, 8a.4.

273 dMu dge bsam gtan (*brDa sprod*, p. 61) nonetheless says that although the fifth case is over-used nowadays as a substitute for the third (especially in let-ters, which are written *from* someone rather than *by* someone), this practice is extremely rare in older texts.

274 Both this and the next example are from *Lam rim chen mo*, 228b.6.

275 In certain cases grammatical particles combine with suffixless syllables at the ends of words and thus do become parts of words. Examples of particles combining in this way with the word མདོ་ are མདོས་ (**dö>**, *by the sutra*), མདོར་ (**dor**, *in the sutra*) and མདོའི་ (**dö**, *of the sutra*). Although these particles never become part of the **lexical word** མདོ་, they do form parts of the **grammatical word**—the word མདོ་ marked for use in a sentence.

276 Tsong-kha-pa, *Lam rim chen mo*, 228b.5.

277 *Lam rim chen mo*, 165a.4-5.

278 *sKu tshab lam rim*, 5a.5.

279 lCang skya, *Grub mtha'*, p. 13.8-10.

280 *bLo gsal gling blo rig*, 6b.

281 *sKu tshab lam rim*, 15a6.

282 *Grub mtha' rin chen 'phreng ba*, p. 3.

283 *sKu tshab lam rim*, 2b.3.

284 *Lam gtso khrid yig*, p. 40.

285 *sKu tshab lam rim*, 4b2.

286 *Lam gtso khrid yig*, p. 47.

287 Ibid., p. 54.

288 *sTon pa'i rnam thar*, p. 4.

289 *Grub mtha' rin chen 'phreng ba*, p. 3.

290 *Bar do 'phrang sgrol gyi 'grel pa*, 2b.4.

291 This example abridges a passage from dbYangs can dga' ba'i blo gros, *Bar do 'phrang sgrol gyi 'grel pa* (6a.3): ལུས་འདི་ལ་ཆགས་པ་དང་། ཐུལ་གྱིས་དོགས་པས་ འཇིགས་པ་དང་། སྒུག་བསྐལ་མི་བཟོད་པའི་ཞེ་སྡང་དང་། རྔང་དོར་ལ་མོངས་ཤིང་ སྡང་ཆད་བདེན་པར་འཛིན་ པའི་གཏི་མུག་སྟེ་དུག་གསུམ་གྱི་མཚན་གྱིས་ རང་སྲོག་རང་གིས་གཏོད་པ་ལ་ཐུག་པའི་ཚེ.

292 *sKu tshab lam rim*, 14a.2.

293 *Grub mtha' rin chen 'phreng ba*, p. 29.

294 *Lam gtso khrid yig*, p. 40.

295 Ibid., p. 41.

296 Modified from a sentence found at *Lam gtso khrid yig*, p. 44.

297 *bLo gsal gling blo rig*, 5b.

298 *Lam rim tshigs bcad ma*, verse 34 (p. 4a).

299 *Lam gtso khrid yig*, p. 44.

300 Modified version of a sentence found in *sKu tshab lam rim*, 8a.4.

301 Tsong-kha-pa, *Lam rim chen mo*, 227a.1.

302 *Lam rim tshigs bcad ma*, verse 253 (p. 17b).

303 *sKu tshab lam rim*, 14a.1.

304 *Lam rim chen mo*, 157b.6.

305 Adapted from *Lam rim tshigs bcad ma*, verse 263 (p. 18a).

306 *Lam gtso khrid yig*, p. 52-53.

307 *Lam gtso khrid yig*, p. 46.

308 Adapted from a passage in *Grub mtha' rin chen 'phreng ba*, p. 14.

309 dKon mchog 'jigs med dbang po, *Sa lam*, 2b.3-4.

310 Modified from a sentence in *Grub mtha' rin chen 'phreng ba*, p. 26.

311 This is based on a sentence in *Lam gtso khrid yig*, p. 40.

# *Bibliography*

This bibliography lists the English and Tibetan works cited throughout *Translating Buddhism from Tibetan*. In addition, it includes—for the sake of those who may wish to read further—a selected list of the sources that were consulted or that played a role in the formation of the analyses and explanations employed in this book. It is arranged in the following order:

1    works in Tibetan on Tibetan grammar and lexicography (including Tibetan-Tibetan dictionaries);

2    works in English on Tibetan grammar and lexicography (including Tibetan-English and English-Tibetan dictionaries);

3    western works on language and linguistics;

4    works on Buddhism in Tibetan;

5    works on Buddhism in western languages.

## Tibetan Grammar and Lexicography
### *Tibetan and other Non-Western Works*

Angdu, Sonam
    *Tibeto-Sanskrit Lexicographical Materials*
      —includes the སྐུ་སྦྱོར་བཀ་པོ་གཉིས་པ།
        Leh: Basgo Tongspon, 1973

*Bod rgya tshig mdzod chen mo*
    See *Great Tibetan-Chinese Dictionary*

Chandra, Lokesh
  *Tibetan-Sanskrit Dictionary*
      Kyoto: Rinsen Book Company, 1976—reprinted from the first edition (New
        Delhi: International Academy of Indian Culture, 1959)

Ḍayap Loden Shérap (*Brag g'yab bLo ldan shes rab*)
  *Dictionary of Tibetan Terminology*
   *Bod brda' i tshig mdzod*
      Dharamsala: Library of Tibetan Works and Archives, 1989

*Dag yig gsar bsgrigs*
  See *New Compilation Lexicon.*

*Great Tibetan-Chinese Dictionary*
  *Bod rgya tshig mdzod chen mo*
      Beijing: *Mi rigs Dpe skrung khang*, 1986

Kharto, Dorje Wangchuk
  *Thumi: dGongs gTer (The Complete Tibetan Verb Forms)*
  *Dus gsum re'u mig thu mi'i dgongs gter*
      Delhi: C. T. Kharto, n.d.

Lhasawa Losang Thonden
  *Modern Tibetan Language* (Volume I)
      Dharamsala: Library of Tibetan Works and Archives, 1980

*New Compilation Lexicon*
  *Dag yig gsar bsgrigs*
      Mtsho-sngon: Mtsho-sngon Mi-rigs-dpe-skrun-khang, 1979

Samden, Mugé— M̄u-gé S̄am-d̄ën (*dMu dge bsam gtan*)
   *brDa sprod blo gsal dga' ston*—cited as dMu dge bsam gtan, *brDa sprod*
      Kan-su'u Mi-dmangs-dpe-skrung-khang, 1980

Sérdok Panchen—S̄ér d̄ok l̄o sang tshül ṭhrím gya tsho (*gSer tok bLo bzang tshul
  khrims rgya mtsho*, b. 1845)
   *Sum-chu-pa and Rtags-kyi-hjug-pa (A Wonder Key to the Tibetan Grammar)*—
      a codex printing of the *Bod kyi brda' sprod pa sum ju ba dang rtags kyi 'jug*

*pa'i mchan 'grel mdor bsdus te brjod pa ngo mtshar 'phrul gyi lde mig*
—cited as gSer tog, *Sum rtags mchan 'grel*
Kathmandu: Guru Deva Lama, 1962

Sidu Panchen—Si-du Paṇ-chen (*Si tu paṇ chen*)
*Commentary on (Tön-mi Sambhota's) "Thirty Stanzas" and "Application of Grammatical Marks"*
*Sum ju pa dang rtags kyi 'jug pa'i 'grel pa*
Edited in Tibetan in Sarat Chandra Das, *An Introduction to the Grammar of the Tibetan Language* (originally published in 1915, reprinted in 1972 by Motilal Banarsidass, Delhi)

Tshaḍul Ngawang Losang—Tsha ḍül ngak w̄ang l̄o s̲ang (*Tsha sprul ngag dbang blo bzang*)
*Sum cu pa'i snying po legs bshad ljon dbang gi slob deb*
New Delhi: 1985

Tshédën Shapḍung—Tshé dën s̲hap ḍung (Tshe tan zhabs drung
*Bod gangs can gyi sgra rig pa'i bstan bcos le tshan 'ga' phyogs bsdus.*
Kokonor: Mtsho sngon mi rigs dpe skrun khang, 1988

## Tibetan Grammar and Lexicography
### Western Works

Bacot, Jacques
*Grammaire du Tibétaine Littéraire*
Paris: Librarie d'Amérique et d'Orient, 1946

Bloomfield, Andrew and Yanki Tshering
*Tibetan Phrasebook*
Ithaca: Snow Lion, 1987

Das, Sarat Chandra
*An Introduction to the Grammar of the Tibetan Language*
Delhi: Motilal Banarsidass, 1972 (reprint edition—originally published in 1915)

Das, Sarat Chandra
 *A Tibetan-English Dictionary with Sanskrit Synonyms* (revised and edited by
 Graham Sandberg and A. William Heyde)
  Calcutta: Bengal Secretariat Book Depot, 1902—reprinted in a compact
  edition (Kyoto, Japan: Rinsen Book Company, 1977)

Goldstein, Melvyn
 *Tibetan-English Dictionary of Modern Tibetan*
  Kathmandu: Ratna Pustak Bhandar, 1975

Goldstein, Melvyn C. and Ngawangthondup Narkyid
 *English-Tibetan Dictionary of Modern Tibetan*
  Berkeley: University of California Press, 1984

Hahn, Michael
 *Lehrbuch der klassischen tibetischen Schriftsprache*
  Bonn: Indica et Tibetica Verlag, 1985

Hannah, H. B.
 *A Grammar of the Tibetan Language. Literary and Colloquial. With copious
 Illustrations, and treating fully of Spelling, Pronunciation and the Construction
 of the Verb, and including Appendices of the various forms of the Verb*
  Delhi: Motilal Banarsidass, 1978.

Jäschke, H. A.
 *A Tibetan-English Dictionary, with special reference to the prevailing dialects*
  London: Routledge & Kegan Paul, 1968  (first published in 1865, reprinted
  in 1883)

Jäschke, Heinrich August
 *Tibetan Grammar*
  New York: Frederick Ungar Publishing Co., 1965 (first published, 1881)

Miller, Roy Andrew
 "A Grammatical Sketch of Classical Tibetan"
 In *Journal of the American Oriental Society* 90.1 [1970]:  pp. 74-96

Miller, Roy Andrew
"Review of A. Róna-Tas, *Tibeto-Mongolica*"
In *Language* 44.1 [1968]

Miller, Roy Andrew
*Studies in the Grammatical Tradition in Tibet*
Amsterdam Studies in the Theory and History of Linguistic Science:
Studies in the History of Linguistics, Vol. 6
Amsterdam: John Benjamins B. V., 1976

Miller, R. A.
"Text Structure and Rule Ordering in the First Tibetan Grammatical Treatise"
In *Silver on Lapis: Tibetan Literary Culture and History*
Bloomington: The Tibet Society, 1987

Napper, Elizabeth (compiler and editor)
*Grammar Summary Materials Developed for Use at the University of Virginia Tibetan I*
Charlottesville: n.d.

Parfionovich, Y. M.
*The Written Tibetan Language*
Moscow: Nauka Publishing House, 1982

Wylie, Turrell
"A Standard System of Tibetan Transcription"
*Harvard Journal of Asiatic Studies* 22 [1959]: 261-267

## Language and Linguistics

Apte, Vaman Shivram
*The Practical Sanskrit-English Dictionary*
Delhi: Motilal Banarsidass, 1975 (fourth revised and enlarged edition)

Curme, George O.
*English Grammar*
New York: Barnes and Noble, 1970

Ducrot, Oswald and Tzvetan Todorov
    *Encyclopedic Dictionary of the Sciences of Language*
        Baltimore and London: Johns Hopkins University Press, 1979

Quirk, Randolph, Sidney Greenbaum, Geoffrey Leech, and Jan Svartik
    *A Grammar of Contemporary English*
        New York: Seminar Press, 1972

*Webster's Ninth New Collegiate Dictionary*
    Springfield, Massachusetts: Merriam-Webster, 1989

## Works on Buddhism in Tibetan

Candrakīrti
    *Commentary on "An Introduction to the Middle Way" (Madhyamakāvatāra-
    bhāṣya)*
    *Dbu ma la 'jug pa rang 'grel*
        Dharamsala: Council of Cultural and Religious Affairs, 1968

Gönchok Jíkmé Wangbo—Gön chok jík mé wang bo (*dKon mchog 'jigs med
    dbang po*)
    *Grub pa'i mtha'i rnam par bzhag pa rin po che'i 'phreng ba*
    *Presentation of Tenets: A Precious Garland*—cited as *Grub mtha' rin chen
    'phreng ba*
        Mundgod, India: printed for Gomang College at the Drepung Loseling
        Printing Press, 1980

Gyëlrong Chödzé—Gyël rong chö> dzë' Lo sang thok mé' (*rGyal rong chos
    mdzad blo bzang thogs med*)
    *dMar khrid thams cad mkhyen par bgrod pa'i myur lam bzhin khrid skyong ba
    la nye bar mkho ba'i zhal shes 'ga' zhig gi brjed tho of rGyal rong chos
    mdzad blo bzang thogs me*—cited as *sKu tshab lam rim*
    In *Two Instructions on the Lam-Rim Teachings, the Lam Rim Myur Lam and
    the Lam Rim Bde Lam, of the Bkra-Shis-Lhun-Po Tradition*
        New Delhi: Ngawang Sopa, 1979

Jambë Sampel—Jam b̄ël s̄am phêl (*'Jam dpal bsam 'phel*, dGe bshes, d. 1975)
  *bLo rig gi rnam bzhag nyer mkho kun 'dus blo gsar mig 'byed*
  —translated in *Mind in Tibetan Buddhism* as *Presentation of Awareness and
  Knowledge, Composite of All the Important Points, Opener of the Eye of New
  Intelligence*—cited as *bLo gsal gling blo rig (Loseling Awareness and
  Knowledge)*
    Modern blockprint—n.p., n.d.

Jamyang Shéba—Jam ȳang shé b̄a (*'Jam dbyangs bzhad pa*, 1648-1721)
  *Grub mtha' i rnam bshad rang gzhan grub mtha' kun dang zab don mchog tu
  gsal ba kun bzang zhing gi nyi ma lung rigs rgya mtsho skye dgu' i re ba kun
  skong*
  *Great Exposition of Tenets: Explanation of 'Tenets', Sun of the Land of
  Samantabhadra Brilliantly Illuminating All of Our Own and Others' Tenets
  and the Meaning of the Profound [Emptiness], Ocean of Scripture and
  Reasoning Fulfilling All Hopes of All Beings*
    Musoorie: Dalama, 1962

Jang-gya—J̄ang ḡya Röl b̄ë dor jé (*lCang skya rol pa' i rdo rje*, 1717-86)
  *Grub mtha' i rnam par bzhag pa gsal bar bshad pa thub bstan lhun po' i mdzes
  rgyan*—cited as lCang skya, *Grub mtha'*
  *Clear Exposition of the Presentations of Tenets, Beautiful Ornament for the
  Meru of the Subduer's Teaching*
    Sarnath: Lama Guru Deva, 1970

Jikmé Lingba—Jík mé' l̄íng b̄a (*'Jigs med gling pa*)
  *Yon tan rin po che' i mdzod kyi rgya cher 'grel pa bden gnyis shing rta*
  —cited as *bDen gnyis shing rta*
    Volume I of *The Collected Works of Kun-mkhyen 'Jigs-med-gling-pa*
    Gangtok: Sonam T. Kazi, 1971

Losang Bëldën Dën-bë Nyima (Fourth Paṇ-chen Lama)—L̄o sang b̄ël dën d̄ën b̄é
nyí ma (*bLo bzang dpal ldan bstan pa' i nyi ma*, 1781-1852/4)
  *gSung rab kun gyi snying po lam gyi gtso bo rnam pa gsum gyi khrid yig gzhan
  phan snying po*

*Instructions on [Tsong-kha-pa's] 'Three Principal Aspects of the Path: Essence of All the Scriptures, Quintessence of Helping Others'*—cited as *Lam gtso khrid yig*
   Manuscript—n.p., n.d.

Losang Chökyi Gyëltsën—Lo-sang-chö-gyí-gyël-tsën (*bLo bzang chos kyi rgyal mtshan*)
   *bLa ma mchod pa*
   In *bLa ma'i rnal 'byor dang yi dam khag gi bdag bskyed sogs zhal don gces btus*
   *Selected Brief Recitation Texts: the Guru Yoga and the Self-Generations of Various Meditational Deities*
      Dharamsala: Tibetan Cultural Printing Press, n.d.—codex edition

Mokjok [Rinboché]—Mok jok (*rMog lcog [Rin po che]*)
   *Lam gyi gtso bo rnam gsum gyi mchan 'grel*
   *A Commentary of Annotations on [Tsong-kha-pa's] 'Three Principal Aspects of the Path'*

Ngawang Bëldën—Ngak wang bël dën (*Ngag dbang dpal ldan*, b. 1797—also known as *dPal ldan chos rje* [Bën dën chö jé])
   *Grub mtha' chen mo'i mchan 'grel dka' gnad mdud grol blo gsal gces nor*
   *Annotations for [Jam-yang-shé-ba's] 'Great Exposition of Tenets', Freeing the Knots of the Difficult Points, Precious Jewel of Clear Thought*
      Sarnath: Pleasure of Elegant Sayings Press, 1964

Ngawang Ḍashi—Ngak wang ḍa shi> (*Ngag dbang bkra shis*)
   *Tshad ma'i dgongs 'grel gyi bstan bcos chen po rnam 'grel gyi don gcig tu dril ba blo rab 'bring tha ma gsum du ston pa legs bshad chen po mkhas pa'i mgul rgyan skal bzang re ba kun skong*
   *Necklace for the Wise, Fulfilling All Hopes for the Fortunate: An Explanation in which the topics of [Dharmakīrti's] Great Treatise Unravelling the Thought of Valid Cognition, [His] "Commentary on [Dignāga's] 'Compendium on Valid Cognition'," Are Brought Together and Shown to those of Best, Middling, and Least Intellect*)—cited as *sGo mang bsdus grva* (*Go-mang Doctrinal Primer*)

Tsong-kha-pa—D̄zong kha b̄a L̄o ṣang ṭak b̄a (*Tsong kha pa bLo bzang grags pa*)
  *dBu ma dgongs pa rab gsal*
  *Illumination of the Thought, [An Explanation of Candrakīrti's "Introduction to
  the] Middle Way"*
      Sarnath: Pleasure of Elegant Sayings Printing Press, 1973

Tsong-kha-pa
  *Lam rim chen mo / Great Exposition of the Stages of the Path*
      blockprint—n.p., n.d.

Tsong-kha-pa
  *Legs bshad snying po*
  *Essence of the Well Explained*
      Sarnath: Pleasure of Elegant Sayings, 1973 (codex edition)

Yangjën Gawë Loḍö—Yang j̈ën ga wë l̄o ḍö> (*dbYangs can dga' ba'i blo gros*)
  also known as *A kya yongs 'dzin* (A ḡya yong ḍzîn)
  *Bar do 'phrang sgrol gyi gsol 'debs 'jigs sgrol gyi dpa' bo zhes bya ba'i 'grel
  pa gdams ngag gsal ba'i sgron me*
  In *The Collected Works of A-kya Yongs-'dzin*, Vol. I, sides 336-363
      New Delhi: Lama Guru Deva, 1971

Yéshé Dzönḍu—Yé s̄hé> dzön ḍu (*Ye shes brtson 'grus*)—known as *Kong po Ye
  shes brtson 'grus*
  *Lam rim bdud rtsi'i snying po*
  *Essence of Ambrosia: Stages of the Path to Enlightenment*—cited as *Lam rim
  tshigs bcad ma (Stages of the Path in Verse)*
      Handwritten copy—n.p., n.d.

Yéshé Gyëltsën—Yé s̄hé> gyël tshën (*Ye shes rgyal mtshan*)
  *Lam rim bla brgyud thub bstan mdzes rgyan las ston pa'i rnam par thar pa*—
  cited as *sTon pa'i rnam thar (Biography of the Teacher).*
      Mundgod India: Drepung Loseling Printing Press, 1978

## Works on Buddhism and Tibet in Western Languages

Bdud-'joms 'Jigs-bral-ye-śes-rdo-rje [Dudjom Rinpoche]
   *The Nyingma School of Tibetan Buddhism: Its Fundamentals and History*
      Boston: Wisdom Publications, 1991

Beckwith, C. I. (editor)
   *Silver on Lapis: Tibetan Literary Culture and History.*
      Bloomington: The Tibet Society, 1987

Dri-med-'od-zer, Kloṅ-chen-pa
   *Buddha Mind: An Anthology of Longchen Rabjam's writings on Dzogpa chenpo*
      Ithaca: Snow Lion, 1989

Griffiths, Paul
   *On Being Mindless*
      La Salle: Open Court, 1986

He-ru-ka, Gtsan-smyon
   *The Life of Milarepa*—translated by Lobsang P. Lhalungpa
      New York: E. P. Dutton, 1977

Hirakawa, Akira
   *A History of Indian Buddhism from Śākyamuni to Early Mahāyāna*
      Honolulu: University of Hawaii Press, 1990

Hopkins, Jeffrey
   *Compassion in Tibetan Buddhism*
      London: Rider and Company, 1980

Hopkins, Jeffrey
   *Meditation on Emptiness*
      London: Wisdom Publications, 1983

Hopkins, Jeffrey
   *The Tantric Distinction*
      London: Wisdom Publications, 1984

Klein, A. C.
*Knowledge and Liberation: Tibetan Buddhist Epistemology in Support of Transformative Religious Experience*
Ithaca, Snow Lion, 1986

Klein, Anne Carolyn
*Knowing, Naming, and Negation: A Sourcebook on Tibetan Sautrāntika*
Ithaca: Snow Lion, 1991

Lati Rinbochay, Denma Lochö Rinbochay, and Leah Zahler, with Jeffrey Hopkins
*Meditative States in Tibetan Buddhism*
London: Wisdom Publications, 1983

Lati Rinbochay
*Mind in Tibetan Buddhism*—translated by Elizabeth Napper
Valois: Snow Lion, 1980

Lopez, Donald
*The Heart Sūtra Explained: Indian and Tibetan Commentaries*
Albany: State University of New York Press, 1988

Lopez, D. S. (editor)
*Buddhist Hermeneutics.*
Honolulu, University of Hawaii Press, 1988

Nakamura Hajime
*Indian Buddhism, A Survey with Bibliographical Notes*
Delhi: Motilal Banarsidass, 1989—first edition, Japan 1980)

Nebesky-Wojkowitz, René de
*Oracles and Demons of Tibet*
Graz/Austria: Akademische Druck-u.Verlagsanstalt, 1975 (reprint edition—first published, 1956)

Obermiller, E.
*History of Buddhism (Chos-hbyung) by Bu-ston: The Jewelry of Scripture*
Heidelberg: O. Harrassowitz, 1931

Obermiller, E.
  *History of Buddhism (Chos-hbyung) by Bu-ston: The History of Buddhism in India and Tibet*
      Heidelberg: O. Harrassowitz, 1932

Perdue, Daniel
  *Debate in Tibetan Buddhism*
      Ithaca: Snow Lion, 1992

Rabten, Geshe
  *The Essential Nectar: Meditations on the Buddhist Path*
      London: Wisdom, 1984

Rabten, Geshe
  *Treasury of Dharma*
      London: Tharpa Publications, 1988

Rhie, Marylin M. and Robert A. F. Thurman
  *Wisdom and Compassion: The Sacred Art of Tibet*
      New York: Asian Art Museum of San Francisco and Tibet House (New York) in association with Harry N. Abrams, 1991

Ruegg, David Seyfort
  *Buddha-nature, Mind and the Problem of Gradualism in a Comparative Perspective*
      London: School of Oriental and African Studies, 1989

Sangharakshita
  *A Survey of Buddhism*
      London: Tharpa Publications, 1987 (revised edition)

Sangpo, Khetsun
  *Tantric Practice in Nying-ma*
      Ithaca: Snow Lion, 1986

Schmithausen, Lambert
  *Ālayavijñāna: On the Origin and Early Development of a Central Concept of Yogācāra Philosophy*

Tokyo: International Institute for Buddhist Studies, 1987
(Studia Philologica Buddhica, monograph series IVa-b)

Snellgrove, David
*Indo-Tibetan Buddhism: Indian Buddhists and Their Tibetan Successors*
Boston: Shambhala, 1987

Sopa, Geshe Lhundup and Jeffrey Hopkins
*Cutting Through Appearances*
Ithaca: Snow Lion, 1989

Tenzin Gyatso
*The Dalai Lama at Harvard*
Ithaca: Snow Lion, 1988

Tenzin Gyatso (Fourteenth Dalai Lama)
*Opening the Eye of New Awareness*
London: Wisdom Publications, 1985

Tucci, Giuseppe
*The Religions of Tibet*
Bombay: Allied Publishers, 1980

Tulku Thondup
*Buddhist Civilization in Tibet*
New York: Routledge and Kegan Paul, 1987

Williams, Paul
*Mahāyāna Buddhism: The Doctrinal Foundations*
London: Routledge, 1989

Wilson, Joe
*Chandrakirti's Sevenfold Reasoning: Meditation on the Selflessness of Persons*
Dharamsala: Library of Tibetan Works and Archives, 1986 (originally published in 1980)

# *Glossary*

Verbs are marked by the Roman numeral indicating the class to which they belong—that is, the syntax they require.

| | | | | |
|---|---|---|---|---|
| **I** | nominative-nominative | **V** | agentive-nominative |
| **II** | nominative-locative | **VI** | agentive-objective |
| **III** | nominative-objective | **VII** | purposive-nominative |
| **IV** | nominative-syntactic | **VIII** | locative-nominative |

The first part of the name of each class identifies the case of the subject and the second, that of the object, complement, or principal qualifier.

[HON] means honorific.

| | | |
|---|---|---|
| ཀ་ཁ་ | ḡa-kha | alphabet |
| ཀ་བ་ | ḡa-wa | pillar |
| ཀུན་མཁྱེན་ | ḡün-khyên | omniscient one |
| ཀུན་དུ་འབྱུང་བ་ | ḡün-ḏu-jung-wa | source, origin |
| ཀུན་དུ་བཟང་པོ་ | ḡün-ḏu-ṣang-ḇo | Samantabhadra |
| ཀུན་ནས་ཉོན་མོངས་པ་ | ḡün-në>-nyön-mong-ḇa | thoroughly afflicted |
| ཀུན་རྫོབ་པ་ | ḡün-ḏzop-ḇa | conventional [lit. 'thoroughly covered'] |
| ཀྱང་ | ḡyang | even, also, but |
| ཀྱེ་རྡོ་རྗེ་ | ḡyé dor-jé | Hevajra |
| ཀླུ་ | ḹu | *nāga* |

| ཀློང་ | ḷong | expanse |
| དཀའ་ | ḡa | difficult |
| དཀར་པོ་ | ḡar-b̄o | white |
| དཀོན་མཆོག་གསུམ་ | ḡön-chok s̄um | three jewels |
| དཀོན་པོ་ | ḡön-b̄o | rare |
| དཀྱིལ་འཁོར་ | ḡyíl-khor / ḡyín-khor | mandala |
| བཀག་ | ḡak | [past of དགག་] |
| བཀའ་ | ḡa | speech, words  [**HON**] |
| རྐྱེན་ | ḡyên | condition |
| སྐོག་པ་ | ḡok-b̄a | hidden |
| སྐད་ཅིག་མ་ | ḡë'-ĵîk-ma | momentary (made of moments) |
| སྐུ་ | ḡu | body [**H**] |
| སྐོར་ | ḡor | turn  **v** |
| སྐྱབས་ | ḡyap | refuge |
| སྐྱབས་འགྲོ་ | ḡyam-ḍo | going for refuge |
| སྐྱེ་ | ḡyé> | is born, arises, is created  **III** |
| སྐྱེ་མཆེད་ | ḡyém-ché' | source  [Skt. *āyatana*] |
| སྐྱེ་བ་ | ḡyé-wa | birth, arising |
| སྐྱེད་ | ḡyé' | create, generate, give birth to  **v** |
| སྐྱེས་པ་ | ḡyé>-b̄a | born, arisen, created |
| སྐྱེས་བུ་ | ḡyé>-bu | being, person |
| སྐྱོ་ | ḡyo | is sad, depressed, disheartened  **II** |
| སྐྱོང་ | ḡyong | nurture, sustain  **V** |

| | | |
|---|---|---|
| སྐྱོན་ | ḡyön | fault |
| སྐྱོབ་ | ḡyop | protect, provide refuge **V** |
| སྐྱོབ་པ་ | ḡyop-b̄a | protector, refuge |
| བསྒོར་ | ḡor | [future of སྒོར་] |
| བསྒོརད་ | ḡor | [past of སྒོར་] |
| བསྐྱངས་ | ḡyang | [past of སྐྱོང་] |
| ཁ་ | kha | mouth |
| ཁ་ཅིག་ | kha-j́ík | someone, a certain person |
| ཁ་དོག་ | kha-dok | color |
| ཁང་པ་ | khang-b̄a | house, building |
| ཁམས་ | kham | constituent |
| ཁམས་ | kham | Kam [in eastern Tibet] |
| ཁས་བླང་ | khë>-lang | [future of ཁས་ལེན་] |
| ཁས་བླངས་ | khë>-lang | [past of ཁས་ལེན་] |
| ཁས་ལེན་ | khë>-lên | assert **V** |
| ཁོ་ | kho | she, he, it |
| ཁོ་ན་ | kho-na | only |
| ཁོ་བོ་ | kho-wo | I, me |
| ཁོ་བོ་ཅག་ | kho-wo-j́ak | we, us |
| ཁོ་བོ་ཅག་རྣམས་ | kho-wo-j́ak-ñam | we, us |
| ཁོ་ | kho | he, it |
| ཁོ་རང་ | kho-rang | he, he himself, itself |
| ཁོགས་ | khok | [imperative of དགག་] |
| ཁོང་ | khong | he, she, it [HON] |

| ཁོང་ཁྲོ་ | khong-ṭho | anger |
| ཁོང་དུ་ཆུད་ | khong-du-chü' | understand V |
| ཁོང་ཚོ་ | khong-tsho | they [HON] |
| ཁྱད་དུ་གསད་ | khyë'-du-sē' | disparage, despise V |
| ཁྱད་པར་ | khyë'-b̄ar | attribute, feature, and quality |
| ཁྱད་པར་ | khyë'-b̄ar | in particular |
| ཁྱབ་ | khyap | pervade, cover, spread VI |
| ཁྱབ་པ་ | khyap-b̄a | pervasion |
| ཁྱབ་བྱ་ | khyap-ja | that pervaded, object pervaded |
| ཁྱབ་བྱེད་ | khyab-jé' | pervader |
| ཁྱེད་ | khyé' | you [HON] |
| ཁྱེད་ཅག | khyé'-j̄ak | you [HON] |
| ཁྱོད་ | khyö' | you |
| ཁྱོད་ཚོ་ | khyö'-tsho | you [plural] |
| ཁྱོད་རྣམས་ | khyö'-ñam | you [plural] |
| ཁྱོད་རང་ | khyö'-rang | you, you yourself |
| མཁན་པོ་ | khën-b̄o | abbot |
| འཁོར་ | khor | turn III [present & future] |
| འཁོར་འདས་ | khor-dë> | cyclic existence and nirvana |
| འཁོར་བ་ | khor-wa | cyclic existence [samsara] |
| འཁོར་ལོ་ | khor-lo | wheel |
| འཁོར་ལོ་སྡོམ་པ་ | khor-lo-dom-b̄a | Chakrasamvara [Cakrasaṃvara] |
| འཁོརད་ | khor | [past and imperative of འཁོར] |
| འཁྱམ་ | khyam | wander III |

| | | |
|---|---|---|
| ཁྲོ་ | ṭho | is angry **II** |
| མཁས་ | khë> | is skilled, is learned [in] **II** |
| མཁས་པ་ | khë>-b̄a | skill, scholar |
| མཁྱེན་ | khyên | know [**H**] **V** |
| མཁྱེན་པ་ | khyên-b̄a | knowledge, wisdom [**H**] |
| འཁྲུལ་ | ṭhül | is mistaken **II** |
| འཁྲུལ་བ་ | ṭhul-wa | mistake, error |
| ག་ | ka | what, which |
| གང་ | kang | what, which, that which, who |
| གང་ཞིག་ | kang-shík | what, which |
| གང་ཞིག་ | kang-s̱hík | [punctuational syntactic particle] |
| གང་ཡང་ | kang-yang | any |
| གང་ཡང་ | kang-yang | none [with negative] |
| གང་རུང་ | kang-rung | either |
| གངས་ | kang | snow |
| གུས་ | kü> | trusts, respects **II** |
| གྱི་ | gyí | although, but [disjunctive—following verb] |
| གྱུར་ | gyur | [past and imperative of འགྱུར་] |
| གྲང་བ་ | ṭang-wa | cold |
| གྲུབ་ | ṭup | is established, is accomplished, is achieved, is proven, exists **III** |
| གྲུབ་ཐོབ་ | ṭup-thop | [tantric] adept |
| གྲུབ་མཐའ་ | ṭup-tha, ṭum-tha | tenets [*siddhānta*] |
| གྲོགས་ | ṭok | friend, companion |

| | | |
|---|---|---|
| གྲོང་ཁྱེར་ | ṭong-kyér | city |
| གྲོལ་ | ṭöl | is free **IV** |
| གྲོལ་བ་ | ṭöl-wa | liberation |
| གླང་པོ་ཆེ་ | lang-b̄o-ché | elephant |
| གླིང་ | líng | island, continent |
| དགག་ | gak | refute, stop, cease **V** |
| དགའ་ | ga | delight in, enjoy **II** |
| དགའ་ལྡན་ | gan-dën | Tuṣhita [a pure land] |
| དགའ་བ་ | ga-wa | happiness, joy |
| དགུ་ | gu | nine |
| དགེ་བསྙེན་ | gé-ñyên | layman |
| དགེ་བསྙེན་མ་ | gé-ñyên-ma | laywoman |
| དགེ་འདུན་ | gén-dün | spiritual community |
| དགེ་བ་ | gé-wa | virtuous, wholesome |
| དགེ་ཚུལ་ | gé-tshül | novice monk |
| དགེ་ཚུལ་མ་ | gé-tshül-ma | novice nun |
| དགེ་སློང་ | gé-l̄ong | monk |
| དགེ་སློང་མ་ | gé-l̄ong-ma | nuns |
| དགེ་སློབ་མ་ | gé-l̄op-ma | probationary nuns |
| དགེ་བའི་བཤེས་གཉེན་ | gé-wë-s̄hé>-nyén | spiritual friend |
| དགོངས་ | gong | consider, think about [HON] **VI** |
| དགོངས་པ་ | gong-b̄a | thought, intention [**HON**] |
| དགོན་པ་ | gön-b̄a | monastery |
| དགོས་ | gö> | must, require **VII** |

| དགོས་ཆེད་ | gö>-ché' | purposive-beneficial [case] |
|---|---|---|
| དགོས་པ་ | gö>-ba | purpose |
| དག྄ | ḍa | enemy |
| དག྄་བཅོམ་པ་ | ḍa-jom-ba | arhat |
| མགོ་ | go | beginning, head |
| མགོན་པོ་ | gön-bo | protector |
| འགལ་ | gël | contradicts **IV** |
| འགལ་བ་ | gël-wa | mutual exclusion, exclusive |
| འགོག་ | gok | [future of དགག་] |
| འགྱུར་ | gyur | becomes, changes, is **III** [present & future] |
| འགྲུབ་ | ḍup | is established, is proven, exists **III** |
| འགྲེལ་པ་ | ḍél-ba | commentary |
| འགྲོ་ | ḍo | go **III** [present and future] |
| འགྲོ་བ་ | ḍo-wa | going, migration [rebirth], migrator [sentient being] |
| རྒོད་པ་ | gö'-ba | excitement |
| རྒྱ་གར་ | gya-gar | India |
| རྒྱ་མཚོ་ | gya-tsho, gyam-tsho | ocean |
| རྒྱགས་པ་ | gyak-ba | haughtiness |
| རྒྱལ་པོ་ | gyël-bo | king |
| རྒྱལ་བ་ | gyël-wa | conqueror |
| རྒྱལ་མོ་ | gyël-mo | queen |
| རྒྱས་ | gyë> | extends, expands **III** |
| རྒྱུ་ | gyu | cause |

| རྒྱུད་ | gyü' | continuum, tantra |
| རྒྱུན་ཞུགས་ | gyün-shuk | stream enterer |
| སྒོ་ | go | door |
| སྒོམ་ | gom | meditate, cultivate **V** |
| སྒོམ་པ་ | gom-ba | meditation [Skt. *bhāvanā*] |
| བསྒོམ་པ་ | gom-ba | meditation |
| རྒྱུར་ | gyur | change, transform, transmute **V** |
| སྒྲ་ | da | sound |
| སྒྲ་བཤད་ | da-shë' | etymology [literally 'explanation of word'] |
| སྒྲིབ་པ་ | díp-ba | obstruction |
| སྒྲུབ་ | dup | establish, achieve, accomplish, prove, complete **V** |
| སྒྲོལ་ | döl | liberate **V** |
| སྒྲོལ་བ་ | döl-wa | liberation |
| སྒྲོལ་མ་ | döl-ma | Tara (*Tārā*) |
| བསྒོམས་ | gom | [past of སྒོམ་] |
| བསྒྱུར་ | gyur | [past and future of རྒྱུར་] |
| བསྒྲལ་ | dël | [past and future of སྒྲོལ་] |
| ང་ | nga | I, me |
| ང་རྒྱལ་ | nga-gyël | pride |
| ང་ཅག་ | nga-jak | we, us |
| ང་ཚོ་ | nga-tso | we, us |
| ང་རང་ | nga-rang | I, I myself |
| ངག་ | ngak | speech |

| ངང་གིས་ | ngang-gí> | naturally |
| ངན་པ་ | ngën-b̄a | bad |
| ངེས་པ་ | ngé>-b̄a | definite, certain; certainty, definiteness, ascertainment |
| ངེས་པར་འབྱུང་བ་ | ngé>-b̄ar-jung-wa | renunciation |
| ངེས་པར་ཤེས་པ་ | ngé>-b̄ar-s̄hé>-b̄a | ascertainment, certain knowledge |
| ངོ་བོ་ | ngo-wo | entity, nature |
| ངོ་བོ་ཉིད་ | ngo-wo-nyí' | identity, entity |
| ངོ་མཚར་ | ngo-tshar | amazing |
| ངོས་ | ngö> | side, surface |
| དངོས་པོ་ | n̄gö>-b̄o | functioning thing |
| མངའ་ | n̄ga | exist, have **II VIII** |
| མངལ་ | n̄gël | womb |
| མངོན་པར་རྟོགས་པ་ | n̄gön-b̄ar-d̄ok-b̄a | realization |
| མངོན་པར་ཤེས་པ་ | n̄gön-b̄ar-s̄hé>-b̄a | clairvoyance, paranormal knowledge |
| རྔ་ | n̄ga | drum |
| ལྔ་ | n̄ga | five |
| ལྔ་སྡེ་ | n̄ga-dé | group of five |
| སྔགས་ | n̄gak | mantra |
| སྔོན་འགྲོ་ | n̄gön-ḍo | preliminary, preparation |
| སྔོན་པོ་ | n̄gön-b̄o | blue |
| ཅི་ | j̄í | what, which |
| ཅི་ཡང་ | j̄i-yang | at all, in any way |
| ཅིང་ | j̄íng | [continuative syntactic particle] |

| | | |
|---|---|---|
| ཅུང་ཟད་ | j̈ung-s̠ë' | a little |
| ཅེ་ན་ | j̈é-na | [question marker]<br>if one says / were I to be asked |
| ཅེས་ | j̈é> | [close quote (syntactic particle)] |
| གཅིག | j̈ík | one, identical |
| གཅིག་པ་ | j̈ík-b̄a | similar |
| གཅེས་པ་ | j̈é>-b̄a | dear, cherished |
| བཅལ་ | j̈ël | [past of འཇལ་] |
| བཅས་ | j̈ë> | possesses, is together with **IV** |
| ∗ དང་བཅས་པ་ | dang-j̈ë>-b̄a | possessing ∗ |
| བཅིངས་ | j̈íng | [past of འཆིངས་] |
| བཅུད་ | j̈ü' | essence |
| བཅོམ་ | j̈om | [past of འཇོམས་] |
| བཅོམ་ལྡན་འདས་ | j̈om-dën-dë> | Transcendent Victor |
| བཅོས་མ་ | j̈ö>-ma | artificial |
| ཆོས་ | chö> | religion; phenomenon |
| ཆོས་ལུགས་ | chö>-luk | religious order |
| འཆད་པ་པོ་ | chë'-b̄a-b̄o | explainer |
| ལྕགས་ | j̈ak | iron |
| ལྕེ་ | j̈é | tongue |
| ཆ་ | cha | part, factor |
| ཆ་ཤས་ | cha-s̄hë> | part |
| ཆགས་ | chak | is attached to **II** |
| ཆུ་ | chu | water |

| | | |
|---|---|---|
| ཆུ་བུར་ | chu-bur | bubble |
| ཆེ་བ་ | ché-wa | great, greater |
| ཆེད་ | ché' | purpose, [for] the sake [of] |
| ཆེན་མོ་ | chên-mo | large, great [feminine] |
| ཆོས་ཀྱི་དབྱིངས་ | chö>-ḡyí-yíng | sphere of truth, expanse of reality [Skt. *dharmadhātu*] |
| ཆོས་སྐུ་ | chö>-ḡu | truth body |
| ཆོས་ཅན་ | chö>-jën | [logical] subject |
| ཆོས་ཉིད་ | chö>-nyí' | nature, reality [Skt. *dharmatā*] |
| མཆི་ | chí | go **III** [present and future] |
| མཆིས་ | chí> | [past and imperative of མཆི་] |
| མཆིས་ | chí> | exist **II** |
| མཆོག་ | chok | highest, best |
| མཆོད་པ་ | chö'-ḇa | worship |
| འཆི་ | chí | die [verb] |
| འཆད་ | chë' | say, explain, present, proclaim **V** |
| འཆར་ | char | appears, rises **III** |
| འཆིངས་ | chíng | tie, bind **V** |
| ཇ་ | c̱ha | tea |
| ཇི་ལྟར་ | jí-ḏar | how, what sort, what |
| ཇོ་བོ་ | jo-wo | lord |
| མཇུག་ | juk | end, conclusion [of text] |
| འཇིག་པ་ | jík-ḇa | disintegration |
| འཇིགས་ | jík | fears **II** |
| འཇམ་དཔལ་ | jam-ḇë(l) | Manjushri [Mañjuśrī] |

| | | |
|---|---|---|
| འཇལ་ | jël | measure, assess, comprehend **V** |
| འཇལད་ | jël | imperative of འཇལ་ |
| འཇིག་ | jík | disintegrates **III** |
| འཇིག་པ་ | jík-ba | disintegrating |
| འཇིག་རྟེན་ | jík-dën | world |
| འཇིགས་ | jík | fears, is afraid of **II** |
| འཇུག་ | juk | enter **III** |
| འཇོག་ | jok | put, posit, present **V** |
| འཇོམས་ | jom | destroy, conqueror **V** |
| རྗེ་ | jé | master, foremost one |
| རྗེས་ | jé> | after |
| རྗེས་ཁྱབ་ | jé>-khyap | positive pervasion |
| རྗེ་བཙུན་ | jé-dzün | revered one |
| རྗེས་སུ་དཔག་པ་ | jé>-su-bak-ba | inference |
| ཉ་ | nya | fish |
| ཉན་ཐོས་ | nyën-thö> | hearer, audiant [Skt. *śrāvaka*] |
| ཉན་རང་ | nyën-rang | hearers and solitary conquerors |
| ཉམས་ | nyam | degenerate, fall from **III** |
| ཉམས་སུ་བླང་ | nyam-su-lang | [future of ཉམས་སུ་ལེན་] |
| ཉམས་སུ་བླངས་ | nyam-su-lang | [past of ཉམས་སུ་ལེན་] |
| ཉམས་སུ་ལེན་ | nyam-su-lën | practice **V** |
| ཉེ་བ་ | nyé-wa | near |
| ཉེ་བར་ལེན་པ་ | nyé-war-lën-ba | appropriation, appropriated |
| ཉེས་སྐྱོན་ | nyé>-gyön | fault |

| ཉེས་པ་ | nyé>-ḇa | fault |
|---|---|---|
| ཉེས་དམིགས་ | nyé>-m̄ík | danger |
| ཉོན་མོངས་ | nyön-mong | affliction, mental distortion |
| གཉིས་ཀ་ | ñyí>-g̱a | both |
| གཉིས་སུ་མེད་པ་ | ñyí>-s̄u-mé'-ḇa | nondual |
| གཉེན་ | ñyén | friend, relative |
| གཉེན་པོ་ | ñyén-ḇo | antidote |
| མཉན་ཡོད་ | ñyen-yö' | Shravasti [*Śrāvastī*] |
| མཉམ་པར་བཞག་པ་ | ñyam-ḇar-s̱hak-ḇa | meditative equipoise [Skt. *samādhi*] |
| རྙིང་པ་ | ñyíng-ḇa | old |
| རྙིང་མ་ | ñyíng-ma | *Nying-ma* Order |
| རྙེད་ | ñyé' | find **V** |
| སྙིང་རྗེ་ | ñyíng-jé | compassion |
| སྙིང་པོ་ | ñyíng-ḇo | heart, essence, pith |
| སྙོམས་པར་འཇུག་པ་ | ñyom-ḇar-juk-ḇa | meditative absorption [Skt. *samāpatti*] |
| བརྙེས་ | ñyé> | [past form of རྙེད་] found |
| ཏིང་ངེ་འཛིན་ | ḏing-ngé-dzîn | concentration (*samādhi*) |
| དེ་ | ḏé | [continuative syntactic particle] |
| གཏན་ཚིགས་ | ḏën-tshík | reason |
| གཏི་མུག་ | ḏí-muk | delusion, obscuration |
| བཏགས་ | ḏak | [past of འདོགས་] |
| བཏང་སྙོམས་ | ḏang-nyom | equanimity |
| རྟ་ | ḏa | horse |

| རྟ་མགྲིན་ | ḍan-ḍin | Hayagriva [Hayagrīva] |
| རྟག་པ་ | ḍak-b̄a | permanent, static |
| རྟགས་ | ḍak | sign, reason |
| རྟེན་ | ḍên | basis, support, [bodily] support |
| རྟེན་ | ḍên | depend on, rely on **II** |
| རྟེནད་ | ḍên | [imperative of རྟེན་] |
| རྟེན་ཅིང་འབྲེལ་བར་འབྱུང་བ་ | ḍên-jíng-ḍél-war-jung-wa | dependent arising |
| རྟེན་འབྲེལ་ | ḍên-ḍél | dependent arising |
| རྟོག་བཅས་ | ḍok-jë> | conceptual |
| རྟོག་པ་ | ḍok-b̄a | thought, conceptuality |
| རྟོག་མེད་ | ḍok-mé' | nonconceptual |
| རྟོགས་ | ḍok | realize, understand **V** |
| རྟོགས་པ་ | ḍok-b̄a | realization |
| བརྟེན་ | ḍên | [future and past of རྟེན་] |
| བརྟེནད་ | ḍên | [past of རྟེན་] |
| ལྟ་ | ḍa | view, look at **VI** |
| ལྟ་བ་ | ḍa-wa | view, viewpoint; [wrong] view |
| ལྟར་ | ḍar | [adverb marking syntactic particle] |
| ལྟུང་ | ḍung | fall **III** [present and future] |
| ལྟོས་ | ḍö> | relates to, is contingent on **II** |
| བལྟ་ | ḍa | [future of ལྟ་ (*look at*)] |
| བལྟས་ | ḍë> | [past of ལྟ་] |
| བལྟོས་ | ḍö> | [past of ལྟོས་] depends on |

| སྟག་ | ḍak | tiger |
|---|---|---|
| སྟེ་ | ḍé | [continuative syntactic particle] |
| སྟེང་ | ḍéng | top, [on] top [of] |
| སྟེར་ | ḍér | give **V** |
| སྟོང་པ་ཉིད་ | ḍong-ḅa-nyí' | emptiness |
| སྟོན་ཀ | ḍön-g̱a | autumn |
| སྟོང་ | ḍong | is empty of, lacks |
| སྟོང་པ་ | ḍong-ḅa | empty |
| སྟོང་པ་ཉིད་ | ḍong-ḅa-nyi' | emptiness |
| སྟོན་ | ḍön | teach, indicate, demonstrate **V** |
| བསྟན་ | ḍën | [past and future of སྟོན་] |
| བསྟེན་ | ḍên | use [medicine], serve [a guru] |
| ཐ་དད་ | tha-dë' | different |
| ཐ་མི་དད་ | tha-mí-dë' | non-different, not different |
| ཐང་ | thang | plain [geographical] |
| ཐབས་ | thap | means, method, technique [*upāya*] |
| ཐར་ | thar | is liberated, is freed **IV** |
| ཐར་པ་ | thar-ḅa | liberation |
| ཐལ་ | thël | logically follow **III**, go too far **III** |
| ཐལ་འགྱུར་ | thën-gyur | consequence |
| ཐལ་འགྱུར་བ་ | thël-gyur-wa / thën-gyur-wa | Consequentialist (Prāsaṅgika) |
| ཐལ་བ་ | thël-wa | consequence |
| ཐལ་རང་ | thël-rang | Prāsaṅgika and Svātantrika |
| ཐིམ་ | thîm | dissolve **III** |

| | | |
|---|---|---|
| ཐུགས་ | thuk | mind [**H**] |
| ཐུགས་རྗེ་ | thuk-jé | compassion [**H**] |
| ཐེ་ཚོམ་ | thé-tshom | doubt |
| ཐེག་པ་ | thék-b̄a | vehicle [Skt. *yāna*] |
| ཐེག་པ་ཆེན་པོ་ | thék-b̄a-chên-b̄o | great vehicle [Skt. *mahāyāna*] |
| ཐེག་པ་དམན་པ་ | thék-b̄a m̄ën-b̄a | modest vehicle [Skt. *hinayāna*] |
| ཐོ་བ་ | tho-wa | hammer |
| ཐོག་མ་ | thok-ma | beginning |
| ཐོགས་ | thok | [imperative of འདོགས་] |
| ཐོབ་ | thop | is obtained, is attained **III** |
| ཐོབ་ | thop | [past of འཐོབ་] |
| ཐོས་པ་ | thö>-b̄a | hearing |
| མཐའ་ | tha | end, extreme |
| མཐུ་ | thu | power |
| མཐུ་ཅན་ | thu-jën | potent |
| མཐུན་ | thün | accords, is in harmony **IV** |
| མཐོ་ | tho | high, higher |
| མཐོང་ | thong | see **V** |
| འཐད་ | thë' | is correct **III** |
| འཐོབ་ | thop | is obtained, is reached **III** |
| ད་ | ta | now |
| ད་ལྟ་ | tan-d̄a | now |
| དག་ཞིང་ | tak-s̱híng | pure land |
| དང་ | tang | and, or |

| དང་པོ་ | tang-b̄o | first |
| དད་ | të' | trusts **II** |
| དད་པ་ | të-b̄a | faith |
| དམ་བཅའ་ | tam-j̇a | thesis |
| དམ་པ་ | tam -b̄a | holy, superior, ultimate |
| དར་ | tar | silk |
| དུ་བ་ | tu-wa | smoke |
| དུ་མ་ | tu-ma | many |
| དུག་ | tuk | poison |
| དུང་ | tung | conch |
| དུད་འགྲོ་ | tün-d̦o | animal [literally, 'bent goer'] |
| དུས་ | tü> | time |
| དུས་འཁོར་ | tü>n-khor | Kalachakra [Kalacakra] |
| དེ་ | té | that, that one |
| དེ་ཁོ་ན་ཉིད་ | te-kho-na-nyí' | suchness [reality] |
| དེ་ཉིད་ | té-nyí' | that itself, reality, adverbial identity [grammar] |
| དེ་ལྟ་བུ་ | té-d̄a-bu | such |
| དེ་ལྟར་ | té-d̄ar | thus [adverbial pronoun] |
| དེ་དག་ | té-dak | those |
| དེ་འདྲ་ | té-d̦a | such, 'like that' |
| དེ་ཕྱིར་ | té-chír | therefore |
| དེ་བས་ | té-wë> | more than that, beyond that |
| དེས་ན་ | té>-na | therefore |
| དོན་ | tön | goal, aim, purpose, object, meaning |

| ོ ་ ་ | tön-jík | equivalent |
| དོན་གཅིག | tön-jík-ba | equivalent |
| དོན་དམ་པ་ | tön-tam-ba | ultimate<br>[lit. 'highest object'] |
| དོན་དུ་གཉེར | tön-du-nyér | seek **V** |
| དྲི་ | ṭí | odor, scent |
| དྲི་མ་ | ṭí-ma | stain, defilement |
| དྲི་མ་མེད་པ་ | ṭí-ma-mé'-ba | stainless |
| གདགས་ | dak | [future of འདོགས་] |
| གདའ་ | da | exist **II** |
| གདུལ་བུ་ | dül-ja | disciple |
| བདག | dak | I, me, self [*ātman*] |
| བདག་ཅག | dak-jak | we, us |
| བདག་ཉིད | dak-nyí' | being, nature |
| བདེ་བ་ | dé-wa | bliss |
| བདེན་པ་ | dên-ba | truth |
| བདེན་པར་གྲུབ་པ་ | dên-bar-ḍup-ba | truly established |
| བདེན་པར་ཡོད་པ་ | dên-bar-yö'-ba | truly existent |
| མདུན་ | dün | front, [in] front [of] |
| མདོ་ | do | discourse  [Skt. *sūtra*] |
| འདའ་ | da | is beyond, transcends **IV** |
| འདས་ | dë> | [past form of འདའ་] |
| འདི་དག་ | di-dak | these |
| འདུ་ | du | [future of འདུད་] |

| | | |
|---|---|---|
| འདུ་བྱེད་ | du-jé' | compositional factor |
| འདུས་མ་བྱས་ | dü>-ma-jé> | uncompounded phenomenon |
| འདུ་འཛི་ | du-dzí> | commotion |
| འདུ་ཤེས་ | du-shé> | discrimination |
| འདུག | duk | exist **II** |
| འདུད་ | dü' | is gathered, is included **III** |
| འདུད་ | dü' | pay homage **V** |
| འདུལ་ | dül | tame, subdue, train |
| འདུས་ | dü> | [past and imperative of འདུད་ ] |
| འདོགས་ | dok | designates, imputes **V** |
| འདོད་ | dö' | wish, assert, claim **V** |
| འདོད་ཁམས་ | dö'-kham | Desire Realm |
| འདོད་ཆགས་ | dö'-chak | attachment |
| འདོད་པ་ | dö'-ba | desire, desired; assertion |
| འདུ་མོ་ | da-mo | like |
| འདྲི་བ་ | di-wa | question |
| རྡུལ་ | dül | atom |
| རྡོ་ | do | stone |
| རྡོ་རྗེ་ | dor-jé | diamond [Skt. *vajra*] |
| རྡོ་རྗེ་འཇིགས་བྱེད་ | dor-jé-jík-jé' | Vajrabhairava [Vajrabhairava] |
| རྡོ་རྗེ་རྣལ་འབྱོར་མ་ | dor-jé ñël-jor-ma | Vajrayogini [Vajrayoginī] |
| རྡོ་རྗེ་ཕག་མོ་ | dor-jé pha-mo | Vajravarahi [Vajravarāhī] |
| རྡོ་རྗེ་ཕུར་པ་ | dor-jé phur-ba | Vajrakila [Vakrakīla] |
| བརྡ་ | da | sign, convention |

| | | |
|---|---|---|
| ལྡན་ | dën | possesses **IV** |
| ལྡན་ | dën | [lexical particle: possession] |
| * དང་ལྡན་པ་ | dang-dën-b̄a | possessing * |
| ལྡན་མིན་འདུ་བྱེད་ | dën-mîn-du-jé' | nonassociated compositional factor |
| ལྡེ་མིག་ | dé-mík | key |
| ལྡོག་ཁྱབ་ | dok-khyap | counter-pervasion |
| སྡང་ | dang | hates, is averse to **II** |
| སྡིག་པ་ | dík-b̄a | misdeed, evil, sin |
| སྡུག་པ་ | duk-b̄a | pleasant, attractive |
| སྡུད་ | dü' | include, gather **V** |
| སྡོད་ | dö' | dwell, remain, sit **II** |
| སྡོམ་པ་ | dom-b̄a | vow |
| བསྡད་ | dë' | [past and future of སྡོད་] **II** |
| བསྡུ་ | du | [future of སྡུད་] |
| བསྡུས་ | dü> | [past of སྡུད་] |
| བསྡུས་གྲྭ་ | dü>-ḍa | doctrinal primer |
| * ན་རེ་ | na-ré | according to * |
| ནགས་ཚལ་ | nak-tshël | forest |
| ནང་ | nang | inside, within, among; inner, internal |
| ནད་པ་ | në'-b̄a | ill person |
| ནམ་མཁའ་ | nam-kha | space |
| ནས་ | në> | [continuative syntactic particle] |
| * ནས་བཟུང་སྟེ་ | në>-ṣung-d̄é | beginning with * |
| ནུབ་ | nup | west |

| ནུས་པ | nü>-b̄a | ability, power, energy |
|---|---|---|
| གནས | ñë> | live, stay, continue **II** |
| གནས་བརྟན | ñë>-d̄en | elder [Skt. *sthavira*] |
| གནས་ལུགས | ñë>-luk | mode of abiding, reality |
| གནོད | ñö' | harm **VI** |
| གནོད་པ | ñö'-b̄a | harm, refutation |
| རྣ་བ | ña-wa | ear |
| རྣམ་པ | ñam-b̄a | aspect, type, form |
| རྣམ་པར་གྲོལ་བ | ñam-b̄ar-ḍöl-wa | liberated |
| རྣམ་པར་རྟོག་པ | ñam-b̄ar-d̄ok-b̄a | conceptuality, thought |
| རྣམ་པར་དབྱེ་བ | ñam-b̄ar-ȳé-wa | distinction, declension [case] |
| རྣམ་པར་སྨིན་པ | ñam-b̄ar-m̄in-b̄a | fruition |
| རྣམ་པར་གཡེང་བ | ñam-b̄ar-yéng-wa | distraction |
| རྣམ་པར་བཞག་པ | ñam-b̄ar-s̲hak-b̄a | presentation |
| རྣམ་པར་ཤེས་པ | ñam-b̄ar-s̄hé>-b̄a | consciousness [vijñāna] |
| རྣམ་སྨིན | ñam-m̄in | fruition |
| རྣལ་འབྱོར | ñël-jor, ñën-jor | yoga |
| སྣ | ña | nose |
| སྣང | ñang | appears, is perceived **III** |
| སྣོད | ñö' | vessel, receptacle |
| དཔེ | b̄é | example |
| སྤང | b̄ang | [future of སྤོང་] |
| སྤངས | b̄ang | [past of སྤོང་] |
| སྤངས་པ | b̄ang-b̄a | elimination |

| སྤོང་ | b̄ong | eliminate, abandon **V** |
| སྤོངས་ | b̄ong | [imperative of སྤོང་] |
| སྤྱན་རས་གཟིགས་ | jën-rë>-s̱í(k) | Avalokiteshvara [Avalokiteśvara] |
| སྤྲུལ་སྐུ་ | ḍül-g̱u | emanation body |
| སྤྲུལ་པ་ | ḍül-b̄a | emanation |
| ཕ་རོལ་ | pha-röl | other, far |
| ཕ་རོལ་ཏུ་ཕྱིན་པ་ | pha-röl-ḏu-chîn-b̄a | perfection, transcendence |
| ཕག་པ་ | phak-b̄a | pig |
| ཕན་ | phën | help, aid, benefit **VI** |
| ཕན་པ་ | phën-b̄a | help, assistance |
| ཕན་ཡོན་ | phën-yön | benefit |
| ཕུན་སུམ་ཚོགས་པ་ | phün-s̄um-tshok-b̄a | marvel; marvelous, consummate |
| ཕུང་པོ་ | phung-b̄o | aggregate [Skt. *skandha*] |
| ཕོངས་ | phong | is destitute, is devoid of **IV** |
| ཕྱག་ན་རྡོ་རྗེ་ | cha-na-dor-jé | Vajrapani [Vajrapaṇi] |
| ཕྱག་འཚལ་ | chak-tshël | bow down |
| ཕྱག་འཚལ་བ་ | chak-tshël-wa | prostration [bowing down] |
| ཕྱི་ | chí | external |
| ཕྱི་མ | chí-ma | subsequent |
| ཕྱི་རོལ་ | chí-röl | outside, external |
| ཕྱིན་ | chîn | [past of འགྲོ་] |
| ཕྱོགས་ | chok | side, direction; position [in debate] |
| ཕྲ་མོ་ | ṭha-mo | subtle |
| ཕྲག་དོག་ | ṭhak-dok | jealousy |

| ཕྲད་ | ṭë' | meet with **IV** |
| འཕགས་པ་ | phak-b̄a | superior [Skt. *ārya*] |
| འཕངས་ | phang | past of འཕེན་ **V** |
| འཕེན་ | phên | propel, throw, shoot **V** |
| འཕྲུལ་ | ṭhül | magic |
| འཕྲོས། | ṭhö> | spreads **III** |
| བ་གླང་ | pa-lang | ox |
| བག་ཆགས་ | pak-chak | latency, predisposition |
| བར་ | par | up to, through |
| བལ་ཡུལ་ | pë-yül | Nepal |
| * བས་ | wë> | more than *, rather than * |
| བུ་ | pu | child, son |
| བུ་མོ་ | pu-mo | daughter |
| བུམ་པ་ | pum-b̄a | pot |
| བེམ་པོ་ | pém-b̄o | [physical] matter |
| བོད་སྐད་ | pö'-ḡë' | Tibetan language |
| བྱ་ | cha | bird |
| བྱ་ | cha | [future of བྱེད་] |
| བྱང་ | chang | north [also verb meaning *purify*] |
| བྱང་ཆུབ་ | chang-chup | enlightenment |
| བྱང་ཆུབ་སེམས་དཔའ་ | chang-chup-sêm-b̄a | bodhisattva |
| བྱམས་པ་ | cham-b̄a | love, Maitreya |
| བྱས་ | chë> | [past of བྱེད་] |
| བྱས་པ་ | chë>-b̄a | produced, made, product |

| ཁྱེས་པ་ | c̱hí>-b̄a | child, immature person |
| བྱུང་ | c̱hung | [past of འབྱུང་] |
| བྱེ་ཐང་ | c̱hé-thang | desert |
| བྱེ་མ་ | c̱hé-ma | sand |
| བྱེད་ | c̱hé' | do, make, perform, serve as **V** |
| བྱེད་པ་པོ་ | c̱hé'-b̄a-b̄o | agent ['doer'] |
| བྱོན་ | c̱hön | come, arrive **III** |
| བྱོས་ | c̱hö> | [imperative of བྱེད་] |
| གྲོལ་ | ṭël | is free of **IV** |
| * དང་གྲོལ་བ་ | dang-ḍël-wa | free from *,  lacking * |
| བླ་མ་ | l̄a-ma | guru |
| ལང་ | lang | [future of ལེན་] |
| ལངས་ | lang | [past of ལེན་] |
| བློ་ | l̄o | mind |
| བློ་གྲོས་ | l̄o-ḍö> | intelligence, intellect |
| བློ་རིག་ | l̄o-ŕík | minds and awarenesses |
| དབང་ | āng / w̄ang | empowerment / initiation |
| དབང་པོ་ | wang-b̄o | empowerment, sense power |
| དབུ་ | ū | head |
| དབུ་མ་ | ū-ma | center, middle, middle way |
| དབུ་མ་པ་ | ū-ma-b̄a | Mādhyamika |
| དབེན་ | én / wén | is isolated from, lacks **IV** |
| དབེན་པ་ | én-ba / w̄én-ba | isolation, solitary place |
| དབྲལ་ | ül | lacks, is devoid of **IV** |

| | | |
|---|---|---|
| དབུས་ | <u>ü</u> | U [central Tibet] |
| དབྱིབས་ | yíp | shape |
| དབྱེ་ | yé | divide **VI** |
| དབྱེ་བ་ | ȳé-wa | division, category |
| འབད་ | b̄ë’ | strive to, make effort in **VI** |
| འབའ་ཞིག་ | ba-<u>sh</u>ík | only |
| དབྱིངས་ | yíng | sphere, expanse |
| འབྱུང་ | jung | occurs, arises **III** [present & future of འབྱུང་] |
| འབྱུང་ཁུངས་ | jung-khung | origin, source |
| འབྱུང་བ་ | jung-wa | arising, element |
| འབྱེད་ | jé’ | separate, open, reveal **V** |
| འབྲེལ་ | ḍél | is related **IV** |
| འབྲེལ་བ་ | ḍél-wa | connection, relation |
| སྦྱོར་བ་ | jor-wa | application, connection, endeavor, preparation, syllogism |
| སྦྲུལ་ | ḍül | snake |
| མ་ | ma | mother |
| མ་འོངས་པ་ | ma-ong-b̄a | future |
| མ་རིག་པ་ | ma-rík-b̄a | ignorance, unawareness |
| མན་ཆད་ | mën-chë’ | that and below |
| མར་ | mar | butter |
| མར་མེ་ | mar-mé | butter lamp |
| མི་ | mi | human being |
| མི་དགེ་བ་ | mí-gé-wa | non-virtuous, unwholesome |

| མི་འཇིག་པ་ | mí-jík—ba | non-disintegrating |
| མི་རྟག་པ་ | mí-ḏak-ba | impermanent |
| མི་འདོད་པ་ | mín-dö'-ba | undesired, unaccepted, unwanted |
| མི་སྡུག་པ་ | mí-duk-ba | unpleasant |
| མིང་ | míng | name |
| མིང་ཚམ་ | míng-ḏzam | nominative [case] |
| མིན་ | mîn | is not  **I** |
| མུ་ | mu | boundary, permutation, possibility |
| མེ་ | mé | fire |
| མེད་ | mé' | does not exist  **II** |
| མོ་ | mo | she |
| མོ་གཤམ་ | mo-šham | barren woman |
| མོས་ | mö> | is interested  **II** |
| མྱ་ངན་ལས་འདས་པ་ | nya-ngën-lë>-dë>-ba | nirvana (*nirvāṇa*) |
| མྱུ་གུ་ | nyu-gu | sprout |
| མྱོང་ | nyong | experience  **V** |
| མྱོང་བྱ་ | nyong-ja | object of experience |
| དམན་པ་ | m̄ën-ba | lesser, inferior, low |
| དམར་པོ་ | m̄ar-bo | red |
| དམིགས་ | mík | observe, visualize |
| དམིགས་པ་ | m̄ík-ba | observation, object of observation |
| དམྱལ་བ་ | ñyël-wa | hell |
| རྨུགས་པ་ | m̄uk-ba | lethargy |
| རྨོངས་ | m̄ong | is confused  **II** |

| | | |
|---|---|---|
| སྨན་ | m̄ën | medicine |
| སྨན་པ་ | m̄ën-b̄a | doctor |
| སྨྲ་ | m̄a | says, propounds, claims **VI** |
| སྨྲ་བ་ | m̄a-wa | speaking, propounding |
| གཙང་ | d̄zang | Dzang [west central Tibet] |
| གཙོ་བོ་ | d̄zo-wo | main, chief, principal |
| བཙལ་ | d̄zël | [past and future of འཚོལ་] |
| རྩ་བ་ | d̄za-wa | root, basis, principal; basic |
| ཙམ་ | d̄zam | only, merely, just |
| རྗེ་ | d̄zé | point |
| རྩོལ་བ་ | d̄zöl-wa | effort |
| བརྗེ་བ་ | d̄zé-wa | love |
| བརྩོན་ | d̄zön | makes effort, is energetic **VI** |
| ཚ་བ་ | tsha-wa | heat |
| ཚང་ | tshang | is complete **III** |
| ཚད་ | tshë' | measure, extent |
| ཚད་མ་ | tshë'-ma | valid cognition, prime cognition |
| ཚད་མེད་ | tshë'-mé' | without measure, immeasurable |
| ཚིག་ | tshík | word |
| ཚིག་ཕྲད་ | tshík-ṭhë' | particle |
| ཚུལ་ཁྲིམས་ | tshul-ṭhim | ethics (*śila*) |
| ཚེ་དཔག་མེད་ | tshé-b̄ak-mé' | Amitāyus |
| ཚོར་བ་ | tshor-wa | feeling |
| མཚན་ཉིད་ | tshën-nyí' | definition, characteristic |

| མཚན་གཞི་ | tshën-<u>sh</u>í | illustration, instance |
| མཚོན་བྱ་ | tshön-ja | that which is defined |
| འཚོལ་ | tshöl | seek, search for **V** |
| མཛད་ | <u>dz</u>ë' | do, make, perform **V** [**HON**] |
| མཛོད་ | <u>dz</u>ö' | [imperative of མཛད་] |
| འཛམ་བུའི་གླིང་ | <u>dz</u>am-bü-líng | Jambu Continent |
| འཛིན་ | <u>dz</u>în | hold, apprehend, grasp, conceive **V** |
| རྫ་ | <u>dz</u>a | clay |
| རྫོགས་པ་ | <u>dz</u>ok-b̄a | completion; complete |
| ཝཱ་ར་ན་སི | wa-ra-na-si | Vāraṇāsi [city in India] |
| ཞལ་བཞེས་ | <u>sh</u>ël-<u>sh</u>é> | HONORIFIC of ཁས་ལེན་ |
| ཞི་གནས་ | <u>sh</u>í-ñë> | calm abiding [Skt. *śamatha*] |
| ཞི་བ་ | <u>sh</u>í-wa | peace, pacification |
| ཞིང་ | <u>sh</u>íng | [continuative syntactic particle] |
| ཞིང་པ་ | <u>sh</u>íng-b̄a | farmer |
| ཞིབ་ཏུ་ | <u>sh</u>íp-d̄u | in detail |
| ཞིབ་མོ་ | <u>sh</u>íp-mo | subtle, fine |
| ཞེ་སྡང་ | <u>sh</u>é-dang | aversion, hatred |
| ཞེ་ན་ | <u>sh</u>é-na | [question marker]<br>if one says / were I asked |
| ཞེན་ | shên | clings, determines, conceives **II** |
| ཞེས་ | <u>sh</u>é> | [close quote (syntactic particle)] |
| ཞོག་ | <u>sh</u>o | [imperative of འཇོག་] |
| གཞག་ | <u>sh</u>ak | [future of འཇོག་] |

| གཞལ་ | shël | [future of འཇལ་] |
|---|---|---|
| གཞལ་བྱ་ | shël-ja | object of comprehension |
| གཞན་དུ་ན་ | shën-du-na | otherwise |
| གཞན་ཕན་ | shën-phën | altruism |
| གཞན་ཡང་ | shën-yang | moreover, furthermore |
| གཞི་གྲུབ་ | shi-ḍup | established base (basic existent) |
| གཞུང་ | shung | text, classic |
| བཞག་ | shak | [past of འཇོག་] |
| བཞིན་ | shîn | [marks continuing present after verbs] |
| བཞུགས་ | shuk | live, remain, sit **II** [HON] |
| ཟག་པ་ | sak-b̄a | contamination |
| ཟག་བཅས་ | sak-j̈ë> | contaminated |
| ཟངས་ | sang | copper |
| ཟབ་མོ་ | sap-mo | profound |
| ཟིན་ | sîn | conjoins **V** |
| ཟུངས་ | sung | [imperative of འཛིན་] |
| ཟེར་ | sér | says **V**, is called **VIII** |
| ཟླ | da-wa | moon, month |
| གཟུགས་ | suk | form |
| གཟུགས་ཁམས་ | suk-kham | Form realm |
| གཟུགས་མེད་ཁམས་ | suk-mé'-kham | Formless Realm |
| གཟུང་ | sung | [future of འཛིན་] |
| བཟང་པོ་ | sang-b̄o | good, auspicious, meritorious |

| བཟུང་ | ṣung | [past of འཛིན་] |
|---|---|---|
| བཟོད་ | sö' | is patient, bears |
| ཡང་ | ang | even, also, but |
| འོག་མ་ | ok-ma | lower, later, following |
| འོག་མིན་ | ok-mîn | Akaniṣṭha [a pure land] |
| འོང་ | ong | come **III** |
| འོང་བ་ | ong-wa | coming |
| འོངས་ | ong | [past form of འོང་] |
| འོད་ | ö' | light |
| འོད་ཟེར་ | ö'-ṣér | radiance, luminance ['light rays'] |
| ཡི་དམ་ | yí-dam | personal deity |
| ཡང་ | yang | even, also, but |
| ཡན་ལག་ | yën-lak | branch, limb, part |
| ཡི་གེ་ | yí-gé | letter |
| ཡི་དྭགས་ | yí-dak | hungry ghost [Skt. *preta*] |
| ཡིག་ཆ་ | yík-cha **or** yîk-cha | textbook |
| ཡིད་ | yí' | mind, mentality |
| ཡིད་ལ་བྱེད་ | yí-la-ché' | attends to **V** |
| ཡུན་རིང་ | yün-ring | long time |
| ཡུལ་ | yül | object [*viṣaya*] |
| ཡུལ་ | yül | place, area, country [*deśa*] |
| ཡུལ་ཅན་ | yül-jën | subject |
| ཡེ་ཤེས་ | yé-ṣhé> | wisdom, pristine awareness |
| ཡོངས་སུ་གྲུབ་པ་ | yong-ṣu-ḍup-b̄a | thoroughly established [also adj.] |

| | | |
|---|---|---|
| ཡོངས་སུ་དག་པ་ | yong-su̱-tak-b̄a | thoroughly pure [also adj.] |
| ཡོན་ཏན་ | yön-d̄en | good quality, virtues, qualities |
| གཡག་ | yak | yak |
| གཡང་ས་ | yang-s̱a | abyss |
| ཨེ་ཤེས་ | ye-s̄hé> | knowledge, wisdom |
| ཡོད་ | yö' | exist, have **II VIII** |
| རག་ལས་ | rak-lë> | depend on, rely on |
| རང་ | rang | own, our own, its own, self |
| རང་རྒྱལ་ | rang-gyël | solitary conqueror |
| རང་རྒྱུད་ | rang-gyü' | autonomy |
| རང་རྒྱུད་པ་ | rang-gyü'-b̄a | Autonomists (Svātantrika) |
| རང་ཅག་ | rang-j̄ak | we, ourselves |
| རང་ཉིད་ | rang-nyí' | oneself, itself |
| རང་སྡེ་ | rang-dé | own group |
| རང་དབང་ | rang-wang | independence ('self-power') |
| རང་དབང་ཅན་ | rang-wang-j̄en | independent |
| རང་བཞིན་ | rang-z̲hîn | nature, inherent nature |
| རང་རང་ | rang rang | each their own, each of them |
| རབ་ཏུ་བྱུང་བ་ | rap-d̄u-jung-wa | going forth [becoming a monk] |
| རི་ | rí | mountain |
| རི་བོང་ | rí-bong | rabbit |
| རིག་ | rîk | know, experience **V** |
| རིག་པ་ | rík-b̄a | knowledge, awareness |
| རིགས་ | rík | family, lineage, type |

| རིགས་ | rík | is correct **III** |
| རིགས་པ་ | rík-b̄a | reasoning |
| རིང་པོ་ | ríng-b̄o | long |
| རིན་པོ་ཆེ་ | rîn-b̄o-ché | precious |
| རིམ་པ་ | rîm-b̄a | stage |
| རུང་ | rung | is suitable, is admissible, is correct **III** |
| རུང་བ་ | rung-wa | suitable, proper |
| རེག་བུ་ | rék-ja | tangible object |
| རེས་འགའ་ | rén-ga | some people |
| རོ་ | ro | taste; corpse |
| ར་ | ra | horn |
| ར་སྟོད་ | ra-d̄ö' | [name of monastery] |
| རླུང་ | l̄ung | wind; energy wind (*prāṇa*) |
| * ལ་སོགས་པ་ | la-s̄ok-b̄a | * and so on, such as * |
| ལགས་ | la, lak | is **I** |
| ལས་ | lë> | action (*karma*) |
| ལས་སུ་བྱ་བ་ | lë>-s̄u-cha-wa | object, objective [case] |
| ལུགས་ | luk | system, mode, [doctrinal] positions |
| ལུང་ | lung | scripture, tradition |
| ལུང་མ་བསྟན་ | lung-ma-d̄ën | neutral |
| ལུས་ | lü> | body |
| ལེ་ལོ་ | lé-lo | laziness |
| ལེའུ་ | lé-u | chapter |
| ལེན་ | lên | take **V** |

| | | |
|---|---|---|
| ལོངས་སྐུ་ | long-ḡu | complete enjoyment body |
| ལོངས་སྤྱོད་རྫོགས་པའི་སྐུ་ | long-j̇ö'-dzok-b̄ë-ḡu | complete enjoyment body |
| ལོངས་སྤྱོད་ | long-j̇ö' | resources |
| སློབ་དཔོན་ | l̄o-b̄ön | *ācārya* |
| བསླབ་པ་ | l̄ab-b̄a | training |
| ཤར་ | s̄har | appear, rise **III** |
| ཤར་ | s̄har | east |
| ཤིང་ | s̄híng | [continuative syntactic particle] |
| ཤིང་ཊ་ | s̄hing-d̄a | chariot |
| ཤེ་ན་ | s̄hé-na | [question marker] if one says / were I asked |
| ཤེས་ | s̄hé> | know, realize, understand **V** |
| ཤེས་ | s̄hé | [close quote (syntactic particle)] |
| ཤེས་པ་ | s̄hé>-b̄a | consciousness, knowledge |
| ཤེས་པ་པོ་ | s̄hé>-b̄a-b̄o | knower |
| ཤེས་བྱ་ | s̄hé>-ja | object of knowledge |
| ཤེས་རབ་ | s̄hé>-rap | wisdom (*prajñā*) |
| ཤོད་ | s̄hö' | [imperative of འཆད་] |
| གཤིན་རྗེ་ | s̄hîn-jé | Yama (lord of the dead) |
| གཤིན་པོ་ | s̄hîn-b̄o | those who have passed, the dead |
| གཤེགས་ | s̄hék | go, come [HON] **III** |
| གཤེད་མ་ | s̄hé'-ma | slayer |
| བཤད་ | s̄hë' | [past and future of འཆད་] |
| ས་ | s̄a | earth, ground, stage |

| ས་བོན་ | ša-bön | seed |
| སངས་ | šang | be dispelled, be purified |
| སངས་རྒྱས་ | šang-gyë> | Buddha |
| སུ་ | šu | who, whom |
| སེང་གེ་ | šéng-gé | lion |
| སེམས་ | šêm | think about, reflect on, consider **VI** |
| སེམས་ | šêm | mind |
| སེར་སྣ་ | šér-ña | miserliness |
| སེར་པོ་ | šér-b̄o | yellow |
| སོ་སོ་ | šo-šo | individual |
| སོ་སོའི་སྐྱེ་བོ་ | šo-šö-ḡyé-wo | ordinary person |
| སོ་སོར་ཐར་པ་ | šo-šor-thar-b̄a | individual emancipation [Skt. *pratimokṣa*] |
| སོགས་པ་ | šok-b̄a | so forth, so on [only in * ལ་སོགས་པ་] |
| སོམས་ | šom | [imperative of སེམས་] |
| སོང་ | šong | [past and imperative of འགྲོ་] |
| སྲས་ | šë> | son or child [**H**] |
| སྲིད་ | ší' | is possible **II** |
| སྲིད་པ་ | ší-b̄a | existence; cyclic existence |
| སྲུང་མ་ | šung-ma | guardian deity |
| སྲོག་ | šok | life, vitality |
| སྲོག་གཅོད་པ་ | šok-j̄ö'-b̄a | killing |
| སླེབ་ | lép | arrive **III** |
| གསང་བ་ | šang-wa | secret |

| གསང་བ་འདུས་པ་ | śang-wa-dü>-ba | Guhyasamaja [Guhyasamāja] |
|---|---|---|
| གསལ་པོ་ | śel-b̄o | clear |
| གསལ་བ་ | śel-wa | clear, bright |
| གསུང་ | śung | say **V** [**HON**] [present and future] |
| གསུང་ | śung | speech [**H**] |
| གསུང་འབུམ | śung-bum | collected works |
| གསུངས་ | śung | [past and imperative of གསུང་] |
| གསུམ་ག་ | śum-ḡa | all three |
| གསེར་ | śér | gold |
| བསགས་ | śak | accumulated **V** |
| བསམ་ | śam | [future of སེམས་] |
| བསམ་པ་ | śam-b̄a | thinking, reflection |
| བསམས་ | śam | [past of སེམས་] |
| བསམ་གཏན་ | śam-d̄ën | concentration [Skt. *dhyāna*] |
| བསམ་པ་ | śam-b̄a | thought, thinking, reflection |
| བསླབ་པ་ | l̄ab-ba | training, precept |
| ལྷ་ | hla | god, deity |
| ལྷ་མ་ཡིན་ | hla-ma-yîn | demigod [Skt. *asura*] |
| ལྷ་ས་ | hla-śa | Lhasa [city in Tibet] |
| ལྷག་མཐོང་ | hlak-thong | special insight [Skt. *vipaśyanā*] |
| ལྷུང་ | hlung | [past of ལྷུང་] |
| ལྷུངས་ | hlung | [imperative of ལྷུང་] |
| ལྷོ་ | hlo | south |
| ཨ་ལི་ཀ་ལི་ | a-lí-ḡa-lí | alphabet |

# *Index*

linking verbs, 230, 596
locative-nominative verbs, 609
logical sequence, 310, 349
nominative action verbs, 478, 601
nominative-syntactic verbs, 520
purposive-nominative verbs, 609
rhetorical verbs, 509, 602
separative verbs, 603
verb classes, 370
verbs of absence, 604
verbs of dependence, 375, 599
verbs of existence, 254, 257, 597
verbs of living ,598
verbs of motion, 470, 600
verbs of possession and existence, 294
Tacit dimension, xxxvii, xxxviii, 84
Technical dimension, 82
Technical usage of terms, 101
Tenet systems, 102-103, 394
Terminating dots, 29
Terminating particles, 158-59, 328, 664
Terminating particles, list of, 666
Thesis, 313, 444
Third case, agentive, 636
Third person pronouns, 382
Three categories and eight classes of verbs,
    outline of, 531
Three criteria of a rhetorical statement, 491
Tibetan alphabet, 3, 5, 547
Tibetan Buddhist language and literature,
    periods of, xxviii
Tibetan texts, 436
Time, locative of, 269, 654
Tone, 5, 6, 19
Topical locative, 270, 439, 654
Topical nominative, 220, 631
Transformed identity, 512, 636
Transitive action verbs, 453, 454, 590-91
Transitory collection, 316
Translation, 102
Translations of Sanskrit, 238-42
Transliteration, 11, 20, 21, 545, 547, 554
Transmission, 197
True paths, 357
True sources, 314
True sufferings, 277
Truth body, 245
Type connective, 645
Types of verbs, 407, 531
Uncompounded space, 146
Understood elements, 236
Understood particle, 574
Understood subject, 303, 489

Vajra, 56, 57
Vajrapani, 246
Vehicles, 243, 398
Verb classes, listed, 370
Verb followed by imperative or syntactic
    particle, 616
Verb forms, 129, 611, 615
Verb modifying particles, 330, 664, 678
Verb syntax, 583
Verbal adjectives, 583
Verbal infinitives, 424, 612, 614
Verbal lexical particles, list of, 274-75
Verbal nouns, 583
    and adjectives, 156
Verbal phrases, 373
Verbals, 125, 189, 371, 567, 583
    creation of from nouns, pronouns, and
    adjectives, 131
Verbs and adverbs, dots with, 571
Verbs expressing attitudes, *see* Attitude
    verbs
Verbs of absence, 521, 522, 592, 603, 604
Verbs of dependence, 227, 332, 374, 375,
    591, 597, 599
Verbs of existence, 219, 227, 253, 261, 291,
    293, 331, 591, 596, 597
    negation of, 259
    syntax of, 257
    uses of, 296
Verbs of living, 227, 332, 333, 591, 597
    indicating duration, 335
    special uses of, 338
Verbs of motion, 273, 301, 469, 592, 599,
    600
    list and syntax of, 470
Verbs of necessity, 290, 298
Verbs of possession, 256, 290, 291, 293
Verbs,
    alternate classifications of, 589
    categories, classes, and types, 127, 225,
    228, 407, 453, 587-89
    function in sentences, 125
    honorific, 133
    irregular, 592
    outline of, 531
    specialized, 287
    tenses of, 375
Vocative, 573, 655
Vowels, 549
Vowel markers, 30-33
Vowel sounds, 24
Vows, types of, 358
Weak auxiliaries, 620-21

# *Errata*

Page 170 should read

"Non-objectifying compassion is compassion that does *not* take inherently existing sentient beings as its objects"

Page 196:

In སངས་རྒྱས་ཀྱི་ཆོས་ནི་ལུང་དང་རྟོགས་པའི་ཆོས་ཡིན།, the subject is a phrase, not a clause.

In Drill 12.1, on page 224:

(12) should read རྒྱུད་སེམས་ཀྱི་འགྲེལ་པ་.

On pages 268–270, the locative of inclusion should be included: see p. 653.

On page 448, the verb འཁོར་ is a class III verb.

Page 520 should read:

nominative      syntactic particle

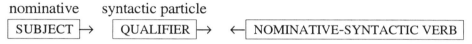

SUBJECT $\rightarrow$    QUALIFIER $\rightarrow$    $\leftarrow$ NOMINATIVE-SYNTACTIC VERB